Toronto Architecture:
A City Guide

Toronto Architecture:

A City Guide

Patricia McHugh & Alex Bozikovic
Photographs by Vik Pahwa

 McClelland & Stewart

Library and Archives Canada Cataloguing in Publication

McHugh, Patricia, author
Toronto architecture : a city guide / Patricia McHugh and Alex Bozikovic.
—Revised edition.

Includes bibliographical references and index.
Issued in print and electronic formats.
ISBN 978-0-7710-5989-6 (paperback).—ISBN 978-0-7710-5990-2 (epub)

1. Architecture—Ontario—Toronto—Guidebooks. 2. Historic buildings—Ontario—Toronto—Guidebooks. 3. Buildings—Ontario—Toronto—Guidebooks. 4. Toronto (Ont.)—Buildings, structures, etc.—Guidebooks. I. Bozikovic, Alex, author II. Title.

FC3097.7.M26 2017   720.9713'541   C2016-904560-9
                                                  C2016-904561-7

ISBN: 978-0-7710-5989-6
ebook ISBN: 978-0-7710-5990-2

Design: CS Richardson

Printed and bound in the USA

McClelland & Stewart,
a division of Penguin Random House Canada Limited,
a Penguin Random House Company
www.penguinrandomhouse.ca

1 2 3 4 5   21 20 19 18 17

Contents

vii *Preface to the Guide*
1 *Introduction*
9 *Architectural Styles of Toronto*

38 **Area I**
  Walk 1: Old Town
  Walk 2: Front Street East

38 **Area II**
  Walk 3: New Town and South Core
  Walk 4: King Street West

59 **Area III**
  Walk 5: Yonge Street

77 **Area IV**
  Walk 6: Financial District

92 **Area V**
  Walk 7: University Avenue
  Walk 8: University of Toronto

123 **Area VI**
  Walk 9: Don Vale
  Walk 10: "Old Cabbagetown" and
    Regent Park

144 **Area VII**
  Walk 11: Sherbourne Street
  Walk 12: Jarvis Street
  Walk 13: Church Street

169 **Area VIII**
  Walk 14: The Grange
  Walk 15: Queen Street West and
    Kensington Market

189 **Area IX**
  Walk 16: Old Yorkville
  Walk 17: West Yorkville
  Walk 18: Bloor Street

211 **Area X**
  Walk 19: Annex East
  Walk 20: Annex West

232 **Area XI**
  Walk 21: Southwest and
    North Rosedale
  Walk 22: Southeast Rosedale

255 **Area XII**
  Walk 23: Waterfront West
  Walk 24: Waterfront East

270 **Area XIII**
  Walk 25: Suburbs West
  Walk 26: Suburbs East

298 *Glossary*
303 *Suggested Reading*
305 *Photo Credits*
306 *Acknowledgements*
307 *Index of Architects*
314 *Index of Buildings*

Preface to the Guide

This book is a guide, for locals as well as visitors, to a city always in the making.

Since 2015 Toronto has been the fourth largest city in North America, after Mexico City, New York, and Los Angeles; a statistical fact that reinforces the truth, obvious to Torontonians, that something dramatic is happening here. What was once "Hogtown" or "Muddy York" has evolved into a sweeping and profoundly multicultural metropolis, and it continues to get denser, more populous— and more sophisticated.

Yet if you look at the history of Toronto after about 1880, you will often find someone claiming the same thing: the city is coming into its own. Looking at Toronto's architecture has convinced me that this is the case. Reshaped by the port, the railways, and the automobile, and progressively larger waves of immigration, Toronto has in fact rebuilt itself over and over again.

This book is, in part, a tool to understand that story. The brick, stone, and concrete of Toronto record its metamorphoses from the little Georgian town of the 1850s to the master-planned modern city of the 1950s, and to today's evolving hybrid—shaped by architects and other professionals who have shown sensitivity, creativity, and brilliance.

When Patricia McHugh (1934–2008) completed the second edition in 1989, she might not have imagined how different Toronto would be 28 years later. Even though the 1980s had brought a "tremendous surge of building" to the city, what's happened since 1996 dwarfs it. In 1989, old industrial neighbourhoods near the downtown core were in decline; today they are booming with residential development, packed with office workers, apartment dwellers and their babies. Cities across North America have seen an influx of people to their centres in the past two decades, and this shift has been dramatic here; while the city began to add tall buildings in the 1950s, it now has many more of them.

Also, the map has changed. The six municipalities of Metropolitan Toronto became, in 1998, simply Toronto. Walkable neighbourhoods from the years before 1930 and the car-oriented suburbs built after World War II are all part of the same political territory. And those suburbs are no longer entirely bastions of prosperity; they are increasingly older and poorer, and it is there that many new Canadians settle.

Conversely, central neighbourhoods that were still gentrifying in the mid-80s are now highly desirable and accordingly expensive.

That would have made sense to McHugh. Born in Los Angeles in 1934, she had lived for a decade in New York and London before landing here with her family in 1972—following the trajectory of Jane Jacobs, and sharing Jacobs's love for a walkable and diverse cityscape. When McHugh, a journalist and editor, began working on this guidebook in the early 1980s, that sort of urbanism was out of fashion in many places; but it had continued to hold sway in the former City of Toronto (the core of the present city). Architects, planners, and citizen activists had remained in these older neighbourhoods, and defended them against too many dangerous big ideas. One of the distinct threads in Toronto architecture is a respectful conversation between the past and present.

Today, those central neighbourhoods are perhaps too well-defended against modest change. But other areas of Toronto have become improbably lively. In her introduction to the second edition, McHugh wrote that "the look of Toronto" will turn "upon the ways in which Toronto's patterns of diversity are nourished in the years to come."

A Note to the Reader

On this point she would have been, I think, pleased. Neighbourhoods from the core all the way to Brampton have been reshaped by new arrivals from across the world. And while that diversity has not really penetrated the world of architecture—the profession is still ruled by Canadian-born white men—there's no question that the city and the region are more open to new ideas.

Toronto, and the Greater Toronto Region, have a much more confident sense of their own identity. McHugh wrote: "A great city is one where differences not only *exist*, but where differences *create* lively encounter and open discourse. It is only through such discourse that Toronto can genuinely acquire a sense of itself as a good and fruitful place to be." Today, the city is getting closer than ever to that ideal.

The book is organized into a series of discrete tours. The first 22 of these roughly follow Patricia McHugh's itinerary in the 1989 second edition, and can each be covered on foot in an afternoon.

I have added one section on the waterfront, which in the 1980s was far less developed; today it is filled with sites of interest. The second new section covers what I call "The Suburbs"—the vast and mixed zone beyond the edges of the old City of Toronto. This goes from streetcar suburbs such as Leslieville to the work-in-progress of downtown Mississauga. This section of the book is far from comprehensive, but gives a flavour of the architectural and planning history of the past century.

Like McHugh I have mixed architectural observations and commentary on the architecture of the city with some thoughts on the social and cultural history that shaped the buildings. I have also added references to planning ideas and works of landscape architecture, which play an increasingly important role. I hope you will use this book to explore, enjoy, and argue about what Toronto is and what it should become.

AB
2017

Entries originally written by Patricia McHugh for the first and second editions of this book conclude with the initials *PM*. Entries written by Alex Bozikovic for this edition are initialled *AB*. Where necessary updates have been made to the text, entries are marked *PM/ updated AB*. Entries marked *PM/AB* are mutually authored.

Introduction

What is Toronto? In 2017 it is a global city: economically stable, culturally sophisticated, extremely diverse. Yet many Torontonians, new as well as long-established, have trouble explaining the essential qualities of this place.

Above all, people will tell you that this is "a city of neighbourhoods."

The phrase seems inadequate—doesn't every city have neighbourhoods? And yet it says much about the culture of the place: This is a metropolis that privileges the small, the local, and the domestic, not the agora or the café but the front lawn and the sidewalk. These attitudes are closely linked with the city's physical form: Toronto began as a city of houses, and for most of its powerful and influential people it remains that. A red-brick Victorian house is the city's architectural emblem.

But there is another symbol, too: the CN Tower. It is barely 40 years old today, the product of modern technology, a symbol of the city's aspirations toward bigness and primacy.

The low, brick, bottom-up city of 1800 through 1930, and the modern, skyscraping, concrete city of big plans: Toronto contains both of these. And the current boom—plus some quirks of planning and politics—has brought these two scales together, creating hundreds of mid-rise and high-rise buildings in places including the downtown. With investment and human capital flowing in, the manner in which Toronto will continue to grow is an open question, and the answer will depend on political will as much as the genius of the city's urbanists. Its architectural future will reflect Torontonians' collective sense of what the city is and what it should be.

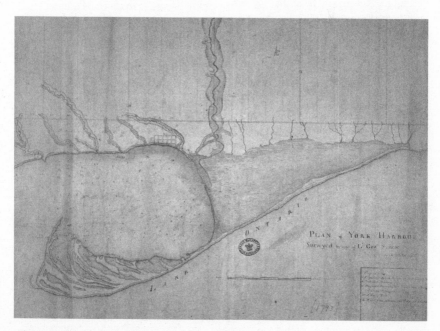

Plan of York Harbour by the surveyor Alexander Aitkin, 1793.

"Surely no city in the world with a background of three hundred years does so little to make that background known," wrote the architect and historian Eric Arthur in *No Mean City* in 1964. Fifty years later, this remains true: Toronto is much older than we think. After tens of thousands of years of aboriginal occupation of the Lake Ontario shore, the Seneca established a town called Teiagon near the mouth of the Humber River. (It stood near today's Jane Street and Baby Point Road.) In 1701 the Mississauga took over the site—the details of the transition are unclear. But this spot allowed access to rich fishing on the Humber, and it lay on the trail that would be known as the Toronto Carrying Place, a long portage north toward Lake Simcoe. When French fur traders arrived here in the 17th century, the importance of the place was clear to them: the French established three forts along the trail, the last the short-lived Fort Rouillé in 1751. By 1759, it was clear that a British victory was coming, and the retreating French burned Fort Rouillé.

Thus the early architectural history of the city can be found only through fragments and ruins; the site of Fort Rouillé remains visible, just barely, on the Exhibition Place grounds. But the Carrying Place trail is, more or less, Highway 400; Davenport Road, too, follows an ancient aboriginal trail along the base of an escarpment.

This approach to the land, responsive to natural features, was overtaken by the very different sensibility of the British colony and the town grid. Today's city was born in 1793 as a colonial outpost named York. Upper Canada's first lieutenant-governor, John Graves Simcoe, chose the site as his capital for its defensibility and its distance from the American border. Loyalist American exiles had pushed for the established town of Kingston; instead Simcoe chose this isolated location, and named it after King George's son the Duke of York, not the last time that a British aristocratic name would be applied to this place. In 1793 Simcoe sent home a map by the surveyor Alexander Aitken, titled "Plan of York Harbour." It does not show Fort York, which lay at the mouth of the harbour to the west, but it depicts in some detail the Don River and its estuary, and the peninsula that would become Toronto Island. This well-protected harbour promised safety, and the river, for Simcoe, access to the interior. And then there is the town itself: ten square blocks, just west of the river, in a grid pattern that drew from four centuries of European practice and the precedents of Roman city-building. This perfect Cartesian geometry responded not at all to the presence of beach, swamp, or hill. This standard layout would define Toronto's development through the next century; the concession grids that extended beyond it would shape British and Canadian settlements across a vast area. As the architect and theorist George Baird put it in the 1970s, Toronto is essentially a grid on a lake.

In the early days the grid was small and its architecture modest, clustered in those original ten blocks and then a "New Town" laid out to the west. Wooden houses were replaced by brick ones in the symmetrical Georgian style; grand churches expressed the spiritual aspirations of the community (the Anglican spire being of course the tallest). The town's nickname, "Muddy York," distinguished it from the other, more impressive Yorks.

The War of 1812, in which Toronto was thoroughly sacked and looted by American invaders, paradoxically helped create a sense of local pride, and wartime spending established a local class of merchants who challenged the class of minor aristocrats and aspiring aristocrats who had ruled the place. Trade, which birthed Teiagon, became central to Toronto; the growth of the port, and then the arrival in the 1850s of the railroads, connected the city consistently with the outside world for the first time.

Influxes of immigrants made the small town much larger, to about 30,000 by 1854, and then 86,000 in 1881. Industry grew rapidly, the financial sector along with it; Toronto soon had ranks of factories and warehouses along Front Street East, while a financial hub grew up to the west as banks competed in stone and brick to show their strength. Boom times always mean building,

King Street East: south side, looking west [1856 or 1857]. (City of Toronto Archives.)

and the oldest of the city's current landmarks went up in this era: William Thomas's St. Lawrence Hall, Cumberland & Storm's University College, Cumberland & Ridout's Cathedral Church of St. James. Small business became big business, and distillers and retailers constructed grand houses for themselves on Jarvis Street or Queen's Park.

The material of the age was brick, much of it drawn from the city's own clay pits; this was not just culture but bylaw. Like other cities of the era Toronto was worried about fire, and indeed was hit by two "Great Fires" in 1849 and in 1904. Brick became the signature of the city, both red and "white" (actually yellow) brick. The interweaving of these two shades of brick allowed for a handsome and reasonably inexpensive type of ornament, on grand public buildings and on the skinny façades of workers' housing.

The double house, also known as semi-detached houses, sprang up here as almost nowhere else—capped usually with a bay window, gable, and bargeboard, which carried the English-old-money connotations of the Gothic style. This form proved a good solution for building densely, and for filling the city's long and skinny residential lots. With small lawns in front, each of these

houses kept its distance from the sidewalk, and yet crouched against its twin and not far from its neighbours. Back lanes captured the smells and messes of the household; the street was the place to see the neighbours before retreating to the privacy of your own house. All this formed the DNA of Toronto's neighbourhood character, with its important but cramped public realm.

The configuration of those neighbourhoods, with their narrow lots, also reflects the capitalist mindset of early Toronto. Simcoe laid out 32 "park lots," running north from the present Queen Street to Bloor Street, which were granted to men in the first generation of colonial officials. Initially they were expected to build grand estates here, helping to establish a quasi-aristocracy for Upper Canada. A few did: D'Arcy Boulton Jr.'s Grange, now part of the Art Gallery of Ontario, remains as proof. Yet most of them bought and sold, and sold; then their heirs sold some more, subdividing the original 100-acre estates into smaller and smaller parcels. This unplanned development left the city with north–south slices, built out in different patterns, whose streets did not always connect. (Some of this was resolved in the 20th century, but not perfectly; the twists of Dundas Street and College/Carlton Street tell the story.) In this way, untrammeled commerce gave us the residential districts from Parkdale to Riverdale that are now so beloved. Served by horse-drawn trolleys and then electric ones, they were built to be walked; yet their back lanes and stables allowed space for the arrival of the car. They are a successful and adaptable form.

The same ad-hoc attitude also kept Toronto from realizing any grand plans in the years after 1900, when other cities were building impressive Beaux Arts public buildings and networks of parks. Toronto did get grand civic structures, such as Queen's Park and Old City Hall in the 1890s, the Royal Ontario Museum in 1914, and the Art Gallery of Toronto in 1918. Yet most of these were centred on the few places in the city, the university campus and the remaining fragments of park-lot estates, that had space for grand gestures. Union Station, completed in 1920, was conceived as part of a scheme to give a ceremonial character to the crowded downtown. It didn't happen. Later, University Avenue acquired some grandeur, but has always been a one-off in the workaday grid of downtown. Mostly the city continued to grow incrementally, through the addition of streetcar suburbs in which many houses were actually built by their owners. Downtown, E.J. Lennox's City Hall sat next to the workshops of Eaton's on one side, and St. John's Ward, the city's arrival point for working-class migrants, on the other; reformers decried The Ward's crowding and lack of sanitation. Just to the south, King and Bay streets became the locus for a cluster of skyscrapers. The Canadian Bank of Commerce, completed in 1929, was the tallest building in the British Empire.

The collision of visible poverty, civic grandeur, and capitalist ambition was

"Bird's eye view" of Toronto, published by Barclay, Clark & Co. Lithographers, in 1893.

"The Ward" and City Hall, 1913. Photograph by Arthur Goss. (City of Toronto Archives.)

typical in North American cities of this period. But in Toronto, such juxtapositions would become less visible in the transformative decades to come.

World War II changed Toronto's built landscape, though it was fought an ocean away. The war effort engendered new factories in the rural hinterlands of the city, in Mimico and Ajax; some of these would become the hubs of new communities as the city began to expand on an unprecedented scale. There were two driving forces. First was another wave of immigration, the largest yet—half a million migrants, largely from southern and eastern Europe, arrived in Toronto in the 20 years after the war, providing both demand for housing and labour, particularly in construction, along with a challenge to the city's Anglo character. At the same time, the growth of car ownership created new demand and new possibilities for suburban expansion.

As with many cities in North America, this happened fast. The brewery magnate E.P. Taylor saw the potential of large-scale suburban development, and created Don Mills, seven miles from downtown. His development company insisted on modern architecture, and a crop of young local designers were able to respond; by this time

Toronto's architects were belatedly embracing the ideas of the Modernist movement which had been born in Europe between the wars. The early impact of Modernism was felt through planning. The CIAM, or the International Congresses of Modern Architecture, articulated a vision of a new city that would employ new technology—the high-rise, the highway—to sort the city into distinct clusters: industry in one place, retail in another, and homes set apart in high-rises surrounded by green space. This set of ideas, intended first for Europe, was picked up in North America by alliances of politicians and developers under the name of "urban renewal."

Toronto was no exception, but its version of urban renewal was modest and in some ways unique. The Metropolitan Toronto government, introduced in 1954, advocated for a network of those crucial modern amenities, expressways—the Gardiner and the Don Valley Parkway were built quickly, the latter continuing a long pattern of treating the Don Valley as a dumping ground. And Metro oversaw the expansion of the city into the largely rural municipalities of Etobicoke, North York, and Scarborough. This top-down planning was somewhat enlightened. In order to justify the costs of new amenities and infrastructure, Metro insisted that single-family houses be mixed with denser forms of housing. Apartment towers, intended for the middle class, went up across the metropolis, establishing a pattern that exists nowhere else on the continent. These were built using the local building industry's expertise in concrete, the European high-rise technology of choice. Within 30 years some of these buildings would become pockets of poverty, housing new Canadians and others who are often carless; the economic and physical integration of these "tower neighbourhoods" is today a significant challenge, while they continue to provide important, relatively affordable rental housing.

Meanwhile, the central downtown was rebuilt, like its counterparts all over North America, with tall towers that blended Modernist thinking with corporate swagger. The big banks, which ruled the economy, had and still have a similar role on the skyline; Toronto-Dominion led the way with its project by Mies van der Rohe. And governments, in a few places, pursued the goal of "slum clearance." Regent Park, between the 1940s and the 1960s, remade a huge swath of Victorian working-class housing with modernist towers-in-the-park. And yet this was the exception. A few other social-housing projects were completed, but the aging neighbourhoods around the core survived intact.

Why? For one thing they had never been forsaken; working-class and middle-class homeowners remained proud of their districts, and while some of the wealthy did certainly head for the suburbs in the 1960s, they were quickly replaced by gentrifying "white-painters." While developers won the ear of Toronto's city council in the 1960s, the young progressive David Crombie ran for mayor in 1972, attacking the official plan as "a hunting license for developers." He and his reform faction won. Their agenda: protecting central Toronto's blend of leafy residential streets and commerce through controlled development and community consultation. The arrival in 1968 of the writer Jane Jacobs added intellectual support to this movement, which shaped a generation of architects and urbanists and the city's planning department.

"Context" became, and remains, an important buzzword: even ardent fans of Modernism came to cherish the historic patterns by which the city was laid out and built. When the Eaton Centre went up in the late 1970s, it was as urbane and sensitive as a downtown shopping mall could be. And Toronto got the CN Tower, which was for three decades the world's tallest structure and rules the skyline to this day; but the city avoided a calamity by rejecting the megaproject that was slated to go with it.

Bold modern architecture has had its moments. Toronto's new City Hall opened in 1965, the result of an international design competition. The Finn Viljo Revell won with a scheme that used concrete to its full sculptural potential. It reflected the beginning of a new era. Its champion was Nathan Phillips, the city's first Jewish mayor (his predecessors, for 130 years, had all been

New City Hall under construction (with neo-classical Land Registry).

Protestant), in a city where 40 percent of residents were foreign-born. The square in front of City Hall was named after Phillips, and it was Toronto's first real agora. Since then, Harbourfront, Yonge-Dundas Square, and a new set of parks on the eastern waterfront have all expanded the city's sense of the public realm.

City Hall did not exactly reshape Toronto architecture—there have been few buildings so ambitious before or since—but the design competition that created it did attract talented young foreigners, including John Andrews. They joined an architectural culture that was studying how to create a denser 20th-century city without destroying the 19th-century fabric. The South African Jack Diamond and the American Barton Myers made a crucial contribution to this infillism. Since then, Toronto architecture at its best has sensitively integrated the new with the old. (Though it must be said

that the city has had a mediocre record of preserving specific heritage buildings, and things are only a bit better today.)

In one important sense the city's built form does not reflect its identity: more than half of Torontonians are foreign-born, and the white, British city of a century ago is gone. Neighbourhoods from Little Italy to Agincourt and Brampton have been reshaped by the cultures of successive immigrant populations. It will only be a matter of time before the building culture of Toronto reflects that reality. The Aga Khan Museum, a spectacular gift that came through the presence of Toronto's Ismaili Muslim community, suggests how that might look.

Meanwhile, four decades of focusing on the small and incremental have had their downsides. For one, a lack of drama. Toronto has had few flashy buildings, despite its considerable public and private wealth. Diamond's opera house is not very operatic, and even Frank Gehry's renovation to the Art Gallery of Ontario is relatively quiet. Will Alsop's Sharp Centre at OCAD University is the newest icon, unpretty and surprising.

But the larger challenge is social and economic. Much of the discussion of house Neighbourhoods (the word has a capital N in the city's official plan) assumes that those areas are essentially middle-class. But what is happening in Toronto, as in other desirable global cities, is that these districts are becoming forbiddingly expensive. The current development boom has been running for nearly two decades and shows no sign of slowing down. Provincial projections now imagine that Toronto will have added 700,000 new residents between 2011 and 2041, 225,000 of them coming to the downtown core and doubling its population. The city's political and planning culture is in no way prepared for this scale of change: both in the postwar suburban areas and in the old city of Toronto, there remains a visceral resistance to new development of all kinds. Age-old cultural conservatism and 1970s progressivism have joined forces.

Where the growth is going, instead, is into previously empty pockets of downtown. The former railway lands and King-Spadina have absorbed tens of thousands of people, packed together very densely. Opaque and complex planning mechanisms are partly responsible for this; the city can be overruled by the province's Ontario Municipal Board, in a lawyerly process that no average citizen understands. But if you were to evenly spread out the presence of new neighbours, many of them would belong in the capital-N Neighbourhoods—the places well-served by parks, schools, transit, and shopping that have always been so beloved. Local architects are very good at infill. Perhaps the politicians will let them at it and Toronto will figure out how to reinvent itself, bit by bit.

One place the city is changing for the better is along the waterfront. In the 1980s, the parks and cultural centres of Harbourfront brought urban Toronto to the lakefront as never before; a barrier of wharves and factories was partially peeled away to reveal Lake Ontario as (yes!) beautiful. The ongoing work of revitalizing the eastern waterfront and the lower Don River is extending that project, and doing so with some of the smartest urbanism and landscape architecture in Toronto's history. This overlooked, underdeveloped quarter could be home to tens of thousands, a workplace for many more, and a place of communal delight for the city as a whole. It might well reconnect Torontonians with the waterfront, reminding them of where this city came from, that it is a grid on a lake. This is a return to where the city began, and it could offer what Toronto has been missing: a big dream, and a bold answer to what this place is all about. *AB*

Sugar Beach.

One of the most efficient ways to describe a building is to attach a stylistic label to it—a word or two that may denote not only physical properties but also historical period, geographical source, building method, even cultural determinant. Labels are far from precise and universal. Terms vary from epoch to epoch ("Gothic" was once "modern"), and from writer to writer (one scribe's "Second Empire" is another's "French Renaissance"). Styles with the same name vary from place to place as well. A Queen Anne house in Toronto is not identical to one in New York, nor does a New York example mimic its London counterpart.

One way to sort out changes in architecture is to think of the various styles in cycles that alternate between classical and picturesque. Symmetrical, orderly classical styles are countered by asymmetric, dynamic picturesque styles, and so on. (An intermediate classical and picturesque style such as Italianate may intervene, and of course there is always overlap.) Following are the names of styles as used in this guide and a few notes on the what, where, and why. Definitions apply specifically to Toronto buildings, as do relevant dates. And remember, some buildings are so idiosyncratic and eclectic as to defy classification by style. They're often the most interesting of all.

Architectural Styles of Toronto

Georgian: 1800–1875
The Georgian style derived from an Anglo-Dutch simplification of Italian Renaissance and Baroque architecture. Especially influential were the buildings and writings of 16th-century Northern Italian architect Andrea Palladio. It was named for the first four King Georges, whose reigns—1714 to 1830—coincided with the style's major period of popularity in England. Toronto was settled by the British near the end of the Georgian period and this small-scale classicism was the young colony's first real architectural expression.

The Georgian style was used for both two-storey detached houses and two-, three-, and four-storey row houses and shops. It was also adapted for public buildings, churches, factories, and warehouses. Toronto's Georgian buildings followed British example but were simpler and plainer. They are characterized by a rectangular box-like shape with a symmetrical façade organized horizontally and centred on a formal entrance bay (except in side-hall plans). Cladding is wood, roughcast, or red or yellow brick (called white brick at the time). Roofs are either hipped or end gable, with plain or dentilled cornices, large tall chimneys, and often dormer windows. Door-cases may be elaborate with toplights and sidelights. Raised basements, columned porticoes, and centre pediments are typical Palladian-evolved features. Windows are generally straight-topped of sliding-sash type with from six to 12 panes of glass in each sash. Sills and lintels are of wood or stone, or there may be relieving arches of radial brick set flush with the wall. Decorative brick quoins may appear at corners of brick houses.

Toronto continued to build in Georgian style long after it had passed out of fashion in the homeland. In later versions, however, picturesque features were appended to the classical Georgian, notably cladding of yellow brick with red-brick accents, or red with yellow; windows with a gently rounded curve at the top and fewer panes; and perhaps a decorative brick corbel table enriching the cornice.

Neo-Classicism or Classical Revival (Greek and Roman): 1825–1860

There are no buildings remaining in Toronto that can properly be called Roman Revival. As for Greek Revival, although it was considered symbolically apt for the new American nation where it dominated residential architecture in the 1830s and '40s, it gained little following among the citizenry of Toronto. Only a few Greek Revival houses are known. Its chaste, formal look did appeal, however, to Toronto's city fathers, who considered it appropriate—just as they had in Regency England—for important commercial and civic buildings. Greek

Revival buildings are characterized by a symmetrical and boxy shape, sometimes with Greek columns and entablature; smooth stone or yellow-brick cladding (to approximate the colour of stone); and low-pitched or flat roofs. Windows and doors are straight-topped and lintelled. Greek-inspired decorative motifs include floral anthemia and meanders.

Gothic Revival and High Victorian Gothic: 1845–1890

The Gothic Revival style first appeared in England in the late 1700s, part of the same nostalgic impulse that prompted the Middle Ages settings of Sir Walter Scott's chivalric novels. The style's appeal blossomed with the Victorians, who saw it as a way to recapture both medieval romance and a sense of national and ecclesiological "appropriateness."

Still in thrall to British tradition and example, Toronto was quick to embrace the picturesque style. English prototypes were closely followed for Gothic Revival churches. In fact, actual prescriptions sent out by the Anglicans' Camden (later Ecclesiological) Society in Cambridge were used. Three forms were revived: squat, high-steepled **Early English**, with masonry cladding and pointed single-light windows; complicated **Decorated** or **Middle Pointed**, featuring windows of curvilinear tracery; and attenuated **Perpendicular**, marked by slender spires, elongated pinnacles, and crenellations.

For later High Victorian Gothic churches, Toronto architects used the general shapes and pointed arches of Gothic Revival but added a variety of cladding materials for a rich polychrome effect. These were also inspired by English models, which in turn had been influenced by John Ruskin's writings on the application of colour in architecture.

Sources for Gothic Revival residential architecture came more directly from the United States, where the style was promoted for single detached houses through builders' guides, notably those of Alexander Jackson Davis and Andrew Jackson Downing. Toronto's Gothic Revival houses are typically symmetrical one-and-a-half-storey cottages with centre gable or asymmetric two-storey L-shaped structures. Cladding may be roughcast or red or yellow brick. Roofs are steeply pitched and multiple-gabled with curvilinear bargeboard trim. Windows are tall and slender, either straight-topped or pointed-arched, sometimes protected by decorative drip-moulds.

Later High Victorian Gothic houses featured two colours of brick, usually red with yellow for decoration; fatter, heavier ornament, especially bargeboards; and corbel tables running under the eaves as well as other decorative brick patterns and panels.

revival of dignified early Renaissance forms to heroically illumine gentlemen's club buildings. The style was broadly adopted in the United States for detached houses, but upon transatlantic translation became freer and less classically self-contained. American pattern books illustrated vague, romantically expansive Italian country villas by the score. Americans liked the flexible style because an Italianate house could be made to look as picturesque as a Gothic one without Gothic's burden of "Englishness." Toronto had no such aversion to seeming English, however, and Italianate houses here are spiked with not a little Gothic Revival dash.

Italianate houses may be symmetrical or asymmetric. They sometimes feature a tall, off-centre tower and often a long veranda. Cladding is usually yellow brick. Roofs are flat or low-pitched with extended eaves, generally set with ornate brackets. Windows are round-headed with projecting window heads or flush relieving arches. In the period, wooden detailing was most often painted a creamy white or very dark green.

Toronto Bay-n-Gable: 1875–1890

The facility with which local builders achieved a graceful marriage of Italianate and Gothic Revival modes is abundantly visible in Toronto's Bay-n-Gables, a distinctive form of double and row house that appeared all across the city in the fourth quarter of the 19th century. Characterized by polygonal end bays atop of which spring pointy gables edged in decorative bargeboards, these pleasing rhythmic

Italianate: 1845–1885

What has come to be called "Italianate" style actually was conceived first in England as a

compositions are virtually Toronto's architectural trademark. The oldest known example standing is at 404 Jarvis St., by Gundry & Langley in 1862 **[12/13]**.

Typically, Bay-n-Gable houses are of soft orangey-red brick with yellow-brick accents. Earlier examples tend to have Italianate round-headed windows, angled bays, and steep gables. Those dating from the late 1880s show more Queen Anne influence, with rectangular bays, straight-topped windows, and lower pitched gables.

Renaissance Revival: 1845–1890

A more ambitious, full-blown Renaissance Revival (French and English as well as Italian) than that sprinkled on Italianate houses was embraced by mercantilist Toronto for commercial blocks, warehouses, and factories. In this, it was following the example of the United States and its mid-century cast-iron architecture. Though whole cast-iron façades never enjoyed much favour in Toronto, iron was common for interior supporting columns as well as for selected exterior ornamentation. The Renaissance Revival style also appealed to Victorians as a way to project both classical tradition and a fashionable look for civic and bank structures. It was not rigidly proscribed and allowed builders and architects a relatively free hand.

Two modes are seen. Conservative Renaissance Revival buildings are symmetrical and boxy, without columns. They are clad in smooth-looking brick or stone. Roofs are low-pitched or flat. Windows are straight-topped with cornice, segmental-, and/or triangular-pedimented window heads. The more flamboyant examples are also symmetrical and rectangular, but they are usually taller than they are wide. Cladding may be stone, but is more often brick. Roofs are flat with ornate cornices. Windows are round-headed in a variety of arch forms, with bold window heads. Decorative details, classically inspired and frequently rendered in cast iron, are rich and profuse.

Second Empire: 1866–1890

Prominent during the contemporaneous reign of Emperor Napoleon III (1852–1870), this was not a revival style *per se,* although the French were certainly drawing on Baroque and Renaissance tradition. The Second Empire style came to Canada from France via the United States and to a lesser extent via England. It was first used here in 1866 by Toronto architect Henry Langley for Government House [demolished] and then dominated major public architecture during the 1870s and domestic architecture through the 1880s. It then fell from favour as quickly as it had risen. For that key period, however, the impressive and ornamental style perfectly captured the air of entrepreneurial ambition that characterized Toronto in the years following Confederation.

Second Empire buildings typically take the shape of symmetrical square blocks that are richly decorated for a highly sculptural profile. Cladding is usually yellow brick with red-brick decorative touches, less often red with yellow. Roofs are always of the mansard type—straight, convex, or concave—pierced by dormer windows. Doors and windows are round-headed and often paired, with moulded window heads. Decorative details may include brackets at eaves, quoins, and belt courses. The brick was sometimes painted for protection, usually in a colour to match its natural hue.

Romanesque Revival: 1870–1910

The descriptive label "Romanesque" refers to the reintroduction of classical Roman architecture after the Dark Ages had all but extinguished it, especially the Roman arch as it appeared in the massive-walled abbeys that rose across Europe in the 10th and 11th centuries. The Victorians revived the form, calling it the "round-arched style." Architects here occasionally used Romanesque Revival for churches (especially Presbyterian), but like Britain and unlike the United States, Toronto preferred Gothic. Romanesque Revival structures may be symmetrical or asymmetric, the latter sometimes with towers of differing heights. Cladding is smooth-looking brick or stone. Windows and all openings are round-arched. Decoration may include arcaded corbel tables, buttresses, and parapeted towers.

Richardsonian Romanesque: 1886–1900

Henry Hobson Richardson, considered one of America's greatest architects, created a version of the Romanesque so distinctive and personal that buildings inspired by his designs have come to be called Richardsonian Romanesque. The style was first used in Toronto at Queen's Park by Buffalo architect Richard A. Waite. This was followed in the next decade by all manner of fine buildings in the weighty and massive-looking style, notably by Toronto architects David Dick, E.J. Lennox, David Roberts, and William Storm.

Richardsonian Romanesque buildings have a chunky shape, either symmetrical or asymmetric, often with a tower. Cladding is rock-faced ashlar, sometimes with red brick. Roofs are high with broad planes. The characteristic wide, round arches occur over entry porches and sometimes windows. Otherwise the deep-set windows are straight-topped with a single pane of glass in each sash and perhaps a transom. Decorative elements include stubby stone columns and the stone or terracotta foliate ornamentation called Byzantine leafwork.

Queen Anne: 1880–1915

This revival style was initiated by Richard Norman Shaw and fellow British architects who set about re-creating the mix of Italian classicism (symmetry, pilasters) and Dutch picturesqueness (red brick, curly gables) that had marked English dwellings of the mid 17th century (for Shaw to call them Queen Anne, who ruled 1702–14, was really inaccurate). In North America, the style's popularity spread rapidly after the British erected two widely publicized Queen Anne buildings at the 1876 Centennial Exposition in Philadelphia. Queen Anne houses are typically detached. Shaw's white-trimmed Queen Anne buildings often appeared serenely classical, but on this continent an exuberant manipulation of space and detail weighted the style toward a more decided picturesqueness. Utilizing an abundance of towers, turrets, gables, dormers, and bay windows, their form is self-consciously asymmetric. Cladding is complicated, combining stone; hard, dark red brick; terracotta tile; and wood. Roofs are high, hipped or gabled, with high chimneys. Windows are generally single-pane sash; transoms and round-arched toplights are common. Decoration includes wooden spindlework, terracotta panels, and stained glass.

After about 1895, Queen Anne houses became boxier-looking, with classical columns replacing turned posts and Palladian windows and dentil mouldings common. This adaptation (like Shaw's early version) is sometimes labelled **Free Classic**.

The Annex House: 1888–1899

For the Lewis Lukes house of 1888–90 [19/9], E.J. Lennox combined the rock-faced ashlar and solid appearance of Richardsonian Romanesque with the asymmetry and picturesque detail of Queen Anne. The result was a hybrid form that was soon copied for single and double houses throughout Toronto's Annex area and elsewhere in the city.

Second Classical Revival: 1890–1930

Repeating the time-honoured seesaw of traditional/picturesque styles, architects returned to classical forms at the turn of the century, especially for public commercial buildings such as railway stations, hotels, and banks. Of the various approaches, the most prominent in Toronto were the massive and austere **Neo-Classical Revival**, with buildings parading Greek orders and lintelled windows and doors; the dramatic as well as ornamental **Edwardian Baroque**, emphasizing plastic, sculptural qualities; and the **Second Renaissance Revival**, a reworking of the logical, serene motifs and forms of the Renaissance, most notably to articulate the tripartite division of Toronto's early skyscrapers into "base, shaft, and capital." All three versions are sometimes, loosely, termed "Beaux Arts" (see Glossary).

Georgian Revival or Neo-Georgian: 1895–1940

The classical tradition reasserted itself in this period with Georgian Revival, a replay of Toronto's first attachment to a style of comforting domesticity. Georgian Revival houses are similar to original Georgian, but they are generally larger and almost always of red brick picked out with light-coloured wood or stone details. The style was also popular for clubhouses and small apartment houses.

Late Gothic Revival or Neo-Gothic: 1895–1935

In the early 20th century, a period of rapid and confusing change, Gothic was marshalled as a style of reassuring "pastness," especially efficacious for its aura of moral and social order. Late Gothic Revival was most often used for churches and school and university buildings, the latter sometimes called **Collegiate Gothic**. This style is plainer, less self-consciously picturesque, and more substantial-looking than Gothic Revival or High Victorian Gothic.

English Cottage Style, Jacobethan, or Neo-Tudor: 1895–1940

The label Neo-Tudor identifies sundry picturesque reincarnations of English 16th-century cottages and manor houses. As in that post-medieval century, the first decades of the 20th saw feverish housebuilding with whole suburbs appearing almost overnight. Neo-Tudor structures were appreciated for their relative simplicity with just enough picturesque detail to suggest a "period house." The most noteworthy examples were the early **English Cottage Style** houses of Arts and Crafts architects C.F.A. Voysey and Edwin Lutyens, whose free, modern rendering of Tudoresque vernacular forms was much copied in North America (in Toronto especially by Eden Smith. Later designs often lacked the earlier originality, and, bandaged in yards of expensive but false half-timbering, have been dubbed "Stockbroker Tudor." Another tag, **Jacobethan**, is applied to large, formal structures such as school buildings, notably those that sport Jacobean curved parapeted gables. Obviously diverse, Neo-Tudor buildings share a blocky but asymmetric shape, usually dominated by one or more bold front-facing cross gables. Cladding may be stucco, brick, stone, or a combination thereof. Roofs are prominent and steeply pitched, usually side-gabled, with elaborate chimneys. Windows are typically mullioned and transomed casement type, frequently arranged in strings of three or more.

Commercial Style: 1895–1930
This term is used to describe the first tall buildings—five storeys or higher—whose flat roofs and orderly, sleekly framed, and many-windowed façades frankly represented their commercial purpose as well as skeletal construction. Conceptualized as a plain two-way grid, these "skycages" were celebrated for their "rationality" and "honesty." Applied ornament is usually minimal but may take the form of classical, Gothic, Romanesque, Sullivanesque, and/or Art Deco decorative touches. The style was first and most fully developed in Chicago. In Toronto, Commercial Style was more than competently explored in the Spadina Avenue loft buildings of the 1910s and '20s.

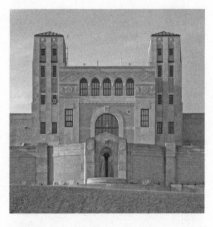

Art Deco, Art Moderne, or Style Moderne: 1925–1955
This style was appropriated for both multi-storey skyscrapers and low-slung two-storey commercial buildings and residences. Art Deco high-rises can be identified by their massive, relatively smooth square forms, often with roofline setbacks; vertically emphasized fenestration; colourfulness; and flattened geometric, abstract, often exotic and fantastic ornament. Low Art Moderne structures are more likely to feature rounded curves and horizontally streamlined fenestration. Toronto's Moderne influence came via the United States, especially New York City where the Art Deco skyscraper was born. Though primarily associated with the 1920s and '30s, in Toronto Moderne rounded corners and setbacks continued to appear on new buildings after World War II, and one large enterprise, the Bank of Nova Scotia, was constructed in 1949–51 using Moderne plans first drawn up in 1929 **[6/31a]**.

Modernism: 1945–1985

A catch-all term for the 20th-century architecture, largely with roots in Europe, that attempted to use new technologies (such as elevators and steel-frame construction) to match the social currents of the age. The International Style is the main, but not the only, stream of Modernism; the city hosted other regional variants, particularly the organic forms and natural materials favoured by Scandinavian Modernists. Toronto architects also adopted these new ideas incrementally; some buildings, especially in the 1950s, combined Modernist details with familiar materials such as brick and smooth-cut stone, and Classically informed composition, such as the Bank of Canada **[7/13]** on University Ave.

International Style: 1947–1975

A term coined in 1932 for an exhibition at the Museum of Modern Art in New York, this concept brings together Modernist ideas formulated in Europe during the 1920s by such architects as Le Corbusier, Walter Gropius, and Ludwig Mies van der Rohe. It is understood to represent an aesthetic appropriate to a new industrial age, employing technologically advanced materials and rejecting Classically derived symmetry. Characteristic elements include steel and reinforced-concrete construction; "curtain walls" that are not structural, but express the volumes that they enclose; open plans; flat roofs; little if any ornament; and an absence of any historical references. While much of the early work so described had a progressive political bent, this style—purely as style—became the default for American corporate architecture in the 1950s onward, and in Canada soon afterward. Toronto's International Style masterpiece, the Toronto-Dominion Centre **[6/34]**, dates to 1964.

Neo-Expressionism: 1950–

This term is applied to individual, sculptural buildings whose sweeping curves and surprising juxtapositions of form are meant to confront the more common rectangularity of the built environment. Because the style is inherently exhibitionist, most Neo-Expressionist buildings are well known: New City Hall **[7/18]**, O'Keefe Centre **[1/24]**, Roy Thomson Hall **[3/6]**, the apartment houses of Uno Prii **[20/7]**.

Brutalism: 1960–1980

Emerging from Britain in the 1950s as "the New Brutalism," this style of modernism emphasized frankness of materials— especially exposed concrete—and bold, sculptural form-making. Toronto has many examples, thanks to the 1960s coincidence of strong concrete trades, European-trained engineers, and a building boom. Brutalism was the default style for cultural projects around Canada's 1967 centennial, such as the St. Lawrence Centre for the Arts [1/22]; it is also seen in Toronto in apartment towers and often in educational buildings such as York University's Ross Building [25/22c] and Scarborough College [26/21a], which appeared in publications around the world.

Late-Modernism: 1975–

Buildings that take as their departure point the modern International Style are collected

under the heading Late-Modern. Often constructed for big business or large institutions, these tend toward unexpected forms, with curves, zigzagging façades or chamfered corners; building façades tend to be smooth and often reflective. Hydro Place [7/31] and Metropolitan Place [7/5] are good examples.

Post-Modernism: 1977–1995

Promoted as a movement to reintroduce many of the traditional elements that modernists had cast aside, Post-Modern buildings use forms and ornament abstracted from past architectural styles to create symbolic, historic, and cultural references. These are rarely straightforward quotations, but often touched with irony or unexpected juxtapositions, as at Mississauga City Hall [25/5a].

Neo-modernism: 1995–

The contemporary architectural mainstream draws from the Modernism of the 1950s through the 1970s.

Ten square blocks. That was how York began, as drawn by surveyor Alexander Aitkin in 1793: the germ of the metropolis, overseen by governor John Graves Simcoe, was planted between today's George, Berkeley, Adelaide, and Front Streets. Four years later there were 241 residents here, and few hints of the future potential of the place. When York officially replaced Niagara as the new capital of Upper Canada in 1798, there was grumbling from the colony's acting surveyor-general David Smith: "How peculiarly hard is the lot of the Civil Officers of Upper Canada, and how carefully they seem selected to be the sport of fortune!"

Yet the settlement of a new town meant the granting of land, and the so-called Family Compact, the colony's insular elite of Anglican officers, gentlemen, businessmen, and speculators, found life here to be profitable. (Smith was criticized for allegedly choosing the best land for himself.) In 1805, the crown revised its previous treaty with the Mississaugas of the New Credit to settle the important question of title to Toronto—in exchange for some cash and 149 barrels of goods, mostly rum. In British eyes, the land had been bought and sold; the Mississaugas would see it otherwise for centuries to come.

Meanwhile, "Muddy York" had little in the way of real economic activity, and accordingly little in the way of a town: a market square on what is now Jarvis Street, a wooden jail, 107 houses of wood and one of brick. The only other brick buildings in town were for the parliament of Upper Canada, located south of the town grid at the foot of today's Berkeley Street. Then, in 1813, invading Americans burned the parliament buildings. (The British would respond in kind the next year by torching the White House.) Parliament would be rebuilt, and many other things changed in the wake of the war: a flood of military spending goosed the economy and York gained a new merchant class. Even as New Town **[Area II]** became more fashionable, what was now called Old Town got a crop of brick Georgian houses, a stone St. James' Church, and more. King Street acquired long rows of distinguished brick shops **[1/5c]**. When Toronto was incorporated as a city in 1834, its heart was here.

Area I
Walk 1: Old Town
Walk 2: Front Street East

The Great Fire of 1849 destroyed many of the oldest buildings in Old Town; today only a few relics remain from that era, including the Bank of Upper Canada and its neighbour, the first post office. In the 1850s ambitious stone and brick buildings began to appear, spurred by the need to rebuild what had burned and the growing prosperity and population of the town—now a port and railway town, and nascent financial centre **[see Introduction, Area III]**. This boom generated the city's first truly fine buildings, St. Lawrence Hall **[1/4]**, an ambitious Anglican cathedral [1/13], a grand Greek Revival post office [1/30a], and an equally serious courthouse [1/31]. Still, the smallness of the place meant that nearly all of its components—market, churches, taverns, shops, courthouse, homes—sat cheek-by-jowl, with few elements of formal planning or indeed of public space. This was not a town for ceremony. A public corridor along the waterfront, the Walks and Gardens Reserve, was gradually eaten up by the needs of industry, and became sandwiched between wharves and railways. Front Street, which marked the original shoreline, was lined with gracious warehouses [1/18a, 1/18b] but the waterfront kept shifting with new landfill [see Introduction, Area XII].

Industrialization in Victorian Toronto chipped away at the mixed-use character of Old Town. Mills and factories sprang up [2/6 and 2/7]; the gas company built great works [2/8, 2/11], filling even the site of the first parliament buildings. That pattern would only continue through the middle of the 20th century; the oldest buildings in town [1/11] got taken over by manufacturing companies, occupied by downscale tenants—and then, as industries abandoned the central city, torn down. By the 1950s this was a district of parking lots and scrapyards between dusty Victorian buildings. It was ripe for modern urban renewal in a developer-friendly city.

Except it didn't quite turn out that way, thanks to some half-measures and the force of cultural memory. The O'Keefe Centre [1/24] was envisioned as part of a cultural complex to rival New York's Lincoln Center, with two halls, convention space, and an office tower, but the city only built the one hall. A few blocks away, St. Lawrence Hall became a rallying point for those who valued the city's history; it was restored in 1967, and a new market building [demolished] built to knit the historic market complex back

together. Then came 1972. Mayor David Crombie's election signalled a new era in city politics and a profound rethinking of what downtown was for and how it should be treated. Community consultation, a respect for history, and a disdain for the high-rise: this was the ethic shared by young planners and politicians. One product here was the St. Lawrence Neighbourhood [2/1], a physical expression of the era's urbanism which stands up very well today. Market Square [1/17] brought market housing back into the area. Now this was a slightly sleepy mixed-use neighbourhood, home to people of all classes, welcoming to tourists, sheltering to designers and artists at its fringes.

The boom that began in 2000 has changed that recipe. While most of the development action has been to the west [see Area II], high-rise housing has altered this part of the city at an increasing rate. The "Two Kings" policy [see Introduction, Area II] opened the gates for new construction and for conversions of loft buildings [2/20]. The corner of King and Sherbourne, once the heart of Muddy York, now has three tallish condo buildings, and that's becoming typical of the district. New retailers have joined a few pioneers [2/23], branding the King East Design District.

More people and more investment are giving the area's public realm something of a polish; the rebuilds of Market Street [1/2] and of Berczy Park [1/26] suggest that this area could be as pretty and sophisticated as a marquee historic neighbourhood ought to be. Yet the co-ops providing affordable housing aren't going anywhere; and new offices [2/23, 2/24] are bringing hundreds of workers into Old Town. What's emerging is a blend of homes, workplaces, culture, and even a courthouse [1/3]. The buildings are taller, the materials different, but this is a mix the people of Muddy York would recognize.

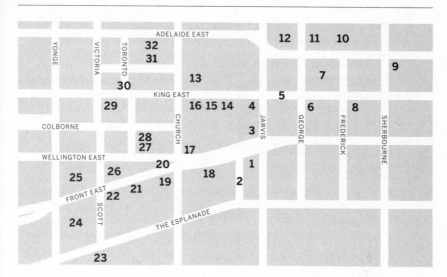

Walk 1: Old Town

1 South St. Lawrence Market, incorporating the second Toronto City Hall, 91 Front St. E., Henry Bowyer Lane, 1844–45; remodelled, J. Wilson Siddall with Beaumont Jarvis, 1901–02. A giant yet tidy structure, this red-brick behemoth neatly ingests its predecessor—the city hall of 1845—leaving part of that building's stone and yellow-brick outline and portals to form the only real decoration here. The city hall, a large pedimented three-storey affair, had done quintuple duty: arcaded market hall on the ground floor, shops and offices in the wings, council chamber on the second floor, police station in the basement.

All served well enough until the 1890s when city fathers moved to a more architecturally up-to-date and fashionably located edifice **[7/17]**. Rather than abandon this old civil servant, it was decided to make of it a large unified food hall, the South St. Lawrence Market. The cupolaed pediment and wings were all but eliminated and sweeping new arched walls built to boldly envelop the remaining shell. In need of refurbishing by the 1970s, this remarkable adaptation was given yet another lease on life when the former council chamber was imaginatively renovated to serve as a civic art gallery, and the elegantly classical rear façade of the original 1840s city hall uncovered to create a historical set for the modern-day market. *PM*

2 Market Street (The Esplanade to Front), DTAH (landscape architects), Taylor Smyth and Goldsmith Borgal, 2013. A bold act of city-building. Developer Paul Oberman **[see 1/14]** assembled the buildings on this historic block, and saw the potential to improve the street itself. He hired DTAH to do so, and they reconceived the sidewalk and roadway as one surface that could be used flexibly as patio, walkway, and parking depending on the season with the use of removable bollards. After Oberman's sudden death, his widow and partner Eve Lewis spent years seeing it through with the city. No doubt it has paid dividends for the developers; it continues to pay off, in comfort and pleasure, for thousands of market visitors each week. *AB*

2 | Market Street redevelopment

3 North St. Lawrence Market, Rogers Stirk Harbour & Partners and Adamson Associates, ongoing.
In 2010 the city held an international design competition for this, the fifth market building in this site's history, to replace an unloved 1967 Brutalist shed. The firm of Richard Rogers won with a scheme for a pair of linked sheds, wrapped in vertical fins and featuring their High-Tech detailing. Sadly, it was too good to be true. The city is also cramming in courthouses, a car-intensive use which does not belong on this block; and the Rogers design was simplified and cheapened before construction began. Still, what's being built retains an intelligent plan and a big architectural move: a glassy atrium will visually link the South Market **[1/1]** and St. Lawrence Hall **[1/4]** for the first time. *AB*

4 St. Lawrence Hall, 151 King St. E., William Thomas, 1850–51.
St. Lawrence Hall is Toronto's Victorian classicism at its very best. What is so memorable here is not just the exquisite carved stone and cast iron—perhaps the finest in the city—but the way in which the whole composition projects both delicacy *and* power. Thomas was one of a handful of accomplished British architects who came to Toronto in this period, bringing with him the ability to design in a multiplicity of appropriately evocative styles. The energy that flows through this, Thomas's municipal gem, made it the supreme representation of the booming town's new civic pride. With

majestic Corinthian-columned front and domed cupola, St. Lawrence Hall stands out grandly from its neighbours; yet, built right up to the sidewalk in line with shopfronts along King Street, it joins the streetscape too.

Like the city hall, St. Lawrence Hall housed a variety of services: municipal offices, shops, public market, and most notably, a sumptuous 100-foot-long Great Hall for public gatherings. Boasting an elaborate plaster ceiling, gleaming crystal chandeliers, and an abundance of gilt decoration, this third-floor assembly room hosted the city's most gala social, political, and cultural events for almost 75 years. Then, with the rest of the area, St. Lawrence Hall was sadly neglected in the 20th century. It was not until Canada's 100th birthday in 1967—and due to no little agitation by architect/historian Eric Arthur—that the building was finally recognized and then restored as Toronto's official Centennial project.

Today, with Market Street transformed into a pedestrian mall, St. Lawrence Hall shines anew as a distinguished symbol of the city's 19th-century past. *PM*

4 | St. Lawrence Hall

The rows of shops on the blocks proceeding from King Street East and Jarvis are among Toronto's most enduring, providing a nostalgic glimpse of the 19th-century commercial setting of St. Lawrence Hall and her sister civic structures.

5a 150–154 King St. E. (three-unit commercial block), 1850; rehabilitated, Clarke Darling Downey, 1988. Nicely restored examples of the quietly formal Georgian style which marked Toronto's architectural beginnings. Built as shops with residential flats and offices above, such buildings occasionally rose to five storeys, though even the four seen here were unusual for low-scale Toronto. This row replaced an earlier one of 1833 which had burned in the Great Fire of 1849. New safety bylaws enacted at that time dictated construction of the brick party walls rising above the roof. Yellow brick was employed to suggest the look of stone; very popular in the 1850s and '60s, the idea probably came from St. Lawrence Hall [1/4]. *PM*

5b King George Square (condominium apartments and retail), 168 King St. E., Burka Varacalli, 2000. Incorporates Sovereign Bank, 172 King St. E., George W. Gouinlock, 1907. A sensitive condo tower from the early days of the current boom, when 15 storeys was tall enough. The design of the three-storey podium does recall the Georgian era, albeit with quoins of precast concrete; better, the building steps around its Classical Revival neighbour, leaving Gouinlock's Ionic pilasters and the rooms behind them intact. A pleasant courtyard connects it to 150–154 King St. E. **[1/5a]**, and holds a statue of the shoemaker-capitalist-politician James Beaty. *AB*

5c 167–185 King St. E. (one-, two-, and four-unit commercial blocks), 1834–43. Though constructed at different times, the buildings in this block are similar, displaying considerate Georgian sensibility for the *streetscape entire*. The style follows the pattern seen across the street at no. 150–154 **[1/5a]**, but with more expensive stone lintels and sills. The attention-getting mansard roofs at nos. 173 and 185 were added in 1880 when the Second Empire style was all the rage and neighbourly good manners didn't seem so important. The same goal undoubtedly prompted the other, less felicitous alterations as well. This is the oldest *line* of buildings standing in Toronto. *PM*

6 Originally Little York Hotel, 187 King St. E., Langley Langley & Burke, 1879–80. Sculpturally rich Second Empire, with high mansard, elaborate dormers, and rhythmic fenestration to make the Little York profitably inviting. The hotel's name harks back to the town's early 1800s appellation when it was sometimes referred to as *little* York to differentiate it from *New York*. *PM*

7 George Brown College/originally Christie, Brown & Co., 200 King St. E. thru to Adelaide St. E., 1874; warehouse addition, 235 Adelaide St., Gouinlock & Baker, 1902; factory addition, Frederick near Adelaide St., Vaux Chadwick, 1907; King St. at Frederick St., factory and warehouse addition, Sproatt & Rolph, 1913; remodelled, Alan E. Moody, 1977. This picturesque architectural assortment, which once housed a venerable Toronto maker of biscuits, is now the St. James campus of George Brown College. Rehabilitation at its contextual best. *PM*

8 George Brown Chefs' House, 215 King St. E., Wickson & Gregg, 1914; renovations, Kearns Mancini with Gow Hastings, 2009. An open kitchen where the stakes are high: This is a place of learning for chef school students (there are classrooms upstairs). The building is likewise open to the street, with a light installation and elegant steel-and-glass canopies that give the utilitarian architecture a bit of spice. *AB*

9 Paul Bishop's Buildings, 363–365 Adelaide St. E., c. 1842. Restored, 2006. Built by the blacksmith Paul Bishop, these are among the few buildings to have survived the 1849 fire; they had been dramatically altered before being cleaned up to something like their original state. *AB*

10 George Brown School of Hospitality, 300 Adelaide St. E., Carruthers Shaw & Partners, 1986–87; alterations and addition, Kearns Mancini with Gow Hastings, 2009. The 1987 building is very much of its time, with quasi-Victorian façades of red and yellow brick, quasi-copper roof edge, and (of course) an atrium.

But it works—and works better with a new wing that adds rainbow-hued windows and puts a teaching kitchen on display at the sidewalk. *AB*

11 Post House Condos, 105 George St., Wallman Architects, 2015. Incorporates Bank of Upper Canada, 252 Adelaide St. E., William W. Baldwin, 1825–27, altered, John Howard, 1843–44, 1846; originally De La Salle Institute, 258 Adelaide St. E., Henry Langley, 1871–72; originally J.S. Howard house and First Post Office, 264 Adelaide St. E., 1833–34. Another condo tower that, like 168 King **[1/5b]**, tries to disappear and succeeds wonderfully. The tower itself is spandrel-glassy and anodyne, sitting on a hefty base of buff brick. You're unlikely to look up, anyway, as you explore the intimate courtyard it has created behind the three aged structures to the south. First, Toronto's first bank building, a neo-classical castle of well-wrought limestone that began with a flat roof; probably the best building in 1820s York. The bank had its head office here until it failed in 1866; at that point the building was purchased by the Christian Brothers for use as a Catholic boys' school. The school added Langley's Second Empire building to the east, and then in 1874 bought the third building in the sequence, built for the town's postmaster. After De La Salle went uptown in 1916, the buildings were bought by Christie's and later rescued by preservationist Sheldon Godfrey. The First Post Office at no. 264 is a museum and, again, a post office. *AB*

12 Vu (condominium apartments and retail), 112–116 George St., Hariri Pontarini and Young & Wright/IBI Group, 2010. Look east along Adelaide from downtown and you see this tower completing the vista. The high-rise here acknowledges that position in the city by tapering to a point. And the limestone-clad townhouses to the east are well-handled. But cheap materials kill the architecture: so much green glass! *AB*

13 Cathedral Church of St. James, 106 King St. E., Cumberland & Ridout, 1849–53; additions, Langley Langley & Burke, 1874. Sober English Gothic and utterly dignified, St. James' perfectly proclaimed its ties with the British homeland and with its conservative, elitist bishop, John Strachan, who for a time practically ran the province. This is the fourth St. James' on the site; construction began after the Great Fire of 1849 destroyed its predecessor. The design by transplanted British architect Frederic Cumberland tried to follow dogma of the day in drawing on English prototypes with a porch/aisled nave/chancel plan that was studiously expressed on the exterior. The idea was to assert architectural correctness—and thereby religious superiority—for all to see. But the chancel ended up being shorter than the theorists would have it, and the tower, spire, porches, and finials were not added for "all to see" until 20 years later. At 306 feet, the tower and spire are the tallest in Canada, second tallest in North America after New York's St. Patrick's.

The monochromatic exterior—the stone dressings stand out hardly at all from the yellow brick—and the blunt aspect of the Gothic forms combine to make St. James' very stolid and serious-looking. The interior is more dramatic, with an elaborate hammer-beam ceiling, marbled apsidal chancel (where Bishop Strachan is buried), impressive Queen Anne organ cases, and a stained glass window (to the Hon. William Jarvis) by Tiffany & Co. of New York, c. 1900. *PM*

14 King James Place (offices and retail), 145 King St. E., Kuwabara Payne McKenna Blumberg, 1991. Incorporates façade of shop, possibly John G. Howard, c. 1850. A firmly Modernist office building that harmonizes with the Georgian streetscape. The tall three-storey front picks up some horizontal alignments from the neighbour **[1/15]**, but its façade is limestone and a pinkish-red brick, expertly detailed. (Architects call those shallow channels "reveals.") The façadectomy in the middle is deftly handled; the octagonal tower turns the corner into pedestrian Market Street. This

14 | King James Place

16b Toronto Sculpture Garden, 115 King St. E., opened 1981. From 1938 to 1981 this was a parking lot. Ever since, with a brief hiatus, it has been a place for contemporary art and contemplation—and also a link from St. James, via Market Square **[1/17]**, to Front Street. The waterfall and ivied walls, designed by city staff, owe a debt to Zion & Breen's Paley Park in Manhattan. *AB*

17 | Market Square Condominiums

fine project, which won a Governor General's Award for KPMB in 1991, is also a credit to the developer, the late Paul Oberman. There's no great architecture without a great client. *AB*

15 Originally Army & Navy Clothing Store. York Belting Building, 133–135 King St. E. (two-unit commercial block), possibly William Thomas, 1842; altered, Langley & Burke, 1887–88. This is one of Toronto's most alluring buildings, juxtaposing the decorative virtuosity of brick and terracotta with surprising and dramatic proportions in an adventurous design by Langley & Burke. The two-storey-high double windows—great arches of multi-paned, metal-framed glass springing from a heavy metal beam—had probably never been seen in the city before this. The drama is even more pronounced today with new glazing stretching clear across the ground-storey front. A valuable gem. *PM/AB*

16a 107–111 and 125 King St. E. (commercial blocks), 1841; no. 109 remodelled, c. 1885. These four shops remained standing after the Great Fire of 1849 and so predate some of those on King Street east of St. Lawrence Hall, but they differ little in style. The elegance of the Georgian design—handsomely revived at nos. 111 and 125—depends on the careful proportions and unerring placement of the windows in the façade. Joseph Rogers, a furrier and hatter, presided at no. 109 for over 30 years. *PM*

17 Market Square Condominiums, 80 Front St. E. and 35 Church St., Jerome Markson, 1982. One of the best buildings of the era in Toronto: dense mid-rise housing dressed in the red and yellow brick of the 19th-century city. (The masonry even came from the Don Valley Brick Works.) By borrowing the massing and window patterns of the nearby lofts, it fits in, and yet the complex retains a residential attitude through its chamfered corners, bay windows, and pedestrian walkways **[see 1/16b]**. The two buildings surround a private raised courtyard; this configuration is common in Europe and makes a good city, and yet the politics and economics of Toronto development mean such projects will be rare. *AB*

The warehouses along the south side of Front Street East form one of the most compelling streetscapes in Toronto. Virile, flamboyant, yet solid, these three- and four-storey buildings perfectly represented the prosperity and self-confidence of the 19th-century mercantile city. They were put up in a period when there was much commercial activity, and they included space for offices and showrooms as well as storage. Although interiors were generally unadorned, exteriors drew on several styles for architectural embellishment, including Georgian, Second Empire, and Renaissance Revival. The latter especially, with its vision of a vigorous Venetian commerce—not to mention its profusion of windows—greatly appealed to the practical merchants. The buildings were covered in flashy red and yellow brick or august stone, with a few in newly useful cast iron.

18a LCBO/originally Edward Leadlay Co., 87 Front St. E. (warehouse), 1865; additions, including mansard, 1871; altered later. A fine warehouse with Georgian proportions plus a Second Empire mansard roof. Leadlay was a dealer in "Wools, Hides, Skins & Tallow," which paid for a grandly picturesque house in the west end [15/15]. *PM*

18b St. Lawrence Lofts, 81A Front St. E. Incorporates 81–83 and 85 Front St. E. (warehouses), 1861; originally Alexander M. Smith Co., 77–79 Front St. E. (warehouse), 1861. Condominium apartment conversion, ERA, 2002. Five old lofts converted into new residences, with hardly any outward sign of the change. The western three are Renaissance Revival in a staid red brick, the eastern two much more glamorous with deep brick piers and round-topped windows. *AB*

18c 71 Front St. E. (offices), Moriyama & Teshima, 1981. One of the city's most gracious infill buildings. *PM*

18d 67–69 Front St. E. (warehouse), 1877; restored, 1987. The meticulous restoration of this ornate Renaissance Revival building received a Toronto Historical Board award of merit. *PM*

19 The Berczy (condominium apartments), 63 Front St. E., Young & Wright/ IBI Group with ERA, 2014. Arguably the most famous corner in Toronto, and we get this muddle? The base is precast concrete pretending to be stone, not convincing anyone; the brick middle tries to copy the neighbour lofts, not very well; the top is a cloud of pale, grim spandrel, perhaps trying to disappear into the sky. If only. Visit Paul Raff's *Shoreline Commemorative* on the Church Street side, and then avert your eyes. *AB*

20 Gooderham Building, 49 Wellington St. E., David Roberts, 1891–92. Toronto's very own "flatiron" building, predating its larger, more famous New York cousin by ten years. The triangular shape was dictated by the awkward site where Wellington and Front Streets intersect (the first street followed the city's grid pattern, the second the line of the waterfront). Built by a scion of the influential

20 | Flatiron (Gooderham) Building

distillery family as headquarters for his financial empire, this theatrical endeavour owes its eye-catching appeal to more than just shape. With a richly textured façade and kingly chateau-esque towered roof that still dominates this busy corner, the building stands as apt symbol of the Gooderham family's powerful position in the community. Roberts also designed a number of the distillery buildings and many prominent Gooderham residences about town [12/21a, 19/31].

The punning trompe l'oeil artwork on the rear of the Gooderham Building entitled "Flatiron Mural," created by Derek Besant in 1980, is a famous Toronto landmark in its own right. The windows depicted are not those of the Gooderham Building; they are copies from the Perkins warehouse across the street at 41–43 Front Street East [1/21b]. PM

21a Originally Dixon Building, 45–49 Front St. E. (three-unit warehouse), possibly Walter R. Strickland, 1872–73. Toronto's only remaining building with a totally cast-iron façade and a tribute to architectural illusion. This building really does look as if it were constructed of painted wood and stone, but the whole front—except for windows—consists of units of cast iron fabricated at the Toronto foundry of W. Hamilton & Son. (Cast-iron aficionados will be able to tell by the crisp, hard-edged quality of the detail; the rest of us might look for telltale signs of rust!) The landlord was real estate speculator B. Homer Dixon [see 15/2]. His first tenants were, west to east: John Smith & Co.; Copp, Clark & Co.; and the Canada Vinegrowers' Association. PM

21b Originally F. & G. Perkins Co./ formerly Perkins, Ince & Co., 41–43 Front St. E. (two-unit warehouse), Macdougall & Darling, 1874–75. An exuberant Victorian warehouse redolent of Venetian *palazzi* with its variety of arched windows and red and yellow brick standing in for the colourfulness of Renaissance marble. The Perkinses were wholesale grocers. PM

21c Beardmore Building/originally T. Griffith Co., 35–39 Front St. E. (three-unit warehouse), David Roberts, 1872–73. Yet another flamboyant façade to enhance mundane warehousing. Griffith was a wholesale grocer; Beardmore a manufacturer of leather goods and owner of one of Toronto's most notable houses [14/11]. PM

22 St. Lawrence Centre for the Arts, 27 Front St. E., Gordon S. Adamson & Associates, 1967–70; interior remodelled, Thom Partnership, 1982; lobby, theatre, and exterior alterations, Paul Syme with 3rd Uncle, 2007. Around the Centennial year of 1967, Brutalism was the language of cultural buildings across Canada. Here, too, with this complex of two theatres forming a tough, asymmetrical companion to the O'Keefe [1/24]. The problematic larger theatre was soon rebuilt by Ron Thom, and 3rd Uncle added a friendlier character to the street face and interiors, but this is a period piece and a handsome brute. May it escape the indignity visited upon its neighbour [1/24] across the street. AB

23 The Esplanade (hotel and residences), 25 The Esplanade, Matsui Baer Vanstone, 1989. Post-Modernism at its most ridiculous: a slab of 19th-century Paris stretched out to 33 storeys, melted into the shape of a flatiron, and dropped into 1980s Toronto. The attached Novotel Hotel is at least the right height, but still the wrong country and century. AB

24 Sony Centre for the Performing Arts/ originally O'Keefe Centre for the Performing Arts, 1 Front St. E., Earle C. Morgan with Page & Steele (Peter Dickinson, design architect), 1956–60; renovations, Kuwabara Payne McKenna Blumberg, 1995. The L Tower (residences), 8 The Esplanade, Daniel Libeskind with Page & Steele/IBI Group, ongoing. Plaza, Claude Cormier, ongoing. A cautionary tale. This hall is full of architectural drama, courtesy of the ambitious Brit Dickinson and engineer Morden Yolles, from its grandiose lobbies to the broad spans of the hall itself. When it opened in 1960, it promised a glamorous new Toronto: its cantilevered canopy welcomed crowds to the premiere of the musical *Camelot* with Richard Burton. And yet the house proved less than ideal for the Canadian Opera Company and the National Ballet of Canada, who eventually left **[7/12]**. What remained was a big city-owned theatre running a deficit, and a 40-year-old building unloved by politicians.

After sketchy plans for new cultural institutions fell through, what was left in the mid 2000s was the valuable site and a residential developer. Daniel Libeskind, then at the height of his fame, added some cachet to the scheme. The curvy tower is formally interesting and well-detailed up top, though its base is extremely poor. It features the architect's trademark shards **[8/43]**, now stripped of any symbolic meaning.

The problem is the relationship between theatre and tower: there isn't one. Materially they are in two different worlds, and the 50-storey volume utterly upsets the integrity of Dickinson's composition. All this for a payoff that now looks paltry. To pay the bills, the city of Toronto has melted down its silverware into shards. *AB*

25 A.E. LePage Building, 33 Yonge St. thru to Scott St., Webb Zerafa Menkes Housden, 1982. In the canonical postcard view of the city, looking at the Gooderham Building **[1/20]**, this is the shiny thing in the background. It belongs there. *AB*

26 Berczy Park, Front to Wellington St., Scott to Church St., opened 1975; renovation, Claude Cormier (landscape architect), 2017. This block was once filled with a cluster of well-wrought warehouses like those across the street; these were demolished for parking in the 1960s. (There was a time when this neighbourhood had a *lot* of parking lots.) In the '70s it became a welcome green space of undistinguished design. The fine redesign by Cormier includes a crisp plaza, new streetscape inspired by Market Street **[1/2]**, and a cast-iron fountain ornamented with sculptures of dogs. A tribute to our four-legged friends, or a poke at Toronto's willingness to let yappy canines rule our public spaces? *AB*

27 Originally Hutchison Building, 36–42 Wellington St. E. (four-unit commercial block), 1854–55. A genteel Greek Revival quartet of shops parading an unusual band of half-windows at the attic storey (at no. 42, the windows became full-size when the roof was raised). In 1855, shop tenants included a saloonkeeper and a dry goods merchant. The landlord was John Hutchison, soon to become Toronto's 13th mayor, after which the depression of 1857 forced him to leave the province. Better times followed, however, and Boyd and Arthurs, prominent wholesale grocers, next assumed all four premises. *PM*

28a Originally Milburn Co., 47–55 Colborne St. (five-unit warehouse and commercial block), E.J. Lennox, 1887–89. Lush Richardsonian Romanesque by Toronto's master practitioner. Cast-iron columns alternating with those of masonry at the ground storey made possible large expanses of glass for the shopfronts. Owner Milburn was a wholesaler of patent medicines and occupied two shops; other tenants purveyed beer supplies and wine and liquor. A heady brew here, architectural and otherwise. *PM*

28b Originally McRae Co., 41–45 Colborne St. (three-unit warehouse and commercial block), 1888–89. The same rich red brick and deep-set windows as next door, but here smooth light-coloured stone is the decorative contrast. Such crisp icing on a Romanesque cake makes for a very unusual morsel, indeed. *PM*

29 Le Meridien King Edward Hotel, 37 King St. E., Henry Ives Cobb with E.J. Lennox, 1901–02; 18-storey addition, Esenwien & Johnson, 1920; alterations, ERA, ongoing. Fashionable Edwardian classicism to herald a new monarchy and a new era of metropolitanism for Toronto (the design was by one of America's leading architects). The King Eddie reigned supreme as the city's de luxe establishment hostelry for almost 60 years before the steady decline of the neighbourhood finally overtook it. Today, thanks to the area's renaissance, the celebrated plasterwork captivates anew in the restaurant. *PM*

Toronto Street was once among the city's most beautiful, a block-long tout ensemble of gracious three- and four-storey office buildings. "Progress" has replaced most of the early structures and what remains is of mixed quality.

30a Morgan Meighen & Associates/ originally Seventh Post Office/formerly Department of Customs/formerly Bank of Canada, 10 Toronto St., Cumberland & Ridout, 1851–53. In the 1850s this was lauded as a "plain but commanding" building, and it's still true. Dignified with a chaste four-columned Ionic portico recessed between side piers, the one-time post office confidently projects harmony and order in the best tradition of the Greek Revival. The grace of the design extended to a Doric-columned screen and counter in the interior, prominent royal arms of England at the roofline, and curved rear corners accommodating a carriageway that originally circled the building. Mail delivery was not general then and most people had to come to the post office to get their mail. But it was open seven days a week, daily 8 a.m. to 7 p.m.; Sundays 9–10 and 4–5! *PM*

30b 20 Toronto Street/originally Excelsior Life (offices), Marani, Morris & Allan, 1964. 36 Toronto St./originally Excelsior Life (offices), E.J. Lennox, 1914; incorporates Millichamp Building, 31 Adelaide St. E., Smith & Gemmell, 1875; renovation and addition, Strong Associates, 1987. Toronto's insurance companies have never built innovative architecture, but at times they have built well. Lennox's 11-storey terracotta skyscraper, at the time the tallest on the street, employs a three-part composition of base, shaft, and what Lennox called "frieze"—a 2-storey quasi-temple studded with Corinthian columns. This was later joined to a new tower on Victoria Street with a late-modernist atrium in the middle. Robert Morris's **[7/13]** 1964 tower follows the same three-part strategy as Lennox's building: its rooftop temple houses mechanicals. With punched windows in otherwise flat façades of Queenston limestone, this embodies a certain strain of Toronto architecture: bland, conservative but deeply competent. *AB*

30c Counsel Trust/originally Consumers' Gas Company of Toronto Chambers, 17 Toronto St., Grant & Dick, 1876; additions, David B. Dick, 1882, 1899. Pedimented doorway, polished red granite columns, fluted Corinthian pilasters, scalloped lunettes, velouted keystones, modillioned cornice, bosses and friezes, string courses and garlands—this is Toronto's flamboyant Renaissance Revival palace *par excellence*. That David Dick was one of Toronto's best late 19th-century architects can well be seen with this masterful conception. *PM*

30d Originally Trust & Loan Co., 25 Toronto St. (office building), Henry Macdougall, 1870–71. Toronto's Victorian version of a dignified 16th-century Florentine *palazzo*, the reticent strain of Renaissance Revival that seldom garners the attention it deserves. This is truly one of the city's most refined buildings, though it does need its cornice and parapet, removed some years ago for fear they would fall on someone's head. *PM*

31 Courthouse Square (park), 10 Court St., Janet Rosenberg & Associates (landscape architects), Carruthers Shaw and Partners (architects), 1995. A landscape rich with evocative smells, textures, and visual detail. Falling water; a cobbled pathway between espaliered crab apple trees; a jumble of herbs that grew here in the early days of York; smooth concrete and a slab of granite on which to rest or declaim. This new square suggests a rich public realm, and imagines a powerful role for the courthouse once again. *AB*

32 Terroni (restaurant)/originally York County Magistrates Court, 57 Adelaide St. E., Cumberland & Ridout, 1851–53; interior renovations, Giannone Petricone, 2008–15. Drawing on the same repertoire as for his Seventh Post Office [1/30a], Cumberland here made the Greek Revival not only commanding but downright awesome. The weighty square Doric columns still dominate this block, much as they must have done in the 1850s when the building boasted two long brick side wings. The formidable building now houses the grandest of the local Terroni restaurant chain—who have commissioned interiors from Giannone Petricone that offer a very Italian blend of history, humour, and *sprezzatura*. The curves of that red chandelier are based on a plan of the racetrack that hosts the Italian Grand Prix. *AB*

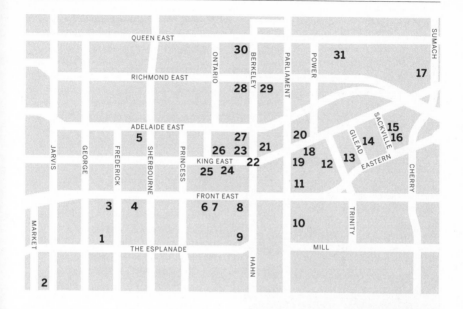

Walk 2: Front Street East

1 St. Lawrence Neighbourhood, Phases I and II, Canadian National railway tracks to Front St., Jarvis to Parliament St. (housing complex), Irving Grossman, Klein & Sears, Vaclav Kuchar & Associates, Boris A. Lebedinsky, Jerome Markson, Matsui Baer Vanstone Freeman, Robinson & Heinrichs, J.E. Sievenpiper, Sillaste & Nakashima, Thom Partnership, 1977–82. In early-'70s Toronto, so-called reform politicians under David Crombie rejected the big ideas of urban renewal **[see Walk 10]**. They answered with this: an entire neighbourhood that was radical in its own way, rejecting every point of Modernist city planning. It is not a superblock but extends the city's historic grid, and places houses, community services, and retail to provide "eyes on the street." It is mixed-use, putting housing and schools within metres of St. Lawrence Market. Parkland does not surround the buildings, but forms a central strip lined by roads and sidewalks. And, crucially, it is neither entirely market-rate nor subsidized housing, but a mix, in mid-rises of similar size that define the edges of the blocks and provide courtyards. All this was

1 | St. Lawrence Neighbourhood

the product of extensive community consultation.

The result was novel; there was zero historic precedent for this building form in Toronto. Yet the place now fits with the city, a tribute to the planners. (Allan Littlewood oversaw the planning, with major input from Baird & Sampson, and collaborators including Jane Jacobs.)

The individual buildings do suffer from a sameness of scale and material: this is 50 shades of red brick, just as the West Don

1 | David B. Archer Co-op

Lands area [see Introduction, Area XII] built four decades later is 50 shades of grey. But there is finesse. Jerome Markson's David B. Archer Co-operative, a U-shaped perimeter block that bridges two streets, is permeable and pleasantly complex for the pedestrian, and yet navigable. Irving Grossman's Crombie Park Apartments buffer the neighbourhood against what was an industrial site on Jarvis, forming a dignified defensive wall of gridded brick. More of that boldness—and more retail and workplaces—would in retrospect have helped, but this was all the same a visionary project. *AB*

2 Market Wharf (condominium apartments and retail), 1 Market St., architects-Alliance, 2013. At a glance, this continues the St. Lawrence Neighbourhood **[2/1]** — the base responds to the Crombie Park Apartments across the street—but there's a tall tower on top, reflecting the realities of market housing in contemporary Toronto. It is an interesting scheme, with sixth-floor townhouses facing a courtyard. Don't miss Paul Raff's sculpture *Wavelengths* in the parking garage. *AB*

3 Originally W. Davies & Co./formerly Toronto Safeworks, 139–145 Front St. E. (factory), Gundry & Langley, 1866–67; rebuilt after fire, William W. Blair, 1883; additions, 1890, 1907. Typical Toronto Victorian factory, with yellow-brick relieving arches and piers standing out as both structural members and simple decoration against red-brick walls. In 1867, this corner was the William Davies pork packing plant. The premises were taken over in 1871 by J. & J. Taylor Toronto Safeworks, which was responsible for the buildings we see today, including the 20th-century all-red-brick extension. Safes were big business in the 19th century: fireproof, burglarproof, and lovely pieces of iron to decorate the office. *PM*

4 Young People's Theatre/originally Toronto Street Railway Co. stables/ formerly Toronto Street Railway Co. electric power house, 165 Front St. E., David Roberts, 1887–88; remodelled, Zeidler Partnership, 1976–77. This handsomely rehabilitated building, boldly reminiscent of a medieval fortress, is what remains of a much larger complex designed to house the nucleus of municipal transport, the horse-drawn streetcar. (The horses were stabled on the first two floors; the hayloft was on the third.) *PM*

5 | Mozo

7 | Joey and Toby Tanenbaum Opera Centre

5 Mozo (condominium apartments), 333 Adelaide St. E., architectsAlliance, 2003. To the south and east, this is warehouse-scaled red brick with punched windows; behind and to the west, an all-glass tall apartment tower. The double-height retail space makes a beautiful corner. Peter Clewes of aA and Howard Cohen's Context Development **[see 2/2]** set an excellent precedent here; too bad other developers haven't copied it very well. *AB*

6 219–221 Front St. E. (factory), 1885. Yellow-brick decoration in brisk splashes across the front, with waves of round-headed Renaissance Revival windows lighting deep interiors. Originally woollens were made at no. 219; cigar boxes at 221. *PM*

7 Joey and Toby Tanenbaum Opera Centre/originally Standard Woolen Mills, 223–237 Front St. E. (factory), E.J. Lennox, 1882; three-storey addition, 1893; additions, including fourth storey, 1904; renovated, Bregman & Hamann with Arcop Associates, 1987. How lovingly detailed the 19th century made a factory: curved relieving arches accenting windows, prominent piers standing out from walls, decorative brick panels, corbelled friezes. And how lovingly detailed the 20th century has rehabilitated it: conscientious cleaning,

accurate restoration including black creosote highlighting yellow brick, sparky 1800s-looking sign. Inside all are offices, archives, and library for the Canadian Opera Company **[see 7/12]**. *PM*

8 Joey and Toby Tanenbaum Opera Centre/originally Consumers' Gas Co. purifying house, 239 Front St. E., probably David B. Dick, 1887–88; rehabilitated, Arcop Associates, 1985. Consumers' Gas Company began generating coal gas here in the late 1860s, eventually occupying all the Front Street blocks between Berkeley and Trinity Streets. Most of the complex has been demolished, but these buildings remain as striking reminders of how architecturally accomplished utilitarian factories can be. Rows of great stone-capped piers, pinnacles, fancy brickwork, stepped gables—none of these were necessary to make gas, but they did announce corporate pride and confidence. No less so for the Canadian Opera Company, whose architects have orchestrated here one of Toronto's grandest comebacks. Rehabilitated as a huge, handsome rehearsal hall, no. 239 stars again as a significant building in the life of the city. *PM*

9a Berkeley Street Theatre, 26 Berkeley St., Strickland & Symons, 1887; renovated 1976. These were engine houses and condensing houses for Consumers' Gas **[2/8]**. Their Romanesque pomp and grand interior spaces have suited them well for theatre, and the brick ornament of the façades is awfully dramatic. *AB*

9b Berkeley Castle/originally Toronto Knitting and Yarn Factory/formerly Toronto Storage Co., 2 Berkeley St. and 250 The Esplanade, c. 1866; additions, Charles J. Gibson, 1896, 1898, 1905, 1909, 1910; remodelled, A.J. Diamond & Partners, 1979–82. Joseph Simpson brought his knitting and yarn works to this corner in 1874, expanding piecemeal over the next 30 years as the need arose, with scant interest in architectural uniformity. Today, the six-building complex is a congenial commercial and office addition to the St. Lawrence Neighbourhood, having been smartly homogenized by A.J. Diamond & Partners, who moved in for a while. *PM*

Ontario's first parliament buildings were located on the west side of Parliament Street, at the foot of what is now called Berkeley Street, from 1797 until they burned in the War of 1812 and then, again, in 1824. Much of the site is now government-owned and there are plans for an interpretive centre.

10 45 Parliament St. (data centre), WZMH, 2016. Does the Internet have a street address? It has many, and this big box is among them, housing private servers next to a spring of bandwidth. The porcelain panels on the façade are meant to recall the punch cards used in early computer programming. They don't, but they are interesting to look at. *AB*

11 Toronto Police Service 51 Division/ originally Consumers' Gas Co. purifying house, 51 Parliament St., Bond & Smith, 1898–99; additions, Frederick H. Herbert, 1902, 1904; renovated, Stantec and ERA, 2004. Another industrial stunner for the gas

company, converted into a police station that is encouragingly more urban and less fortress-like than the force's earlier architecture **[5/29b, 7/24]**. *AB*

Workers at the Gooderham & Worts Distillery **[23/9]** populated this Victorian neighbourhood, which had gentrified slowly and has now gotten a boost in prosperity and visibility from the redevelopment of the Distillery District.

12 Enoch Turner Schoolhouse/originally Trinity Street School/formerly Trinity Church Sunday School, 106 Trinity St., Gundry & Langley, 1848. Addition, 1869. Spunk and charm in soft yellow banding and exclamation-point Gothic windows, this is Toronto's oldest standing school building. The Protestant Irish in this working-class district were too poor to send their children to the school at St. James', and the city council balked at public education, so a beneficent neighbourhood employer, the brewer Enoch Turner, paid for Trinity Street School to be built on the grounds of Little Trinity Church. When free education was finally instituted, the school board took the facility over in 1851. Never happy with its coeducation and church-related programs, however, the board built Palace Street School in 1859 and in fact as well as deed this became Trinity Church Sunday School. *PM*

12 | Enoch Turner Schoolhouse

13a 105–109 Trinity St. (three-house row), 1885. Workers' cottages built in Second Empire style and delightful for their immodest—and successful—aims at all the grand effects: decorative slate roof, sawn curlicues in dormer pediments, yellow brick patterning the red. *PM*

13b 115–127 Trinity St. (seven-house row), 1886–87. A very old-fashioned Georgian style for this late date, but two full storeys high and all brick. The white-painters of the '80s are being joined by the black-painters of the '10s. *PM/AB*

14 7–15 Gilead Place (townhouses), Brian Kucharski, 2009. The nicest houses in the neighbourhood are hidden in this laneway. Designed and developed by an experienced architect, this Modernist row is thoroughly detailed and looks good both from a distance and nose-to-brick. The orange spandrel panels are a very 1960s touch. *AB*

15 21–33 Sackville St. (seven units of original eight-house row), 1890. Another row of Second Empire cottages for workers, radiantly strung together by yellow-brick necklaces. Though flatter and less sculptural than many "French-roof" houses, they are exciting for their colour contrast. A knifed-off eighth house originally completed the ensemble. *PM*

16 Inglenook Community High School/ originally St. Lawrence Ward School, 19 Sackville St., William G. Storm, 1887. Unadorned yellow brick, tall light-giving windows, girls on one side, boys on the other—what could be simpler? *PM*

17 52 Sumach St./19–21 Bright St. (condominium apartments and houses), Quadrangle, 2010. One of three small mid-rise buildings built here around 2010 by a young entrepreneur, Les Mallins of Streetcar Developments. This one is the most interesting for the way it reaches onto charming Bright Street. As with the other buildings at 510 and 569 King St. E., its design could be refined, but the scale and terraced form make for friendly intensification. Toronto should have hundreds more buildings like this—and has tried to encourage them—but they remain rarities. *AB*

18a Little Trinity Anglican Church, 425 King St. E., Henry Bowyer Lane, 1843–45; restored after fire, F. Hilton Wilkes, 1961. Built after Anglicans in this neighbourhood complained that they could not afford pew rents at St. James', and without any great Ecclesiological pretensions, Little Trinity turns out to be one of our most captivating churches. The building is beautifully proportioned, but it's the scenic Tudor Gothic details that really make it sparkle: octagonal corner buttresses, crenellated tower, energetic wishbone drip-moulds. *PM*

18b Little Trinity House, 417 King St. E., Cumberland & Storm, 1853. The rectory: a Georgian box lightly dusted with Gothic details. With the church, an idyllic setpiece. *PM*

18c Little Trinity Annex/originally Francis Beale Buildings, 399–403 King St. E., c. 1850; renovations and additions, DTAH with ERA, 2015. Two Georgian shops here were long owned by the church **[2/18a]**; now their spruced-up façades front a new building that provides event space and community services. *AB*

19 The Derby (condominium residences and retail), 393 King St. E., Ron Thom and Dermot J. Sweeny, 1988. Perhaps the first new-build in Toronto to create "lofts" for residential or live/work use. The vaguely historicist idiom stands up well. *AB*

20 | 334 King St. E.

20 334 King St. E. (offices and retail)/ originally Aluminum and Crown Stopper Co., Frederick H. Herbert, 1911–12; renovated 2007. Ornamented industrial for the early 20th century, with a lovely Edwardian entrance sited to take advantage of the angled street corner. The company made "wood bungs, tops, spikes, caps, bottling wire, wax cork," and their own invention, the Crown Stopper. *PM*

21 55–79 Berkeley St. (thirteen-house row), 1871–72; renovated, Joan Burt, 1969. These simple 19th-century workmen's cottages were among the first in Toronto to be recycled. Architect Burt became known for her rehabilitated grey-stucco rows **[see 3/23]**. *PM*

22a Italinteriors/originally Reid & Co. Lumber, 359 King St. E. (commercial block), 1891–92; renovated, Peter Hamilton, 1984; store interior, Bruce Kuwabara, 2005; additions, 2005. The block's one Victorian building, and very Victorian it is: a great red-brick construction assembled with a sparkling assortment of window types—Gothic, Romanesque, Queen Anne—and strings of swirling ornament. This was all surely wonderful advertisement for the first owner, a purveyor of building supplies. Now the shop sells fine European furniture. *PM/AB*

22b Originally Garibaldi House, 302 King St. E. (commercial block), 1859. In the 1800s, this jogged corner signalled the last street in town and the point at which travellers headed their horses northeast along the road to Ottawa. Many an inn and tavern stood nearby to help ease the arduous cross-province journey. No. 302 was a roughcast hotel called Garibaldi House in the 1860s. *PM*

23 Klaus by Nienkamper/originally Small Row/formerly James Greenshields Grocery, 298–300 King St. E. (two units of original three-house row), 1845; store renovation, Joan Burt, 1967. A very old red-brick Georgian row, featuring yellow-brick quoins and belt courses, stone lintels and sills, and huge double chimneys. The row was owned by Charles Small, son of Simcoe's fellow officer Major John Small. (Their large family villa, Berkeley House, stood across King Street until 1891 when no. 359 **[2/22a]** was built.) Charles Small's first tenants in this grand three-storey ensemble were Henry Sullivan, professor of anatomy at King's College; John Marling, a "gentleman"; and brother James Small, provincial solicitor-general. In 1879, no. 300 was enlarged by thrusting the front wall out to the sidewalk, at which time the houses acquired their shopfronts. Greenshields purveyed groceries to the carriage trade from this site until 1956, one of the city's longest-lived enterprises. And now the Nienkamper family has been here half a century, purveying their furniture and the best in contemporary global design. *PM/AB*

24 Globe and Mail Centre, 351 King St. E., Diamond Schmitt, 2016. Into the *Sun's* former parking lot comes the *Globe and Mail*—having left its own long-time head-quarters **[3/28]** across town. No presses here, but the building includes a top-level conference space instead. The architecture is rather showy for Diamond, with cantilevered blocks of light-blue and dark-blue glass sliding this way and that. *AB*

25 King East Centre/formerly Toronto Sun Building, 1975–91; renovations and addition, Pellow Associates, 2013. The upstart *Sun* newspaper settled here in the 1970s with both its newsroom and presses. In the 2000s, the declining paper eventually shrank to one floor and then left entirely. The Post-Modern building has been split between George Brown College, Coca-Cola Canada's head offices (moved from Don Mills), and retail. The renovations look cheap and half-baked, especially the curvy glass office addition and the Front Street retail. *AB*

26 SAS Canada (offices and retail), 280 King St. E., NORR, 2006. A pioneer in bringing corporate offices to this area; among the very first commercial buildings in Toronto to be certified under the LEED environmental ratings system; and not a bad neighbour. The tall retail spaces have attracted home-design showrooms and added some grace to the block. *AB*

27 Alumnae Theatre/originally Firehall No. 4, 70 Berkeley St., 1859; alterations and additions, Grand & Irving, 1871; altered, A. Frank Wickson, 1903; remodelled for theatre, Ron Thom, 1971. The once-familiar firehall tower has been missing since 1952, but probably the boldest window in Toronto is still here, bursting with stone voussoirs and crowned with a boisterous shaped gable. Quite appropriate for Canada's oldest theatrical company, originally the University Alumnae Dramatic Club. *PM*

28 106–108 and 110–112 Berkeley St. (two double houses), 1886. Two splendid examples of Toronto's native Bay-n-Gable design, an inspired marriage of bay windows and gingerbread gables that was consummated all across the city in the late 1870s and early 1880s. *PM*

29 Originally Sheldon Ward house, 115 Berkeley St., 1845; altered, 1881. The 1880s remodelling, which altered this large Georgian-chimneyed single house to resemble its neighbours, has long hidden the fact, but this is one of the oldest houses standing in Toronto. It was put up as his own showy bichrome house by Sheldon Ward, a brickmaker and prominent city councilman. Poor Ward only lived here one year. In 1846, he "lost his life by a scaffold on a building in process of erection giving way with him." *PM*

30 Berkeley Church/originally Berkeley Street Wesleyan Methodist Church/ formerly Berkeley Street United Church, 315 Queen St. E., Smith & Gemmell, 1871–72. A bulky Methodist "preaching box" spiked with energetic Gothic windows and drip-moulds that are especially crisp for being rendered in cast iron. It's now an event venue; the two buildings to the west, which formed an interesting courtyard space, are targeted for high-rise intensification. *PM/AB*

31 St. Paul's Roman Catholic Church, 93 Power St. at Queen St. E., Joseph Connolly, 1887–89. One is not prepared to come across the serene grandeur of a Renaissance basilica in Toronto—the Roman Catholics were the only denomination to try it—and that St. Paul's is such a poised version complete with 129-foot bell tower is all the more remarkable. This church has been likened to the 15th-century Santa Maria Novella in Florence, with the green and white marble of that edifice re-created here in rough Credit Valley stone and smooth Cleveland limestone. The light-filled interior displays all the lucidity and sense of visual order inimitably associated with the Renaissance: a barrel-vaulted nave separated from the aisles by a graceful Ionic arcade; short mural-graced transepts; and a lovely triple-apsed chancel. The church we see today replaced an earlier St. Paul's built for this working-class community in 1826. Power Street was named for Bishop Michael Power, first Roman Catholic bishop of Toronto, who died in 1847 while nursing the sick in a cholera epidemic. *PM*

Area II
Walk 3: New Town and South Core
Walk 4: King Street West

Welcome to the Wild West. What began as a genteel extension of the Town of York is now Toronto's Entertainment District and a hotbed of high-rise development—the densest, fastest-changing part of the metropolis, and still far from complete.

York was founded in 1793 in a compact square east of here **[see Area I]**. A few years later, when Peter Russell had taken over as the Administrator of Upper Canada, he extended the town west and north to what is now Queen and Peter Streets. (He gave his own name to the latter.) Past Peter was military land: Fort York **[23/18b]** ensured the British presence here, and the stretch from what is now Peter Street to Dufferin Street was the Military Reserve or Garrison Reserve, a buffer at the harbour mouth to protect the fledgling town.

After the War of 1812, with York no longer under threat, a "New Town" grew up along King Street West. By the 1830s the military lands had been laid out for development, with the sequence of Clarence Square and Victoria Square defining a planned upscale residential neighbourhood. New Town held the most important and architecturally distinguished buildings in Toronto, including the general hospital and new parliament buildings (the third; the previous two, in Old Town, had burned). Later in the century, a popular phrase had King and Simcoe as the corner of "Legislation, Education, Salvation, and Damnation": Government House, the lieutenant-governor's residence, on the southwest corner; Upper Canada College on the northwest; St. Andrew's church on the southeast; and a tavern on the northeast.

That delicate colonial blend would be thoroughly disrupted by the arrival of massive, noisy, and dirty new infrastructure: the railways, which cut the city off from Lake Ontario and remade New Town. Toronto, now with about 30,000 people, welcomed the arrival of rail, which would allow the economy to keep working year round, and in 1851 the first railway—the Ontario, Simcoe, and Huron—broke ground near the waterfront. The original shoreline was extended over and over; instead of government and gentility, this area got fuel tanks and lumber yards. And hotels **[3/38]**, too, to serve rail passengers. Great new factories went up along King **[4/3a]**, and this concentration only grew after the Great Fire of 1904 burned out the city's previous warehousing district **[see Walk 7]** near Bay and Wellington.

When John Lyle's Royal Alexandra Theatre **[3/4b]** went up in 1907, it was the last gasp of the old neighbourhood. Five years later, Government House across the street was torn down by Canadian Pacific

Railway to make room for marshalling yards and a terminal. This was a place for industry.

The architectural results were impressive: manufacturers hired some of the city's best architects to create showpiece buildings in brick and terracotta. At the turn of the century, George Gouinlock **[4/4a]** or Burke & Horwood **[4/5]** were building grand residences uptown and grand factories downtown, sometimes for the same clients. After the 1910s, manufacturing buildings got taller and began to have multiple tenants; Spadina Avenue was the heart of the garment district, and a number of the Jewish entrepreneurs who were thriving in that business built their own monuments. The pioneering Jewish architect Benjamin Brown, in works like the Commodore Building **[4/9]** and the Balfour Building **[4/16]**, combined flourishes of historical ornament with up-to-the-minute structural innovation and grand windows. In the 1950s, manufacturing began to disperse to the suburbs and along highways; the shmatte business survived into the 1980s, but King-Spadina fell into a long, gradual decline.

As did the railways' presence here; those massive yards began to look more attractive for other purposes. The Metro Centre scheme of the 1960s would have remade much of the railway corridor as a Modernist megaproject; in the end only the CN Tower **[3/16]** directly came out of it, but the Convention Centre **[3/17]**, Roy Thomson Hall **[3/6]**, and Metro Hall **[3/19]** were lesser products of the railways' wheeling and dealing. Then, of course, there was SkyDome **[3/15]**, which city planners wisely placed near the existing city fabric in anticipation that it would grow south.

And grow it did, with what became known as CityPlace. This predominantly residential neighbourhood imported a developer and urban design ideas from Vancouver, and sadly it doesn't match its West Coast counterparts in quality; it did, however, create homes for thousands of people in what had been a wasteland for over a century. Something similar would happen to the east a decade later, a mix of homes, offices, and entertainment in the just-add-water district called South Core.

Meanwhile, those lofts to the north were acquiring a new lease on life. As late as the 1980s there were about 30,000 people working in the garment industry downtown; by the early '90s that number was just a few thousand, and property owners couldn't find tenants. In 1994 a garment-business veteran told the *Globe and Mail* that he didn't know what to do with his money-losing loft

building and was ready to "blow it up." Then two things happened: Loft offices became more fashionable and pricier, and the city did something radical. In 1996, then Toronto mayor Barbara Hall unveiled a new policy for the Two Kings, King-Parliament [see walk 2] and King-Spadina. Led by the planner Paul Bedford with help from Jane Jacobs, the new policy was hands-off; instead of defending manufacturing jobs, the city would loosen up the rules and let these lofts find new purposes. It worked in ways nobody could have predicted. First there were modest new mid-rise residential buildings [3/32], and then bigger ones, and then even bigger ones. Fifteen storeys [3/46] gave way to 45 storeys [3/42] and, with the Mirvish + Gehry proposal, 92 storeys and the demolition of sizeable loft buildings. The one square kilometre of King-Spadina is on track to have 40,000 residents.

How did this happen? For one thing, there were no neighbours to complain. Fewer than 1,000 people lived in King-Spadina in 1996; the dominant presence was night-clubs. Accordingly, the first rounds of development displaced no one's homes and made no political waves. This growing cluster of towers reflected the city's planning realities too. Toronto's land-use decisions are subject to provincial policy, which encourages intensification of downtown, and the Ontario Municipal Board often overrules city council on matters of density and height. The radical growth here, and in Liberty Village to the west, seems illogical when you look at the swaths of low density and fine local amenities that surround central Toronto—and yet Toronto's cult of the neighbourhood [see Introduction, Area X] means those areas are not changing much. In order for Toronto to grow, this place has to go sky-high.

And that is not, by any means, all bad. The area's identity as the Entertainment District, started by the Mirvishes, took off with the (temporary) era of the dance clubs and the arrival of what's now the Scotiabank Theatre. A few architects, principally Peter Clewes of architectsAlliance, have been able to create novel and beautiful buildings [4/14]. Some heritage buildings are being retained, while others are being updated or rebuilt in very interesting ways [4/13 and 4/3b]. The megaproject called The Well [3/28] promises to create a whole new district of office, retail, and residential in itself.

And yet Toronto has never seen anything like this, not at such scale—even in St. James Town. Are there enough parks, schools, community centres, or hospitals to serve all these new residents and workers? Not yet. But things can change fast. If you'd predicted in the 1980s that this area would be bustling with hip entrepreneurs and new moms, no one would have believed it. 21st-century Toronto will be full of surprises.

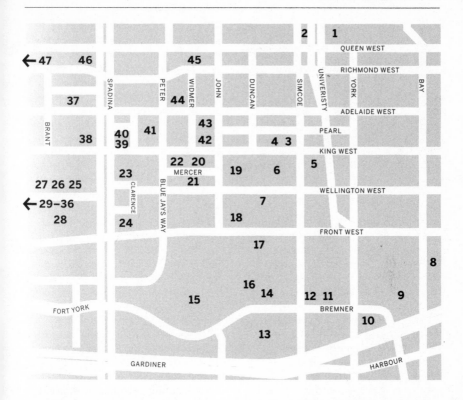

Walk 3: New Town and South Core

1 Osgoode Hall, 116–138 Queen St. W.
East wing, John Ewart, 1829–32; portico
added, Henry Bowyer Lane, 1844; altered,
Cumberland & Storm, 1856–59; law
school addition, William G. Storm,
1880–81, 1890; interior altered, Edmund
Burke, 1894; interior altered, Vaux and
Bryan Chadwick, 1923–24; rear additions,
Saunders & Ryrie, 1937, Mathers &
Haldenby, 1958, NORR Partnership, 1990.
Centre block, Henry Bowyer Lane, 1844;
altered, Cumberland & Storm, 1856;
additions, Kivas Tully, 1876; rear addi-
tions, F.R. Heakes, 1910–12; additions and
alterations, Page & Steele with Eric
Arthur, 1972. West wing, Henry Bowyer
Lane, 1844; altered, Cumberland &
Storm, 1856–59; Chancery Court, offices
and judges' rooms additions, Kivas Tully,
1884; interior altered, Burke & Horwood,

1894; rear addition, F.R. Heakes, 1910–12;
renovated and rear addition, Page &
Steele, 1972–73; addition, Page & Steele,
1984. Fence and gates, William G. Storm,
1866. General restoration, Taylor Hazell,
1996–99. Built at the head of York Street
north of Queen Street, then the town limits,
Osgoode Hall was a harbinger of New Town's
architectural eminence. In 1832, it consisted
of the front east wing only, a small portion
of the grand building we see today.
Nevertheless, it was an ambitious showcase
for Toronto's elitist colonials (specifically the
Anglican Tory governing class, many of
whom were lawyers). Osgoode Hall was built
as headquarters of the Law Society of Upper
Canada, the lawyers' fraternity, and duly
named for the first chief justice of the
province, William Osgoode. Today it still
serves the society, and houses the Court of
Appeal for Ontario as well.

Three architectural firms contributed to
the design before 1860. Surprisingly, the
result is a classical building of great

1 | Osgoode Hall

presence, though an architectural hybrid. The scheme of temple-fronted wings flanking a centre pavilion is that of a Palladian villa. The central façade ornamented with rooftop urns owes much to the garden front of Versailles. And the interior vestibule, glass-roofed court, and paired stairway resemble nothing so much as an Italian Renaissance palazzo—a form then being explored in London for aristocratic clubhouses. In fact, the building preserves the air of a private club, rather forbidding behind that impressive iron fence. Actually, the fence is only gated against wandering cows—a problem in the early years—and visitors are welcome to look inside and visit the library, perhaps the noblest room in Canada. Beautifully proportioned, it is 122 feet long with a 40-foot-high vaulted and domed ceiling that virtually dances with rich plasterwork.

Additions and alterations since 1860 have been many. The west wing was extended in a sympathetic classical mode in 1884, and again—not so sympathetically—in 1910–12, the same time the rear of the centre block was enlarged. A Romanesque law school was appended to the east wing in 1880–81, then hidden by nondescript cast-stone extensions in 1937 and 1958, the former lightly dusted with Moderne detail. Classical forms were also used for the final northwest addition, part of massive renovations completed in 1973. The Law Society originally had its own Osgoode Hall Law School in this building, which moved and amalgamated with York University in 1958. *PM*

2 Campbell House, 160 Queen St. W., c. 1822. William Campbell came out from Scotland to fight in the Revolutionary War, after which he settled in the Maritimes. After being named a judge in frontier Upper Canada in 1811 and transferred to York, the man who was to become chief justice and the first Canadian judge to be knighted built himself a large Georgian house overlooking the harbour from high ground at Frederick and Adelaide Streets in the heart of Old Town **[Area I]**. One of the earliest brick houses built in Toronto, it boasted such late Georgian refinements as a fanlighted door-case, oval-windowed pediment, and elegantly tall windows ornamenting the front. Threatened with demolition in 1972 (before Old Town began its resurgence), the 300-ton house was put on wheels and moved with great fanfare to its present, not entirely inappropriate site, for other such fine Georgian houses stood in New Town in the 1830s and '40s. Campbell House has been renovated and partially restored; it operates as a house museum. *PM/updated AB*

3 Union Building, 212 King St. W. (office building and warehouse), Darling & Pearson, 1907. Built for the Canadian General Electric Company, this is a fine example of the miniature Classical Revival palaces which prosperous manufacturers were erecting all along King Street in this period **[see Walk 4]**. The moulded terracotta window surrounds, stone portico, and elaborate pressed-metal and terracotta cornice are all remarkably well preserved. The 1980s mansard added on top is suitably subtle. *PM*

4a Theatre Park (mixed-use), 224 King St. W., architectsAlliance, 2016. A rule-breaker, in its mid-block tallness and its setback behind a quasi-public plaza. The plaza and syncopated glass lower façade provide a fine complement to the Royal Alexandra **[3/4b]**. For now a standalone, it's exceptionally handsome. *AB*

4b Royal Alexandra Theatre, 260 King St. W., John M. Lyle, 1906–07. Built as a series of three graduated boxes (lobby, auditorium, stage), but it is the small first box that catches the eye with elegant balustraded windows and paired pilasters sparkling across the front beneath a crested stone parapet—a fine legacy of Lyle's Beaux Arts schooling and his Carrère & Hastings training. The Royal Alex was rescued from demolition in 1963 and restored to its Edwardian splendour by merchant "Honest Ed" Mirvish—and now will be protected as part of his son David's massive development next door. **[4/6]**. *PM/updated AB*

The corner of Simcoe and King Streets was the heart of Toronto's extravagant New Town in the early 19th century. Here, in the block north of King Street, stood Upper Canada College (1829–1900); Government House (1815–62 and 1866–1912) was in the next block south between King and Wellington Streets; and south of that, covering the whole block between Wellington and Front Streets, stood the third parliament buildings (1829–1900).

5 St. Andrew's Presbyterian Church, 189 King St. W., William G. Storm, 1874–75. St. Andrew's Manse, 73 Simcoe St., Robert Grant, 1873; third-floor addition, David B. Dick, 1895; condominium addition, Northgrave Architect, 1988–89. Looking more florid every day as sleek new structures rise all around it, St. Andrew's poses theatrically in a Romanesque Revival costume borrowed from medieval Scotland. Typical of this "Norman Romanesque" are the arcaded corbel tables, tower finished off with parapets, broad stone wall surfaces, and novel decoration—the name and date interspersed on protruding stone bosses along the west façade for instance.

This revival style, which adherents pronounced more "democratic" and less ostentatious than Gothic but equally picturesque, would have held special appeal for this congregation, for it was they who counselled moderation in the split—over

organ music for one thing—that saw a few of the members break off to build their own (organless) St. Andrew's on Jarvis Street **[12/10]**.

In the late 1980s, St. Andrew's sold its air rights to the Sun Life Centre across the street **[7/7]**, and sold the space above and below the manse, which has been dug under, shored up, and cantilevered over to accommodate a 25-storey condominium. At least it's all still there. *PM*

6 Roy Thomson Hall, 60 Simcoe St., Arthur Erickson with Mathers & Haldenby, 1982; altered, Kuwabara Payne McKenna Blumberg, 2002. Toronto has never been a hospitable place for showy buildings. But here's one: this hall by Erickson is round, it is glassy, and it quite literally stands by itself. Why? The "New Massey Hall," as it was first known, found this site on CP Rail's former freight yards through a development deal between the city and the railway. Erickson's scheme for the block included a multi-levelled civic square with a prominent water feature. In the end, the hall went up by itself, and was joined years later by the bland Metro Hall **[3/19]** and what is now David Pecaut Square.

The building, thanks to this history, is awkwardly sited: it huddles too close to Simcoe Street, the parking lot to the south is an eyesore, and the sunken garden to the north feels like a moat (though it does open up the underground PATH). And yet the hall

6 | Roy Thomson Hall

is a handsome object. The triangular grid of the glass façades neatly resolves its sloped-and-curved geometry—no easy feat—and the payoff comes in the lively dance of light across its facets. All this pales against the fantastic lobby that encircles the concert hall. You can promenade here as you can few other places in Toronto. The hall itself is underwhelming; it delivers a large seat count (about 3,000) at the expense of intimacy. The sound too was originally unimpressive. A 2002 renovation removed the original acoustic devices—reflective discs, and 2,000 wool tubes in shades of greige and purple and scarlet, overseen by the talented interior designer Francisco Kripacz. These were visually grand, a counterpoint to the hall's restrained character. KPMB's hardwood canopy and panels have toned it down but left the hall much improved acoustically, so the drama is left to the orchestra—at least until intermission. *AB*

7 Residences at the Ritz-Carlton, 181 Wellington St. W., Kohn Pedersen Fox with Page & Steele/IBI Group, 2011. RBC Centre, 155 Wellington St. W., Kohn Pedersen Fox with Sweeny, Sterling, Finlayson & Co and Bregman & Hamann, 2009. Tall, glassy, and subtle. Each of the towers is pierced by a wedge-shaped division, for a quietly sculptural effect. More importantly, the lobby of the office complex is agreeably transparent, and it achieved a LEED Gold certification for such features as sunshading and efficient climate-control systems. The Ritz shows some flair by suspending its ballroom above the street, though in a slightly Wile E. Coyote manner. The pedestrian connections through the block are victories for the city. *AB*

8 Bay Park Centre (offices), 81–131 Bay St., Wilkinson Eyre with Adamson Associates and PUBLIC WORK (landscape architects), proposed. The rail corridor has been a barrier for much of Toronto's history [see Introduction, Area II], and occasionally someone promises to bridge it; this proposal's elevated privately-owned public space would do that beautifully. It would also

house a new GO bus terminal, badly needed. The two towers above, with their strong sustainability agenda and subtly folded façades, would be among the city's best. *AB*

9 Air Canada Centre (arena and office tower), 40 Bay St., BBB, 1999; altered later. Incorporates façades of Toronto Postal Delivery Building, Charles B. Dolphin, 1939–40. An arena built on a tight site to accommodate the Raptors and then, with the end of Maple Leaf Gardens [13/20], the Leafs. The interior, much renovated, is comfortably cramped, and fits within two façades of its predecessor. Dolphin's sorting plant is interesting: the strip windows are firmly International Style, the composition Moderne, and the ornament a Canadian Deco. Limestone bas-relief panels trace the history of communication in Canada—drumming, smoke signals, the stagecoach, and so on, culminating in the mail van. *AB*

9 | Air Canada Centre

The zone around the Air Canada Centre has gone from a sea of parking lots, as late as the 1990s, to a dense mixed-use neighbourhood. The proximity to Union Station has helped, as does the presence of the arena and the adjacent Maple Leaf Square. But with hotels, offices, and residences, there's a genuinely urban quality that is rare for an instant neighbourhood—aided by wide brick-paved sidewalks, which would be even busier if those PATH connections weren't sucking people and retail off the streets.

10 Maple Leaf Square, 55 Bremner Blvd., Kuwabara Payne McKenna Blumberg with Page & Steele/IBI Group, 2011. This has the ambition of a 1960s megaproject, combining apartments, hotel, offices, daycare, and curvy shopping arcade. The façade-and-crown composition works well on the skyline, and the complex frames the adjacent square—Jurassic Park—with activity and a fine streetwall. *AB*

11 Southcore Financial Centre, 120 Bremner Blvd., KPMB, 2015; 18 York St., Kuwabara Payne McKenna Blumberg, 2012. Two well-tailored, high-performing towers, now attracting financial and tech tenants who will gain some killer views to the old financial district. The two towers meet on an elevated, planted plaza—take the glowing stairs to get up there. *AB*

12 Delta Hotel Toronto, 75 Lower Simcoe St., Page & Steele/IBI Group, 2014. A lively glass skyscraper with playful nips and tucks in its curtain wall. The massive granite-clad base houses a gracious lobby and is surrounded by an equally gracious sidewalk and forecourt. *AB*

The bridge to the north connects the Southcore buildings with the PATH system and Union Station. The black ribbon that wraps it and more camouflage within are a public art installation by Jennifer Marman and Daniel Borins, who worked with design architect James Khamsi and Page & Steele/IBI Group.

13 Originally Canadian Pacific Roundhouse, 255 Bremner Blvd., 1929. These days, you might hardly imagine that the railways dominated this zone of the city for a century. This majestic relic, which includes the Toronto Railway Museum, recalls the brawn and scale of those enterprises. The adjacent park (capping a garage) contains a collection of railway outbuildings, weirdly thrown together. *AB*

14 Ripley's Aquarium, 288 Bremner Blvd., B+H, 2013. A great shark, its glass mouth ready to gobble up tourists leaving the CN Tower. This is a welcome attraction, but a grim presence on the street—windowless, as aquariums must be, but only lightly dressed up with some desultory folds and grey spots. The lobby is small and mean, the stairs steep and awkward, and the sequence inside designed to rush you back out. The most prominent features are two logos, one facing the Gardiner Expressway and another on the roof for Tower-goers. *AB*

15 | Rogers Centre

15 Rogers Centre/originally SkyDome, 1 Blue Jays Way, RAN International, 1989. The CN Tower **[3/16]** and the SkyDome are well matched in their Brutalist heft and technological sophistication. Here the design force was the English expat Rod Robbie, who won a 1985 design competition nearly on his own and then formed RAN International— the partnership of his office Robbie, Young and Wright, the structural engineers Adjeleian Allen Rubeli, and the Toronto architectural firm NORR Partnership, who collectively pulled it off. Robbie and Michael Allen patented the retractable roof design, which continues to work, creakily, almost 30 years later.

The building is not handsome. But now that the city has grown up around it, it seems less of a hulk than it once did. And indeed it was deliberately placed near Front Street in

16 | CN Tower

order to allow future growth; the John Street Pumping Station was moved south out of the way. The stadium relies heavily on transit and on downtown garages to accommodate fans, and so it is not surrounded by oceans of parking lots. This, in the 1980s, was something of a miracle. The pedestrian bridge to the north, designed by Montgomery Sisam, is now named after Robbie. *AB*

16 CN Tower, Webb Zerafa Menkes Housden Partnership with John Andrews and Quinn Dressel (structural engineers), 1976; altered, c. 1993; alterations and entry pavilion addition, IBI Group, 2016.
The city's defining architectural icon: a 553-metre tower that is both gawky and majestic. It's the product of local expertise, the enduring presence of the railroads, and wild visions brought sensibly down to size.

In the 1960s, CN Rail and CP Rail came together to propose Metro Centre, a redevelopment of their yards between Yonge and Bathurst. The scheme, led by John Andrews **[26/21a]** and Roger du Toit, would have moved the rail corridor south; demolished Union Station, and replaced it with a new transit hub; created a cluster of octagonal towers sitting on an elevated platform; and provided a new CBC head-quarters, along with a communications tower. The tower would have been three separate cylinders, joined by bridges that would provide stability.

In the reform era after 1972 **[see Introduction]**, most of this scheme was scotched, except the tower—its design was revised by the local firm WZMH and the Andrews office, led by Andrews partner Ned Baldwin. It began construction in 1973 and soon became less a piece of infrastructure than a tourist attraction, which is now surrounded by others **[3/15, 3/14]**. It retains its public role (and its antennae) today, but lost its status as the world's tallest free-standing structure to the Burj Dubai in 2007. Owned by the federal government, it is shoddily maintained; the new entry pavilion is the latest indignity. And yet: When the most famous Torontonian in history, Drake, imagined himself on top of the city for the cover of his 2016 album, the image placed him sitting on the edge of the CN Tower. This is, and will always be, the top of Toronto. *AB*

17 Toronto Convention Centre. North Building, 255 Front St. W., Crang & Boake, 1984; South Building, 222 Bremner Blvd., Bregman & Hamann, 1998. On Front, a dull monolith—conceived in the wake of Metro Centre **[see 3/16]** when this part of downtown was dead. Today, it still does its best to kill street life. Criticism of the design from the Toronto Society of Architects, Jane Jacobs, and John Sewell made little difference. The next phase, thanks to a welcome push from city planners, went largely underground, allowing the creation of Bremner Boulevard, Roundhouse Park, and the partial preservation of the CP Roundhouse **[3/13]**. *AB*

Simcoe Park is a product of the 1980s redevelopment of this block. It features three works of public art including *Mountain* (1995) by the British artist Anish Kapoor.

18 CBC Broadcast Centre, 250 Front St. West, Barton Myers Associates (development guidelines), 1987; Johnson/Burgee with Bregman & Hamann and Scott Associates, 1992. The product of a partnership between CBC and developers Cadillac Fairview, this gargantuan centre marked a hubristic high point for the public broadcaster and its architects. Among the latter was Philip Johnson—designer, patron, curator, and tastemaker to New York architecture through the eras of high Modernism and Post-Modernism. In the late 1980s, Johnson was trying to articulate a new style: He had recently curated the show *Deconstructivist Architecture* at the Museum of Modern Art, which included Daniel Libeskind and Frank Gehry **[4/6, 14/10]** exploring "the pleasures of unease." As a text for that show put it, these architects "intentionally violate the cubes and right angles of modernism." That's what happens here: blue-glass and glossy red volumes bust out of the box's white and red grids, which were conceived by Barton Myers. Another

non-conforming slab, this one green, pierces the atrium inside. And yet the place's massive scale and general uniformity are anything but edgy; many CBC staffers since have longed for the days of their previous buildings **[12/11]** with all their mess and soul. *AB*

19 Metro Hall (offices), 55 John St., Brisbin Brook Beynon, 1992. The head-quarters for the regional government of Metro Toronto, completed only six years before a hostile Queen's Park abolished this level of government. Metro looked to developers for partnerships, and one proposed a complex by Frank Gehry on Queen's Quay. Instead we got this, vague High-Tech but capped with weakly Decoesque glass hats. Only the rotunda and art installations mark this as a public building. More practical than City Hall **[7/18]** but without a hint of its symbolic heft; the former Metro council chamber is now, aptly, a customer-service call centre. *AB*

20 Originally John B. Reid house, 24 Mercer St., John Tully, 1857. One of Georgian Toronto's few Greek Revival strays. Characteristic Greek Revival features are the attic-storey half-windows in a "frieze" above the ornamental brackets (which likely terminated an applied cornice), the crisp rectangular windows with stone lintels and sills, and the sharply cubistic look to the whole. When built, this was the only brick house on a street of one- and two-storey roughcasts. Reid was a lawyer; Tully lived one door down. *PM*

21 Originally Verral Cab, Omnibus and Baggage Transfer Co./formerly Pilkington Bros. Ltd., 15–31 Mercer St. (originally stables), Langley Langley & Burke, 1878; addition, David B. Dick, 1894; factory and warehouse addition, Burke Horwood & White, 1909; office building addition, 1938–39. Nobu Residences, Teeple Architects, proposed. Pilkington Brothers, manufacturers of "Polished Plate and Window Glass, Plain and Bevelled Mirror Plates, Rolled Plate, Fancy Cathedral, Colored Glass etc.," came to Mercer Street in the early 1900s, first occupying the two-storey brick stables building to the east, later enlarged with a four-storey addition. The real excitement, however, is the two-storey Art Moderne office building they appended in 1939. Befitting a maker of glass, it boasts a streamlined glass-block exterior. The whole ensemble could soon become the front for a double-towered condo and hotel branded by the Nobu chain. *PM/AB*

22 Hotel Le Germain, 30 Mercer St., Lemay Michaud, 2003. Red brick, punched square windows, and a double-height ground floor with real stone and lots of glass. Quietly excellent. *AB*

Clarence Square was one of Toronto's first public parks when laid out in the 1830s; it was intended as the focus of an exclusive residential neighbourhood, which was never built. The fountain that's now at the centre stood for decades in the Art Gallery of Ontario's Walker Court as the Signy Eaton Fountain.

23 Clarence Terrace, 5–16 Clarence Square (twelve units of original sixteen-house row), likely Langley, Langley & Burke, 1879–80; renovated, Joan Burt with Douglas Swan, 1964. Building did not begin around Clarence Square until the late 1870s, and these middle-class row houses (one of which, when new, housed architect Edward Langley) are less than the 1830s planners had in mind. Nevertheless, the long Second Empire ensemble was distinguished enough to become one of Toronto's first downtown house-rehabilitation projects, led by the pioneering Burt. *PM/AB*

24 Originally Steele, Briggs Seed Co. Ltd., 49 Spadina Ave. (factory and warehouse), Sproatt & Rolph, 1911. This neighbourhood began skidding from residential to industrial after the 1904 great fire; in 1911, the Canadian Pacific Railway built a spur to Simcoe Street. Steele, Briggs were among the first manufacturers to take advantage of the change, building this unobtrusive five-storey red-brick commercial box. *PM/AB*

This stretch of Wellington Street West, originally called Wellington Place, was designed as a stylish residential avenue formally linking Clarence Square to Victoria Memorial Square. It never became as fashionable as expected, however, and beginning in the 1910s it was built out with factories.

25 Originally Smith/Powell house, 422–424 Wellington St. W., 1889. Condominium tower addition, architects-Alliance, ongoing. This mighty Queen Anne double house is a last reminder of Wellington Place's residential intentions. Originally at no. 422 was John C. Smith of Cooper & Smith Boots and Shoes [for Mr. Cooper, see 11/17]; at no. 424 lived Charles Powell, manager of the Temperance Colonization Company, whatever that was. Both houses will become tower bases in an approved redevelopment, part of the area's rapid transition to high-rise. *PM/AB*

26 Monarch Building/originally Croft Building, 438 Wellington St. W. (factory), Charles J. Gibson, 1914; residential conversion, Richard Hodgins Architect, 1998. William Croft & Sons manufactured something enigmatically listed as "small-wares" in the city directories, but there is nothing small about this precise six-storey red-brick cube with its simple but well-placed stylized classical ornamentation. *PM*

27 Originally Houlding Knitwear, 462 Wellington St. W. (factory), Yolles Chapman & McGiffin, 1916. More "modern classical" decoration with smooth stone base and the slimmest of capitals at the top fifth floor to turn piers into square columns. Very handsome—and now home to architects and a Herman Miller showroom. *PM/updated AB*

28 The Well (mixed-use), 410 Front St. W. to Wellington, Spadina to Draper St., Hariri Pontarini (master plan), Claude Cormier (landscape architect), ongoing. A massive intensification of a 7.7-acre site, which housed the *Globe and Mail* from 1974 to 2016. Low, terraced buildings would face

Wellington, while four towers step up along Front to an office building at the corner of Spadina. Many details of the architecture remain unclear. But anyway, this would be most interesting for its high-quality public realm: the design promises to bury all parking, create pedestrian-only streets paved with brick, and widen Wellington Street with a pedestrian promenade. *AB*

Draper Street, full of winsome mansard-roofed and Bay-n-Gable houses, is one of the city's little-known treasures.

29a 20–24, 26–28, 30–32 Draper St. (one triple and two double houses), 1890. Late-blooming Bay-n-Gables, with solid, squarish forms derived from Queen Anne style. Closely built and looking at first blush like a row, these are actually three separate buildings. *PM*

29b 4–6, 8–10, 12–14, 16–18 Draper St. (four double houses), 1882–83. Second Empire cottages, one and a half storeys high and sweetly detailed with bay windows and panelled brick. *PM*

29c 3–5, 7–9 Draper St. (two double houses), 1882–83. More of the same. *PM*

29d 11–13, 15–17, 23–25 Draper St. (three of original five double houses), 1881–82. The expansive Second Empire mansard provided much needed space to attic bedrooms in small houses such as this, not to mention an eye-appealing roofline. *PM*

30a Originally M. Granatstein & Son Ltd., 482–488 Wellington St. W. (warehouse), James A. Harvey, 1907; west addition, Hynes Feldman & Watson, 1916–18. The addition is a Commercial Style stunner much talked about in its day. Decoration is minimal but bold and incisive. Note how piers rise to little Aztec observatory domes instead of

cutting off at the roof, for example. In 1918, the real news, however, was those steel-sashed windows occupying the entire space between piers on all four sides of the open-plan building. *PM*

30b 500 Wellington West, 500 Wellington St. W. (condominium apartments), CORE, gh3 (landscape architects), 2011. Not another warehouse, but a stack of full-floor luxury units expertly finished with grey brick, ipe, and frameless glass balconies. An excellent building thanks to such details, the forecourt, and the scale that matches the older neighbours. It will soon be surrounded by much bigger newcomers. *AB*

30b | 500 Wellington West (on left)

30c Offices/Originally Copp, Clark Publishing Co. (factory), 495 Wellington St. W., Wickson & Gregg, 1912. 517 Wellington St. W., Wickson & Gregg, 1928. Altered and combined, Jurecka, Lobko, Tregebov Architects, 1989. Smooth red brick for two early Commercial Style buildings, one decked out in classical detail, the other lightly streaked with stylized Gothic. Unfortunately, the industrial sash windows—which originally set the tone for both these buildings—have been removed. *PM*

31 Victoria Memorial Square, 10 Niagara St.; restoration, The Planning Partnership (landscape architects) and ERA, 2001–09. This was once a military cemetery, located near Fort York and the centre of the large military reserve which ran from Peter to Dufferin Streets. The memorial in the centre of the square sits on a 1901 plinth by Frank Darling; the bust by Walter S. Allward, added in 1906, is dedicated to those who served in Upper Canada in the early years. The remaining gravestones have been thoughtfully gathered into a new monument; the neighbourhood's small children and yappy dogs give it life for the first time in ages. *AB*

32 | Twenty Niagara Condos

32 Twenty Niagara Condos, 20 Niagara St. (condominium apartments), Wallman Clewes Bergman, 1998. The first collaboration between Peter Clewes and developer Howard Cohen of Context, who was then working with Lloyd Alter. At a glance it's nothing fancy—it addresses the park with a terrace and very well-proportioned façade. Within, however, this mid-rise is profoundly innovative. The apartments are floor-through, with west and east exposures; pairs of units each share a tiny lobby and elevator access, so almost no space is wasted. The balconies on the west side provide access (when an alarm is triggered) to an emergency stair, the second exit required for fire safety. *AB*

33 Thompson Hotel and residences, 550 Wellington St. W., architectsAlliance with ERA, 2010. Incorporates façade of Crangle's Collision/originally International Harvesters' Building, Norman A. Armstrong, 1940. Hotel and residences in a complex, intriguing ensemble of tall and low slabs. Townhouses greet Stewart Street on the north side; to the west, a dubious tribute to heritage, with the rebuilt façade of a Moderne body shop. *AB*

34 66 Portland St., CORE, 2004; 20 Stewart St., CORE, 2007; 32 Stewart St., CORE, 2003. A set of reasonably good mid-rise condo buildings, all for Freed Developments. Their consistent massing and materials establish a rare quality in contemporary Toronto building: coherence. *AB*

35 38 Stewart St. (condominium apartments), ZAS Architects with Saucier + Perrotte, 2016. To end the row, a flashy and beautiful black slab by Montrealers S&P. The in-and-out rhythm of the façades, and the interesting through-block lobby and pedestrian walkway, help obscure the fact that the building is too tall for its small, tight site. *AB*

36 75 Portland St. (condominium apartments), CORE with Philippe Starck, 2011. A generic U-shaped slab. The presence of the star French designer added some pops of colour, the outscaled furniture, and the interesting long table that seems to slice through the wall from lobby to the lively courtyard. *AB*

37a Ace Hotel, 51 Camden St., Shim-Sutcliffe, ongoing. North America's hippest hotel chain favours repurposed old buildings; here, instead, a bespoke structure by local heroes. This will be a rare publicly accessible building by Shim-Sutcliffe, and they are designing intricate façades of brick, weathering steel, and glass that will make it a landmark. The haute-craft branch of Canadian architecture has rarely had such a visible presence. *AB*

37b Brant Park Condos, 39 Brant St., architectsAlliance, 2016. A sleek essay in less-is-more Modernism, with windows and balconies set back behind an unyielding white-square grid. When all that white stucco starts to discolour, though, every drip will mar that composition. *AB*

37c 29 Camden St. (condominium apartments), Oleson Worland and CORE, 1999. A new-build "live/work" condo that aimed to copy the red brick and mid-rise scale of nearby lofts, with raw concrete floors and tall ceilings within. It still holds the streetwall admirably. *AB*

38 460 King St. W., formerly Spadina Hotel/originally Richardson House, 1875; additions, 1884, 1890; altered, Gensler, 2015. This place has seen it all: it's gone from respectable hotel to flophouse and bar, to backpacker's hostel, to "innovation centre" and real estate sales office. The current renovation reveals the unusual half-timbering of the front wing and carves out a lovely double-height space behind. *AB*

39 The Hudson (residences and retail), 438 King St. W., Diamond Schmitt, 2007. Jack Diamond often speaks of the importance of "background buildings" to a city. His firm has made a fine one, with a veneer of buff brick, that holds the corner very well. The glass on the supermarket clearly needs some shading, though. *AB*

40 Glas (condominium apartments), 25 Oxley St., architectsAlliance, 2010. Yes, glass, going straight up from the sidewalk, with no balconies to mess up the lower façades. Sharp. *AB*

41 King Charlotte (condominium apartments), 11 Charlotte St., architectsAlliance, 2016. Peter Clewes and aA play with blocks: an abstract composition of glass, concrete, and then glass again in an off-kilter stack of cantilevers. The glass slab up top has some very fine proportions and façades that neatly wrap the balconies. Replace the cheap precast cladding with limestone, and this would be one for the ages. *AB*

39 | The Hudson

42 TIFF Bell Lightbox (mixed-use), 350 King St. W., Kuwabara Payne McKenna Blumberg with Kirkor, 2010. This was the site of Toronto's first general hospital from 1829 to 1862. The city's marquee festival moved here from Bloor Street **[Walk 18]**, and its collection of theatres, shops, and restaurants—accessed via a lucid and welcoming ground floor—gives a lot to King Street. The podium façade is artful, and on its top, a stepped rooftop terrace alludes to the Villa Malaparte in Capri, which plays a starring role in Godard's *Contempt*. The architecture otherwise fails to capture the visual creativity that's promised by a cinematheque. *AB*

43 Cinema Tower, 21 Widmer St., Kirkor with Page & Steele/IBI Group, 2014. The non-profit Artscape has a performance space here, a rare amenity born from the condo boom. But the architecture is an orange assault on the eyes. The canopy over the front door, an installation by artist Peter Powning, looks like something out of a dinosaur ride at a theme park. *AB*

44 Peter Street Condominiums, 338 Adelaide St. W., architectsAlliance, 2015. Above the storefront are offices (on the podium floors) and residences (above that). The base, with irregular windows set deep in a cladding of purple brick, sets an example for bottom-line developer buildings: inexpensive, unfussy but well detailed, with the city's capable bricklayers allowed to do their thing. Maybe it helped that the architects have their offices across the street [4/9]. *AB*

45 Picasso (condominium apartments), 318 Richmond St. W., Teeple Architects, 2016. Teeple here manages the difficult task of making art within a developer's balance sheet. The tower's skin is not the customary all-glass but panels of cement board, which is more energy-efficient and in this case more beautiful. The window openings are skilfully composed, in combination with cantilevered boxes that make the building resemble a stack of blocks assembled by a particularly brilliant child. Like 60 Richmond East [13/1], it also includes planted terraces. *AB*

46 The Morgan (residences and retail), 438 Richmond St. W., Quadrangle, 2002. An attempt to echo the language of the nearby Tower Building and Fashion Building [4/18 and 4/19]. The half-hearted base ornament doesn't carry its weight. *AB*

47 Edition Richmond (condominium apartments), 850 Richmond St. W., Audax, 2015. Somewhere between apartment building and townhouse complex, this savvy building sticks 20 two- and three-level units, 1,000 to about 2,000 square feet, on a tight site between two private walkways. The fine detailing of the architecture and the public realm, plus its relatively low height, make it a good neighbour in this mixed district or most anywhere. If the density at King and Spadina ever spreads out, it might look like this. *AB*

45 | Picasso

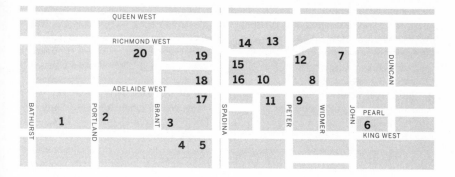

Walk 4: King Street West

1a Originally Mason and Risch Piano Manufactory, 642 King St. W., 1879.

Mason and Risch projects a neat, conservative, almost domestic image with its four storeys of carefully laid red Georgian brick picked out with yellow-brick quoins, relieving arches over windows, and string courses between storeys. The company, with a combined annual output of 4,000 instruments, was one of ten in Toronto making pianos and organs in the 19th century. This enduring little manufactory employed 45 hands in woodworking, varnishing, and finishing; actions and keyboards were imported. *PM*

1b 636 King St. W. (office building),

c. 1955. Two-storey no. 636 displays the experimentation of the post–World War II building boom: glass curtain walls, black-glazed brick, decorative panels. Inside is a stylish *retardataire* Art Deco steel stair rail. *PM*

1c 620 King St. W. (offices and residences), Hariri Pontarini, in progress. Incorporates Parisian Laundry Building, 602 King St. W., Henry Simpson, 1904.

A new brick slab—dressed up with plenty of ornament and corbelled arches—topped with an office tower and rental apartments. This is a deep and complicated site, on a deep and complicated block; the designers plan to wrap the whole thing in a continuous woonerf paved with brick. It will be interesting, and maybe wonderful. *AB*

2a Originally Beatty Manufacturing Co., 600 King St. W., Chadwick & Beckett, 1900–01.

Subtle red-on-red brick with crisp details woven in like a piece of fine damask worthy of Mr. Beatty's bindings, tapes, and braids which were made within. The Classical Revival composition proceeds with a base of horizontally rusticated brick for the first storey; a middle of two many-windowed floors; followed by a top attic storey decorated with columns blocked in brick; the whole finished off with a deep cornice, elliptical pediment, and finally, a flagpole. A majestic little factory. *PM*

2a | 600 King St. W.

2b Fashion House (condominium apartments and retail), 560 King St. W. and 461 Adelaide St. W., CORE Architects, 2014. Incorporates Toronto Silverplate Co., 572 King St. W. (factory), 1882; ground-floor addition, 1983. One of the first factories in the area, Toronto Silverplate featured a forward-looking design for 1882, with its brick punched by many windows. Badly run-down by the early 2000s, it was rescued by this condo project—whose form defers nicely to the older building, packing density into the middle of the block. Excellent public realm here: the front plaza, the woonerf at the east side, and the private courtyard joining the complex's two buildings are coherent and well-detailed. Building residents are supposed to use only one shade of red curtains to close off their walls of glass. We'll see whether that lasts. *PM/AB*

2b | Fashion House

3a Originally E.C. Gurney & Co. Stove Foundry, 500–522 King St. W., 1873. This was the first factory on King Street West, its various buildings covering more than half the block. An experienced hand was at work here, enlivening the façade with a buoyant moulded impost course following the curve of windows and an extravagant brick corbel table at the cornice, the whole punctuated by brick piers every two windows. It's now in great shape; even Shoppers Drug Mart has revealed the brick-and-beam guts of the place. *PM/updated AB*

3b Westbank King Street (mixed-use), 489–539 King St. W., Bjarke Ingels Group with Diamond Schmitt and PUBLIC WORK (landscape architects), proposal. Incorporates Hart Building (warehouse), 489 King St. W., 1918; American Watch Case Co., 511 King St. W. (factory), George W. Gouinlock, 1893. A radical break from Toronto tradition, this project would be a downtown version of Moshe Safdie's Habitat 67. "Mountains" of apartments would rise across the site, their terraces lined by greenery and overlooking a courtyard planted with a "secret forest" of hemlock. Retail would sit at and below ground level, and visitors could walk through the site in several directions on public pathways. This scheme fuses utopian form-making with a walkable, fine-grained streetscape (which already exists on this deep block riddled with courtyards). If built, likely in scaled-down form, it will show that innovation is possible in developer housing. How it includes fragments of the existing buildings is an interesting problem, yet to be resolved. *AB*

4a Originally Dominion Paper Box Co., 469 King St. W. (factory), George W. Gouinlock, 1903; addition, J. Francis Brown, 1907. Classical Revival, but with too many fussy light-coloured "stone" details, all looking as if they were pasted on to the red brick. In contrast to the busy base, the attic storey and roofline look unfinished, as if the architect were worn out by the time he got up there. No denying, though, the charm of winged cherubs decorating Ionic capitals at the entrance. *PM*

4b Originally Toronto Lithographing Co./ formerly Stone Ltd. Lithographers/ formerly Salada Tea, 461 King St. W. (factory), Gouinlock & Baker, 1901. A firm red-brick factory building with Classical Revival details massively and organically in place. Though the Dominion Paper Box building **[4/4a]** is a failure compared to this, the two together—joined by common scale and a decorative iron fence—do create a Beaux Arts *environment entire,* something sadly missing on most of the street. *PM*

4b | 461 King St. W.

5 Samuel Building, 431 King St. W., Burke & Horwood, 1908. Originally Imperial Bank of Canada, 441 King St. W., Darling & Pearson, 1906. Krangle Building, 445 King St. W., J. Francis Brown, 1906. Originally Toronto Pharmacol Building, 455 King St. W., J. Francis Brown, 1904. This wonderful set of four designated heritage properties is owned, like many buildings in the area, by Allied REIT; they are slated for retention even as the complicated Westbank project (on which Allied is a partner) remakes the block. These date from a moment when this area was rapidly shifting from residential to industrial; they'll now see the opposite happen. *AB*

6 Mirvish + Gehry (mixed-use), 260–270 King St. W. and 274–322 King St. W., Gehry International and Page & Steele/IBI Group, proposed. Incorporates Eclipse Whitewear, 322 King St. W. (factory), Gregg & Gregg, 1903, renovated, A.J. Diamond & Barton Myers, 1970; Princess of Wales Theatre, 300 King St. W., Lett/Smith, 1993; Anderson Building, 284 King St. W., William Fraser, 1915. The largest project in the career of the world's most famous architect—that's the promise of Mirvish + Gehry. First, Mirvish: It's David, art collector and developer, whose father "Honest Ed" **[20/31]** bought these warehouses after he rescued the Royal Alexandra Theatre **[3/4b]** in 1963. (The Eclipse Whitewear Building was first bought and renovated by architects Diamond Myers in the 1970s.) In time, Ed opened a string of corny, popular restaurants that brought life to his theatre and to the block. In 1993, he built the Princess of Wales Theatre here too.

But now comes Gehry: Born in Toronto, and still attached to the place after 70 years in Los Angeles, he has been passed over for local projects **[3/19]** and, in the case of the Four Seasons Centre **[7/12]**, courted unsuccessfully. In 2012 Mirvish revealed the architect's scheme for three very tall residential towers, which Mirvish said would become "a symbol of what Toronto can be." In the end the hyper-dense proposal was condensed to two towers of 92 and 82 storeys atop a base of shopping, space for OCAD University, and an art gallery. That gallery, atop the Eclipse building, would house Mirvish's private collection; funding its operation is part of the rationale Mirvish has given in pushing for such skyscraping density. But really these buildings, like all supertall towers, are about money and sheer ambition, and they promise to be worthy showpieces. As with many Gehry buildings, they express a conflict between the conventional—boxy towers, maybe clad in terracotta—and the subversive: the forms of the towers would be cut by irregular "waterfalls" of glass. Down on the ground, the scheme has evolved into something sculptural, nuanced, and respectful of the streetscape, ready to mark a proposed cultural corridor along John Street. If and when it's built, this project will be Toronto architecture at its biggest and boldest. *AB*

7 RioCan Hall/originally Festival Hall, 259 Richmond St. W., Kirkland Partnership, 1999. Incorporates façade of Turnbull Elevator Manufacturing Co./ originally John Burns Carriage Works, 126–132 John St., 1886; addition, Wickson & Gregg, 1906; additions, 1909, 1919. Turnbull Elevator moved into John Burns's factory building in 1900 when it was one of four companies in Toronto making elevators. Today fragments of its factories remain as part of this retail-entertainment complex, which was a welcome sign of life in 1999 but already seems both garish and clunky. That long escalator ride up to the movie theatres does pay off in a rich skyline vista. *AB*

8 Manufacturers Building, 312–318 Adelaide St. W. (loft), Baldwin & Greene, 1927–28. Hailed at the time as the "greatest year in the history of Canadian construction," 1928 saw hundreds of open-plan Commercial Style loft buildings spring up. Flat roofed and forthright, their primary feature was abundant light-giving windows. (In buildings where decorative fenestration seemed desirable, it usually appeared only on front or corner walls, with large industrial sash covering less conspicuous sides.) Stylistic touches were minimal; the three-tone brickwork is subtly handsome. *PM/AB*

9 Commodore Building, 317–325 Adelaide St. W. (loft), Benjamin Brown, 1929. The metal-frame technology that made tall, many-windowed Commercial Style buildings possible in large part determined their aesthetic as well—precise, regular, clean, and mechanistic. In the hands of the best architects, however, this characteristic façade was never less than human: the scale of the individual window was that of the worker inside; the base storeys that of the pedestrian on the street. Here Benjamin Brown has created a fine, inviting, vaguely

historical—and thereby reassuring—ground storey and portal. A graduate in architecture at the University of Toronto in 1913 and member of the Ontario Association of Architects, Brown designed many of the distinguished loft buildings in the garment district in this period. Today the terrazzo in the lobbies and stairs remains intact. *PM/updated AB*

10 Capitol Building/originally Hobberlin Building, 366 Adelaide St. W. (loft), Yolles & Rotenberg, 1920. In 1920, this seven-storey structure for the garment industry was one of the ten largest loft buildings ever constructed in Canada. It remains among the most outstanding. It used steel columns on side walls and the lightest possible brick bearing piers on front and rear to provide the absolute maximum of light—90 per cent of the walls are glass. It also featured four high-speed elevators, a sprinkler system that lowered the insurance rate, one of the fastest construction periods on record—78 days—and terracotta Gothic detailing handsomely capping the top. (Sad to say, ghostly new glazing has taken some of the life out of it.) *PM*

11 MacLean Building, 345 Adelaide St. W., George Gouinlock, 1913–14. Gouinlock had a chance to show off on this rare long-and-skinny corner site, and did; the façade artfully weaves delicate bays with thick brick piers. *AB*

12 Tableau (mixed-use), 125 Peter St., Wallman Architects with Claude Cormier (landscape architects), 2015. Like QRC West across the street [4/13], this hoists new floorspace up in the air; but rather than preserve an older warehouse, it offers a simulacrum of its front façade in today's fashionable purple brick. A bizarre landing—and too bad, because the syncopated tower is quite fine. *AB*

13 QRC West, 134 Peter St., Sweeny & Co., 2015. Incorporates 134 Peter St./ originally George Weston Biscuit Co., George Robinson Harper, 1910; 364 Richmond St. W. (loft). Not since the 1970s [see 11/4a] has Toronto seen such a creative response to heritage retention. This complex raises a new 11-storey building up high in the air on a dramatic steel structure, keeping three façades of the loft at the corner and preserving the neighbouring building intact. The atrium between these new and old volumes is breathtaking. *AB*

13 | QRC West

14 District Lofts (condominium apartments), 388 Richmond St. W., architects-Alliance, 2000. A creative product of the 1990s, when most anything was possible here as long as it wasn't too tall. A veneer of buff brick nods to the scale of nearby loft buildings, fronting a parking garage; retail adds life to the car-choked stretch of Richmond; above, two towers of floor-through units face each other across a deep, narrow courtyard. The city's current focus on "separation distances" would kill such an idea today, but it works, well. *AB*

15 | 401 Richmond

15 401 Richmond (offices and retail)/ originally Macdonald Manufacturing Company, John Wilson Siddall, 1899; additions, 1903–23, converted to studios and offices, 1994–ongoing. "New ideas must use old buildings." This complex bears out that axiom of Jane Jacobs: its five buildings house a community of artists, galleries, designers, artisans, film festivals, and the odd architect. That's due to the foresight and generosity of the Zeidler family; Margaret, daughter of Eb [see 23/24], oversaw the purchase of the complex as this area hit its nadir in the 1990s, and runs the place with artificially low rents for creative tenants. The brick-and-beam bones have been sandblasted and windows restored—but the complex is wonderfully creaky and atmospheric, topped with a rooftop garden. A place worth venerating not for how it was built, but for what it has become. *AB*

16 Balfour Building, 119–121 Spadina Ave. (loft), Benjamin Brown, 1930. Another loft by Brown, this time 12 storeys spelled out with geometric zigzags, fans, and lettering of the Art Deco vocabulary. The building was named to honour British Prime Minister Arthur James, the Earl of Balfour, who in 1917 pledged his government's support for a Jewish homeland in Palestine. *PM*

17 Darling Building, 96–104 Spadina Ave. (loft), 1909. One of the area's first lofts, this nine-storey Commercial Style building is remarkable for its balanced vertical/horizontal design with large regularly placed steel-sash windows and practically no ornament, not even a cornice. The battlemented projections at the corners might be rooks on an empty chess board. *PM*

18 Tower Building, 106–110 Spadina Ave. (loft), Benjamin Brown, 1928. A carefully composed loft building with design devices marshalled to accentuate the ten-storey height: tall windows with long narrow triple sash; shallow unbroken piers rising the height of the building; spiky Gothic ornament around the entrance; and of course that landmark pyramidal-roofed tower (really a disguise for rooftop mechanicals). *PM*

18 | Tower Building

19 Fashion Building, 130 Spadina Ave. (loft), Kaplan & Sprachman, 1927. More vague medieval details for the garment makers, especially in heavily encrusted base storeys and the lobby—which is tiny, and almost comically stuffed with ornament. Above rise six floors of what might be mistaken for a yellow-brick apartment building. *PM/AB*

20 The Waterworks, 505 Richmond St. W. (condominium apartments, food hall, and YMCA centre), Diamond Schmitt, ongoing. Eva's Phoenix (youth centre), 60 Brant St., LGA Architectural Partners, 2016. Incorporates city waterworks maintenance buildings, Kenneth Stevenson Gillies, 1932–33. Surprising things can happen when market forces are reined in a bit. This site, thanks to a discerning city policy, is now being redeveloped by Woodcliffe **[see 1/2]** and MOD **[see 5/38b]** with a modestly scaled tower, badly needed recreational centre, and the non-profit Eva's Phoenix. Plus, most of the existing buildings will be retained and made accessible. The Moderne buff-brick and limestone complex was designed by Gillies, long-time city architect and at the time commissioner of buildings, on St. Andrew's Square, which had been this area's public market square from the 1830s onward. Part of the development scheme is for a food hall, offering prepared meals and fresh food—bringing this block back to life. *AB*

This is the axis of the city. Toronto street numbers march outward east and west from Yonge—and as that fact suggests, Yonge has had a central place in the city's development. Yet the street has changed dramatically more than once, from being a rural track on the fringe to a retail main street to—if today's trends continue—a largely residential strip of tremendous height and density.

It began, in the early days of York, as a dirt road running through forest. As the town grew up to the east, the zone along Yonge was undeveloped and privately owned; as attention shifted rapidly west, Yonge was finished with macadam, an early form of paving, in the 1830s. (It was probably in place in 1837, when William Lyon Mackenzie's rebels were overcome by Sheriff William Botsford Jarvis and 27 riflemen at Yonge and Maitland.) The downtown growth of warehouses and banks, south of King Street **[Area IV]**, was met by retail and residential north of it only slowly. An 1858 map shows just a scattering of buildings on the blocks below Bloor; this changed over the next two generations, as the lands either side of Yonge were subdivided and filled with housing, accompanied by neighbourhood retail on the main street. As King Street's commerce declined **[Walk 1]**, Yonge was lined with increasingly prosperous shops, designed by some of the better architects in town. (A good number of these, like E.J. Lennox's 664–682 Yonge **[5/41]**, are still around, at least for now.)

The decisive factor was the growth of Eaton's and Simpson's, the twin Torontonian examples of the emerging department-store type. Two dry-goods merchants, Timothy Eaton and Robert Simpson, put their money on this new business model, creating stores that would become institutions for a century to come—and grand buildings to match **[5/6]**. "The opening of Simpson's handsome new structure in the fashionable Romanesque style was an event of 1894," according to a company brochure.

The next round of grand plans came again from Eaton's, with the development of College Park **[5/25]**. The retailer counted on College Street to be the next prime address, and tried to help this process along by

Area III
Walk 5: Yonge Street

donating land for the widening of Yonge Street and a shifting of College to meet Carlton. But as with other schemes of the era **[see Introduction, Area V]**, the Depression and World War II cut it down to size. Toronto Hydro's headquarters **[5/26]** was among the few new buildings in this never-quite-chic district. The real money, and attendant retail, went north to Bloor Street and into the suburbs.

At that point, development on Yonge more or less stalled, to the benefit of the city's architectural heritage. Simpson's and Eaton's remained behemoths, while some small upscale stores such as Fairweather's **[see 5/1b]** remained for many years as vestiges along lower Yonge. The arrival of the subway in 1954 brought some disruption and a bit of demolition; but generally, as on Queen Street West **[Walk 15]**, the narrow street fronts of the Victorian city endured and became less desirable. This former main street took on a marginal character, dominated by car traffic; seedier retail, including porn theatres and sex shops; and loud neon signs. (One of those signs, for Sam the Record Man, was a civic landmark; it is in storage awaiting a new home, while the store's site is now home to the Ryerson Student Learning Centre [5/21].)

This downscale turn had its upside. For one thing, Yonge Street became a haven for the gay community, the one place for "out" gay culture in a city frankly homophobic well into the 1980s. This was also the birthplace, in the 1960s, of the Toronto Sound, a local fusion of rock and R & B: The Mynah Birds, featuring Neil Young and Rick James, played here. Friar's Tavern at 283 Yonge (now the Hard Rock Cafe) was where Bob Dylan first met The Band.

But the building stock remained in place until Eaton's shook things up again. The store's development proposal of the mid 1960s nearly created a huge Modernist superblock at the expense of Old City Hall [7/17] and the Church of the Holy Trinity [5/12a]; instead, Toronto got the Eaton Centre [5/11], a relatively sensitive piece of massive urban renewal. The prospect of further big projects left Yonge in a state of uncertainty for a generation to come, which only ended with the creation of Yonge-Dundas Square [5/16a] in the 1990s. That civic space became the hub of the Luminato Festival and other cultural events, and gave a new character to this zone. The expansion of Ryerson University [5/21] has also changed the tone around Yonge and Dundas, and that change is far from complete.

In the post-2000 building boom, Yonge began to undergo a dramatic physical shift. Its central location and lack of a loud residents' association have made downtown Yonge a prime target for condo development. The city's tallest residential building is already here [5/21], for better or worse. But three more major high-rise developments are already in the ground by mid 2016, with at least four more approved and several more being promoted by developers [5/20d]. These represent a serious threat to

the remaining heritage buildings along Yonge, and could mean a string of mediocre and very big towers in a part of the city that's been largely commercial for 100 years. Two of the city's best infill projects, Massey Tower [5/7d] and Five Condos [5/38b], suggest how heritage can be incorporated into dense new development; it's uncertain whether future projects will show similar finesse, and whether the city can provide the community services to meet the needs of thousands of new residents. The answers to those questions will determine the success of Yonge Street for the next two generations.

Walk 5: Yonge Street

1a Originally Hiram Piper & Brother Hardware/formerly Toronto World Newspaper building, 83 Yonge St. (commercial block), probably Joseph Sheard, 1857; addition, Charles J. Gibson, 1895; altered later. Yonge Street's earliest shop buildings were simple Georgian boxes, most now gone. The next generation of stores aspired to a more elaborate and commercial look. The cut-stone capitals on the pilasters and radiating brick lintels over the windows rank among the city's finest. The Pipers became prominent businessmen

and politicians, and one family member ran Toronto's first zoo. The city's third morning daily, the conservative *Toronto World*, took over the building in 1892. *PM*

1b 100 Yonge St. (office building), Quadrangle Architects, 1988–89. Incorporates front façade of Fairweather Building, Charles S. Cobb, 1918–19. 102–104 Yonge St. (commercial block and nursery school; part of Scotia Plaza), Webb Zerafa Menkes Housden, 1988–89. Incorporates front façade of Bible & Tract Society Building, Gordon & Helliwell, 1885–86; altered, Burke Horwood & White, 1910. Champions of one-wall preservation call it better than nothing; detractors, "façadism," "façadectomy," or "façadomy." We preserve old buildings to impart a sense of the past, which should help us to understand the present and future. But what precedent, what inspiration, is provided by these token remnants slapped onto new construction? What consolation? Are we reminded here of Robert Fairweather's ultra-sophisticated ladies' fine furs and specialty shop, of a time when coming downtown to buy a pair of gloves, not to mention a fur, was an act of some occasion? Is there anything left to signal the Bible & Tract Society's rousing mansarded, proselytizing presence on 1880s Yonge Street? And how can we begin to appreciate the sense of place these structures once evoked when their historic neighbours have been levelled? As to their neighbours, no. 100's 15-storey granite-clad office tower is spare and elegant, making the attached historic façade all the more incongruous. New construction behind the façade of no. 102 is fortuitous; no. 104 is pathetic Post-Modernism. As seen in this whole sequence, façadism makes for superficial preservation; flawed new design; and an incoherent, deceptive streetscape. *PM*

2a Lumsden Building, 2–6 Adelaide St. E. [See Walk 6/11a.]

2b Ontario Heritage Centre, 8–12 Adelaide St. E. [See Walk 6/11b.]

2c 20 Adelaide St. E. [See Walk 6/11c.]

3a Dineen Building, 140 Yonge St. and 2 Temperance St. [See Walk 6/13a.]

3b 9 Temperance St. [See Walk 6/13b.]

4 Arcade Building, 137 Yonge St., Wilfrid Shulman, 1960. Replaced Toronto Arcade, Charles A. Walton, 1884. Long before the Eaton Centre, Toronto's first shopping mall stood here, a glass-topped arcade behind a Renaissance Revival façade. It came down in the 1950s and was replaced with this, a building of quiet quality outside and down-at-heel mid-century patina inside. *AB*

5 Confederation Square, 20 Richmond St. E. [See Walk 6/14.]

6 Hudson's Bay Co. and Saks Fifth Avenue/originally Robert Simpson Co., 160–184 Yonge St. (department store), Edmund Burke, 1894; rebuilt after fire, Burke & Horwood, 1895–96; addition, Burke Horwood & White, 1907; addition, Horwood & White, 1923; restored and entrance remodelled, 1977; interior alterations FRCH Design Worldwide and SAKS Fifth Avenue team, 2016; Richmond/Bay addition (store and office building), Chapman & Oxley, 1928. Simpson Tower, 401 Bay St. (office building), John B. Parkin Associates with Bregman & Hamann, 1968–71; alterations, Pellow Associates and WZMH, ongoing. Robert Simpson began selling dry goods in Toronto in 1872, moving to this corner in 1881 where his two-storey business could claim 13 clerks and two display windows. Today the buildings, under new ownership, blanket the block. The most stunning is the six-storey structure at Queen and Yonge, which was put up as the city's first entry in a daring new enterprise: the high-rise "departmental" store. Not only was the idea revolutionary, so was the architecture—a polished translation of avant-garde modes then being explored in the United States by Louis Sullivan and other express-the-steel-skeleton pioneers. The steel skeleton bore the weight of the building and permitted open interior

6 | Simpsons

spaces as well as large light-giving windows—perfect for a department store. Torontonians loved Simpson's, not least for its newfangled escalators, baby-minding facilities, "writing rooms, waiting rooms, and toilet rooms." With the 1907 nine-storey addition along Queen Street, it became the largest retail establishment in Canada.

The 1928 Art Deco addition at Richmond and Bay Streets influenced storewide alterations, including creation of a broad interior concourse lined with Moderne display windows. Little of this era remains inside, but the exteriors of both wings have been well cared for. Not so Parkin's interesting 1971 tower at Queen and Bay. For now, its bronze-hued glass and metal base speaks a different language than its precast-concrete top. But the current recladding will wrap it all in anodyne blue glass. *PM/AB*

7a 2 Queen St. E., WZMH, 2001. Incorporates Bank of Montreal, 173 Yonge St., Darling & Pearson, 1909–10. The aluminum and glass tower is both fussy and forgettable. It does, however, preserve the fine fruit-and-leaves plaster ornament of the banking hall, and the terracotta wreaths and garlands on the outer façades. *AB*

7b Elgin Theatre/originally Loew's Yonge Street Theatre and Winter Garden Theatre, 189–191 Yonge St., Thomas W. Lamb with Stanley Makepeace, 1913–14; interior remodelled, H.N. Stillman, 1934; restored, Mandel Sprachman, 1989. Swathed in Adamesque plasterwork, gold leaf, and red plush, Loew's Yonge Street originally exuded vaudeville house opulence. The upstairs Winter Garden was—and now is again—even more enticing: one of the world's first "atmospheric theatres," decked out with a ceiling of real leaves, supporting columns in the form of tree trunks, and trellised walls. It is one of Toronto's most whimsical and memorable rooms. Both houses were restored in the 1980s and now welcome live theatre again, under the ownership of the Ontario Heritage Trust. *PM/AB*

7c Originally J.F. Brown Furniture/ formerly Heintzman Hall, 193 Yonge St. (warehouse and commercial block), Henry Simpson, 1903; altered, J. Wilson Gray, 1910; altered later. This is probably the closest Toronto ever came to the spacious, crisp vocabulary of Frank Lloyd Wright and his followers. Buff-coloured brick and three-part Chicago windows are lessons learned from the Prairie School master. *PM*

7d Massey Tower, 197 Yonge St., Hariri Pontarini with ERA, ongoing. Incorporates Canadian Bank of Commerce, 199 Yonge St., Darling & Pearson, 1905. This complex and creative piece of development and architecture will retain most of the Beaux Arts bank branch, inside and out, while a thoughtful 60-storey tower slides in behind mid-block. New balconies will be lined by fritted white glass with a sinuous pattern; the tower promises to be as graceful as the architects' One Bloor **[18/21]**. But at ground level, the renewal of the bank (which will be the condo lobby) promises a fine dialogue between new and old. Another service to city-building: the developers have given a chunk of land for the expansion of Massey Hall **[5/9]**. *AB*

8 Toronto-Dominion Bank/originally Bank of Toronto, 205 Yonge St., E.J. Lennox, 1905–06. A small lavish Pantheon, squeezed onto the site with the same energy as that colossal model of antiquity in Rome. Lennox's interest in organic, integrated detail seems to have deserted him in this florid number

8 | Old TD Bank, 205 Yonge St.

(really more Greek than Roman), but one can't help admiring the panache with which he goes at it. If the bank doesn't look entirely prudent, it certainly looks prosperous. *PM*

9 Massey Hall, 15 Shuter St., Sidney Rose Badgley with George M. Miller, 1889–94; alteration and addition, KPMB and Goldsmith Borgal, ongoing. Massey Music Hall was built as a gift to the city by farm machinery magnate Hart Massey. Today looking the worse for wear and the safety regulations that have draped ever-larger fire escapes across the front, the hall is still renowned for its superb acoustics. Actually, the flat-chested red-brick exterior never had any great architectural pretensions; it was criticized from the first (chauvinistically, in part, because the plans were by an architect practising in Cleveland). Long the home of the Toronto Symphony Orchestra, Massey Hall (the word "Music" was dropped in the 1930s when "music hall" began to convey more salacious interests) continues as a Toronto institution even with the symphony ensconced elsewhere [see 3/6]. The current six-storey addition—replacing an older wing at the rear—will solve some of the hall's many technical deficiencies by providing a loading dock at street level, accessibility to all levels, and back-of-house spaces. It may also add another hall and glassed-in passages that run along the outside of the old Massey, which will itself get a cleanup. *PM/AB*

9 | Massey Hall

10 Originally John Catto Co. Ltd., 221–223 Yonge St. (two-unit commercial block), 1920; altered later. Very modern for its day. There is no question here where the supporting steel piers are located, nor that the wall of glass is a curtain hung between those piers, bearing no weight but its own and admitting as much light to the interior as possible. *PM*

11 Eaton Centre, Queen to Dundas St., Bay to Yonge St., Bregman & Hamann with Zeidler Partnership, 1977–78 (E.L. Hankinson with Parkin Millar & Associates for Eaton's store). Bell Trinity Square, 483 Bay St., Parkin Partnership, 1983. Mall additions, 1990; additions and alterations, 1999; alterations, 2015, Giannone Petricone; Nordstrom renovation, Queen's Quay Architects International Inc., 2016. Arguably the most important building in post-1950 Toronto, this is an oddity: a shopping mall in the middle of a pedestrian downtown, a profoundly North American building that alludes to Europe, a big-business big project with the blessing of Jane Jacobs. It is, in short, a modern Toronto compromise.

The Eaton's retail empire began imagining some sort of redevelopment in the early 1950s, as the shopping mall gained traction in the fast-growing suburbs [see 25/24]. Eaton's had assembled much of the block to serve its retail and mail-order operations; then city planners came to them in 1958 to suggest a shopping centre as a suitable neighbour for the new City Hall [7/18]. After working with New York developer William Zeckendorf and architect I.M. Pei [6/32b], Eaton's joined E.P. Taylor [26/5a] in assembling land and then went on its own. Eaton's 1965 proposal involved levelling Holy Trinity church [5/12a], and buying Old City Hall [7/17] from Metro Toronto's government and demolishing all but the clock tower. The design, by locals Mathers & Haldenby with Skidmore, Owings & Merrill, was a superblock including five towers and a half-underground mall. It almost happened before Eaton's abruptly cancelled the scheme in 1967.

The Fairview Corporation, the Bronfman family's development arm, cooked up a new scheme after Phyllis Bronfman **[6/34]** called upon architect Eberhard Zeidler. City planners insisted on keeping the mall engaged with the street grid and the larger neighbourhood. The Bauhaus-educated Zeidler found a precedent in Milan's Galeria Vittorio Emanuele II, which "functioned like a lively outdoor street, yet was protected from the weather," Zeidler wrote later. And it came to pass: 900 feet long and 60 feet wide, lined by stores and upstairs offices, capped by a glass roof that brought sunlight down through the mall via large atria. The architectural language was what came to be known as High-Tech, with exposed ducts and the steel structure painted white. (This effect has been heavily eroded through renovations.) The geese of Michael Snow's *Flight Stop* quickly became beloved public art.

The mall itself had a more mixed impact. Its largely closed front on Yonge Street was criticized for killing quality retail on the street. Jane Jacobs, a Zeidler friend and ally, thought otherwise: "In effect, the Galleria is an extra street dropped between Yonge and Bay for the length of a few blocks," Jacobs wrote. "Successful streets downtown strengthen one another." Was she right? The successful creation of Dundas Square **[5/16a]** suggests so: Yonge Street itself needed a shakeup, and today both the mall, a genuine urban place, and the street are doing just fine. *PM/AB*

12a Church of the Holy Trinity, Trinity Square, Henry Bowyer Lane, 1846–47; School addition, William Hay, 1856–57. Stout, corner-buttressed Holy Trinity looks more impressive today than it did as the centrepiece of Macaulaytown, later St. John's Ward, a working-class community **[see Introduction, Area V]**. The church was built with funds donated anonymously by a woman in England who, the story goes, greatly admired Toronto's visiting Bishop Strachan. Rather plain Gothic Revival, Holy Trinity nevertheless manages a good measure of finesse thanks to its cruciform plan and distinct chancel—supposedly a requirement of the gift, as was free seating. How misguided was Eaton's plan to demolish this church; it forms one of the most appealing vistas in the centre. *PM*

12b Church of the Holy Trinity rectory, Trinity Square, William Hay, 1861. Looking as comforting and picturesque as a Victorian parsonage should, the rectory and garden of Holy Trinity today provide a setting of enviable repose for lunch-hour office workers and weary shoppers. *PM*

11 | Eaton Centre

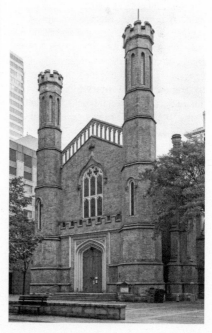

12a | Church of the Holy Trinity

12c The Rev. Henry Scadding house, originally at 10 Trinity Square, William Hay, 1857; third-floor addition, c. 1875; moved and restored, 1977. Henry Scadding was the first rector of Holy Trinity and the well-regarded author of two early histories of Toronto. His eclectic Georgian/Gothic house originally stood east of the rectory. The mansarded top floor containing Scadding's study was probably added in the 1870s; its intriguing balcony is said to have commanded a view down to the harbour and all around the town in the reverend's day. *PM*

13 Ryrie Building, 229 Yonge St. (commercial block and office building), Burke Horwood & White, 1913–14; restoration, ERA, 1997–2005. The Chicago architect Louis Sullivan's terracotta-ornamented skyscrapers of the 1890s deeply influenced architects including Frank Lloyd Wright [5/7c]. This building, though designed two decades later, harks back to that work while adding Edwardian neo-classical touches. This was an investment for jeweller Harry Ryrie, whose store (now demolished) was down the street. Ryrie's son Jack became an architect and worked on Maple Leaf Gardens [13/20]; perhaps he was inspired by this building, which—while no skyscraper—is, to borrow a Sullivan phrase, "every inch a proud and soaring thing." *AB*

14 Originally Art Metropole Ltd., 241 Yonge St. (commercial block), Mitchell & White, 1911. Yonge Street's narrow frontages were parcelled out with modest Georgian shops in mind. When later builders wanted to put much taller structures on the same narrow lots they were hard put to create buildings of similarly pleasing proportion and grace. Mitchell & White admirably met the challenge here, however, treating their four-storey curtain wall like a blank canvas on which to sketch elaborate and lovely windows and classical details. Inside, Art Metropole ran a picture gallery, blueprinting facility, and art supply store. *PM*

15a | Mirvish Theatre

15a David Mirvish Theatre/originally Pantages Theatre/formerly Imperial Theatre/formerly Imperial Six Theatre, 263 Yonge St. to 244 Victoria St., Thomas W. Lamb, 1920; remodelled, Mandel Sprachman, 1972; restored, David K. Mesbur, 1988–89. The vicissitudes of the Pantages echo those of many theatres in North America in the 20th century. When built, it was the largest vaudeville house in the British Empire, a lavish place of plush upholstery and Adamesque detail. With the advent of talkies and huge Depression-era audiences, it became a grand picture palace. When double features disappeared and large crowds with them, it was divided into six theatres fronted by a sleek "stripscape" façade of video machines on Yonge Street. A real-estate battle of two giant distributors had it severed in half for a time until one acquired the whole for come-full-circle restoration to a legitimate theatre once again. A generation of Torontonians know this as the home of *The Phantom of the Opera. PM/updated AB*

15b Hard Rock Cafe/originally Childs Restaurant, 279–283 Yonge St. (commercial block), John C. Westervelt, 1918. Childs was a large New York chain with a reputation for simple but stylish premises where the average wage-earner could sit down to a speedy, reasonably priced meal. Designed by Childs's New York architect, this Toronto branch (there were eventually three) was typical of Manhattan restaurants of the era with its many windows and bold white terracotta face. In 1918, Yonge Street office workers and shoppers would have found the interior equally direct and sparkling. *PM*

16a Yonge-Dundas Square, Brown + Storey, 2002. A decades-long effort to clear out some of Yonge's downscale retail culminated—through expropriation and an international design competition—in this, the first major public space downtown in generations. Like Nathan Phillips Square [7/18] it is a grass-free zone atop a public parking garage. But its surface is made of granite, and it slopes, rising up toward a stage that's put to frequent use. The north-side canopy provides shade and a café; a water feature provides sound, visual stimulation, and an opportunity for play. But mostly the design stays out of the way, establishing a finely polished blank slate for urban life. *AB*

16b 10 Dundas Square/originally Metropolis, Baldwin & Franklin, 2009. The companion to Yonge-Dundas Square [5/16a], this massive pile-on of cinemas and billboards has almost no architecture to speak of. The theatres are sometimes used by Ryerson University for classes; the signage shows a conceptual debt to the 1990s cleanup of New York's Times Square. *AB*

16c Hermant Building (offices and retail), 19 Dundas Square, Bond & Smith, 1913. HNR Building, 21 Dundas Square, Benjamin Brown, 1929; restoration, ERA, ongoing. Velocity at the Square (rental apartments), 252 Victoria St., Diamond Schmitt, Page & Steele/IBI Group and ERA, ongoing. Toronto's diamond dealers, gold dealers, and jewellers gather in this pair of Deco-ish towers—a tall warren of small, beat-up offices that seems to belong in mid-block Manhattan. The smaller of the two, at no. 19, has wonderful terracotta ornament; the larger, at no. 21, was designed by Benjamin Brown [4/9] with a lack of ornament that was remarkable for 1929 Toronto. The new apartment building at the corner, developed by the same owners, will help keep these gems polished and set in place. *AB*

17 Ted Rogers School of Management, 55 Dundas St. W., Zeidler Partnership, 2006. Business school and big boxes, poorly packaged. *AB*

18 Atrium on Bay, 20–40 Dundas St. W. to 595 Bay St. (retail and office building), Page & Steele, 1982–83; altered, 2000. Not one atrium but actually three atria, connecting to all sides of the block. This type of space, so common in office towers of the 1980s, serves quite well here as a gathering place—although the idea of putting a quasi-street inside a massive, street-killing building was and remains perverse. The three buildings, two of 13 storeys and one of nine storeys, are Late-Modernist glass boxes with the era's *de rigueur* chamfered corners and highly reflective façades. *AB*

19 Toronto Camera Centre/originally Thornton-Smith Co., 340 Yonge St. (commercial block), John M. Lyle, 1921. One of Toronto's most amiable small shop buildings. Lyle won first place in an Ontario Association of Architects competition for this "modernized Italian" treatment, complete with (originally red) tile roof. The large display windows on two floors were a requirement of the client, an antiques dealer and interior decorator. *PM*

Named for a solitary elm tree that once dominated the corner at Yonge, Elm Street is still of interest for its landscaping. An attractive row of ash trees and the widened and handsomely paved sidewalk make this a very appealing detour.

20a Barberian's Steak House, 7–9 Elm St. (double house), 1868.
Georgian, the first style to enjoy favour in colonial Toronto, featuring a carefully proportioned, formal façade invigorated with picturesque round-arched windows and a brick cornice. These were built as dwellings, but the style served equally well for shops, a few of which still survive on Yonge Street. *PM*

20b Arts and Letters Club/originally St. George's Hall, 14 Elm St., Edwards & Webster, 1891; interior remodelled, Sproatt & Rolph, 1920.
A late Victorian smorgasbord with enough Old World historicizing to make members feel right at home. (The St. George's Society was founded to foster British traditions in Canada.) Inside is the *pièce de résistance,* a wood-panelled Tudor dining hall with great baronial fireplace and fanciful heraldic crests invented in 1920 for members of the Arts and Letters Club. *PM*

20c | Elmwood Club

20c Elmwood Club/originally YWCA, 18 Elm St., Gordon & Helliwell, 1890–91; rear addition, André Ostiguy, 1982.
A rich and rotund Richardsonian Romanesque club building with fine detail outlining the mass. The new addition in the rear for a women's health and social club is first-rate: large, but not overpowering; modern, but not incompatible. *PM*

20d 8–12 Elm Street (shops), 1889–90; proposed redevelopment, Page & Steele/IBI Group, ongoing. Chelsea Hotel/originally Delta Chelsea Inn, 33 Gerrard St. W., Crang & Boake, 1975; addition, 1990; proposed redevelopment, architectsAlliance, ongoing.
The quick and stealthy growth of Yonge Street after 2000 may come to a head on this block. The Elm Street site, small and adjacent to the national historic site of the Arts and Letters Club [5/20b], is being eyed for an 80-storey tower. Just to the north, the massive hotel could be replaced by an even more massive complex with three towers of 88, 88, and 49 storeys, respectively, containing housing, retail, and a hotel.

Why such a radical clustering of density? Blame Toronto's opaque development process [see Introduction] and the precedent set by the adjacent Aura [5/24]. Something will probably come of these proposals, with mixed news in terms of urban design and architecture: architectsAlliance reliably build good developer buildings, while in this era Page & Steele/IBI reliably build poor ones. Details aside, this is a sign of policy dysfunction: it would make much more sense to spread out this density across downtown, but that's not how Toronto is being built these days. *AB*

21 Ryerson Student Learning Centre, 341 Yonge St., Snøhetta with Zeidler Partnership, 2015.
One of the flashiest, and best, buildings in Toronto of the past two decades. With a growing student body and cramped campus [see Area VI], Ryerson commissioned this stack of study spaces as an adjunct to its Library Building [see Walk 13]. Where its neighbours are opaque concrete, this building dons glass fritted

21 | Ryerson Student Learning Centre

with a varied triangular motif; its interiors offer a masala of intense colours, odd angles, and nooks and crannies designed to welcome different kinds of chat, browsing, and study. The people-watching here is fascinating.

Each level has a visual theme and implied narrative ("The Forest" is green, and so on), culminating in "The Beach." The latter's enormous room slants down across a double-height volume, its slope finished in warm wood, zigzagged by ramps and dotted with colourful lounge chairs. There's an important caveat, though: since the ramps are constantly being blocked by sitting figures, the room is largely inaccessible by people with physical disabilities, and that's true also of the ceremonial stair that brings people in from the street. This is a building for everyone—or almost everyone. *AB*

22a YSL (residential and retail), 385 Yonge St., KPF, proposed. Incorporates 363–365 Yonge St. (three-unit commercial block), Denison & King, 1890; Gerrard Building, 385–395 Yonge St., Sproatt & Rolph, 1924. Another wildly tall proposal, this one at 98 storeys. If built, its smooth façades and sculptured massing could be very handsome. Meanwhile, the loosely

Richardsonian block at 363–365 remains a delight, with Moorish windows and a profusion of ornament; the Gerrard Building's austerely Gothic face sets a forward-looking example. *PM/AB*

22b Elephant & Castle/originally Dominion Bank, 378 Yonge St., John M. Lyle, 1930. One of the great surviving works by Lyle, who aspired to create a regional Canadian architecture in the age of the International Style. His method: "new combinations of old forms and a new language of ornament . . . symbolism in the form of fresh, vital, contemporary decoration." Here, the ornament includes pine cones, owls, and a depiction of labourers on the Toronto harbour, while French and English coins have equal place on the Yonge Street façade. The two-storey banking hall retains much of its ornament and lovely proportions. Ironically, this product of Canadian nationalism is now a London-themed pub, complete with red phone box and street sign to Leicester Square. *AB*

22b | 378 Yonge St.

23 401–405 Yonge St. (three-unit commercial block), 1873. Much taller than Georgian-style predecessors and employing all the facile shadow-producing details of the Renaissance Revival, these row shops must have appeared very grand in their day. Now the façades have been beautifully restored. *PM/updated AB*

24 Aura (condominium apartments and retail), 386 Yonge St., Graziani & Corazza, 2014. Toronto's tallest residential building, highly visible and titanically bad. The base has two masses visually crashing into one another; above that a squared-off stack of balconies and spandrel extends into the sky, capped by an ovoid shaft that ends in a scoop and an icy-bright light feature. But what's worse is the ground level: the sidewalk-facing retail spaces are cramped and cluttered, overshadowed by an ominous cantilever, and walled in by patio seating. This project might have seemed like a victory when the area was in transition—all those condo dwellers need mattresses and trash cans, and the big-box stores on levels 2 and 3 supply those needs—but it makes for a junky skyline and a mean street. The next round of very tall towers had better improve on this. *AB*

25 College Park/originally Eaton's College Street, 444 Yonge St. (department store and office building), Ross & Macdonald with Sproatt & Rolph, 1928–30; apartment and office additions, Allward & Gouinlock, A.M. Ingleson & Associates, Joseph Bogdan, Webb Zerafa Menkes Housden, 1983. Barbara Ann Scott Park, renovation, Toronto Parks, Forestry and Recreation with RAW Design, MBTW/ Watchorn Architect and Project for Public Spaces, ongoing. The seven-storey 1920s Art Deco building is a fraction of the 40-storey-plus skyscraper that Eaton's expected would replace its hodgepodge of Queen Street stores, workrooms, and offices. The Depression and construction difficulties

interfered and the building never proceeded further than this, but monumental scale, superb materials, and distinctive detailing made it an architectural event anyway. (Contemporary writers dubbed the stylized half-naturalistic/half-classical ornament "floral Ionic.")

When the first stage of Eaton Centre opened in 1977 **[5/11]**, Eaton's sold this facility to developers, who have turned it into individual shops and offices. Much of the Art Deco interior in the shopping levels designed by French architect René Cera is in place, as is an extraordinary seventh-floor Deco concert hall and restaurant created by another Frenchman, Jacques Carlu. Adjacent new buildings on the College Park site are huge but forgettable, neither enhancing nor detracting from the 1920s centrepiece. *PM*

26 Toronto Hydro-Electric System, 14 Carlton St. (office building), Chapman & Oxley, 1931–33. Built as the head office of the city's hydro system in what was considered Toronto's up-and-coming business section, this ten-storey skyscraper was the last word in suave Deco styling. Few glass buildings can match the smoothness of its meticulously laid limestone face, sleekly graced with Moderne bas-reliefs and four female heads peering precipitously down over the sidewalk. Inside, Hydro ran a Home Institute featuring lectures on "the use of electrical appliances for interested housewives." *PM*

27 2 Carlton St. (offices), Edward I. Richmond and Alan Moody, 1958; proposed redevelopment, IBI Group, ongoing. An International Style tower with several curious features. It mixes white and black brick; its façades cant apart to meet the angle of the street corner; it's lined with brick projections that suggest apartments but actually provide shade for offices. All this and a parking garage whose grid of offset rectangles channel Le Corbusier via Peter Dickinson. Well worth a second look—but targeted for demolition. The owners' initial proposal for two 72-storey towers is preposterous. *AB*

25 | College Park

College Street, like University Avenue [Walk 7], was originally a private road leading to the University of Toronto grounds, complete with pre-emptive gate at Yonge Street. The area south of this road was the site of the Hon. J.B. Macaulay estate built in 1841. It later served as Bishop Strachan School from 1870 to 1915, at which time Eaton's acquired the land for their new store [5/25]. To the north another solitary villa dominated until 1881 when the O'Brien house was constructed. The university removed its gate in 1882 and officially conveyed the thoroughfare to the city as a public street in 1889.

28a YC Condos, 460 Yonge St., Graziani & Corazza, ongoing. The same architects as Aura, again for the developer Canderel, and no better but much gaudier—black and white and loud all over. *AB*

28b Originally Oddfellows' Hall, 2 College St. (commercial block and office building), Dick & Wickson, 1891–92. The Independent Order of Odd Fellows owned and met in this building, and there certainly is a feeling that mystical rites were carried on behind the elaborate chateau-roofed, Gothic-ornamented fourth storey. "Going to lodge" was a popular leisure activity in Toronto at the turn of the 20th century, with scores of branches of various fraternal societies located around town, some in money-making edifices such as this. *PM*

28c Originally Upper Canada Bible Society, 14 College St. (office building), Gordon & Helliwell, 1910. The Bible Society unabashedly borrowed an Ionic portico from the repertoire of the banks to front this building. The office block atop is a later addition. *PM*

28d Superior Loan/originally Canadian Order of Foresters, 22 College St. (office building), William R. Gregg, 1908–10. Comfortable buff-brick Classical Revival, following no rigid rules but coming together in a pleasantly dignified structure. The quasi-residential character of College Street at this time seemed to appeal to fraternal societies. *PM*

29a Native Child and Family Services, 30 College St. Building, Kirkor, 1989; interior alterations, Levitt Goodman, 2010. This building's corporate box is now a welcoming home for an agency that provides social services. Levitt Goodman strived to find common references among Canadian Aboriginal peoples; they added colour, natural materials, and plant life, plus a contemporary take on the longhouse and, on the roof, a healing lodge and fire circle. *AB*

29b Metropolitan Toronto Police Headquarters, 40 College St. (office building), Shore Tilbe Henschel Irwin Peters, 1987–88. The eighties-est building in Toronto: grand forecourt, quasi-classical columns, a dome up top, a giant atrium, and the inevitable pink granite everywhere. Some design attributes of the building might come back into fashion; for instance, part of it is massed like a mountain **[4/3b]**. But whatever is in style, this will unfortunately reflect an era when police felt the need to build fortresses **[7/24]**. Bonus: the police museum in the front varies from hokey to seriously macabre. *AB*

30a 480 Yonge St. (detached house), 1864. Initially the home and office of a "corn dealer," this was among the first buildings erected on Yonge Street north of College. In the 1870s, it served as an inn, and the unusual pliant-looking stone quoins and window surrounds might have been affixed at that time. *PM*

30b Halo (condominium apartments), 484 Yonge St., Quadrangle, proposed. Incorporates tower of Firehall No. 3, James Grand with William Irving, 1870–72. If this condo is built as planned, the Victorian firehall tower—previously hidden behind storefronts—will come out to the sidewalk to ornament a bulky, bland slab. Some rescue. *AB*

31a YMCA of Greater Toronto, 20 Grosvenor St. thru to 15 Breadalbane St., A.J. Diamond & Partners, 1984. Sleek with rosy-red brick, trim stonework, smooth glass blocks, and bold muscular shapes, this building glows with health and vigour. The materials and aesthetic are assuredly those of the 1980s, but this is no flimsy Post-Modern exercise. It is a challenging, meticulous balance of cubes and spheres, flat planes and curves, all rendered with extraordinary skill. The building is large but never overwhelms its through-block site, and the composition is as intriguing viewed from the rear street or even through the parking lot from the side street as from the front. One has the feeling this building will still be winning kudos 100 years from now. *PM*

31a | YMCA, 20 Grosvenor

31b George Drew Building, 25 Grosvenor St., Ludlow & Fleury, 1975. A sober and spare Brutalist slab for the province's coroner and other offices, with remarkably few details executed remarkably well. This is the work of Eric Arthur's former office **[8/47]**. *PM/updated AB*

32a Originally Clarke's Buildings, 502–508 Yonge St. (four units of original six-unit commercial block), 1860. These were the first three-storey brick shops on this stretch of Yonge. One unit served as a boarding house, another as a saloon, and the others for an organ maker and stonecutter. The showy Renaissance Revival pediment and cornice window heads are later additions intended to give a second generation of stores a sophisticated, up-to-date character. Today they would benefit from a cleaning. *PM/updated AB*

32b 526–528 Yonge St. (two-unit commercial block), McCaw & Lennox, 1881. This is one of E.J. Lennox's first-known buildings, designed when he was in partnership with William F. McCaw. This pair of shops in fact replaced a brick house put up on the site only ten years prior. Yonge Street's burgeoning commercial potential made rebuilding desirable, and the flashy Second Empire style was just the ticket to attract customers. The first shopkeepers sold furniture and stationery and lived upstairs. *PM*

33 Offices/originally William Galbraith house, 37 Maitland St., 1868. Flour merchant Galbraith built himself one of the most radiant houses in Toronto. He must have liked it, too, for he lived here 30 years, 1868–98. The well-laid courses of red brick, the handsome chimneys and hipped roof, the contrasting yellow-brick quoins, string courses, and relieving arches all make for a beautifully articulated and civilized composition, now in fine repair. *PM/updated AB*

34 527–529 Yonge St. (two-unit commercial block), 1876. 531 Yonge St. (commercial block), 1883–84. 533 Yonge St. (commercial block), 1880–81. 535 Yonge St. (commercial block), 1881–82. These five shops were variously owned and rented out by the four Sharpe sisters, spinsters whose family had held the land hereabouts from before 1834. While the different styles might point to varying proclivities among the Misses Sharpe, they also indicate the period's rich architectural repertoire: Second Empire, Renaissance Revival, Queen Anne. In 1883, shopkeepers were, south to north, a druggist, spice dealer, furniture dealer, butcher, and marble worker. *PM*

35 Wellesley On the Park (condominium apartments), 11 Wellesley St. W., KPMB and Page & Steele/IBI Group, ongoing. Park, DTAH, ongoing. What promises to be an interesting tower of white-glass curves; the negotiation between developers and city produced the adjacent L-shaped park, which will sit atop the building's parking garage. *AB*

36 Originally "Somerset House" (residence of Hon. James Cox Aikens)/ formerly J.W.L. Forster house, 27 Wellesley St. E., 1876; apartment house addition, Jerome Markson, 1979. Wellesley Street was originally lined with fashionable residences, much like those on nearby Church and Jarvis Streets **[see Area VII]**. One of the few to survive was Somerset House. James Aikens, secretary of state under Sir John A. Macdonald, built this tall-gabled country-house-style manor. The apartment building in back is a modestly scaled 1970s triumph of Toronto infillism. *PM/AB*

37a 588 Yonge St. (commercial block), 1879. Big roof, little window; but the bracketed cornice is lively enough to handle any deficiencies. In 1879, Charles Barnsley, a wig-maker, had these premises; today, it's a hairdresser. *PM/updated AB*

37b 590–596 Yonge St. (four-unit commercial block), 1888. Fine commercial buildings with crisply detailed cornice and pilasters—a very unusual touch is the alternating wide and narrow bays and windows. In 1892, no. 596 was a "locksmith and bell-hanger's" store and works. *PM*

37c 565–571 Yonge St. (four units of original six-unit commercial block), 1887–88. Today bleakly "blackwashed," this commercial block was once as ruddy as its Richardsonian Romanesque details suggest. Such a weighty look was not much used for shops; its massive rough-cut ashlar and deep-set windows were just too expensive for speculative builders. *PM*

St. Joseph Street, like other saintly thoroughfares in this neighbourhood, was laid out and named by John Elmsley, a wealthy landowner and Roman Catholic convert. The rise of sandy ground which dominated his holdings and accounted for the curve of St. Joseph Street as well as Irwin Avenue (originally St. Charles) one block north, he called Clover Hill. In the early 1850s, Elmsley donated a choice parcel atop Clover Hill for the building of St. Basil's Church and St. Michael's College [8/48a].

38a 6–14 St. Joseph St. (five-house row), 1879. A proud and brassy Second Empire quintet, built when the mansard-roof style was at the peak of fashion in Toronto. Usually Second Empire houses were of yellow brick, not the red seen here, but all the other rich effects are typical. *PM*

38b Five Condos, 5 St. Joseph St., Hariri Pontarini with ERA, 2017. Incorporates 606–612 Yonge St., 1884–85; 614 Yonge St., 1885; 616 Yonge St., 1885, altered, Kaplan & Sprachman, 1929; 618 Yonge St.; originally Marmaduke Rawlinson Storage, 5 St. Joseph St., Wickson & Gregg, 1905–07. How can the high-density development of 21st-century Toronto coexist with modestly scaled Victorian architecture? If there's a way, this is it. Nine buildings have been skilfully restored in place, not just their façades but most of their masses; this saves the scale and to some degree the fine-grained commercial character of Yonge Street, and the grandeur of the warehouse on St. Joseph, heart of the Rawlinson Cartage operation here for more than 80 years.

The local architect Robert Allsopp calls this approach "urban taxidermy," complaining about the reduced number of businesses, the displacement of long-time tenants, and the inevitable dulling presence of a bank. But tenants can change, and with genuine street-facing stores, this approach represents a huge step up from the stage-set façades of Brookfield Place **[6/2]** in the late 1980s. The tower above is interesting too: the balconies, aesthetic bugbears, are here fronted with a snaky ornamental screen of fritted glass. The public art by Eldon Garnet includes a fitting aphorism: "FROM ONE NARRATIVE TO THE NEXT." *AB*

38b | Five Condos

38c Eleven Apartments, 11 St. Joseph St., Taylor Hazell with Young + Wright, 2004. Incorporates façades of Marmaduke Rawlinson Storage, 11–19 St. Joseph St., Dick & Wickson, 1895–96; fourth-storey addition, A. Frank Wickson, 1898–99. An earlier version of "urban taxidermy," also quite fine, with an earlier warehouse for the same company as next door—though its rebuilt brick façade looks thoroughly ersatz. *AB*

38d Canadian Music Centre, 18–20 St. Joseph St. (double house), 1892. A Queen Anne/Romanesque medley in a form that Toronto made its own, especially in the Annex **[Walk 19]**. This harmonious gable/turret duet now enlivens Chalmers House, the Canadian Music Centre. *PM*

38e Cloverhill Apartments, 26 St. Joseph St., J. Gibb Morton, 1939. This Art Moderne building nearly fills its site, and has flourishes—showy brickwork and handsome corner windows—yet is retiring and extremely handsome. Toronto could use another few hundred of these, or their contemporary equivalents. *AB*

38e | Cloverhill Apartments

39 634–644 Yonge St. (six-house row), 1860; remodelled as commercial block, c. 1870–80; nos. 642 and 644 renovated with rear addition, G.S. Baldine Associates, 1983–84. Wooden sills and six-light sash windows betray the early date of these simple two-storey brick row houses, built in a period when Yonge Street was still partly residential. They had all probably been converted to shops by 1880. The two corner units got a careful 1980s restoration and Post-Modern addition. *PM/updated AB*

40 Gloucester Mews/originally Masonic Hall, 601 Yonge St. (commercial block and office building), Richard Ough, 1888; renovated with rear addition, Gordon S. Adamson & Associates, 1972. For many years the tallest building on Yonge Street north of Dundas, this red-brick and stone five-storey structure stands as one of Toronto's best late 19th-century commercial blocks, bringing dignity *and* energy to the street. The whole building is well represented by the complicated yet clean-looking wood and iron shopfronts with rope-turned posts. Grocer Alexander Patterson, a member of the Scottish Rite Freemasons, commissioned the building with the guild in mind; they met here in a hall on the fourth floor for 33 years until 1921 when a new Masonic building was constructed at Davenport and Yonge.

The Adamson office's immaculate renovation in 1972 included a Bay-n-Gable house on Gloucester Street sensitively linked to the Masonic Hall by a modern but complementary two-storey glass structure. A development proposal, stalled but likely to return, would put a 34-storey residential tower here. *PM/AB*

41 664–682 Yonge St. (ten-unit commercial block), E.J. Lennox, 1883. These shops rival Lennox's gracious houses, except that they are splendidly bigger and bolder. Architecturally, they mark a short but interesting interval between a time when Yonge Street stores could pass for houses and when they became no-nonsense commercial fronts. Lennox designed this row for the Scottish Ontario and Manitoba Land Company, a name recalling days when developers forthrightly spelled out their aims. *PM*

42 6–14 Irwin Ave. (five-house row), 1892. A Queen Anne quintet nimbly grouped around a central tower for added pizzazz on this curved street. *PM*

43a 45–63 St. Nicholas St. (ten-house row), 1884–86. Situated on what was once a back lane, this delightful row of small houses—each with a name marker for a different tree or flower—is unknown to most Torontonians. Bargeboarded Bay-n-Gable was unusual for such a long terrace, but it works just fine. *PM*

43b Nicholas Residences, 75 St. Nicholas St., CORE with Goldsmith Borgal, 2014. A tower of some elegance, most notable for the handsome lobby and townhouses flush to the street. It's a sharp contrast to the Modernist tower-in-the-park across the street, which shows no awareness whatsoever of where it is. *AB*

44 Originally Robert Barron Provisions, 726–728 Yonge St. (two-unit commercial block), George Gouinlock, 1889. Behind the paint and signage are lavish Richardsonian Romanesque arches and terracotta detail plus an elegant Queen Anne oriel window hanging over the corner. Toronto provisioners—they sold liquor and wine as well as foodstuffs in those days—often seemed to command the handsomest buildings on their blocks. *PM/updated AB*

45 Originally Postal Station F, 675 Yonge St., David Ewart, Department of Public Works, with Samuel G. Curry, 1905–06. In contrast to Yonge's more usual brick, terracotta, and ground-level entries, massive rock-faced ashlar, cut-stone Ionic columns, and a stepped-up first floor were used to signify the postal station's important civic function. The early 1900s date would also have dictated such formal, classical architecture. *PM*

46 764 Yonge St. Originally Loew's Uptown Theatre, 764–766 Yonge St. thru to Balmuto St., Thomas W. Lamb, 1918; remodelled, Mandel Sprachman with Marvin Giller, 1970. Uptown Residences, 35 Balmuto St., Burka Architects, 2011. This storefront was once the front door and conduit to a 2,000-seat vaudeville house, later converted to movie use. The bulk of the theatre itself, on Balmuto Street to the west, has been replaced with a tall neo-Deco mediocrity. *AB*

Yonge Street north of Bloor Street was part of the independent Village of Yorkville [see Area IX], dominated by the Yorkville Town Hall that stood just north of Yorkville Avenue until 1942.

47 | Toronto Reference Library

47 Toronto Reference Library, 789 Yonge St., Raymond Moriyama, 1973–77; alterations and additions, Moriyama & Teshima, 2009. If Toronto's City Hall **[7/18]** expressed the ambitious, far-reaching spirit of the 1960s, this public building equally captures the inward-looking and less prosperous 1970s. And yet it is excellent on those terms: large but retiring, novel in form (a mountain pierced by a 45-degree opening) but wrapped in familiar brick. This was a compromise. Moriyama's first proposal was glass. Moriyama's design balances the building's competing uses as a research centre (on the upper floors) and public gathering place (on the ground floor). The latter mandate was well served by the renovation carried out by Moriyama's firm 30 years later, which complements the original water features with a now-requisite café.

The literal and poetic centrepiece is the atrium, which recalls Moriyama's Scarborough Civic Centre **[26/17]**, as well as the work of the Post-Modern pioneer James Frazer Stirling. Such grand interior spaces became a bombastic cliché in hotels and public buildings **[see 5/29b]**; this one works, its scale softened by warm nubbly carpet, greenery, and Scandinavian curves. You can read here while feeling very much a citizen of the city. *AB*

In early York, it was church spires that ruled the skyline; in today's Toronto, it is bank towers. The big Canadian banks play an outsize role in the city's economy, and likewise in its urban form: the familiar logos of those institutions and their nearly-as-familiar towers rule the skyline from King and Bay. Yet that corner and this district are, like so much of the city, in a subtle and fascinating state of flux.

The banks go back a long way in this district. While the city's first bank, the Bank of Upper Canada founded in 1822, was in the Old Town of York **[Area I]**, its successors wound up clustering here. In the 1840s and 1850s, the area emerged as a warehousing and wholesale district quite apart from the Old Town or New Town **[Area II]**. The Bank of Montreal **[6/1]** and the Bank of British North America **[6/3]** were joined by a string of competitors—all of whom used architecture to send messages about their solvency and solidity. The careful stonework and classical mien of the former Commercial Bank of the Midland District, now on display within the galleria of Brookfield Place **[6/2]**, suggest the effort and expense that went into these temples of capitalism.

They didn't last long. Since these buildings were showpieces, the banks were constantly upgrading them with newer, bigger, and finer iterations. That process continued through the 19th century, accompanied by other forces that pushed architecture literally to new heights. From the 1860s to the 1880s, the building type of the skyscraper grew up in Chicago and New York, spurred by the innovations of cast-iron and then steel structure, the passenger elevator, and electric power. Toronto—and it might not be surprising to hear this—had a very ambivalent relationship with this new ethos of tallness; there was considerable public opposition to it. A few buildings of masonry reached new heights at seven storeys, including Confederation Life's **[6/14]**, and, in 1896, George Gouinlock's remarkable 12-storey Temple Building at Bay and Richmond [demolished in 1970]. But high-rise Toronto took off with the Traders Bank building **[6/5]**, whose 15 storeys were equalled by the Canadian Pacific Building

Area IV
Walk 6: Financial District

[6/6]. These structures, ambitious though they were, shared the conservatism of their low-rise predecessors: They favoured a classical idiom, and often mimicked the three-part composition of a classical column: base, shaft, and capital.

The next wave of towers, starting in the 1920s, embodied a different aesthetic and set of values: not solidity and heft but modernity and sheer verticality. One innovation, as seen in the Sterling Tower on Bay Street **[6/16]**, was the ziggurat form: buildings stepped back at the top to allow light down to the street and to express an upward thrust [6/18]. Inspired by New York's 1916 Zoning Resolution, the form was used in Toronto for poetic effect—as were forms of ornament developed by architects such as Raymond Hood, which were often abstractions of older styles. At the Concourse Building [6/24], Baldwin & Greene and artist J.E.H. MacDonald put a Canadian spin on the exterior ornament and lobby. John Lyle's Canadiana shaped the new home of the Bank of Nova Scotia [6/31a], designed in the late 1920s and built after World War II. By the 1930s, the thoughtful Lyle aspired for his work to be "modern but not crazy," a very Torontonian ambition.

Nonetheless, modern architecture, undiluted, would soon arrive in Toronto. The young British expatriate Peter Dickinson helped bring the downtown into the new era with a small office building on Richmond Street West in 1954 [6/25], and John C. Parkin, at the firm led by his namesake John B. Parkin, [7/9] followed; the decisive shift came with the new Toronto-Dominion Centre [6/34], designed by that giant of Modernism, Ludwig Mies van der Rohe. The complex itself was literally giant, its first two black towers suddenly dominating a skyline that had heretofore been ruled by the Royal York. "Familar in form to the architectural profession, it nevertheless manages to confound its critics by inviting comparison with its neighbouring buildings," Canadian Architect wrote in 1967. Those buildings were mostly short, with masonry bones and skin of stone. That changed, as the other banks followed TD's lead in commissioning their own grand headquarters [6/33, 6/36]. It took until the end of the 1980s for that process to be completed with Scotia Plaza [6/31b], by which time a kind of historicism— Post-Modernism—was back in fashion. The singular megaproject of the 1980s, now Brookfield Place [6/2], paid at least lip service to historic preservation, turning several century-old buildings into ornaments on its great mass.

But the fabric of this neighbourhood had by now undergone a dramatic change. For one thing, TD Centre had launched the network of underground shopping malls that would be known as the PATH, taking retail and pedestrian activity away from the streets. At the same time, TD and the bank projects that followed it, including Commerce Court [6/32b], had disrupted the street grid with new superblocks, and added an increasingly monolithic character to the area. A growing movement of progressive planners and architects saw dangerous implications in this homogenization and sorting of the city. The 1974 report On Building Downtown introduced urban design guidelines for the downtown core, and called for a more mixed character, including residences; this call was answered only in fits and starts in the 1970s and 1980s.

Today, however, residences have pushed to the east edge of the Financial District [Walk 2], to the west edge [Walk 3], and even to its heart [6/19]. Meanwhile, the core itself continues to build on the economic strengths of finance and professional services. Yet the architectural preferences of Bay Street have changed. The first generations of skyscrapers, including one of Dickinson's [6/25], have acquired a vintage charm; the behemoths of the 1960s and '70s are aging and require updates; and a new boom is creating fresh space nearby. The towers of South Core, just outside of the Financial District [3/10 to 3/12], offer shiny new space in a district that includes homes and entertainment, the sort of mixed-use downtown that attracts today's white-collar workers. The towers of the Financial District aren't going anywhere—the PATH is busier on a winter's day than any street in the city—but their granite and steel have lost a bit of their lustre.

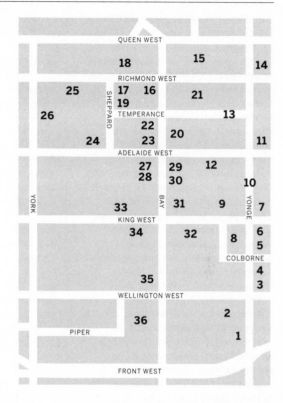

Walk 6: Financial District

1 Hockey Hall of Fame/originally Bank of Montreal, 30 Yonge St., Darling & Curry, 1885–86; altered, Bregman & Hamann with Spencer R. Higgins, 1993. This rich and lovely rococo gem is surely the most spirited, self-assured building erected in 19th-century Toronto. Put up in a prosperous period of national optimism, it abounds with vigorous stonework, grand plate-glass windows, and exuberantly carved trophies announcing verities to make the country great: Agriculture, Architecture, Music, and Commerce on the south side; Science, Industry, Literature, and Art on the east. The interior boasts a 45-foot-high banking hall (now Esso Great Hall) topped by a vibrant stained glass dome depicting more allegory: a dragon guarding gold from an eagle! The wing to the west housed the manager's office, boardroom, and private apartment. This bravado building, which replaced a restrained straight-fronted High Renaissance–style bank put up in 1845, was the Bank of Montreal's head Toronto office until 1949, then its most magnificent branch until 1982. Today it is a temple to the national game. *PM/updated AB*

1 | Hockey Hall of Fame

2 Brookfield Place/originally BCE Place, 181 Bay St. Canada Trust Tower, 161 Bay St., Bregman & Hamann with Skidmore, Owings and Merrill, 1990. Bay-Wellington Tower, 181 Bay St., Bregman + Hamann with Skidmore, Owings and Merrill, 1992. Galleria and Heritage Square, 181 Bay St., Santiago Calatrava with Bregman + Hamann and Spencer Higgins, 1992. Incorporates Commercial Bank of the Midland District, formerly 13–15 Wellington St. W., William Thomas, 1845. Outer façades incorporate 36 Yonge St. (warehouse), 1844–45, altered, 1928; 38–40 Yonge St. (two-unit warehouse), 1852, no. 40 altered, c. 1865; 42–44 Yonge St. (two-unit warehouse), 1850–51, altered, c. 1880–85; originally Argyle Hotel, 46 Yonge St., 1844, altered, Frederick H. Herbert, 1901; 5 Wellington St. W. (warehouse), 1858–59; 7 Wellington St. W. (warehouse), Smith & Gemmell, 1871; 9 Wellington St. W. (warehouse), Smith & Gemmell, 1871, altered, Bond & Smith, 1919; 11 Wellington St. W. (warehouse), possibly William Hay, 1854–55; Gowans Kent Building, 18–22 Front St. W., MacVicar & Heriot, 1923. The top of every business cycle generates its monuments, and this complex crowned the 1980s boom in style. Thanks to "the postmodern condition and our newfound attraction to complexity," the *Star*'s Christopher Hume wrote in 1990, "a development such as this can embrace new and old, big and small." The "big" included two towers with Modernist granite skins (new) but vaguely Deco crowns (old) up top. The "small" included a string of buildings from the 1850s through the 1870s, whose façades were preserved or rebuilt mostly in their original places, their brick and stonework preserved for future generations. These choices show more respect for architectural history than evident in the tabula rasa superblocks of the 1960s **[see 6/34]**. And yet . . . these façades are grafted onto a shopping mall: they have doors that don't open, windows with no one behind them. This is not urbanism but decoration. Inside is a real architectural gift to the city: a galleria and "heritage square" by the Spanish architect and engineer Santiago Calatrava. Built to satisfy the city's public art requirement, this bravura arcade of white steel evokes by turns whale bones, an ancient forest, and Victorian engineering feats such as the Eiffel Tower. Looking on from one side is the Greek Revival façade of the Merchant's Bank, out of place in this novel scene but somehow looking comfortable. *AB*

3 Irish Embassy Pub and Grill/originally Bank of British North America, 49 Yonge St., Henry Langley, 1873–74; altered, Burke & Horwood, 1903. Henry Langley brought the sophistication of Baron Haussmann's Parisian boulevards to Toronto with this richly decorated Second Empire bank of Ohio sandstone. Langley had introduced the French-derived style to Toronto with his 1866 Government House and it took the city by storm, but nowhere was the style's message of grandeur and power more appropriate than here, the most prestigious corner of the financial district at the time. (The doorway originally stood on Wellington, but after Yonge Street became the more important thoroughfare, it was moved to that façade in 1903.) Today the ground floor houses a pub called the Irish Embassy, a fate that would have raised some eyebrows among the bank's original customers. *PM/updated AB*

3 | 49 Yonge St.

4 55 Yonge St. (offices), Page & Steele (Peter Dickinson, design architect), 1958.
Dickinson designed this fine speculative office building wrapped in limestone and terrazzo for developer Walter Zwig. This investment was spurred by the nascent O'Keefe Centre [1/24] nearby. *AB*

5 Originally Traders Bank of Canada, 61–67 Yonge St. (office building), Carrère & Hastings with Francis S. Baker, 1905.
Designed by New York architects Carrère & Hastings, this 15-storey tower was Toronto's first real skyscraper. The architects would later create such extravagant Beaux Arts masterpieces as the New York Public Library, but here they are responding to more cautious concerns with a conservative three-part classical composition that emphasizes horizontal movement and hides the uppermost floors behind a deep cornice, thus diminishing any visual sense of height. "A virtue of the projecting cornice for the people of Toronto," wrote a contemporary skyscraper-shy critic, "is that it will reduce the building in appearance to 12 storeys." The building was planned with the main banking hall on the second floor, a concept new to Toronto but thought to be very sensible, for the centrally located stairway led the public into the middle of the floor space and kept tellers together around the window-lighted perimeter. The hall was long ago demolished, but the dignified exterior of this benchmark tower has been cleaned up. *PM*

6 Canadian Pacific Building, 1 King St. E., Darling & Pearson, 1911–13; altered, 1929.
Built for the Canadian Pacific Railroad with a grand marbled and columned ticket office on the ground storey and floors and floors of rentable offices above, this building replaced the Traders next door as "The Tallest Building in the British Empire." At the time, it was one of some 200 structures in North America with 15 storeys or more. Frank Darling, who only 15 years prior had been doing such rococo palaces as the Bank of Montreal [6/1], seemed right at home with skyscraper style, creating a skeletal vertical composition that lifts the eye

upward from a granite base via emphatic ribbons of double windows, piers, and corner end bays that rise uninterrupted through arcaded attic storeys until they are capped at the top by shapely cupolas. The original cladding was a more exuberant terracotta; it was replaced in 1929 with the bland limestone we see today. *PM*

7 Royal Bank, 2 King St. E. (office building), Ross & Macdonald; banking hall, Carrère & Hastings with Eustace G. Bird, 1913–15. The 20-storey Royal Bank building quickly upstaged the Canadian Pacific structure as "The Tallest Building in the British Empire." Headquartered in Montreal, the Royal selected hometown architects Ross & Macdonald, who perhaps relied on Carrère & Hastings (credited with the interior of the banking hall) for the magnificent Corinthian-columned granite and limestone base. By contrast, the shaft is stark with plain windows set into smooth terracotta cladding and the crowning attic storeys hardly noticeable. One reached Carrère & Hastings' ornate main-floor banking room by walking up a short marble stairway. Steps descended to the savings department on the King Street side and to four retail shops on the Yonge Street elevation. This banking hall ensemble was demolished in 1964 when the Royal moved its Toronto headquarters to 20 King Street West, and 2 King became just another branch. Today the main tenant is a mattress store. *PM/updated AB*

8 One King West (hotel/apartments)/ originally Dominion Bank, 1 King St. W., Darling & Pearson, 1913–14; altered and tower added, Stanford Downey with Allan Seymour, 2005. It's a hotel lobby now, but the banking hall of this one-time head office of the Dominion Bank remains a treat. As one enters, a wide central stair leads dramatically down a few steps to the savings department and its monumental, theatrical vault. (At the time, this was the largest vault in Canada and was said to be protected by the heaviest doors ever built. The bank's literature explained that the vault was equipped with a telephone for anyone accidentally locked in at night!) At the west end of the foyer, off which originally was a ladies' waiting room, an even more ceremonial marble stair with bronze balustrade beckons to the main banking hall on the floor above—two storeys high, ringed by an 18-pier arcade, and lined with sumptuous marble from floor to ceiling. The Dominion Bank, 50 feet shorter than the Canadian Pacific Building across the street, was never The Tallest anything, but its architectural reputation was assured by the sophistication and beauty of its Renaissance Revival design. The new tower is a feat of engineering, remarkably tall and skinny; as architecture it is also "thin." *PM/AB*

9 Originally Prudential Building, 2 King St. W., Page & Steele (Peter Dickinson, design architect), with Barott, Marshall, Merrett and Barott, 1961; altered, Stevens and Burgess Architects, 1986.
A fine expression of Dickinson's innovative office-building language: a façade of steel fins, glass, and precast concrete panels inset with shiny chips of quartz. The lobby shimmered with three kinds of stone, including Gibraltar stone, since the Rock of Gibraltar was the client's symbol. This space is now compromised by a silly Post-Modern intervention, but the tower stands up. *AB*

9 | 2 King St. W.

10a Originally Hiram Piper & Brother Hardware, 83 Yonge St. [See Walk 5/1a.]

10b 100 Yonge St. [See Walk 5/1b.]

11a Lumsden Building, 2–6 Adelaide St. E., John A. Mackenzie, 1909. In 1909, this extraordinary waffle was said to be the largest concrete-faced building in the world, an unusual application in an era when structural steel skeletons were clad in brick or terracotta, with stone-looking concrete restricted to selected ornament. That the architect so dramatically expressed the decorative possibilities of his material with a modular repetition of husky blocked window surrounds makes the essay all the more interesting. Built as a profit-making venture by the Lumsden Estate of Ottawa, the rental units were identical, including striped awnings at each window and a wash basin in each office. Whether tenants could equally avail themselves of the swimming pool and Turkish baths in the basement is unknown. Such amenities are long gone, as is, unfortunately, the rich modillioned cornice which handsomely completed the original composition. *PM*

11b Ontario Heritage Centre/originally Canadian Birkbeck Investment & Savings Co., 8–12 Adelaide St. E. (office building), George W. Gouinlock, 1907–08; renovated, 1986–88. Lavish classical pomp for a five-storey miniature treasure by one of Toronto's master Beaux Arts evocateurs. Thanks to consummate restoration, the radiant exterior as well as rich banking hall and other interior spaces gleam anew for the heritage organization that now inhabits the place. *PM*

11c 20 Adelaide St. E. (office building), Francesco Scolozzi and Page & Steele, 1987–88. A dashing standout in the cityscape, no. 20 Adelaide is Toronto's best Post-Modern office building to date. With its polychromy, sleek surfaces, and segmentally curved pediment, the building has an air of the 1920s about it, but even more of the Renaissance (whose rigorous geometry was the touchstone for Art Deco). *PM*

12 11 Adelaide St. W. (office building; part of Scotia Plaza), Webb Zerafa Menkes Housden, 1988–89. Incorporates front façade of original John Kay Co./formerly Wood Gundy & Co., 36–38 King St. W., Samuel G. Curry, 1898; altered, Ferdinand H. Marani, 1922. Its wealth of Renaissance Revival terracotta detail made the John Kay carpet store worthy of preservation. Critics are uncertain of the value of transporting its front wall here to the back of Scotia Plaza [6/31b], however, especially as the façade we see is a confusing mix of two architectural impulses anyway. The ground "floor" owes its staid investment-banker classicism to a 1922 remodelling. *PM*

Temperance Street was laid out and named by Jesse Ketchum, a Toronto settler who owned the land from just north of King all the way to Queen between Yonge and Bay Streets. A political reformer, temperance advocate, and generous philanthropist, he later donated much of his land to "worthy causes," including the Yonge Street tannery plot to the Bible & Tract Society [5/1b], and here on Temperance Street, a large lot for a temperance hall [demolished]. Ketchum's deed covenants on Temperance Street forbade licensed inns or other places where "spiritous liquours" might be sold, a restriction that remained until the 1960s.

13a Dineen Building, 140 Yonge St. and 2 Temperance St., Frederick H. Herbert, 1897; restoration and addition, George Robb; café interior, Pencil Design, 2012. Furriers W. and D. Dineen's building is playful Late Victoriana, now in fine fettle despite the clumsy top-floor addition. The new café's eclectic fixtures and boldly multi-coloured floor tiles would have pleased Herbert. Meanwhile, the Chase Fish & Oyster's ground-floor dining room gains some vibe from the exposed bones of the building. This is what retaining heritage buildings does for a downtown: it supplies brio and soul in a district of big and slick. *AB*

13b 9 Temperance St. (offices), Webb Zerafa Menkes Housden and Inger Bartlett and Associates, 1996. Incorporates façade of Comet Bicycle Co., 17 Temperance St. (factory), E.J. Lennox, 1894–95; remodelled as commercial block, E.J. Lennox, 1905. This office block maintains the front of the Comet Bicycle Company building, erected during the 1890s' North American cycle craze. In 1895, there were 19 companies in Toronto manufacturing bicycles, and a traffic count that year recorded 395 cyclists in one half-hour passing the corner of Yonge and King. Enthusiasm didn't last, however, and faced with competition from the United States many Canadian companies folded. In 1905, Lennox remodelled his bold bicycle building for Aikenhead's Hardware, who lasted there most of the century. *PM/ updated AB*

14 Confederation Square/originally Confederation Life Building, 20 Richmond St. E., Knox Elliot & Jarvis, 1890–92; altered, J. Wilson Gray, 1898–1900; addition, J. Wilson Gray, 1908; renovated, Thom Partnership, 1981–82; altered and restored, Thom Partnership, 1984. 1 Queen St. E., Page & Steele, 1990. The fairy-tale Confederation Life Building has held Toronto's imagination from the day the design competition was announced in 1889, through completion in 1892 when its six storeys plus towers marked it as one of the city's four tallest buildings, to the fire that almost destroyed it in 1981, and now in a splendid restoration. Adding towers, steep hipped roof, wishbone window surrounds, and other chateauesque touches to the period's popular Richardsonian Romanesque style, Knox Elliot & Jarvis came up with a bold, massive structure enlivened

14 | Confederation Life Building

16 Sterling Tower, 372 Bay St., Chapman & Oxley, 1928–29. Twenty storeys of smooth height with the squared mass of the building stepped at the top in an arrangement of setbacks. Bay Street was getting into 1920s skyscraper swing here. Narrow piers provide vertical oomph, and stylized Gothic quatrefoils, exotic dragons, and similar appliqués perk up the ground and attic storeys. Though the big-windowed base still makes use of classical square columns, they are so zingy as to thrust antique impulse into the jazz age. *PM*

16 | Sterling Tower

with the sort of fanciful detail that was being lavished on Fifth Avenue millionaires' mansions at the time. Confederation Life loved the image of solidity plus richness, and publicized it widely.

The structure is actually two units, separated by the middle tower, which stood originally over an open carriageway leading to a lane behind. In 1900, the ground floor of the Yonge/Richmond unit was altered considerably to provide larger window openings and a prominent corner entrance, a transformation that entailed prodigious shoring and balancing of the weighty upper floors. The more conventional-looking office block along Victoria Street was appended in 1908. Today the building is joined to the office tower behind it at 1 Queen Street East. *PM/updated AB*

15 Hudson's Bay Co. and Saks Fifth Avenue/originally Robert Simpson Co., 160–184 Yonge St. [See Walk 5/6.]

17 Graphic Arts Building, 73 Richmond St. W., Francis S. Baker, 1913. A beauteous Greek temple built to house not commerce but culture, this was the home of *Saturday Night,* the debonair magazine intent on bringing insight and wit to Canada in the 1910s (and on through the end of the century). Cultivated refinements remain intact in the marble and wood lobby: elaborately carved wooden doors sporting knights and damsels, deep coffered ceiling. *PM/updated AB*

18 Victory Building, 80 Richmond St. W., Baldwin & Greene, 1929–30. An inventive Art Deco version of a traditional three-part skyscraper, the Victory Building uses contrasting brown brick in horizontal bands at the second and top floors to create a veritable base and cornice for its 20 stretched storeys of tan brick. Especially zippy are elongated pyramids decorating spandrels and the Art Deco chrome and marble lobby. Baldwin & Greene had come a long way from their mushy Central Building at 45 Richmond St. W. *PM*

19 INDX condos, 70 Temperance St., Page & Steele/IBI, 2017. A rare residential high-rise in the area, but in every other way ordinary: It brings the cheap window systems and mediocre detailing of the contemporary condo into a quarter of well-built office towers. The clear balcony glass exposes the residents' clutter, and awkward illuminated rectangles in the façade (clearly visible from Nathan Phillips Square) mess up the skyline. Still, it could have been much worse; the developer Harry Stinson earlier tried to build a much taller blue-glass tower by Turner Fleischer capped with a giant ball. *AB*

20 Bay Adelaide Centre, 333 Bay St., West tower, WZMH, 2009. Incorporates façades of National Building, 347 Bay St., Chapman & Oxley, 1925–26. East tower, KPMB with Adamson Associates and ERA, 2016–17. Incorporates façades of Elgin Building, 118 Yonge St., 1850; altered, James L. Havill, 1910. The epic tale of this office complex began in the late 1980s, with a scheme by WZMH for two towers that was killed by an economic bust. Left behind were an underground parking garage, Cloud Gardens **[6/21]**, 11 Temperance, and a six-storey stump of elevator shaft. After a "stump-busting" ceremony in 2006, the final version rose without incident: two Neo-Modernist glass towers with meticulously proportioned curtain wall, the urban equivalent of a fitted navy suit. Within, the lobbies lined with pale marble and granite feature grand proportions that make even a junior associate stand taller. Yet the new development differs from its 1980s neighbours in how it meets the street: frankly and up close, without forecourts or atria. Instead the new towers embrace a small courtyard and another hidden one that wraps around 9 Temperance. Two strong works of public art add some poetry: James Turrell's *Straight Flush* in the west tower, Micah Lexier's transformative *Two Circles* in the east.

The rebuilt and relocated façade at Yonge and Temperance recovers part of the Elgin Building, once home to Holt Renfrew and jewellers Ryrie-Birks. ERA have designed three bays of the façade to evoke, but not copy, sections lost long ago. Nearby is the complex's one clunker, a restaurant closed to the public. Professional services firm Deloitte occupies much of this building, and its staffers enjoy their lunches behind glass. You can't join them, though people often try, drawn in by the architecture only to be stiff-armed. *AB*

20 | Bay Adelaide East

21 Cloud Gardens and Cloud Gardens Conservatory, 14 Temperance St., Baird Sampson with WZMH, Milus Bollenberghe Topps Watchorn (landscape architects), Margaret Priest and Tony Scherman (artists), 1993. Rich in architectural ideas and fantasies, this park is like no other place in the city. The competition-winning scheme caps a parking garage **[see 6/20]** with a garden, a pool, a copse, and a set of eroding terraces leading up through waterfalls to a belvedere. Behind this rises a steel structure that seems caught, as the city always is, between rise and ruin; this is artist Margaret Priest's *Monument to Construction Workers*, the steel grid establishing a sampler of 25 different trades from brick to glass to plumbing. And then there is the conservatory, a humid and verdant redoubt that provides refuge (when it's open) from the stresses of office politics—or, today, cramped high-rise living. The park won a Governor General's Award of Merit in 1994. *AB*

22 Originally Atlas Building, 350 Bay St., S.B. Coon & Son, 1928. The façade sports a little of the old heavily classical skyscraper vocabulary and some of the new vertical emphasis, but most noteworthy here is the splendid 1930s elevator lobby glowing with polished-brass roped columns and a frieze of half-lion/half-eagle griffins. *PM*

23 Originally Northern Ontario Building, 330 Bay St., Chapman & Oxley, 1924–25; addition, Webb Zerafa Menkes Housden, 1982. With the exception of exotic griffins (again griffins?) flanking second-floor windows, the Northern Ontario Building is an unassuming 1920s skyscraper: just a dab of classical detail to ornament the ground floor (originally six separate shops), only darker-coloured spandrels to relieve the clean-limbed shaft, and the slightest of cornices "waving" along the broken-cornered eaves course. The 1982 addition to the north is interesting for its stepped horizontal profile in contrast to the verticality of the Northern Ontario Building. It is not a bad marriage. *PM*

24 EY Tower, 100 Adelaide St. W., Kohn Pedersen Fox with WZMH, Goldsmith Borgal, and ERA, 2016. Incorporates Concourse Building, Baldwin & Greene, 1928. Almost a century after Mies van der Rohe was imagining an all-glass skyscraper, the type still has some life in it. This building looks generic at a glance, but its curtain wall has some interesting chamfers and folds, achieving a very fine sculptural effect despite its generally squared-off floors. Handsome protruding sunshades and fins help moderate the hothouse impact of all that glazing.

24 | EY Tower

However: this worthy new tower has shattered Toronto's best Deco building, a skyscraping brick shaft ornamented with bright tiles up top and mosaics down below. These features have been carefully reconstructed in a façadectomy; the mosaics by Group of Seven painter J.E.H. MacDonald and his son, Thoreau MacDonald, still depict an array of Canadian wildlife and vegetation in colourful style. But the façade is bogus—step inside and it's revealed as backless and hollow, a theatrical flat. What's more, the architecture is distorted, its 16 floors of brick and stone reconstructed as 13 in the broader rhythm of the new tower. J.E.H. MacDonald imagined the Concourse would spur other ambitious buildings; its ornaments would be "a brightly illuminated letter in a fine manuscript, beginning, perhaps, some greater chapter in our future development." This is probably not what he had in mind. *AB*

25 111 Richmond St. W. (offices), Page & Steele (Peter Dickinson, design architect), 1954; alterations, WZMH and ERA, 2012. One of the city's first and best modern office buildings has gotten the respectful restoration that so many of its contemporaries have been denied. New windows mimic Dickinson's design, and the polychromatic stone decoration of the lobby is all cleaned up; upstairs one floor has been stripped down to the concrete for a loft effect, while Google's five levels include the *de rigueur* band room and arcade games. *AB*

26 Drake 150 (restaurant interior), 150 York St., Martin Brudnizki, 2013. After 2000, the Drake Hotel presaged the decade's dominant hipster aesthetic: it updated a flophouse hotel with salvaged furniture, rustic custom cabinets, and Canadiana kitsch. This downtown outpost is a Bay Street–friendly version of that vibe, a brasserie with cork ceiling, industrial windows, and lots of art. Loosen your tie. *AB*

27 Canada Permanent Building, 320 Bay St., F. Hilton Wilkes with Mathers & Haldenby and Sproatt & Rolph, 1928–30; banking hall renovations, SGH Design Partners, 2003. The architect said he wanted to avoid "restless outlines," and by combining massive bulk with delicate ornament, that is exactly what he did. He also avoided any possibility of architectural distinction. The two design impulses cancel one another and the Canada Permanent Building ends up with neither power nor grace—a stout matron in too-thin ingenue's finery. Only the deeply vaulted entrance and its bold coffered ceiling speak with any vigour, pronouncing the solidity and weightiness that "The Permanent" undoubtedly hoped to evoke. The interior lobby and banking hall are another matter—rich extravaganzas of satiny marble and burnished metal in the best Art Deco manner, now ignobly repurposed but largely intact. Don't miss the bronze elevator doors whereon are portrayed kneeling antique figures, one holding out a model of the company's medievally quaint former headquarters and another a replica of this skyscraper—self-congratulatory offerings to the gods of commerce. *PM/updated AB*

28 Originally Trust and Guarantee Co. Ltd./formerly Crown Trust, 302 Bay St. (office building), Curry & Sparling, 1916–17; addition, 1929. The somewhat incoherent architecture of this building reflects skyscraper design as it was conceived before and after 1920. The sculptural Corinthian temple front shows the rich classicism of the earlier period; the attic storeys added 12 years later are in the smooth, angular, stepped fashion then popular. The exquisite marble and plaster-work banking hall is from the earlier period before 1920, when fine craftsmanship and materials were still the order of the day. (You can peek from the front foyer into what is now office space.) *PM/updated AB*

29 Trump International Hotel and Tower (hotel and residences), 325 Bay St., Zeidler, 2012. Before Donald Trump upended U.S. politics, he didn't do any favours for Toronto architecture as the front man for this development. The tower is weak-sauce Post-Modernism, long after there was any intellectual excuse for it. Artist Michael Snow's installation *Lightline* is garishly Trumpian. *AB*

30 National Club, 303 Bay St., Curry Sproatt & Rolph, 1906–07. The four-storey red-brick Neo-Georgian National Club, with its self-consciously domestic air, probably appeared less alien to its surroundings in 1907, when Bay Street still consisted mainly of 19th-century commercial blocks, houses, and churches. The National Club was founded in 1874 as a counter to growing sentiment for union with the United States. *PM*

31a Bank of Nova Scotia, 44 King St. W. (office building), designed, John M. Lyle, 1929; built, Mathers & Haldenby with Beck & Eadie, 1949–51; altered, 1988–89. Office buildings erected in Toronto after World War II took up where their pre-war brethren left off. The Bank of Nova Scotia was built using actual pre-war Deco plans (shelved during the Depression). Lyle had been a prolific architect of banks notable for their crisp planarity and stylized decoration based on Canadian themes **[see 5/8]**. In 1949, Alvan Mathers found that Lyle's scheme was "the best solution of the problems," and his office worked with Lyle's former associates to build it, making small alterations that slightly simplified the façades. (The Bank of Montreal's now-demolished headquarters on the northwest corner, by Marani & Morris with Chapman Oxley & Facey, was completed in 1948 to a similar scale and style.) Hard to believe this is nearly a contemporary to TD Centre **[6/34]**.

Yet the 23-storey bank still stands resolutely on this key corner, its massive smooth stone base punctuated by elegant metal-mullioned Deco windows and 1930s style bas-reliefs (executed by Fred Winkler). Lobbies and the banking hall are further decked out in Moderne streamlining, marbles, metals, and Lyle's iconography (north-wall mural by Jacobine Jones). The hall was "opened up" as part of the Scotia Plaza complex **[6/31b]**, which tries and fails to equal its textured grandeur. *PM/AB*

31b Scotia Plaza, 30 King St. W. (complex of office and commercial buildings), Webb Zerafa Menkes Housden, 1985–88. The last of the five major banks to build a less-is-more tower in the financial district, Scotiabank opted for red cladding in contrast to the black, white, silver, and gold of the others'. It is not a boring box; it's a 68-storey boring trapezoid, with two of its parallel sides stepped. (Read, more corner offices.) Actually, at ground level the project is in many ways commendable. It fits into the tight site elegantly and the forecourts on King and Adelaide Streets are ceremonial and gracious. The legible punched windows, referencing 1920s and '30s skyscrapers, add human scale to the monumental. The fact that older buildings were retained **[6/30, 6/31a]** makes the block seem more alive and natural. The façade shenanigans **[5/1b, 6/12]** are definitely unreal, however. *PM*

31b | Scotia Plaza

32a Canadian Imperial Bank of Commerce/originally Canadian Bank of Commerce, 25 King St. W. (office building), York & Sawyer with Darling & Pearson, 1929–31. Mighty monumentality and soaring grace in a 34-storey structure of unquestionable presence. York & Sawyer were New York's leading bank architects, and they obviously knew a thing or two about image-making as well as composition. If one's money isn't safe inside the awesome Romanesque stone block that forms the building's base, where then? If that massive, smooth shaft gliding upward in a series of subtle setbacks does not connote architectonic movement and skyscraping height, what then? And at the top, if that Romanesque diadem-cum-observation-deck thrusting gigantic heads over the city of Courage, Observation, Foresight, and Enterprise is not the way to pronounce richness and bold endeavour crowning the

32a | Canadian Imperial Bank of Commerce

Bank of Commerce, how then? Similar grandeur suffuses the interior of the ground-floor banking rooms and lobbies, especially the immense main banking hall, executed in roseate stone with gilt mouldings and roofed with a deep blue coffered barrel vault. There is a dusky, hushed tone of reverence here that is the closest the financial district comes to ecclesia. *PM*

32b Commerce Court, 243 Bay St. (complex of office buildings), I.M. Pei & Partners with Page & Steele, 1968–72; additions and alterations, Zeidler Partnership, 1994. Commerce Court comprises York & Sawyer's 1931 skyscraper [6/32a], five- and 14-storey limestone buildings, and, on the fourth side of the plaza, a slick 57-storey glass and stainless-steel towering box. The tower is International Style at its cleanest and most rational, with horizontally emphasized layers of office floors rising one atop another, unadorned, undifferentiated, and precision-perfect. Pei's tower is distinguished from similar packages by its fragile-looking three-storey glass base, a telling contrast to the impenetrable stone of the adjacent 1931 building. In fact, contrast and contradiction are the name of the game at Commerce Court: old and new, high and low, steel and stone, void and solid, axis and cross-axis. Unfortunately, the cerebralizing doesn't add up to hot architecture, but to cold plazas—the chilliest corner in Toronto, they say. Originally the banking hall's rectangle was pierced by a circular void, opening a route below ground; 1990s interventions by Zeidler unwisely closed this up, and added mannered pavilions between the 1920s stone and 1960s steel. *PM/AB*

33 First Canadian Place, 100 King St. W. (office building), Edward Durell Stone Associates with Bregman & Hamann, 1972–75; alterations, Moed de Armas & Shannon with B+H, 2012; BMO main branch interior, Kearns Mancini, 2014. For its headquarters, the Bank of Montreal chose one of the most-lauded architects of the era, Edward Durell Stone, who was (very controversially) reviving elements of classical architecture. This is how Toronto's tallest skyscraper came to be clad in white Italian marble. Outside, the marble panels cracked and were replaced by fritted glass; inside, they survive in the groovy time-capsule main lobby. The corner bank branch, now with sofas and corporate carpet, is a pathetic counterpoint to TD's temple [6/34] across the street. *AB*

33 | First Canadian Place

34 Toronto-Dominion Centre, 55 King St. W. (complex of office buildings), Ludwig Mies van der Rohe with John B. Parkin Associates and Bregman & Hamann, 1963–69. TD West Tower, 100 Wellington St. W., Bregman & Hamann, 1974. TD South Tower, 79 Wellington St. W., Bregman & Hamann, 1985. Ernst & Young Tower, 222 Bay St., Scott Tan de Bibiana with Bregman & Hamann, 1991. A central figure in the European avant-garde of the 1920s and '30s, Mies—as he was singularly known—emigrated to Chicago in 1938 and redefined the high-rise tower. His Seagram Building, on Park Avenue in New York, was among the most influential structures ever built, combining two Modernist dreams: a glossy column of glass, "the quintessential material of the future," shimmering and immaterial; and "skin and bone construction," revealing the succinct poetry of modern steel building. The TD towers and Seagram shared a patron, Phyllis Lambert of the Bronfman family [see 5/11], who were developers here. Like Seagram, these buildings are clad in dark glass and mullions that evoke structural I-beams, though here they are steel and not bronze.

The complex of two towers and one-storey banking hall was among the largest of Mies's career, and the pavilion is a gem, a sculpture in steel, glass, marble, granite, and English oak that holds the symbolic corner of King and Bay with austere elegance. (It replaced a fine Beaux Arts temple by Carrère & Hastings.) The evolution of the complex after his death is another story: Mies had planned for a possible third tower, but the fourth and fifth towers [6/35] disrupt the composition of the ensemble and dilute his design language.

34 | Toronto-Dominion Centre

The urbanism of the complex was also highly influential. The granite plaza that fills most of the block—and is humanized by artist Joe Fafard's cows—inspired inferior imitations. Also, this is where Mies did the city the dubious favour of pioneering the underground shopping concourse. The Miesian signage and detailing are now gone from underground, but the PATH system continues to grow, turning office-dwellers into moles and emptying the streets. *PM/AB*

35 Ernst & Young Tower, 222 Bay St., 1992; incorporates Design Exchange/ originally Toronto Stock Exchange, 234 Bay St., George & Moorhouse with S.H. Maw, 1937; altered, Kuwabara Payne McKenna Blumberg, 1994. A Miesian tower, with a few "improvements," impaled upon an Art Deco box. This building project should have been spiked for both its impact on the block and its muddled design. Ironically, it helped birth a design museum here, in the very fine old granite-and-limestone stock exchange. (The traders moved out in 1983, and trading went purely online in 1997.) While Design Exchange has little on show these days, its space remains handsome. On the façade, a stone frieze designed by Charles Comfort shows workers in Canadian industry; inside, the trading floor retains much of its marble, metal, and wood Deco details. The renovation, led by Shirley Blumberg of KPMB, knits together Deco and Modern with stone, steel, and sandblasted glass. *PM/AB*

36 Royal Bank Plaza, 200 Bay St. (office building), Webb Zerafa Menkes Housden, 1973–77; altered, WZMH, 2009. Any building in Toronto that makes it look as if the sun is shining on a dreary winter day has a lot going for it. The faceted gold-enriched mirror-glass of Royal Bank's Late-Modern jewel seems to reflect a warm sunny glow no matter what the weather. This is a very showy building all around. The triangular 41- and 26-storey gold-glass towers are linked by a 12-storey clear-glass atrium, now perversely closed off. Otherwise the building is lively hijinks on the skyline as well as in the streetscape, and best of all, it manages its joie de vivre with respect for very proper dowager neighbours **[Area V]**. *PM/updated AB*

35 | Design Exchange

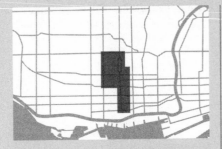

Area V
Walk 7: University Avenue
Walk 8: University of
          Toronto

If you transported a Torontonian from the 1850s to the present day, there are few places in the city she would recognize. The University of Toronto's St. George campus is one: even as the town has become a metropolis, the school has maintained its position and its ambitious early architecture. Yet the university has also evolved in dramatic fashion, particularly since the 1960s. The result is the greatest compilation of architecture in the city—Gothic Revival and Romanesque and Brutalist in a rich and evolving conversation.

When it began, it was King's College, and its site was rural: 150 acres on the fringe of York, purchased for £3,750 for the establishment of a school for "the education of youth in the principles of the Christian Religion, and for their instruction in the various branches of Science and Literature." The plans for the Anglican university came with grand urbanistic ambitions. The campus was imagined as the meeting place for two new streets, College Street **[see Walk 5]** and a broad College Avenue, today's University Avenue, with a carriageway and treed walkways suitable for promenading. The university's classical building went up in 1843 north of that intersection, but its site was soon coveted by the province; it became a park in 1860 and the Ontario legislature's buildings **[7/35]** were opened there a quarter-century later.

Meanwhile, the Romanesque University College **[8/1]** was completed in 1859 as the school moved west and became a secular institution. Those two trends, a move to the west and toward religious and cultural pluralism, continue even now.

Between 1880 and 1910 the university brought the other Christian denominational colleges, which had sprung up around its campus, into the fold. Among them were St. Michael's **[8/48a]**, Knox **[8/18]**, Wycliffe **[8/40]**, Victoria **[8/47]**, and Trinity **[8/39]**—the latter founded as a breakaway institution by U of T's first president, the Anglican bishop John Strachan. While the Romanesque style ruled at Victoria **[8/47]** and the new university library **[8/4]**, the different origins of these institutions showed up in the architecture, from Trinity's pompous neo-Neo-Gothic to the varieties of Catholic architectural grandeur and modesty at St. Michael's.

Torontonians retained fairly conservative ideas of what a university building should look like through the first decades of the 20th century: the Collegiate Gothic of Oxford and Cambridge, as in the sublime Hart House **[8/3]**; Beaux Arts **[8/7a]**; or staid Neo-Georgian **[8/26]**.

In the years after World War II, a new wave of building changed those ideas dramatically. "The chatter of thousands of young voices . . . competed with the shouts of workmen and the roar of construction machinery," wrote a *Globe and Mail* reporter in 1961, noting a record enrolment of 16,500 and the opening of the new Sidney Smith Hall **[8/25]**. Facing the reality of the Baby Boom and postwar economic growth, the university's leaders envisaged two suburban campuses, and began looking to the west. St. George Street, a grand residential boulevard, had been the border. Now U of T pushed through it with a grand scheme for a pedestrian-only West Campus, including playing fields and reaching the border of the planned Spadina Expressway.

This plan was never entirely carried out; instead the university worked largely within the existing streetscape and built out one new building after another, including New College **[8/22]**. There was one enormous exception: Robarts Library **[8/27]**, designed as a provincial stronghold for academic books, open only to faculty and graduate students. Quickly nicknamed "Fort Book," it occupied three acres of what had been Victorian streetscape, and was tall, dark, opaque, and alien in its form and attitude. "There is something about the library that offends every sense," wrote *Canadian Architect* managing editor Robert Gretton. "It resembles not so much a place of learning as a World War II gun emplacement. Instead of a warm, humane place for the pursuit of studies, the library is a cold storage unit for paper and print." Infill this is not. And yet, in the years since, it has found admirers for its boldness and coherence, its profoundly un-Torontonian indifference to context. Certainly it represents a moment in architectural practice, one that's decisively over; the new addition to the building promises a much more transparent and friendly character, though it's unclear whether that is the appropriate architectural response. Meanwhile, Ron Thom's Massey College **[8/36]** was beloved when new, and remains so, one of Toronto's gems.

While the university has made some bad buildings, it has usually found ways to engage with thoughtful contemporary architecture. The two champions of Toronto infillism built here well: Jack Diamond, with Innis College **[8/31]**, and Barton Myers, with Woodsworth

College **[8/33a]**, a quietly wonderful building that marked the emergence of KPMB from Myers's office. Later, in the 1990s, a further building boom was shaped by the university's design review panel, and the stewardship of then architecture dean Larry Wayne Richards; Graduate House **[8/23]** is the most visible and provocative in a crop of excellent builds and renovations, its hanging steel O stretching the university right to its Spadina Avenue edge.

Today the university is looking further west for more building projects along Spadina Avenue, but also improving the green heart of its campus. A 1990s Open Space Master Plan inspired some improvements to the historic Front Campus, south of Convocation Hall; now that zone is the heart of a new project, led by KPMB and Michael Van Valkenburgh Associates (MVVA), that will bury this zone's car parking underground and create a new network of finely detailed plazas and quads. This important public space might finally get back the quality landscape it deserves.

University Avenue, that other outgrowth of the campus, should be so lucky: it has been shedding its horticultural beauty for 150 years. It was first laid out in 1829 by André Parmentier, an early figure in the nascent field of "landscape gardening." Charles Dickens visited Toronto in 1842, and later wrote that "the Avenue is *one* of, if not *the* finest in the Dominion, or perhaps on this Continent." It was "120 feet wide, arranged with a central carriageway and boulevards and walkways on either side, and shaded by double rows of pink flowering chestnuts (used here for the first time in Toronto)."

It couldn't last. Toronto has never been a fertile place for grand urbanism. In the City Beautiful era of the 1910s, John Lyle proposed a new Federal Avenue, running straight north from Union Station **[7/2]** to end in a grand civic precinct at Osgoode Hall **[7/15]** and the then City Hall **[7/17]**. This didn't come to pass, beyond the station itself, the Dominion Public Building **[7/1]**, and Canada Life's headquarters **[7/20]**. In 1929, the plan was revived in slightly

different form, as a southern extension of University incorporating a traffic circle, with a war memorial, and Cambrai Avenue. This idea, too, fizzled: with the onset of the Great Depression, University was extended down to Front in modest, curving form. In the 1950s and 1960s the avenue was built up largely with office and hospital buildings, initially in a consistent coat of limestone and then **[7/9]** in various Modernist idioms.

Since University Avenue was widened in the 1940s, it has been an uncomfortable place to walk, dominated by roaring car traffic. And yet it retains a certain elegance, thanks to its scale and the careful landscape of its medians. Along with the completion of the University subway line, in 1963, came a new set of plazas, gardens, and fountains—a complete, coherent Modernist landscape by the Dunington-Grubb office **[7/16]**. This design is often overlooked, but remains in place and reasonably well-maintained; if and when the emphasis shifts from cars to pedestrians, it will make an important contribution to the place.

Toronto's truly grand civic space is nearby: Nathan Phillips Square **[7/18]**, which is now receiving a slow rebuild and rejuvenation. At the same time, local writers have brought fresh attention to the history of the neighbourhood that used to be there: St. John's Ward, home to the city's African-Canadian community as early as the 1840s and then to a polyglot assembly of immigrant groups, including Chinese, Italians, and European Jews. After almost 100 years, "The Ward" was expropriated, assembled, levelled, and then wiped from the map of the city. Grand plans often come at the expense of marginalized groups; big urban schemes can ruin people's lives. Such events have been rare in Toronto's history—for worse and for better.

Walk 7: University Avenue

1 Dominion Public Building, 1 Front St. W., Thomas William Fuller, east and centre blocks, 1929–31; west block completed, 1935–36. The starting point of the grand Beaux Arts scheme planned for Front Street and University Avenue in the late 1920s, the Dominion Public Building is typical of hundreds of buildings whose impressive classical countenances were sent marching across North America in the service of public architecture in the early years of the 20th century. The monumentality of this, originally Toronto's customs house, is additionally enhanced by the sweeping arc of its Ionic-columned front, rhythmically keeping step with the curve of the street. *PM*

2 Union Station, 65–75 Front St. W., Ross & Macdonald with Hugh G. Jones and John M. Lyle, 1915–20; opened, 1927; renovations, Zeidler Partnership, NORR, FGMDA, ERA, RDH, and PARTISANS, ongoing. With this grandiloquent Classical Revival building, a style then synonymous with progress and prosperity, Toronto architecturally entered the 20th century. It was not an easy birth, nor has its life since been secure. Begun in 1915, the building was not opened until 12 years later, construction having been thwarted first by World War I and then by a bureaucratic feud over a planned viaduct. Threatened demolition in the early 1970s for the Metro Centre scheme **[see 3/16]** inspired no laughter, however, and the station was saved.

If any building in Toronto can be described as monumental, this is it. More

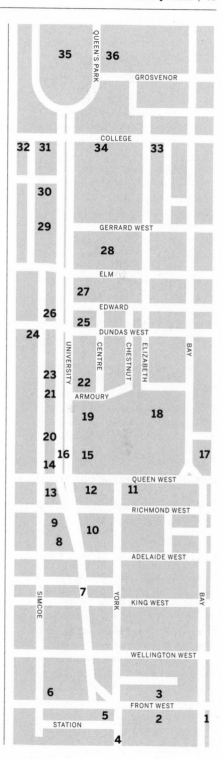

2 | Union Station

than 750 feet long and set well back along its Front Street block, Union Station borrows from antiquity its elongated form and colossal colonnade to create a magnificently powerful yet simple structure. It is a fitting gateway for a great metropolis.

As mighty as the exterior is, the architectural glory is the interior, the Great Hall. Considered by many the finest room in Canada, this majestic space features a vaulted ceiling that gently curves down to rows of clerestory windows that bathe the hall in natural light, illuminating walls of sand-coloured Missouri Zumbro stone and a floor paved in muted grey-and-pink Tennessee marble. The impression is of soft light and serene surfaces, a grand and tranquil background for the bustle of arrivals and departures.

Yet the station was rundown and over-capacity. Starting in 2010, a $1-billion-plus municipal-provincial megaproject has been expanding the station to handle 50 million passengers a year. To the south, the train shed is getting a restoration by ERA and RDH, and part of it a glass roof by Zeidler, a fine counterpoint to the stony original building. A green roof will cover the rest of the shed. The main building's underground departure concourse is being tripled in size; a new level is being dug below it, a remarkable engineering feat, to accommodate new retail.

The station's shopping area will be dramatically larger and, it is promised, more interesting and upscale; developers Osmington have hired the ambitious young firm PARTISANS to detail the interiors. The highlight will be the addition of an oyster bar and restaurant in the Great Hall, a reason for locals to linger in this grand, central civic room. *PM/AB*

3 Royal York Hotel, 100 Front St. W., Ross & Macdonald with Sproatt & Rolph, 1928–29; east addition, Ross, Townsend, Patterson & Fish, 1956. Skyscraper-cum-chateau overlooking not the Loire, but the railways, which took their role most seriously. If the railways' stations resembled classical temples through which travellers were intended to enter the city like Caesars,

3 | Royal York Hotel

their hotels became fairy-tale castles in which guests were invited to live like kings. (In fact, members of the Royal Family often stay here when they visit Toronto.) The Canadian Pacific Railway's "castle" mode—a pleasing but vague mix borrowed from 16th-century France, Venice, and Lombardy—was used by other hotel builders in North America, but the Royal York is an especially refined version. For many years, it was the largest hotel in the British Commonwealth, and its picturesque verdigris-tinged roof still contributes a note of grace to Toronto's skyline. *PM*

4 Canadian National Express Building, 20 York St., John S. Schofield with Hugh G. Jones, 1929; Skywalk, IBI Group, 1989; Union Pearson Express terminal, Zeidler with Hosoya Schaefer and Winkreative, 2015; proposed Union Centre (office tower), Sweeny & Co., ongoing. Originally the lean Beaux Arts structure on York Street received goods to be carried by horse-and-wagon into Union Station; now it is pierced by the SkyWalk, which carries Blue Jays baseball fans at game time, and is lined by the sleek station for the Union Pearson Express. A proposed office tower would turn Station Street into a long, covered public promenade, giving access to a bean-shaped glassy office tower at the west end. Office tenants will be drawn by not just the rail connection but the adjacency of 151 Front Street West, now a data centre that is the hub of Internet traffic in downtown. *AB*

5 Metropolitan Place, 1 University Ave. (office building), Brisbin Brook Beynon, 1985–86. A wise and gentle comment upon the nature of this site and of University Avenue, this building avoids aggressive gestures but has its own monumentality. By using airy glass and subtle shape, this 19-storey structure does not compete with the Royal York **[7/3]**, knows its place, but suffuses that place with rare elegance. The overall impression of lightness and grace is enhanced by the serenely stepped landscaping which floats the building above the busy intersection, and by the sensuous bluey-green glass and weathered bronze. *PM*

6 160 Front St. W. (warehouse), 1905; office tower, AS + GG with B+H, ongoing. This 1905 relic of an older, lower downtown is slated to become part of a curvy office tower overseen by Chicago's Adrian Smith and Gordon Gill. It promises to be one of the tallest, and one of the best, towers in downtown. *AB*

7 Sun Life Centre, 150 and 200 King St. W. (two office buildings), Webb Zerafa Menkes Housden, 1983–84. A giant matched pair that brings to University Avenue a vision more grandiose than any the wildest Beaux Arts dreamers could have conceived. In some ways, the structures are praiseworthy: the two towers sit firmly on their corner sites flanking the avenue;

stepped setbacks, used to such dramatic effect by 1920s skyscrapers to lighten their tops, do the same for Sun Life's shafts; the envelopes are handsome, with small-gridded glass skins and precisely grooved elongated shapes. Sun Life gained its size, extraordinary for the time, in a density trade with St. Andrew's church **[3/5]**. *PM*

8 Shangri-La Hotel and Residences, 188 University Ave., James K.M. Cheng with Hariri Pontarini, 2012. Incorporates Bishop's Block, 192–194 Adelaide St. W., 1833. Where University bends, an awkward site provided an opportunity for B.C. developer Westbank to slip a luxe 67-storey tower into downtown. The blue-glass building is conscious of its role as a visual terminus of the street—they take view corridors seriously in Vancouver—and meets the street well. Cheng, the architectural force behind the tower-and-podium model in downtown Vancouver, places the lobby behind a double glass screen to balance transparency and distance from the river of traffic; nearby, the floating glass-box restaurant speaks to the adjacent Parkin tower **[7/9]**, and Zhang Huan's *Rising* is one of the better public-art projects in downtown. The forecourt on Simcoe Street is far

7 | Sun Life Centre

8 | Shangri-La Hotel and Residences

prettier than it needs to be, down to the granite paving. The rebuilt Georgian buildings on Adelaide now house the private club Soho House Toronto. *AB*

9 Originally Sun Life, 200 University Ave., John B. Parkin Associates with A.J.C. Paine, 1961.
A fine building by the Parkin office that looks just as good, and even contemporary, 55 years on. The firm's design leader, John C. Parkin, fought the city's requirements for setbacks and a stone façade, winning the right to build with curtain wall and anodized aluminum. A one-storey banking pavilion originally lay to the southeast. The design of the façade clearly derives from Skidmore, Owings & Merrill's Inland Steel Building in Chicago. *AB*

9 | 200 University Ave

10 Hilton Toronto, 145 Richmond St. W., Searle, Wilbee, and Rowland with Reno C. Negrin Architects, 1975; renovation, Kuwabara Payne McKenna Blumberg, 2000.
A well-tailored piece of Brutalism, with deep-set gridded windows that recall Gropius and Erickson. (Negrin was a hotel specialist based in Vancouver.) The elevated plaza with swimming pool is a fascinating space, much like the Sheraton Centre gardens. *AB*

11 Sheraton Centre, 123 Queen St. W., John B. Parkin and Associates with Searle, Wilbee, and Rowland, and Seppo Valjus, 1972.
City Hall's commercial counterpart, this 1.5-million-square-foot complex was designed by members of the design team—including City Hall architect Viljo Revell's close associate Valjus—to share a colour and texture of concrete (not to mention an elevated pedestrian connection) with the new civic complex. Within the hotel, the terraced, elevated outdoor gardens by J. Austin Floyd are remarkable. *AB*

12 Four Seasons Centre for the Performing Arts, 145 Queen St. W., Diamond Schmitt, 2006.
On the night of a performance by the Canadian Opera Company or National Ballet of Canada, this is the warmest and liveliest spot on the avenue: through a great transparent façade, patrons proceed across the hall's "City Room" lobby and up stairs of glowing glass. Unfortunately, the south and east façades on this crowded site are tough, without detail or activity, and this is nearly as true for the Queen Street façade facing Osgoode Hall. Jack Diamond's office set out on a tight budget to deliver an excellent venue, and on that front they succeeded. The woodsy, horseshoe-shaped R. Fraser Elliott Hall is congenial, with fine sightlines and, more importantly, fine acoustics. At its genesis, the house prompted complaints from those who wanted this cultural building to showcase architecture as a cultural pursuit; some courted Frank Gehry to design it. In the end, it is no icon. But—at least if you

12 | Four Seasons Centre for the Performing Arts

only look at the front—it is both beautiful and generous to the street, giving life to arid University Ave. (A side note: This building was singularly responsible for introducing the fashion of dark brick to Toronto.) *AB*

13 Originally Bank of Canada (offices), 250 University Ave., Marani & Morris, 1958. A transitional building. This represents an older generation of Toronto architects bringing Modernism to their conservative clients. The design light here was Robert S. Morris, who received the prestigious Royal Institute of British Architects Gold Medal in 1958. The building is nearly free of ornament—but it does bear the Coat of Arms of Canada, designed and carved by Alexander Scott Carter, above the front door, and relief sculptures by Cleeve Horne on the south and north façades. Similarly, the building employs a Classical tripartite composition on its main façade, and the north side is lined with evenly spaced piers that suggest engaged columns. This style is now known as "stripped classical." At the time it was seen as regressive. Now that Modernism has long since won the battle for stylistic supremacy, we can appreciate the elegant proportions and materials of this stolid but solid edifice. *PM/AB*

14 Campbell House, 160 Queen St. W. [See Walk 3/2].

15 Osgoode Hall, 116–138 Queen St. W. [See Walk 3/1].

16 University Avenue landscape, Dunington-Grubb & Stensson, landscape architects, 1960–62. "The opportunity of designing the most important street in a city of one and a half million people does not often arise," wrote the landscape architects J.V. Stensson and Janina Stensson. Or, in this case, redesigning: this Modernist work was meant to give a new identity to the street after the median had been torn up for the construction of the subway beneath. The Dunington-Grubb firm had long been Toronto's leading landscape architects; this project appears to have been largely designed by the next generation in the firm

(and family), the Stenssons. The design includes 12 islands, each with benches and a variety of annuals, hedges, and trees; these islands, while different, share a common vocabulary of strong geometric forms, and a material palette of aggregate concrete, granite, limestone, slate, and brick. The volume of car traffic on University Avenue makes it hard to appreciate the considerable subtlety and beauty of this work. *AB*

17 Old City Hall, 60 Queen St. W., E.J. Lennox, 1889–99; altered, E.J. Lennox, 1926. This is one of Toronto's most rousing architectural testaments, expressing not only the confidence of the late 19th-century city but also the prowess of one of its most accomplished architects. In the 1890s in North America, the style of public dignity was unshakably Richardsonian Romanesque, with courthouses and town halls rising all across the continent in the massive, robust solidity of Henry Hobson Richardson's seminal 1884 Allegheny County Court House in Pittsburgh, Pennsylvania. When it came to building a new courthouse here, Toronto chose native-son E.J. Lennox's own bold Romanesque design.

By the time construction started in 1889, city hall functions had been added and the plan much expanded. The basic form of the building resembles Richardson's—both are designed with rough masonry of immense scale, legible corner pavilions, and great mansard roofs ranging around a courtyard—but Lennox's building is no mere imitation. Old City Hall is pictorial and ornamental in ways not found in Richardson's more intellectual, abstract granite composition. Here the bell tower, placed to terminate the vista up Bay Street, is off-centre, and the façade is handled as a surface to be decorated, either by contrasting textures and colours of brown and beige sandstone or by intricate foliate and grotesque carvings.

The interior is equally picturesque, featuring intricate bronze and iron detailing, painted murals by George Reid, as well as a huge allegorical stained glass window by Robert McCausland. Such elaboration was not without cost: the resulting $2.5-million figure brought the architect lawsuits,

17 | Old City Hall

investigations, and untold imbroglios, the most notorious being the affair in which his name was revealed carved in corbels below the eaves. The letters, interspersed along the sides, spell out "E J LENNOX ARCHITECT."

When New City Hall [7/18] was opened in 1965, there was much concern about the future of this older building, which almost disappeared in the development of the Eaton Centre [5/11]. But preservationists rallied to save this distinguished structure, a campaign that was instrumental in developing Toronto's awareness of its architectural heritage. Someday, this should be a museum of Toronto. *PM/updated AB*

18 New City Hall, 100 Queen St. W., Viljo Revell with John B. Parkin Associates, 1965; altered, Kuwabara Payne McKenna Blumberg, 1999. Nathan Phillips Square alterations and green roof, PLANT Architect Inc., Shore Tilbe Irwin & Partners, Peter Lindsay Schaudt Landscape Architecture, Blanche Lemko van Ginkel, and Adrian Blackwell, ongoing.
One of Toronto's very best buildings, and one of the boldest leaps forward in the city's history. The Modernist ensemble resembled nothing else in gridded Toronto: two curved, asymmetric towers surrounding a saucer-shaped amphitheatre for council and embracing a grand civic square.

It could have turned out much differently. In the 1950s, the immigrant neighbourhood of St. John's Ward [see Introduction] was expropriated and levelled for a new city hall and parking garage. City Council asked three establishment firms—Marani & Morris,

Mathers & Haldenby, and Shore & Moffat—to collectively design a scheme, and in 1955 they presented a limestone slab-and-podium that impressed nobody. That became, more or less, Mathers and Haldenby's stately Imperial Oil Building [25/33], but citizens agitated for something more innovative; they were rallied by a letter signed by U of T architecture students that called it "a monstrous monument to backwardness." (This bit of agitprop was strongly encouraged by Eric Arthur.)

Mayor Nathan Phillips successfully pushed for a global competition that would produce "a symbol of Toronto, a source of pride and pleasure to its citizens." Among the 500 entrants were I.M. Pei [6/32b], Kenzo Tange, and a slew of students and young graduates: several settled in the city and made lasting change, including John Andrews [26/21a, 3/16] and Macy DuBois [8/22].

This came a year after the global competition for Jorn Utzon's Sydney Opera House, led by the great Modernist architect Eero Saarinen; he was on this jury too, with

18 | New City Hall

Arthur, and again helped select an obscure Scandinavian. The Finn Viljo Revell collaborated with the Parkin office until Revell died in November 1964, in the middle of construction. There were compromises and cutbacks, of course, but many of Revell's details remained: marble set into the outer façades and inner floors, silk-smooth curved concrete, teak and mahogany handrails. And most importantly the design's public spirit was maintained. Councillors and the mayor have offices fronting the square; there is nowhere for politicians to hide here. (The madness around the revelation in 2013 of then mayor Rob Ford's crack use proved the point.)

The square, named after Phillips, spent decades becoming increasingly cluttered and poorly maintained. A design competition in 2007 selected a team of locals led by the multidisciplinary PLANT. Their scheme fell victim to cost cuts and remains incomplete, but it effectively cleared out the square while greening its upper podium level and adding the Peace Garden to the west—two very fine civic spaces. Their work won a Governor General's Medal in 2016 and gave new life to the city's central gathering place. *AB*

19 Metropolitan Toronto Court House, 361 University Ave., Marani Morris & Allan, 1964-66; landscape, Michael Hough, 1966; addition, 1987; south wing, 1985. Understated, formal modernism in an appealing composition with wide plaza that bows both to the scale and classical façade of Osgoode Hall **[3/1]** and the Neo-Expressionism of New City Hall **[7/18]**. The polygonal tunnel that directs pedestrians between University Avenue and Nathan Phillips Square is an interesting architectural conceit, accommodating a courtroom above. It should be noted, however, that this "artistic" ensemble does neglect its street-affirming duties to University Avenue. A memorial plaque in front of the courthouse commemorates the largest armoury in Canada which stood on this site from 1890 to 1963, once an architecturally distinguished and important building in the life of the city. *PM*

20 | Canada Life Assurance Building

20 Canada Life Assurance Building, 330 University Ave., Sproatt & Rolph, 1930–31. Rising resolutely from the street line to a cornice height of 100 feet and formally framed by swatches of manicured lawn, Canada Life was the first—and only—building constructed on University Avenue in accordance with visions of 1929 Beaux Arts planners. As originally designed, the "tower" was to have climbed higher in a series of dramatic setbacks, which probably would have made the solid, almost excessively scaled bulk of the Classical Revival "base" less formidable. The deepening Depression cut back on the height and other construction on the avenue as well. Even truncated, the tower with its neon weather beacon has become the company's trademark: a steady green beacon predicts fair weather, red means cloudy skies; white flashes are for snow, red flashes for rain. *PM*

21 University Club of Toronto, 382 University Ave., Mathers & Haldenby with F. Hilton Wilkes, 1928–29. The University Club was founded in 1906 in premises near King and Bay Streets. Members, who had to be university graduates, were mostly from the nearby business and legal communities but also included several prominent architects. After purchasing land on University Avenue for a new building, the club held a design competition for architect-members, drawing six entries. Mathers & Haldenby won with this elegant Palladian-windowed Neo-Georgian design borrowed from the illustrious clubhouses of London. F. Hilton Wilkes came a close second, and the comradely jury named him associate. When built in 1929, the University Club was flanked by office buildings of comparable scale and style. *PM*

22 375 University Ave. (offices); altered, Page & Steele, 1988. Many people looking back on the 1980s regret their hairstyles. Similarly, this 1960s limestone box would no doubt like to lose its blue-glass pompadour. *AB*

23 Residences at the Royal Canadian Military Institute, Zeidler, 2014. Incorporates 426 University Ave., c. 1890; altered, Chadwick & Beckett, 1907, 1913; altered, Mackenzie Waters, 1930; altered, Fisher Tedman Fisher, 1955. Altered and tower addition, Zeidler, 2014.
Preservation—or is it? This clubhouse for Canadian Forces officers, largely designed by members and architects Capt. Vaux Chadwick and Lt.-Col. Mackenzie Waters, retains a visual presence on University thanks to a fragment of rebuilt façade. Unfortunately, it has the air of a hapless Looney Tunes character about to be crushed by a falling anvil. The anvil is a 35-storey slab of condo apartments, capping the institute's seven-storey club, library, and collection of artifacts. *AB*

22 | Residences at the RCMI

24 52 Division Headquarters, Toronto Police Service, 255 Dundas St. W., Shore Tilbe Henschel & Irwin, 1977; renovations, Cannon Design, ongoing. Very 1977, with its upside-down massing and somewhat Post-Modern quoting of Moderne glass-block and pinstripe ornament. Its defensive posture is also a product of its time—it's a fortress against the mean streets of the city, almost impossible to see into. The current renovation will replace the glass block with a fritted curtain wall—incredibly, maintaining the building's grim opacity. Perhaps one day a redesign of the concrete forecourt will make this feel more like peaceful downtown and less like a war zone. *AB*

25 | 481 University Ave.

25 McClelland and Stewart Building/ originally Maclean Publishing Co., 481 University Ave. thru to Centre St. (office building), Sproatt & Rolph, 1911; addition, Marani & Morris, 1961; altered, William Strong Associates, 1984; proposed addition and alterations, B+H, ongoing. 210 Dundas St. W. (printing plant), probably Murray Brown, 1928.
The Maclean Publishing Company moved to University Avenue in 1911. Theirs was the first commercial building on the street, situated among houses and a few churches. The rear of that original building still shows off striking red-brick and stone buttresses along Centre Street. The front was consumed in 1961 by the edifice that now occupies the University Avenue frontage, later updated with a sassy Post-Modern entrance. The 1928 eight-storey printing plant at Dundas and Centre Streets

still intrigues for its fine "modern classical" details and handsome tall ground-storey windows—unusually high to accommodate printing presses. A proposed condo project would bring the taller building to 55 storeys and add a few floors to 210 Dundas. *PM/ updated AB*

26 The Residences of 488 University Avenue, CORE, ongoing. Incorporates Global House, 480 University Ave. (office building), Webb Zerafa Menkes, 1968. A tower on top of a tower: across the street **[7/25]** it's just an idea, but here it's happening. The developers Amexon began with a very good 18-storey International Style office tower, and have added 37 storeys of condos on top. How? By stripping the cladding of the old building and inserting new steel structure, engineered by Sigmund Soudack—all while the offices inside remained occupied. An unfortunate loss of built heritage, a virtuoso piece of engineering and construction, and a so-so new work of architecture. *AB*

27 Originally Shell Oil Building (offices), 505 University Ave., Marani & Morris, 1958; addition, Marani Rounthwaite & Dick, 1966. A conservative building for the time, in keeping with the city's aspirations for University Avenue. Yet its limestone skin and fine proportions have aged well. This sort of thing might not be good enough for City Hall **[7/18]** but was and remains just fine for corporate Canada. The ornamented, windowless mechanical floor midway up used to be the topmost; the upper seven levels were added in 1966. *AB*

28 Hospital for Sick Children, 555 University Ave., Govan Ferguson Lindsay Kaminker Maw Langley & Keenleyside, 1949; addition, Zeidler Partnership, 1993. The staid 1949 wing is now effectively the back of this world-renowned institution; the main entrance is to the east through Zeidler's addition and its atrium. That is a winning space for kids and adults alike, with kitschy Post-Modern decor suggesting a city-in-a-building, burbling fountains and cheerful public art, High-Tech

elevators and cantilevered benches that offer thrilling peeks over the edge. *AB*

29 Mount Sinai Hospital, 600 University Ave., Bregman & Hamann, 1974; additions, BBB and Stantec, 2012–14. The architect and critic George Baird once said that Toronto has "some of the best second-rate architecture in the world," and he was thinking of this building wrapped in nubbly precast concrete. Seen from along Gerrard Street, its front elevation does reveal a certain elegance. The newly added Hennick Family Wellness Gallery, a street-front lobby space for patients and visitors showing work by the artist Sorel Etrog, places a welcome focus on the experience of patients and families. *AB*

30 Princess Margaret Cancer Centre, 610 University Ave., Zeidler Roberts, 1995. Incorporates Hydro-Electric Building, George W. Gouinlock, 1915. Ontario Hydro Building, 620 University Ave., Sproatt & Rolph, 1935; ten-storey addition, Sproatt & Rolph, 1945. Another atrium hospital by Zeidler, incorporating two very different expressions of Ontario Hydro's

30 | Princess Margaret Cancer Centre

corporate ambition. Hydro chairman Adam Beck (whose effigy by Emanuel Hahn stands a few blocks away, in the median south of Queen Street) commissioned the first Neo-Classical Revival building. Of that, only a façade remains, including Hydro's coat of arms (wheels for power, wavy chevrons for running water, stars for light, a locomotive for electric railways). The second—which began at six storeys, then topped up to 16—is a very fine Moderne tower that remains intact. Look for the water streaming over a dam on either side of the front entrance. *AB*

31 Hydro Place, 700 University Ave. (office building), Kenneth R. Cooper, 1975. Hydro's current head office, a massive and inscrutable curved-glass box, is much harder to love, but such Late-Modernist monumentalism is starting to look better with age. Its sunken front garden and all-underground retail are period pieces, too, but less salvageable—they kill the pedestrian experience on the block. *AB*

31 | Hydro Place

32 Stewart Building/originally Toronto Athletic Club, 149 College St., E.J. Lennox, 1891–94; interior renovation, Bortolotto, 2009. Round-arched Richardsonian Romanesque without the usual rugged sandstone, but still a very stalwart building and a tribute to 19th-century brickwork. Lennox lavished a good deal of care here—the subtle incline or batter of the west tower and taut equilibrium of disparate window shapes and sizes, for

example. The exterior continues to demonstrate Lennox's mastery, while the latest of many renovations reveals good bones. *PM/AB*

33 Canadian Blood Services (originally Victoria Hospital for Sick Children), 67 College St., Darling & Curry, 1889–91; renovation and addition, Parkin, 1993. Sick Kids began as the first hospital in North America designed exclusively for children, and after a few moves settled in this brawny Richardsonian Romanesque structure, with the support of John Ross Robertson, owner-editor of Toronto's *Evening Telegram* [see 11/6b]. It boasted a deft E shape to provide cross-ventilation and maximum light to wards, as well as a rooftop playground. Though the building is compact and tightly packed onto its city lot, the façade is energetic, almost playful. The cheery carved angels above the round-arched entry set the tone. *PM*

34 MaRS Centre, 101 College St. South Tower and Toronto Medical Discovery Tower, Adamson Associates, 2005–06; Heritage Wing/originally Toronto General Hospital, 101 College St., Darling & Pearson, 1909–19, altered 2005; West Tower, 661 University Ave., B+H, 2014. The original building of Toronto General Hospital, a warm Georgian Revival number, has found a new purpose and slightly

34 | MaRS Centre

ridiculous new name as home and co-working space for tech companies. Behind it is a wonderful atrium linking three buildings that have a very contemporary mix of programs—hospital research programs, private medical research, tech start-ups, and pharmaceutical companies, along with public-sector offices meant to bring them together and spur innovation. Sadly, the architectural envelope is far from radical, ranging from the handsome but anodyne curtain walls of the first two towers to the incoherent mishmash of the west tower. *AB*

35 Provincial Parliament Building, 1 Queen's Park, Richard A. Waite, 1886–92; west wing rebuilt after fire, E.J. Lennox, 1909–10; library addition, George W. Gouinlock, 1909–10. Torontonians don't take this amiable Richardsonian Romanesque building as seriously as they should. Perhaps it is the usual city-slicker disdain for the country bumpkin—the Ontario legislature has historically been associated with rural interests—and there *is* something slightly cloddish about this reddish-brown behemoth. But the mono-chromatic palette hides a wealth of beautiful carved detail, and the interior boasts exquisite decoration. The grand ceremonial staircase leading from lobby and entrance vestibule to the legislative chamber above is of delicate ornamental iron, and the red, blue, and cream chamber itself is adorned with bronze-coloured ironwork and intricately carved woodwork. In the rebuilt west wing, grey and white marble piers and balustrades grace walls and stairwells. And the white and gold library wing in the rear introduces luxurious marble detailing. (On the exterior as well, these two additions, though generally following Waite's Romanesque, can be seen to display their architects' own distinctive imprint.)

The Provincial Parliament Building was surrounded by controversy from its beginning, possibly because its architect was not only English-born and Buffalo-based, but also had been one of the judges in the inconclusive design competition that at first had awarded the commission to a Canadian firm. Or possibly because it was so

expensive. Waite's building eventually cost nearly $1.3 million, well above his estimates. But this edifice and Lennox's city hall of about the same date **[7/17]** are undeniably the two buildings that carried Toronto out of the small-town category architecturally and gave the city the imprimatur of an urban metropolis. *PM*

36 Whitney Block, 23 Queen's Park Cres. E., F.R. Heakes, 1925–27; Frost Building North, 95 Grosvenor St., George N. Williams, 1955; Frost Building South, 7 Queens Park Cres. E., Mathers & Haldenby, 1966. Macdonald Block complex, 900 Bay St. and 77 Wellesley St. W., Gordon S. Adamson Associates, Allward & Gouinlock, Mathers and Haldenby, and Shore & Moffat, 1968–71. Landscape, Sasaki Strong and Richard Strong Associates, 1967; restored, The Planning Partnership with Ian Dance, 2004. "Queen's Park," in architectural terms, also includes these fine and varied buildings. The Whitney Block was one of the last buildings that Heakes designed in his three-decade run as the province's chief architect; his Gothic-accented Deco rises to an exclamation point 16 storeys tall, its Queenston stone carved with figures by Charles Adamson representing ideals of Justice and Truth. The Frost Buildings, across the street, are low-key Toronto Establishment modernism, forced by the curved site to loosen up for an almost Brazilian effect. The provincial government also grew to the east in the 1960s with with four refined International Style towers, ornamented by a strong public art program; the landscape that surrounds them, originally overseen by Hideo Sasaki, has been sensitively restored. *AB*

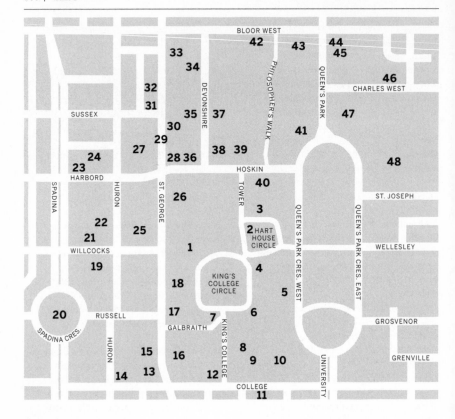

Walk 8: University of Toronto

1 University College, 15 King's College Circle, Cumberland & Storm, 1856–59; restored after fire, David B. Dick, 1892; restoration and renovation, Wilson Newton, Roberts Duncan, and Eric Arthur, 1979. Laidlaw Library addition, Mathers & Haldenby, 1964; renovation, Kohn Shnier and ERA, ongoing. Part Romanesque cathedral, part Ruskinian college; part picturesquely medieval, part symmetrically classical; part colourful and flamboyant, part commanding and formal—University College confounded reviewers from the start. (At the unveiling, the *Globe* reporter surmised that the tower was unfinished and would soon acquire three additional turrets. It is to this day asymmetrically graced with but one.) The architects had first drawn an English Gothic design, but the governor-general of the provinces, perhaps mindful of Gothic's ecclesiastical flavour and the new university's avowed secularism, countered with something more "Italian." Back and forth they seem to have gone, with one of the most exciting, inventive structures ever created in Canada the magnificent result.

1 | University College

Dick's restoration after the devastating fire of 1890 is evident only in the interior where brightly tiled floors and robust wooden gargoyles speak of the late 19th-century Arts and Crafts movement. On the exterior the superb carved stone details—no two alike—and grand stone masses and profile of 1859 stand much as before. The library wing added to the north in 1964 to close the quadrangle is nondescript and will soon be renovated; the outdoor space, designed by Michael Hough, is remarkably refined in itself. *PM/AB*

3 | Hart House

2 Originally Louis B. Stewart Observatory, 12 Hart House Circle, Cumberland & Storm, 1855; reconstructed, 1908. A charming Victorian miniature, this towered relic incorporates the stones as well as the style of the 1857 Toronto observatory, one of three in the world established by the British government for geodetic survey in the mid 19th century. The building was moved from its original site on the other side of the Front Lawn in 1908 to make way for new buildings. *PM*

3 Hart House, 7 Hart House Circle, Sproatt & Rolph, 1911–19; altered, Mathers & Haldenby, 1949. Soldiers' Memorial Tower, Sproatt & Rolph, 1924. Hart House was a gift to the University of Toronto from the Massey Foundation, overseen by Vincent Massey and intended as an undergraduate men's activity centre. It was designed in the Late Gothic Revival style then in favour for "scholastic work," admired for its evocation of ancient centres of learning, specifically the English universities of Oxford (which Massey attended) and Cambridge. Henry Sproatt, who counted this his master-piece, gave Hart House a bold, undulating façade with strongly defined fenestration.

The centre went co-ed in 1972, and has seen other changes since: among them the arrival of the Justina M. Barnicke Gallery and the end of the shooting range, which survived until 2007. But many of the rooms remain with their character intact, among them the Map Room and Music Room—and most of all the Great Hall, with its double hammerbeam roof and stained glass windows.

Soldiers' Memorial Tower was added to Hart House to commemorate students and alumni who lost their lives in World War I (and later World War II). It is a fine, firm tower that turns what might have been an uneasy meeting between Romanesque University College and Gothic Hart House into an exciting architectural juncture. *PM/AB*

4 Gerstein Science Information Centre/ originally University of Toronto Library, 7 King's College Circle, David B. Dick, 1892; south wing, Darling & Pearson, 1909; north wing, formerly Sigmund Samuel Library, Mathers & Haldenby, 1953–54; Morrison Pavilion addition, Diamond Schmitt, 2003. Dick designed this "New University Library" even as he restored University College **[8/1]** in the wake of an 1890 fire. His Richardsonian Romanesque composition includes a grand, round reading room and a tower influenced by Kelso Abbey in his native Scotland. Darling & Pearson's bookstack addition to the south is remarkable: glass floors allow light to filter down to the lowest levels, while cast-iron bookstacks pierce the floors and keep going. Mathers & Haldenby's 1950s expansion to the north features solid materials and strong proportions that look better with age. Finally, Diamond Schmitt's wing wraps open study space in the requisite limestone and slightly mannered massing that relates very comfortably to what came before. *AB*

5 Canadiana Building, 14 Queen's Park Crescent W., Mathers & Haldenby, 1951.
Some Toronto architects adopted Modernism slowly and incrementally, and this slate-roofed box is a relic of the transition period, stone-garbed but with windows that show an awareness of the International Style. The statues of Champlain, Wolfe, Simcoe, and Brock were designed by Jacobine Jones and carved by Louis Temporale. *AB*

6 Medical Sciences Building, 1 King's College Circle, Govan Kaminker Langley Keenleyside Melick Devonshire & Wilson with Somerville McMurrich & Oxley, 1966–69. A big and forceful example of late-1960s Brutalism, this block was designed by hospital specialists and has the inward-looking quality of contemporary medical facilities. But its precast concrete cladding is something special: project architect Peter Goering asked the artists Ted Bieler and Robert Downing for some ornament that would also contain reinforcing bars in the panels. Bieler's *Wave* and *Helix of Life* ornament the building and courtyard. *AB*

7a Convocation Hall, 31 King's College Circle, Darling & Pearson, 1906–07; renovation and restoration, ERA, 2007–10. One of the great large rooms in Toronto, capacious yet intimate with a handsome domed skylight at the centre. The Ionic columns add grandeur, while the bulk of the structure is a very restrained Beaux Arts classicism. The brick is grimy, but the building has a pleasant patina after marking many thousands of tearful graduations. *AB*

7b Simcoe Hall, 27 King's College Circle, Darling & Pearson, 1923–24. The home of the university's top administrators and Governing Council has a pretty, temple-like entrance tucked, somewhat awkwardly, into its armpit. *AB*

8 Mechanical Engineering Building, 5 King's College Rd., Darling & Pearson, 1909; new wing, Allward & Gouinlock, 1947–48. Darling & Pearson's energetic yellow-brick Romanesque sits to the rear, its grand three-storey arches of glass as powerful as the machinery glimpsed inside. By contrast, the very smooth yellow-stone walls and slim ribbons of industrial sash employed by Allward & Gouinlock for the street addition of 1948 appear unusually sleek and serene. That date makes their structure one of the very first Modern Movement buildings in Toronto. The clockface set on a protean tower was a trademark of the Bauhaus style. *PM*

9 Mining Building, 170 College St., Francis Riley Heakes with Frank Darling, 1901–05; addition, Baird Sampson Neuert, 2011. Paid for by the province to boost Ontario's burgeoning mining industry, this beautifully executed red-brick structure with imposing elevated Ionic portico illustrates the high seriousness placed on science and technology in the period. (Heakes also designed the nearby Whitney Block at Queen's Park.) The interior brickwork is spectacular. A characterful attic renovation and rooftop addition house a centre for "mining innovation." *PM/AB*

7a | Convocation Hall

10a | Leslie Dan Pharmacy Building

10a Leslie Dan Pharmacy Building, 144 College St., Foster + Partners with Moffat Kinoshita, 2006.

A crisply Modernist addition to the city from a father of High-Tech that manages to be both rational and a bit wild. Underground are two lecture halls; at ground level, a five-storey glassed-in atrium that lines up with the cornices of adjacent buildings; up top, seven more storeys with a wrapper of ceramic-fritted glass. But those upper floors are cut by a breathtaking atrium, and two round volumes float off-kilter in the middle of the atrium, illuminated at night in candy hues. While distinctly of its time, it has a vaguely '70s reticence that speaks well to Hydro Place across the street [7/31]. *AB*

10b Haultain Building/originally Mill Building, 170 College St. (rear), Francis R. Heakes with Frank Darling, 1903; rebuilt, Craig & Madill, 1930–31.

Originally one storey, the Mill Building served the mining engineering department under Prof. H.E.T. Haultain. The 1930s reworked it into four storeys of Georgian red brick which, today, are rich in character. *PM/updated AB*

10c Donnelly Centre for Cellular and Biomolecular Research, 160 College St., architectsAlliance and Behnisch, Behnisch and Partner, 2005. Rosebrugh Building/originally Electrical Building, 164 College St., Darling & Pearson, 1920.

The Rosebrugh Building once faced onto Taddle Creek Road; around the turn of the millennium, the university converted that nub of a road into a building site, and the Stuttgart firm of Behnisch was selected for this new interdisciplinary research centre. The loft-like lab floors, wrapped in a highly insulated glass envelope, glow at night with a rainbow of coloured accents. Downstairs in the lush atrium garden, Frank Darling's amazing Romanesque brick façade for the Rosebrugh sits like the piece of art that it is. *AB*

10c | Donnelly Centre for Cellular and Biomolecular Research

10d FitzGerald Building/originally Hygiene and Public Health Building, 150 College St., Mathers & Haldenby, 1926.

Behind this unassuming red-brick Georgian Revival façade some of the most notable advances in the history of Canadian public health were achieved. Under the direction of Prof. J.G. FitzGerald, work leading to the virtual extinction of diphtheria and other contagious diseases was carried out, and from 1937 to 1969, the entire nation's insulin was produced. The top floor and gently balustraded roof originally contained houses and runs for rabbits, cats, and guinea pigs. *PM*

11 University of Toronto Health Sciences Building/originally Education Centre, Toronto Board of Education, 155 College St., Page & Steele (Peter Dickinson, design architect) with F.C. Etherington, 1961. Renovation, Stantec, 2006. 263 McCaul St., Charles H. Bishop, 1916. Two beautifully crafted buildings, evidence that this city once took public education very seriously. On College, the syncopated windows show Dickinson's exuberant sensibility, expressed in a conservative vocabulary of Deer Island granite on the first floor and limestone above. Inside, a wild variety of stones and artwork channel the modernism of the Festival of Britain. U of T preserved much of this after buying the building for a song; inside, a lobby mural by Stefan Fritz remains intact, as does Elizabeth Hahn's relief carving in the limestone on the west end, a figure holding a lamp of learning. Upstairs, incised figures of Confucius, Maria Montessori, and John Dewey look out from the walls of the auditorium. Behind is Bishop's Beaux Arts headquarters of 45 years earlier, which once faced College Street but was moved south—into hiding—to make room for its successor. *AB*

12 Wallberg Memorial Building, 184–200 College St., Page & Steele, 1947–49. A simple modern red-brick façade with smooth stone details and dignified twin entrance-pavilions disconcertingly bombarded by a fusillade of rooftop mechanicals. *PM*

13 Koffler Student Services Centre/ originally Public Reference Library, 214 College St., Alfred H. Chapman with Wickson & Gregg, 1908; addition, Chapman & Oxley with Wickson & Gregg, 1928–30; theatre renovation, Irving Grossman, 1961; renovations, Howard D. Chapman with Howard V. Walker, 1985. One of the best Second Classical Revival buildings in Toronto, rich in sculptural stone ornament but poised and firm, with graceful large windows set deep into smooth yellow-brick walls and a gradually stepped

13 | Koffler Student Services Centre

approach to dignify the entrance. The City of Toronto accepted $350,000 from library benefactor Andrew Carnegie to build this reference facility (albeit reluctantly; one Canadian scion thought the offer from an American "impertinent"). The winner of the resulting national architectural competition was this enlightened Beaux Arts composition by Alfred Chapman. The north façade has now been incorporated into the Bahen Centre **[8/15]**. *PM/updated AB*

14 Originally Dentistry Building, 230 College St., Burke, Horwood and White, 1909; north addition, Molesworth, West and Secord, 1920; renovation and front addition, Kohn Shnier, 2000; renovation and additions, Superkul, ongoing. Edmund Burke, also responsible for the Bloor Street Viaduct and Simpson's **[5/6]**, designed this as a dentistry school; U of T's architects moved in from 1961 to 2017, adopting the loft-like upper floors for studio space and making some interesting interventions and additions. Kohn Shnier's audacious front bay, once part of the architecture library, will survive the current adaptation to a "student commons" and be joined by new additions on the west. *AB*

15 Bahen Centre for Information Technology, 40 St. George St., Diamond Schmitt, 2002; café renovation, Gow Hastings, 2014. A big building full of surprises and nuance. A somewhat moody glass-topped atrium extends a long way west, touching a round volume that contains a stair and circular meeting rooms. Shaded, gridded windows and occasional glass bays pierce the pale-brick façade; the south side faces an interesting courtyard between adjacent structures. *AB*

15 | Bahen Centre for Information Technology

16 Cumberland House, 33 St. George St., Frederic W. Cumberland, 1857–60; renovations, William Storm, 1883. Architect Frederic Cumberland built himself this refined residence at the same time he was working on spectacular University College **[8/1]**. The style is indeterminate, but forms and details are very pleasing. (The principal façades were originally those looking south and east; a long front path ran south to College Street.) This became the official home of Ontario's lieutenant-governors in the 1910s at a time when St. George Street was primarily residential and the large lots were held by well-to-do Torontonians on 21-year renewable leases from the university. *PM*

17 Physical Geography Building/originally Forestry Building, 45 St. George St., Darling & Pearson, 1925. A handsome red-brick Georgian cube with, as reported at the opening, "no suggestion of extrava-gance." The building was moved south to make way for the 1960 Galbraith Building by Page & Steele. *PM*

18 Knox College, 59 St. George St. thru to 23 King's College Circle, Chapman & McGiffin, 1911–15. A typical North American Collegiate Gothic building of the period, with blocky, rather dry forms in a quadrangular plan that encompasses library, chapel, dining hall, and student residences. Rough sandstone walls and leaded casement windows are quite appealing, though, and the Gothic-detailed interiors among the most evocative in all the university. *PM*

19 Earth Sciences Centre, Bregman & Hamann with A.J. Diamond, Donald Schmitt and Co., 1989. An enormous building that somehow, to its credit, does not overwhelm. The complex spans nearly two blocks, bridging the pedestrianized Bancroft Avenue and creating a double quadrangle lined by a long, gracious colonnade. Its mass is artfully broken down with different materials (pink and yellow cast stone) and forms, including Post-Modern cylinders and gabled roofs. This is clearly kin to the office's Toronto Central YMCA **[5/31a]**. The plantings inside the courtyards, the work of landscape architect Michael Hough, are a boreal forest and a Carolinian forest—fragments of seeming wilderness magically present in the heart of the city. *AB*

20 Daniels Faculty of Architecture, Landscape and Design/originally Knox College, 1 Spadina Crescent, Smith & Gemmell, 1875; renovations and addition, NADAAA with Adamson Associates and ERA; landscape architects, PUBLIC WORK, ongoing. Once among the most visible buildings in the city, this very Gothic structure bristles with gables and turrets. The spectacular new addition responds in kind, with pointy, mannered volumes that dig into an angular, bermed landscape. To the north, studios and a meeting hall sit under a columnless 110-foot span enjoying a wash of north light. Meanwhile, the original building begins another of its many lives: built as a seminary for Knox College **[8/18]**, it has housed a military hospital, Connaught

Laboratories, and the Eye Bank of Canada, along with university departments and a works yard. Its long period of decrepitude has come to an end and its Victorian grandeur restored, providing a lesson to young architects about how the venerable and the innovative can fit together. *AB*

21 New College Residence, 40 Willcocks St., Saucier + Perrotte, 2003. Facing the city and the west, red brick with syncopated punched windows; facing campus, zinc cladding and a rational grid. In between, a covered grand stair leading to a set of residences, an auditorium, lightwell, and sky gardens. The architects are often more audaciously sculptural **[24/16]**, but this context-sensitive building contains a complex and intriguing set of spaces. *AB*

22 New College (Wetmore and Wilson Halls), 300 Huron St., Fairfield & DuBois, 1964 and 1969; addition and renovation, Dunker Associates, 1999; renovations, Van Elslander & Associates, ongoing.
A product of the university's 1960 western push, this undergraduate college is square and fortress-like on the outside (the Spadina Expressway threatened to push past the walls); the inner quadrangle is snaky and organic, its curves and brown brick recalling Alvar Aalto's Baker House Dormitory at the Massachusetts Institute of Technology. *AB*

22 | New College

23 | Graduate House

23 Graduate House (residences), 60 Harbord St., Morphosis with Teeple Architects, 2000. The university sticking its neck out—and sticking a giant cantilever over Harbord Street. This 120-suite building was the controversial winner of an international, limited design competition; its protruding corridor-slash-sign, intended as a gateway to the campus, had some locals ostensibly worried about snow and ice falling onto the street. (This never seems to have happened; they would have better protested the poor typography that runs two storeys high.) Its varied façades are of stucco, precast concrete, and perforated aluminum, including a screen on the south side that seems to come apart from the mass of the building. Arguably successful, surely provocative, the building spurred the architectural discourse in Toronto and prefigured later Morphosis buildings in Los Angeles and San Francisco. Morphosis principal Thom Mayne won the Pritzker prize, architecture's highest honour, in 2005. *AB*

24 Early Learning Centre, 7 Glen Morris St., Teeple Architects, 2003. Ramps, protrusions and overlapping plans, peekaboo windows and rooftop play areas: this is a building to inspire preschoolers toward a life in architecture. Teeple was clearly opening a dialogue with the more aloof Graduate House **[8/23]**. *AB*

25 Sidney Smith Hall, 100 St. George St., John B. Parkin Associates, 1961; cafeteria addition, Irwin/Beinhaker Associates, 1984; infill additions and renovation, Ian MacDonald, 2002–04. Among the first Modernist buildings on campus, this International Style complex looked radical when new; today the artful façades of Parkin's six-storey office block look retro but retain their dignity. The project helped establish the language of the 1960s west campus, which was imagined as a pedestrian-only superblock with underground loading docks—hence the building's high siting and surrounding plazas. Additions by Ian MacDonald elegantly filled in some gaps with boxes of corrugated stainless steel. *AB*

25 | Sidney Smith Hall

26 Whitney Hall, 85 St. George St., Mathers & Haldenby with John M. Lyle, 1930–31; addition, Mathers & Haldenby, 1960. Sir Daniel Wilson Residence, 73 St. George St., Mathers & Haldenby, 1954. Morrison Hall, 75 St. George St., Zeidler Partnership, 2005. "Sir Dan" and Whitney Hall are two self-conscious Neo-Georgian ensembles erected three decades apart— well into the Modernist era on campus—as University College **[8/1]** residences. Zeidler's tower, crammed into a tight site, takes next door's yellow brick and slate-blue skyward, trailing off in half-hearted quasi-Gothic setbacks. *PM/AB*

27 John P. Robarts Research Library, 130 St. George St., Warner Burns Toan & Lunde with Mathers & Haldenby, 1971–73; renovations, Diamond Schmitt, 2011; west addition, Diamond Schmitt, ongoing. Forceful, mannered, and aloof, "Fort Book" is a love-it-or-hate-it proposition. Ron Thom called it a "dictionary of architectural miseries," and many locals continue to dislike it, but in its fifth decade it has acquired a fan base among younger architects and aficionados.

Its boldness was no accident. In the building craze leading up to Canada's 1967 centennial, the university under president Claude Bissell set out to build a badly needed new library—and to do so in a dramatic way. Four blocks of houses were cleared with eminent domain to establish a site. Then Bissell chose the boldest of five schemes by New York library specialists WBTL, for a 14-storey tower of stacks and reading rooms and two smaller appendages. The seven-storey Bissell Building houses the library and information science department, and the six-storey wing holds the Thomas Fisher Rare Book Library. (The latter's central atrium is one of the best Modernist spaces in the city.) These buildings share a geometry of equilateral triangles, from details of ceiling slabs right up to the shape of the buildings themselves, and a peculiar material and formal palette: precast and poured-in-place in various textures, accented with West African mahogany and lit through castle-like slot windows. In a 2011 renovation, Diamond

27 | John P. Robarts Research Library

Schmitt took an appropriately gutsy response to the building, with new millwork of a grainy beech. Their new west addition, largely for study space, will be glassy, but might just have enough personality to stand proudly by its Brutalist neighbour. *AB*

28 89 St. George St. Newman Centre of Toronto/originally Wilmot D. Matthews house, 89 St. George St., possibly David Roberts Jr., 1890. Ballroom addition, George M. Miller, 1901. St. Thomas Aquinas Church, Arthur W. Holmes, 1927. One of the grandest remaining of St. George Street's grand homes, this is a rather upscale—and exuberant—example of an Annex house. The Newman Foundation, a Catholic outreach group, bought the property and added the quaint Gothic church in the 1920s. *AB*

29 St. George St., Wilson Gate and Perly Rae Gate (streetscape design), Brown + Storey and van Nostrand DiCastri, with Corban & Goode (landscape architects), 1996. Widened in 1948 to accommodate more car traffic, this central spine of the campus was dangerous to pedestrians. This scheme undid the damage by widening sidewalks, adding hundreds of trees, and installing concrete elements that serve both as benches and retaining walls. This important precedent for a more walkable downtown was championed by planner and philanthropist Judy Matthews, who would go on to seed The Bentway **[23/19]**. *AB*

30 Joseph L. Rotman School of Management, 105 St. George St., Zeidler Partnership, 1995; addition, Zeidler Partnership, 2006; south wing, Kuwabara Payne McKenna Blumberg, 2011, incorporating the J. Downey House, 97 St. George St., 1888–89, and addition for the Canadian Missionary Society, Sproatt & Rolph, 1930. A fascinating assemblage. First, Zeidler's 1990s ersatz loft, sliced up by Deconstructivist zinc shrapnel; then KPMB's made-to-measure black boxes wrapping a Victorian house. The ensemble works, and the atria of the new and old wings connect. But most of the finesse is found in

30 | Rotman School of Management

the KPMB wing. It crams 150,000 square feet of floor space onto, above, and below a tight site—while keeping the ground level transparent and finely integrated with the rest of the block. (The broad, shallow central stair, with its hot-pink accents, and the fifth-floor terrace are some of the highlights of the interior.) That wing won a Governor General's Medal in 2014. *AB*

31 Innis College, 2 Sussex Ave., A.J. Diamond & Barton Myers, 1975. Residence, 111 St. George St., Zeidler Partnership, 1994. In the wake of Robarts **[8/27]**, this home for a new college promised modesty and a light touch toward the city's Victorian fabric—the emerging Toronto style and ethic of infillism **[see 11/4a]**. Jack Diamond and his office worked with an existing house and added a new building of the same height that employs a friendly Modernism: reddish-brick cladding, a colonnade, and hints of gabled roof. The atrium linking new and old is an inviting social space that opens to the quiet, green courtyard to the north. The Zeidler residence

31 | Innis College

hall across the street displays a similar set of values but is more mannered and less successful. *AB*

32 Max Gluskin House, 150 St. George St., Hariri Pontarini, 2008/originally William Crowther house, 1889; south wing for Canadian Medical Association, Allward & Gouinlock, 1960. This sensitive addition wraps a Bay-n-Gable house and a fragment of a Georgian Revival office building with a new L-shaped pavilion clad in glass and weathering steel. A pleasant bookend to the Innis College courtyard **[8/31]**. *AB*

> The block between Hoskin and Bloor, St. George and Devonshire, is perhaps the single best collection of architecture in Toronto.

33a Woodsworth College, 119 St. George St., Barton Myers Associates and Kuwabara Payne McKenna Blumberg, 1992. Incorporates Alexander McArthur House, David B. Dick, 1892; altered, Francis S. Baker, 1911; Kruger Hall, Allward & Gouinlock, 1947. One of the great Toronto buildings of the 20th century: an act of infill that ennobles older buildings with new construction that's finely detailed and built to last. It was started by Myers and completed by his former associates, led in this case by Thomas Payne and including Siamak Hariri.

They began with a grand Annex Style house, and a drill hall and officers' quarters built for the Canadian military's officer training program. The architects integrated them into one complex, which extended across the backyards of two houses to the north, forming a quadrangle. (These houses, completed in 1888 by Langley & Burke and 1899 by Burke & Horwood, are not actually part of the college.)

The outer façades of the college are clad in red brick and ashlar granite, while doors and windows are of mahogany and glass—an idiom borrowed from Louis Kahn that would become central·for KPMB and other high-design Toronto practices, including Hariri Pontarini **[see 8/46]**. The rich interior employs limestone, Quebec granite, brick, and teak—solid materials unlikely to go out of fashion. What makes the place remarkable, though, is the artful linking of indoor and outdoor spaces, old and new architecture, found façades and artfully wrought interventions. *AB*

33b Woodsworth College residence, 321 Bloor St. W., architectsAlliance, 2004. High-rise, clad in a checkerboard and stripes of clear and opaque glass panels; the base creates a pleasant courtyard that links with the adjacent Woodsworth College **[8/33a]** and Goldring Centre **[8/34]**. *AB*

34 Goldring Centre for High-Performance Sport, 100 Devonshire Pl., Patkau Architects and MacLennan Jaunkalns Miller, 2014. Most people consider architectural design in its horizontal dimension; think of a floor plan, which resembles a map. But architects also

33a | Woodsworth College

34 | Goldring Centre for High-Performance Sport

think in section—imagine a vertical slice through a building, which reveals the arrangement of spaces above and below each other. This masterful piece of design by the great Vancouver architects the Patkaus and local luminaries MJMA works its magic in this "sectional" dimension. The Kimel Family Field House, a competition space with seating for 2,000, is stashed below ground. The Strength and Conditioning Centre is raised above, supported by dramatic steel trusses that display their strength through street-front windows. Meanwhile, a glassy ground floor with a pedestrian through-street knits together the block. *AB*

35 St. Hilda's College, 44 Devonshire Pl., George & Moorhouse, 1938, 1960; addition, Rounthwaite, Dick & Hadley, 1982. In the allotment of architectural styles, women's residences seem habitually to receive neat domestic Georgian. This one serves the ladies of Trinity. *PM*

36 Massey College, 4 Devonshire Pl., Ron Thom (for Thompson Berwick Pratt), 1963; renovations, Shim-Sutcliffe, 1998, 2001, 2002, 2005. Arguably *the* greatest Toronto building of the 20th century. It began with a medieval model, as a small residential college for male graduate students. This was proposed and funded by the Massey Foundation. Along with Vincent Massey **[see 8/3]** the foundation included his son Hart and his nephew Geoffrey, both architects and the latter an early partner of Arthur Erickson.

A private design competition brought together Erickson and Ron Thom from the

West Coast, and Carmen Corneil **[25/35]** and John C. Parkin **[26/7]** from Toronto. Three of the four responded with straightforwardly Modernist schemes. But Thom, then little known outside Vancouver, had a different response, and he won. The plan was inward-looking, the main cladding was Ohio brick, and there were elements—such as the finials atop the south wing—that were clearly ornamental. All of these elements were criticized as regressive. Yet, as critics have observed, the massing and forms recall Dutch de Stijl Modernism, while many aspects of the building owe a debt to Frank Lloyd Wright. It was, and remains, gorgeous: the low, multi-levelled Junior Common Room and the dining room, Ondaatje Hall, are among Toronto's finest rooms. Thom's manipulation of light and space and fusion of Gothic grammar with a very personal Modernism create the qualities the Masseys asked for: "dignity, grace, beauty and warmth." *AB*

37 Gerald Larkin Academic Building, 15 Devonshire Pl., Somerville McMurrich & Oxley, 1961. A quietly modern version of Trinity stone and stance, without the flounces but with all the flair. Beautifully sited and landscaped, it is home to the George Ignatieff Theatre, offices, and a buttery. *PM*

38 Trinity College Library and Munk Centre for International Studies/ originally Devonshire House, 3 Devonshire Pl., Eden Smith & Son, 1908–09; renovation, Kuwabara Payne McKenna Blumberg, 2000. Gardens, Martin Lane Fox, 2000. Smith's Jacobethan residences were transformed into academic and library space with an agreeably domestic character. KPMB's Thomas Payne oversaw the linking of the three wings with new meeting rooms wrapped in vaguely historicist envelopes of sandstone, brick, and wood. The three-sided courtyard-and-passageway ensemble recalls Woodsworth College **[8/33a]**. *AB*

36 | Massey College

39 | Trinity College

39 Trinity College, 6 Hoskin Ave., Darling & Pearson, 1925; residence west wing addition, George & Moorhouse, 1941; chapel addition, Sir Giles Gilbert Scott, 1955; residence wing addition, Somerville McMurrich & Oxley, 1961. Quadrangle landscape, gh3, 2007. A third-hand evocation of England's ivied halls, this grandiose stone building is a copy of the original Trinity College of 1851 on Queen Street [demolished], which in turn had borrowed its Tudor Gothic garb from Oxford and Cambridge. Trinity did not affiliate with the University of Toronto until 1904 and did not arrive on campus, having reconciled itself to a secular university, until 1925. Of special note is Trinity's distinctive chapel, designed in 1955 by Sir Giles Gilbert Scott, of Liverpool Cathedral renown. Built of bright, crisp stone with luminous clear glazed ornamentally leaded windows sparked by brilliant touches of colour, the chapel is almost mystically "light." The quadrangle, meanwhile, is shady, but has been redesigned to wonderful effect with a concrete-and-grass pattern that uses the Greek letter *chi*, an early Christian icon for Christ. *PM/AB*

40 Wycliffe College, 5 Hoskin Ave., David B. Dick, 1888–91; Convocation Hall, George M. Miller, 1902; dining hall and dormitory, Gordon & Helliwell, 1907; principal's residence and new chapel, Gordon & Helliwell, 1911; Leonard Library addition, Chapman & Oxley, 1929–30. Founded in 1877 as a "low church" Anglican college to train clergy in the evangelical ways of John Wycliffe, the school sits directly opposite Trinity [8/39], representative of

the "high church." Wycliffe federated with the U of T in 1889 and its unpretentious but well-made building was one of the many Richardsonian Romanesque structures designed by Dick for the early campus. The Leonard Library addition to the rear ignores Wycliffe's red-brick richness, lining up instead with stony Late Gothic Revival Hart House [8/3]. *PM*

Running from Hoskin Avenue to Bloor Street, Philosopher's Walk follows the course of Taddle Creek, which once meandered through these fields. More crowded by buildings than it once was, it remains a trace of the picturesque 19th-century campus.

The iron and stone Alexandra Gates at the north end originally stood at Bloor and Queen's Park. Designed by Chadwick & Beckett for the Imperial Order of the Daughters of Empire, they were officially opened by Queen Alexandra's son, the future King George V, and his consort on their visit in 1901.

41 Flavelle House/originally "Holwood" (Sir Joseph Flavelle residence), 78 Queen's Park, Darling & Pearson, 1901–02; addition for Faculty of Law, Hart Massey with William J. McBain, 1961; altered with addition, Moffat/Kinoshita, 1988–89; addition replaced by Jackman Law Building, Hariri Pontarini with B+H, 2016. Flavelle House, one of Toronto's grandest mansions, was built by meatpacker and philanthropist Joseph Flavelle at a time when Queen's Park was a very prominent residential quarter. Today the house—with its portico supported by Corinthian columns, and two wings connected at a very un-classical angle—serves U of T's Faculty of Law. (The fine Georgian hall with Art Nouveau ceiling painted by Gustav Hahn remains intact.) The house has been increasingly overshadowed by new buildings for the faculty. The newest of three iterations responds poetically to the curve of Queen's Park Circle with an arc of limestone fins. Unfortunately, the design has suffered what construction types call "value engineering," and it shows in the awkwardly fortress-like ground floor, the density of the façade, and the interior's utilitarian materials. Compare McKinsey & Co. **[8/46]** to see what Hariri Pontarini can do with enough freedom and budget. *PM/AB*

42 Royal Conservatory of Music/ originally Toronto Baptist College/ formerly McMaster Hall, 273 Bloor St. W., Langley Langley & Burke, 1880–81; Mazzoleni Hall, Burke & Horwood, 1901; renovations, Kuwabara Payne McKenna Blumberg, 2007; TELUS Centre for Performance and Learning addition, 2009, KPMB. What was a High Victorian theology school for the Baptists, and then home to McMaster University, has spent the last 54 years filled with the sounds of music. In the 1990s, the RCM began working with KPMB under Marianne McKenna to renew its remarkable but crumbling campus for teaching, rehearsal, and performance. The result was a brilliant restoration and addition, including the acoustically and architecturally fine 1,135-seat Koerner Hall. The "Great Court" between old and new sections offers up-close views of the Romanesque college's stone skin. Try not to lay your hands on it. *AB*

42 | Royal Conservatory of Music

43 | Royal Ontario Museum

43 Royal Ontario Museum, 100 Queen's Park, Darling & Pearson, 1912–14; east wing addition, Chapman & Oxley, 1930–32; infill additions, Moffat Moffat & Kinoshita with Mathers & Haldenby, 1978–83; Michael Lee-Chin Crystal addition, Studio Daniel Libeskind with B+H, 2009. Roof garden, PLANT Architect, 2010. Any discussion of contemporary architecture in Toronto has to include a look into the Crystal. Daniel Libeskind's scheme beat out 51 other submissions in an international competition at the height of the "starchitecture" frenzy. It was audacious and novel; as a journalist put it at the time, it was "a colossal gamble" by museum CEO William Thorsell on the work of a silver-tongued academic. The gamble failed. The crystal went from 50 per cent glass to 20 per cent during the design process, so that in the end its highly complex steel structure is mostly wrapped in metallic cladding. Inside, the pricey project is cheaply finished, and its angular spaces have proved impractical for display and circulation. Even its rhetorical connection to the museum's gem collection proves false; its form echoes Libeskind's earlier Jewish Museum in Berlin and equally his later shopping mall in Las Vegas. The museum is planning a renovation of the lobby after less than a decade, clear evidence of the project's poor planning.

And yet it makes a fascinating ensemble with the older, better wings of the museum. (To Libeskind's credit, his renovation cleaned up the confusing internal circulation scheme.) The ROM began facing Philosopher's Walk, with a Romanesque gem by Darling &

Pearson. Its west façade, like that of the architects' Rosebrugh Building **[8/10c]**, is a treasure: elaborate corbelling, grand arched windows below, Venetian Gothic windows up top. Chapman & Oxley's addition along Queen's Park, much more visible, was joined at the middle with the original wing to form an H. Their 1932 façade has Romanesque windows and rough limestone, but is Art Deco in its ornament: visit with the seated female figure in the tympanum above the entrance, standing between Old World obelisk and New World totem pole.

The south side of the H retains a mediocre office building, and faces the McLaughlin Planetarium, a Modernist work by Allward and Gouinlock that will soon come down for a university building designed by Diller Scofidio + Renfro with architectsAlliance. That new arrival could be, and hopefully will be a gem. *AB*

44 Originally Lillian Massey Department of Household Science, 157 Bloor St. W., George M. Miller, 1912. A distinguished example of Neo-Classical Revival, this building features a pedimented Ionic portico centring beautifully proportioned wings with giant engaged columns, all of smooth Indiana limestone. The facility was intended to educate young women in the scientific running of a household; a gymnasium and swimming pool in the basement served women students from across the campus. Today the south side is an apt home for the university's classics department, while the north side houses the luckiest Club Monaco in the city. *PM/updated AB*

45 | Gardiner Museum of Ceramic Art

45 Gardiner Museum of Ceramic Art, 111 Queen's Park, Keith Wagland, 1984; renovation and addition, Kuwabara Payne McKenna Blumberg, 2006. A small museum full of delicate treasures now has an equally fine building. Wagland's pink-granite Post-Modernism has largely disappeared under a renovation by KPMB that favours buff limestone and minimal detailing. A fine place also to admire the neighbouring buildings. *AB*

46 McKinsey & Co. (offices), 10 Charles St. W., Taylor Hariri Pontarini, 1999. In moving here, the management consultants chose to borrow some intellectual gravitas from the university precinct, and in exchange they delivered a spectacular piece of

46 | McKinsey & Co.

architecture by a young and talented local firm. (Michael Taylor soon left the partnership to begin Taylor Smyth.) The three-storey structure snakes across its site, wrapping a courtyard to the west; this is the best place from which to admire its mix of rough-cut and smooth Owen Sound limestone, mahogany, and teak, and its low, daylit volumes. The heart of the building is a three-storey atrium nicknamed "the Hive," where staff can come together, impromptu—foreshadowing the corporate-design dogma of 15 years later. The company's confidentiality requirements mean you're unlikely to ever see it, though. *AB*

47 | Victoria College

47 Victoria College, 73 Queen's Park Crescent E., William G. Storm, 1892. Annesley Hall, 95 Queen's Park, George M. Miller, 1901–03. Burwash Hall, 89 Charles St. W., Sproatt & Rolph, 1909–12; additions, Sproatt & Rolph, 1930. Birge-Carnegie Library, 75 Queen's Park, Sproatt & Rolph, 1908–11. Emmanuel College, 75 Queen's Park, Sproatt & Rolph, 1929–31. Isabel Bader Theatre, 93 Charles St. W., Lett/Smith, 2001. Wymilwood, 95 Charles St., Fleury & Arthur, 1953; Goldring Student Centre, Moriyama & Teshima, 2013. E.J. Pratt Library, 73 Queen's Park Crescent E., Gordon S. Adamson & Associates, 1961; renovation, Kohn Shnier with Shore Tilbe Irwin & Partners, 2001. Northrop Frye Hall/originally New Academic Building, 73 Queen's Park Crescent E., Gordon S. Adamson & Associates, 1967. Singly and as a group, the buildings of Victoria University are probably the best of their type on campus. Certainly the Brobdingnagian creation that is Victoria College—hard to believe this giant is only three storeys high—is as solid, as rich, as consummately crafted and energetically balanced as any Richardsonian Romanesque structure in the city. It doesn't look like an institutional building at all—more like a colossal house eager to shelter its 1890s family of scholars.

Burwash Hall, the Late Gothic Revival 1910s assembly of men's residence houses that rims the site to the east and north, is superb, neither stiff nor quaint, with fluid ashlar walls and clean stone window surrounds. It was paid for by the Masseys, as was the earlier domestic-looking Jacobean Annesley Hall for women residents located on Queen's Park.

Victoria's Modernist student union building, Wymilwood, was designed by the influential Eric Arthur with partner William Fleury; its folded-plate roof, warm wood structure, and sinuous spiral stair express a humane and nuanced Modernism. The 2010 addition is capable but makes a clumsy attempt to echo the rough-and-smooth stonework of the McKinsey building next door [8/46].

American library benefactor Andrew Carnegie and Canadian steel magnate Cyrus Birge were responsible for endowing the 1930s Late Gothic Revival building on the northwest corner of the site. Originally the college library, this romantic church-like edifice now houses the central archives of the United Church of Canada—a luminous place to dig for facts. The United Church's divinity school, the 1931 Emmanuel College, compatibly finishes off the west wing of Victoria's Gothic quadrangle.

To the north, the Isabel Bader Theatre is a handsome building whose height and rough-cut Owen Sound limestone speak cordially to its neighbours.

The Pratt Library and Northrop Frye Hall, exquisitely terraced and sited to border Victoria College to the south, are quiet, immaculate 1960s boxes floating in space, never obtrusive to the grand mansion that still towers over the elegant ensemble. When Methodist Victoria College elected to federate with the University of Toronto and left its Cobourg home in 1890, it was a grand day for scholastic architecture in Toronto. PM/AB

47 | E.J. Pratt Library

48a St. Michael's College, 50 St. Joseph St., William Hay, 1856; additions, William T. Thomas, 1862; addition, 1872 (demolished); addition, 1903 (demolished). St. Basil's Church and Odette Hall, 50 St. Joseph St., William Hay, 1856; southeast wing, William T. Thomas, 1862; north extension, 1878; southern extension and tower, A.A. Post, 1887; spire addition, Arthur W. Holmes, 1895; Odette Hall renovations, Carlos Ott, 1996. Queen's Park Building (Pontifical Institute for Mediaeval Studies, More House, Fisher House, Teefy Hall), 53–59 Queen's Park Crescent E., Arthur W. Holmes, 1935–36. Brennan Hall, Elmsley Place, 81 St. Mary St., Arthur W. Holmes, 1938; north wing addition, Frank Brennan, 1967. Carr Hall, 100 St. Joseph St., Ernest Cormier with Brennan & Whale, 1954. St. Basil's College, 95 St. Joseph St., Ernest Cormier, 1951; addition to fourth storey, John J. Farrugia, 1982. John M. Kelly Library, 113 St. Joseph St., John J. Farrugia, 1969. Muzzo Family Alumni Hall/originally Ontario Research Foundation laboratories, 121 St. Joseph St., Mathers & Haldenby, 1930; two-storey addition, Mathers & Haldenby, 1946; renovated, John J. Farrugia, 1983. Sam Sorbara Hall, 70 St. Joseph St., Carlos Ott, 2001. Situated on a quietly dignified site east of Queen's Park, the buildings that make up the University of St. Michael's

College seem unlike any others on the U of T campus, beginning with French Gothic St. Basil's Church and attendant college buildings designed by William Hay in 1856. In fact, it was only coincidental that St. Michael's was located so near the University of Toronto campus at all. The Basilian Fathers, who had come to Toronto from France to found the Catholic school, objected to the obvious east-end location around St. Paul's because of its proximity to the unhealthy Don River **[see Introduction, Area VI]**, and accepted instead this commanding site atop Clover Hill proffered by wealthy landowner and Roman Catholic convert John Elmsley **[see Walk 5]**. Propinquity undoubtedly influenced St. Michael's early decision to affiliate with the U of T in 1881, the first outside school to do so.

St. Michael's College, then, can claim the oldest buildings on the U of T campus, predating completion of University College **[8/1]** by three years. It was supposedly at donor Elmsley's request that a parish church was put up here along with school buildings, perhaps so he wouldn't have to walk as far as St. Michael's Cathedral **[13/4a]** for his daily devotions (Elmsley's house, also called Clover Hill [demolished], was situated within a stone's throw). St. Basil's is a fine Gothic Revival church: lithe, tense, almost prickly-looking. The attached St. Michael's wing displays some of the same energy, with pointy dormers and lovely spired turrets sprouting along the high roof. But there is also a cautious, flattened dignity here,

48a | Carr Hall

characteristics that reappear in later college buildings as well. Subsequent easterly additions to St. Michael's were expropriated by the city and demolished in the 1920s during Bay Street's northward march.

Holmes's Queen's Park Building and Brennan Hall are 1930s Late Gothic Revival, built of limestone and stone-textured light-coloured cement blocks. Again picturesque Gothic detail is rendered coolly French and precise, an impression reinforced especially at the Queen's Park Building with its formal open quadrangle and decorous "stone" and iron fence. A world centre for medieval studies, this building also contains student residences (More and Fisher Houses) and classrooms (Teefy Hall). Brennan Hall, named for Father Laurence Brennan, who was pastor of St. Basil's, 1880–1889, 1891–1904, is a student and faculty activity centre.

Carr Hall, the classroom building added along St. Joseph Street in 1954, was designed by Montreal architect Ernest Cormier, author of the Supreme Court building in Ottawa. Cormier's transitional Gothic is refined and subtle; the hexagonal stair tower and arched windows defer to the historicism of the surrounding buildings, while the gridded windows on the west side are decisively Modernist.

Cormier's yellow-brick St. Basil's College was once rather plain; John Farrugia's concrete additions to the front have all the grace of a cyst. Farrugia, however, also designed the Brutalist John M. Kelly Library next door, which rewards a second look.

The most recent addition to campus, Ott's Sorbara Hall, is competent historicism with neither the craft nor personality of its older neighbours. *PM/AB*

48b 1 Elmsley Pl., Langley & Langley, 1896. 3 Elmsley Pl., Langley & Langley, 1897. 5 Elmsley Pl., possibly John M. Lyle, 1897. Maritain/Gilson House, 6–8 Elmsley Pl., A. Frank Wickson, 1901. 2 Elmsley Pl. and 96 St. Joseph St., Marshall B. Aylesworth, 1892–93; additions, Burke & Horwood, 1897, 1903. Now part of St. Michael's campus, Elmsley Place was laid out in 1890 by Remigius Elmsley, son of John Elmsley, as an exclusive residential precinct. The land was conveyed by leasehold, and in the 1920s, St. Michael's was able to buy up the attractive enclave with its bevy of distinguished turn-of-the-century houses, most of which stand now as student residences. Illustrious early residents included a famous portrait painter, a university president, and an Ontario attorney-general, senator, judge, and premier. *PM*

This is the land of the Bay-n-Gable house.
That Victorian type—described by the term
coined by Patricia McHugh in the first edition
of this book—was probably born in Yorkville
[17/20b]. But it was here, in the 1870s and
'80s, that the type blossomed and multi-
plied, in strings of modest houses often built
for working-class tenants. Cabbagetown is
also where, in the 1960s and '70s, the
Bay-n-Gable acquired its cultural status: a
generation of middle-class gentrifiers began
to restore these modest buildings, eventually
to treat them with reverence, and to
establish in Don Vale one of Toronto's few
consistent pockets of historic preservation.

This zone is also the home of Toronto's
one grand urban renewal project—Regent
Park, which wiped out another working-class
Victorian quarter to replace it with two
massive "superblocks." That piece of
Modernist urbanism reflected the ideals of
professional planners in the 1940s and
'50s—against which the gentrifiers and
activists of Don Vale would define themselves. The battle produced a consensus on
city building that continues to shape the
area, and the city, in the 21st century.

Once, though, this was simply a
woodland, near the river known to the
Mississauga people as Wonscotonach. They,
like the Seneca who occupied the area
before them, seem not to have established
permanent settlements along the narrow
and marshy river. John Graves Simcoe, the
lieutenant-governor of Upper Canada from
1791 to 1796, was attracted to the site, a
judgment that was not always shared by
the next generations of Torontonians.
He set aside the area east of town—400
acres as "King's Park" for government
buildings, the northern half for his own use.
Simcoe and his wife Elizabeth established
their summer residence here, and named it
Castle Frank after their son, Francis. (It was
"built on the plan of a Grecian Temple," as
Elizabeth put it in her diary in 1796, with a
colonnade of four peeled pine logs. The
house was incomplete when the Simcoes left
Toronto forever in 1798.)

When the city grew to reach the Don
Valley, the relationship between architecture
and nature changed: the woods proved a good

Area VI
Walk 9: Don Vale
Walk 10: "Old Cabbagetown" and Regent Park

hiding place. In the 1850s, the city began
assembling land along the lower Don, and
placed in it certain institutions that belonged
away from the city: the Don Jail **[9/16]**; an
isolation hospital; and a "house of refuge,"
colloquially a poorhouse. St. James' Cemetery
[9/1a] and the Necropolis **[9/14]** were
established early on, the former through a
donation from the Scadding family, who had
acquired Simcoe's land.

Riverdale Park, spanning both sides of
the river, opened in 1880. Then, starting in
1888, the Don was channelized, making
room for rail lines and (in theory) a deeper

and more navigable waterway. The lower Don became more heavily polluted and a gathering place for industries **[see Area XII]**.

Those distilleries **[see Walk 24]**, brewers, slaughterhouses, and tanneries needed workers, and those workers needed housing. Beginning in the 1840s, Toronto received welcome waves of potential labourers: Irish migrants escaping the Potato Famine, who settled along the Don, unafraid of its apparently malarial marshlands. The area along Dundas, what is now Regent Park, became predominantly Irish for a century and at some point acquired the unflattering epithet "Cabbagetown," likely after the vegetables that these newcomers grew in their gardens.

The 1870s brought more people to the city, and the area saw a boom in specula- tively built housing, for the middle class and, especially, the working class. "Building societies" and individual developers built houses or groups of them. The row house and the double house, in particular, served well as discrete small projects that could crowd plenty of housing onto small sites. In the process, these many projects created a complexity and density that would be seen first as "slum" and later as "charming."

Many of these houses were Bay-n-Gable, a style that managed to be both classy- looking and inexpensive. Tall ceiling heights helped the narrow rooms feel gracious. The façades of decorative brickwork and woodwork employed Gothic Revival motifs, a language that alluded to Britain and old-money good taste; but the other surfaces of the houses could be covered in cheaper stucco or lime render. (As the designer of an 1820s pattern book put it, "Houses built in couplets are not only attended with less expense in their erection than when detached, but they are calculated to present an appearance of consequence which singly they might not possess.") En masse, they look coherent and pretty; today's gentrified Don Vale, where most of the houses' Victorian faces have been cleaned and restored, has some of the most attractive streets in the city.

These 3,000 or so buildings, erected by small-business people and largely rented, became the basis for a stable community that lasted into the 1930s. Then, with those houses run down and more crowded than ever in the Depression, the neighbourhood was, as Hugh Garner described it in the preface to his novel *Cabbagetown*, "the

largest Anglo-Saxon slum in North America." Reformers saw the need for change. Lieutenant-governor Herbert Bruce's 1934 report on housing in Toronto examined working-class dwellings in areas including Cabbagetown and (quite reasonably) found three-quarters of them unhealthful.

In 1947, voters approved the "clearance, replanning, rehabilitation and modernization" of what became known as Regent Park. Between that year and 1960, the redevelopment took over two massive "superblocks" that disrupted the street grid from Gerrard to Shuter, Parliament to River; the modest low-rise apartment blocks and houses of the north half [10/22] were succeeded by firmly Modernist high-rises in the southern half [10/30] by 1960. The latter, by the young Brit Peter Dickinson, were clever but orthodox expressions of Modernist social-housing dogma: homes should be in new buildings, with much light and fresh air, surrounded by green space.

By this time the large ambitions of Modernist planning and its government-corporate offspring "urban renewal" had begun to attract criticism in North America. Jane Jacobs published *The Death and Life of Great American Cities* in 1961 and assailed "projects" like Regent Park for their "monotony, sterility, and vulgarity." In Toronto, Regent Park was already losing its appeal. "It has an institutional character you don't find in most neighbourhoods," *Maclean's* reported in 1965. "In some people's mind a stigma attaches to anyone who lives there."

At the same time, Don Vale—the area known today as Cabbagetown—was looking better, the "peculiar, at times bizarre variety of form and detail" possessing an "honest, human, unpretentious feeling," as the young architect Irving Grossman put it in 1965. Young professionals were drawn here as to

Yorkville [see Area IX], settling in these cheap, largely decrepit houses and often painting them white. When two pockets of Don Vale were targeted for renewal, the "white painters" fought back and won. They would win, too, at Trefann Court [10/28]—where the activists and policy-makers included three future Toronto mayors: John Sewell, David Crombie, and June Rowlands. They helped birth the ethos of bottom-up planning and protection for local communities that came to rule the old City of Toronto.

Today in the amalgamated Toronto, 19th-century districts such as Cabbagetown are designated "stable residential neighbourhoods" in the official plan, and are more or less off limits to development. The Cabbagetown Residents Association (established 1967) is going strong, and helped the neighbourhood acquire four Heritage Conservation Districts protected by the city. The Bay-n-Gable, here, is safe.

While Don Vale has seen its façades restored—a good thing in many ways—the houses behind these fronts are often expensively renovated and enlarged, and home to fewer, and wealthier, people than ever before. Such reverent preservation must be seen as the counterpart to the breakneck growth that is remaking the industrial fringes of downtown. In a growing city, people have to live somewhere.

One place where new arrivals can settle is Regent Park, where the grand project of the 1950s is being comprehensively replaced by a new grand project. The new buildings mix market and social housing, and the architecture is firmly Modernist. But the urban design is firmly traditional: buildings face the streets, and those streets that were erased 60 years ago have been restored. The human, unpretentious wisdom of the 19th century can, perhaps, live in towers, too.

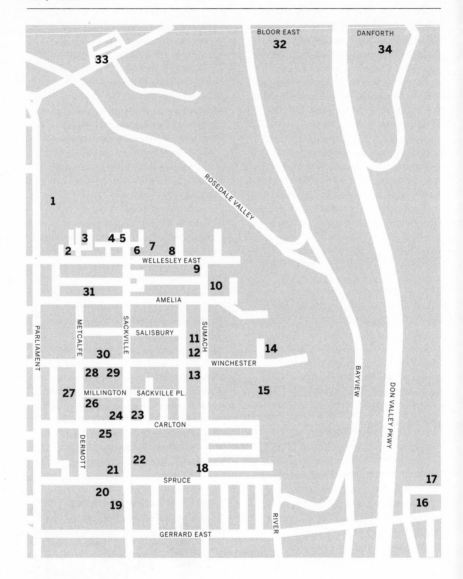

Walk 9: Don Vale

1a St. James' Cemetery, 635 Parliament St., John G. Howard (grounds), 1845; Darling & Pearson (fence and gate), 1905.
A 19th-century guidebook called it a "garden of graves," and the meandering roads and lush landscaping designed by Howard for the rolling, heavily wooded site still make for a richly scenic spot. The first graveyard for the Anglicans had been adjacent to St. James'

Church on King Street **[1/13]**, but by the 1840s, that was filled and this remote site acquired on the hills overlooking the Don Valley. At 65 acres, this was the largest cemetery in Toronto, and it was here that the leading families of the 19th century came to rest; among their grand mausoleums is Sir Casimir Gzowski's, a rare instance of Egyptian Revival. (His descendant Peter has joined him there.) Over 89,000 interments and 75,000 cremations have taken place here. *PM/AB*

**1b St. James-the-Less Chapel,
635 Parliament St., Cumberland & Storm,
1858.** Built in a decade when many superb
structures designed by immigrant British
architects were rising in the city, this is one
of the choicest buildings in Toronto, if not in
all of Canada. Although it may suggest a
simple 13th-century English parish church,
there is nothing primitive about the bold
massing and tense outlines seen here, with a
squat masonry base playing against the
swoop of a steep roof punctuated by a sharp,
soaring spire. Intended only as a mortuary
chapel, St. James-the-Less did hold public
services for a period in the mid 1860s before
nearby St. Peter's was built. *PM*

1b | St. James-the-Less Chapel

**2 Originally Thomas Harris house,
314 Wellesley St. E., 1889–90.** This joyful,
informal house is emblematic of Don Vale's
Queen Anne architecture of delight, with
irregular massing and fenestration, a variety
of materials, ingenuity of shapes, and lively
surprises, provided here by a veritable
catalogue of terracotta and carved stone
ornament. Mr. Harris was, appropriately,
proprietor of a stone-cutting firm. As a result
of new row houses sneaked in behind, no. 314
gained a garage but lost some garden. *PM*

**3a 316–324 Wellesley St. E. (five-house
row), 1888–89. 326–334 Wellesley St. E.
(five-house row), 1888–89.** Many Don Vale
houses were built in a rush of speculation by
a few contractors, offering an unusual
opportunity to create large and ambitious

ensembles—including these by Frank
Armstrong. On Wellesley, twinned five-house
rows with bristling corner towers keeping
watch over Laurier Avenue have few equals in
Toronto for bravura planning. *PM*

**3b 1–21 Laurier Ave. (ten-house row),
1889. 2–22 Laurier Ave. (ten-house row),
1889.** More Armstrong projects: Queen Anne
row housing that is repetitious but never
static. Working with a basic repertory of
factory-made parts—bargeboards, wooden
slatted porches, stained glass windows—
builders like Armstrong were somehow able
to adapt features of a style known for variety
and asymmetry to long Bay-n-Gable rows of
look-alike houses. Part of the trick was the
exuberant sunbursting detail that went with
the style; part was the undulating rhythm of
the façade. *PM*

**4 1–7 Wellesley Cottages (seven-house
row), 1887; rear additions, 1985.** This
district—and particularly this block on the
north side of Wellesley—is packed with a
surprising number of separate dwellings, far
more than would be permitted by contemporary planners. And yet these once-modest
cottages are desirable: the row served as
inexpensive rental housing until the 1980s
but has been thoroughly gentrified and
grandly renovated to take advantage of the
cemetery views. *AB*

4 | Wellesley Cottages

5 1–17 Alpha Ave. (nine-house row), 1888. 2–18 Alpha Ave. (nine-house row), 1888.
After the peaked-roof one-and-a-half-storey cottage came the mansard-roof one-and-a-half-storey cottage, here with brickwork adding as much ornament as possible on the tiny façades. Alpha Avenue was another instant 1880s street, which was remade by "white painters;" since the early 1970s, no. 1 and no. 3 have been joined to form one dwelling. *PM/AB*

6 483–485 Sackville St. (double house), 1889–90. 376–380 Wellesley St. E. (triple house), 1889. These dwellings sitting around the corner from one another are uncommonly commercial-looking, flaunting flat roofs, pressed-metal cornices, and brick belt courses. Potential residents didn't much take to them either and they stood vacant for many years, even though they were expensively built entirely of brick instead of the roughcast with brick front more usual in this area. The owner was Nathaniel Baldwin, who ran a dairy store on the corner between the two. *PM*

7a Owl House Lane, 390 Wellesley St. E. (complex of 20 row houses and one rehabilitated house), Peter Turner, 1978–79. A fine, unobtrusive condominium development boasting one of Toronto's better courtyards and an 1892 house tucked in a corner of the complex that was once home to artist C.W. Jefferys and his parents and brothers. *PM/AB*

7b 398–402 Wellesley St. E. (three-house row), 1886. This trio well represents the Bay-n-Gable houses that rose in great numbers across Toronto in the 1870s and 1880s. The curved bargeboard embroidering the gable, polygonal bay window, and red brick sparked with yellow continue to spell picturesque at its most sprightly. *PM*

8a 414–416, 418–420, 422–424, 426–428 Wellesley St. E. (four double houses), 1887–88. Displaying vigorous patterns and textures associated with the burgeoning Queen Anne style, these slam-bang double houses are later versions of Toronto Bay-n-Gable. Tall and flat with dynamic rectangular bays and boldly geometric ornament in the gable, they loom large and loud in the streetscape. *PM*

8b 1–15 and 2–16 Wellesley Ave. (eight double houses), 1888. 17–19, 18–20 Wellesley Ave. (two double houses), 1889. Wellesley Avenue was created by developer Frank Armstrong, also responsible for the houses framing it on Wellesley Street **[9/8a]** and the similar Laurier Avenue project **[9/3a, 9/3b]**. Armstrong was an inventive speculative builder, deploying prefabricated parts and forms in different combinations. Here the double houses feature a single, centred gable. The land at the end of this narrow cul-de-sac did not belong to Armstrong; the two double houses there were built in a different style one year later. *PM*

8b | Wellesley Ave.

9 442–444, 446–448, 450–452, 454–456 Sumach St. (four double houses), 1886–87. The Second Empire mansard roof was practical for providing space to attic bedrooms and these straight-sided mansards were the most practical of all. *PM*

10a 437–439 and 441–443 Sumach St. (two double houses), 1892. Weighty Richardsonian Romanesque loners in this nimble precinct, these double houses parade the heavy stone bases and voluminous round-arched windows of houses built in Toronto's Annex neighbourhood during this period. *PM*

10b 425–435 Sumach St. (six-house row), 1904–05. An idiosyncratic row still enjoying a Victorian passion for the strange and exotic. The half-timbered oriels suggest medieval England; the lilt to the gabled dormers is almost Chinese. *PM*

About Wellesley Park and Hillcrest Avenue abutting the Toronto Necropolis originally stood a dozen factory buildings of Peter R. Lamb & Company, makers of glue, ground bone, lime, animal charcoal, and a popular shoe and stove lustre known as Lamb's Penny Blacking. Begun here in 1848, this was Don Vale's first and only real industry, and while it may have drawn some settlement to the area, it is likely the sooty, malodorous enterprise kept more potential development away than it attracted. The main building burned down in 1888 and the factory was never rebuilt, although the family retained this large parcel of land until it was built up with houses and the park created in the early 1900s.

11a 420–422 Sumach St. (double house), 1886. Sporting four sprightly pointed dormers skipping across a mansarded roof and a harmonious ornamental porch, this red-brick Second Empire pair makes a handsome contribution to the streetscape. *PM*

11b 410–412 Sumach St. (double house), 1884. Well-made Bay-n-Gables with pleasantly curved yellow-brick details sparking the red. *PM*

11c 404–408 Sumach St. (triple house), William L. Symons, 1902. The English cottage found its way to Toronto in the early 20th century. Its fresh, quaint half-timbered look was typically used—paradoxically enough—for large, expensive single-family dwellings, but it also worked well for this winsome miniature triple house. *PM*

12 Originally Daniel Lamb house, 156 Winchester St., 1867; altered and major additions, 1877. Daniel Lamb was the son of Peter Lamb, founder of the glue and blacking factory at the end of Amelia Street [see aside]. When Daniel moved into no. 156 on his marriage in 1867, it was a single-storey frame dwelling. Over the years, many additions and a few subtractions led to the substantial, albeit picturesque Victorian mien we see today. Daniel, who was twice alderman for this area, lived here until his death in 1920. *PM*

13 384 Sumach St. (detached house), 1866; altered later. The quintessential "Victorian" house with its wooden gingerbread and Eastlake bric-a-brac. Ironically, such flavour was achieved over many years, the house having been much added to and altered. *PM*

14 Toronto Necropolis Chapel, 200 Winchester St., Henry Langley, 1872. The Toronto Necropolis cemetery dates from the early 1850s, when a group of concerned citizens banded together in search of a new site for the town's nonsectarian burying ground and potter's field, which then stood dangerously close to the burgeoning Town of Yorkville [see Introduction, Area IX]. (Graveyards were considered unhealthy, and indeed did pose a threat to the water supply.) The solicitous group paid the City of Toronto $16,000 for these 18 acres and

14 | Toronto Necropolis

proceeded to transfer the remains from the potter's field. In the mid '60s, they purchased an adjacent 15 acres, but the municipality bought them back when landowners in the area objected to expansion by the necropolis; a spreading "City of the Dead" was little spur to real estate development.

Langley's High Victorian Gothic mortuary chapel ensemble with porte cochère and superintendent's lodge was added in 1872, and is today one of the city's unspoiled architectural treasures. Elaborated with all the panoply of the decorative style—multi-coloured and patterned slate roof, complicated tracery and bargeboards, crockets, finials, ironwork—the chapel also manages a quality of ground-hugging repose, even simplicity, that admirably suits its function and site. *PM*

15 Riverdale Park, Carlton to Winchester St., Sumach St. to the Don Valley, opened 1880; zoo addition, 1898. The City of Toronto created Riverdale Park from land which it had begun purchasing in the 1850s. At one time, the park encompassed 162 acres on either side of the Don River. Today, much diminished in size and beauty—and divided by the Don Valley Parkway and rail lines—it needs some attention but retains its spectacular topography.

The zoo, brainchild of Alderman Daniel Lamb, got off to a slow start in 1898 with only two prairie wolves and a few deer. In 1901, a polar bear was added. One year later, however, success seemed within reach with the arrival of an elephant—a gift of the Toronto Street Railway, which not incidentally was the means by which most visitors would travel here.

In 1978, with the opening of a new metro zoo **[26/23]**, the Riverdale facility transformed into a bucolic farmyard zoo with 19th-century barns removed from Markham, Ontario, and a replica of a Markham farm house, named after its restoration architect, Napier Simpson House. *PM*

16 The Toronto (Don) Jail, 550 Gerrard St. E., William Thomas, 1858; rebuilt after fire, William T. Thomas, 1865; restoration, ERA and the Ventin Group, 2013. For the Victorians, prison was a place for reform, and they took their prison buildings very seriously. Leading architects were called upon to design them, expensive materials and methods were utilized to construct them, and every care was given to meet functional concerns of security, supervision, ventilation, and heating.

Such was the case with Toronto's stately Don Jail. Designed by William Thomas, who also created St. Lawrence Hall **[1/4]**, the classically inspired Don Jail sits serenely on a rise, its entrance one of the noblest doorways in the city. Manipulating vermiculated quoins, piers, half columns, and cornice window heads, the architect has made four storeys look like two, a complicated façade look calm, a massive building seem humane. The precisely fitted courses of fine Queenston and Ohio stone, the neatly laid brick, and the beautifully carved stone details are all superb. The layout followed 19th-century thinking by putting prisoner accommodations in wings radiating from a core that was the heart and hub of surveillance.

Prisoners occupied this structure until 1977 (and the last hangings in Canada took place here in 1962), while a later jail operated operated through 2013. In a long-awaited restoration, the building became administration space for Bridgepoint Health **[9/17]**, with the central atrium and some cellblocks preserved and finely restored. *PM/AB*

16 | Don Jail

17 Bridgepoint Health, 1 Bridgepoint Dr., KPMB with Stantec (planning phase) and Diamond Schmitt with HDR (design-build phase), 2013. A rehab hospital designed by many hands emerges as a strong piece of design. This is no icon—the punch-card pattern on the prominent west façade is hardly beautiful—but it is an urbane building and a humane place for patients, many of whom are here for long stays. Patient rooms are designed for actual comfort, importantly including visual connections with the outdoors; time outside is possible too, on a public open-air terrace and green roof from which some of the best views in Toronto can be enjoyed. The surrounding public realm, thoughtfully detailed by PFS Studio and MBTW (if cheaply built), helps the huge building reach to the surrounding city in a way that few hospitals ever attempt. The adjacent park is named for William Peyton Hubbard, a City of Toronto alderman from 1894 to 1914 and Toronto's first black elected official. *AB*

17 | Bridgepoint Health

18 Spruce Court Apartments, 1–32 Spruce Court, Eden Smith & Sons, 1913; additions, 330 Sumach St., Mathers & Haldenby, 1926. This trim, spacious two-storey complex was the city's first government-sponsored housing project, built to provide decent accommodation for low-income families at reasonable rents. Enjoying many salutary features associated with the period's experimental housing— grassy communal courtyards, private entrances, intimate scale, plenty of windows for air and light—it also respects the street and neighbourhood. A similar experiment,

18 | Spruce Court Apartments

Riverdale Courts, was designed by Eden Smith one year later at 100 Bain Avenue on the other side of the Don Valley. *PM*

19 298A and 298B Sackville (infill houses), Baird Sampson Neuert, 1999. Peanut Factory Lofts (apartments), 306 Sackville St., renovation, John Cowle, 1987. More hidden housing. The first project at no. 306 reflects its 1980s birthdate with its stuccoed surfaces and cupola: this is Post-Modernism *alla* Aldo Rossi. It's also good urbanism, with a row of houses facing a semi-private mews. The later project by Baird Sampson Neuert adroitly fills in a smaller site with two crisply detailed houses, linked to the street by a skinny six-foot-wide lane—a configuration that could be repeated on many other lots. *AB*

Gifford and Nasmith Streets were laid out in the 1920s following demolition of Toronto General Hospital, which had occupied the four-acre site between Sumach and Sackville Streets from 1855 to 1913. The two short streets were built up with simple, unassuming bungalows typical of the period throughout North America. The style was very popular in Southern California and should be familiar to Hollywood movie buffs of the era. Early 20th-century bungalows line many a street in the near suburbs of Toronto as well.

20a Trinity Mews, 41 Spruce St. (complex of seven row houses and rehabilitated Trinity College Medical School), Ferdinand A. Wagner, 1979. Established in 1859 as part of Trinity College on Queen Street [see Introduction, Area V], Trinity Medical School moved to this bold brick facility close to the general hospital in 1871. In 1903, the school was absorbed by the University of Toronto Faculty of Medicine and this building fell to a variety of owners, including a maker of mattresses, before it was salvaged as the showpiece of Trinity Mews. The houses in behind try to borrow the older building's idiom and fail. *PM/AB*

20b "Janus House," 39 Spruce St., 1886; renovation, Studio NminusOne, 2012. Victorian in the front, modern in the back. A Dutch family of homeowners imported a European approach to preservation here: restoring the Bay-n-Gable with most of its interior features, while adding an entirely new wing that is bright and spatially complex. The architects have named it after the two-faced Roman god. From the lane next door, you can see the addition clad in Cor-Ten steel, and the glassy atrium between old and new. *AB*

20c Originally Charles B. Mackay house, 35 Spruce St., 1867. An early house endowed with the dignity of a deep setback and orderly red-brick Georgian façade, although the front gable is unusual for a Georgian design. Mackay clerked at the customs house on Front Street [demolished], and so lived a long way from work at a time before the horse-drawn street railway ran up dirt and gravel Parliament Street. *PM*

21 56 Spruce St. (attached house), 1872; restored, 1983. A simple roughcast cottage of the 1870s, more endearing than ever thanks to its honest restoration. *PM*

22 Originally Francis Shields house, 377 Sackville St., 1876; altered later; restored, Monica Kuhn and James M. Davie, 2014. Mr. Shields, a drover, chose the Second Empire style as did his neighbours at 373–375. However, the stone front—sandstone with marble quoining—made his home unique in the district, then and now. *PM/AB*

23 Originally Benjamin Brick house, 314 Carlton St., 1874. A neat mansard-roof brick cottage enjoying formal repose and grandeur more typical of its larger Second Empire brethren. At the time he built his house, Mr. Brick was listed in the assessment rolls as—what else?—a bricklayer. He later became a full-time contractor for several fine houses on this street. *PM*

24a 294–296 and 298–300 Carlton St. (two double houses), 1889. Late Bay-n-Gables plumbing all the diverse details the Queen Anne style had to offer. The double doors and stained glass transoms are stunners, never mind that they were repeatable prefabs. The porches contribute to the happy scale. Modern-day renovators who shear off porches on Victorian houses willy-nilly are making a big design mistake, as well as a practical one. *PM*

24b Originally William Lumbers house, 288 Carlton St., 1881. A formal 1880s Second Empire house built for a medicine manufacturer, today looking a little silly with the addition of a 1980s Second Empire garage! The smooth stone window lintels set flush with the wall seem to have been popular in this neighbourhood for all manner of houses. *PM*

24c Originally Frederick Nicholls house, 286 Carlton St., 1884. Bowed bay, end-wall porch, and gabled slate roof for a merchant, whose original front door is now "boxed" and daintily bracketed. *PM*

25a 297 Carlton St. (detached house), 1892. A sober late Queen Anne house whose narrow, frontal emphasis is misleading; the house is huge. The reticence is real, however, signalling new turn-of-the-century Classical Revival architectural directions. *PM*

25b Originally Hugh Neilson house, 295 Carlton St., 1878. A handsome Gothic Revival survivor with fine details. The bargeboards edging a perfectly proportioned gable borrow from church tracery for their trefoil profile, which is scrupulously repeated in cresting atop the bay. Neilson, who was associated variously with the Dominion Telegraph Company and the Telephone Dispatch Company, had installed in this house one of the first residence telephones in the city. (Telephones were first used in Toronto in 1877. In 1883, there were 700 lines from 14 switchboards, and records indicate approximately 3,400 telephones were in service by 1890.) *PM*

Sloping, narrow Metcalfe Street is surely one of the city's loveliest, graced with a series of gentle late Victorian rows, all tied together with new delicate iron fencing and a concern for the streetscape.

26a 1–3, 5–7 Metcalfe St. (two double houses), 1889. 9–11, 13–15 Metcalfe St. (two double houses), 1885. A long, neat Queen Anne string of houses put up in two different years. Builder Thomas Bryce did the assembling here, shopping for doors, windows, and other parts at the same factory from whence had come 294–296 and 298–300 Carlton Street **[9/24a]**. The roof-like projection overhanging the first storey, called a pent eave, is a distinctive feature of this neighbourhood. *PM*

26b 17–25 Metcalfe St. (five-house row), 1888–89. A neatly composed all-red row with two bowed bays framing three straight arrows. *PM*

26c 7 Millington St. (stable converted into housing), renovation, CORE, 2006. Down the lane hides another 1980s loft conversion, this one in the former stable for 28f. The wood slats on the façade give away one unit, no. 7, as a more recent architecty reno. *AB*

27a 6–18 Metcalfe St. (seven-house row), 1883. A Bay-n-Gable row with three curious eyelid dormers winking from the roof and lighting what must be a shared attic. Removal of shadow-producing details and new homogenizing stucco covering the brick reveal how much these Victorian abodes need those eye-catching furbelows. *PM*

27b 20–32 Metcalfe St. (seven-house row), 1886. Bay-n-Gable details in the service of congenial urban housing: red-with yellow-brick trim, polygonal bays, peaked gables, and scroll-sawn gingerbread. *PM*

28 Formerly James L. Morrison house, 37 Metcalfe St., 1875; remodelled, J. Wilson Gray, 1891; altered, 1912. What's going on here? This looks like a showroom for decorative mouldings, or maybe an over-the-top movie set. In 1875, Capt. John T. Douglas owned the southeast corner of Metcalfe and Winchester Streets, on which he built a large rambling Italianate villa facing north onto Winchester. He rented and then sold it to Joseph Reed, an insurance man, who enjoyed the comfortable house, spacious grounds, and quiet neighbourhood until 1882. Enter a new owner, James L. Morrison, one-time president of the Brilliant Sign Company. Morrison expanded the Victorian villa into a much grander mansion complete with the latest classicizing details: modillioned cornice, dentils, Ionic columns, leaded glass transoms, scrolled pediment, even carved lions. Then, in 1910, a new owner sold the front lawn and Winchester Street address as the site for an apartment building **[9/29a]**, leaving the house with an address on Metcalfe Street. Not wanting to waste any of Morrison's expensive touches, he transferred those hidden by the apartment to the new Metcalfe Street front, ergo the lately spruced-up Classical Revival billboard on view today. *PM*

29a Three Streets Co-op/originally Hampton Mansions, 77 Winchester St. and 39–43 Metcalfe St., Simpson and Young, 1910. This grand buff-brick apartment building—with exterior fire escapes, a rarity in Toronto—was built for middle-class tenants; it shared in the neighbourhood's downturn but not in its subsequent gentrification, since tenant activists succeeded in getting the federal housing agency to make it a co-op in 1981. *AB*

29b Formerly Charles Parsons house, 85 Winchester St., 1857. Formal Georgian proportions and decorous deep setback mark this as one of the first houses in the area; in fact, it is Don Vale's oldest building still with its original bearing. *PM*

30a 92, 94–96, 98 Winchester St. (two single and one double house), 1898. After the fidgety demeanour of so many Victorian houses, the passive mien of these turn-of-the-century abodes comes as a welcome relief. With barn-like girth and a great roof sliding down and enveloping all, they epitomize "hearth and home." *PM*

30b Toronto Dance Theatre/originally St. Enoch's Presbyterian Church/ formerly St. Enoch's United Church/ formerly Don Vale Community Centre, 80 Winchester St., Gordon & Helliwell, 1891; Robert Pogue Hall addition, Molesworth West & Secord, 1927. Designed in monochromatic Romanesque Revival style, St. Enoch's is undramatic but decent in the manner of many Presbyterian churches of the time. The building is almost a square, with identical end walls coming together at the compulsory, and here perfunctory, corner tower. *PM*

31 John Lennox House, 50 Amelia St., 1875; renovation and addition, John O'Connor, 2004. This little Gothic Revival cottage dressed in cement board has been thoroughly rebuilt as an office, with a three-storey modern house concealed behind it. The changes to the front façade would be forbidden now that a Heritage Conservation District designation is in effect; the much more consequential change behind is fine with everybody. In today's Cabbagetown, appearances matter. *AB*

32 Prince Edward Viaduct, Bloor Street at the Don Valley, Edmund Burke, consulting architect, 1915–19. Luminous Veil barrier, Dereck Revington, 2003–15. One of Toronto's greatest and most forward-looking pieces of civic infrastructure, the viaduct was memorably mythologized in Michael Ondaatje's *In the Skin of a Lion*. The structure connected the Danforth and eastern suburbs to the city as never before and also, thanks to the foresight of public works commissioner R.C. Harris, included a lower deck for a future subway—which came into use almost half a century later. Burke's hybrid of concrete and steel achieved a Beaux Arts symmetry and handsome ornament up top, which was altered in 2003 with the addition of a suicide prevention barrier by the artist-architect Revington. *AB*

33 Castle Frank subway station, 600 Bloor St. E., John B. Parkin Associates and A.G. Keith, 1966. Bridge, John B. Parkin Associates with DeLeuw, Cather & Co. (engineers), 1966. The architecture of the Bloor-Danforth subway line reflected a Toronto that had just built its radical City Hall. Designed by the Parkin office with TTC architect Keith, the line featured a consistent vocabulary of signage, materials, and architectural details. These are preserved very well at this station, one of the least busy on the line: brown and grey brick laid in a stack bond, terrazzo flooring and lintels, and the TTC's signature typeface (which is now getting something of a revival from the agency). Castle Frank also has features that other stations lack, including the flying-saucer-shaped entry pavilion and the bus bay's leaning columns and round skylights. "It's a sign of the way Metro is facing the future," Prime Minister Lester B. Pearson said on the line's opening day. The project also included the graceful concrete bridge that brings trains across Rosedale Valley to join the Prince Edward Viaduct **[9/32].** *AB*

34 City Adult Learning Centre/formerly Parkway Vocational School, 1 Danforth Ave., Toronto Board of Education, design architect Peter Pennington, 1963. Rosedale School of the Arts/formerly Castle Frank High School, 711 Bloor St. E., Fleury Arthur & Barclay, 1963. Two grand and exuberant buildings, one on either side of the Don Valley, began as vocational high schools. The former Parkway, to the east, includes three wings—the tallest for a library, academic instruction and trades including barbering and upholstery, six storeys high "to conserve land on the restricted site," as a contemporary article put it. It is in fact more than six acres! The complex displays a remarkable variety of materials and textures—brown and white-glazed brick, raw cast-in-place concrete and white precast, insets of Mondrian-esque coloured glass—the work of Board architect Peter Pennington. Across the valley, the former Castle Frank school is slightly more modest, but includes a sculptural pavilion for a pool, fan-shaped auditorium, and two internal courtyards. Both warrant protection and maintenance, or thoughtful reuse. Each showed, as a Board official wrote in 1964, that "schools need not be sterile, box-like structures, but should add something to the look and feel of a city changing and growing as it never has before in its history." *AB*

34 | City Adult Learning Centre

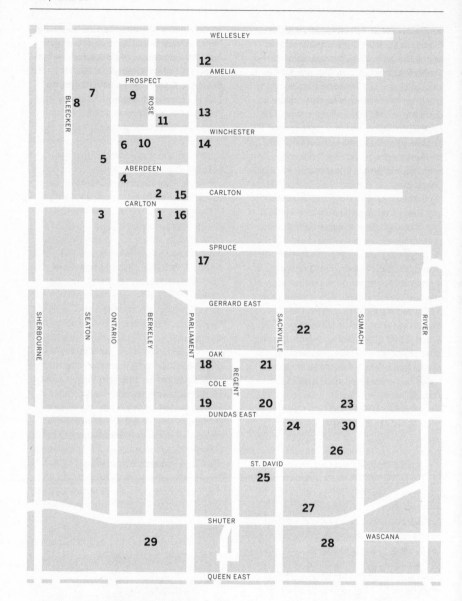

Walk 10: "Old Cabbagetown" and Regent Park

This stretch of Carlton Street was laid out in the late 1850s, shortly after which modest frame and roughcast cottages began to sprout. More ambitious dwellings followed, Georgian in style and set out along the street in a tidy urban string. Later Gothic Revival and Second Empire neighbours did not detract from the mannerly streetscape, and today, though some houses have become offices or shops and the street has been widened, an air of courteous restraint continues to prevail.

1 219 Carlton St. (detached house), 1882.
Big bays and little gables in exuberant red and yellow brick with a pointy High Victorian Gothic Revival air. Look to the side for other well-executed, well-cared-for details. Stone lintels were much favoured in this neighbourhood. *PM*

2a 230–232 Carlton St. (double house), 1864. Rather awe-inspiring these days, with a tall mansard addition looming on top, this double house started out as a tasteful two-storey Georgian rectangle, undoubtedly with a low-pitched roof and dormer or two. Yellow brick—called "white" when new—was popular in Toronto in this early period. The owner, jeweller James Ellis, who lived in a large house on the street behind, tore down two frame dwellings that had been constructed only four years earlier to put up these more stylish and remunerative rentals. *PM*

2b 226–228 Carlton St. (double house), 1879. Gorgeously decorative Second Empire, built when the style was at its peak in Toronto. Yellow brick lost out to red in the early and mid 1870s, but it returned to popularity later when red was reserved for glittery accents. Bold wooden trim provided further drama. The arcaded second-floor sun porch with starchy rope-turned mouldings and bent corner windows looks extremely inviting. *PM*

2c 218, 220, 222–224 Carlton St. (two single houses and one double house), 1878. Variations on a yellow-brick theme, with some houses subtly changed over the years and some seemingly not at all. When Oscar Wilde, the "Apostle of Aestheticism," lectured here in 1882, he remarked on Toronto's "horrid white brick with its shallow colour spoiling the effect of the architecture." Yellow (white) brick was equal in price and availability to red, so its use was simply a matter of fashion. *PM*

3a 195 Carlton St. (half of original double house), 1858. This was among the first of the Carlton Street buildings, originally a roughcast double house with straight-headed six-light sash windows. Storefront appendages work particularly well on these ancient Georgian boxes, so it seems misguided that half this building was replaced. *PM*

3b 191 Carlton St. (detached house), 1892. Virile brick and stone in the city's *last* Victorian style, the Queen Anne/Romanesque hybrid that filled up empty lots across Toronto in the 1890s. *PM*

3c Originally William Jamieson house, 185 Carlton St., 1861; altered, 1988.
Hipped-roofed and quietly formal, with an assured repose typical of early Georgian houses in this district. The splendid wooden door-case was fitting for Mr. Jamieson, a lumber dealer. *PM*

3d 187–189 Carlton St. (double house), 1878. 181–183 Carlton St. (double house), 1878. Chamberlin Block, 165–179 Carlton St. (eight-house row), 1877–78. A bevy of townhouses assembled by builder Charles Chamberlin in the best richly sculptural tradition of Second Empire. The concave curve of the mansards is properly animated, and curved doors just as refined. Chamberlin, who liked to attach his name to buildings, was also responsible for Chamberlin Terrace nearby on Parliament Street. *PM*

3d | 165–179 Carlton St.

4 481–483 Ontario St. (double house), 1877. Pointed arches and lacy bargeboard for an appealing yellow-brick Gothic Revival number, straight out of a builder's pattern book, which probably would have labelled it a "double-detached villa." *PM*

5 484–490 Ontario St. (four-house row), 1877. A handsome yellow-brick Bay-n-Gable row still boasting heavy hammerbeams in gables and peaked overdoors for entrances. Only blank new windows detract from the overall felicity. The less said about the gauche new pastiches next door, the better. *PM*

6 497–503 Ontario St. (four-house row), 1885. 505–511 Ontario St. (four-house row), 1884. Two identical Bay-n-Gable rows seasoned with spicy details: polygonal bays, rickrack trim, stained glass transoms, and creosoted black bricks to pepper the front. *PM*

The superblock between Carlton, Wellesley, Bleecker, and Ontario Streets was the site of a bitter redevelopment struggle in the 1970s, pitting residents and politicians against Meridian, developers of St. James Town to the north [11/17]. Originally Meridian had sights on a much larger area, to be called South St. James Town. However, public outcry combined with the reform city council slowed matters down and eventually achieved a compromise whereby Meridian got only this block and the city assumed Meridian-acquired neighbourhood properties for conversion to city-run housing.

7a Winchester Square, 55, 85, 101 Bleecker St. (housing complex), Klein & Sears, 1980–81. Not as high as high-rises can get, nor as charmless as government-run

7a | Winchester Square

housing can be, Winchester Square manages a decent, European matter-of-factness. The complex weaves unassuming red-brick buildings of differing heights and small details in a casual layout that is quite inviting. Covered pedestrian bridges linking the taller buildings are practical and pleasing. *PM*

7b Hugh Garner Housing Co-operative, 550 Ontario St., Klein & Sears, 1981–82. Named for the Canadian novelist who made Cabbagetown his special purview, the Hugh Garner Co-op, with its colourful orange and blue ornamentalist design, was built at a moment when safe and serious architecture would no longer do. *PM*

8 Fieldstone Co-op, 135 Bleecker St., Klein & Sears, 1981. A co-op complex that is a pleasant place to live. Four bar-shaped midrise buildings encircle private court-yards—and unlike so many such spaces, these courtyards are beautiful, verdant, and well used by kids playing and gardeners at work. Large apartments engage the street and the green space within. *AB*

9a | Winchester St. Junior PS

9a Winchester Street Junior Public School, 15 Prospect St. thru to Winchester St., Charles H. Bishop, 1898, 1901. "Massive dignity and good old-fashioned academic atmosphere" was the description in the early 1900s, and it still rings true. The secular Queen Anne style was popular for public school buildings; not only did it seem "democratic," but those many tall windows gave perfect light for studying.

A school has stood on this block since 1874. This particular building began in 1898 as a preliminary one-storey red-brick affair. So rapid was student population growth, however, the slowly staged expansion was accelerated and completed in one fell swoop three years later. *PM*

9b 15 Prospect St., Winchester Street Senior Public School, Toronto Board of Education (design architect Peter Pennington), 1959. A fine piece of 1950s Modernism by school board architect Pennington—the sober, rational grid of windows and brick spiced up by turquoise and yellow accents, angled concrete brises-soleil and a cheery mosaic-tile mural. To appreciate the craftsmanship, head to the front doors and look down: the diamond motif of the paving continues on the two-tone terrazzo inside. *AB*

9b | Winchester St. Senior PS

10a 7–11 Winchester St. (triple house), 1885; porch additions, c. 1900. Heavy stone lintels and sills, as well as the stone bases and capitals of the square pillars gracing the front, make this Queen Anne triple house an unusual standout. *PM*

10b Formerly the Rev. Samuel Boddy house, 21 Winchester St., 1858. This is what is left of an early tall-chimneyed Georgian house that for many years served as the rectory for St. Peter's on nearby Carlton Street. Despite disfiguring surgery as well as grafts, it remains appealing for its

English garden and inviting setback from the street. *PM*

11 Winchester Block, 1–11 Rose Ave. (six-house row), 1879; demolished no. 5 replaced, 1979. A creative 19th-century brick mason was at work here, with a lovely border of yellow brick embroidering the red on a six-house row built for John Winchester, a local landowner. A fine latter-day brick mason has been at it as well, seamlessly stitching in a new no. 5 to replace that torn out by Meridian in its redevelopment manoeuvres. *PM*

12 583–585 Parliament St. (two-unit commercial block), 1889. With corner oriel, finialed tent-roofed tower, and big broad gables, this building looks more like a lavish Queen Anne house than a retail block. It was probably trying to be a good neighbour on its then residential street. Originally at no. 583 was Arthur Squires, a butcher; at no. 585, Benjamin Playter sold shoes. *PM*

13 Brougham Terrace, 549–563 Parliament St. (eight-house row), 1875–76. Comfortably plump red- and yellow-brick row houses, now mostly with ground-floor shops. The wishbone sweep of the bargeboard edging the gables is grand. *PM*

14a Hotel Winchester/formerly Lake View Hotel, 531 Parliament St., Kennedy & Holland, 1888; restored, 2005. A tavern and/or hotel has stood on this site since the 1860s when an establishment called the Santa Claus held sway. The present

14a | Hotel Winchester

three-storey building was constructed in 1888 for the Lake View—a belvedere once perched atop the corner tower and one could indeed view the lake from that aerie. The Lake View was highly recommended in guidebooks of the era. It was at the end of the omnibus route and advertised a bucolic resort atmosphere with a "good lawn" and beer garden, plus "electric bells and bathrooms" on every floor. Nothing to write home about today, though the old fire escape is wonderfully decorative. *PM*

14b Maple Terrace, 519–527 Parliament St. (five units of original six-house row), 1875–78. There are gables hiding up there. What's left of the brick façade at no. 519 shows traces of a red beer wash, an early technique to turn unfashionable white brick red. *AB*

15 242–250 Carlton St. (five-unit commercial block), 1889. A theatrical three-storey commercial row, richly tapestried with stone sills and lintels, semicircular-arched windows, keystones, panel brick, and lots more. No. 244 retains its original shopfront. *PM*

16 Canadian Imperial Bank of Commerce/ originally Canadian Bank of Commerce, 245 Carlton St., Darling & Pearson, 1905. Auspicious Classical Revival with weighty Doric columns framing a deep vault-like entrance; above, a domestic Queen Anne bay window—curtains and all. These small branch banks were often built with residential flats on the second floor. *PM*

17 Lepper's Block, 433–443 Parliament St. (six-unit commercial block), 1885–86. Flat roof and bracketed projecting cornice to signal another early commercial entry on Parliament Street. Originally purveyed, south to north, were groceries, barbering, hardware, plumbing, stationery, and more groceries. Lepper was vice president of Union Loan & Savings Company and had a large house on Winchester Street. *PM*

18 Regent Park. 1 Oak St. (housing), Kearns Mancini, 2010. This 12-storey apartment building, housing mostly family-sized units, borrows the language of early 20th-century loft buildings, with punched windows in a field of matte red brick and matching mortar. The window pattern confuses the scale. *AB*

19 One Cole and 25 Cole St. (housing), Diamond Schmitt with Graziani + Corazza, 2009. An agreeable assemblage of towers and townhouses, with red brick camouflaging the podiums and a generous green-roof courtyard. The grocery store and the bank opened in 2010; Regent Park hadn't had either amenity since the 1950s. *AB*

20 246 Sackville St. (housing), architectsAlliance, 2009. Two stacks of good new housing, urbane and well-dressed in purple brick. The 22-storey point tower to the north contains seniors' residences, plus the neighbourhood's district energy plant in a sub-basement; the eight-storey mid-rise tower to the south holds family-sized apartments with a daycare centre on the ground floor. Each tower has a hospitable, transparent lobby, and residents of both towers come together on a planted terrace. *AB*

21 One Park West (housing), 260 Sackville St., CORE, 2011. Private housing that's inferior to its social-housing neighbour [10/20], with a poorly detailed ground level and messy façades. The white precast concrete slabs already look ragged and dirty. *AB*

22 Regent Park North, Gerrard to Oak St., Parliament to River St. (apartments and row houses), John E. Hoare Jr., 1947. About a dozen of these buildings remain, for now—uniform in their low height, cruciform

22 | Regent Park North

plan, mean brown brick, and seemingly deliberate lack of visual interest. Hoare was Toronto-born and -raised, and capable of more handsome work, including the modern Roycroft and Crofton Apartments at 707 and 717 Eglinton Avenue West. *AB*

23 Regent Park Aquatic Centre, 640 Dundas St. E., MacLennan Jaunkalns Miller, 2012. One of Toronto's best public buildings of this or any era. An angular slab of charcoal zinc shelters a big, bright, kid-friendly pool facility. At ground level, it is a pavilion, with glass walls opening to the street and the adjacent park; some sections open entirely in the summer months, and a wood ceiling extends to the soffit outside to reinforce this sense of connection. The universal change rooms, a first in the city, allow all visitors to change in private cubicles, a feature that serves conservative ideas about gender segregation and allows people to self-identify. When it opened, the centre boldly signalled the city's commitment to quality in the rebuilding of Regent Park—and it continues to attract visitors from far beyond the neighbourhood. *AB*

23 | Regent Park Aquatic Centre

24 Daniels Spectrum (community and cultural centre), 585 Dundas St. E., and Paintbox Condos, 225 Sackville St., Diamond Schmitt, 2012. Fittingly, the most colourful building in Regent Park. The rainbow hues on the Spectrum's vertical cladding panels and protruding panels allude to the flags of dozens of countries; it's a subtle nod to the area's cultural diversity, a quality that's enhanced by the office space

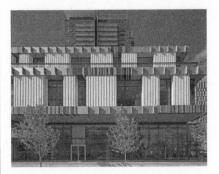

24 | Daniels Spectrum

and teaching studios for neighbourhood arts groups within. The residential tower is handsomely detailed and benefits from its own coloured accents. Both structures are uncharacteristically flashy for Diamond Schmitt, and successfully so. Both also share access to the café, an important mixing place for the neighbourhood's different constituencies. *AB*

25 180 Sackville St. (apartments), St. David St. and Sutton Ave. (townhouses), 180 Sackville St., Giannone Petricone, 2015. Here is brick doing some unfamiliar exercises—folding in and out with the façade of the mid-rise building, laid in alternating courses of smooth and rough to establish subtle ornament. The squarely street-facing houses benefit from hits of hot colour and a nearly Victorian polychromic brick. *AB*

25 | 180 Sackville St.

26 | One Park Place

26 One Park Place (condo apartments, office and retail), 55 Regent Park Blvd., Hariri Pontarini, 2014. So far, the best residential building in the area. The base places well-proportioned retail spaces against a generous sidewalk; it also attractively mixes red brick (clearly visible as a veneer, not structural material) with white fins of precast concrete. The towers, whose façades are only 50 per cent glass, use white concrete mullions for a novel and handsome effect. *AB*

27 Regent Park Community Recreation Centre and Employment Centre, 402 Shuter St., CS&P, 2016. Nelson Mandela Park Public School, 440 Shuter St., C.H. Bishop, 1915–17; renovations and addition, CS&P, 2013. A transparent multi-purpose recreation centre, cut through the middle by a top-lit passageway and stairs. Clear in plan, it is uninspired in its details and materials; the north and south faces have grids of red, white, and grey aluminum that have little to do with the rest of the building.

27 | Regent Park Community Recreation Centre

The centre links up with the adjacent public school, which makes use of the centre's gym and other facilities. (It is an embarrassing truth that the school board and the city don't usually cooperate in this manner.) That school is one of the few buildings in this precinct to have survived the clearance of Regent Park in the 1940s. A renovation preserved much of the Beaux Arts envelope while updating the interior. *AB*

28 Trefann Court, Queen to Shuter St., Parliament to River St. (row houses, apartments, and rehabilitated houses), 1971, 1973, 1978. In the 1960s, this was a densely populated pocket of 185 houses, in mixed condition—a prime target for urban renewal, and the city revealed a scheme to replace it all with public housing in 1966. But its working-class homeowners rose up to demand otherwise, aided by community organizers including the future Toronto mayor John Sewell. (Tenants were represented by another future mayor, June Rowlands.) After Sewell was elected to council in 1970, the city created a planning office in the neighbourhood, led by Howard Cohen **[see Area XII]**. The result: Many existing houses were retained; new houses and walkup apartments of a similar scale and undistinguished Victorian-ish design were added in between. Public housing coexisted alongside privately owned homes. This was "infill," in the 1970s Toronto sense, architecturally modest and highly consultative. *AB*

29 Moss Park Apartments, Queen to Shuter St., Sherbourne to Parliament St., Somerville McMurrich & Oxley with Gibson & Pokorny and Wilson & Newton, 1961. As the Regent Park superblock disappears, this one—another urban renewal project that displaced a working-class neighbourhood—remains. The 15-storey, V-shaped buildings are being examined for "Tower Renewal," the city's effort to improve the urban design and energy performance of its tower neighbourhoods; they are good candidates. Get rid of the moat of parking and this pocket could become fully a part of the city again. *AB*

30 Regent Park South towers [demolished], Page & Steele (Peter Dickinson, design architect), 1957. As the 20th-century Regent Park was demolished, this set of five 14-storey towers was an unfortunate casualty. The towers featured large two-storey apartments in a skip-stop configuration, with entrances on alternate floors; that pattern was legible in a grid pattern of brick and window on the façade. Dickinson, one of the most important Toronto architects of the 20th century **[see 25/34a]**, used the most modern of ideas. Bearing the clear mark of Le Corbusier, the towers won a Massey Medal in 1961 and were highly regarded by architects. Tenants liked them less, especially after decades of poor maintenance. The Toronto Community Housing Corporation (TCHC) originally planned to retain one of the towers, and then failed to properly account for it in the new urban design. In the end, the lack of accessibility within the units made them unworkable as social housing, while their very large size made condo conversion unprofitable. And yet these were clearly important pieces of architectural heritage, and their abandonment will be noted by future generations. Here, high-rise Modernism is history. *AB*

The first neighbourhood to take the name "Cabbagetown" lay here, along Dundas Street, but it has been utterly erased: between 1948 and 1957, the City of Toronto expropriated 69 acres of Victorian workers' housing, and replaced its "slums" with the latest in urban-renewal thinking.

The plan, initiated by the Modernist planner Eugene Faludi, consolidated the area into massive "superblocks." These featured towers floating in a no-man's-land of green "park" space, surrounded by parking and psychologically cut off from the rest of Toronto. The resulting social and economic isolation did no favours for the residents, initially WASP multi-generational Torontonians and later a mix of new Canadians from around the world: the area was affected by the drug trade and related street crime. The 7,500 people who lived here, by the 1990s, were increasingly poor and cut off from the wealthy, leafy precincts to the north [Walk 9].

After 2000, Toronto Community Housing saw a solution to the area's urban-design and social woes, as well as to the large backlog of repairs on the buildings in the area—a partnership with private development that would add about 5,400 market housing units, bringing investment to build out some of the empty land in the district. A 2002 plan, led by Markson Borooah Hodgson and Ken Greenberg, called for the area to be linked with the surrounding area, and residents to be welcomed into new apartments. Plans now call for 5,400 market units and about 2,300 affordable-housing units.

It was a very big vision, big enough to erase the earlier big vision entirely. TCH signed on with the socially minded developer Daniels, which took a proactive and philanthropic approach; among other moves they helped fund the Daniels Spectrum [10/24] and have provided financial support for Regent Park residents to buy market-rate housing.

The results, so far, have been good—the street grid restored; buildings oriented to provide "eyes on the street," as Jane Jacobs put it; public buildings added or improved. And, for the first time, there is a park in Regent Park, with playground and pizza oven. (The open spaces and sidewalks are cheaply paved and meanly planted, typical for Toronto.)

This new crop of buildings is of mixed architectural quality—in some cases, mediocre; in others, innovative and beautiful.

Area VII
Walk 11: Sherbourne Street
Walk 12: Jarvis Street
Walk 13: Church Street

"Of all the avenues extending south from Bloor Street to the Bay, the noblest are Church, Jarvis and Sherbourne Streets," Charles Pelham Mulvany wrote in a Toronto guidebook of 1884. "Church Street is somewhat less aristocratic.... Jarvis and Sherbourne are lined on either side through most part of their extent by the mansions of the upper ten."

Today, to put it mildly, things have changed: the area contains Toronto's largest concentration of shelters and substance-abuse treatment facilities, along with modern apartment towers and renovated middle-class Victorian housing. Yet for Torontonians from the 1880s on through the 1910s, these were grand streets, their northern reaches lined with the homes of prominent families. That era didn't last long, but "aristocratic" houses remain as part of a varied architectural mix, which today is being significantly altered yet again.

These three streets, like downtown's other north–south arteries, reflect the "park lots" of 100 acres that John Graves Simcoe doled out to his early officials after 1793 **[see Introduction, and Area VIII]**. As the town grew rapidly, these plots were converted into sterling by members of the Family Compact. In 1845, Samuel P. Jarvis began to sell off his father's holdings: He'd been removed in disgrace from his position as superintendent of Indian affairs over financial irregularities, and was deeply in debt. He hired John G. Howard **[see 25/17a]** in 1845 to lay out a subdivision along a new tree-lined avenue—Jarvis Street. But Jarvis's own house, "Hazelburn," stood in the way: Jarvis had it torn down, and sold off the salvaged joists, bricks, and black walnut panelling. (Jarvis's debts would soon also include Howard's bills for the work, which Jarvis never paid.)

Howard's scheme laid out small lots to the south, near downtown; middling ones near the centre; and mansion sites at the suburban edge of the city, Bloor Street. To the east, George William Allan subdivided *his* father William's grant in the 1850s, following a similar pattern—and keeping a site for his horticultural gardens **[11/1]** right in the middle, an act of philanthropy that paid dividends. Allan also laid out the curves on Dundas and Wellesley, and Homewood and Pembroke Avenues connected the family's manors, William Allan's "Moss Park" and George Allan's "Homewood."

By the 1860s the new grand houses that John Howard had anticipated were in place north of Shuter Street—along Jarvis for the prominent Cawthra, Massey **[12/20]**, and Gooderham **[12/21a]** families, and on Sherbourne **[11/17]** for "many leading

merchants and manufacturers," as a contemporary observer put it.

To the west, Church Street evolved with more modest housing but, as the name suggests, several houses of worship: John McGill's former estate made room for the grand churches of Toronto's Catholic **[13/4a]** and Methodist **[13/2]** communities, joining St. James' Church **[1/13]**.

This district's high times came to an end early in the 20th century. As Toronto grew north and west, the area—which was close to, but not quite in, the downtown—suffered. Its large houses became too expensive for single-family use, while the rich retreated to the Annex **[Area X]**, Parkdale, the nascent Forest Hill, and Rosedale, which was being developed by Sam Jarvis's cousins **[Area XI]**. Institutions began to move in, drawn by the increasing concentration of poverty in the area and inexpensive, big buildings. In 1922, a children's charity, Dr. Barnardo's Homes, took over Cawthra Mulock's house at 538 Jarvis, starting a trend. The city-run homeless shelter Seaton House was founded nearby in 1931 and remains a major presence in the area.

By the end of the Depression, the quarter had gone downscale. The *Globe* wrote in 1946, a bit dramatically, that Jarvis Street was "long past its prime, and stripped of its youthful grandeur . . . Bootleggers,

prostitutes and dope peddlers have made their headquarters in its big old rooming houses and apartments."

At the same time, this reshuffling of the social deck also made room for a new white-collar middle class, and a new type of housing—apartments—that catered to them. Between 1870 and 1920, the city shifted to an industrial economy, which came to dominate the downtown **[Area IV]** with increasingly bigger companies, operations, and buildings. And a good number of the clerks, telephone operators, and salespeople who made those offices hum lived around here. Or, at least, those of British or Irish descent, largely unmarried, did. This crop of middle-class singles, living outside the norms of family life, aroused suspicion. The city's Medical Officer of Health complained in 1918 that the district was "crowded to capacity with young men and women, who may be said to herd together."

They were living in grand old houses redefined as hotels or pensions **[12/21b]**, and in purpose-built apartments—some of the first of this kind in Toronto, where civic leaders generally resisted this building type. Such buildings went up in the Classical Revival style in the 1910s and '20s **[13/22b]**, or Art Moderne later **[12/9]**.

A larger variety of apartment towers would shake up the area, after the city upzoned swaths of land here in 1953 to make room for large, modern housing. The most visible child of this policy was St. James Town **[11/13]**, assembled through predatory "blockbusting" beginning in the late 1950s, then systematically blockbusted and rebuilt in grand modern style in the late '60s. Towers in the park, surrounded by (vaguely defined) open space: this was a private-sector version of what the city had done for itself at Regent Park and nearby at Moss Park.

But that radical mutation of the city fabric was stopped by the progressive wave of the early 1970s. The "reform Council" of 1971, which had strong support from young gentrifiers here and in nearby Cabbagetown, put the brakes on redevelopment plans **[10/7a]**. Activists helped stop one high-rise scheme **[see 11/4a]** on Sherbourne in 1973—and instead Barton Myers and Jack Diamond designed and built low-but-dense "infill" housing. That idea, of mid-rise scale and the full retention of historic buildings, was highly influential during the late 1970s and early '80s, especially for public housing.

On the other hand, certain tall modern apartment towers such as City Park **[13/21a]** fit in somewhat better to the city, and served their residents well. They provided, along with the older, smaller

apartment buildings, a place for Toronto's gay community to cluster. Where once queer men and women had gathered in bars on Yonge Street in the 1960s and '70s, the community now settled along Church and became louder in the early '80s. With the opening of The 519 **[13/25]** in 1975, Church and Wellesley became the focus of the Village, and it remains so 40 years later.

But some of these features—particularly the identity of the Village—are subject to change. The gay community today is more widely dispersed, and many others want in to this very central neighbourhood. After the rapid intensification of development in west downtown began in the early 2000s **[Area II]**, first eastern downtown **[Area I]** and then this quarter started to catch the attention of developers. A set of tall, architecturally undistinguished residential towers **[12/4]** is catering to the growing presence of Ryerson University **[see Walk 13]**. And the ambitious redesign of Moss Park will show, in plain sight, how the neighbourhood's current residents, wealthy and poor, gay and straight, old and young, can get along—a design project that is very noble.

Walk 11: Sherbourne Street

1 Allan Gardens, Gerrard to Carlton St., Jarvis to Sherbourne St., opened, 1860; Palm House, Office of City Architect of Toronto, 1910, 1913; Children's Conservatory, Mathers & Haldenby, 1931–32. In true botanical garden fashion, there has always been an eye-catching pavilion here. The first, a large open-air affair of rough-hewn logs, was erected in 1860. The second, a more ambitious endeavour put up in 1878, was an exotic pagoda-like extravaganza that boasted the late 19th-century city's finest ballroom and concert place. Destroyed by fire in 1902 along with its extensive greenhouses, it was replaced in 1910 by the present structure designed by the Office of the City Architect under Robert McCallum. (A civil engineer by training, McCallum did little designing; one of his assistants and future successors, either John J. Woolnough or George F.W. Price, is likely responsible for the Palm House.) Palm House, which borrows both construction and name from British prototypes, is a bubble of glass and metal tracery. The Children's Conservatory began its life later and on a different site; it was moved here in 2004, from the corner of College and University, where it served as the greenhouse for the University of Toronto's botany department. *PM/AB*

2a Moss Park (park and community centre), MacLennan Jaunkalns Miller, LGA and landscape architects West 8, ongoing. Moss Park began as the site of William Allan's manor; today it is a busy public park serving a community of economic extremes. As thousands of new condo apartments are approved in the vicinity, the city is getting ahead of growth with a comprehensive redesign of the park and recreation facilities, with the cooperation of the 519 **[13/25]** and a private donor. The architects' scheme for an integrated rec centre is three-dimensionally complex, recalling MJMA's work on the Goldring Centre for High-Performance Sport at U of T **[8/34]**, and it's brilliant. West 8's new "common" will be robust and flexible, and designed to be inclusive. How it actually

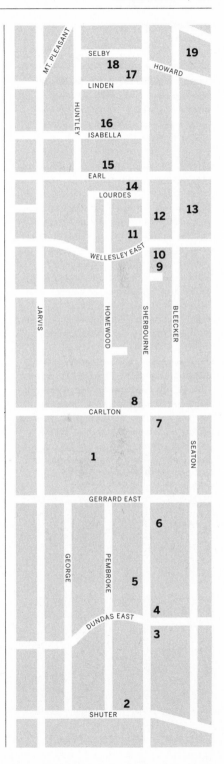

works as a social condenser remains to be seen. *AB*

2b Row houses: 142–152 Shuter St., 1871; altered, 1985. 138–140 Shuter St., 1987. 122–136 Shuter St., 1876–77. 112–120 Shuter St., 1891. Shuter Street between George and Sherbourne is lined with row houses of all persuasions. No. 142–152, built during the 1870s economic slump, is the simplest of two-storey rows embellished only with gently curved windows, and doorways with rectangular toplights. No. 122–136, slightly later and more ambitious, demonstrates how ideal the newly popular Second Empire mansard style was for row housing, providing an animated and inexpensive third storey. No. 112–120 follows the Queen Anne prescription that each house in a row have an air of exciting individuality. The 1980s additions at no. 138–140 should be noted for their very plain—and dull—face. *PM/updated AB*

3 All Saints Church-Community Centre, 223 Sherbourne St., Richard C. Windeyer, 1874; Sunday school addition, Richard C. Windeyer, 1883. Homes for Tomorrow Society Housing, 319 Dundas St., Howard Walker and Howard Chapman, 1988. The rector had been to England and knew the score—not only was democratic ecumenism favoured, so was High Victorian Gothic.

Inspired by the writings of John Ruskin, whose models were Italian buildings of multi-coloured marble, High Victorian churches flaunted smooth, highly decorated surfaces, most typically red with black or yellow with red brick. All Saints perfectly captured their effect, which—depending on one's bias—was dubbed either "constructional polychromy" or "streaky bacon."

The church was equally adventurous in its ministry. An accommodating spirit in the 1870s mixed high and low church practices and welcomed parishioners of whatever means by offering free seats in an age when pew holders paid for their spaces. Today this space houses a drop-in centre for the neighbourhood, and helped build the 60-unit affordable-housing building tucked in at the rear. *PM/updated AB*

4a | Sherbourne Lanes Housing

4a Dan Harrison Social Housing Complex/originally "Sherbourne Lanes," 241–285 Sherbourne St. (complex of four apartment houses and 17 rehabilitated houses), A.J. Diamond & Barton Myers, completed by Barton Myers Associates, 1976. A seminal project of the "reform era" of the 1970s. Jack Diamond and Barton Myers landed in Toronto with lessons they'd absorbed as students in Philadelphia—a city that was attempting large-scale "urban renewal" that also respected, to a degree, the city's historic fabric. Here, they applied their approach to a site assembled by a developer and targeted for redevelopment with two high-rises. In early 1973 a group of activists, including Jane Jacobs **[20/28]**, blocked the developer's demolition crews, and the city

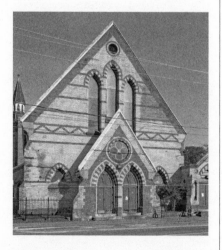

3 | All Saints Church

bought out the site for social housing, launching the non-profit housing authority CityHome.

The result, from Diamond and Myers, was the preservation and renovation of 17 houses including no. 241 **[11/4b]** and no. 283–285 **[11/6a]**, and new development in their backyards in the form of five- and six-storey apartment buildings lining a private pedestrian street. With a total of 376 units, it was dense—and yet it was and remains largely hidden from the street, leaving the Victorian rhythm of Sherbourne intact **[see 14/17]**. Myers wrote in 1978: "Through infill development, a 'high-rise on its side' in rear of site, existing buildings are conserved rather than demolished; neighbourhood street patterns and social fabric are respected; more people can be successfully and feasibly housed on the same land without high-rise apartment buildings." The architectural expression of the new buildings, with exposed concrete frames filled in with brick and diagonal setbacks that evoke Victorian gables, recalls the Philadelphian master Louis Kahn. *AB*

4b Originally "Allendale" (Enoch Turner residence), 241 Sherbourne St., 1856.

This glowing gem was the home of Enoch Turner, a successful and beneficent brewer who paid for beer for his horses and the city's first school for the poor **[2/12]**. His fine-looking red-brick Georgian house is bedecked with quoins and cornice of yellow brick, a showy bichrome effect that was repeated again and again in Toronto. *PM*

4b | 241 Sherbourne St.

5a 260–262A Sherbourne St. (two attached houses), northern house, 1872; altered and southern house added, Knox & Elliot, 1889–90.

Stones and bricks, semicircles and rectangles, towers and gables, carved panels, finials, even an emblematic carved stone crane for a striking example of Richardsonian Romanesque. Architects Knox & Elliot, newly arrived from Chicago, created this extraordinary amalgam for Edward Hewitt, an alderman and busy speculative builder. *PM*

5b 280 Sherbourne St. (complex of 11 row houses and one rehabilitated house), Ferdinand A. Wagner, 1979.

A new "Victorian" pastiche, taking its red and yellow bichrome cue from the Enoch Turner house across the street at no. 241 **[11/4b]**, but here the effect is gaudy baubles rather than polished gemstone. *PM*

6a Originally Ritchie/Forneri house, 283–285 Sherbourne St., 1856–57.

A row should be more than two houses, but this large handsome pair clearly bears the imprint of decorous English or New York rows with its flat blocky shape, neat multi-light sash windows, and low-pitched roof. These were expensive houses, but well-to-do Torontonians—unlike their fellows in Montreal—did not much take to row houses and no. 283–285 stood alone, unimitated, and surrounded by vacant land for almost two decades. Earliest residents were John Ritchie, a merchant; and James Forneri, professor at University College **[8/1]**. *PM*

6b Robertson House/formerly "Culloden" (John Ross Robertson residence)/ originally Capt. John T. Douglas house, 291 Sherbourne St., 1875; veranda addition, Samuel G. Curry, 1903; renovations and rear wing, Hariri Pontarini, 1998.

This vaguely Italianate house is primarily of interest as the home from 1881 to 1918 of John Ross Robertson, muckraking publisher of the Toronto *Evening Telegram*, a liberal philanthropist who endowed the first hospital in North America for children **[7/33]**, and compiled six volumes of Toronto history. Robertson also owned the house at no. 295. Both have been incorporated into the present complex, which serves as a shelter for homeless women and their children. The new rear wing and courtyard, largely hidden from the street, recall KPMB's similarly arranged addition to Woodsworth College **[8/33a]**, on which Siamak Hariri played a leading role, and the emerging Casey House a few blocks north **[12/23]**. *PM/AB*

7 Saint Luke's United Church/originally Sherbourne Street Methodist Church, 355 Sherbourne St., Smith & Gemmell, 1871; Sunday school addition, Langley Langley & Burke, 1876; remodelled, Langley & Burke, 1886; porch and south wing addition, Parrott Tambling & Witmer, 1960. Sherbourne Street Methodist started out in 1871 as plain brick Gothic. Enlarged and re-dressed in grey and brown sandstone in commanding new Richardsonian Romanesque style in 1886, the church was called "the handsomest in central Toronto" at the turn of the century. Admiring its carefully wrought checkerboard stonework and dramatic tiled conical tower, one can envision what a rich and powerful presence it must have been on this corner before the nondescript porch and south wing were grafted on, insidiously sapping the strength and integrity of a bold composition. *PM*

8 Originally Abram M. Orpen house, 380 Sherbourne St., Henry Simpson, 1900. A perfect turn-of-the-century expression, this large house sophisticates 1890s picturesque (rough-cut stone, round arches, decorated brackets) by smoothing out the edges with smart 1900s classical (Palladian windows, keystones, dentil mouldings). Orpen was president of a contracting and paving company in 1900. In 1899, he too seemed to have had a more picturesque profile; the city directory listed him as a "book maker." *PM*

9 Rosar-Morrison Funeral Residence, 467 Sherbourne St. (detached house), possibly David B. Dick, 1877–78. Classical frets and pilasters, even leaves on the Corinthian capitals, rendered in picturesque red and yellow brick. Dick is known to have designed a house of the same date that once stood next door, and he may have been responsible for this handsome, playful endeavour as well. Rosar-Morrison have occupied the premises since 1929. With records to 1861, they are one of Toronto's oldest firms. *PM*

10 Ernescliffe, 195 Wellesley St. E. (apartment house), Redmond & Beggs, 1914–16. Designed in the Classical Revival style of the moment, the Ernescliffe took the axiom of "building as column" more literally than most, with a rusticated cast-stone base at ground storey, modillioned cornice capping the top, and giant Ionic pilasters at every turn of the five storeys of shaft. The double entrances on Wellesley Street are grand little temple fronts. *PM*

11 Tony DiPede Residence (housing), 490 Sherbourne St., regionalArchitects, 2008. Run by Woodgreen Community Services and Fife House, this building offers 112 units of housing for people living with HIV and AIDS. The skinny tower's façade offers a handsome composition of windows, spandrel glass, and buff brick—the latter clearly a surface veneer, and yet a welcome gesture to the area's architectural history. *AB*

12 Wellesley Community Centre and Toronto Public Library, St. James Town Branch, 495 Sherbourne St., MacLennan Jaunkalns Miller and ZAS in joint venture, 2004; pool addition, MJMA, in progress. In a district that had been starved for public amenities, City Hall and the Toronto Public Library teamed up to provide an efficiently planned new facility, with a shared lobby that links residents with all sorts of public services. It is highly transparent—walk up Sherbourne and you can see kids playing dodgeball in the gym—which serves two

12 | Wellesley Community Centre and Toronto
Public Library St. James Town Branch

purposes: beckoning residents into the
centre, and connecting passersby with what
has been a physically and socially isolated
community. The overhangs, generous
sidewalk, and cheerful mosaic tile all send
messages of welcome. The planned pool
addition should continue that theme, if it is
nearly as good as MJMA's Regent Park
Aquatic Centre [10/23]. *AB*

13 St. James Town, Wellesley to Howard St., Sherbourne to Parliament St. (housing complex), George Jarosz with James Murray, 1965–68.

Toronto's densest
neighbourhood and one of its most diverse,
this is a place like no other in the city. Its
7,000 generously sized apartments are
home to at least 17,000, but that's merely a
guess: about two-thirds of the population are
immigrants, among them family groups and
roommates that could add up to a total of
25,000 people. (The most widely spoken
languages as of 2006 were Tagalog, Tamil,
and Chinese, among dozens of others.)

Architecturally, the cluster of 18 towers,
rising 16 to 33 storeys, is typical of the 1960s
private-sector apartment boom, with
concrete structure and white glazed-brick
cladding (the latter borrowed from the
fashions of New York apartment houses). Yet
St. James Town takes the logic of that boom,
and the consequent challenges, to a radical
extreme. This nine-block site of more than
30 acres was once a mixed Victorian
streetscape, much like the blocks to the
south and west. But speculators sent it into a
downward spiral of disinvestment and
decrepitude, and—with the support of the
city and the federal government—the area
was almost entirely levelled and rebuilt,
before the province commissioned the last
four buildings as affordable housing. It began
as a dream of local politicians in the 1960s,
new housing for an emerging crop of
downtown young professionals ("a small city
in itself, having a private club with dining
room, discotheque, heated indoor pool," as
an ad had it). But it emerged as a nightmare
of the progressive 1970s: tall, isolated from
the surrounding city, and increasingly poor
and dysfunctional. Today the social fabric is
stronger, but the built fabric is ragged. The
network of private streets and underground
parking is, as in many other places,
confusing, ugly, and unsafe; all buildings are
in noticeably poor shape; and residents lack
green space and community facilities,
though the community centre and library
[11/12] have been welcome additions.

And yet: the central location allows
residents good access to transit, shopping,
and the social and cultural opportunities of
downtown. Not so elsewhere: buildings of this
kind and vintage across the city are increasingly sites of "vertical poverty," as a local think
tank puts it, and targets for architectural,
social, and economic renewal. *AB*

13 | St. James Town

14 Our Lady of Lourdes Roman Catholic Church, 520 Sherbourne St., Frederick C. Law, 1884–86; remodelled, James P. Hynes, 1910. When built, this was considered a most glorious jewel: the only domed church in the city and a worthy commemorative to the first Roman Catholic archbishop of Toronto, John Lynch. Lynch was credited with helping quell much of the religious prejudice then prevalent in the province, and in recognition of this and as part of the 25th anniversary of his appointment as archbishop, a fund was raised to build a small memorial church at his official summer residence, St. John's Grove, located near Sherbourne and Wellesley. The Renaissance Revival church that Frederick Law built directly beside the Gothic Revival residence (still visible in the rear) consisted of what is today the wing along Earl Street. The altar was situated to the west beyond the domed crossing and a portico fronted the east entrance. When it came to enlarging Our Lady of Lourdes in 1910, James Hynes was forced to do some juggling. The only space for a new nave was running north/south along Sherbourne Street, and accordingly the altar was moved to the centre of the original structure with the side spaces becoming east and west choirs. Hynes also moved Law's portico to adorn his own new entrance. Unconventional but impressive, outside and in. *PM*

15 Earl Court, 30–38 Earl St. (complex of ten row houses and three rehabilitated houses), Peter Turner, 1982. Well detailed and constructed, the new houses are a felicitous match for the old. In the best tradition of such "mixers," they are not slavish copies but capture the general forms and spirit of the originals, which date to 1879 and 1885. Very nice. *PM*

16 Elementary Teachers' Federation of Ontario (offices), 136 Isabella St., KPMB, 2013. At 121,000 square feet, this institutional building is hardly small, but it is an uncommonly sensitive addition to the neighbourhood. From the sidewalk it appears to match the three-storey scale of the Queen Annes across the street, and the reddish fibre-cement panels on the handsome front façade evoke Don Valley brick. But inside, that conceit vanishes in a grand atrium, linking together a tightly engineered yet highly transparent series of offices, training rooms, and conference space. *AB*

16 | Elementary Teachers' Federation of Ontario

14 | Our Lady of Lourdes

17 Originally James Cooper house, 582 Sherbourne St., 1880–81; addition, Charles J. Read, 1911; James Cooper Mansion, renovation and addition of condo apartment tower, Burka Architects with Goldsmith Borgal, 2011. Domestic Victorian grandeur meets 21st-century developer expediency. First, the house, which was moved forward on its site: the finest Second Empire dwelling remaining in Toronto. The owner of no. 582, a boot and shoe manufacturer, would have understood the aura of power and privilege conveyed by such a palatial building. The design boldly contrasts red-brick walls with light-coloured wood, metal, and limestone details.

These only look better by contrast with the house's new rear neighbour. This condo tower mixes windows with glass spandrel in the standard developer's formula, these components forming a grid that is clumsily proportioned and articulated. The buff-brick-fronted "townhouses" to the side, with their hints of Georgian ornament, suggest too clearly that—in this case—they don't make 'em like they used to. *PM/AB*

17 | 582 Sherbourne St.

18 Originally Charles H. Gooderham house, 592 Sherbourne St., David Roberts, 1883; The Selby, condo, BKL, ongoing. Another marriage of mansion (slightly pushed forward) and high-rise. The former is Victorian picturesque with fanciful sawn bargeboard, tall two-pot chimneys, and informal windowed sun porches; one of the eight sons of the founder of the Gooderham and Worts Distillery lived here for many years with his family. Next it housed Branksome Hall from 1910 to 1913, and then became a hotel; Ernest Hemingway and his wife Hadley lived here briefly. The tower rising in behind, at 50 storeys, will be big, but the promised deep terraces and cladding of red masonry promise to be novel and—if the renderings don't lie—beautiful. *PM/AB*

19 North St. James Town proposal, architectsAlliance, ongoing. The lands between Howard and Bloor and Sherbourne and Parliament are where the St. James Town blockbusting stalled. The developer Lanterra owns three separate pieces of this area, and has begun restoring and moving several Victorian structures (including the Bay-n-Gable houses at nos. 6 to 16 Howard Street) while attempting to win approval for a multi-tower project of more than 1,200 units. The proposal promises a varied set of towers, finely detailed public realm, and crisply Modernist brick-fronted townhouses. We'll see. *AB*

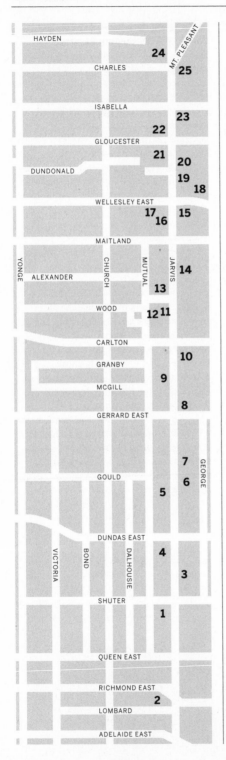

Walk 12: Jarvis Street

1 Salvation Army Harbour Light, 160 Jarvis St., Diamond Schmitt, 2009. The missionary organization has been a patron of ambitious architecture; in the 1950s the Parkin office designed a grand, Corbusian national headquarters on Albert Street (later demolished). This tough, brick-clad complex offers transitional housing and community services. The lantern-like chapel provides a symbolic and literal light at the corner, though its plastic panels are already discolouring. *AB*

2 French Quarter (condominium apartments), 120 Lombard St. and 115 Richmond St. E., Northgrave Architect, 2003. Perhaps the most ridiculous of all Toronto's historicist condo towers: apartments from Haussmann's Paris, supersized, twisted out of symmetry, and wrapped in flimsy-looking precast. *AB*

3a 207–213 Jarvis St. (four units of original six-house row), 1879. Around 1880, Toronto used the Second Empire style for everything from courthouses to row houses. The grandiose courthouses were massed around projecting centre pavilions; here the centrepiece is a double dormer in the convex-sloped mansard roof. *PM*

3b 215–219 Jarvis St. (three-house row), 1863. Probably the closest Toronto ever came to Manhattan's Italianate brownstones, sans the brownstone. Typical features include flattish roof, heavy cornice, round-headed windows with boldly protruding drip-moulds and sills, and prominent doorways with overdoors resting

3b | 215–219 Jarvis St.

on pilasters. The exterior flight of steps leading to a raised parlour floor and the rusticated high basement with access from the outside are the most telling common denominators. *PM*

4 Pace (condo apartments), 155 Dundas St. E., Diamond Schmitt, 2014. Dundas Square Gardens, 200 Dundas St. E., Page & Steele/IBI, ongoing. Grid Condos, 181 Dundas St. E., Page & Steele/IBI, ongoing. Pace, on the southwest corner of Dundas and Jarvis, is the first in a cluster of high-rise condominium towers to rise here in the 2010s. It replaced a suburban-style strip mall; the result is almost as generic, a window-wall tower with *au courant* black brick on the base. The double-height ground level at least meets the sidewalk well. Of the two Page & Steele projects, Grid on the southeast corner promises to be by far the more interesting, channelling the deadpan formalism of the Dutch architects OMA. But developers' drawings often lie. *AB*

5 Simpsons-Sears, 222 Jarvis St. (office building), Maxwell Miller, 1969–71; renovation, WZMH, 2011. Merchandise Building/originally Robert Simpson Co. Mail Order Building, 155 Dalhousie St., N. Max Dunning with Burke Horwood & White, 1916; addition, 1930; residential conversion, Paul Northgrave, 2000.
In 1916, Simpson's department store on Yonge Street **[5/6]** hired American architect Max Dunning to create the last word in a mail order house. And he did. Eleven storeys of precast reinforced concrete and light-refracting windows, the building featured such radical energy-, time-, and space-saving devices as openings in the floor slab

under each parcelling bin to drop orders onto a conveyor belt running just under the ceiling of the storey below. Eighty years on, the building proved its adaptability when it was redeveloped as 504 loft apartments.

The Brutalist upside-down ziggurat next door came later, as headquarters for the merged Simpson's and Sears mail order business. Company architect Miller was clearly inspired by Boston City Hall, opened in 1968; and while that controversial building reveals its Corbusian concrete structure, this one Miller clad in brown brick, "creating perhaps the first example of Victorian Brutalism the world has seen," as architect Jeff Hayes amusingly put it. In renovating no. 222 for the provincial government, WZMH carved out a lobby that places the building's spatial and structural drama on show. *PM/AB*

6 285–291 Jarvis St. (four-house row), possibly Knox & Elliot, 1889–90. Row housing is cheaper and faster to build than detached units so it has always appealed to speculative builders, but this is Toronto's only known row using weighty Richardsonian Romanesque style, and a very skilful application it is. The developer here was Alderman Edward Hewitt, for whom architects Knox & Elliot had just created a distinguished Romanesque two-family house nearby on Sherbourne Street **[11/5a]**, suggesting the talented pair may have also designed this virile composition which even years of neglect can't hide. It is unique and begs to be restored. *PM*

7 Juvenile and Family Courts Building, 311 Jarvis St., Page & Steele, 1955. For this courthouse complex and detention centre, Peter Dickinson provided a grand lobby and a show-stopping front façade: a concave plane of Queenston limestone pierced with

5 | 222 Jarvis St.

7 | Juvenile and Family Courts Building

more than 400 windows, which bring light without compromising privacy. Any redevelopment of this site, which goes all the way through the block, should treat that front wing—at least—as treasure. *AB*

8a Jarvis Street Baptist Church, 130 Gerrard St. E. at Jarvis St., Langley Langley & Burke, 1874–75; renovated and altered, Horwood & White, 1938–39. This Jarvis Street landmark was designed in Decorated Gothic Revival, considered *de rigueur* for ecclesiastical architecture in the 1870s. It boasts a wealth of fluid detailing and a complicated composition, with the animated cater-corner siting of the tower resonating in contours of rough brownstone walls and outlines of jagged buttresses. That these expressive gestures work in a relatively small church on a tight city lot is a measure of Langley's finesse. The west doors, expressively flanked by grinning gargoyles, were inserted in 1939, part of massive renovations carried out by Horwood & White, Langley's ultimate successor firm. *PM*

8b Toronto Baptist Seminary/originally Samuel Platt house, 337 Jarvis St., 1849–50; renovations and third-floor addition, William Irving, 1872. Mr. Platt, a brewer and distiller, must have been thumbing through some architecture books. The pointed detailing on his front door is Gothic; the capitals on the pilasters, Egyptian; the rectangular shape of the doorway comes from Greek Revival; and the symmetrical plan with low hipped roof looks Italianate. (The early 20th-century porch is not Platt's doing.) It all comes together in a very distinctive manner, however. *PM*

9 Essex Park Hotel/originally Frontenac Arms Apartments, 300 Jarvis St., Joseph A. Thatcher, 1930. The Frontenac Arms was the embodiment of a 1930s apartment building with romantic name, salubrious design, and stylish Moderne façade. This was the heyday of apartment construction in Toronto and keen competition flogged features such as superior ventilation, view, sun, and sound insulation. The ten-storey Frontenac boasted all these plus

concrete-block construction and Deco decoration enhancing lower-floor spandrels. Unfortunately, it was too late to rescue Jarvis Street from its downhill slide, and the Frontenac never attracted the tenants it had hoped for. Ten years later, it was an apartment hotel and the sole example in this area of a 1930s high-rise. *PM*

10 St. Andrew's Lutheran Church/ originally St. Andrew's Presbyterian Church/formerly St. Andrew's United Church, 383 Jarvis St., Langley Langley & Burke, 1878; Sunday school addition, Langley Langley & Burke, 1882. In 1894, Toronto historian John Ross Robertson confidently wrote, "St. Andrew's presents a uniform, substantial, real appearance that fittingly symbolizes the character of the religious faith in which it is enshrined." Langley's plain but pleasant façade of Credit Valley freestone has since been called upon to represent the Lutherans, after a 25-year stint for the Uniteds, but it seems to have adapted well enough. *PM*

11 National Ballet School, Kuwabara Payne McKenna Blumberg and Goldsmith Borgal in joint venture, with landscape architects MBTW, 2005. Incorporates 354 Jarvis St., George M. Miller, 1898; 372 Jarvis St., Joseph Sheard, 1856. A profoundly Torontonian collage of old and new. Along Jarvis, the studios of the National Ballet School occupy a set of three linked buildings called the Celia Franca Centre; these wrap their gridded concrete block and glass around courtyards, a lobby dubbed

11 | National Ballet School

"Town Square," and the stately Northfield, designed by Sheard for the young Oliver Mowat, later the long-time premier of Ontario. Northfield would become a residence for Havergal College and then part of CBC headquarters, which occupied this site for decades. CBC also built a 150-metre broadcast tower that stood next door until 2002, but the heart of its operations was in Miller's 1898 Jacobethan pile for Havergal down the block at no. 354. Today the latter contains classrooms for the ballet school's students, linked by bridge to the new additions.

While the National Ballet School is not generally open to the public, the subtlety of the architectural mixture, overseen by urban designers Urban Strategies, makes a walkaround worthwhile. *AB*

12 Radio City (condominium apartment towers and townhouses), 281–285 Mutual St., architectsAlliance, 2006. Some of the funding for the National Ballet School project came through a deal with Context Development, which moved density to the rear of the site; the resulting towers are of middling-to-good quality, but the yellow-brick townhouses are very fine, and the ensemble, including Roland Brener's "Radioville," fits Sirman Lane with great finesse. *AB*

13 Betty Oliphant Theatre/originally Blaikie/Alexander house, 400–404 Jarvis St., Gundry & Langley, 1863–64; no. 404 remodelled, 1882; remodelled with additions, A.J. Diamond & Partners, 1987–88. Even though land was plentiful, some well-to-do Torontonians were not averse to double houses. Pattern books touted their economy, especially when "people can agree and get along together." The first two owners here were partners in a brokerage firm, at which time the houses displayed similar Gothic Revival intentions. By 1882, however, the occupants seem no longer to have been in agreement and no. 404 received a fussy Queen Anne facelift. Today, their front exteriors have been meticulously restored while in behind an attachment creates a large but unobtrusive facility for the National Ballet School. *PM*

14a Maitland Place, 445 Jarvis St. (complex of two apartment houses and four rehabilitated houses), Edward I. Richmond with Spencer R. Higgins, 1983–84. The rehabilitation of these four fine Victorian houses as frontispiece offices for a new high-rise apartment development is unusually honest and well done. *PM*

14b Originally Alfred Mason house, 441 Jarvis St., 1881. Vigorous High Victorian Gothic eschewing facile surface ornament for an organic decoration created by the structural bricks and boards themselves. No. 441 was built for the manager of the city's first savings and loan company, Canada Permanent. *PM*

14c The Blake House, 449 Jarvis St., Knox & Elliot, 1891; north bay addition, David B. Dick, 1897. Vaguely chateauesque, but really more Shakespearean stage set than serious style. Concern for invention did not preclude quality, however; both firms of architects were masters of their art and the house is flamboyant but never flimsy. Built for Edward F. Blake, the Hon. Edward Blake's son [see 12/14d]. *PM*

14d Originally Samuel Briggs house/ formerly Hon. Edward Blake house, 467 Jarvis St., possibly Smith & Gemmell, 1871–72; addition, David Dick, 1897. An eclectic 19th-century house mixing Second Empire mansard with Italianate tower and off-centre plan in a typical Victorian show of the practical and picturesque. No. 467 was bought by one of Canada's leading statesmen, the Hon. Edward Blake, in 1879, the year he became leader of the opposition Liberal party. The previous owner was a lumber merchant. *PM*

15 Jarvis Collegiate Institute, 495 Jarvis St., C.E.C. Dyson, 1922–24. "Collegiate Gothic," the last, recumbent phase of Gothic Revival, is well represented by Jarvis Collegiate Institute with its horizontal solemnity and 20th-century "medieval" mouldings, parapets, and mullioned and transomed windows. Jarvis traces its lineage to Toronto's first secondary school, the publicly owned but tuition-funded Home District Grammar School of 1807. *PM*

15 | Jarvis Collegiate Institute

16 Hincks-Dellcrest Centre, 440 Jarvis St. (office and residential building), Shore & Moffat, 1967. A splendidly designed small-scale psychiatric facility for adolescents and their families. The building's delicacy and reserve along with large trees make it easy to miss, but this is one of the most thoughtful structures on Jarvis Street, clearly inspired by Louis Kahn's 1962 Richards Laboratories at the University of Pennsylvania. *PM/AB*

17 Originally H.D. Warren house, 95 Wellesley St. E., 1892; additions, c. 1900; additions, Symons & Rae, 1908. A large, rambling, slightly Jacobethan manor, no. 95 is one of those houses that just grew, with additions sprouting every few years. Mr. Warren's profits from gutta percha (a 19th-century formulation akin to rubber) paid for it all, another instance of Victorians' longing to live in a picturesque past even as they worked to create the fantastic future. *PM*

Two of the best 19th-century houses in the city are to be found on Wellesley Place, hidden behind hospitals that long ago swept away their neighbours.

18a Originally R.M. Simpson house, 2 Wellesley Pl., Charles J. Gibson, 1899. With its broad flat front elaborated with one finely wrought Richardsonian Romanesque detail after another, this is a virtuoso artist's canvas of plum-coloured stone and red-brown brick. The stepped gable of the stable in the rear (belonging to an earlier, demolished house) is studiously repeated in this house to the side. *PM*

18b Originally Mrs. Mary Perram house, 4 Wellesley Pl., 1876. Reminiscent of Ontario farm houses, this is an Italianate villa minus the typical tall square tower, but all the rest of the picturesque panoply is here. *PM*

19 Keg Mansion Restaurant/originally Arthur R. McMaster house/formerly "Euclid Hall" (Hart Massey residence), 515 Jarvis St., Gundry & Langley, 1868; additions, Langley Langley & Burke, 1882; additions, E.J. Lennox, 1883–85; additions, George M. Miller, 1900–01. The home of farm machinery magnate Hart Massey underwent accretions from several architectural firms before it came out looking like the quintessential Baronial Gothic

19 | The Keg/Hart Massey House

ensemble that it is today. To the initial asymmetric Gothic composition of crenellated tower, bay windows, and high gables, Langley Langley & Burke introduced interior Queen Anne fittings for the Masseys in 1882. Lennox added veranda and conservatory to the south (now gone). Miller's contribution included a domed south turret; inside it, he assembled a Moorish-style smoking room, a favourite turn-of-the-century conceit commissioned by Massey's daughter, Lillian Massey Treble. It is unlikely the abstentious Massey would have approved of its current use. *PM*

20 Originally Charles A. Massey house/ formerly Chester D. Massey house, 519 Jarvis St., E.J. Lennox, 1887; additions, Sproatt & Rolph, 1907. Another Massey mansion, but here too many cooks have spoiled the architectural broth. Lennox's basic recipe for a picturesque Queen Anne house using half-timbered gables, dormers, and decorative bargeboards has been consider-ably diluted by Sproatt & Rolph's classical additions: skylit picture gallery to the north (for Chester's collection of Dutch masters), and columned porte cochère to the south (for his Packard and Peerless motorcars). Today the house is primarily of note as the boyhood home of brothers Vincent Massey, Canada's first native-born governor general; and Raymond Massey, the Broadway and Hollywood actor. *PM*

The west side of Jarvis Street between Cawthra Square and Gloucester is a precious intact block of late Victorian houses, all built during the 1880s, all abandoned by original owners within a few decades, and today all enjoying renewed uses.

21a Originally George H. Gooderham house, 504 Jarvis St., David Roberts, 1889. This house for the 21-year-old son and namesake of distillery magnate George Gooderham was architect Roberts's rehearsal for the more grandiose Richardsonian Romanesque house designed for father George a year later in the Annex [19/31]. A decorous pile of red brick and

21a | 504 Jarvis St.

stone, it is like a Rubik's cube with all the parts twisting precisely into place. Not a bad first house for young George, who had his initials entwined in the expertly carved frieze over the front door. *PM*

21b Originally Thomas Taylor house, 510 Jarvis St., 1888. Attractive scrolled brackets and an unusual stepped gable. The original owner was big in brewing and malting. By 1911 the house was dubbed "The Inglewood" and advertised in the *Globe* as offering "Beautiful rooms in Exclusive Pension, excellent table," to serve a different class of resident **[see Introduction, Area VII]**. Today, it is apartments. *PM/AB*

21c Originally Edward Gallow house/ formerly Charles Band house, 512 Jarvis St., possibly E.J. Lennox, 1889–90. Classical Revival touches for a late Victorian house: Doric columns, dentil mouldings, pedimented lookout. Gallow was a broker; Band a grain merchant well known for his collection of paintings by the Group of Seven (donated at his death to the Art Gallery of Ontario). *PM*

21d Originally Charles R. Rundle house, 514 Jarvis St., E.J. Lennox, 1889–90. If the house at the other end of this block is like an earnest Rubik's cube, no. 514 is more akin to one of those agile wooden acrobat toys that tirelessly somersault down the upended ladder—quick and quirky but executed with supreme skill and confidence. The architect has manipulated the house on this small lot brilliantly, placing the entrance on the interior south side to permit a centre hall and to give over the principal façade entirely to windows and an abundance of lovely Romanesque/Queen Anne ornament. Rundle was a speculative builder for whom Lennox designed several houses in this neighbourhood, none finer than this. *PM*

22 100 Gloucester St., 105 and 108 Isabella St. (apartments), Bregman & Hamann, c. 1958. These yellow-brick International Style slabs are handsome if densely packed; the fact that the original windows are still in place adds much to the design effect (although it's surely drafty in there). Along Gloucester, ground-floor apartments seem to have been refaced with reclaimed brick and industrial-scale windows, for a peculiar loft-cottage effect. *AB*

23 Casey House/originally William R. Johnston house, 571 Jarvis St., Langley Langley & Burke, 1875; renovation and addition, Hariri Pontarini, ongoing. This merchant's house, an eclectic design with hints of Scottish Baronial, has become Casey House, a hospital for people living with HIV or AIDS. The addition provides space for in-patient and outpatient care, with rooms on four levels arranged around a private central courtyard. The new exterior façades evoke a quilt, the long-standing symbol of HIV/AIDS, in brick, tinted glass, and limestone. *AB*

24 X Condos and X2 Condos, 101 and 110 Charles St., architectsAlliance, 2010. A weird quasi-homage to Mies **[see 6/34]**: the Modernist master, who made an art of

24 | X Condos

precisely calibrating the grids of his curtain walls, would not have been impressed with the proportions of these ones, or with the hits of primary colour sprinkled across the façades. An experiment not to be repeated—although the pair of sculptures by Shayne Dark make a strong contribution to the street. *AB*

25 | Rogers

25 Rogers/originally Confederation Life, 1 Mount Pleasant Rd., Zeidler Roberts, 1987–92; internal renovations, Zeidler, 2003. Now part of Rogers's "campus," this is Toronto's grandest project of the Post-Modern moment, and its most ridiculous: a set of stumpy office towers topped with turrets. The goal was to recall Confederation Life's iconic downtown headquarters **[18/28]**, but even the materials aren't true to history: here the walls are wrapped in pink granite, the roofs in green fake copper. The massing is quite smart, on this weirdly shaped site, but the impenetrable street fronts and gaudy cladding obscure that truth.

Zeidler fully endorsed the Post-Modernist premise of ornamental gestures to the past. In a brochure, the firm wrote that the complex would "continue the heritage of Confederation Life's architecture leading back to the beginning of Confederation"; it would also "evoke the emotional reassurance of the past, as well as the translucence, efficiency and precision of the future." Events here would not prove either precise or reassuring: the company collapsed shortly after moving in, and the tallest turret, the very image of Confederation Life, is now capped by the name ROGERS. *AB*

Walk 13: Church Street

1 60 Richmond East (co-op apartments), Teeple Architects, 2010. Toronto Community Housing teamed up with a hospitality workers' union to develop this building of large apartments in the heart of downtown; the main-floor restaurant is a social enterprise that serves as a training site for workers. None of this suggests the budget or mindset for innovative architecture, and yet this building is visually and formally extraordinary: a set of building blocks pierced by a vertical shaft, dabbed with hits of colour, and garnished with terrace gardens. The building is also designed to be energy-efficient, with only 40 per cent glass on the outer walls, and was built remarkably cheaply. A winner on every front, and a 2014 Governor General's Medal laureate. *AB*

1 | 60 Richmond East

2 Metropolitan United Church/originally Metropolitan Wesleyan Methodist Church, 56 Queen St. E. at Church St., Henry Langley, 1870–72; rebuilt after fire, J. Gibb Morton, 1928–29. This majestic "Cathedral of Methodism" was in no small way a symbol of the commercial and social power of Toronto's Methodist community in the 1870s, raised as bold challenge to both

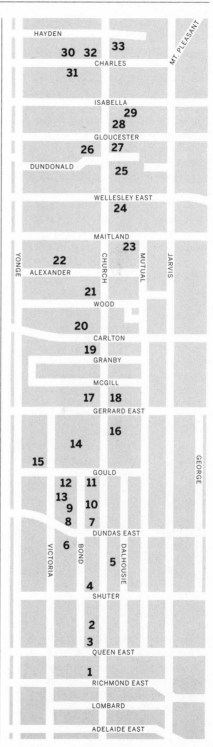

Anglican and Roman Catholic cathedrals [1/13, 13/4a]. All three have towers by Langley but Metropolitan's remains the best, its heroic proportions and firmness restored after a devastating fire in 1928. And even though the rebuilding did not make use of the same High Victorian elaboration as the original, the deeply recessed windows, sharply contoured buttresses, and sweeping rhythm are in similar spirit and give Metropolitan a magnificent sense of space and volume. In 1925, this centre-city church became Metropolitan United. It continues to enjoy a privileged site in the middle of a block-square park. Unfortunately, the cast-iron fence designed by Langley to complete the setting has been removed. *PM*

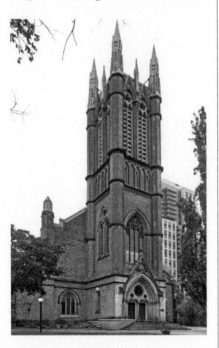

2 | Metropolitan United Church

3 Metropolitan United Church parsonage, 51 Bond St., Curry Sproatt & Rolph, 1906. With its diminutive, rough-hewn character, this stone parsonage looks exactly as we have come to expect from our reading of English novels. *PM*

4a St. Michael's Roman Catholic Cathedral, 57 Bond St., William Thomas, 1845–48; tower and spire additions, Gundry & Langley, 1865–67; dormer additions, Joseph Connolly, 1890; restoration, Ventin Group Architects, 2016. Today, hemmed in by streets and adjacent buildings, St. Michael's lacks the expansive sites of both St. James' and Metropolitan United, and therefore the grand prominence of those two edifices. As well, too many fussy details appended later have sapped whatever drama the 14th-century-derived church with its striking west façade might have originally enjoyed. Langley insinuated three detailed lancets in each face of the tower where Thomas had planned but a single traceried window, and the quirky dormers stapled onto the broad roof—though they do provide a light-enhancing clerestory—destroy the bold sweep of Thomas's roofline. The interior is appealing with lushly painted ceiling and exuberant Gothic arcades and clustered piers. *PM*

4a | St. Michael's Cathedral

4b St. Michael's Cathedral rectory/ originally Bishop's Palace, 200 Church St., William Thomas, 1845–46; north wing addition, Joseph Sheard, 1852; third-floor addition, Frederick C. Law, 1889; renovation, Ventin Group Architects, 2016. The residence for the bishop uses the same stone-dressed brick as the cathedral [13/4a], but here Thomas is flashier, employing decorative buttresses and pinnacles among other evocative medieval memories. The label-stops depict the heads of both bishop and architect. *PM*

5 191–197 Church St. (four-house row), 1852; rebuilt after fire, probably John Tully, 1856; demolished no. 195 rebuilt, Mekinda Snyder & Weis, 1981–82. One of Toronto's finest remaining Georgian rows, actually highlighted by the replacement at no. 195. Before the gap site was filled, it seemed only a faithful reproduction would do. But the properly scaled reinterpretation, announced by decidedly modern fixtures alongside the Georgian, has proved to be more interesting, both in itself and for its commentary on the whole. The wooden door-cases on these houses resemble those around the corner at 68–70 Shuter Street. *PM*

6 William Lyon Mackenzie house, 82 Bond St. (one unit of original three-house row), 1858; addition, 1967. This charming Georgian showplace, once part of a row, is an architectural rarity for Toronto with its high parlour floor reached by a flight of steps inside a vestibule. This was the last home of Toronto's renegade first mayor after he was allowed to return from sanctuary in the United States whence he had fled following an abortive rebellion against the ruling oligarchy in 1837. After Mackenzie's death in 1861, his widow and children stayed on, two of his daughters running the "Misses Helen and Elizabeth Mackenzie Ladies Boarding School" here. Today it is a house museum; the addition on the back, built with salvaged bricks from the Normal School **[13/14a]**, houses an 1845 printing press. *PM/AB*

6 | 82 Bond St.

7a Originally C.E. Goad Co., 105 Bond St., Curry & Sparling, 1912. This three-storey structure isn't as old as it looks. The rusticated ground floor, stone string courses, and alternating segmental- and triangular-pedimented window heads were all part of the Second Classical Revival that around the turn of the 20th century saw Italian *palazzi* again put in the service of private clubs, banks, and small office buildings. This particular palace was for a compiler of insurance atlases, C.E. Goad Company. *PM/ updated AB*

7b John Frank Place (housing), 80 Dundas St. E., Dunker Associates, 1995. A late spinoff of the Eaton Centre's development **[5/11]**, this affordable-housing tower came out of activism by Holy Trinity church **[5/12a]** and other local churches. The base borrows the massing and window dimensions of nearby lofts **[see 12/5]**, with a few compositional flourishes offset by contextual yellow brick. *AB*

8 Originally Piper/Birnie house, 110–112 Bond St., 1862. A fine early Toronto double house in the tall, blocky tradition of Georgian row housing **[see 11/6a]**. Original owners were Noah L. Piper, a hardware merchant, and Mrs. Grace Birnie, who ran a girls' boarding school here. Perhaps that's why Mr. Piper later moved to Yorkville. *PM*

9 First Lutheran Church/originally St. John's Lutheran Church or German Lutheran Church, 116 Bond St., Charles F. Wagner, 1898–99. Described in its time as "modern Gothic," this perky abstraction features smooth stucco walls and elongated windows, buttresses, and corner tower. The congregation, which was founded in 1851, replaced an earlier wooden meeting house on the site. *PM*

10 St. George's Greek Orthodox Church of Toronto/originally Holy Blossom Temple, 115 Bond St., J. Wilson Siddall, 1895; remodelled, 1938; renovated, Allan M. Young, 1982–84. After centuries of emulating the architecture of the community in which they found themselves, Jewish congregations of the late 19th and early 20th centuries tried to develop a distinct synagogue style that they hoped would acknowledge their Middle-Eastern origins. Holy Blossom Temple on Bond Street, the second synagogue of the first Hebrew congregation in Toronto, was typical of these efforts. A Byzantine domed cubicle was given a Romanesque façade, then punctuated at the corners with stair towers topped by shaped domes. A large central dome is also the style of the Eastern Orthodox church, and not a few downtown synagogues have converted to those houses of worship as the Jewish population moved elsewhere. No. 115 Bond Street was purchased by the Greek community in 1938 and is now their Toronto mother church. Meanwhile, Holy Blossom is thriving uptown **[25/29]**. *PM/updated AB*

10 | St. George's Greek Orthodox Church of Toronto

11 Ryerson University Student Campus Centre, incorporating "Oakham House" (William Thomas residence)/formerly Working Boys Home, 322 Church St., William Thomas, 1848; addition, David B. Dick, 1901; additions, George E. Kneider, 1977, addition, Carruthers Shaw & Partners, 2005. For his own house, Toronto's eclectic transplanted English architect William Thomas chose a romantic version of the medieval with an abundance of showy Gothic decoration: pointed arches,

quatrefoil tracery, drip-moulds, pinnacles, crockets. The somber dark-brown-brick addition of 1901 was for working boys; the 2005 addition for Ryerson students. *PM*

12 Ryerson Image Centre, 122 Bond St.; renovations, Crang & Boake, 1969; renovations and additions, Diamond Schmitt, 2012. A nearly lightless warehouse, converted to a home for photography and film—the irony was clear, and continued for decades until the most recent renovation. Diamond Schmitt carved out a slice from the north end of the building, providing transparency into its lobby and toward the public galleries within. The rest of the exterior donned a handsome glass skin, which can be backlit with changeable coloured LEDs that make the building itself into a work of art. *AB*

12 | Ryerson Image Centre

13 Heaslip House, 297 Victoria St., Chapman & Oxley, 1939; renovation and expansion, Rounthwaite Dick & Hadley in association with Lett Architects, 2006. To the south, a fine Moderne office building built for E.P. Taylor's Canadian Breweries (don't miss the reliefs of workers holding sheaves of grain). The building was elegantly repurposed and expanded to reach out toward the adjacent Devonian Square, though furnishings now block up the transparent lobby. *AB*

14a Normal and Model Schools, St. James Square, Cumberland & Ridout, 1851–52; all but folly demolished, 1963. Founded by Egerton Ryerson, the Normal and Model Schools provided the first teacher-training facility in the province. Housed in an imposing Victorian neo-classical edifice in the centre of a landscaped square, the school was a Toronto landmark for many decades. Though the facility had become sorely antiquated by the 20th century, it served briefly after World War II as a veterans' training school and later the first home of Ryerson Institute before it was finally demolished in 1963. A solitary span of porticoed wall was left standing in the middle of the Ryerson quadrangle, however, creating one of those architectural oddities referred to as "follies." *PM/updated AB*

14a | Ryerson quadrangle/the "folly"

14b Ryerson University: Kerr Hall, 50 Gould St., Burwell R. Coon, 1954–63; Recreation and Athletics Centre, Lett/ Smith, 1986–87. Constructed around the old Normal School before it was demolished, Kerr Hall embodies a moment when Canadian architecture was wrestling with how or whether to adopt Modernist precepts, here adding hints of unfashionable classical adornment to a very austere slab. The stone bas-reliefs by Thomas Bowie depict Ryerson students as nude Art Deco–style Greek gods and goddesses: ponytailed reader, gymnast, skater. Another delightful surprise is Ryerson's 1980s

Recreation and Athletics Centre, a high-style facility burrowed two and a half levels under the central quadrangle. *PM/AB*

15 Ryerson University Learning Resources Centre, 350 Victoria St., Webb Zerafa Menkes, 1971. Jorgenson Hall, 380 Victoria St., Webb Zerafa Menkes, 1968; ServiceHub renovation, Gow Hastings, 2016. This pair of galoots puts the "brute" in Brutalism: They are massive, nearly windowless, difficult to enter, and hard to navigate. Built at a time when the city was seen as a hostile environment, they keep activity above or below ground level; once you're inside, the hallways are low and cramped. Rehabilitation will be tough; cosmetic changes such as those to the ServiceHub can't disguise these spatial problems. *AB*

16 Ryerson University Architectural Science Building, 325 Church St., Thom Partnership, 1981. Paul H. Cocker Architecture Gallery, Gow Hastings, 2013. The ingredients here are familiar to the era: exposed concrete, brown quarry tile, exposed ducts. But Ron Thom's office arranged these inexpensive materials artfully, and the central atrium is surprisingly beautiful. *AB*

17 62–66 Gerrard St. E. (three-house row), 1855; mansard addition, c. 1875. The crisp rectangularity of an early Georgian row, with Flemish-bond yellow brick and stone lintels and sills. The Second Empire mansard was added later. In the mid 19th century, Gerrard Street was a prestigious residential thoroughfare. *PM*

18 Gallery Arcturus/originally Green/ Green house, 78–80 Gerrard St. E., 1858. This is one of Toronto's most interesting buildings, a handsome yellow-brick double house, unusual for its three-storey height and bay-windowed front. It does resemble some other early Toronto Georgian double houses, however, in that the units look more like row housing than semi-detached (the entrance to no. 80 has been bricked into a window), and in the high parlour floor reached by a steep flight of steps. At no. 78 lived Columbus

H. Green, a barrister; at no. 80, the Rev. Anson Green. Today the houses have been joined into a public gallery. *PM/updated AB*

19 Canadian Imperial Bank of Commerce/ originally Somerset House Hotel, 432 Church St., Frederick H. Herbert, 1895; remodelled as bank, Langley & Howland, 1930. This branch bank began life as the Somerset House Hotel when Church Street was still a fashionable address. Hotel guests were no doubt attracted by the ample windows and finely detailed Richardsonian Romanesque character of the place as well. *PM*

20 Formerly Maple Leaf Gardens, 438 Church St. (athletic hall), Ross & Macdonald with Jack Ryrie and Mackenzie Waters, 1931; renovation, 2012: base building, Turner Fleischer; store interior, Landini Associates; athletic centre fitout, BBB. One of Toronto's best-loved buildings from the 1930s to the 1990s, scene of the Maple Leafs' glorious and many non-glorious years. Leafs owner Conn Smythe built the "Carlton Street Cashbox" in the Depression, cheaply and quickly—it took less than six months. Yet the results were solid, a workmanlike reinforced-concrete structure wrapped in a Moderne yellow-brick veneer. Today it houses an unlikely mix of uses: Ryerson's Mattamy Athletic Centre up top, near the domed roof, and retail below that serves the neighbour-hood. The Loblaws interior by Australian designer Mark Landini pioneered the chain's

new aesthetic of quasi-retro signage and hot-orange floors. *AB*

21 City Park Apartments, 484 Church St., Peter Caspari, 1954. In the 1950s, City Park was famous as Toronto's first high-rise apartment complex, a daring three-building experiment in the vocabulary of the International Style. Today the precise modular patterning is no longer novel, but the simplicity of the design—which relies on little more than balcony shadows for ornament—remains distinguished. Its European developers and their local architect used a combination of reinforced-concrete frame with poured reinforced-concrete carrying walls between apartments, and cut back by one-third the number of apartments allowed by city council. *PM*

21 | City Park Apartments

22a Village Green, 40 and 50 Alexander St. and 55 Maitland St., John Daniels, 1967. These two slabs and cylindrical tower—tall, but with a remarkable amount of open space—date from the apartment boom of the 1960s. Daniels would become a major developer; at this point he was among the architects who made white brick, then fashionable in New York, a standard material of modern Toronto. *AB*

22b The Maitlands, 36–42 Maitland St. (apartment house), 1911. A typical apartment block of the first decades of the 20th century when classical architecture was in vogue again, the orangey-brick Maitlands sports a handsome cornice at the top, portico of pressed metal and cast stone at the base, and jutting bays at the sides. *PM*

20 | Maple Leaf Gardens

Church and Wellesley is the heart of "the Village," for four decades and counting the soul of queer Toronto. The building on the southwest corner long had a Second Cup and a set of steps that became "the Steps"—the neighbourhood's agora, the place to talk, look, and be looked at.

23 Currie Hall, National Ballet School/ originally Society of Friends Meeting House, 111 Maitland St., John A. Mackenzie, 1911.
An elegant Palladian surprise shining amid Victorian furbelows. With its pedimented Tuscan portico and round-arched multi-light windows, this building is a dignified study in classical simplicity that must have seemed especially appropriate to its Quaker congregation. *PM*

24 77 Wellesley St. E. (apartment house), Larremore V.V. Sweezy, 1926; remodelled, Jedd Jones, 1982.
This apartment building eschewed popular Classical Revival and Art Deco styles, opting for the Gothic touch— clues are "medieval" lettering over the door and the suggestion of a pointed gable at the roof. The remodelling introduced shops to the ground floor. *PM*

25 519 Community Centre/originally Granite Club annex, 519 Church St., Edwin R. Babington, 1906; renovation and addition, Kohn Shnier, 2004.
As erected on the site in 1880, the Granite Curling Club was an exuberant Renaissance Revival building. What we see today was an attached addition of 1906, but when the principal building burned in 1913, this was left. The city

25 | 519 Church St.

bought the building in the 1970s for a community centre to serve the burgeoning gay community in the Village. Kohn Shnier's addition contributes both transparency and a certain flair, using brick in the least traditional way possible. *PM/AB*

26 580–582 Church St. (double house), 1877–78.
A Second Empire double house at its dignified best. The gentle concave curve of the mansard roof, striking dormer windows, brisk classical window surrounds, and harmonious symmetry create a rich design that is both conservative and assertive. Not surprising that the first owner of no. 580 was Robert Simpson, whose dry goods shop at 184 Yonge Street prospered and grew into a vast Canadian department store enterprise. *PM*

27a | 2–36 Monteith St.

27a 2–36 Monteith St. (18-house row), 1887–88.
When this row of economical brick houses was built in the late 1880s, Second Empire was no longer the height of fashion. Nevertheless, its dominant trademark—the mansard roof—was put to good use, providing a practical third storey and rhythmic roofline to the long row of working-class dwellings. The enterprising builder added further cachet to his development by naming the private lane on which the row was built after the Cawthras, then one of the wealthiest families in Toronto. The impulse was prophetic. Roy Thomson, who was born at no. 32 in 1894, the son of a barber and his wife, went on to become newspaper magnate Lord Thomson of Fleet. The street name was changed to Mulock in 1897 and Monteith in 1909. *PM*

27b 551–555 Church St. (triple house), 1888. Displaying a sensitivity to proportion and materials that belies the charge of "frantic excess" sometimes levelled against late Victorian houses, this three-house ensemble projects a quality of repose that still draws attention on the street. Thoughtfully adapted for shops and offices. *PM*

28 Grace MacInnis Co-operative: 561–571 Church St. (six-house row), 1890; 573–575 Church St. (two-thirds of original triple house), 1889. Six harmonious row houses and a building of grab-bag shapes, materials, and colours made more asymmetrically picturesque than necessary by the excision of its northern one-third, now a driveway to the condominium building at 86 Gloucester Street. The condos gained their height in a trade with the city whereby the Church Street houses were renovated as low-cost housing and kept in place as a valuable segment of streetscape. *PM*

29 The Merlan, 81–83 Isabella St. (apartment house), Norman A. Armstrong, 1927; remodelled, 1982. Church-Isabella Co-operative, 72 Isabella St. (apartment house), 1917. The Brownley, 40–42 Isabella St. (apartment house), 1931–32. Star Mansions, 61–63 Charles St. E. (apartment house), 1931–32. Like many apartment buildings of this period, The Merlan displays a ceremonious name on the front (often the date of construction is there too) and a deep, light-giving U shape. Though the ends of the U sometimes presented dissimilar faces to the street, usually the decoration was classical in keeping with the fashion of the new century. Other versions—that at no. 72 Isabella Street, for example—sported projecting bays duplicating those of a bay-windowed house. In a few years, however, to be stylish would mean to be Moderne. The Brownley is representative of many such 1930s apartment buildings in which distinctiveness actually amounts to little more than Art Deco spandrels and entrance fixtures. Star Mansions is another such small Deco declaration. *PM*

30 Casa, 33 and 42 Charles St. E., architectsAlliance, 2010. Two in a string of new towers bringing a new level of density to an already crowded block. At no. 33, the double-height lobby helps conceal a four-storey parking garage, which is used in part by the property's former owners, the Children's Aid Society, who have consolidated office space in a new building just behind this one. No. 42 repeats the design, with less bulk and more ornament on the glass balcony fronts. *AB*

31 Chaz, 45 Charles St. E., Page & Steele/ IBI, 2015. Why all the 45-degree angles? They are an homage to the previous building on this site, a refined Brutalist Fairfield & Dubois office block from 1967. Those fragments of column stuck in the façade? Who knows. The adjacent lane is named after Macy DuBois, but this incoherent lump of a tower is a poor tribute to him. *AB*

32a Manhattan Apartments, 68–70 Charles St. E., James A. Harvey, 1909. One of Toronto's earliest apartment buildings, cleverly consuming an existing house, the entrance of which is still used on Church Street. Now threatened by development on a much larger scale. *PM/updated AB*

32b 634–636 Church St. (double house), 1878. Second Empire in an exuberant mood, with strongly articulated centre pavilion, flanking end bays, and lively mansard roof. Thanks to two of Toronto's more enduring restaurants, this fine double house still stands much as it was. *PM*

33 Traders Building, 625 Church St., Morani & Morris, 1957. This extension of Bloor Street's Insurance Row **[see 18/23]** is easy to miss, a grey-flannel suit of 1950s architecture. But look closely: this is a profoundly well-crafted building, from the carved limestone at ground level to the subtle ornamentation in the brickwork above. A quieter, less expensive variation on the architects' Bank of Canada Building **[7/13]**, hardly innovative but finely tailored. *AB*

Grange Park is an ideal place to ponder Toronto's architectural history. Stand in the centre of the lawn, once the picturesque front grounds of a grand estate, with a carriage path that looped around where people today wheel their strollers. Look north, and you'll see the house that went with it: The Grange **[14/1]**, the Georgian manse that D'Arcy Boulton Jr. built in 1817. The Grange's orchard and tennis courts are gone; what was once a genteel, rural estate has been woven into the fabric of downtown Toronto, with a mixed crop of low housing off to the west on Beverley Street, the Modernist grand project of Village by the Grange **[14/7]** to the east, and a thicket of tall new towers sprouting to the south **[Area II]**.

And rising behind The Grange is the Art Gallery of Ontario **[14/10]**, whose two most recent renovations by Barton Myers/KPMB and Frank Gehry now frame The Grange like a beloved historic artifact. Next door to the east is OCAD University, Will Alsop's box-on-stilts Sharp Centre for Design showing itself both raucous and sensitive in its address to the cityscape.

This conversation between eras, and the mingling of institutions, residences, and commerce, might not have been what John Graves Simcoe had in mind when he granted 32 100-acre "park lots," running from today's Queen Street to Bloor Street, to colonial officials such as Robert Gray, who was granted no. 13. (Boulton, son of Upper Canada's solicitor-general, purchased the land in 1808.)

But the development of The Grange, and the park lots to the west, reflected the characteristic early-Toronto pattern of speculation and development, and their present scrambled vitality reflects the economic prosperity and waves of migration that define the contemporary city.

The Boulton family began selling off their lands in the 1820s, with the north half—from College and Bloor—going to the new King's College at £25 an acre **[see Introduction, Area V]**. The southern half went to building lots, aided by Mr. Boulton's donated lands for Church of St. George-the-Martyr **[14/2]** and St. Patrick's Market **[14/6]**. Grange Road was in place by the 1870s, with a gatehouse

Area VIII
Walk 14: The Grange
Walk 15: Queen Street West
and Kensington
Market

marking the southern expanse of The Grange; a decade later the surrounding streets were filled with houses, and an interloping "Chemical Works" on Beverley Street. Houses went up to the west and north in the 1870s and 1880s, first Second Empire **[14/12]** and then a succession of other fashionable styles.

The lands to the west, between Beverley and Augusta Streets, evolved similarly in the hands of the Baldwin family. In the 1820s William Warren Baldwin **[see 19/1]** began dividing up his several park lots, laying out Spadina Avenue in 1822 and establishing one

of the few grand gestures in Toronto's 19th-century fabric. He laid out the smaller residential streets, with family names like Baldwin and Willcocks, in a deliberately discontinuous fashion, creating the DNA of what became Kensington Market. And further west, ending at Bathurst, the Denison family did the same thing: Denison, Lippincott, and Augusta are all names from the family tree, while their estate was called Belle Vue. (The manor lay just north of the present Bellevue Square.)

Between 1871 and 1911 Toronto's population grew from 56,000 to 376,000. As the city rapidly grew west and north, this area's genteel and residential character rapidly transformed. The Grange itself, with the bequest of its final owners, Harriet Dixon and Goldwin Smith, became home to the Art Museum of Toronto. Industrial lofts pushed up John Street right to the gatehouse.

But what was happening to the west was more radical: starting with the boom of the 1880s, this part of the city became poorer, vastly denser, and filled with Torontonians who were decidedly not Anglican. At the start of the 20th century, European Jews became the city's largest minority—that is to say, non-British—group. In the 1910s they began to leave their initial gathering place, the neighbourhood known as St. John's Ward—the object of much genteel angst for its ethnic mix and crowded conditions—most

settling along Spadina Avenue, near the garment district to the south **[see Walk 4]**, as their Chinese neighbours moved up to Dundas and Elizabeth.

By the 1920s, three-quarters of Toronto's 35,000 Jews lived in and around Kensington Market, establishing synagogues such as the Kiever **[15/24]** to serve populations with common roots in Eastern Europe. They gave a Yiddish accent to the area's Anglo street names, and made it an informal market—colourful, rich in smells and hues, disorganized—for food, spices, and garments.

Spadina itself, with its tall storefronts-and-apartments facing the grand avenue, acquired its own special sense of place, lined with delis and jobbers and haberdashers. "Spadina was Toronto Central," wrote Matt Cohen, "the cosmic spine." In the 1960s Jewish Spadina would become Chinese Spadina, as the Chinatown shifted to a new hub at the corner of Dundas. New waves of ethnic Chinese from the mainland and Vietnam took over as shopkeepers, restaurateurs, and landlords **[15/27]**.

Kensington was what the journalist Doug Saunders has termed an "arrival city," with cheap informal housing and economic opportunity. A stall in the front, a home at the back; this was the model, and it worked well. So well, that the model survived once Jews moved on into the suburbs from the 1940s through the 1970s and were succeeded by other groups. In the postwar period, new arrivals from Hungary and Ukraine and then the West Indies and Portugal—especially the Azores—brought new languages and customs. Kensington today shows signs of gentrification, worrying progressive locals, but that was the case a decade ago and not much has changed.

The fact is that Kensington's chaos—the many small buildings, laneways filled with houses [15/26], and land ownership accordingly chopped up into tiny, often interlocking slices—makes change difficult. Any coherent development vision will be hard to get off the ground.

And sometimes a grand vision can have harsh, unforeseen consequences, as Alexandra Park [15/16] demonstrates: well meant though it was, the radical remaking of the block structure and urban design had negative effects, and much of the plan is being reversed after 40 years.

Right next door, Queen Street West is undergoing its own subtler transformation. The mile-long stretch between University and Bathurst became a solid commercial street during the boom of the 1880s, and the grandiose-but-small Victorian buildings [see 15/1 through 15/12c] that sprang up in that period remained in use and largely intact. Because they housed small businesses, most remained in separate ownership and

survived a period of hardship in the mid 20th century, so that by the early 1980s this was "a forlorn stretch of rundown businesses, neglected storefronts, seedy diners and . . . second-hand and antiquarian bookstores," as a journalist put it later. The edgier art galleries were here, too, on Queen and in loft buildings just off it. And, of course, music venues, of which the Rivoli at no. 334, the venerable Horseshoe Tavern at no. 370, and the Cameron House at 408 survive.

But downtown's revival of fortunes [see Introduction] brought what we now call gentrification: loft buildings fell to development [see Area II] and rising rents on Queen brought chain retailers and a shopping-street atmosphere. In a familiar pattern, artists and galleries were pushed further and further west; the term "Queen West," in the strange linear logic of Toronto, began applying to the area past Bathurst and then west of Ossington. Today, galleries are moving on even from there, to the (for now) scruffy Dupont and Dufferin. The gracious Victoriana of Queen and Spadina might be the last lovely place in Toronto that ever belongs to the artists. But the city's great art museum endures, with its grand new wing designed by a Jewish boy from the neighbourhood [14/10], overlooking the lawn of a country estate that is now surrounded, noisily but happily, by the city.

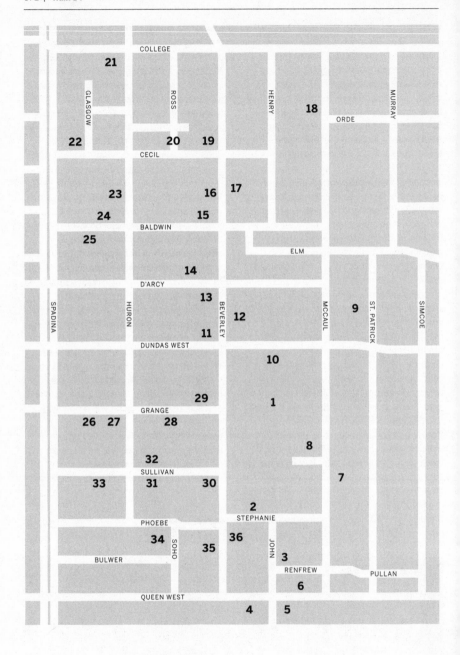

Walk 14: The Grange

1 "The Grange" (D'Arcy Boulton Jr. residence), Grange Park at John St., c. 1817; bathroom wing addition, c. 1840; library wing addition, probably Walter R. Strickland, 1885; restored, Peter John Stokes, 1973; renovated, Gehry International and ERA, 2008. One of the four oldest buildings in Toronto, The Grange was the quietly imposing residence of the pioneer Boulton family, who named it after their ancestral home in England. It was built of red brick at a time when most buildings in the town were of wood or roughcast plaster, and it took as its design the harmonious Georgian box that was standard for the English gentry.

D'Arcy Boulton Jr., who built it, later added a short wing to the west for indoor plumbing and turned three bedrooms into a music room on the second floor and two others into a breakfast parlour on the first. (When built, The Grange was far in the country and the many socially and politically important visitors often stayed overnight, ergo many bedrooms.) D'Arcy's son and next Grange occupant was William Henry Boulton, a sportsman and two-time Toronto mayor. William Henry let the house be, though he did cut up some of the 20-acre backyard for a racecourse. In 1875, a year after William Henry died, his widow married Anglo-American academic Goldwin Smith. Smith appended a sympathetic library wing, rebuilt the wooden portico in stone, and Victorianized the colonial interiors. The Smiths willed the house to the Art Museum of Toronto, which exhibited here from 1913 to 1918, when a new gallery was built adjacent **[14/10]**. The Grange was then relegated to offices until 1973, at which time it was restored and opened as a house museum; in 2008 it became principally a members' lounge for the gallery. The look-alike building to the east was the first Ontario College of Art on this site **[14/8]**. *PM/updated AB*

2 Church of St. George-the-Martyr, 203 John St., Henry Bowyer Lane, 1845; Sunday school addition, Kivas Tully, 1857; all but tower and Sunday school destroyed by fire, 1955; parish hall addition, Gerald Robinson, 1987–88; rectory, 205 John St., Gundry & Langley, 1865. Dignified Perpendicular Gothic, attested by the bell tower of the steeple that alone stands after a devastating fire of 1955. Once celebrated for its beautiful stained glass windows and soaring spire atop the bell tower—it was the second highest in Toronto—St. George's was at the centre of a thriving west-end community. Today services continue in the former Sunday school and the orphaned tower carries on as bold symbol of church and district. The complex is completed by the rectory of 1865, a polite Victorian structure of a type common throughout Ontario, and a porticoed stone parish hall and cloister. *PM*

3 Umbra showroom, 165 John St., Kohn Shnier, 2007. Sometimes beauty is skin-deep, and sometimes a beautiful skin wraps an equally alluring building. Kohn Shnier reskinned a steel-framed loft building,

1 | The Grange

3 | Umbra showroom

then wrapped it with a showy veil: 300 translucent panels of iridescent polycarbonate. (Umbra made its name working with plastics, and the architects used a similar material for the company's Scarborough headquarters **[26/15]**.) The store itself is three-dimensionally complex, with stairs-slash-display cases connecting its levels and a view-framing window at the rear. But this is first and foremost an object, a delicious one. *AB*

4 315 Queen St. W. (office building), Zeidler Roberts Partnership, 1983.

Designed by Zeidler Roberts, this was among Toronto's first Post-Modern forays, filled with self-conscious abstractions of historical forms. Typical of the era's play on past architectural modes are four-part square windows, colourful golden-hued square ceramic tiles, and a centre-stage Deco-curved bay of square glass blocks. The architects have their own offices on the mansarded top floor. *PM/AB*

5 | 299 Queen St. W.

5 Bell Media/originally Wesley Buildings, 299 Queen St. W. (factory and office building), Burke Horwood & White, 1913–15; interior altered, Quadrangle, 1986–87.

An early 20th-century contribution to the neighbourhood that seems to have strayed outside factory precincts to the south **[Walk 4]**. Built for the Methodist Book and Publishing Company (later Ryerson Press), the Wesley Buildings are garbed in Gothic fervour appropriate to the publishing company's early church association. The architects were not above a little Gothic fun as well, pinning grotesque readers and

scribes along the second-storey horizontal band. Yet the technology was entirely modern: steel framing, terracotta cladding, and plenty of windows for air and light. Interior alterations in 1986 for ChumCity were even more avant-garde, creating the world's first television facility without formal studios. The freewheeling style of Citytv and MuchMusic made the building a national TV star, and this continues though the corporate consolidation has changed the ownership. *PM/AB*

6 Originally St. Patrick's Market, 234–240 Queen St. W., G. F. W. Price, 1912–13.

In 1836, D'Arcy Boulton Jr. of The Grange donated some of his park-lot land for a St. Patrick's Market, so-called because it was in St. Patrick's Ward, one of the five saintly political precincts created when the city was incorporated in 1834. The first market structure built by the city was a simple wooden Georgian design. Its replacement was more grandly brick Italianate. And the present building, now privately owned, is all utility, enclosing market space with long brick and wooden walls and the meekest of classical motifs. *PM*

7 Village by the Grange, 49–105 McCaul St. thru to St. Patrick St. (complex of apartment houses and commercial blocks), Webb Zerafa Menkes Housden, 1980; apartment conversions, Kirkor Architects, 1998.

A homely mega-scale development of the 1970s, which in the progressive climate of the era retained a reasonable height and urban porosity. (Its new neighbours on St. Patrick Street will be vastly higher.) The "village" offers a surprising mix of units, from one-bedrooms to "houses" in an elevated courtyard. What's more, it has proven itself uncommonly able to adapt. In the 1990s developers converted part of the ground-level shopping mall to condo apartments, one of the oddest such conversions in Toronto's history; nearby, forlorn mid-block retail space is serving well as extensions of the OCADU campus. If, as Jane Jacobs said, new ideas must use old buildings, perhaps 35 years is old enough. *AB*

8 OCAD University/originally Ontario College of Art, 100 McCaul St., Horwood & White, 1926; addition, Govan Ferguson Lindsay, 1957–61; altered, Moffat Moffat & Kinoshita, 1980–81; renovations and addition, OCAD Sharp Centre for Design, Alsop Architects with Robbie/Young + Wright, 2004. Addition, Morphosis with Teeple Architect and Two Row Architect, ongoing. The Ontario College of Art began on this site in 1913, using part of the second floor of The Grange **[14/1]** until its own new premises were constructed in complementary Georgian Revival. That two-storey red-brick structure now sits behind the street-facing addition of 1957–61. That tentatively Modernist façade hides spaces created inside by Moffat Moffat & Kinoshita in 1980–81; the whole volume is now subject to a planned major revamp led by Morphosis **[see 8/23]**.

The highlight is up high: the Sharp Centre, a flying box 88 feet off the ground. Few buildings have dominated Toronto's cultural conversation like this one, which in the early 2000s became an instant showpiece not just for its ambitious institution but for the city. Alsop's unforgettable design creates a volume for studio and gathering space; wraps it in a pixellated skin of aluminum; then hoists it all up on 12 diagonal struts of oil pipeline, painted in Crayola-bold hues. (The black elevator core does a lot of the heavy lifting.) A public square beneath, which will one day soon connect to Grange Park, is a bonus of all this structural drama. *PM/AB*

8 | Ontario College of Art

9 Our Lady of Mt. Carmel/originally St. Patrick's Church, 196 St. Patrick St., Gundry & Langley, 1869–70. Redemptorist Fathers residence, 141 McCaul St., 1886. St. Patrick's Church, 131 McCaul St., Arthur W. Holmes, 1905–08. Named after the fifth-century cleric who carried Christianity to Ireland and only coincidentally after the political ward in which it was located, St. Patrick's was among the first Roman Catholic churches in Toronto. A small frame chapel stood on the site as early as 1860; when this burned in 1864, the amiable French Gothic house of worship we see today on St. Patrick Street was put up, followed by a schoolhouse to the north and the stolid Gothic priests' residence fronting on McCaul Street.

The larger St. Patrick's was erected in 1908 in a placid Romanesque Revival of rather pasty stone, partly reclaimed by the vigorous arcaded portal and saintly niche at the top. *PM*

Dundas Street West between McCaul and Beverley was cut through The Grange's back gardens in 1877 when the last acres from the estate were sold off. Among the first houses to go up in 1878 were paraphrases of the Second Empire mansions on adjoining Beverley Street. A number of 1870s houses in the centre of the block are remnants of Toronto Bay-n-Gable with fine sawn woodwork enlivening the gables. The most ambitious house is no. 344–346, a tall 1896 Queen Anne boasting lavish wooden detail and terracotta panels.

10 Art Gallery of Ontario, 317 Dundas St. W., Darling & Pearson, 1918; additions, Darling & Pearson, 1926, 1935; altered with additions, Parkin Partnership, Architects and Planners, 1974 and 1977; altered with additions, Barton Myers Associates, 1993; altered and expanded, Gehry International and ERA, 2008. Weston Family Learning Centre, Hariri Pontarini, 2010. Hands-on Centre, 3rd Uncle, 2010. Founded in 1900 as one of the city's first cultural institutions, the Art Museum of Toronto made its first home in the Grange mansion **[14/1]**. In 1918, it moved into new galleries constructed in an austere Renaissance Revival style adjacent to the Georgian house. Enlarged in 1926 and again in 1935, this building, with its dignified, classically detailed Walker Court, served the city for close to 50 years.

In 1966, with provincial support and renamed the Art Gallery of Ontario, the institution turned to thoughts of expansion. The project was given definite shape four years later when Henry Moore was persuaded to donate a major collection of his work. This work determined much of the interior design of the new building, along with a neighbourly desire to maintain a low scale by situating many facilities below grade. The same impulse undoubtedly dictated much of Barton Myers's 1993 expansion plans, which added a new Dundas façade of brick and sandstone topped with a symbolic tower and pyramid.

The gallery's most recent and most famous renovation project came just 15 years later. The Pritzker Prize–winning Gehry, who grew up nearby **[14/36]**, oversaw a thorough reshuffling of the building capped by the glass-and-timber Galleria Italia along Dundas—one of Toronto's great public rooms. Some observers were disappointed not to see an icon like Gehry's world-changing Bilbao; instead the AGO became a bigger, more rational, and more easily navigable building that retains moments of magic, such as the lobby's winding ramp and the corkscrew stair, which offers some of Toronto's best views before landing, dramatically, above Walker Court. It also embodies Gehry's resistance to the neutral

white-box gallery; check out the varied spaces, short and tall, on the new top floors, and look for Douglas fir plywood and veneers, a favourite material of Gehry's from the experimental 1970s, in both rough and refined guises. *PM/AB*

11 Italian Consulate/originally "Chudleigh" (George Beardmore residence), 136 Beverley St., 1872; additions, Eden Smith, 1890, 1900, 1901. The first of the Beverley Street mansions and still the most impressive house on the street, this is a bold asymmetric design accentuated by picturesque off-centre tower with oval picture-frame windows. Beardmore was a leather merchant with an equally striking warehouse on Front Street **[1/21c]**. No. 136 owes its distinction in part to its size—it was enlarged several times by Beardmore's son, who joined old stables to the house; and to its spacious grounds ringed by an imposing stone, brick, and iron fence. In the 1930s, the house became the Italian consulate; it was confiscated during World War II; given back in 1958 to become an Italian language centre; and now, spruced up, serves again as consulate. *PM*

12 Beverley Mansions: 133–135 Beverley St. (double house), 1877; 137–139 Beverley St. (double house), 1876–77; 141 Beverley St. (detached house), 1877; 145–147 Beverley St. (double house), 1878. The name seems a bit pretentious for this block renovated by the city's non-profit housing corporation as a 58-unit project, but in the 1870s these houses would have been thought quite grand indeed, if only for their expansive garden settings. No. 145–147 also boasts elegant one-storey mansarded kitchen pavilions to either side instead of more common rear service wings. *PM*

13 Originally John Cawthra house, 152 Beverley St., 1874; additions, Sproatt & Rolph, c. 1920; rehabilitated with additions, 1985–86. Subdued Second Empire for a third-generation scion of the millionaire Cawthra family (grandfather Cawthra had come to Canada from Scotland in 1803 as an apothecary merchant and had gone on to

10 | Art Gallery of Ontario

become the principal importer of dry goods in the province). This house, restored after a damaging fire in 1984, now serves as community housing. *PM/updated AB*

14 84–100 D'Arcy St. (nine-house row), Frederick H. Herbert, 1893. Flamboyant anarchy and undeniably the city's most original row. During the 1890s and the height of the Queen Anne style in Toronto, the architectural rule was individuality and visual excitement. Insurrection against rectangular sameness was especially tested in a long row like this, but the ever-inventive Herbert met the challenge, creating an impression of nine distinct houses, each with its own peculiar bit of business. *PM*

15 Originally "Lambton Lodge" (George Brown residence), 186 Beverley St., William Irving with Edward F. Hutchins, 1875–76; restored, 1987–88. A formal red-brick mansard-roof house with powerful carved-stone portico and window surrounds, built for George Brown, founder of *The Globe* newspaper. Brown was also a Father of Confederation, having served in the United Provinces parliament from 1851 to 1865. In 1880, the high-principled radical was shot by a disgruntled *Globe* employee; the wound became gangrenous and he died in this house six weeks later. Used as a soldiers' rehabilitation centre by the Canadian National Institute for the Blind from 1919 to 1956, the place is now the property of the Ontario Heritage Foundation, which uses George Brown House for conference and office space. *PM*

15 | George Brown House

16 196 Beverley St. (detached house), possibly George M. Miller, 1889. 198 Beverley St. (detached house), possibly George M. Miller, 1889; altered, David B. Dick, 1894. 200 Beverley St. (detached house), possibly George M. Miller, 1888. Designed with true distinction (if slightly ill-maintained), nos. 196 and 198 are outstanding examples of Richardsonian Romanesque style, with carved and moulded terracotta ornament among the most original in the city. The powerful stonework and brickwork are enough to make one feel at once the weight and depth of walls and dark openings. They were built by James T. McCabe, also responsible for no. 200 in a somewhat less commanding idiom. We know Miller designed other, similar houses for this contractor, and it is conceivable he was the architect here too. *PM/updated AB*

17 | Beverley Place

17 Beverley Place, Baldwin to Cecil St., Beverley to Henry St. (units of housing and nine rehabilitated houses), A.J. Diamond & Barton Myers (completed by A.J. Diamond & Partners), 1978. Another seminal infill project from Diamond & Myers **[see 11/4a]** combining restored houses with hidden density. In the new building to the east, two sets of units—duplexes on the basement and ground levels, and floor-through apartments on the third—each with their own front doors, bring life and community outdoors; likewise the mid-block yards and recreation area, which have many overlooks and remain well used. The project grew out of a plan by Ontario Hydro to level the block for a transformer station; it's still known to some Torontonians as the Hydro Block, and represents a grand victory for progressive activism and architects closely allied with it. *AB*

18 Ronald McDonald House (short-term family housing), 240 McCaul St., Montgomery Sisam, 2011. This long, low, elegant building houses 81 children and their families during treatment at the nearby Hospital for Sick Children. Snaking around a series of courtyards, it borrows its red brick and (more or less) its domestic scale from adjacent Henry Street. *AB*

19 Polish Combatants' Hall, 206 Beverley St., Wieslaw Wodkiewicz, 1973. Its corduroy concrete façades standing in radical contrast to its Second Empire neighbours [14/20a], this meeting hall channels the Brutalism that was the dominant style of Canadian cultural buildings at mid century. (That category arguably includes Parkin's 1974 and 1977 additions to the Art Gallery of Ontario [14/10] down the block.) Wodkiewicz was a member of this veterans' group, based here in an older building since 1947, and his scheme, with its concealed parking and modest massing, is surprisingly sensitive in its own way. *AB*

20a 20–22, 24–26, 28–30 Cecil St. (three double houses), 1881; demolished no. 24–26 rebuilt, Peter Turner, 1980–81. Three trim Second Empire double houses of very congenial proportions attractively situated on generous-sized lots. Originally three more such houses ran to Huron Street, making these two blocks among the few in Toronto to approximate the expansive siting typical of American middle-class suburbs in this period. A close look at no. 24–26 reveals that it is a rebuilt copy of its neighbours, instructive for what the 1980s included and what it omitted of an 1880s house. *PM*

20b 37, 39, 41, 43, 45 Cecil St. (five detached houses), 1886. A quintet of speculatively built houses in decorative Queen Anne style making the most of irregular massing, rooflines, colours, textures, and elaborate *japonesque* woodwork, best preserved is no. 45. *PM*

21 Lillian H. Smith Branch Library, 239 College St., Phillip H. Carter, 1995. This late and very good example of Post-Modernism houses a library branch with a strong children's collection. The chunky massing and large windows make it hard to read the scale—it resembles a Renaissance Revival house blown up to four times its natural size, which is fitting for a building stocked with fairy tales. With its typically Postmodern grab bag of stylistic references, it's hard not to like: How many Toronto buildings are guarded by pairs of bronze griffins? *AB*

22 Cecil Community Centre/originally Church of Christ/formerly Cecil Street Synagogue, 58 Cecil St., Knox & Elliot, 1890; remodelled, 1922; remodelled, Matsui Baer & Vanstone, c. 1978. Built of sturdy brick and stone in Romanesque Revival, the original Church of Christ structure as designed by Knox & Elliot was dominated by an angled corner tower dramatically decorated with conical top and circular turret buttresses. In 1922, the building was bought by the Congregation Anshei Ostrovtze (Men of Ostrovtze) and became known as Cecil Street Synagogue. Several changes were made, including replacement of the Church of Christ's tower with one more in keeping with synagogue design **[see 13/10]**. The synagogue moved away in 1956 and after years of desultory use the building was skilfully altered to serve as a community centre. *PM*

23 122 Huron St. (detached house), 1889. 124–126 Huron St. (double house), 1889. Queen Anne again, this time with character-istic tile-hung gables and walls the outstand-ing feature. The Queen Anne style enjoyed a long vogue in Toronto. That singularly American form, the Shingle Style, succeeded Queen Anne in the United States, but Toronto's fire regulations—which outlawed wooden shingles unless backed by brick—forestalled any tile-less tangents here. *PM*

24 110–112 Baldwin St. (double house), 1890–91. A severe brick double house with one of the flossiest wooden porches in town—woodturning raised to art. *PM*

25a 123–125 Baldwin St. (double house), 1873. Like many in the area, this double house boasted expensive brick only on the front façade; the sides and rear were roughcast. The builder was not sparing in other niceties, however: vermiculated keystones and tall crest-like wooden finials. *PM*

25b Originally Consolidated Plate Glass Co. Ltd., 241 Spadina Ave. (factory), William Steele & Sons Co., 1910; altered, 1982. This small five-storey factory is something to feast your eyes on, one of the city's most appealing creations. There is a rousing firm base with lovely iron grillwork at the entrance, a simple smooth shaft, and most wonderful elaborate cornice, all the more extraordinary for having been done in moulded and carved warm red brick and terracotta. These were materials of the picturesque, but the idiom here is clearly classical. This building is also a lesson in sympathetic alteration: stores have been slipped into the ground floor, but without cutting big jarring windows in the façade, thereby amending hardly at all Spadina Avenue's most stunning architectural essay. *PM*

26 Originally George M. Evans house, 69 Grange Ave., 1871. One of the finest early houses left in the area and a good demonstration of how eclectic Toronto architecture could be. No. 69 handily mixes hipped roof, tall end chimneys, and brick quoins from Georgian ancestors with Italianate round-arched window heads and projecting bays. Evans, a popular Toronto lawyer and five-time alderman, lived here for 20 years until his death in 1891. *PM*

27 Grange Triple Double (multifamily house), 51 Grange Ave., Williamson Chong, 2015. Toronto's Victorian and Edwardian housing stock has always adapted into different unit configurations. This ambitious multifamily building aims for more of the same flexibility. A single-family house hugs the courtyard and steps up three levels, with a semi-autonomous grandparents' suite within; separate rental units can be carved out of the first floor and basement. Artfully placed

27 | Grange Triple Double

windows and roof gardens allow these and many more possibilities. *AB*

28a 27–29 Grange Ave. (double house), 1885. Plastic, energetic Second Empire with not a few standout flourishes: convex curved mansard, bowed bays with incised details, bold brackets, and busy dentil moulding. *PM/updated AB*

28b 13–17 Grange Ave. (triple house), 1886. 19–21 Grange Ave. (double house), 1886. 23–25 Grange Ave. (double house), 1885. Toronto's trademark Bay-n-Gable form is given idiosyncratic appeal on this string of houses by carved and knobbed wooden "jaws" angling the gables. The speculative developer, Alexander Mitchell, was a carpenter by trade. *PM*

29 Pachter House, 22 Grange Ave., Teeple Architects, 2005. In the 1970s, the artist Charles Pachter returned to the neighbour-hood where his grandparents had once lived; he remains there, now at this highly sculptural house/studio/gallery that does a lot, formally, within a long-and-skinny Toronto site. Transparent front façades reveal the house's public functions. *AB*

30 Toronto Chinese Baptist Church/ originally Beverley Street Baptist Church, 70 Beverley St., Langley & Burke, 1886; Sunday school hall, 1880. A neat, spiky composition with slender piers, narrow windows, and attenuated brick corbel table bringing zesty energy to this Baptist bastion. Wealthy merchant William McMaster, a member of illustrious Jarvis Street Baptist [12/8a], donated land and money for this mission church, which counted Goldwin Smith of The Grange as an early member. The egalitarian Smith probably liked the idea that there were no pews to buy—Beverley Street Baptists sat on folding opera chairs.

In tandem with ethnic changes in the neighbourhood, the church has accommodated English, Swedish, German, Czechoslovakian, Hungarian, Finnish, Estonian, Russian, and Ukrainian congregations. At one time in the 1960s, there were four different congregations holding services in four languages. *PM*

31 Originally Rubberset Co. Ltd./formerly RCMP building, 11 Sullivan St., 1919; remodelled as apartment house, Annau Associates, 1983. About all that's left of the turn-of-the-century factory is the bold cast-stone classical entry, looking equally important and formal today as frontispiece for a 31-unit city-assisted housing project. *PM*

32 24–26, 28–30, 32–34 Sullivan St. (three double houses), 1886. These likeable ditties are from the hand of C.R.S. Dinnick, a dean of moderate-priced, standard-plan houses in Toronto. *PM*

33 53–83 Sullivan St. (16-house row), 1880–81. Even though individual units in this grand row have undergone idiosyncratic remodelling over the years, the effect is still one of dignified cohesion. Following the Second Empire style axiom of classical symmetry, the row is arranged about a

33 | 53–83 Sullivan St.

centre pavilion with identical wings to the sides, except that on the east sits a single, useful grocery store instead of a residence. Margaret Atwood and Graeme Gibson lived at no. 73 for five years in the 1980s, when neighbours included Barry Callaghan. *PM/ updated AB*

34 Soho Square, Soho and Phoebe Sts. (complex of 14-, ten-, and six-house rows), Howard M. Greenspan, 1982–83. 14–24 Soho St. (six-house row), 1888. In the late 1970s in Toronto, it became chic to live in a Victorian house. Economics being what they are, developers started building new Victorian houses—with garages. Few are as good as these red-brick numbers, whose inspiration can be seen a few doors south at 14–24 Soho Street. *PM*

35 The Phoebe on Queen (condominium apartments), 18 Beverley St. and 11–25 Soho St., Burka Architects with Wayne Swadron and Ferris & Associates (landscape architects), 2002. One project, three buildings, three quasi-historical dialects—the most successful the warehousey red brick to the southwest. The large, private green space at the centre is a rarity in the long-and-skinny logic of Toronto lots. *AB*

36 12 Degrees Condos, 25 Beverley St., CORE Architects, 2015. An attempt at formal novelty in the budget-crunched world of condo development, this twisted Rubik's cube is halfway successful—but the artful glassy mass lands inexplicably in a grey stone cladding worthy of the Flintstones. The house that once stood at 15 Beverley was long home to Sam and Lillian Caplan; their grandson, the future Frank Gehry, would remember playing with live carp in the bathtub as inspiration for the curves of his late career. *AB*

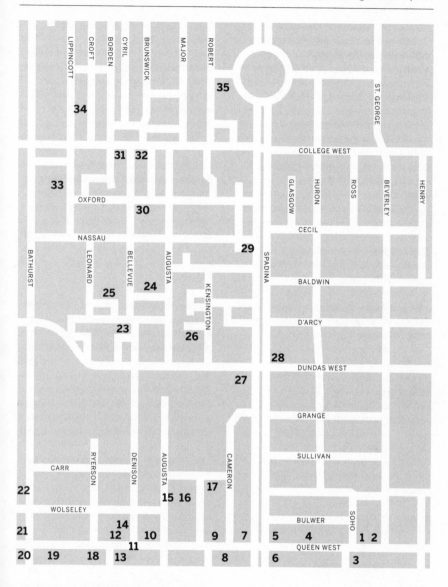

Walk 15: Queen Street West and Kensington Market

Queen Street West began in the early 19th century as a street of modest houses interspersed with small frame and roughcast shops. Later, these first buildings were replaced with more distinguished brick structures, at most four storeys high. Amazingly, most of these commercial blocks are still with us, and protected by a Heritage Conservation District. Above the messy storefronts, the legacy of Victorian ornament and invention is usually intact on floors above—look up.

1 Black Bull Tavern, 298 Queen St. W., c. 1833; rear additions and alterations, 1886, 1889; altered, c. 1910. An inn has stood on this site almost since York began and many an early traveller must have stopped the night at this unassuming roughcast structure before the last leg of the journey into town. By the 1880s, the town had spread to the tavern, but business was good and the proprietor built bold brick extensions to the rear and added a Second Empire mansard roof to the original two-storey front. (Hotels had discovered that a mansard was an easy and inexpensive way to create more accommodations, and across North America the style survived for these buildings long after it had otherwise been abandoned.) Brick cladding and wooden pilasters were added to the front in the 1910s. *PM*

2 Originally Mara's Groceries and Liquors, 280 Queen St. W. (commercial block), 1881. Making the most of this unusual "corner" site, no. 280 is a grand plastic composition of ornamental brick piers, bracketed cornice, mansard roof, and dormer windows. Mara's Groceries and Liquors was the first to display its wares behind the plate-glass windows. The landlord was B. Homer Dixon, consul-general of the Netherlands in Canada and brother of Mrs. William Henry Boulton of The Grange, the former owner of this choice piece of real estate. *PM*

2 | 280 Queen St. W.

3 371–373 Queen St. W. (two-unit commercial block), 1890. Two neat shopfronts with more 19th-century trim in place than most, including some nice stained glass. No. 373 began as Bird's Provisions in 1890, incorporating a branch post office; in the 1980s, Peter Pan Restaurant here pioneered the gentrification of the strip. *PM/ updated AB*

4a 328–330 Queen St. W. (two-unit commercial block), James Avon Smith, 1864. A three-storey brick building whose early date is affirmed by dignified windows with stone lintels and sills, gently sloping roof with dormers, tall end chimneys, and yellow brick under the paint. The druggist and the milliner who first had the shops lived upstairs. *PM*

4b The Noble Block, 342–354 Queen St. W. (seven-unit commercial block), Smith & Gemmell, 1888. 356–356A Queen St. W. (two-unit commercial block), c. 1895. A dazzling Victorian package ornamented with corbelled brick, Romanesque arches, classical keystones, and irrepressible oriel windows, among other flourishes. Mrs. Emma Noble, widow, owned six units, and Mrs. Mary Ann Harvard, widow, held the last unit plus the property to the west. The widows must have planned a symmetrical nine-unit block, but Widow Harvard dropped out and the new owner didn't go along with the scheme, ergo the different look to no. 356 put up some time later. The first tenants purveyed, east to west: furniture, musical instruments, jewellery, barbering, men's clothes, tailoring, fruits, and drugs. *PM*

4b | The Noble Block

5 Canadian Imperial Bank of Commerce/ originally Bank of Hamilton, 378 Queen St. W., George W. Gouinlock, 1902–03. Overbearing blocked rustication and exclamation-point stone keystones for a turn-of-the-century office/bank combo. Such decorative rhetoric was often marshalled by banks to convey their corporate message of wealth and permanence. *PM*

6 Originally Devaney Bros. Dry Goods, 441–443 Queen St. W. (commercial block), Langley & Burke, 1886. In the 1880s, this structure was illustrated in all the Canadian periodicals, acclaimed for its lush Victorian dome that still draws attention on this corner. Classical window heads and cornice were equally splendid. A delicious building. *PM*

7 Originally Cockburn Building, 388–396 Queen St. W. (five-unit commercial block), William G. Storm, 1881–84. A workmanlike quintet with cleaned no. 388 giving a hint of the original zest; the other units are too flattened by paint or grime. The mansard roof was mostly for show here, being too shallow and sloping to make a useful attic storey. First tenants were a druggist, bootmaker, provisioner, photographer, and grocer. The owner listed himself in assessment rolls as a "professor." *PM*

8 489–491 Queen St. W. (two-unit commercial block), 1890. 493–495 Queen St. W. (two units of original four-unit commercial block), 1889. Semicircular Romanesque Revival parading a handsome arcaded fourth storey and arched oriel windows. Trophy panels at the third storey allegorize art and science, with lyres, compasses, gears, violins, and the like trying to lend a touch of class to original emporia: a billiard hall, barber shop, grocery, tailoring establishment, furniture store, and undertaking parlour. *PM*

9 Originally Richie & Stratton Block, 440–450 Queen St. W. (six-unit commercial block), William Irving, 1876. An early mansard-roof composition featuring elaborate brackets at the eaves and classically distinguished open-pediment dormers. *PM*

10 472–474 Queen St. W. (two-unit commercial block), Francis R. Heakes, 1893. A tall, crisp commercial block embroidered with elegant Classical Revival ornament and delicate angled oriel windows. Two ladies first rented the shops: Mrs. Booth, millinery; and Mrs. Bachrack, dry goods. *PM*

11 484 Queen St. W. (commercial block), 1879. An early, big commercial block, put up at a time when most of its neighbours would have been smaller and less formal. Deeply modelled pedimented window heads draw from the conservative Renaissance Revival, a refined rectangular-windowed style rare in Toronto. The owner-occupant George J. St. Leger first sold books here, adding shoes to the line the following year. Two years later, the shoes had completely replaced the books. *PM*

12a 486–492 Queen St. W. (four-unit commercial block), 1880. Another unusually large commercial block for this date and district, displaying careful concern for distinguished detail. Note for example the incised stone capitals at the impost of the arcaded third storey. *PM*

12b Originally second Cockburn Building, 500–504 Queen St. W. (three-unit commercial block), William G. Storm, 1884. A rousing Victorian trio decked out in enormous mansard, bursts of decorated dormers, and heroic cresting, designed by Storm for the same client as nos. 388-396. The West Branch of the Ontario Bank did business at no. 500 for a time. *PM*

12c Originally Crocker's Block, 506–514 Queen St. W. (five-unit commercial block), William Stewart, 1874–75. One of the first commercial blocks in Toronto to essay a Second Empire mansard roof, though Mr. Crocker must not have thought the new style entirely adequate for letting in light to the attic storey. Why else the row of glazed lunettes winking underneath? *PM*

12c | 506–514 Queen St. W.

13 Originally Bank of Montreal, 577 Queen St. W., Frederick H. Herbert, 1899. A splendidly enduring little corner bank, infused with robust details and crisp pressed brickwork and terracotta. *PM*

14 St. Stanislaus Roman Catholic Church/originally West Presbyterian Church, 12 Denison Ave., Gordon & Helliwell, 1879–80. Presbyterian churches often seem overly reticent, but this monochromatic broad and smooth Gothic/Romanesque design is saved by its octagonal spire, a vigorous statement on this corner and in the neighbourhood. This was the west end's second Presbyterian church on this site, serving until 1911 when demographic changes dictated a Polish Roman Catholic congregation. *PM*

15 St. Felix Centre/originally Edward Leadlay house, 25 Augusta Ave., 1876. One of the most Victorian of Toronto's Victorian houses, with all the romantic bric-a-brac picturesquely in place: bonnet dormers, canopied windows, bracketed eaves, filigreed veranda, and gabled tower. Leadlay's was the single house of this size and grandeur built in the neighbourhood. A dealer in "Wools, Hides, Skins & Tallow" with

15 | St. Felix Centre

a warehouse on Front Street **[1/18a]**, he originally had his "sheepskin pulling" factory on this site. The building later became Salvation Army housing, then a convent, and now serves as transitional housing. Its façade has been maintained with remarkable care. *PM/updated AB*

16 Alexandra Park, Queen to Dundas St., Augusta to Cameron St. (apartments and row houses), Jerome Markson with Webb Zerafa Menkes and Klein & Sears, 1967–69. Revitalization plan, Urban Strategies (urban design), 2011. Another of Toronto's few neighbourhood-clearance projects of the urban-renewal era, this came a decade after Regent Park South **[10/30]**; more modest in scale, it shares the same, failed urban-design ideas. It breaks the street grid in favour of walled, intimate pedestrian lanes, which allowed neighbours to mix and their kids to play, free of cars. ("It's not *de rigueur* now," Markson told the *Globe and Mail* in 2003, "but we separated

16 | Alexandra Park townhouses, 1967–69

people and cars. . . . We hated cars.") This worked, in part—residents formed a strong community here, and indeed took over management of the site as a co-op in the 1990s. Yet as at many similiar developments in Toronto and in the United States, the lack of transparency and the vague ownership of shared spaces allowed street crime to flourish. The "revitalization" will retain the apartment buildings and many townhouses, which are handsomely and efficiently designed, while restoring most of the missing streets. *AB*

17 Alexandra Park townhouses, 41–97 Vanauley St. and 1–25 Paul Lane Gardens, LGA, 2016. SQ2 (condo apartments), 20 Cameron St., Teeple Architects, ongoing. Together with the neighbours **[15/16]**, these new additions provide a stark display in how much has changed in urban design and planning over 50 years. The new houses provide a continuous streetwall and "eyes on the street," as Jane Jacobs put it, much like their 19th-century predecessors across the city. Yet the detailing is firmly Modernist and very crisp—the hints of colour and fine, subtle brick ornament have survived community housing's low budgets and demands for total durability. Most importantly, each resident family enjoys three or four bedrooms in well-designed, well-lit interiors, plus their own (small but private) backyard. The 14-storey condo behind the houses shares their visual language, and promises to be one of the most attractive such buildings of its time. *AB*

17 | Alexandra Park townhouses, 2016

18 Queen Portland Centre (shopping centre and residences), 589 Queen St. W., Turner Fleischer with Fournier Gersovitz Moss, 2011. A condo tower and shopping mall, attempting half-heartedly to conceal itself at the low 19th-century scale of Queen West. The streetwall is the right height, but everything else is wrong: the profusion of materials (those odd, extra-large bricks) and the string courses that almost, but don't quite, rhyme with anything on the block. What are those odd bay windows doing here? Serving the needs of a suburban-scaled grocery store, that's what. The back end of this complex, wrapped in garish blue-glass snakeskin, is best avoided completely. *AB*

18 | Queen Portland Centre

19 Burroughes Building, 639 Queen St. W., Herbert George Paull, 1906–09; restored, 2007. Quite a radical building for its time, when the high-rise department store was growing in popularity. The F.C. Burroughes Furniture Co. constructed this seven-storey edifice just as Simpson's was adding to its own complex **[5/6]** at Yonge and Queen. Paull's façade is much more stripped-down than Burke Horwood & White's on Queen, a confident rendering of Louis Sullivan's innovations in Chicago. *AB*

20 Originally Occident Hall, 651 Queen St. W., McCaw & Lennox, 1878. This Second Empire confection began life as a Masonic hall, and was an early project by Lennox in his brief partnership with William Frederick McCaw. It originally had a third floor and a mansard roof, as the style demanded; these disappeared around 1950 when the building became the Holiday Tavern; later, as an important music venue called the Big Bop, it was painted bright purple. The current modern-on-the-inside restoration shows how it should be done. *AB*

21 West Neighbourhood House, 588 Queen St. W., Darling & Pearson, 1901; renovation, Levitt Goodman, 1996. Darling & Pearson conjured some busy but likeable Classical Revival for this Bank of Commerce branch, which included basement vaults and a top-floor apartment for the branch's manager. Levitt Goodman's renovation converted the structure into a drop-in centre and parking spaces into a courtyard. *AB*

22 Origami Lofts (condominium apartments), 202 Bathurst St., Teeple Architects, 2016. Toronto has never had many small apartment buildings, and the post-2000 development boom has grown increasingly tall ones. This is a counterpoint, just 21 units over seven storeys with civil setbacks—and its small developer, Symmetry, has managed, despite the economic challenges of working at this scale, to achieve interesting formal and material effects. *AB*

Kensington Market is, as it has been for a century, the least-planned place in downtown Toronto—messy and gloriously so. The houses built here around 1900 have remained relatively affordable and highly adaptable; a laissez-faire attitude from city inspectors and do-it-yourself modifications have helped keep the place welcoming to newcomers and fertile for commerce.

23 Originally Charles R. Peterkin house, 29 Wales Ave., 1884. One of the Denisons' outbuildings stood on this site before the family began to parcel out their land for development. Peterkin, a fledgling lumber dealer, moved in in 1876, and eight years later built this stout house of his own. The bold wooden turnings of the porch bespeak his calling. In the 1920s the house belonged to a Kiever congregation member named Mr. Silverman, and hosted services while the synagogue **[15/24]** was being built. *PM/AB*

24 Kiever Synagogue, 28 Denison Square, Benjamin Swartz, 1927; restoration, Martin Mendelow, 1975. The currents of shifting population in this neighbourhood are especially vivid here. Where once dominated a grand manor of the pioneer Denison family, the vista up Denison Street is now commanded by the exotic synagogue of Congregation Rodfei Sholom Anshei Kiev. The building's pastel and white trim colours, geometric stained glass, and Byzantine stair towers recall a time when there were as many as 30 synagogues in the area, each used by a homogeneous group from a particular part of Europe.

Today Kiever Synagogue itself is an anachronism, almost the last of its kind in this quarter. It was saved from adaptive use by the Ontario Jewish Archives Committee, which has beautifully restored it. *PM*

25 Stinson House (detached house), 5 Leonard Pl., Jeffery Stinson, 1989. The very first of the architect-built laneway houses downtown, this preceded Shim-Sutcliffe's **[26/12b]** by several years. Architect and academic Stinson bought a 14-by-15-yard lot, containing garages for Perlmutar's Bakery, in the lee of Toronto Western Hospital. He self-built a 2,200-square-foot house, "a really elegant barn," he wrote, of concrete block and galvanized metal. It shows the potential of such sites, and their attendant real-estate value: despite its DIY origins, it sold for nearly one million dollars after Stinson's death in 2008. *AB*

26 Gradient House (detached house), 1 Fitzroy Terrace, Superkul, 2012. Fitzroy Terrace, a pocket of laneway houses that dates to the 1880s, gets a fresh addition. A couple inspired by the wild creativity of Japanese urban houses commissioned this house in place of a burned-out cottage, and the product—with a pitched roof, radically rectilinear façade and crisp grey cement-board skin—slides into the block quietly and elegantly. *AB*

27 Dragon City Mall, 280 Spadina Ave., Michael K. Wong, Architects, 1987. The biggest thing to happen on Spadina in a generation, this indoor shopping mall was the work of Shiu Pong Group, a family development company with roots in Hong Kong. (They would have great success with similar malls in Markham.) The design by Wong is choppy Post-Modern—the loft-like front façade doesn't seem to be speaking with the glassy corner stair. But the interior, with multiple levels of small businesses largely run by ethnic-Chinese entrepreneurs, reveals a distinct take on a North American building type: the market in a mall. *AB*

28 Originally Standard Theatre, 285 Spadina Ave., J.M. Jeffrey with Benjamin Brown, 1922; altered later; interior alterations, c. 1970, Mandel Sprachman. The secular heart of 1920s and 1930s Jewish Spadina, the Standard opened as a venue for Yiddish live theatre, including for a time its own stock company. (The Scottish-born Jeffrey designed several movie houses in Toronto, and later worked with the firm of Schultze & Weaver on the Los Angeles Biltmore Hotel and grand New York hotels including the Waldorf Astoria.) The 1,500-seat auditorium also hosted labour rallies, boxing matches, and other expressions of secular Jewish life before it became a movie house in 1934; it later evolved into the Victory Burlesque and a Chinese-language theatre, undergoing various renovations. Today, the upper floors lie empty, and the façade is ragged and marquee-less, but otherwise in its 1930s state. *AB*

29 | Kensington Market Lofts

29 Kensington Market Lofts (condominium apartments)/incorporates Houston Public School, 21 Nassau St., 1924 and Provincial Institute of Trades, 160 Baldwin St., c. 1957; residential conversion by R.E. Barnett with Paul Oberst and Kohn Shnier, 1999. This complex, like much of Kensington, has a history of renovations and reuse: the brick volume to the northeast was an elementary school, later joined by two larger, terracotta-clad buildings when the complex became a trade school—the precursor to George Brown College [1/7]. The ensemble was converted by the nascent Context Development [20/24, 4/14] into grand, quirky, high-ceilinged apartments, among the few real lofts in the city. *AB*

30 91 Oxford St. (offices), William John Carmichael, 1907; converted to offices, 2016. Overdressed for Kensington, this is a sturdy box in Renaissance Revival style. Bell Canada chief architect Carmichael designed it, as a switching centre, with Beaux Arts symmetry and rigour. Bell moved out in the 1930s and the building survived 75 years in other industrial uses, including half a century of plastics manufacturing, before the long-time owners converted it to office space. *AB*

31 Firehall No. 8, 132 Bellevue Ave., 1877–78; addition Mark Hall, 1899; rebuilt after fire, 1973–74. The tall belvedere-capped towers of the city's fire stations, rising resolutely like medieval lookouts, must have been very reassuring to the fire-plagued Victorian city. One of the most evocative of these early fire houses is No. 8, a working station completely rebuilt in 1974—after a fire! (The station was empty and in the course of restoration at the time.) *PM*

32 St. Stephen-in-the-Fields Anglican Church, 103 Bellevue Ave., Thomas Fuller, 1858; rebuilt after fire, Gundry & Langley, 1865; transept additions, Richard C. Windeyer, 1878; parish house addition, and alterations, William A. Langton, 1890.
The simplest and most primitive of revived medieval styles, Early English Gothic was recommended by the Ecclesiological Society for remote parish churches, and that's exactly what St. Stephen's was in 1858. But this is not just any country church. Its architect was soon to win the competition for the Houses of Parliament in Ottawa, and this sophisticated composition of sweeping roof and broad brick front broken only by a slim open belfry attests to his talent. (The gabled dormers were not part of the original plan.) In 1926 the church became notewor-thy as the "Radio Church," from whence came the first regular religious broadcasting in Canada. *PM*

32 | St. Stephen-in-the-Fields Church

33 56 Lippincott (townhouses), Netkin Architect, 2010. These three-and-a-half-storey townhouses have been slipped in sideways to a long lot, with an unusual arrangement: parking spaces at ground level and elevated, hedged courtyards a few steps up. The front (that is, side) façade is unfriendly, but this is not a bad urban-design tradeoff. *AB*

34 54 Croft St. (detached house), Kohn Shnier, 2004. Croft is an extension of Kensington's loose urbanism: it feels like a lane but has the infrastructure and legal status of a street. Houses have been here for a long time, as you can see up the block at nos. 92–96. This fine one, replacing an older occupant, uses its site masterfully, putting the public rooms upstairs to enjoy surprising long views. *AB*

34 | 54 Croft St.

35 Lord Lansdowne Public School, 33 Robert St., Toronto Board of Education (design architect Peter Pennington), 1961. In the boom years of the 1960s, the Toronto Board of Education's own architects designed schools that embodied the ambition of public education in the era. None more so than this, which combines a nine-sided pavilion with a serrated roof and outward-leaning steel columns. Materials are equally cheerful: three tones of brick, intensely coloured spandrel panels and a rainbow spiral on the main chimney stack. These reflect the influence of the Festival of Britain on the Toronto Board of Education staff architect Peter Pennington. *AB*

Yorkville. The name has different reso-
nances to Torontonians of different vintages:
a low-rent residential district; a fragrant
haven for hippiedom; a hub for art dealers
and chic cafés; Toronto's premier place to
buy designer bags and bump into movie
stars. And today another identity is
emerging—a moneyed redoubt of Victorian
quiet, surrounded by an increasingly tall and
ambitious cityscape.

Remarkably, much of this social change,
from the 1940s to the 1990s, took place
within the same built fabric of Victorian
houses. The progressive architects Jack
Diamond and Barton Myers wrote in 1972,
"Although the older buildings provide a
framework for what is there, present
functions are almost completely new.
Yorkville is entirely a creature of today, and it
is the continual 'recycling' process that
makes the area as fascinating as it is." That
"recycling" sensibility, so important to
Toronto's 20th-century architectural history,
was in part formed here.

The code for Yorkville's built form dates
back to the 1790s. Bloor Street was laid out
by John Graves Simcoe as the First
Concession Line, separating the Town of York
and Simcoe's "park lots" **[see Introductions,
Areas I, VII, and VIII]** from farmland and
wilderness beyond. Where Yonge Street **[Area
III]** crossed the First Concession Line, a toll
gate was erected in the early 1800s to tax
farmers bringing produce to town from the
north. Two inns to serve travelling farmers,
the Red Lion and Tecumseh Wigwam [both
now demolished] grew up nearby. From 1825
until about 1850, the Town of York's large
nonsectarian burying ground and potter's
field was also situated near these crossroads
[see 9/14 and 18/10].

Joseph Bloor's brewery, located in the
Rosedale Ravine **[21/1]**, first brought
workers to the area in 1830, followed by
Severn's Brewery near Yonge and Davenport
Road in 1835, and the brickworks northwest
of Yonge and Davenport. In the early 1850s,
the surrounding land was subdivided into
streets and building plots by speculators,
chiefly John Elmsley.

The community was incorporated as the
Village of Yorkville in 1853; a splendid High

Area IX
Walk 16: Old Yorkville
Walk 17: West Yorkville
Walk 18: Bloor Street

Victorian town hall went up in 1860 [now
demolished], and an impressive firehall in
1876 **[16/3]**. The village extended from
Sherbourne Street to near Bedford Road—a
much larger area than the Yorkville of today,
including sections that are now parts of the
Annex **[Area X]** and Rosedale **[Area XI]**.

In the next decades, Yorkville prospered
as a small, bedroom community. The
horse-drawn Toronto Street Railway ran cars
every 20 minutes from Yorkville Town Hall to
St. Lawrence Hall **[1/4]**. In addition to
labourers and shopkeepers, residents of
more substantial means were attracted by

the village atmosphere and low taxes, which were half those of Toronto. Architecturally, Yorkville was not unlike other Toronto neighbourhoods of the era, with a variety of 19th-century designs built close to one another and to the street.

The City of Toronto annexed Yorkville in 1883. At the time, Bloor Street (by this date named after Yorkville's entrepreneurial brewer) numbered few buildings: on the south were St. Paul's Church [18/27] and a handful of row and double houses, some functioning as laundries, groceries, and the like; on the north sat a few largish houses between Sherbourne Street and Avenue Road, on the corner of which the Church of the Redeemer had settled in 1879 [18/7]. In the next ten years, this pattern greatly accelerated, with row houses filling in the south side, and grand houses with large grounds similar to those on upper Jarvis Street [Area VII] completing the north. When the street railway, now electrified, added Bloor Street to its route in 1894, it took in "scores of the town's finest private mansions," according to a guidebook of the period.

By the turn of the century, however, wealthy residents moved on. Mansions on Bloor Street were turned into osteopaths' and dentists' offices, along with premises for dressmakers, antiques dealers, and tearooms. Yorkville quietly settled back as a working-class streetcar suburb, a role it was to enjoy through the 1940s.

For Bloor Street, the quiet was not to last. As a major cross street strategically located between downtown and burgeoning suburbs, it looked very appealing to 1920s city planners. There was talk of widening the thoroughfare, and in anticipation of this, in what must have been a daring gamble, Manufacturers' Life Insurance Company began constructing a majestic six-storey office building on regally landscaped grounds [18/26] across from St. Paul's Church in 1924. Other construction took off: apartment houses and medical buildings, and Moderne storefronts, now largely vanished.

The street widening was completed in 1929, but the Depression and World War II effectively stalled further building projects.

Bloor Street again sat quietly as a decorous shopping street, with the annual Easter Parade its most exciting event. (Things did liven up a little at night at the Embassy Ballroom on Bellair Street, where the big bands played.)

The postwar years, however, brought dramatic shifts. Immigrants began to occupy the area's dense, inexpensive housing, bringing such novel European ideas as the sidewalk café. To some, the area looked like another slum to be cleared: the influential Modernist planner Eugene Faludi drew a scheme for a full demolition and redevelopment of the neighbourhood as towers-in-the-park.

But that pessimistic view did not prevail, and the area soon became livelier and more commercial. Pioneering restaurateurs and retailers including interior designer Budd Sugarman saw opportunity in the rundown streets north of Bloor, especially with the arrival of the subway in 1963.

Then came the hippies. By the mid 1960s, the heart of the area (just a few blocks along Cumberland and Yorkville, from Avenue to Bay) was "a magnet for the young, freedom-loving set," in the contemporary words of two academics: "In a few square blocks north of Bloor congregate the youthful swingers and would-be swingers, drug-takers and pushers, teenyboppers, bikers and greasers." Coffee houses such as the Riverboat (located in two Victorian houses on Yorkville Avenue) became the centre of the Canadian folk music scene, out of which came Joni Mitchell, Gordon Lightfoot, and Ian and Sylvia. Yorkville became a buzzword for the real and imagined excesses of Canada's hippie generation, with blocks of 19th-century houses sporting psychedelic shopfronts and a particular herbal odour.

Those houses proved highly "recyclable," to use Diamond and Myers's term, proving Jane Jacobs's dictum from *The Death and Life of Great American Cities*: "New ideas must use old buildings." While Yorkville's top end, north of Scollard, remained largely residential (Myers built his own radical house here [16/24]), the two high streets of Cumberland and Yorkville saw old houses assume new uses. What had been cafés and clubs in the 1960s were soon rebuilt as more upscale commercial spaces. The courtyard complexes that emerged here made a unique contribution to the urbanism of Toronto. Webb Zerafa Menkes's Lothian Mews **[see 18/10, demolished]** and George Robb's Old York Lane **[16/11]** evoked the "romantic, human, friendly, populous markets of the past," Robb wrote in 1963, a powerful counterexample to the "gleaming, shoddy and conformist" shopping malls that were in fashion. This was a defence of venerable urban forms. At the same time, Diamond and Myers's York Square **[16/13]** showed how the "fabric" of the city could be retained in part even while making room for more density. Diamond and Myers would further explore this approach with housing at Beverley Place **[14/17]** and Sherbourne Lanes **[11/4a]**. And the sensitivity that they displayed, respecting the proportions and property lines of the intricate 19th-century streetscape, became a central idea in Toronto architectural discourse into the 1980s and beyond. The resistance to tabula rasa urban renewal **[see 2/1]** went along with a tendency to bridge Modernism and preservation as KPMB would later do nearby at the Royal Conservatory of Music **[8/42]**, showing values learned from George Baird **[see Area IV]** and from Barton Myers.

Along the way, Yorkville was transformed by what we would now call gentrification, and many loyalists were not pleased (indeed some haven't entirely gotten over it four decades later). The truth is that the flavours of both bohemian-hippie-downscale and gallery-upscale disappeared by the end of the century, replaced by ever wealthier residents, high-end retail, and a more glamorous vibe on the shopping streets. This was aided by the presence of the Toronto International Film Festival in the area from the late '70s until about 2010. (The festival's old venues, including the University Theatre **[18/10]** and the Uptown **[5/46]**, have largely disappeared.)

High-fashion Yorkville found its clearest expression on Bloor Street, whose status as a dense and high-rent commercial district began with the construction of the

Colonnade **[18/8]** in 1964. The city's first large mixed-use building combined residences, offices, shops, and restaurants. This mix, the building's relatively low height but big size, and its partial setback from the street set the tone for subsequent development on Bloor through the 1970s. The 1980s and 1990s brought taller and denser buildings, which have been succeeded by a much larger new wave of development in the years since 2010. The Four Seasons Hotel and Residences **[16/4]** defined this new scale, and the emerging pair of very tall towers at Bloor and Yonge **[18/18 and 18/21]** will punctuate it. Development is pushing into the neighbourhood.

And yet: both commercial Yorkville and the nearby stretch of Bloor are highly walkable and hospitable. Bloor Street has received a privately funded facelift, and its elegant granite paving and healthy street trees (designed by The Planning Partnership) show just how good Toronto's public realm might look with enough attention and money. More importantly, there are people. The wealth of retail and restaurant draws, combined with a high density of local residents, leave these streets agreeably buzzy at all hours. The Village of Yorkville Park **[16/8]** includes a new public piazza; together, such robust public and quasi-public spaces, including the many restaurant patios, sustain the kind of urban energy that Jane Jacobs, and the young Diamond and Myers, liked to see. Cities keep changing, and so do the villages within them.

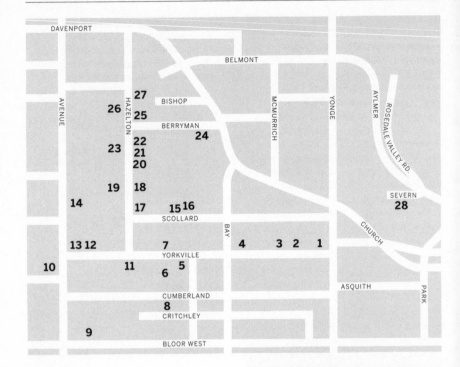

Walk 16: Old Yorkville

1 18 Yorkville, architectsAlliance with landscape architect Janet Rosenberg, 2008. A fine example of the tall-and-skinny "point tower" that Toronto has borrowed from Vancouver. The shaft of this tower has artfully composed window walls, and it hits the ground with much more finesse than most of its peers: the low podium, clad in granite and brick, looks fine from a pedestrian's viewpoint. The parking garage is capped by Rosenberg's Town Hall Square, a Modernist twist on French formal gardens that looks good from up high. *AB*

2 Yorkville Public Library, 22 Yorkville Ave., Robert McCallum, 1906–07; addition and interior remodelled, Barton Myers Associates, 1978. One of the hundreds of "Carnegie Classical" libraries built across North America with funds from the Andrew Carnegie Foundation. Though the library is small in size, an appropriately bold porticoed entrance announces its civic

2 | Yorkville Public Library

importance, as does its high first storey and foursquare stance. Myers's 1978 remodelling brilliantly lightened the interior—the space seems to literally glow—while leaving the public impress of the structure unchanged. *PM*

3 Firehall No. 10, 34 Yorkville Ave., Hancock & Townsend, 1876; all but tower rebuilt, Mancel Willmot, 1889–90; addition, 1975. Though it might look like a child's anthropomorphic Lego-set creation with bright features of yellow and red brick smiling out at us, this firehall has served as a suitably serious hose house for over 100 years, with the high tower used to hang and dry fire hoses and to sound the alarm to volunteer fire fighters and the community at large. The coat-of-arms on the tower is that of the Town of Yorkville, removed to the firehall from the town hall when the latter suffered a fire in 1941 and was demolished. Represented are initials of the town's first councillors and symbols of their vocations: beer barrel for the brewer, jack plane for the carpenter, brick mould for the builder, anvil for the blacksmith, and bull's head for the butcher. *PM*

3 | Firehall No. 10

4 Four Seasons Hotel and Residences, 60 Yorkville Ave., architectsAlliance with Claude Cormier (landscape architect), 2012. From the fifth floor up, these tall blue visions are Toronto's most beautiful towers in decades. But their clunky, opaque bases appear to belong to other, much worse buildings. The landscape is likewise a mixed bag. The driveway and fountain find Cormier in playful Post-Modernist mode with a "carpet" of pavers; the adjacent labyrinth of shrubs is gorgeously planted and detailed, and should be more clearly marked as the publicly accessible space that it is. *AB*

4 | Four Seasons Hotel and Residences

5 Originally John Daniels house, 77 Yorkville Ave., c. 1867. An early Yorkville cottage built by John Daniels, erstwhile saloonkeeper of the popular Tecumseh Wigwam inn which stood nearby at Bloor and Avenue Road in the mid 19th century. When he lived here, Daniels was constable of the village and tradition has it that his "overnight guests" were entertained in sheds at the back. Actually, being constable was only a sometime job, although Daniels was empowered to carry a gun for six weeks in hot summer to shoot stray dogs. His house retains congenial Georgian proportions while introducing such zesty Victorian touches as curved relieving arches of slightly raised brick. The first-rate adaptation to present-day commercial use added an unobtrusive glass showroom of compatible scale to the rear without at all diminishing the character of the house. *PM*

6 | Cumberland Court

6 Cumberland Court, 99 Yorkville Ave. thru to Cumberland St. (commercial complex), Webb Zerafa Menkes, 1973.

They're called courts, mews, squares, or lanes, and Yorkville abounds in them. Basically they're commercial complexes that contrive to combine shops and restaurants with landscaped outdoor spaces plus appealing traffic courses on several levels in an atmosphere that is variously described as lively, informal, and—at their worst—quaint. Cumberland Court gathers 19th-century gabled houses on Yorkville and Cumberland and boldly infills around them with a strikingly modern structure containing shops, cafés, art galleries, and offices. The long, relatively narrow passage that angles in and out of doors through the complex is probably the most interesting in Yorkville for its variety and surprise. *PM*

7 80 and 100 Yorkville Ave., Hariri Pontarini, 2009.

This unusually configured infill project occupies linked sites with a pair of set-back towers. You're unlikely to notice this, however; the two-storey retail podium along Yorkville, wrapped in sumptuous limestone and perfectly scaled to the street, is as good as condo bases get in Toronto. It also incorporates the Georgian Revival façade that Benjamin Kaminker and Edward Richmond designed for the old Mt. Sinai Hospital in 1934. (Pay no attention to the "traditional" townhouses around back on Scollard by another architect.) *AB*

8 Village of Yorkville Park, 115 Cumberland St., Oleson Worland with landscape architects Schwartz/Smith/Meyer, 1994.

The product of a design competition, and one of Toronto's finest public spaces. The park is divided into slices, which allude to the historic pattern of property lines in the area; each of these symbolizes a different element of the Canadian landscape, including a marsh, a waterway, a wildflower garden, and a massive hunk of Canadian Shield granite. The design has been criticized as being too fussy, but the constant crowds lingering here suggest otherwise. *AB*

8 | Village of Yorkville Park

7 | 80 and 100 Yorkville Ave.

9 155 Cumberland St./originally CIL House, Bregman & Hamann, 1960; addition and alterations, Quadrangle, 2009. A novelty: a tower on top of a tower. Developers KingSett preserved the International Style office building, including its 13th- and 14th-floor penthouse that was the home of society couple Noah and Rose Torno. That apartment may (the evidence is unclear) have been designed by the American architect and provocateur Philip Johnson; in any case, it was successfully preserved and resold, along with seven levels of luxury condos in the new limestone-clad volume on top. *AB*

9 | 155 Cumberland St.

10 The Prince Arthur, 38 Avenue Rd., Page & Steele, 2000. This social-climbing condo tries to borrow the language of 1920s New York uptown apartment houses—which is a good strategy for "traditional"-minded builders, as demonstrated at 1 St. Thomas [18/12]. The problem is execution: with its messy precast-concrete detailing and preposterous drive-through arcade, this one gets it all wrong. *AB*

11 Old York Lane, 117 Yorkville Ave. thru to Cumberland St. (commercial complex), George A. Robb, 1963. A discreet block of one-storey shops set along a brick-paved pedestrian way, Old York Lane was the first commercial complex in Yorkville. Its ground-hugging low scale, contrasting surface textures, rhythmic façade, and inviting atmosphere still make it a standout. *PM*

12 Hazelton Hotel and Residences, 118 Yorkville Ave., Page & Steele with Yabu Pushelberg (interior designers), 2007. A Neo-Whatever wedding cake, brick on the bottom and limestone up top. The interior vastly exceeds the architecture in quality and refinement—a sad equation that's much too common in Toronto and in this district. *AB*

13 York Square, Yorkville Ave. at Avenue Rd. (commercial complex), A.J. Diamond & Barton Myers, 1968; redevelopment, Zeidler Partnership, ongoing. Here, Diamond and Myers showed Toronto how to add hidden density while also retaining a set of Victorian houses (and updating them with Louis Kahn-ish brick flourishes). This scheme is distinguished by its delicately controlled scale and massing; the planned redevelopment will preserve some of the building forms at ground level, while destroying their legacy with a high-rise on top. Talk about missing the point. *AB*

13 | York Square

14 Yorkville Village, 55 Avenue Rd. thru to Hazelton Ave. (commercial complex and apartment houses), Webb Zerafa Menkes Housden, 1976; interior alteration, Johnson Chou, 2016. A laudably gentle piece of 1970s urbanism (formerly Hazelton Lanes), which squeezes in two residential mid-rise towers while holding the streetwall on Avenue Road and staying relatively low to the ground. The mall itself, once brown-on-brown and mazy, has gotten a white-on-white minimalist upgrade that suits its increasingly upscale self-image. *AB*

Scollard Street is a mixed bag—despite the intrusion of large-scale condo development, it still hints at the 19th-century village that cheek-by-jowl built labourers' cottages, bank clerks' row houses, and "gentlemen's" semi-detacheds.

15a 94–104 Scollard St. (six-house row), 1893. Rebuilding for speculation is nothing new to Yorkville. This cheerful Queen Anne row of 1893 replaced an 1871 sextet of one-and-a-half-storey cottages, each ensemble a rental enterprise of Larratt Smith, prominent Toronto lawyer and vice-chancellor of the university. The latest conversions to retail and office use have been unobtrusive, maintaining the picturesque rhythmic gables that still highlight this block. *PM*

15b 92 Scollard St., Shim-Sutcliffe, 2016. This skinny infill project captures the scale and the heavily ornamented front façades of the area's Victorian fabric, employing the classic Toronto material of red brick in decidedly novel fashion. *AB*

16 72–76 Scollard St. (triple house), 1888–89. Triple houses are fun to puzzle out for the way they do-si-do an unequal number of parts. Here the architectural dance choreographs identical end units with a flopped version centrestage. The builder seems to have been a little uncomfortable with his Second Empire mansard roof, altogether too high and stiff, and certainly on its way out of fashion at this late date. *PM*

17 Hazelton House/originally Olivet Congregational Church, 33 Hazelton Ave. at Scollard St., Dick & Wickson, 1890; remodelled as commercial block, Sheldon Rosen, 1972–73. A 19th-century church given a 1970s update as shops, galleries, and offices. Skilful adaptive reuse of a church building, a kind of architectural challenge that is everywhere in 21st-century Toronto. *AB*

17 | Hazelton House

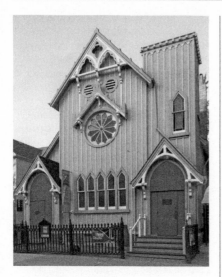

18 | Toronto Heliconian Club

18 Toronto Heliconian Club/originally Olivet Congregational Church, 35 Hazelton Ave., 1876. A rare Toronto example of delightful Carpenter Gothic style wherein the humble woodworker is able to parade sophisticated medieval intentions. Using nail and board instead of mortar and masonry, Gothic details are invented anew: lancet arches become triangular; vertical buttresses, battens; bold decoration, filigreed. This church originally stood on the corner, but—being wooden—was easily moved when the congregation decided to build a larger, red-brick edifice [16/17]. The interior, today used by a venerable women's arts and letters group, is a simple auditorium with apsidal chancel. *PM*

Though much changed, Hazelton Avenue retains enough of its early buildings to hint at the area's quiet suburban origins. The considerable wealth on the street has, so far, tended toward preservation rather than mansionification.

19 Originally St. Basil's School, 30 Hazelton Ave., James M. Cowan, 1928; addition and alteration as condo residences, Quadrangle and Goldsmith Borgal, 2016. The buff-brick Gothic Revival façade of the former St. Basil's School gets a new life as the face of a luxury condo building. It is a façadectomy, to be sure, but one of the best examples of that dubious form of preservation. The stepped building conceals its bulk well. *AB*

20 49–51 Hazelton Ave. (double house), 1874. Looking slightly unreal after a remove-all-the-warts renovation, no. 49–51 nevertheless is one of Yorkville's most interesting houses, having dipped into the Victorian architectural costume box for seldom-seen Baronial Gothic accessories: bulbous-roofed tower, stringy drip-moulds, pointed-arch porches. *PM/updated AB*

20 | 49–51 Hazelton Ave.

21 53–55, 57–59, 61–63 Hazelton Ave. (three double houses), 1875–76. After serious, boxy Georgian style, the next Yorkville double houses were playful, pointy centre-gable numbers, pleasing in their prickly insouciance. These variously clad free-spirits are typical. *PM*

22a Originally George Daws house, 65 Hazelton Ave., 1875. This diminutive mansarded gem is one of Yorkville's most attractive houses, with its high parlour floor—and therefore high basement—reached by a tall flight of steps. The bell-cast roof and gingerbread of the bay window are especially appealing touches articulated by the first owner, a bricklayer and contractor. He probably looked through a builder's pattern book to find this "French-roof cottage." *PM*

22b 77–81 Hazelton Ave. (triple house), 1881. An engaging centre-gable trio of typical Yorkville houses sporting High Victorian red- with yellow-brick decoration. *PM*

23 Originally George Lee house, 68 Hazelton Ave., 1878. A wonderful Gothic Revival house and garden built by the village registrar, and seemingly untouched by time. The centre gable with bargeboarded fascia, windows framed by shutters and raised brick, graceful iron-crested porch, and fine iron fence continue to spread Victorian delight. *PM*

24 Originally Barton Myers house, 19 Berryman St., A.J. Diamond & Barton Myers (designed by Barton Myers), 1970. Not just a champion of Yorkville, Myers actually settled here, and designed this High-Tech house of steel and glass that set the template for his later Wolf House **[21/32]**

and a series of grander, later projects in Southern California. Modest in scale and clear in its language, the house has survived well for 47 years, though the current owner has lamentably removed the Supergraphic "19" that once covered the garage door. *AB*

25 85 Hazelton Ave. (detached house), 1879. This commodious-looking house planted firmly on the corner site is an eclectic design that marries ornament and form from several styles to come up with an engaging example of Victorian picturesque. Modern eclecticism has turned it into three separate units plus a boring attachment to the east. *PM*

26 88–90 and 92–94 Hazelton Ave. (two double houses), 1885. Looking like delectable frosted cake with their white-painted trim, these late Bay-n-Gables parade sure proportion and fine detail. *PM*

27 101–105 Hazelton Ave. (four attached houses), 1880–81. The slick modernization (which turned four houses into twice that number of apartments) has robbed this Second Empire ensemble of its resonance, but it is of interest for the arched carriage-way that originally led to stables. *PM*

28 Studio Building, 25 Severn St., Eden Smith, 1914. This is where the Group of Seven and Tom Thomson came together, in a building partly owned by Lawren Harris **[25/31]** and rented out to his colleagues and friends. Smith's design was radical for 1914 Toronto: the tall floors and steel sash windows evoke a factory, while flooding the six studios within with ideal north light. The setting has changed dramatically, but this is a crucial location in Canada's cultural history, and has been recognized as a National Historic Site. *AB*

24 | 19 Berryman St.

Walk 17: West Yorkville

Cut off from the rest of Yorkville by traffic-choked six-lane Avenue Road, the enclave between Avenue and Bedford Roads exists more sensibly today as part of the Annex [Area X], though quieter, lower, and more uniformly affluent than areas to the west. Nevertheless, the short east–west streets, architectural styles, and construction dates confirm this district's Village of Yorkville pedigree. Originally owned by the Anglican Church and then sold to real estate speculators, the land had been carved out for streets and building lots by the 1860s. Construction began on Avenue Road, Prince Arthur Avenue, and Lowther Avenue, followed by development on Elgin, Victoria (now Boswell), Dufferin (now Bernard), and finally Tranby—a narrow afterthought. In 1882, on the eve of annexation by the City of Toronto, this western section of the village contained approximately 100 dwellings, housing close to one-tenth of Yorkville's population of 5,200. Avenue Road remained residential and of moderate width well into the 1920s.

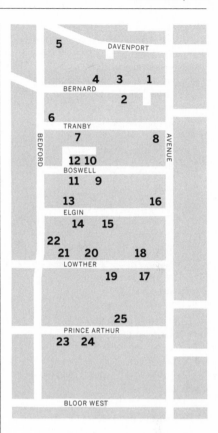

1 10 Bernard Ave. (detached house), 1881.
A firm Gothic Revival villa with fine proportions under a steeply pitched roof and pointed gable. Expensive detail is quiet but effective: stone lintels and sills bridging rectangular windows, bell-cast roof capping bay window, and raised brick quoins neatly turning the eye in to the tidy composition. The present door-case is an alteration. *PM*

2 Originally Noah L. Piper house, 19 Bernard Ave., 1875. One of West Yorkville's standout houses, this large, gracious Georgian box was the home of

2 | 19 Bernard Ave.

well-to-do Yonge Street hardware merchant Noah L. Piper. Very late for a Georgian design, the sedate style was enlivened with colourful High Victorian brick detailing. Piper moved to this then-bucolic precinct—his was the only house on this block for over two years—from "downtown" Bond Street [13/8]. *PM*

3 18–20, 24–26, 28–30 Bernard Ave. (three double houses), 1877–78; no. 18–20 remodelled, c. 1915. When this section of Yorkville was developing in the 1870s, Second Empire was the height of fashion in Toronto. Described in periodicals of the day as befitting "aspiring gentlemen," it was a sophisticated urban style whose use for these handsome, plastic houses suggests that at least some builders had "citifying" ambitions for the area. Yellow brick—called white brick at the time—was preferred for Second Empire houses, perhaps to approximate the colour of expensive stone. The wood trim was probably originally painted creamy white or dark green. *PM*

3 | 24–26 Bernard Ave.

4 32–34 and 36–38 Bernard Ave. (two double houses), 1889. In the late 1880s, the new Annex area west of Yorkville was in the throes of wholesale development in a Richardsonian Romanesque/Queen Anne mode; it is not surprising the activity filtered eastward into Yorkville. These identical double houses clearly draw from that massive, solid tradition, with cave-like round-arched entries and an intriguing trick of the form that sequesters one window of each of the polygonal bays inside the "cave." *PM*

5 277 Davenport Ave., Hariri Pontarini, 2016. This little luxury condo only ten units over six storeys suggests a novel approach to high-end housing in the city. It gentrifies what is still a scruffy stretch of Davenport with limestone and good glass, while its stepped form should be compatible with the protected neighbourhood behind it. *AB*

6 123, 121 Bedford Rd. and 70 Tranby Ave. at Bedford Rd. (three detached houses), 1892–93. Put up by one speculative builder, these three late 19th-century houses are instructive for the variety of ways they use similar brick, stone, and wooden details, and mix up form and fenestration for an individual look. *PM*

Tranby Avenue, cut through the centre of a single large property during a prosperous period of mass construction in Toronto, provided developers with a real chance to show their stuff. Although several builders were responsible for the houses we see here, the same machine-made parts appear in various guises, and massing and silhouettes all come together in a harmonious whole. A great street, fine and pleasing, and a perfect example of architecture as the art of assemblage.

7a 66–68 and 71–73 Tranby Ave. (two double houses), 1891–92. The sentinel-like towers on these once-twinned double houses dramatically mark the end—or beginning—of the street and set its ensemble tone. *PM*

7b 33–35, 37–39, 43–45, 47–49, 51–53 Tranby Ave. (five double houses), 1889–90. Although they look alike at first blush, these five late Bay-n-Gable double houses have gone to some pains to relieve the monotony with a variety of fenestration, gable decoration, and ornamental brick panels. The bracketed shed roofs over the entrances are practical and pleasing. The ten units were built for $1,800 each, which would have made them relatively expensive middle-class housing in 1890. *PM*

8 Tranby Terrace, 11 Tranby Ave. and 102, 104, 106 Avenue Rd. (complex of nine row houses and three rehabilitated houses), Klein & Sears, 1981. The agile layout of this infill complex can best be appreciated from its handsome flagstoned courtyard, as can

8 | Tranby Terrace

the careful renovations of the three 1880s houses incorporated on Avenue Road. The newer row houses manipulate the same ingredients as their Victorian forebears: red brick, peaked gables, round-headed windows, even shed roofs over the entries—sleekly interpreted in glass. *PM*

9 Originally Phillipe Grandjean house, 41 Boswell Ave., 1881; renovation, Superkul, 2006. A tiny, spirited accumulation of Victorian details that continues to spell visual pleasure. The gable still suspends its decorative pendant (long gone in most houses of this period). The gabled wall dormers to the sides were to light the attic storey, no longer an issue after a Neo-Modernist renovation has expanded and opened up the interior, invisibly from the street. Grandjean was a watchmaker and engraver. *PM/AB*

10 46–48 Boswell Ave. (double house), 1884. An eclectic, well-mannered double house distinguished by formal-looking symmetry, rectangular windows with trim shutters, cornice window heads, and a graceful two-storeyed porch that adds much to the polite effect. *PM*

11 49–51 Boswell Ave. (double house), 1875. A pair of simple, earthy-looking houses sitting close to the ground with an exterior of roughcast plaster rather than more expensive brick. The pediment-shaped wooden window and door heads are an endearing carpenter's touch. *PM*

12 54–56, 58, 60–62 Boswell Ave. (two double and one single house), 1889. This five-unit ensemble deploys an abundance of wooden trim to enliven the façade. By this date such elaborate detail could be mass-produced, but factory provenance made it no less fancy. Yorkville was annexed by the City of Toronto in 1883, signalling the beginning of developer construction such as this. *PM*

13 52 Elgin Ave. (detached house), Frederick H. Herbert, 1897–98.
The barnlike girth, gambrel roof, and tile-hung walls embracing this house are derived from American Shingle Style dwellings, a simple, hearty form which sought to evoke warmth and shelter within. Fire regulations prohibited wooden shingles in Toronto (unless backed by brick), resulting in forays like this into what might be dubbed Tile Style. *PM*

13 | 52 Elgin Ave.

14 45–47 Elgin Ave. (double house), 1875.
A Gothic Revival "double detached villa" as picturesque as any the pattern books ever illustrated. The tall chimneys, bargeboarded gables, pointed windows, drip-moulds, bichrome relieving arches, and spandrel panels are especially evocative touches articulated by the busy Toronto builder Thomas Snarr, who himself resided at no. 45. *PM*

15 27 Elgin Ave. (detached house), 1885. 27A Elgin Ave. (detached house), 1985. 25 Elgin Ave. (detached house), 1878.
These three preserve the early character of Elgin Avenue as a street of medium-sized houses sprinkled lightly with picturesque details to evoke the virtues of hearth and home in a simpler age, this despite the fact no. 27A dates to the 1980s. It is one of the

most successful Victorian copies in the city. How unfortunate then that greed dictated its being squeezed in here, because the houses on Elgin Avenue were also once appreciated for their large lots! *PM/updated AB*

16 Originally George Booth house, 2 Elgin Ave., 1879; veranda and portico additions, Darling & Pearson, 1909. Built for painter George Booth, this is one of West Yorkville's most attractive houses, its abundance of rich Italianate detail playing over a plastic, strongly textured form that accommodates with insouciance the portico and corner veranda added in 1909. At that time, the house sat on more generous grounds, still surveying a modestly wide, residential Avenue Road. *PM*

16 | 2 Elgin Ave.

17 Originally Albert Locke house, 9 Lowther Ave., 1876. This delightful, picturesque house can't help but intrigue. On one hand it is so unassuming, narrowly squeezed between neighbours as if an afterthought; and on the other, so self-dramatizing, confidently parading all kinds of saucy ornament. *PM*

18 Originally William Luke house, 16 Lowther Ave., 1881. Of no pronounced style, but with gentle balanced proportions, human scale—not too large, not too small—thoughtful economy of detail, and intimation of commodious space within, this is one of those affectionate buildings that has well stood the test of time, as appealing today as it must have been 100 years ago. William Luke was listed in assessment rolls as a "gentleman." *PM*

19 23–29 Lowther Ave. (three attached houses), 1875; altered, c. 1970. Old photographs reveal that these three were originally similar-looking Victorians with bow windows and a veranda snaking across the front. More interesting than *style,* however, is the unusual *form,* with an arresting carriageway—once doored—topped by a Gothic gable and oriel window. (The oriel lights a front room belonging to no. 25; the room behind goes with no. 29.) Inspiration for no. 23's Georgian Revival brick redo came via Boston or Philadelphia. *PM*

20a Formerly Barbara Gordon house, 26 Lowther Ave., 1878. Connections—the mucilage of details that joins one part of the exterior envelope to another—played a big role in the look of 19th-century buildings. This lovely Victorian villa has superb connections: turned, pierced, and sawn woodenwork stringing porch, veranda, and eaves; corbelled, panelled, and raised brickwork hemming door, windows, belt courses, and cornices. Built for Barbara Gordon, who in the 1880s married the founder of the Parker cleaning empire. *PM/updated AB*

20a | 26 Lowther Ave.

20b Originally Struthers/Ross house, 30–32 Lowther Ave., Grant & Dick, 1875. This generous double house may have been the prototype for Toronto's popular Bay-n-Gable form, that felicitous marriage of Gothic Revival and Italianate forms and motifs. Designed by the distinguished firm of Grant & Dick, this perky pair vividly displays the projecting polygonal end bays and lively bargeboarded gables that soon began to inform red-and-yellow-brick semi-detacheds put up all across the city. *PM*

20b | 30–32 Lowther Ave.

20c Originally Mrs. William Augustus Baldwin house, 36 Lowther Ave., 1888–89.
William Augustus Baldwin, brother of Robert the reformer and son of Dr. William the doctor/lawyer/architect/politician, died in 1883. Five years later his widow and second wife built this firm mansion adjacent to her eldest stepson's residence at no. 50 [17/22]. The Richardsonian Romanesque/Queen Anne style of the house was borrowed from the neighbouring Annex, as was—in a way—the money to build it, for the Baldwin fortune was in part based on the sale of Annex lands to speculators. Mrs. Baldwin lived here with another stepson, Robert Russell Baldwin, and his family, but they were not cramped for space: the house boasted 20 rooms, eight with tiled fireplaces. In addition, there was central heating from a coal-burning furnace, gas lighting, and indoor plumbing. Today, there's a garage slipped into the basement too. *PM*

21 Originally William Garside house, 46 Lowther Ave., Charles J. Gibson, 1897–98.
Eclecticism gone berserk, this house contrives to combine Queen Anne tile-hung front gable, classical Palladian window, chateauesque door surround, even a Gothic trefoil. This was the year Queen Victoria celebrated her Diamond Jubilee and perhaps Mr. Garside, a wholesale boot and shoe manufacturer, wanted architect Gibson to go all out in a show of architectural imperialism. *PM*

22 Originally Henry St. George Baldwin house, 50 Lowther Ave. at Bedford Rd., c. 1878; renovated and remodelled, 1986–87.
Henry St. George Baldwin was the eldest son of William Augustus Baldwin who at one time owned all the land between Lowther and Davenport from Huron to just beyond Bedford Road. In 1878, Henry St. George was given this parcel on the southeast corner of the family property on which he built himself a large red-and-yellow-brick house, today serving rather niftily without too many exterior alterations as a multi-unit dwelling. *PM*

23 Originally Alexander Macdonald house, 35 Prince Arthur Ave., 1896.
Built by a barrister on the eve of Victoria's 60th reigning year, no. 35 is an exuberant red-brick extravaganza with not a few histrionics harking back to 1066 and all that: crenellations, bartizans, traceried windows. *PM*

24 25–27 and 29–31 Prince Arthur Ave. (two double houses), 1888.
Carefully remodelled for art galleries and offices, these four sparky Bay-n-Gable abodes are still fastidiously decked out in raised-brick string courses, bracketed shed roofs, and iron cresting. The architect Charles Gibson rented at no. 27 for a period early in his career. *PM*

25 Prince Arthur Towers, 20 Prince Arthur Ave. (apartment house), Uno Prii, 1965.
Swooping grand gestures for a 22-storey Neo-Expressionist apartment house. Situated on an appropriately large lawned site, and with a clean, dramatic look, this represents one of architect Prii's more sculpturally handsome designs. Nevertheless, neither grounds nor grandiosity belong here on intimate, small-scale Prince Arthur Avenue. *PM*

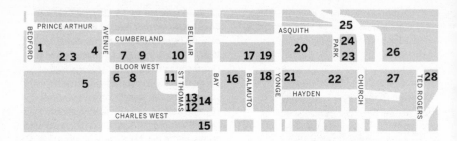

Walk 18: Bloor Street

1 One Bedford, KPMB with Page & Steele, 2009. Incorporates fragments of John Lyle studio, John Lyle, 1921. A high-rise condo with good urban manners. The courtyard, strongly massed podium, limestone cladding, and double-height ground floor create a sense of quality. Then there's a peculiarity: the façade of John Lyle's studio, which once stood in a backyard on this site. KPMB, who have expressed great respect for their predecessor, have placed it as a fragment in the courtyard, fronting a Starbucks. Love it or hate it. *AB*

1 | One Bedford

2 Museum House, 206 Bloor St. W., Page & Steele/IBI Group, 2012. A demure luxury tower that, with its precise gridded façade of windows and I-beams, does a lot of things right. It's betrayed by the clunky base. The manicured set of balcony gardens, no doubt labour-intensive, garnish the architecture to wonderful effect. *AB*

3 Exhibit Residences, 200 Bloor St. W., R. Varacalli Architect, interior design by Diego Burdi of Burdi Filek, landscape design by NAK Design Group, ongoing. In drawings, this scheme of four staggered cubes, lined by continuous milky-white balconies, looked great. The reality, surprisingly, matches the promise. The rare condo tower that aims for crisp and sculptural and gets there. *AB*

4 Park Hyatt Hotel/originally Queen's Park Plaza Hotel, 4 Avenue Rd. at Bloor St., Hugh G. Holman, 1926–29; addition, Page & Steele, 1956; proposed renovation, KPMB and ERA, in progress. Along Bloor, an apartment/hotel constructed when skyscrapers were giving up on the look of florid classical palaces but had yet to become Deco ziggurats. A thin arcade of double-height windows with slim frieze

4 | Park Hyatt Hotel

running above marks the Park Hyatt's reticent base; a brief balustraded parapet suffices for cornice; in between, long streams of windows and incipient setbacks hint at new streamlining. In their eagerness to occupy a fast-improving address in the 1920s, the Queen's Park Plaza Hotel built over an underground finger of meandering Taddle Creek. The building began to sag and elevators would not function. After frustrated efforts at bracing, a solution was found, the story goes, to "permafreeze" the ground. The connected 12-storey annex of 1956, designed in jaunty Modernist style by Peter Dickinson for Page & Steele, has been mutilated beyond recognition. The current redevelopment proposal would carefully restore the south tower's façade (and make that tower into apartments), while remaking the north tower and the low-rise link between with a new bronzed Modernist cladding. *PM/AB*

5 Royal Ontario Museum, 100 Queen's Park. [See Walk 8/43.]

6 Originally Lillian Massey Department of Household Science, 157 Bloor St. W. [See Walk 8/44.]

7 Renaissance Centre, 150 Bloor St. W. (mixed-use complex), Webb Zerafa Menkes Housden with Page & Steele, 1982. Church of the Redeemer, 162 Bloor St. W., Smith & Gemmell, 1879. This hulking, expensively solid shops/offices/ condominium complex does resemble a Renaissance building: the glum, inward-looking *palazzi* beloved of the Medicis and their fellow Florentine bankers. Actually, the real "rebirth" here is that of the Church of the Redeemer, its stout no-nonsense visage revealing startling grace and power against Renaissance's incongruous backdrop. Sweeping slate roof, rough stone walls, and looming belfry now form a commanding presence on this busy corner. Built in the 1870s for a new parish carved out of what had been St. Paul's territory, the Church of the Redeemer is a High Victorian interpretation of the medieval: larger, more solid, less intricate and rustic. The interior is pure High Victorian, flourishing coloured bands of red and yellow brick on walls, bold wooden brackets at the ceiling, and rich granite columns to mark the transept. *PM*

8 The Colonnade, 131 Bloor St. W. (mixed-use complex), Gerald Robinson with Tampold & Wells, 1961–64; altered, 1986–87. The 12-storey Colonnade was Toronto's first building to purposefully combine residences, offices, and retail, including restaurants and a theatre. The multiplicity of functions was spelled out in the design, a complicated composition focused on a row of slender square columns and segmental arches—the colonnade. Apartment floors are signalled by the small concrete waffle grid of the upper storeys. This contrasts to the larger scale of the shops, which curve out from under the colonnade to form a semicircular forecourt. The forecourt, in turn, is punctuated by a "floating" concrete staircase that leads to commercial space on the second and third floors. A 1980s remodelling sought to make major changes. Interior alterations have not been kind; thankfully, on the exterior the Colonnade still retains its landmark 1960s aura. *PM/updated AB*

7 | Church of the Redeemer / Renaissance Centre

8 | The Colonnade

9 110 Bloor St. W. (mixed-use complex), Daniel Li, 1980; altered, 1987–88. The epitome of gilt-edged—or, more accurately, stainless-steel-edged—Late-Modern stylishness, this is one of Toronto's most self-consciously elegant buildings. Every sleek detail spells luxury, from the discreet shops with their tasteful signs to the steel-trussed glass canopy to the way the envelope of residences rises in a smooth sweep of silky reflecting glass. Before the 1988 remodelling, the composition was surprisingly similar to that of the Colonnade [18/8]—even down to a floating staircase— making for a neat comparison between the architectural vocabulary of the 1960s and that of the 1980s. *PM*

10 100 Bloor St. and 10 Bellair, Burka Architects, 2003. Incorporates front façade of University Theatre, Eric Hounsom, 1946–49. This site was long the subject of controversial redevelopment plans, which finally produced a thoroughly bland and underwhelming building. The most important site of contention here was the 1,328-seat University Theatre—put up just after World War II using 1930s Art Moderne curves, silvery chrome, and black granite—whose façade now caps a multi-level retail space. Other presences here left no trace, including a potter's field which operated from 1826 to 1856, the mid-rise 1922 Physicians and Surgeons Building, and Lothian Mews, Toronto's first courtyard-and-retail complex, which was a place to be seen from 1962 until its decline in the 1980s. *PM/AB*

11 Windsor Arms Hotel, 18 St. Thomas St., Kirk Hyslop, 1927; renovation and addition, Page & Steele, 1999. Hyslop put a rather austere Gothic Revival face on this hotel at the height of the Roaring Twenties; after a period as a landmark of bohemian Yorkville, the place went under in 1991. Upon its reopening, Page & Steele reconstructed the old façade, and added a high-rise addition with its own, half-hearted Gothic flourishes. *AB*

12 1 St. Thomas, Robert A.M. Stern Architects with Young + Wright, 2008. The finest historicist high-rise in Toronto. Stern knows the New York precedents for this building type as well as anyone alive; he establishes a strong composition of base-shaft-and-tower, and borrows the terracing and quiet materiality of Rosario Candela to a truly Manhattanish effect. The precast concrete up high looks very much like the pricey limestone at the base. *AB*

12 | 1 St. Thomas

13 7 St. Thomas, Hariri Pontarini, ongoing; incorporates 1 Sultan St. (house), c. 1885, and 3–11 Sultan St. (houses), built for Charles R. Rundle, 1887. Six good Victorian houses—one Second Empire and five Richardsonian Romanesque—are folded into this office-condo building as Hariri Pontarini's addition of curvy, fritted glass establishes a lovely counterpoint of form and material between new and old. *AB*

14 1166 Bay St. (apartment house), H.D. Burston; completed, Paul H. Northgrave, 1979–81. A very distinguished 22-storey condominium building with lovely gleaming polygonal bays stepping out neatly in file along the front. This undulating, many-windowed look is remarkably reminiscent of one of architectural history's great early skyscrapers: Burnham & Root's 1889 Monadnock Building in Chicago. *PM*

15 Bay/Charles Tower, 55–57 Charles St. W. (apartment house), Klein & Sears, 1979–80. An eccentric design that seems to work, Bay/Charles Tower features a polygonal shape with shafts of bay windows jutting out at different floor levels, rather like so many glass-enclosed elevators scurrying up and down the walls. *PM*

16 Manulife Centre, 55 Bloor St. W. thru to Charles St. (mixed-use complex), Clifford & Lawrie, 1974; remodelled, Clifford Lawrie Bolton Ritchie, 1984; addition, Clifford & Lawrie, 1988; addition, Crang & Boake with MCA, 1996; renovation, B+H with MdeAS, in progress. One of those Brutalist buildings that have fallen out of fashion and then back in again, Manulife's two rugged towers retain a formal and material strength after four decades. (Not to mention relatively good structural and energy performance, since they lack the balconies that have become Achilles' heels to many of their contemporaries.) The 51-storey apartment building in back,

16 | Manulife Centre

Toronto's tallest at the time of its construction, remains in high demand; likewise the offices in the Bloor-front tower. The original base, which included a courtyard, waterfall, and reflecting pool, has been much altered by the addition of new retail, theatres, and glassy façades; this trend is likely to continue with the latest planned alterations, which will leave the sturdy towers above (and the raised private garden) in good shape. *AB*

17 Holt Renfrew Centre, 50 Bloor St. W. (commercial block), Crang & Boake, 1978. No doubt very chic in the Late-Modern 1970s with its Bianco Carrara cladding, this building is now being overshadowed by very tall towers; and indeed the property has now been approved for a 71-storey replacement, so it's only a matter of time before the marble crumbles. *AB*

18 The One, 1 Bloor St. W., Foster + Partners and CORE with landscape architects The Planning Partnership, ongoing. One of the most audacious developments in Toronto since the 1960s, this could, if all goes to plan, be Toronto's tallest building aside from the CN Tower. It will place 70-odd levels of luxury condos on top of a multi-levelled retail mall that is, in itself, nearly as tall as the nearby Manulife Centre **[18/16]**. Luckily, size promises to come with savvy: the design so far suggests the city will gain a brassy icon in Foster's refined High-Tech mode, plus fine public realm at the base of the tower. The architects are also drawing fashionable green walls and groves-in-the-sky, which will be nice if the landscape architects can bring them to life. This complex will represent intensification of the city, no doubt, but in just the right place. *AB*

19 2 Bloor St. W. (office building), Ogus & Fisher with Peter Caspari, 1971; altered, 1987–88. Late-Modernism gone awry. The glass-clad "boring box" obviously needs more than vertical "suspenders" and a striped "belt" around the middle to smarten it up, especially if the suit is as big, brown, and blah as this 34-storey tower. Changes to the ground level have made it a bit friendlier but no more elegant. *PM/updated AB*

20 Hudson's Bay Centre, 2 Bloor St. E. (office building and department store), Crang & Boake, 1974. The skeletal pattern of the 35-storey Hudson's Bay Centre building is only a little less impoverished than that of its fuzzy neighbour across the street **[18/19]**. And the double abomination of a shrouded, seemingly inaccessible banking pavilion taking up this important corner plus the mausoleum-like face of the Bay's department store walling the rest of the block make this complex one of the most deadly pieces of architecture in Toronto. *PM*

21 One Bloor, 1 Bloor St. East, Hariri Pontarini, 2016. At 76 storeys, this condo/retail tower already dominates the skyline, and should form a pair with The One **[18/19]**. Its architectural expression is entirely different, though: the base is wrapped in glass that ripples (a bit too fussily) like a set of sails, while the irregularly swoopy balconies above invite similar metaphors. Deeply derivative of Studio Gang's 2009 Aqua Tower in Chicago, but like that building it manages to dress up a condo block in grand, yet economical, style. *AB*

21 | One Bloor

22 New York Life Centre, 121 Bloor St. E. (office building), Page & Steele, 1983. St. Andrew's United Church, 117 Bloor St. E., Page & Steele, 1983. When St. Andrew's United offered up the whole Bloor Street plot which their Romanesque Revival edifice had occupied since 1890, the deal specified a replacement church along with the developer's high-rise heaven. Page & Steele's bluish-tinted glass skyscraper with precise layers of cloud-white banding is a Late-Modern version of the horizontally emphasized tall building. The beautifully sited church uses the same stepped massing and mirror cladding as the office block but punctuates it with verticals of warm beigey brick, two of which stand in for a charismatic bell tower. *PM*

23 Crown Life Insurance Co., 120 Bloor St. E. (office building), Marani & Morris, 1956. 160 Bloor St. E. (office building), Bregman & Hamann, 1984. That Bloor Street East would become the major venue of Toronto's insurance companies seemed assured when both Crown Life and Confederation Life **[18/28]**. joined pioneering Manufacturers' Life **[18/26]** here in the 1950s. Crown Life's first building at 120 Bloor is typical of postwar 1950s architecture, splendidly executed by Robert Morris **[7/13]**. In 1969, the company erected an adjacent high-rise, notable only for the fact it was torn down just a little over ten years later to make way for the mirrored giant that now dominates the site. Crown Life's newest building, despite its uninspiring stubby shape, boasts such a sophisticated, fragilely scored smooth skin that the structure invites a careful look for the unique qualities that mirror glass can bring to architecture: the visual paradox of a wall that is constantly changing depending on viewpoint, light, weather; a wall that backlit at night changes to the point of disappearing. No. 160 gained its extraordinary size by trading property it owned between Asquith and Church Streets for city-sponsored housing **[18/24]** and a public park. *PM*

24 Asquith Park, 14 Asquith St. thru to Church St. (apartment house), Hiro Nakashima, 1984. The City of Toronto deserves praise for its architecturally distinguished non-profit housing. This tower's interesting curved shape accommodating an awkward site as well as sweep of balconies on Church Street and asymmetric fenestration on Asquith make it a lively addition to the neighbourhood. *PM*

25 Central Christadelphian Church, 728 Church St., John B. Parkin Associates, 1948. 50 Park Road, John B. Parkin Associates, 1954; later alterations, du Toit Architects, 1992. The L-shaped building on Church St. is principally an ecclesia, as Christadelphians call their places of worship; its stripped geometry and brick cladding presage many Ontario church buildings of the '50s and '60s, though few of them share this one's Modernist rigour. Down the hill, the Parkin office would design a fine Miesian steel-and-brick box as headquarters for the Ontario Association of Architects. That building, while altered and expanded, serves elegantly as offices for the design firm DTAH; the OAA moved out to Don Mills in 1992 **[26/2]**. *AB*

26 Manufacturers' Life Insurance Co., 200 Bloor St. E. (office building), Sproatt & Rolph, 1924–26; additions, Marani & Morris, 1953. 250 Bloor St. E. (office building), Marani Rounthwaite & Dick, 1968. North Tower, 200 Bloor St. E. (office building), Clifford Lawrie Bolton Ritchie, 1983. The various office buildings of Manufacturers' Life erected on this stretch of Bloor Street over some 60 years are a lesson in corporate architecture at its well-bred best. Each building was designed in the style of its time, rendered with such thoughtful reserve and outstanding quality that there never could be a question but that one's equities were safe and solvent at Manufacturers' Life. The first edifice of 1926, the majestic six storeys fronting no. 200, used cut stone and refined Roman Doric detail to convey an air of urban gentility then appropriate to Bloor Street. Later large additions to the rear showed similar good

taste. The 1960s building, no. 250, was built of crisp, three-dimensional concrete modules in the manner of Marcel Breuer to form a forceful, sculptural structure. With careful siting to close the vista up Jarvis Street, this building quickly became a further landmark on Bloor Street. Manufacturers' Life's newest building used Late-Modern reflective glass cladding—gold in colour— innovatively hung *behind* a giant concrete frame. It is a bravura design of High Renaissance grandeur, a comparison brought to mind by the elegant domed pavilion (unfortunately overly baroque inside) that connects this building to the older one. And of course all three buildings benefit from a park-like setting on the crest of Rosedale Ravine carpeted with the finest lawns in Toronto. *PM*

26 | Manufacturers' Life Insurance Co.

27 Maurice Cody Hall/originally St. Paul's Church, 227 Bloor St. E., Edward Radford & George Radford, 1861; addition, George M. Miller, 1900; addition, E.J. Lennox, 1903. St. Paul's Anglican Church, 227 Bloor St. E., E.J. Lennox, 1913; addition, Black & Moffat, 2006. This adventurous translation of a medieval English village church ranks among the best architecture in Toronto, as much a standout today among skyscrapers on Bloor Street as it was 120 years ago when it actually was a village church, serving newly incorporated Yorkville and other outlying residential communities. The Radford brothers had studied well that ardent Victorian Gothicist Augustus Welby

27 | Maurice Cody Hall

Northmore Pugin; no doubt the master would have approved their sturdy stone edifice, albeit the spirited composition and sophisticated stone tracery of windows and bell tower were not entirely in keeping with staid formulas for houses of worship sent from mother country to colonial hinterlands. The Radfords, who had come from England, departed Toronto soon after this commission. More's the pity. This building is now known as Maurice Cody Hall in memory of the drowned son of a prominent rector. Next door looms E.J. Lennox's 1913 Gothic re-revival, built at a time when the Anglican congregation had outgrown its little country church—already twice altered and enlarged. Lennox's St. Paul's presents an imposing bulk, but it lacks the vigour of its earlier neighbour, perhaps because planned towers and decorative carving were never completed. The interior is radiant, however, with Lennox's "scenic quality" glowing in place. Knitting all these structures together is Black & Moffat's fine, glassy set of atria. *PM/ updated AB*

28 Confederation Life Insurance Co., 321 Bloor St. E. (office building), Marani & Morris, 1954–56; additions, Marani Rounthwaite & Dick, 1973. Rogers headquarters/formerly Confederation Life office building, Zeidler Roberts, 1988. Formerly offices of Shaw & Begg, 350 Bloor St. E., Parkin Partnership, Architects and Planners, 1970. On Bloor, this discreet, domestic-looking structure—Georgian in style, small in scale, and distinguished in detail—was Confederation Life's contribution to insurance company land. Marani & Morris's nine-storey tower features orangey-coloured Flemish-bond brick, stone window surrounds with the slightest of metal-capped cornice heads, balustraded parapet, and a smooth stone base with grand pillared entrance. The 1973 addition to the rear is neatly compatible. Zeidler Roberts's much more grandiose contribution behind marked the final heights of Confederation Life before the firm collapsed. These buildings now form the heart of Rogers's corporate "campus," along with a little-noticed gem on the north side by the Parkin office that shares a vocabulary with I.M. Pei's concrete work at Commerce Court **[6/32b]**. *PM/AB*

"The Toronto Annex." The name began as a sales pitch and a plea, from the land developer Simeon Janes. He was advertising 259 lots available between Bedford and Spadina Roads, Bloor and Dupont Streets. This was still township land, not part of the city: Janes was presenting his development, a suburb that would enjoy a bit of healthful distance from the city . . . but that certainly needed the city's services in order to proceed. It needed to be annexed.

And it was, in 1887, as far west as Kendal Avenue. By 1888, Toronto's borders pushed much farther west, and the Annex as it's known today, from Avenue to Bathurst, was part of the city. [Adjacent Yorkville had been annexed in 1883; **see Area IX.**] Served by horse-drawn trolleys, these areas were within commuting distance of downtown and affordable to a growing professional class, who would occupy much of the Annex.

Janes's successful pitch marked the start of commercial development here. The land had already been sold and divided from the hands of the Baldwin family **[see 19/1]** and those of military officer and legislator Joseph Wells. As elsewhere in Toronto, these elite families benefited handsomely from developing the land they had bought cheaply or been granted. The Baldwins had already laid out Spadina Avenue south of Bloor **[see Area VIII]** and subdivided the land; in 1875, they extended Spadina Road and also laid out a curvy block of Walmer Road.

But the bulk of the Annex's streets, and many of its houses, would be built in fairly quick succession, lending a coherence to its planning and architecture. Janes, and the builders to whom he sold lots, bought into a consistent vision. Houses would be large, on relatively small lots, either detached or semi-detached; there would be essentially no laneways, nor any commercial or industrial uses, though room was found for numerous churches.

The houses of the Annex display very consistent urban design: their scale, setbacks, and height remained similar over time, while tight green lawns in front created visual continuity and put the houses' façades on display. This effect is somewhat reduced

Area X
Walk 19: Annex East
Walk 20: Annex West

now by mature street trees, shrubbery, and the chaotic impact of parking, fences, and recycling bins, especially in multi-unit and residential buildings. But on streets such as Admiral Road, this agreeable consistency remains intact.

Stylistically, many of the houses were shaped by the picturesque complexity of the Queen Anne mode, an 18th-century revival style then in fashion: their varied cladding, and asymmetrical compositions of bays and turrets and gables **[20/14d]**, remain lively. But others evoke a different current style, the Romanesque of H.H. Richardson, with its weighty, rough stone, round arches, carved ornament, and multi-toned façades. The key Toronto building of this style is Old City Hall **[7/17]**, and its architect, E.J. Lennox, played an important role in the development of the Annex. With the Lewis Lukes house **[19/9]**, he blended Richardsonian Romanesque with the wild decoration and looser spirit of Queen Anne. This blend became characteristic of the Annex House, often built from Credit Valley sandstone and Don Valley brick and clay.

The most common vocabulary for later houses is the English Cottage Style: these houses **[19/45, 19/10]** are identifiable by their expansive plain walls, bays clad in stucco, high prominent roofs, tall square chimneys, and multi-light casement windows.

Although most houses constructed in the Annex were put up by speculative builders using variations on stock plans, many well-known architectural firms designed buildings here. In addition to Lennox, they included Charles Gibson, Edmund Burke, Darling & Pearson, and Eden Smith, the master of English Cottage Style. Langley & Burke were responsible for grand Gothic **[20/17]** and Romanesque **[20/19]** churches. A planned Anglican cathedral that would have dominated the district was never fully realized.

From the 1890s through the 1920s, the Annex enjoyed a brief moment as a destination for members of Toronto's economic and social elite; David Roberts's mansion for George Gooderham **[19/31]** remains to testify to this, though Timothy Eaton's grand house at 182 Lowther, on the northwest corner of Spadina Road, is long gone to development. So are most of the lesser-but-still-grand houses that occupied the curvy bottom block of Walmer Road.

The area's decline in fortune between the 1920s and the 1960s was precipitous, the combined result of the age of the housing stock, the desire of wealthy families to move to car-friendly areas in Forest Hill, and the more general middle-class exodus to more distant suburbs. The area's inexpensive large houses were occupied by tenants, including students; by fraternities pushed north of Bloor by the University of Toronto's 1950s expansion **[see Walk 8]**; and by families of lesser means: skilled blue-collar workers, who had always lived on the Annex's western and northern fringes, began also to occupy grander homes. As in Yorkville **[see Area IX]**, this population became increasingly more diverse with the waves of immigration to Toronto post-1945, and the neighbourhood was gentrified by educated progressive types: called "white-painters" for their characteristic choice of façade treatment.

The latter group, including many University of Toronto professors and artists of various disciplines, particularly writers,

would have a decisive influence on the place and a lasting influence on the city. Editor and writer Robert Fulford (an Albany Street resident from 1969 to 1971) wrote that the Annex "has been the most literary section of Toronto." Among the arrivals was Jane Jacobs, who landed here in 1968 and would settle at 69 Albany **[20/28]**. Jacobs was a writer herself but was already famous for her activism in New York, which she had left during the Vietnam War. In New York, she had written *The Death and Life of Great American Cities* and battled the forces of urban renewal. In the Annex, she and her architect husband found a simpatico group of white-painters, and they mobilized to fight the Spadina Expressway, a new addition to the city's highway network that would have extended what is now Allen Road right down Spadina through the heart of the district. Of course, they won; the fight to Stop Spadina became a decisive victory for the reform movement in city politics that was battling to defend the city core from such grand, destructive schemes **[see Introduction]**.

Vocal activists (the Annex Residents' Association goes back to the 1880s) did not, however, fully prevent change from happening in the neighbourhood. The impending arrival of the Bloor Street subway (in 1966) made sites near Bloor and St. George and Bloor and Spadina attractive to developers; many of the area's biggest houses, on big lots, were redeveloped as apartment towers of varying quality, with the blessing of the city. A few of those by the architect Uno Prii **[20/7]** have real architectural character; others clearly don't live up to the standard of the grand 19th-century buildings that they were replacing.

This partial rebuilding, however, did have some advantages. It made the area more diverse, allowing in students and young professionals; and it added population, which makes the Annex, for all its leafy streets, one of the more densely occupied areas in the vicinity. Given the central location and abundance of services, this is good policy, and the Annex has functioned well for everyone for four decades. The challenge now is to avoid stasis. Large-scale development has been mostly prevented by zoning since the early 1970s, and new residential additions to the area have taken the form of conversions **[20/24]** or infill **[20/8]**. Increasingly, the houses of the Annex are becoming single-family homes again, occupied by the white-collar professionals and captains of industry who lived here a century ago. No white-painting writers can buy houses here, nor will they ever be able to do so again.

Where, then, will aspiring middle-class Annegonians settle? New condos **[20/30]** and promised rental housing **[20/31]** are the likely answers, but those particular projects, which destroy no architectural heritage to speak of, have been assailed by some locals for their very height and density. The question for the Annex and adjacent neighbourhoods is this: can they make room for newcomers, or must those arrivals head for more distant Annexes, on the fringes of today's Toronto?

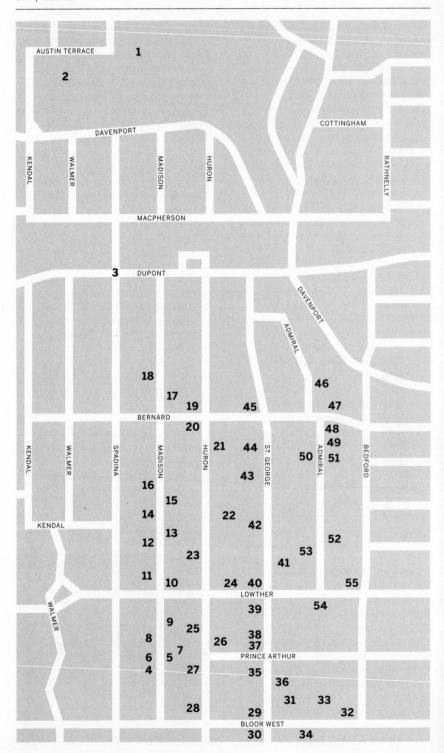

AUSTIN TERRACE

1

2

DAVENPORT

COTTINGHAM

KENDAL

WALMER

MADISON

HURON

RATHNELLY

MACPHERSON

3 DUPONT

DAVENPORT

ADMIRAL

18

46

17

19

45

47

BERNARD

20

48

21

44

ST. GEORGE

49

KENDAL

WALMER

SPADINA

MADISON

HURON

50

ADMIRAL

51

BEDFORD

16

43

15

14

22

42

KENDAL

13

12

23

53

52

41

11

10

24

40

55

LOWTHER

WALMER

39

54

9

25

8

26

38

37

6

5

7

PRINCE ARTHUR

4

27

35

36

28

31

33

29

32

BLOOR WEST

30

34

Walk 19: Annex East

1 Spadina House, 285 Spadina Rd., 1866; altered later. Dr. William Warren Baldwin named this place after an Aboriginal word for hill, and he chose a fine site for an estate, atop the Davenport escarpment. From here, you can see the expanse of the Baldwin family's former lands, a park lot extending down to Queen Street and including much of what's now Forest Hill. Baldwin, a lawyer and doctor, was also a hobbyist architect; it was his plan that defined Spadina Avenue and much of the street grid around it. He also designed a house here, which burned, and then its replacement. The current house went up for businessman James Austin in 1866, in High Victorian style, and was renovated by Austin descendants over the next decades. Today it's a house museum with much to say about the 1920s and 1930s. *AB*

1 | Spadina House

2 Casa Loma, 1 Austin Terrace, E.J. Lennox, 1915. One hundred and eighty thousand square feet of grandiosity. And don't forget the lodge, or the stables, which you can reach through the underground tunnel. (If you're armed with arrows, you will find the stable towers ideal points from which to take aim at any attackers.) By 1905, Henry Pellatt had made his fortune in banking, railways, and hydroelectric power. Pellatt had a stake in the Electrical Development Company of Ontario, which hired E.J. Lennox to design a grand Beaux Arts power station in Niagara Falls. Pellatt soon turned to Lennox to design for him a castle inspired by sketches and clippings he'd gathered during visits to a string of European chateaux. The result was a mixed-bag Gothic Revival, loaded with heraldic beasts and crenellations and arches borrowed (along with the odd fireplace) from Scotland or Normandy or other Old World milieux. Such eclecticism had shaped Victorian buildings like University College **[8/1]**; here, in the Edwardian era, it was rather backward-looking, a patchwork costume for a building with a structure of concrete and steel. It's hard not to see the place as a fable of wealth gone wrong. Pellatt's desire to trumpet his own success produced a building that is the image "of overwhelming lavishness, limitless luxury," the architectural historian Alan Gowans fumed in the 1950s. "Architecturally it is one hundred per cent hopeless . . . its like (we may hope) will never be built again." Gowans, and many others, have taken glee at the fact that Pellatt suffered a reversal of fortunes and surrendered the house for back taxes. Today, with this preposterous building in city hands, it's best appreciated as a venue for fanciful weddings, a place for schoolchildren to think a bit about architectural history, a sign of the fickleness of fortune, and a reminder that staid old Toronto had people capable of grand, spendthrift gestures. *AB*

2 | Casa Loma

3 Dupont subway station, Dunlop Farrow Aitken, 1978. With its expansion of the Spadina Line [see 20/10 and 25/25], the TTC went for grandeur and stylistic flash, aspiring to the drama of the 1960s Montreal Métro construction. Here, a profusion of fashionable browns, mosaic-tile art (*Summer Under All Seasons* by James Sutherland), and a double-height platform—plus a pair of steel-and-glass pavilions that were and remain the most stylish things at Dupont and Spadina. *AB*

4a 12 Madison Ave., 1891. 14 Madison Ave. (detached house), 1891. The four arches wheeling smartly across the front of these twinned houses are emblematic of the Annex. The Romans perfected the round arch almost two millennia ago and it has graced—and supported—buildings ever since. You'll find arches and decorative curves such as these scalloped tile-hangings and segmental bricks throughout the area. *PM*

4b 16–18 Madison Ave. (double house), 1891. "Picturesque" in architecture translates as asymmetry and variety, so perforce the two halves of a picturesque double house would be strikingly different. But, as with any good design, the two halves are in calculated harmony: the gabled porch of no. 16 rehearsed in no. 18's conical roof; the arched entry of no. 18 echoed in the curve of no. 16's attic porch; the corner turret in one balanced by the tower-like projecting bay and gable of the other. *PM*

5 17–19 and 21–23 Madison Ave. (two double houses), 1891. These abodes follow a standard plan for speculative houses with side hall and three principal rooms per floor. The builder did make a stab at having the four appear dissimilar, however: here a round arch, there a straight lintel; here a dormer, there a gable; brick on this, terracotta for that. All in all, a handsome assemblage. *PM*

6 20 Madison Ave. (detached house), 1891. The builder of this house, George Hunter, a carpenter, must have known that brick and stone were *in* for the Annex, but he didn't give up altogether his obvious love for wood. The painted wooden balconies really don't meld into the composition, but they are so exuberant and inviting, one remembers no. 20 long after forgetting better-designed houses. *PM*

7 Huron-Madison Project, 25 Madison Ave. thru to Huron St. (complex of apartment house and nine rehabilitated houses), Paul Martel, 1981. Making good use of the space and vista down a brick-paved entryway, this four-storey infill building cleverly manipulates 12 units in an unobtrusive but distinctive composition. The decision to give each ground-floor occupant a high-walled garden "pen" is a little depressing though. The ensemble is owned, for now, by Toronto Community Housing. *PM/updated AB*

8a 24–26 Madison Ave. (double house), 1891. Typical Annex asymmetry with one-half of this double house dominated by a wide front gable, the other half reciprocating with a tall corner tower. Variations on this gable/tower equipoise occur throughout the district. *PM*

8b 30–32 Madison Ave. (double house), 1889. A nice big house? No, two houses, with the second entrance tucked away at the side. Even if the pretence didn't work, such a design cleverly produced two different interior layouts. *PM*

9 Originally Lewis Lukes house, 37 Madison Ave., E.J. Lennox, 1888–90. This, Lennox's domestic masterpiece, was among the first houses designed for the Annex, and it became a model for much of what followed. The architect had set the stage for a robust Richardsonian Romanesque style in Toronto with his mighty city hall then going up on Queen Street [7/17], but Lennox knew he couldn't put up massive monuments of stone on small residential lots. His solution was to temper the bulk and solidity of Romanesque with the lithesomeness of Queen Anne. Designed for a building contractor who would have appreciated the wit that the invented form demanded, no. 37 revels in a calculated equilibrium of interrelated parts. This disciplined pictur-esque with its aura of stability along with the fashionableness was just what late Victorian suburbia hankered for, and in block after Annex block houses began to go up with the same progression of rock-faced stone, rich red brick, decorative terracotta tile, and intricate woodwork. As a group the houses are impressive, but Lennox's example remains the standout, and not just because today it is flanked by tawdry Tudor boxes. *PM*

9 | 37 Madison Ave.

10 47 Madison Ave. (detached house), Eden Smith, 1903–04. A new century and the beginning of much plainer looking houses. White stucco facing, small windows, and an embracing roof are typical character-istics of the English Cottage Style, a simplified rendering of vernacular Tudor forms very popular in the early 1900s. *PM*

11 St. Thomas House/originally James Henderson house, 54 Madison Ave., Frederick H. Herbert, 1904–05; addition, Armstrong & Molesworth, 1976. A fine Gothic-inspired wall dormer and door-case here, plus wing-like eaves and shooting window heads that make this subtly asymmetric house look as if it might fly away. Definitely a bird of another feather in this neighbourhood. Henderson was a barrister with Henderson, Small and Beaumont. The addition for a nursing home is properly unprepossessing. *PM*

12 64–66 Madison Ave. (double house), 1891; porch addition to no. 64, Chadwick & Beckett, 1893. Stepped gable, stained glass portholes, and artsy-craftsy porch for a change of pace. *PM*

13 69–71 Madison Ave. (double house), 1894. A catalogue of beautifully articulated terracotta. In the 1890s, as much attention was paid to creating designs for terracotta as for stone. Of course, once moulds were made, terracotta decoration could be cheaply reproduced—over and over and over again. *PM*

14 78 Madison Ave. (detached house), 1899. The delightful porches gracing the first and second storeys of this house may be its two best rooms. No doubt many an Annex denizen has sat here behind spooled balustrades to watch the passing parade. *PM*

15 93–99 Madison Ave. (apartment house), Langley & Langley, 1907. Early Toronto apartment buildings, which were introduced after 1900 following the lead in Montreal, Boston, and New York, took great pains to melt into established neighbour-hoods. This one succeeds entirely: its cornice line, setback, red brick, and wide projecting bays all echo those of surrounding houses. Instructive, since today's residents' associa-tion would never countenance the develop-ment of such a building on this site. *PM/AB*

15 | 93–99 Madison Ave.

16 88 Madison Ave. (detached house), Frederick H. Herbert, 1899. Always coming up with something out of the ordinary, Herbert has here made the requisite Annex tower into a wishing well. One wishes he'd made the windows bigger, but the sheltering roof sweeping down over the porch is grand. *PM*

17 145 Madison Ave. (detached house), Frederick H. Herbert, 1895–96. Tower as elfin sun porch, and a long way from Middle Ages antecedents. *PM*

18a Originally "Rivermead" (Percy R. Gardiner residence), 138 Madison Ave., Jocelyn Davidson, 1934. A late version of the Neo-Tudor, with horizontal bands of small casement windows and rough clinker brick to impart a rustic flavour. "Rivermead" replaced an earlier house on this large double lot (now occupied by a pair of infill houses). Gardiner, who was a stockbroker with his own firm, must have fared better than most in the 1929 crash. *PM/updated AB*

18b 140 Madison Ave. (detached house), 1902. Georgian Revival in an American mood. *PM*

19 Originally Stanley C.H. Clarke house, 112 Bernard Ave., Chadwick & Beckett, 1906–07. Georgian Revival at its inventive best, adapting 18th-century forms to 20th-century proclivities. The high first storey, for example, allows for an amiable billiard room in the basement, and the three-part casement windows for much light and air. The height also dramatizes a grand hooded and pilastered entrance. Clarke was branch manager of the Imperial Bank at Yonge and Bloor. *PM*

Huron is a street of well-intentioned Annex houses rendered clumsy in later years by the addition of chain-link fences and shrubs in too many front yards. In a district of large houses close to one another and to the street, the unbroken vista of the front lawns was essential for proper perspective.

20 Originally Thomas A. Lytle house, 610 Huron St., 1891. A Queen Anne smorgasbord paid for by a prominent pickle manufacturer and looking more variety-laden than usual thanks to its corner site: two sides of the building for invention, play, and the hanging of tiles. *PM*

21 571–573 Huron St. (double house), 1894. In a district infatuated by towers and turrets (little towers), one way to make one's own tower stand out was to skew it at a 45-degree angle. Another was to top it with an eye-catching finial. *PM*

22 | Huron Street School

22 Huron Street School, 541 Huron St., 1890; demolished, 1956; new building, Irving D. Boigon, 1958. Huron Street School Annex, Charles H. Bishop, 1914. When this area was annexed in 1887, the city acquired land on centrally located Huron Street for an elementary school, and a fine three-storey edifice with cupola-topped mansard and 12 maple-panelled rooms was built in 1890. As the Annex grew so did the school population, and in 1914 the Board of Education Superintendent of Buildings was called on to design an annex building with a further six classrooms. In the Queen Anne style favoured here and abroad for munici-pally run schools, the Flemish-gabled Huron Street School Annex fit right in with residential neighbours. In 1956, the original structure was deemed substandard and it was replaced by one of Toronto's first Early-Modern buildings, a low-scale ribbon of large-windowed classrooms strung out along the street [25/14]. The annex building was subsequently threatened, but school parents, citing its "big, airy and beautiful" rooms, organized to upgrade and save it. So today the Annex can boast two very distinguished school buildings, one of 1914, the other 1958. *PM*

23a 534 Huron St. (detached house), probably Frederick H. Herbert, 1895. Chateauesque arches and Neo-Tudor half-timbering. *PM*

23b 532 Huron St. (detached house), Frederick H. Herbert, 1896. Classical pediments and keystones saucing Queen Anne flummery. With what relish Herbert went about these Annex houses, and how unpalatable some of them look. *PM*

24 80 Lowther Ave. at Huron St. (detached house), Frederick H. Herbert, 1899–1900. 82 Lowther Ave. (detached house), Frederick H. Herbert, 1895–96. 84 Lowther Ave. (detached house), Chadwick & Beckett, 1900–01. 86 Lowther Ave. (detached house), Frederick H. Herbert, 1899–1900. A turn-of-the-century quartet answering the call of Classical Revival. *PM*

Huron Street south of Lowther Avenue is a block of distinguished Annex houses flung out of scale by high-rise apartment buildings and no-rise parking flats. The park at the southeast corner owes its existence to ground too soft to build on, a function of mysterious Taddle Creek, which meanders under the Annex and surfaces in surprised householders' basements every once in a while.

25a Originally Walter Gaynor house, 500 Huron St., 1889. More austere and crusty than later Annex houses. The first occupant was an estate and financial broker, and his rock-faced manor with looming tower undoubtedly projected an appropriate aura of security and stability. *PM*

25b 496 Huron St. (detached house), Strickland & Symons, 1897. Like an onion, this layered façade peels itself back from scroll-gabled polygonal bay to wide-gabled flat front to deep-set portal. A very poised rendition of the Queen Anne song, with not a few Classical Revival notes typical of this late date. *PM*

26 Originally William Ince house, 94 Prince Arthur Ave. at Huron St., Darling Curry Sproatt & Pearson, 1892–93. Trim Queen Anne with a conspicuous Classical Revival porch and door-case replete with Ionic columns and fanlight and sidelights. William Ince was a partner in Perkins, Ince wholesale grocers on Front Street **[1/21b]**. *PM*

27a 480–482 Huron St. (double house), probably Smith & Gemmell, 1888. A grand and expansive ground-hugging house, graciously accommodating two suburban families. Architect John Gemmell was listed as first owner of this finely crafted and detailed double house, and it is likely his firm designed it. Another architect, David Roberts, took up residence at no. 480 years later. *PM*

27b 478 Huron St. (detached house), probably Smith & Gemmell, 1888. The same windows, brick panels, and front door as at no. 480–482 **[19/27a]**, this time in the service of a single dwelling. The clipped-back gable roof was an interesting design device to make these buildings seem less close together. *PM*

28 Bloor Street United Church/originally Bloor Street Presbyterian Church, 300 Bloor St. W., William R. Gregg, 1889–90; additions, Wickson & Gregg, 1908–09; altered, Wickson & Gregg, 1927. As begun in 1889, Bloor Street Presbyterian was a small and unassuming Decorated Gothic Revival stone structure that the congregation outgrew even before it was finished. Greatly enlarged in similar dry, workaday fashion, the church has little to recommend it, even though it did once enjoy Gothic-arched portals along a narrower Bloor Street. When Presbyterians, Methodists, and

Congregationalists in Canada united in the sweeping, often acrimonious church reform of 1925, the outspoken minister of this church, Rev. George Campbell Pidgeon, was elected the new body's first head. Obviously, voting delegates were not influenced by the architectural pre-eminence of his house of worship. *PM*

29 Originally Medical Arts Building, 170 St. George St. at Bloor St., Marani Lawson & Paisley, 1928–29. When the doctors ran out of mansions on Bloor Street to turn into waiting and examining rooms in the 1910s and '20s **[see Introduction, Area IX]**, they built this circumspect office tower. Part of Toronto's pre-Depression high-rise boom, it was the first tall building in this area. The University of Toronto, always property-hungry, bought it in 2002 and made it the Jackman Humanities Building in 2008. *PM/ updated AB*

St. George Street, as a continuation of an important residential avenue south of Bloor, early attracted those who sought to erect the most imposing of Annex houses. Following World War II, apartment builders began to capitalize on this reputation as well as the avenue's proximity to the planned subway, and today many high-rises share the street with former stately homes.

30 Bata Shoe Museum, 327 Bloor St. W., Moriyama & Teshima, 1995. A shoe museum? Yes, thanks to Sonja Bata, the wife of shoe magnate Thomas Bata and an educated patron of architecture. (Bata Shoe's former Canadian headquarters in Don Mills, demolished for the Aga Khan Museum, was a landmark.) This building sees the Moriyama office flirting with the Deconstructivist movement, and very successfully; the calculated disorder of the façade's limestone planes is pierced by a wedge of glass that points the way to an interesting (and quite orderly) interior. This could be seen as a prequel, and a superior one, to Daniel Libeskind's ROM **[8/43]**. *AB*

31 York Club/originally George Gooderham house, 135 St. George St., David Roberts, 1889–92. The most distinguished Richardsonian Romanesque house in Toronto, and arguably the most distinguished house of any kind, built for a man who was the wealthiest in the province at the time. George Gooderham was president of Gooderham & Worts (an enterprise begun by his father, William, in 1832 that had gone on to become the largest distillery in the British Empire), as well as a leading figure in the world of Canadian banking, railroading, and real estate. His chosen architect, David Roberts, also designed much of the distillery complex **[see Area XII]**, the distinctive Gooderham office building **[1/20]**, and most of the manors around town for this large and influential family (George had 11 children and was brother to 12). But this magnificent ensemble of beautifully executed brick and stone was Roberts's masterpiece. Consummately balancing assertive tower, gables, and chimneys with deep round-arched porch, gallery, and windows, the architect has created a composition so firm, so formal-looking, as to endow the picturesque and asymmetric Romanesque with a majestic classical serenity. The Gooderham house was sold to the York Club in 1909. At the time, adjacent mansions on Bloor Street still served as residences, making this the first secular institution tolerated in the Annex. Through the years the York Club has been a careful custodian, and this building continues to stand as one of the finest in the city. *PM*

31 | York Club

32 Factor-Inwentash Faculty of Social Work/originally Texaco offices, 246 Bloor St. W., Marani & Morris, 1950. Renovated, DuBois Plumb Partnership, 1999. A less luxe and slightly less Classical cousin to the Bank of Canada building at 250 University Ave. **[7/13]**. A bit corporate for its current occupants but very handsome. *AB*

33 Ontario Institute for Studies in Education, 252 Bloor St. W., Kenneth R. Cooper, 1969. One of the best Brutalist buildings in the city: a tough sculptural skin protects a warm and enticingly complex interior of brick, quarry tile and wood. *AB*

34 Munk School of Global Affairs/ originally Dominion Meteorological Building, 315 Bloor St. W., Burke & Horwood, 1908–09. Renovation and addition, KPMB and ERA, 2012. A light-touch renovation modernized the interiors of this, once the headquarters for the Meteorological Service of Canada. The rusticated Miramichi sandstone looks spiffy after the removal of a century's grime. Inside, you can enter the tower, but there is no longer a telescope. *AB*

35 174 St. George St. (detached house), George M. Miller, 1890–92. 176 St. George St. (detached house), George M. Miller, 1890–91. 178 St. George St. (detached house), George M. Miller, 1890–91. A trio of typical detached Annex houses designed by George M. Miller for builder James T. McCabe shortly after the Gooderham house was begun. Miller was at some pains to differentiate the houses one from another by scrambling their picturesque details, but he respected a common setback and eaves line for all three, thereby situating them firmly in the ceremonious streetscape. No. 178, with its corner watchtower, was for many years the home of the sheriff of York Township, Joseph J. Widdifield. *PM*

36 Royal Canadian Yacht Club, 139 St. George St., Crang & Boake, 1984. One of the very best Post-Modern buildings in the city, the RCYC's in-town address captures the Annex recipe of stolid red brick and giddy ornamentation with symmetry of form and some very fine details. (Just look at that corner.) The wall, built in 1892, once surrounded George Gooderham's son-in-law's house. *PM/AB*

37 Originally Thomas W. Horn house, 180 St. George St., Frederick H. Herbert, 1898; west wing addition, Chadwick & Beckett, 1907. Full-blooded Richardsonian Romanesque with an all-stone skin tautly curving around and enveloping the bold structure. The design makes the most of an interesting site, calling up a striking conical-capped tower to mark the corner and a beautiful formal entrance to articulate the long front. This is probably Herbert's best design in Toronto. The west wing is a sympathetic later addition by Chadwick & Beckett. Horn was president of a concern that made light-enhancing glass for shop windows, Luxfer Prism Company. *PM*

38a Originally Harris L. Hees house, 182 St. George St., Eden Smith & Son, 1910–11. A very large formal stone house trying to look "cottagey," with sweeping roof, half-timbered gables, multi-light casement windows, and swelling bays to break up the mass. Harris L. Hees was in the family window shades business. *PM*

38b Originally James O. Buchanan house, 186 St. George St., S. Hamilton Townsend, 1889–90. Built for the manager of the Union Bank of Canada on Wellington Street, this was the first house on St. George Street above Bloor. Though fundamentally a Romanesque/Queen Anne design, the simple massing, flatness, and half-timbering across the second storey anticipate the Neo-Tudor houses constructed in this area later in the early 1900s. *PM*

39 190 St. George St. (condominium apartment tower), Joseph A. Medwecki, 1972. A distinguished essay in Late-Modernism that picks up where the smooth-sided International Style leaves off, with a plastic though still spare form that crisply articulates the layers of floors and punctuates the front with a thrusting, dynamic V. Quality materials and gracious siting on the well-landscaped lot enhance the message. An effective statement on a street of more often weak sisters. *PM*

39 | 190 St. George St.

40 First Church of Christ, Scientist, 196 St. George St., S.S. Beman, 1915. This was the first Christian Science church in Toronto, built here for the large and tranquil site and central location. Like Christian Science churches elsewhere in the world, the atypical ecclesiastical design is that of a large domed auditorium imposingly cloaked in classical detail, in this instance Doric. *PM*

41a Originally Henry Victor Cawthra house, 163 St. George St., Gordon & Helliwell, 1897–98. Subdued Queen Anne with the usual gable/turret litany. Turrets were picturesque of course, but they were also practical, for their bayed windows served to draw more light and air into deep rooms. No. 163 was built as a wedding present for his son by Henry Cawthra of the mercantile and banking dynasty **[see 14/13]**. *PM*

41b 165 St. George St. (detached house), Eden Smith, 1906. Toronto's version of English Cottage Style as interpreted by the prolific Eden Smith, this time with the characteristic tall chimney poised like a sentinel against the broad, plain front. The round-arched, recessed porch with stone voussoirs is very welcome looking. *PM*

41c 169 St. George St. (apartment house), Crang & Boake, 1956. One of the best small 1950s apartment houses in Toronto, no. 169 uses stretches of glass and a Miesian ground-storey setback to very stylish effect. The contained balconies to the sides are infinitely more practical than the toothy ones punctuating so many apartments of this era. *PM*

42 212 St. George St. (detached house), Charles J. Gibson, 1907; apartment house addition, Emslie Eden, 1980. An imposing Neo-Tudor manor felicitously fronting a modern residential complex, demonstrating that there are ways—and ways—to build multiple housing. *PM*

43 228 St. George St., Eden Smith, 1900–01. 230 St. George St., Edwards & Saunders, 1909. 234 St. George St., E.J. Lennox, 1902–03; renovation and new housing at rear, George Popper, 1996. This varied group of three Annex houses, including a Smith and a Lennox, has been knitted together with two hidden backyard additions into a complex of apartments. The treasure here is Lennox's Jacobean confection for Robert Watson, owner of a candy factory. *AB*

44 Chinese Consulate/originally Ontario Medical Association, 240 St. George St. (office building), A.J. Diamond & Barton Myers (designed by Barton Myers), 1968. The neighbourhood's residential red brick, low scale, and recessed entries handsomely translated into the sleek architectural vocabulary of the 1960s in a modish office building designed for the OMA. Its current use has brought protesters, heavy gates, and security, taking away some of its grace. *PM/ updated AB*

45 260 St. George St. (detached house), Eden Smith, 1905. The large suburban Cottage Style house that Eden Smith made famous in Toronto sat particularly well on a corner lot, comfortably meandering down the long frontage poking its tall chimneys up along the way. Very, very cheery. *PM*

Admiral Crescent, as Admiral Road north of Bernard Avenue was first called, was laid out some years after the grid subdivision of the Annex. Its picturesque curve was designed to fit the northeasterly lots to the bend of Davenport Road on which they back.

46 101 Admiral Rd. (detached house), Chadwick & Beckett, 1909. Distinctive Neo-Tudor with pegged half-timbering and the pro forma Annex tower rendered in countrified stone and stucco. *PM*

47 Originally Gamble Geddes house, 62 Bernard Ave., 1891–92. The first house in this block and one of the best English-inspired Queen Anne designs in Toronto. This sprightly, pretty house really does look as if it had emigrated from London's Bedford Park or some other equally salubrious and "Aesthetic" garden suburb. The architect is unknown; Geddes was listed in the assessment rolls as a "general agent." *PM*

48 63 Bernard Ave. (detached house), nkArchitect, 2010. A tall, purely rectangular composition in stone, brick, glass, and concrete, this house could have been uncomfortable. But it isn't: the young studio of Nelson Kwong has filled the corner with a house that is harmonious with its Admiral Road neighbours. *AB*

Admiral Road between Bernard and Lowther is a narrow, quiet enclave laid out around a venerable tree. The tree is gone but the jog in the street remains.

49 Originally Currie house/formerly George Deeks house, 77 Admiral Rd., Darling & Pearson, 1909–10; fence and garage, Darling & Pearson, 1911. In 1910, the Georgian style was again a metaphor for the gracious and comfortable life, especially in the capable hands of a firm such as Darling & Pearson. This large, handsome house was built for the Misses Margaret and Elizabeth Currie, who transferred it the following year to a contractor, George Deeks. *PM*

50 58–60 Admiral Rd. (double house), 1892–93. 62–64 Admiral Rd. (double house), 1892. Same-plan speculative houses by builder Davidson Todd, quietly mixing up Romanesque/Queen Anne details. The lavish modernization at no. 62–64, using expansive panes of glass, is more assertive, but works well. *PM*

51a Originally R. Ross Bongard house, 59 Admiral Rd., Eden Smith, 1905–06. Built for a stockbroker and one of the architect's bravura houses, this is surely one of the most sophisticated structures in Toronto. Smith has here rendered the ingredients of the English Cottage—white stucco walls, ribbons of casement windows, tall chimney, and sweeping roof—almost abstractly modern. *PM*

51a | 59 Admiral Rd.

51b 57 Admiral Rd. (detached house), David Binder, 1987. Just the opposite of the pseudo-Victorian mode prevalent for new houses in old neighbourhoods, no. 57 is a High Modernist model whose ancestry can be traced to the Bauhaus. The pipes, glass blocks, curved wall, and white colour are typical of the form. Slipped into no. 59's side garden, to which it relates very nicely. *PM*

52 13–15 Admiral Rd. (double house), 1891. 14–16 Admiral Rd. (double house), 1892. Twinned double houses by builder Davidson Todd with splendid wooden bric-a-brac frosting porches, balconies, and recessed galleries. *PM*

53 12 Admiral Rd. (detached house), Charles J. Gibson, 1896–97. An eclectic melange of Queen Anne/Romanesque/ Classical Revival forms and details for a very tall house of late date. In the 1920s, Lester B. Pearson toiled on the third floor here as a young history professor at the University of Toronto. *PM*

54 Originally C.J. Holman house, 75 Lowther Ave., Edmund Burke, 1892–93, altered, Bruce Kuwabara, 2010. A particularly fine and well-preserved Annex house with tile-hangings voluminously wrapping upper storeys and brick and stone meticulously anchoring a high first floor and basement. Holman practised law with Holman, Elliott & Pattullo. *PM*

54 | 75 Lowther Ave.

55 Society of Friends Meeting House/ originally Miller Lash house, 60 Lowther Ave., Curry Sproatt & Rolph, 1906; rear addition, John Leaning, 1970. A rousing reincarnation of the red-brick cube with freely adapted Georgian details. *PM*

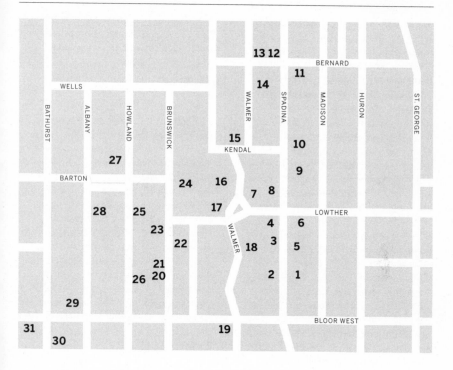

Walk 20: Annex West

The extension of Spadina Avenue north of Bloor Street is called Spadina Road. The extension was first plotted in the 1870s, but most houses did not begin to go up until the 1890s, at the same time and in the same Romanesque/Queen Anne mode as other parts of the Annex. Some 75 years later, Spadina Road was tagged by developers as a prime location for apartment construction because of its proximity to the nascent Bloor Street subway. Many early houses were torn down to make way for these high-rises, as well as for construction of station facilities and of the subway itself (the flat ribbon of parking lots and parkettes that cuts a swath just north of Bloor Street, as far as Christie Street, is that subway's above-ground legacy). Spadina Road fared better with construction of the Spadina line, which was run under the street in this neighbourhood, with an 1899 house rehabilitated as subway station at the juncture of Spadina and Kendal Avenues. Today the area is an interesting mix of the old and new, high and low, and—architecturally—good and definitely not so good.

1 9–11 Spadina Rd. (double house), 1889.
This large double house seems a bit pathetic standing all alone in the parking lot, but it began life all alone in empty fields. The second house to go up on the east side of Spadina Road, it is in the tradition of symmetrical Bay-n-Gables built earlier in older parts of town, with only elaborate wooden balconies to mark it as part of the Queen Anne fancy so inimitably associated with the Annex. *PM*

2 Annex Lane (townhouses), 16 Annex Lane, 2002. A form of infill development that was briefly, inexplicably in vogue at city planning, this places two rows of townhouses tightly face-to-face, lacking light in front and privacy on any side. The architectural veneer, thoroughly incoherent Subdivision Traditional, doesn't help. *AB*

3 Native Canadian Centre of Toronto/ originally Ontario Bible College, 16 Spadina Rd., Mathers & Haldenby, 1928.
Wide gables, rectangular bays, Tudor arch,

and ribbons of neat casement windows to disguise a utilitarian school as Jacobethan manor. *PM*

4 Alliance Française de Toronto, 24 Spadina Rd., c. 1904; addition, Hariri Pontarini, 2014 and in progress. A classic Annex double house, with an addition that expresses itself in a totally different—but equally vigorous—way. The curved wall clad in cedar slats encloses a performance space, while the glass boxes above are classrooms. A planned further addition will provide a grand stair and entrance on Spadina. *AB*

5 25 Spadina Rd. (double house), Frederick H. Herbert, 1897. Splendid rehabilitation of this 1890s Annex house reveals afresh the sumptuous coursed brick, subtle play of windows, superb ornamented stone, and striking pressed-metal balcony. Pressed metal was an inexpensive turn-of-the-century substitute for stone and wood and in those days would have been painted to hide its lowly identity. *PM*

6 Spadina Gardens, 41–45 Spadina Rd. (apartment house), A.R. Denison, 1905–06. One of the best—and best preserved—of Toronto's early apartment houses, with low scale, careful symmetry, and firm Classical Revival details projecting an air of quiet grandeur appropriate to this once prestigious residential thoroughfare (the Timothy Eaton house stood on the northwest corner of Spadina Road and Lowther from 1889 until 1965). The first apartment houses intrigued early tenants in the relative amplitude of their rooms, which on one floor could be laid out in ways

impossible in a narrow multi-level row house. Spadina Gardens—note the stylized "S G" etched on the glass of the front doors—still retains these amenities, having been spared the minimalizing conversions prevalent elsewhere. *PM*

7 35 Walmer Rd. at Spadina Rd. (apartment house), Uno Prii, 1965. The apartment buildings that began to invade the Annex with the coming of the subway, unlike their 1910s, '20s, and '30s ancestors, showed little respect for the scale and spirit of existing streetscape. Many in this area also came under attack for their shoddy materials and garish appearance. Related to the flamboyant hotel architecture being practised by Morris Lapidus in Miami Beach, they were an early attempt to invigorate International Style's "boring box." Yet with the passage of time, these seem clearly expressions of their own period; this building was added to the city's heritage register in 2004. *PM/AB*

7 | 35 Walmer Rd.

6 | Spadina Gardens

8 50 Spadina Rd. (apartments), Roberts & Caunter, 2009. 35 Walmer was conceived as a tower-in-the-park; as with many buildings of its vintage, that "park" proved to be an unused lawn topping a parking garage. Developers are increasingly filling those empty spaces with buildings like this eight-storey rental structure, which restores a streetwall on Spadina. (There is another a block north at 100 Spadina Rd.) Sadly, the architecture—clumsily articulated windows, cheap spandrel glass, unconvincing brick veneer—isn't good enough for the Annex of Lennox or of Prii. *AB*

9 Originally A.R. Boswell house and W.H. Kerr house, 69–71 Spadina Rd. (originally Normal B. Gash house), Frederick H. Herbert, 1894. Typically the two halves of Annex double houses were made to appear quite different in an attempt at picturesque asymmetry, and looking at no. 69–71 one can see why: one absurdly small corner tower popping up at roof level is funny; two are downright ludicrous. *PM*

10 TTC subway station, 85 Spadina Rd./ originally Norman B. Gash house, Robert M. Ogilvie, 1899; remodelled, Adamson Associates, 1977. A Queen Anne subway station, and why not? Advocacy from the Toronto Historical Board allowed this felicitous re-use and preservation of endangered streetscape. *PM/updated AB*

11 Originally M.A. Armstrong house, 151 Spadina Rd. (detached house), James A. Harvey, 1905–06. Zoning laws prohibited it and assessment rolls list only single-family occupancy, but this building suspiciously resembles what in Boston would be called a three-decker: a three-family dwelling disguised as a single house. The higher than normal third storey, stained glass window in the second storey (as if for a second dining room), and bank of porches in the rear are clues. *PM*

12 Originally William Pakenham house, 106 Spadina Rd. (detached house), Arthur C. Barrett, 1905. The architect was no Eden Smith—his façade is too disorganized—but he does use all the English Cottage ingredients: multi-light casement windows (replaced), stuccoed projecting bays, tall chimneys. *PM*

13 Originally James P. Watson house, 109 Walmer Rd., S. Hamilton Townsend, 1901–02. This is one of the most evocative, appealing houses in the Annex. Though built on a relatively small lot, the angled wings and overhanging second storey make the house appear rambling and commodious. In addition, wooden shingles flow from the roof and wrap down over the walls in an expression of snugness and shelter further enhanced by the house's siting low to the ground amid much shrubbery. Watson was president of E.S. Currie Ltd., neckwear manufacturers on Wellington Street, where two years after this house was built the Great Toronto Fire of 1904 was to start **[see Introduction, Area II]**. *PM*

13 | 109 Walmer Rd.

14a 95–97 and 91–93 Walmer Rd. (two double houses), 1893, 1894. Twinned double houses with slightly sluggish façades more than compensated by a sprightly parade of capped dormers marching around the roof. The small-paned windows of no. 91 are replacements; Queen Anne houses were proud of their large plate glass. *PM*

14b 87 Walmer Rd. (detached house), 1907. An English Cottage with swooping ski-jump roof. *PM*

14c 83–85 Walmer Rd. (double house), 1891. A quintessential Annex double house with rocky plum-coloured sandstone foundation, round-arched entries and windows, red brick, and decorative terracotta in a taut composition that balances wide gable with polygonal tower, the latter capped with a lovely finial. *PM*

14c | 83–85 Walmer Rd.

14d 81 Walmer Rd. (detached house), Frederick H. Herbert, 1896–98. A tile-hung Queen Anne house, graciously accommodating a Georgian pilastered triple window and pedimented porch. *PM*

Walmer Road between Kendal and Bloor was conceived as a winding alternative to the grid of most of the city. The houses built here were similar to others in the suburb, but the serpentine course and more generous setback impart to these "villas"—those that remain—an estate-like character.

15a 70 Walmer Rd. (detached house), Langley & Burke, 1891. Closing the vista up lower Walmer Road and once boasting an eye-catching classically detailed porch at its centre, no. 70 could claim a prominence in the streetscape not usually found in a city planned like Toronto. Langley & Burke

further utilized a conspicuous variety of textured and coloured materials—terracotta, brick, sandstone—to draw attention to their spacious concept. The architects also designed nos. 59 and 61 Walmer Road, using similar patterns of masonry. *PM*

15b Originally John A. McKee house, 53 Walmer Rd., Frederick H. Herbert, 1898. The pro forma Annex corner tower is here enlivened by a classical mushroom dome. Adamesque ornament around the tower, below the eaves, and in the pediment crowning the porch is especially notable in this house. It was made of pressed metal, a very useful material that permitted elaborate decorative effect at low cost. McKee was manager of Dodds Medicine Company. *PM*

15b | 53 Walmer Rd.

15c Institute of Child Study/originally the Hon. Leighton Goldie McCarthy house, 45 Walmer Rd., Sproatt & Rolph, 1932; school addition, Gordon S. Adamson & Associates, 1955; rear school addition, Taylor Smyth, in progress. Red-brick Georgian Revival, more interesting for not being wholly symmetrical. Details and orchestration of parts, by Henry Sproatt [see 8/3], are remarkably fine. McCarthy, who was Canadian ambassador to Washington in the 1940s, replaced two earlier houses on this site, one an Eden Smith design of 1894.

On McCarthy's death in 1953, the house was inherited by the University of Toronto, which installed its famous child study institute. *PM*

16 44 Walmer Rd. (apartment house), Uno Prii, 1969. Not as tall as no. 35 [20/7] by the same architect, but no less showy, with waving façade and giant concrete hoops arcing by the entrance. *PM*

17 Walmer Road Baptist Church, 188 Lowther Ave. at Walmer Rd., Langley & Burke, 1888–92. Walmer Road Baptist sits with assurance and solidity on its corner site, yet it is delicate and graceful. This was the largest Baptist church in Canada when it was built, and its distinctive battered tower beckoned some 1,500 well-to-do faithful. The church was founded by the Rev. Elmore Harris, uncle of Group of Seven artist Lawren Harris, and built by his family from the profits of Massey-Harris farm implements. *PM*

18 21 Walmer Rd. (detached house), Frederick H. Herbert, 1894. Another eclectic Herbert house, with too many quick and fussy decorative details for its own good. The "paneful" replacement windows only make matters worse. *PM*

19 | Trinity-St. Paul's United Church

19 Trinity-St. Paul's United Church/ originally Trinity Methodist Church, 427 Bloor St. W., Langley & Burke, 1889; Sunday school addition, Burke Horwood & White, 1909; interior renovations, ERA, ongoing. A structure of considerable grandeur, Trinity Methodist was the only church built in the Annex to use the Richardsonian Romanesque style that was being so liberally sprinkled on surrounding residences. The architects worked with great conviction here, taking equal care on both sides of the corner site, each featuring a wide central gable with rose window. The corner itself is resolutely defined by a tall, firm tower. Seating 2,000, Trinity Methodist was for many years the largest Protestant church in Canada. It was paid for by Eatons and other Methodist merchants who lived in the Annex. *PM*

The Annex area between Brunswick Avenue and Bathurst Street was originally part of Seaton Village. Streets had been laid out as early as the 1850s, but this part of the village remained largely uninhabited until some years after annexation by the City of Toronto in 1888. In fact, most of the houses—stout little affairs with polite façades—date to the turn of the 20th century, when classical details were finding favour anew.

20 324–326 Brunswick Ave. (double house), 1906; no. 324 remodelled, 1981. A timid double house saved by a grand marquee-like stepped gable. *PM*

21 328–330 and 332–334 Brunswick Ave. (two double houses), 1899, 1897; porch additions, c. 1900. Overbearing classical porches (now gone from 328) obscured what these large Queen Anne houses were intended to look like. But the porch salesman was very persuasive—who wants to look old-fashioned?—and the porches are practical. *PM/updated AB*

22a 343 Brunswick Ave. (detached house), 1902. By this date, classically detailed porches came with the houses. There's not another around like this, with its miniature triple columns. *PM*

22b 345 Brunswick Ave. (detached house), 1908. La-di-da Ionic. Only two and a half feet high, but stylishly classical. *PM*

23 348, 350, 352–354, 356, 358–360 Brunswick Ave. (three single and two double houses), 1886–87. There are seven dwellings in a row here that predate all others on this block by some years. A few still retain their distinctive early Bay-n-Gable configuration; others have patched on all kinds of "modernizations," the picturesque tile-hung Queen Anne box enveloping the Gothic gable of no. 356 for example. *PM*

24 The Loretto (condominium apartments), 385 Brunswick Ave., Neil G. Beggs, 1914; additions and renovations, architectsAlliance and Quadrangle, 2008. Beggs employed a very austere sort of Beaux Arts for this Catholic girls' school; its steep stair and rather grand pediment suggested an unbending discipline. The condo-fication of the site added a new set of limestone-fronted townhouses at the back, well-sited and mediated with a handsome walk and driveway; every part of this project speaks of craftsmanship and care. *AB*

24 | The Loretto

25 67–69 and 71–73 Howland Ave. (two double houses), 1902. Double houses in Georgian Revival style are rare and these are quite fine, achieving a clarity and simplicity that make them very appealing. *PM*

26 21–23 Howland Ave. (double house), 1892; renovation, no. 21, Williamson Chong, 2012. An extravagant big double house. Out front at no. 21, the high-end concrete steps, ipe deck, and mahogany windows signal a high-design renovation; the shabbier imitation stairs at no. 19 show that craft is just as important in the 21st century as it ever was. *PM/AB*

27a Church of St.-Alban-the-Martyr, 100 Howland Ave., Richard C. Windeyer with John Falloon, 1885–91. Coming upon St. Alban's, its glorious Norman chancel looming rugged and momentous among flaking Victorian blocks, is like stumbling on a medieval ruin at Hampstead Heath. It was begun with high hopes in the 1880s as cathedral church of the Diocese of Toronto. St. James' **[1/13]** was technically a parish church and paled beside the grandiloquent plan for this cathedral modelled after the great St. Alban's in England. But funds ran out after only this small section had been built, and they still hadn't been raised in 1911 when the eminent American architect Ralph Adams Cram was called on to draw a new plan, nor by 1935 when the whole scheme was finally dropped. Today we are left with one-quarter of a cathedral and three-quarters of a private boys' school, which may or may not have known what it was doing in snubbing the church building when finishing off. *PM*

27b Royal St. George's College/originally St. Alban's see house, 120 Howland Ave., Darling and Curry, 1886. If there's to be a cathedral, there must be a house for the bishop, and this dignified yet delightful Queen Anne house by Frank Darling was it. *PM*

28 69 Albany Ave.; renovated, Bob Jacobs, 1971; altered later. Jane Jacobs's long-time home, renovated by her architect husband in 1971. She lived here until her

28 | 69 Albany

death in 2006, frequently sitting out front to observe "the ballet of the good city sidewalk." *AB*

29 Bloor Hot Docs Cinema, 506 Bloor St. W., Kaplan & Sprachman, 1941; renovation Hariri Pontarini, 2013. Most of Toronto's neighbourhood movie palaces have now disappeared; this one, which has functioned variously as a first-run, "adult," and second-run house, seems to have found rare stability as the home of Hot Docs. The prolific Kaplan & Sprachman designed more than 20 movie houses in the city between 1926 and 1949, and others as far away as Vancouver and Halifax. Here they created a solid and serious Moderne building, with abstractly placed windows and some linear brick ornament on the façade; the much flashier interior, respectfully renewed, is a delightful period piece. *AB*

30 | B.streets condo

29 | Bloor Hot Docs Cinema

30 B.streets (condominium apartments), 783 Bathurst St. and 10–20 Loretto Lane, Hariri Pontarini, 2014. This mid-rise plays an interesting game with materials, switching from dark iron-spot brick to white concrete for its upper levels in an attempt—successful, from most angles—to disguise its bulk. The townhouses at the rear represent a rare

attempt by developers to intensify downtown laneways, an idea often discussed **[see 26/12b]** and rarely implemented. *AB*

31 Mirvish Village (mixed-use development), 581 Bloor St. W., Henriquez Partners with ERA, landscape architect Janet Rosenberg + Studio, ongoing.
There's no place like this place, anyplace! That was the boast of discount retailer and genius pitchman Ed Mirvish, who made his store a landmark for many Torontonians— especially immigrants—in the postwar era. Mirvish assembled the store site (a precursor to chain big-boxes) and the adjacent block of houses over 35 years, initially with plans for parking but eventually for a quaint artists-and-restaurants strip overseen by his wife, Anne. Son David Mirvish's **[see 4/6]** decision to sell the property in 2013 prompted much angst, but the proposed development promises to be better than what it replaced. With rental housing and retail organized in skinny "towers" that mimic the old storefront rhythm on Bloor; the activation of laneways with creative tenants; meaningful retention of most of the heritage buildings on site; a market hall; and a new park, this promises to be a remarkably nuanced, intricate, and neighbourly form of big development. *AB*

Area XI
Walk 21: Southwest and
North Rosedale
Walk 22: Southeast
Rosedale

"Rosedale" is one of those rare Toronto names that serves as a metonym: it is not just the neighbourhood but a congregation of the city's elite, well-ensconced, well-read, and comfortable in the shade of their leafy, curving streets. "Canada both cherishes and loathes the 'Rosedale myth,'" Scott Symons told Peter C. Newman in *The Canadian Establishment*. "Yet, without it, without its quiet embodiment of decent manners and its sense of family and historical continuity, we might be merely Americans."

The fact that Symons was both a boundary-pushing queer artist and a scion of

Rosedale may suggest that there are some gaps in that "myth" of prosperous staidness— and the development of the area does, in fact, reflect affluent good taste modulated by economic and social ups and downs: speculative hustle by members of the colonial elite; failed and then successful development schemes; the influx of a professional upper-middle class; the Depression, suburban flight, and the downmarket exploitation of big aging houses; and then, finally, an influx of wealth and historicism that have brought "decent manners," and costly craftsmanship, back to the streets of Rosedale.

In 1824, this was the countryside far from the fashionable heart of the city **[see Area I]**. But a 25-year-old named William Botsford Jarvis saw opportunity. Jarvis would later become sheriff of the Home District (facing off against Mackenzie's 1837 Rebellion), but as a young man he was, like many well-connected peers, a land speculator. He bought 110 acres, including a farm house (at what is now 30 Rosedale Road), and settled here with his wife. Mary is said to have coined the name Rosedale because of the rich array of wild roses. Yet their lands were isolated from Yonge Street by Rosedale Ravine, a geographic fact that would shape the future of the area.

As Yorkville **[see Area IX]** grew, Jarvis began the first subdivision of the area: Rose Park, as it was called, included 62 sizeable building lots in the western part of what is now South Rosedale. An economic downturn in the late 1850s stalled this scheme; one house **[see 21/4]** was built.

Among the next generation, Jarvis's daughter Sarah **[21/12c]** dabbled in real estate, and most enterprisingly so did Edgar Jarvis, the sheriff's nephew. He and his wife, Charlotte, built Glen Hurst, an Italianate house on Park Road [demolished], to set a standard for the area; he spent much of the 1870s and 1880s acquiring land in South Rosedale. Later, he collaborated with the Scottish Ontario and Manitoba Land Company to bridge the Park Drive ravine and subdivide North Rosedale.

But after a short boom in the 1880s, when the Annex **[Area X]** was being built out, Rosedale did not begin to see real growth until after 1900. In the early 1900s, Toronto real estate went wild, and in Rosedale, four lots became 20. A housing shortage meant that scores of houses were put up and purchased immediately. A newly affluent middle class was eager to grab onto that symbol of their arrival: home ownership. And Rosedale by now had three bridges spanning those barrier ravines, one of them at Sherbourne Street, over which ran electric streetcars to carry businessmen to and from downtown offices. (Automobiles were still an unreliable novelty on the unpaved streets, and many Edwardian homes were constructed here with neither coach nor "motor" house. Today more than one Rosedale house has an underground garage.)

This period of Rosedale's greatest growth was one of architectural confusion. A local journalist, trying to describe these Edwardian residences some years later, wrote, "The main concern in building a house was to make it different. If it was a high house, it was made lower by draping a bit of roof around it. . . . If it was low, strange things happened to the chimney. If the logical place for the doorway was the front, they contrived it on the side." This hectic boom was also responsible for Rosedale's variety of frontage widths and house sizes, plus a few apartment buildings [21/28].

Of interest in this regard is that no matter how narrow or wide the lot, or how small or big the structure, almost all the houses were constructed close to the street and to one another. Even the few owners who acquired fairly large lots built houses off to one side, perhaps in speculation-crazed anticipation of "selling off the garden" (almost all eventually did). In their consistent alignment, Rosedale houses may have been emulating semi-urban British subdivisions such as London's Bedford Park. And like Bedford Park, most houses were for the middle and upper-middle class. A few mansions built here by the very wealthy in this period were the exception. This neighbourly mix set a tone for Rosedale that was to continue through the next, more architecturally distinguished stages of its development.

In 1909, the Canadian trade publication *Construction* pronounced the curving blocks of Rosedale's newly laid out Chestnut Park "Toronto's loveliest suburb." Conceived all of a piece—"both consistent and charming," enthused *Construction*—Chestnut Park [see Walk 21] was a preview of the two styles into which pre–World War I Canadian architecture would sort itself: picturesque Neo-Tudor and classical Neo-Georgian. The influences came primarily from Britain, harking back to post-medieval vernacular cottages and manor houses and to the buildings of Christopher Wren for inspiration. And yet new attitudes about craftsmanship, use of space, and relation to site generated some innovation.

Allied to the notion of national style was the idea of tying a building to the land. An organic relationship between house and surroundings, between city and country, was the goal. This went nicely with the desire to escape a bit from the industrial city. When the last portions of the Drumsnab estate [22/17] were sold off in the 1920s, a brochure proclaimed: "The fine homes which surround the park, and its wonderful trees, give perfect seclusion, yet it lies nearer to the heart of Toronto than any other first class residential location."

Then, in the 1940s, the area began to lose its appeal. Designed to be cared for by servants and with few garages or driveways, the houses were considered by many "unsuitable for modern living." Though a strong sense of community continued to anchor old families (some now into the second generation), high taxes and expensive maintenance turned others away. During World War II, when a housing shortage led to relaxed zoning regulations, some 200 Rosedale homes were converted to rooming houses and nursing facilities. After the Second World War, the old places were increasingly torn down for apartment buildings, about 20 of them between 1951 and 1970 **[21/31]**. Apartments also began to appear on the fringes of the ravines **[22/12]**. Much despised by preservationists and many neighbours, these buildings are now period pieces in their own right, and the neighbourhood did not lose its charm.

Quite the opposite: in the early '60s, the bloom came back to Rosedale. The commodious houses, now relatively inexpensive, began to attract growing numbers of middle-class families with young children. These enthusiastic newcomers joined with the old guard to slow conversions and virtually ban apartment construction. (The Rosedale [Ratepayers] Association is

the oldest in the city, having been founded in 1903.) From the 1980s on, the area became slowly, and then rapidly, more exclusive: as a growing number of affluent Torontonians began to choose the city over postwar suburbs, Rosedale's blend of leafiness, proximity, and old-Toronto-money cachet became a powerful draw. In other neighbourhoods "neo-traditional" builder houses of the early 2000s are often trying clumsily to achieve the Georgian or eclectic-Edwardian look of prime Rosedale, and here it comes with patina.

Today multi-generational Rosedale families and the lucky white-painters have been joined by new arrivals of considerable means. This has brought some friction: Gerald Schwartz and Heather Reisman ruffled feathers with the demolition and rebuilding at their Cluny Drive complex **[21/23]**. But more often Rosedale building and rebuilding leave few visible traces. The odd house has silently disappeared **[21/15b]** for the enlargement of a garden, but the general pattern is toward thorough, expensive, and discreet renovation, remaking the interiors while restoring the façades to something like their original states. Today both South and North Rosedale are designated as Heritage Conservation Districts, ensuring that decent architectural manners and historical continuity will prevail well into the future.

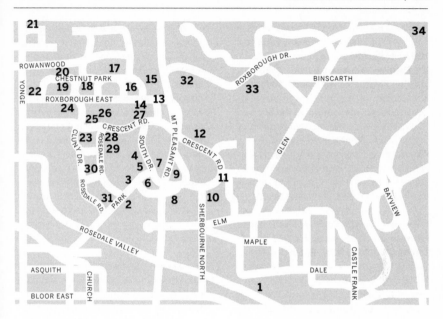

Walk 21: Southwest and North Rosedale

1 Rosedale Ravine was a formidable wilderness in the 19th century. The first rough track to penetrate its heavily wooded terrain crept from Yonge and Belmont Streets through a creek and up to Sheriff Jarvis's homestead **[see 21/30a]**. In 1834 Jarvis cleared a northern approach via what is now Roxborough Street East, while Francis Cayley hacked out an eastern path from Parliament Street to Drumsnab **[22/17]**.

About this time two brewers were attracted to the flowing creek. John Severn established his venture at Davenport Road and Yonge Street, and Joseph Bloor located his southeast of present-day Park and Rosedale Valley Roads. This latter lasted until the 1840s, after which the ravine reverted to playground for adventurous youngsters and hideaway for tramps. The first true road, made of corduroy logs, was installed by Sheriff Jarvis in 1853 on the eve of the Rose Park subdivision, ergo the name Park Road. It served as primary entrance to Rosedale until its creek bridge collapsed in 1872. Three new bridges were erected over the next 20 years **[see Introduction, Area XI]**.

By the turn of the century, this idyllic retreat had become a blighted open sewer, prompting the city to expropriate the "pestilential valley." The creek-cum-sewer was sent underground and Rosedale Ravine Drive widened and paved to become Rosedale Valley Road. The ravine was further tamed by extensive landfill in 1929–31. The city has maintained Rosedale Ravine as parkland ever since. *PM*

2 107 Park Rd. (detached house), Bruce Wright, 1936; addition, David Craddock, 1985. 105 Park Rd. (detached house), c. 1960. Rosedale was virtually begun and finished between 1890 and 1930, after which there was no buildable land left. Later construction has therefore been on the "edges," where fresh lots have appeared now and again. These two moderns (on land sold off by Branksome Hall) are good examples. No. 107 is one of Toronto's first and few Art Moderne houses. In any other city the cladding would have been stucco, but the buff brick used here makes for fascinating quoins, cornice, and belt course. (Many Toronto Art Moderne buildings have this Georgian cast.) At No. 105 is a Modernist number that shows the influence of Alvar Aalto. *PM/AB*

3 100 Park Rd. (detached house), 1888.
104 Park Rd. (detached house), 1888.
108 Park Rd. (detached house), 1890.
110 Park Rd. (detached house), 1888.
114 Park Rd. (detached house), 1888.
A muscular quintet of Richardsonian Romanesque/Queen Anne abodes, these are "city" houses—they seem out of place on this sloping countrified road. Nevertheless, they mark the first consistent development of Rosedale. This depression-plagued push petered out soon after, which is why today Rosedale doesn't look like the Annex. *PM*

4 Formerly George Reginald Geary house, 124 Park Rd., 1855; second storey added, 1863; renovated, 1987–ongoing. This was the first house built in the 1854 Rose Park subdivision, and with demolition of Jarvis's villa in 1905 **[see 21/30a]**, it now ranks as the oldest in Rosedale after Drumsnab **[22/17]**. The house was originally only one storey, but even then it must have spelled gracious living with beautifully proportioned Georgian front and spacious high-ceilinged rooms. First owner in 1855 was lawyer James Davis but the property is more closely identified with one-time Toronto mayor George Reginald Geary, who occupied it 1927–54. *PM*

5 120 Park Rd., A.J. Diamond, Donald Schmitt, and Co., 1996. A house carved out of the garden at no. 124, and designed by Jack Diamond himself for the arts administrator and former Diamond partner Kevin Garland. Its vocabulary echoes Louis Kahn except for its Rosedalian (though low and metal) gabled roof. *AB*

6 Originally "Lorne Hall" (William Davies residence), 3 Meredith Crescent, Langley Langley & Burke, 1876. An elegant amalgamation of invention and order, Second Empire was the perfect architectural expression of entrepreneurs longing to be gentlemen. Here, Second Empire's lofty mansard, swelling bays, and imposing portico provided the aura for pioneering pork packer William Davies. Designed by Henry Langley, this stately mansion still impresses

despite diminished siting. In 1876 it was one of about ten houses in all of Rosedale, grandly surveying uninhabited woodland from its hilltop aerie. *PM*

7 Originally James How house, 48 South Dr., 1876; altered, Gordon S. Adamson & Associates, 1945; addition and restoration, c. 2000. Originally John Thom house, 54 South Dr., 1880. Among the few houses constructed here prior to 1883 and annexation by the City of Toronto, these two High Victorian dandies stand almost alone in Rosedale as examples of this picturesque genre. First owners were a dentist and a lawyer. *PM*

8 Rosedale Presbyterian Church, 129 Mount Pleasant Rd., Chapman & McGiffin, 1909–10; addition, Mathers & Haldenby, 1954–55. Rosedale Presbyterian, solemnly built of stone with smooth craftsmanly details, is unmistakably early 20th-century Gothic. It was planned that the east and centre blocks would be used for services only until a larger church wing could be built to the west. These plans were thwarted—by church union in 1925, which drew off close to two-fifths of the members, and by widening of Mount Pleasant Road in 1948, which took about 55 feet of buildable land. "Temporary" chapel, with resounding hammerbeams and McCausland's stained glass, became permanent church. In 1955 a truncated extension finally provided the long-awaited Sunday school. *PM*

9a Originally James Jermyn house, 74 South Dr., A. Frank Wickson, 1899. Last-gasp 19th-century historismus with heavy charms that are starting to pall. Jermyn was listed in city directories as a farmer but this ain't no farm house. *PM*

9b 67 South Dr. (detached house), J. Francis Brown, 1907–08. Originally Hugh Munro residence, 69 South Dr. (detached house), E.J. Lennox, 1902. Originally Charles May residence, 73 South Dr. (detached house), A. Frank Wickson, 1900–01; altered later. 75 South Dr. (detached house), 1898. 79 South Dr. (detached house), J. Francis Brown, 1902. Although built just after no. 74 across the street, these five are clearly of another era. Victorian furbelows have been lightened up, thinned out, or simply left off. Crisp white-painted details are the order of the day, though in this period of experiment they represent a confusing combo of classical (columned porches, Palladian windows) and picturesque (parapeted gables, half-timbering). This was the decade of the area's greatest growth and these houses are the very stuff of Rosedale. *PM*

10 Formerly "Heyroyd" (Banks Brothers residence), 35 Sherbourne St. N., c. 1866; altered later. This urbane house, today looking almost American Federal with large glazed areas, polygonal bays, and delicate porch, is one of Toronto's most charming. It's relatively old, as many fireplaces, high ceilings, and thick brick walls attest; it was only the seventh or eighth house built in Rosedale. But the original has been much altered and exactly when the house acquired its present polish is unclear. From 1891 to 1895 the place was rented by the Board of Education for classrooms before the area's first public school opened on Scarth Road. *PM*

10 | 35 Sherbourne St. N.

11a Originally George Newman house, 103 South Dr., Robert J. Edwards, 1898–1900. Clear, coherent, and vibrating with earthy directness, this delightful house is in a class by itself. Almost beyond "style," it simply bespeaks "shelter." Newman was a principal at Dominion Express Company. *PM*

11b Originally James Lumbers residence, 182 Crescent Rd. (detached house), Percy H. Finney, 1909. Originally Mark Hall residence, 180 Crescent Rd. (detached house), Mark Hall, 1900–01. Two more houses typical of the transitional early 1900s—the latter designed by Hall as his own home. Often labelled "Free Classic" for their rediscovery of classical details, they might as easily be tagged "Free Picturesque" for their putative love affair with Tudor. The deep protective porches, assuming the social function of Victorian vestibule and entrance hall, represent a new reassigning of space. Look for these attributes throughout Rosedale. *PM/AB*

12a Originally Charles Boone house, 170 Crescent Rd., Symons & Rae, 1907–08. Often illustrated as the epitome of Rosedale, the Boone house is in fact singular, one of only a handful of lavish homes built here. Jacobethan's powerful volumes, impeccable brickwork, and conspicuous stone dressings were just the ticket for those like contractor Boone who wanted reassuring historical copies. Partners William Symons and William Rae designed many Rosedale houses, but none nearly as fine as this regal Neo-Tudor. *PM*

12b Originally Edward Fisher house, 166 Crescent Rd., Burke & Horwood 1899–1900. Through 25 years of partnership between 1894 and 1919, Edmund Burke and John C.B. Horwood were Society's architects of choice, turning out competent if uninspired residences to approximate all the latest trends. In 1899 the trend was uncertain and so is this flighty arrangement of bays and vaults, gables and arches, windows and doors. Fisher was musical director at the Toronto Conservatory of Music, whose new building on College Street the architects were also just polishing off. *PM*

12c Originally Lewis Ord house/formerly Sir Henry Drayton house, 164 Crescent Rd., 1882; altered and enlarged, Mackenzie Waters, 1932. Although Sheriff Jarvis sold his acreage to all and sundry, many parcels found their way into family hands. The sheriff's three daughters all speculated in Rosedale real estate. This splendid lot was acquired by daughter Sarah and her husband, Lewis Ord. Though not constructed until 1882, their stout yellow-brick Victorian country manor was among the first in this slow-to-develop subdivision. The place still impresses with gracious siting and reserved air. *PM*

12d Mooredale House/originally Sir Frank Baillie house, 146 Crescent Rd., Sproatt & Rolph, 1902–03; altered later. Like the similarly Jacobethan extravaganza up the block at no. 170 **[21/12a]**, this is a "big house" anomaly in Rosedale. Here Sproatt & Rolph used meticulous brickwork firmly gripped by stone dressings to turn an asymmetric design into something quietly monumental. Yet there is a Rosedalian lack of hauteur: the proto-colonnade reads more like whimsy than auspicious entry. When captain of industry Frank Baillie died suddenly in 1920, his widow sold no. 146. In 1930 it was slated for demolition to make way for the Jarvis Street extension, but survived to become home to the Rosedale–Moore Park Community Association in the late 1940s. The association now runs the house and adjacent buildings as a community and athletic centre. *PM/updated AB*

Mount Pleasant Road, cutting through the heart of Rosedale, was first planned in 1930. Part of a major public works program that envisioned arteries city-wide, its goal was to whisk drivers between downtown offices and new north suburbs. (The plan originally called for streetcars on the extension as well!) However, local opposition and Depression-era cutbacks stalled the project for decades. Finally opened in 1950, it became Toronto's first expressway. Amazingly, only five houses were demolished in the process.

13a Originally J. Wilson Siddall house, 171 Roxborough St. E., J. Wilson Siddall, 1902–03; enlarged later. English architect Siddall came to Canada to work on Confederation Life **[6/14]**, but most of his practice was residential, no doubt garnered from this Tudoresque advertisement for himself. The house's yellow brick, though popular in the 1850s and '60s as a stand-in for stone, had not been used in Toronto for decades. In Britain, Arts and Crafts architects were specifying light-coloured stucco in similar protest against Late Victorian red brick. *PM*

13b 170 Roxborough St. E. (detached house), 1889. 172 Roxborough St. E. (detached house), 1889. 174 Roxborough St. E. (detached house), 1889–90. 176 Roxborough St. E. (detached house), 1889. Put up during Rosedale's short-lived spurt of the late 1880s, these are the sort of rich, frolicsome Queen Annes that Edwardian architects were eager to renounce. Whitewashing owners at nos. 172 and 176 seem to have renounced them too. Shame. Still glowingly ruddy no. 174 was originally home to the Rev. Benjamin Thomas, pastor of Jarvis Street Baptist Church. *PM*

13b | 174 Roxborough St. E.

14 141–147 Roxborough St. E. (four-house row), 1889–90. After 1904 and introduction of land-use bylaws (an idea borrowed from Germany), Rosedale became almost exclusively an area of single, detached houses. That makes this row of four an oddity even before one considers its nervous front. Actually it's that very Queen Anne lack of row-house repetition that allows it to dance so nimbly in the neighbourhood today. *PM*

Chestnut Park was the name given to his property by Sen. David Macpherson. A purchaser into the northwest quadrant of Rose Park in 1855, Macpherson acquired adjacent lands as well, where he had a villa facing Yonge Street. On his death in 1895, his trustees hired architect Alfred E. Boultbee and his barrister brother Horatio to create and manage the distinctive development we know today. In concert with architect Hamilton Townsend, they laid out Chestnut Park's curving blocks with special lamp standards, brick sidewalks, and no electricity poles (the enclave was planned to run on gas). Boultbee and Townsend also designed many of the houses.

All went well and quickly. By 1909, U.S. city planners visiting Toronto could adjudge Chestnut Park "the most restful and artistic section [of this] model city . . . the epitome of suburban beauty." It still is.

15a Originally James Mickleborough house, 86 Chestnut Park Rd., Burke & Horwood, 1904–05. All the name architects scurried to Chestnut Park, including much-in-demand Burke & Horwood. Here, commissioned by the president of a wholesale woollens company, they drew a textbook design of the "new architecture": good proportions, simple detail, local materials, natural landscaping. In short, unobtrusive. Note for example the way the multi-paned windows enhance the impression of surface smoothness rather than digging holes in the sleek brickwork as single-paned windows might have done. *PM*

15b Originally Harold Gagnier house, 82 Chestnut Park Rd., Langley & Langley, 1904. Publisher Harold Gagnier's frozen-looking confection is quite eccentric, but at least they got the fenestration right. "No one feature imparts so great an element of the picturesque as the casement window," intoned architectural journals such as Gagnier's own *Construction*. But many North Americans were wary, citing difficulty in cleaning, drafts, and burglars! The attached garage is a later addition; garages were generally built separate from houses well into the 1930s. *PM*

16 Originally W.T. Giles residence, 77 Chestnut Park Rd. (detached house), S. Hamilton Townsend, 1906–07. The flat, taut exterior of this daring design reflects a powerful opening-up inside. Townsend's great box seems about to burst. The architect is in step here with Frank Lloyd Wright, who, in the American Midwest, has already pushed the box as far as it will go and broken through with long outstretching wings. Townsend didn't pursue that; instead he melded "Prairie box" with "Cottage naturalness" to create an image all his own. Look for his tautness, horizontality, wide eaves, stretch of windows, and signature front-door canopy throughout Rosedale. *PM*

17a Originally John McCarter house, 56 Chestnut Park Rd., Wickson & Gregg, 1908–09. Termed "modern English" at the time, Neo-Tudor at its best exhibits a cleanness and precision that continues to appeal. Typical features seen here include bold rectangular bay, grand front-facing gable, horizontal fenestration (which should have been casement throughout), and aura of unity between house and garden. McCarter was president of Eclipse Whitewear, for whose premises on King Street West **[4/6]** he also commissioned Wickson & Gregg. *PM*

17b Originally S.B. Gundy house, 50 Chestnut Park Rd., Alfred E. Boultbee, 1905–06. While many Toronto architects were toying with Tudor, another group was seeking to regenerate Georgian. Contemporary magazines highlighted the style, but the wonderful houses that Alfred Boultbee designed in Chestnut Park (including this for publisher S.B. Gundy) look as if they've jumped straight off the pages of an 18th-century pattern book for the gaily elegant Georgian of Robert Adam. *PM*

18a 45 Chestnut Park Rd. (originally detached house), Curry & Sparling, 1915. Altered later. Happily, here original Neo-Georgian symmetry, hipped roof, and harmonious stone portico are all elegantly in place. Conversion to three units meant appending wings to the sides, laudable for their up-front honesty—they look exactly like modern, appended wings. *PM*

18b Originally John McKenzie house, 43 Chestnut Park Rd., Alfred E. Boultbee, 1905–06. Designed for a university professor, this is another of Boultbee's deft Adamesque delights which in 1906 you could have bought for $7,000. Despite the confident revival exterior, these Neo-Georgians were often extremely innovative inside. *PM*

18c Originally Norman McLeod house, 39 Chestnut Park Rd., S. Hamilton Townsend, 1906–07. In its bold shape, sharp definition of smooth surfaces, and low band of ground-floor windows tying structure to site, no. 39 is avant-garde but not anti-histori-cal. The appeal of English Cottage Style was

18c | 39 Chestnut Park Rd.

just this knitting of trendy and traditional. A year or two earlier, architects were designing stables for Chestnut Park, but by 1906 the detached "automobile house" seen here was more usual. *PM*

19 27 Chestnut Park Rd.; renovation GH3, 2015. Not your great-grandfather's red brick. This rare new addition to the street (a full renovation of a 1980s infill house) uses the classic Toronto material to clad its very modernist, precisely symmetrical faces— and to conceal a garage door. *AB*

20 Originally John Falconbridge house, 22 Chestnut Park Rd., Alfred E. Boultbee, 1904–05. Originally Robert Greig house, 20 Chestnut Park Rd., Alfred E. Boultbee, 1905–06. While three-storey Adam houses constitute a sizable and lofty body of American colonial architecture, revival examples are everywhere rare. With correct 12-pane windows, fanlights, porticoed entrances, even iron handrailings, these extraordinarily lovely reproductions deserve universal renown. *PM*

20 | 22 Chestnut Park Rd.

21 Summerhill LCBO/formerly North Toronto Railway Station, 10 Scrivener Square, Darling & Pearson, 1915–16; restoration, Goldsmith Borgal, 2004. Built by CP to a spectacular level of quality, a Beaux Arts temple in Tyndall limestone, this became the city's main rail station until the

1929 opening of today's Union Station. The building was poorly used for many years as a beer and liquor store. Even the 140-foot clock tower, modeled after the campanile at St. Mark's in Venice, acquired a new rectangular clock on its facade, branded by National Bank—"a discredit to the Toronto townscape" and "the work of Philistines," fumed Dennis Warrilow in *Canadian Architect* in 1968. It took a while before the building's grandeur was recognized and restored, yet under cheap tile and paneling much of it had survived: herringbone floors remain in the 40-foot-tall Great Hall along with original light fixtures designed to resemble train wheel, brass ticket wickets and luscious marble on the walls. A very grand place for Rosedale denizens to buy a Barolo. *AB*

22a Originally William Carrick house, 15 Chestnut Park Rd., Langley & Langley, 1910–11. The stone front together with tiled roof and bracketed eaves mark no. 15 as Second Renaissance Revival. Since Georgian style also has roots in the Renaissance, it's not surprising this house shares the symmetry and repose of Neo-Georgians. In the 1970s it was one of Rosedale's many rooming houses. *PM*

22b Originally James Ryrie house, 1 Chestnut Park Rd., Burke Horwood & White, 1912–15. The location of Sen. Macpherson's Victorian villa (which after his death served as St. Andrew's College for a time) was the spot chosen by James Ryrie to put up the most stately home in Chestnut Park. His lovely loggiaed Neo-Georgian gem was perfect foil for the president of the most successful jewellery company in Canada **[see 5/13]**. When Rosedale's large-house appeal began to fade after World War II, there were plans to adapt Ryrie's 30 redoubtable rooms to medical offices, but fortunately that came to naught. Today they comprise condominium units boasting much of the original interior detail and an exterior as ravishing as ever. *PM*

23 Schwartz/Reisman house, 37 Cluny Dr., c. 1903; additions and renovations, Christian Liaigre, 2003. "Fort Schwartz" is how it's known by cranky neighbours, and the compound assembled by Gerald Schwartz and Heather Reisman is discreetly defended by hedges and fencing. The site, originally five houses, was rebuilt under the eye of French designer Christian Liaigre. It now includes four separate buildings, an underground parking garage, and a movie theatre. If Rosedale's early history was about properties being speculatively split and sold, this signals the current trend to buy, not sell. *AB*

24 Originally John J. Dixon residence, 52 Cluny Dr. (detached house), S. Hamilton Townsend, 1902–04. For the ceremonial-entrance crossroads of Crescent and Cluny, Townsend designed one of the estate's most alluring residences. Many of his English Cottage Style orchestrations are here, but rendered in field and cut stone, simplicity was not cheap. The house stood empty for several years before seducing banker John Dixon. No. 50 Cluny Drive was originally his "motor house." *PM*

25 60 Crescent Rd. (detached house), Sproatt & Rolph, 1901. 76–78 Crescent Rd. (originally detached house), 1892. 80 Crescent Rd. (detached house), 1896–97. Originally Robert H. Davies residence, 84 Crescent Rd. (detached house), Langley & Langley, 1899–1900. 88 Crescent Rd. (detached house), 1884. As much as one tries to impart that most Rosedale houses were middle-class moderate, it's the biggies that attract. Here are five of interest for their girth and/or resident go-getters.

No. 60—becoming more grandiose with each renovation—was boyhood home of physicist Charles Wright, remembered for his participation in Scott's ill-fated South Pole expedition of 1912.

Once-Romanesque no. 76–78 first belonged to Arthur Harvey, an insurance agent who built, occupied, and sold a number of Rosedale residences. In the 1920s this house was occupied by Henry Pellatt after he was forced to give up Casa Loma **[19/2]** for back taxes.

No. 80 is best known for occupancy in the early 1900s by Ontario Justice Featherston Osler, one of the four influential Osler brothers **[see 22/26]**.

And no. 84 was designed by eminent Victorian architect Henry Langley in late partnership with son Charles.

No. 88 is a great Victorian villa and the second oldest on Crescent Road, having been built by David Pender, co-owner of a carriage-supply house, shortly after the 1882 Ord house **[21/12c]**. *PM*

26 Originally Lewis/Haldenby house, 68–70 Crescent Rd., Mathers & Haldenby, 1926. Originally Mrs. Peleg Howland house, 95 Crescent Rd., Langley & Howland, 1931. One shouldn't leave Crescent Road without interjecting Eric Haldenby's unique double house for himself (now awkwardly fitted with Modernist black-framed windows) and Langley & Howland's nifty construction for Howland's mother. Rosedale was well built-up by this time and these two Neo-Georgians were slipped into side gardens—Haldenby's that of his in-laws, who later came to share the place. *PM/updated AB*

27 108 Crescent Rd., Superkul, 2004. A rare post-2000 addition to the streetscape, this went up on a lot created in vintage Rosedale style—the owners severed it from the garden of their previous house next door. Its two-and-a-half-storey scale and setbacks match the neighbours'; and its clearly Modernist design language is disguised slightly by the delicate employment of brick and dark wood. The interior is built around an atrium and is much less conformist. *AB*

28 Castlemere Apartments, 75 Crescent Rd., Henry Simpson, 1912; renovated, 1988. "Apartments are a modern necessity," editorialized the *Globe* soon after the Castlemere went up, and—still unacceptable to many—this came to represent the form in Rosedale, being referred to for years as simply "The Apartment." In its experimental layout and mix of classical/Tudor details, the Castlemere is not unlike many houses of the era. *PM*

Rosedale Road, laid out in 1854 as part of the Rose Park subdivision, was the first thoroughfare in Rosedale to attract builders in any number. Early construction took place on the east side of the road as the Jarvis villa and outbuildings dominated the west.

29a 41–43 Rosedale Rd. (double house), 1881. Many Second Empire double houses were being built in the 1880s, but this is the only one to find its way to Rosedale. Essentially an urban form, no. 41–43 must have appeared strange on this rural road. In any event, it was never duplicated. *PM*

29b Originally George Murray house, 47 Rosedale Rd., 1889. Rosedale's first genuine development in the late 1880s featured Richardsonian Romanesque/Queen Anne houses similar to those then taking root in the Annex. This, for gas fixtures manufacturer Murray, was one of the most felicitous anywhere—there is a delicacy and buoyancy here not often seen in this rugged style. *PM*

29c Originally Capt. Samuel Crangle house, 35 Rosedale Rd., Gordon & Helliwell, 1892. This large ship-shape Queen Anne for the superintendent of the St. Lawrence & Chicago Steam Navigation Company replaced an earlier house of c. 1880 on this site. *PM*

29d Originally Charles Niles house, 45 Rosedale Rd., Chadwick & Beckett, 1905. Put up during the area's crucial decade of growth, this Neo-Tudor was one of Rosedale's most architecturally progressive. Today, it still looks wonderfully fresh, with bold windows and sparkling, precise ornament. *PM*

29d | 45 Rosedale Rd.

29e Originally "Idlewold" (Walter Brown residence)/formerly Arthur Harvey house/formerly Henry Osborne house, 23 Rosedale Rd., 1857–58; altered, c. 1890; enlarged, Alfred E. Boultbee, 1911; renovations, B. Napier Simpson, 1977. A charming Italianate house that retains its antique ambience despite many alterations. Brown, a banker, was the second to build in Rose Park. In the 1870s and '80s the owner was insurance agent Arthur Harvey, who broke up the property into 18 lots before moving on to Crescent Road **[see 21/25]**. Boultbee's additions for stockbroker Henry Osborne in 1911 included a large drawing room with Arts and Crafts moulded plaster ceiling. *PM*

30a "Rosedale Villa" (originally Sheriff William Botsford Jarvis residence), near 9 Cluny Dr., 1821; additions, John G. Howard, 1835; further additions later; demolished 1905. Set prominently on the heights above the ravine, Sheriff Jarvis's house must have been an impressive sight to Yonge Street travellers in the 19th century. When acquired by Jarvis in 1824, it was a two-storey roughcast foursquare. With the advent of marriage and a blossoming family of five (not to mention real estate profits), he enlarged it to take in bedroom wings, conservatory, and wide veranda, as well as servants' quarters, and stables.

After his wife's death in 1852, the sheriff moved to Toronto and the villa housed variously his three daughters and their families (Merediths, Nantons, and Ords), or sat empty. In 1878, Sen. Macpherson added it to his holdings **[see aside, p. 239]** and later *his* daughter and her husband, Percival Ridout, lived here until the villa was demolished in 1905. In 1922, Cluny Drive was cut through the property, creating Rosedale's last square block available for development. *PM*

30b Originally R.R. McLaughlin house, 52 Rosedale Rd., Mathers & Haldenby, 1935. Originally Alex Gooderham house, 48 Rosedale Rd., Sproatt & Rolph, 1922–23. Originally John Turnbull house, 44 Rosedale Rd., 1926–27. Originally Samuel McKeown house, 40 Rosedale Rd., Vaux & Bryan Chadwick, 1929–30. Originally Arthur Holden house, 36 Rosedale Rd., Archibald J. Stringer, 1923. The Rosedale Road '20s and '30s "period" houses were intriguing for their old-fashioned show of Renaissance urns, Georgian sidelights, Tudor half-timbering, and such. But these houses *were* modern in their smooth, simple shapes; in their large rooms and expansive interiors; and in their rearrangements, which now might put the kitchen in front to give over the whole of the rear to a large "living room" situated to gain privacy and perhaps open onto terrace or pergola—all new ideas. *PM*

30c Originally Dr. Geoffrey Boyd house, 34 Rosedale Rd., Page & Warrington, 1919–20. Originally Isaac Weldon house, 2 Cluny Dr., Eden Smith & Sons, 1922–23. English Cottage Style houses built in Toronto a decade earlier had been rendered in brick or stone because in a Canadian winter more natural-looking stucco tended to "fall away in spots thereby destroying the wonderful charm." By the 1920s, new technology had made stucco possible even in Canada.

(Ironically, by that date others were already sick of what in Los Angeles they were calling "that stucco rash.") *PM*

30d Originally John Coulson house, 19 Rosedale Rd., 1914; enlarged and altered, John M. Lyle, 1928. Originally John Gibbons house, 30 Rosedale Rd., George Moorhouse & King, 1929–30. In 1930, *Canadian Homes & Gardens* wrote that "the Georgian tradition runs through most of the best architectural work in Canada at the present time." Here are two examples, although no. 19's flat frontage is actually a smoothing out of an earlier, more picturesque construction. *PM*

31 1 Rosedale Rd. (apartment house), Bregman & Hamann, c. 1957. 16 Rosedale Rd. (apartment house), Bregman & Hamann, c. 1958. Built during Toronto's postwar apartment boom, these are two typical unobtrusive constructions, one with bands of Miesian windows, the other with punched ones. But, unobtrusive or no, Rosedale didn't really want apartment houses at all. When a bylaw limiting their height to no more than 35 feet above grade was circumvented by developers—taking advantage of the ravines, they built three storeys above grade and eight or more below, as at no. 16—ratepayers persuaded city planners against further apartments except around subway stations. The battle continues. *PM/updated AB*

31 | 1 Rosedale Rd

While development in South Rosedale began in the 1860s, North Rosedale, the plateau to the northeast—across the deep obstacle of the Park Drive Reservation ravine—remained more isolated and, accordingly, was slower to be built out. In 1908 real estate promoter Harton Walker subdivided the area as a curvy, Olmsted-like suburb, and most of the lots were built out within a generation. Eden Smith and other leading architects of the 1910s and 1920s built here, establishing a similar character to South Rosedale on some streets. But the later history here was different: few apartment buildings, but more construction of new houses on ravine-side sites, including some architectural gems in the 1960s and more recently.

32 Wolf House, 51 Roxborough Dr., A.J. Diamond and Barton Myers, 1974; lower-level addition, 1983; interior renovations, Yabu Pushelberg, 1995, Heather Faulding, 2008. Completed a few years after Myers's own Yorkville house **[16/24]**, this larger house is built around a courtyard, rather than an atrium, but shares its design language—what would come to be called High-Tech. "The contemporary warehouse steel frame, metal decking and open-web steel joists contribute significantly to the lightness, spaciousness and flexibility of the house," Myers wrote in 1976. So too does the sloping, treed site, next to a park and backing on a ravine. The house's quasi-industrial interior has survived many changes, yet the exterior remains remarkably intact, down to the quasi-nautical detail of the front entrance, which brings to mind Paris's Pompidou Centre and the Eaton Centre **[5/11]**. *AB*

32 | Wolf House

33a Fraser Residence, 4 Old George Place (detached house), Ron Thom and Paul Merrick, 1965; renovations, Altius Architecture, 2003. Today little known and nearly invisible from the street, this is one of Toronto's great houses of any period. Designed in the wake of Massey College [8/36], it shares that building's orange brick, deep concern for landscape, and reverence for Frank Lloyd Wright; but the architecture here is, unlike Massey, radically sculptural. As in Thom's West Vancouver houses of the period, its plan employs diamonds and trapezoids, but Merrick—who was largely responsible for the design— added a rare three-dimensional complexity. The rooms tumble vertically down the steep side of the Park Drive Reservation, con- nected by balconies, overhangs, half-walls, and irregularly placed windows that knit the house into the site with profound poetry. *AB*

33b Originally J. Douglas Crashley residence, 3 Old George Place (detached house), John B. Parkin Associates, 1965; renovation, c. 2005; renovation and additions, Giannone Petricone, 2016. When this cul-de-sac was developed in the 1960s, John C. Parkin's response to the site couldn't have differed more from Merrick's. The house for bachelor businessman Crashley was all straight lines, grey brick, and walls of rough-laid granite boulders. The current, much bigger iteration presents a two-storey street frontage that's less mysterious than its neighbour, but very handsomely made. *AB*

34 Integral House, 194 Roxborough Dr. (detached house), Shim-Sutcliffe, 2009. At the far end of Roxborough Drive, on one of the great ravine sites in Toronto, sits this—what former MOMA and AGO director Glenn Lowry called "one of the most important private houses built in North America in a long time." James Stewart, a mathematician and successful textbook author, passed up Frank Gehry before hiring Shim-Sutcliffe for the project, which takes its name and its many curves from within Stewart's discipline of calculus. Facing the street is a two-storey domestic wing wrapped in translucent glass and vertical oak "fins"; the latter continue on the back of the house, a five-storey volume that descends "to become part of the forest," Brigitte Shim has written. This ravine zone includes a double-height performance space that served Stewart, a serious amateur musician. It is lined by a "screen wall," as the architects put it, in which the "fins" modulate the light and views of the ravine. The latter is visible from the Evergreen Brick Works [22/31]. Stewart hoped the house would have a public role; after his death in 2014, it found new owners who have said they will open it to events. *AB*

34 | Integral House

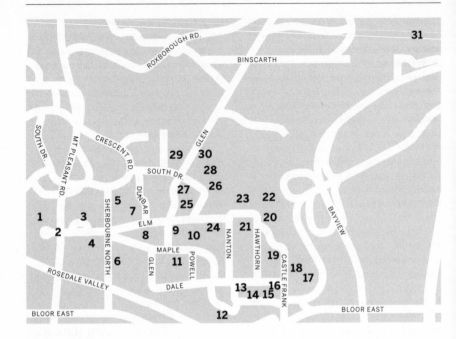

Walk 22: Southeast Rosedale

The first streets in this walk are part of the residential neighbourhood laid out by Edgar Jarvis in the 1870s. It too was isolated and slow to develop, but for over 30 years and despite great financial loss, realtor Jarvis persisted. Building, selling—and at times occupying with family of 14—one house after another, he never gave up on his dream of an enclave for Toronto's wealthy. Sad to say, Rosedale didn't come into its own until after Jarvis's death in 1907, and then with a much more moderate visage than he had anticipated.

ground-floor windows, there was an air of both symmetrical formality and easy grace about it—a persuasive proclamation of the good life Jarvis was angling to sell in Rosedale. The house faced west with access via a winding drive off Park Road. When the Park Road bridge collapsed in 1872, Jarvis replaced it with one at what is now Mount Pleasant Road, making the main approach to his house then from the east. Enlarged and altered by later owners, today 2 Elm serves as classrooms, and what's left of the glen and the hurst as playing fields for Branksome Hall girls' school. *PM*

1 Originally "Glen Hurst" (Edgar Jarvis residence), 2 Elm Ave., Gundry & Langley, 1866; additions, Smith & Gemmell, 1880; rehabilitated, 1948; altered later. When built, Glen Hurst was one of five or so houses in all of Rosedale and—sited prominently on a hill (hurst) above the ravine—it remained the grandest for many years. With high-hipped roof, gabled centre pavilion, and expansive Italianate veranda sheltering tall

1 | 2 Elm Ave.

2 Originally R. Laidlaw Brodie house, 1 Elm Ave., 1881; altered later. Originally William Alexander house, 3 Elm Ave., 1878; addition, Darling Sproatt & Pearson, 1897. Originally William A. Warren house, 4 Elm Ave., 1878. Originally John Blaikie house, 10 Elm Ave., Langley Langley & Burke, 1879; additions later. Edgar Jarvis's new bridge and tree-lined Elm and Maple Avenues inspired but a few timid takers. These High Victorian manors were built within a few years of one another, and, surprisingly, within a few yards of one another as well. With so many lots available, why did Rosedale pioneers cluster so? Oh well, today the grouping helps the four to form a mannerly campus for Branksome Hall school, which arrived on Elm Avenue about 1913, ten years after its founding. *PM*

3 Originally Charles Nelson house, 14 Elm Ave., probably Charles J. Gibson, 1895; veranda added, Charles J. Gibson, 1911. Originally William Alley house, 16 Elm Ave., 1895. Originally Henry Drayton house, 18 Elm Ave., Charles J. Gibson, 1897–98. Originally Mrs. Mary Davies house, 20 Elm Ave., Frederick H. Herbert, 1898. Despite the clutch of financiers at the west end of Elm [22/2], the avenue remained almost empty until the late 1890s. Only then did these Richardsonian Romanesque/Queen Anne houses grandly rise behind lavish iron fences to create one of the most swaggering architectural ensembles in Toronto. Little changed—though the elms are dead and gone—they still impress with mighty brick and stone, rich terracotta and wood, commanding high-pitched roofs and even higher chimneys. All firmly declare these are houses (and by inference, owners) to be reckoned with. Nelson and Alley were manufacturers; Drayton, assistant city solicitor; Mrs. Davies, widow of a scion of William Davies pork packers. *PM*

4 Originally Percival Leadlay house, 21 Elm Ave., Frederick H. Herbert, 1904–05. Originally Robert McLean house, 23 Elm Ave., Frederick H. Herbert, 1908–09. Originally John Rennie house, 25 Elm Ave., Bond & Smith, 1906–07. Originally Thomas Wilkins house, 24 Elm Ave., J. Francis Brown, 1910–11. Originally William Kernahan house, 26 Elm Ave., James P. Hynes, 1914–16. Reviewing these houses in 1910, *Construction* confided that "the 'Stylist' may not find to his entire satisfaction architectural coordination." The Edwardian period was one of disorder, it's true, but, unrecognized at the time, these houses shared a modernizing interest in pushing out interior space to form smoother, flatter-looking exteriors. In fact, the three hipped-roof "boxes" at nos. 21, 23, and 25 come close to progressive Prairie School architecture. First owners manufactured hides and wool (no. 21), stationery and books (no. 23), seeds and bulbs (no. 25), smallwares (no. 24), and beer (Kernahan of no. 26 was manager of O'Keefe Brewery). *PM*

3 | 14–16–18 Elm Ave.

Electric streetcar tracks were installed in Rosedale in 1891. The streetcar looped up Sherbourne Street North, then along Elm Avenue, Glen Road, and South Drive before heading out over the bridge again filled with customs brokers and bookkeepers headed for downtown offices.

5 Originally Edward D. Gooderham house, 27 Sherbourne St. N., Sproatt & Rolph, 1907–09. In the early 1900s, land agent Jarvis attracted the Gooderham clan to Rosedale. They had long been resident in houses adjacent to their distillery **[see Walk 24]**, but in 1903 company secretary William G. Gooderham had family architect David Roberts design a huge house for him here on the corner of Sherbourne and Elm [demolished], and four years later William's son, company clerk Edward D. Gooderham, age 24, built this solemn manor in a corner of the lot. Designed by Sproatt & Rolph (Roberts had died), it was described as "quiet and restful modern Georgian." *PM*

6 Ancroft Place (21-unit housing complex), 1 Sherbourne St. N., Shepard & Calvin, 1927. Ancroft Place is among the best housing ever conceived in Toronto. It came into being at a time of worldwide interest in town planning and especially in the Garden City movement. Few whole garden cities were built, but the theories influenced a range of schemes, as this unique Rosedale complex attests. Made up of three English Cottage Style structures, each with seven houses of varying elevations, plans, and sizes, and arrayed on a

6 | Ancroft Pl.

three-acre site with delightful interplay of communal and private space, the complex today exudes an almost Arcadian sense of bliss. It is all the more remarkable because Shepard & Calvin were bank designers, although Brooklyn-born Shepard had worked for the eclectic New York architect Ernest Flagg. Flagg, however, never did any housing as exciting as this. *PM*

7a 44–46 Elm Ave. (double house), 1875. In 1875, construction of what amounted to lower-middle-class semi-detacheds must have been a disappointing development for Jarvis. Years later, in 1896, he was reduced to living at no. 46 himself, where Mrs. J gave music lessons. *PM*

7b Originally Henry O'Hara house, 50 Elm Ave., Charles J. Gibson, 1898. This great plump dowager of a building comfortably ensconced on a wide stretch of lawn seems reassuringly unchanged by time. Gibson was very good at these well-made, unfussy Queen Annes. Designed for a broker of mining stocks, no. 50 is not at all formidable. *PM*

Although too many houses have been greedily stuffed into this Elm Avenue block, the smorgasbord makes for a quickie menu of Rosedale development.

8a 53–55 Elm Ave. (double house), 1888. The first structure on the block and still a standout thanks to picturesque turret and double-house girth. No. 53–55 was built and probably designed by contractor Jeremiah Bedford at a time when Rosedale was still "too far," and large Queen Anne semi-detacheds almost out of fashion. For years Bedford occupied one of the semis himself, locating his construction office here too. *PM*

8b 51 Elm Ave. (detached house), 1889. It's likely that Jeremiah Bedford constructed this house as well. Put up one year after no. 53–55, it's basically a Queen Anne with Romanesque Revival masonry girding ground-floor front. *PM*

8c 61 Elm Ave. (detached house), 1890.
Also attributed to Bedford, this chubby
cherub is just the sort then aborning in the
Annex **[Area X]**. Though Bedford's array of
Romanesque parts is wobbly, such richly
rendered red brick and terracotta can't help
but appeal. *PM*

**8d Originally Charles H. Francis resi-
dence, 49 Elm Ave. (detached house),
Gordon & Helliwell, 1901–02.** In the
United States, late Queen Anne houses were
rounding themselves out in Shingle Style,
but fire-fearful Toronto discouraged shingles
unless backed by brick—an expensive
proposition. With virtually no local precedent
or practice then, this proto-Shingle isn't half
bad. *PM*

**8e 47 Elm Ave. (detached house),
Chadwick & Beckett, 1905. 45 Elm Ave.
(detached house), Frederick H. Herbert,
1905–06.** A little Tudor gabling, some
classical dormers, Prairie School overhangs,
plus a dab of Beaux Arts doorway—these
houses of no fixed affiliation exemplify those
that suddenly began to go up all over
Rosedale in the early 1900s. *PM*

**9 Originally John Hoare house, 57 Glen
Rd., Designing & Draughting Co., 1911.
Originally Oliver Adams house, 55 Glen
Rd., Chadwick & Beckett, 1901–02.
Originally Ambrose Small house, 51 Glen
Rd., 1903.** No. 57 is a neat, symmetrical
red-brick Neo-Georgian gone picturesque
with Craftsmany porch, eaves, and dormers.
Architectural credit goes to D.C. Cotton and
H.G. Macklin, who respectively filled the roles
of the Designing & Draughting Company.
No. 55 is Second Classical Revival starring a
full-height Ionic-columned entry porch.
Such dramatic designs were inspired by the
Beaux Arts spectacle of the 1893 World's
Columbian Exposition in Chicago. No. 51 is
noteworthy not as architecture but as home
to Ambrose Small, the hated and envied
owner of theatres across the province who
disappeared in 1919 along with $10-million
from his bank account. Neither was seen
again; and yes, the basement has been
excavated! *PM*

**10 Originally Harris Henry Fudger house,
40 Maple Ave., Gordon & Helliwell,
1897–98; additions, Burke & Horwood,
1902–03, 1907.** When the Fudger house was
built, its design represented a grandiose look
back at the 19th century; but its situation,
surrounded by empty lots with open views
to the Don Valley, spelled a step into the
20th and an optimistic commitment to this
new neighbourhood. Fudger had just
become part owner and president of the
Robert Simpson Company **[5/6]**, and his
conspicuously picturesque house with
circular drive and formal gardens was an
elitist spectacle. *PM*

**11 33 Maple Ave. (detached house),
probably James P. Hynes, 1903–04.
35 Maple Ave. (detached house), Langley
& Langley, 1903–04. 39 Maple Ave.
(detached house), 1905–06. 41 Maple
Ave. (detached house), Symons & Rae,
1902.** Taking a cue from the Fudger
extravaganza across the street, these
fat and full Jacobethans break out at
the top in a whimsical file of potted chimneys
and stone-coped gables. No. 37, dating to
1902, is a classical loner in this Neo-Tudor
precinct. *PM*

As late as the 1870s, the whole of southeast
Rosedale was in the hands of just four landowners:
Maunsell Jackson, who lived at Drumsnab
[22/17]; bachelor Edward Nanton, who resided in
a former milkman's cottage near today's Nanton
Avenue; Yorkville developer Walter McKenzie, who
had a house at today's McKenzie Avenue; and
Judge John Hoskin, who presided over The Dale
[22/12] at (where else?) today's Dale Avenue. All
four reached home by a ravine road that began at
Parliament Street, where they jointly maintained
a gatekeeper's lodge.

**12 21 Dale Ave. (originally site of "The
Dale" [John Hoskin residence]; now
apartment building), Crang & Boake,
1951.** In 1891, a guidebook writer advised
that "For its fine sylvan setting and the rare
attractions of its conservatories, The Dale is
well-nigh unsurpassed among Toronto

homes." Today all that remains of Judge Hoskin's 1874 villa is a much-denatured gate lodge (no. 15 Dale). As for the beige-brick apartment building that replaced The Dale, sneaking past the city's 35-foot-height bylaw [see 21/31], it has aged well; its bulk hidden from the street and its trees maturing, it suggests something of the sylvan setting that Hoskin must have enjoyed. *PM/AB*

13 Originally Albert E. Kemp residence, 2 McKenzie Ave. (originally detached house), S. Hamilton Townsend, 1903–05.

The smooth, simplified forms and neatly balanced but asymmetric composition mark this as the powerful, sophisticated work of Ontarian Hamilton Townsend, whose enduring Rosedale houses deserve more recognition. *PM*

14 Originally Mrs. Eleanor Street house, 10 McKenzie Ave., William Langton, 1909.

This house draws our eye for its stately-home grace replete with cut limestone details and expensive slate roof. Langton situated the house farther back than others on the street to give more light to rooms in the rear, and this siting enhances the Georgian formality. But the house did follow romantic ideas of the day in being set, not high above grade, but close to the ground for a "more natural" connection. *PM*

14 | 10 McKenzie Ave.

15a Originally Lewis Grant house, 20 McKenzie Ave., Eden Smith & Son, 1908–09.

Built for painter Lewis Grant, this is quietly radical. Its spare façade and unusually placed windows suggest that architect Smith was paying close attention to currents in European Modernism, as he would demonstrate at the Studio Building [16/28] a few years later. *AB*

15b Originally James Ramsey house, 49 McKenzie Ave., Charles J. Gibson, 1896–97.

The only building that many drivers ever see of Rosedale as they whip off the Don Valley Parkway, this quintessentially Victorian house is very impressive. Imagine what it would have seemed in 1897 when there was no expressway, no viaduct, not even a Bloor Street (which terminated then at Sherbourne). The terracotta "picture frame" was re-created a year later on Elm Avenue [22/3]. This was for a maker of photographers' supplies. *PM*

16 Originally Henry Kelly house, 65 Castle Frank Rd., Chadwick & Beckett, 1912.

Six-over-six shuttered windows, pedimented dormers, and side-lighted entrance spell Georgian. But no. 65, in its flat relief, horizontal emphasis, and siting close to the ground, is akin to Tudor-derived 2 McKenzie [22/13]. Clients might choose appended "style," but architects knew that form-created space was the real challenge. Kelly, manager of Dun & Company, asked Chadwick & Beckett to add a garage almost before the house was finished. The relatively tight site decreed a breach in no. 65's classical good taste: garages were built discreetly out of sight until the 1930s. Witness adjacent Dale Avenue, a whole street of them. *PM*

17 "Drumsnab" (originally Francis Cayley residence)/formerly Maunsell Jackson house, 5 Drumsnab Rd., 1834; second-floor addition, William Thomas, 1856; addition, Eden Smith & Son, 1908.

Drumsnab is one of Toronto's most alluring houses, not only because it's the oldest in town still a private home, but also because it continues to evoke the refreshing charm of a

Regency cottage, those informal country dwellings set in rustic landscapes that were the *beau idéal* of early 1800s England. With simple shape and two-foot-thick fieldstone walls, Drumsnab perfectly embodied the form, and in 1834 the 120-acre site overlooking a Don Valley mound—a drumsnab—would have been rustic territory indeed.

Cayley was brother of politician William Cayley and a bachelor who seems to have whiled away his time painting frescoes on the walls of Drumsnab. On his death the house was purchased by Maunsell Jackson, whose descendants occupied it well into the 20th century. In 1928, 13 years after the Prince Edward Viaduct had been constructed, Drumsnab was still ensconced amid 11 country acres, probably the largest estate then existing within the City of Toronto. *PM*

18 48 Castle Frank Rd. (detached house), Bond & Smith, 1911. As with Georgian forebears, Georgian Revival houses feature classical entrances, cornices, and windows. This sweetly appealing house also boasts prototypical tall chimney and quoins at the corners. But the asymmetry, with off-centre door and single bellying bay, definitely marks it as 20th-century. In 1911, you could have had it for $7,000. *PM*

19 Originally Edward Hay residence, 43 Castle Frank Rd. (detached house), Chadwick & Beckett, 1907–08. Vertical stretch and too-small windows make this early Castle Frank house a tad gawky, but cobbled clinker brick saves all. Once thrown out as seconds, vitrified, misshapen clinkers became popular in the early 1900s and were manufactured specially for their "artistic effect." (Their rough, faux-old descendants are common in today's suburbs.) *PM/AB*

20 Originally "Inchraffay" (Gerald Strathy residence), 32 Castle Frank Rd., Eustace G. Bird, 1911–12. "The rich men in Toronto, and there are obviously a great number of them, build large detached houses on pieces of land which we should think just big enough for a gardener's lodge and potato patch," wrote a British architect visiting

Canada in the 1920s. He could well have had Gerald Strathy's enormous T-shaped Neo-Georgian in mind. In addition to its small lot, the plainness of the house is striking. Nearby, architect Bird had just finished his own, similar house **[22/22a]**. *PM*

21 44 Hawthorn Ave. (detached house), 1906–07. Originally Ernest L. Kingsley residence, 46 Hawthorn Ave. (detached house), Charles J. Gibson, 1905–06. Originally Lawrence Boyd residence, 48 Hawthorn Ave. (detached house), E. Beaumont Jarvis, 1902–04. These three neat and various Edwardian abodes were among the first on Hawthorn Avenue, which was part of an 1885 subdivision of Edward Nanton's land. No. 48 was designed by Edgar Jarvis's son Beaumont. How intriguing that this zealot Rosedale realtor encouraged his eldest child to become an architect. *PM*

The street we know as Hawthorn Gardens was Eustace Bird's driveway until the rest of this prime-spot plot was parcelled out. Today five houses share the cul-de-sac allure.

22a Originally Eustace G. Bird house, 5 Hawthorn Gardens, Eustace G. Bird, 1909–10; additions, Mathers & Haldenby, 1930; altered later, Gordon Ridgely. Ontarian Eustace Bird is little known save as Toronto rep of New York architects Carrère & Hastings **[6/7]**. The clonish design of his own house does nothing to alter that image. Ironically, it would become the long-time home of the very forward-thinking art collector and curator Ydessa Hendeles (the daughter of developer Jacob Hendeles). *PM/AB*

22b Originally "Marbrae" (Melville White residence), 6 Hawthorn Gardens, Burke Horwood & White, 1910. In the hands of Eden Smith or Hamilton Townsend, Tudor vernacular could take on an almost modern look, but less adventurous Burke Horwood & White rendered it straight with all the medieval quaintness prettily in place. Still, no denying the appeal of this dark-trimmed white-stuccoed "cottage." Melville White was manager of Canada Foundry and brother to architect Murray White. *PM*

22c Originally William Gundy house, 4 Hawthorn Gardens, S. Hamilton Townsend, 1910–11. Nowhere in Toronto are the principles of English Cottage Style—simplicity, strength, harmony with nature—better demonstrated than in publisher William Gundy's house. Without symmetry but with such consummate balancing as to seem to be, Townsend's design is both daring and graceful. The pattern of windows clearly expresses the interiors; the sentinel chimney and dormer push briskly through the roof like outgrowths of the canopied entrance below, and tapestry brickwork along with siting low to the ground blend the house beautifully with its surroundings. *PM*

22d Originally Norman Seagram house/ formerly Jesuit Fathers residence, 2 Hawthorn Gardens, Vaux Chadwick, 1929–30. By the late 1920s, the bold English Cottage Style experiment to create non-copyist but still traditional architecture was dead and—in real reversal—reproductions were wholeheartedly embraced. Seagram's dry, lacklustre, although obviously expensive "period" house is a good example. Never in the family distillery business, Norman Seagram made his fortune in his father-in-law's brokerage firm. On his death, the 30-room mansion was acquired by the English-speaking Jesuit Order in Canada. It is now condominium units. *PM*

23 Originally Gerald Larkin house, 8 Castle Frank Rd., George Moorhouse & King, 1926. Salada Tea Company scion Gerald Larkin built this house on Castle Frank Road two years after the Osler property behind was opened as parkland **[22/26]**. Although a classic Palladian design of horizontally emphasized fenestration, raised basement, and pedimented central pavilion, the Larkin house seems not at all formal, thanks in part to the welcoming, congenial entrance. A great and gracious house, best appreciated without the garden wall. *PM*

23 | 8 Castle Frank Rd.

24a Originally John H.C. Durham residence, 93 Elm Ave. (detached house), J. Wilson Siddall, 1901. The most interesting thing about this house is the gorgeous iron porch shielding the front door. Actually a driveway shelter (porte cochère), it was removed here from a house on Sherbourne Street. *PM*

24b 89 Elm Ave. (detached house), E.J. Lennox, 1902–04. Even accomplished E.J. Lennox could be flummoxed by the Edwardian architectural agenda. What a mishmash! *PM*

24c Originally Franklin Kerr house, 88 Elm Ave., Burden & Gouinlock, 1926–27. Unusually, both the Elm Avenue loggia face and South Drive court face are given equal importance. No. 88 won the Ontario Association of Architects 1929 award for "garages, stables, and gatehouses" with its three-car garage for bond dealer Kerr. *PM*

25 Originally "Evenholm" (Edgar Jarvis residence), 157 South Dr., E. Beaumont Jarvis, 1905–06. This was Edgar Jarvis's last Rosedale home; one year after moving in, he died here, age 72. An impressive, unusually symmetrical Jacobethan, it was appropriately designed for Jarvis by his son Beaumont, who by this date had become a reasonably successful architect. *PM*

26 Craigleigh Gardens/originally site of "Craigleigh" (residence of Sir Edmund Osler), 160 South Dr.; gates, Darling & Pearson, 1903. On this scenic ravine site in 1876, Edgar Jarvis shepherded construction of a lavish High Victorian house into which moved, the next year, wealthy businessman Edmund Osler. Osler, it seems, put up most of the money for Edgar Jarvis's bridges, houses, and dreams, and this was probably the beginning of their extensive financial dealings.

Osler resided at Craigleigh for 47 years, eventually overseeing a mansion of some 25 rooms. At his death in 1924, the house was torn down and the 13 acres of manicured grounds presented to the city for a park. *PM*

27 97 Glen Rd. (detached house), probably Chadwick & Beckett, 1901–02. Second Classical Revival houses with full-height "Mount Vernon" porches were very popular in the U.S. during the first half of the 20th century. This imposing Canadian version may have been commissioned by Edgar Jarvis, whom directories list as living next door in the semi-detached at no. 89 in 1901. It would have been consistent with his never-flagging grandiose vision for Rosedale. *PM*

At the intersection of South Drive and Glen Road Edgar Jarvis erected two large houses in 1880 and 1881 in hopes of setting a stately-home stamp on Rosedale. On the northeast corner stood Sylvan Tower, a house the Jarvis family itself occupied until 1889. Then rented for many years to a widow, it was sold in 1908 to James Plummer, president of Dominion Iron & Steel. On the northwest was Norcastle, a towered stone mansion sold to woollens wholesaler Henry W. Darling. It was resold in 1903 to Albert Gooderham, who renamed it Deancroft. Rosedale never became the district Jarvis had envisioned. By the 1930s nobody wanted to live in Sylvan Tower and Deancroft (Lady Gooderham, recently widowed, was moving to Forest Hill Village) and the houses were torn down.

28 Originally Wilmot Matthews house, 146 South Dr., Saunders & Ryrie, 1934–35. Originally S. Temple Blackwood house, 144 South Dr., Mathers & Haldenby, 1935. When the two mansions at Glen Road and South Drive were demolished and the land subdivided in the early '30s, realtor A.E. LePage reported, "Lots will be sold to private parties who wish to erect homes immediately. It is the intention to have the Georgian type of house built. . . ." Note how variously the style could be interpreted. No. 146 is a copy of the classic vernacular side-gabled Palladian as it was built in Britain and the U.S. in the mid 18th century. The firm of Dyce Saunders and Jack Ryrie was well known for these delightful "home-like" houses. This, one of their best, was designed for lawyer Wilmot Matthews.

28 | 146 South Dr.

No. 144 comes from the slightly later, more urban tradition of British Regency and American Federal architecture of the 1810s period. Designed for a stockbroker, this subtly detailed house garnered Mathers & Haldenby an architectural award of merit. *PM*

28 | 144 South Dr.

29 134 South Dr. (detached house), 1936. 132 South Dr. (detached house), 1936.
Georgian "Regency Revival" houses with almost flat roofs and unusually plain roof/wall junctions became popular in the 1930s. Soon even the stone surrounds will be removed and they will be on their way to sleek Modernism [see 21/2]. *PM*

30 Ravine House, 105 Glen Rd. (detached house), Kuwabara Payne McKenna Blumberg with landscape architects NAK and PFS Studio, 2002.
One of the very few houses in Rosedale to show its modernity on its face and also in its landscaping, including the dark teak slats of the fence and broad-brush expanses of groundcover and grass facing the road. Occupying a lot first built out in the 1950s (and which would be off-limits today for its proximity to the adjacent ravine), the house reads as a series of linked rectangular pavilions, buff brick balancing expanses of ravine-ward glass. *AB*

31 Evergreen Brick Works, 550 Bayview Ave., master plan, architectsAlliance; architects Joe Lobko and du Toit Architects; landscape architects DTAH and Claude Cormier + Associés; Centre for Green Cities architects Diamond & Schmitt; heritage architects ERA, 2010. Kiln building renovation, LGA Architectural Partners with ERA, ongoing.
Nineteenth-century

Toronto was a predominantly red-brick city, and much of the red clay (including for Massey Hall [5/9]) came from the earth right here. The Don Valley Brick Works opened in 1889, and continued, remarkably, until 1984. The site was purchased by developers, but conservationists had already begun arguing for a restoration of the valley and of this site. The Brick Works was expropriated and came back into city hands as a 40-acre park, including the adaptive reuse of the site's remaining industrial architecture. Since 2010 the 16 buildings have been managed (in an unusual arrangement) by the non-profit Evergreen; this zone is a hybrid of environmental education centre, event space, commerce, and social enterprise, a place like no other in Toronto.

The new architecture, following a theme articulated by Joe Lobko, works around the existing buildings as precious ruins; Diamond Schmitt's Centre for Green Cities combines sheds and wall fragments into a new structure of offices and public space. But the highlight here is outside in the subtly restored landscape: you can appreciate the scale of the valley, the intensity of the industrial use that carved out the quarry, and (if you look closely) the volatile power of the river itself, which floods this site regularly. The Brick Works has already brought many Torontonians here; it has also inspired a vision of reclaiming more of the Lower Don Valley as parkland, an idea so powerful and logical that it will, in some form, have to be realized. *AB*

31 | Evergreen Brick Works

Toronto has a vexed relationship with its waterfront. It lies "in the broad basin of the lake bed," as Amy Lavender Harris has written, "as if cradled by an ancient hand." And, over 250 years, its Lake Ontario shoreline has been admired for its beauty, exploited by industry, cut off by rail and an expressway, marred by pollution, and then rediscovered as a canvas for city-building.

While John Graves Simcoe chose Toronto's site for strategic reasons—Fort York **[23/18b]** was placed here to command the waters of Lake Ontario—the governor also imagined that the lakefront would serve more poetic purposes: in 1793 his contemporary Peter Russell wrote that Simcoe "has fallen so much in love with the land that he intends to reserve from population the whole front from the Town to the Fort—a space of nearly three miles."

The Walks and Gardens Trust was established in 1818 to implement this vision, which would have linked two planned parks at either end of town: Garrison Reserve, north of Fort York, and King's Park to the east along the Don, whose extensive marshlands were feared as a zone of disease.

But the plan, like many later schemes for Toronto's waterfront, collapsed. Both of the large parks were sold off for piecemeal development, and the Walks and Gardens Lands—including the idea of a public "esplanade" along the water's edge—was overrun by waterfront commerce and then, in the 1850s, the arrival of the railways. The edge of the lake was moved south with fill from Front Street to the Esplanade, and this ground was occupied by railways and industry.

The wharves, piers, and docks of this period were largely obliterated as the lakeshore was pushed even farther south; the oldest structures on the waterfront today date to the early 20th century, when local business leaders pushed for new port infrastructure. "Toronto is to become the Pittsburgh of Canada," an editorial in the *Globe* argued in 1907—referring to the major producer of iron and steel. Meanwhile grain elevators, including Canada Malting's **[23/12]**, dominated the skyline.

The big move came in 1912, with the

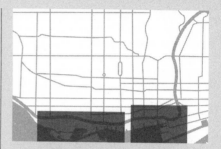

Area XII
Walk 23: Waterfront West
Walk 24: Waterfront East

Toronto Harbour Commission's Waterfront Development Plan: 1,300 acres of marshland was filled and transformed into what is now the Port Lands. But all this sculpting of the landscape never made Toronto into an economic powerhouse; the rise of trucking rendered lake shipping less important, making the port instead a place for large, dirty, low-intensity industry that employed relatively few people. This pattern repeated in the 1950s, when new port infrastructure was built to accommodate bigger ships travelling the St. Lawrence Seaway.

Too late. Containerized shipping made Toronto's port nearly obsolete; the presence of ironworks, oil refineries, and tank farms, and the construction of the Gardiner Expressway helped cut the city off from the body of water that had shaped it. By the 1960s many industries were heading for the suburbs, and yet they'd marred the place; dirty, empty, and in stasis, this was not a waterfront with which one could easily fall in love.

And yet, as developers began to covet the waterfront for high-rise housing, a series of bold schemers tried to reconnect Toronto and the lake. Expansion of the Toronto Island Park created a grand, Modernist landscape design and a generous public getaway from the city.

Meanwhile, Metro's 1967 plan for the waterfront and the Toronto Harbour Commission's 1968 Harbour City scheme each imagined a renewed residential presence on the water; the latter, designed by the young Eb Zeidler, would have moved the Island Airport and replaced it with 500 acres of water-accessible housing, "creating Venice in Toronto," as Zeidler has written. Ontario Place **[23/24]** was the only fruit of this initiative.

But the remnants of the industrial waterfront became attractive for a different sort of revitalization. In the 1972 federal election campaign, the Trudeau Liberals promised a waterfront park for Toronto: this was born the next year as Harbourfront Passage, a pathway through the industrial ruins marked by paint, planter tubs, Douglas fir benches, and flags.

Through the development of what became Harbourfront, the post-industrial waterfront became a site for culture and social gathering. A 1978 plan by Tony Coombes and Michael Kirkland called for the retention of old buildings, in what critic Adele Freedman called "a fascinating architectural experiment." One of them, Zeidler's Queens Quay Terminal **[23/2a]**, opened in 1983 with a mix of retail, offices, and condominium apartments—a mix that still makes sense 30 years later. Nearby, Arthur Erickson's Kings Landing **[23/11]** and Daniel Li's Harbour Terrace **[23/9]** established a mid-rise, water-facing urbanism; other developers continued to build tall condo towers that were widely despised, though the subsequent growth of the South Core district **[see Walk 3]** now makes them seem demure. And while the Harbourfront precinct did not mature until the late 1980s, its community hub **[23/5]**, culture venues **[23/3]**, and robust public realm succeeded in reconnecting downtown Toronto with the lake.

The Port Lands and surrounding area, meanwhile, remained a dead zone, victims of fractured ownership, pollution, and endless bickering among levels of government—what the scholar Gabriel Eidelman calls "a case of waterfront ambitions gone awry."

And then, remarkably, things began to go right. A political alignment between all three levels of government (driven by an Olympic bid) birthed a new joint agency. The group of interests that would become Waterfront Toronto in 2001 controlled 2,000 acres of the Port Lands and eastern waterfront. This agency, despite desperately low expectations, did the plodding work of cleaning up brownfields and consultatively planning the area as a dense new mixed-use district.

Design has been a key ingredient. The agency also used prominent landscape architects to tackle the environmental and urbanistic challenges—making Toronto one of the world's biggest test cases for this sort of post-industrial problem-solving, dubbed "landscape urbanism." Michael Van Valkenburgh Associates designed Corktown Common [24/13] with its "flood protection landform" to keep the Don River in check; they also won the competition to master-plan the port lands and "renaturalize" the mouth of the river, a precondition for future development of the area. That work remains, at this time, unfunded and not yet begun, but the massive potential of the port lands—a largely empty tract nearly as big as downtown, and next door to it—will inevitably lead to its redevelopment.

That will require a psychological shift, and here, too, landscape architecture has begun to play an important role. Waterfront Toronto has relied on a strategy of leading with landscape: building parks and public realm of the highest design quality, and then looking for private partners to develop offices and housing. Sugar Beach [24/3] and Sherbourne Common [24/6] have helped put this zone back on the mental maps of Torontonians. All of the buildings being planned by Waterfront Toronto are at least decent architecture, and all are coherently linked with an urbanism that privileges transit, cycling, and walking, encapsulated on Queens Quay [23/7].

A redesign of the Jack Layton Ferry Terminal and Harbour Square Park, now in the works, promises to add a new standard for public architecture here. In a city that has always been defined by incremental development, the waterfront is now the one place with enough space—physical and political—for grand ideas. The West Don Lands, planned in a hurry leading up to the 2015 Pan American Games, shows Toronto urbanism in a rare coherent state: grey, but also diverse and walkable, with a strong emphasis on the public realm. This creates a grand question for the next 30 years: as intense private development adds tens of thousands of residents to the central and eastern waterfront, will that thoughtful design and public spirit prevail? If it does, Toronto might acquire a beloved new face, and perhaps begin to see itself as it has always been: a lake city.

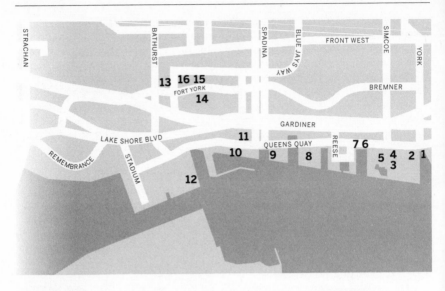

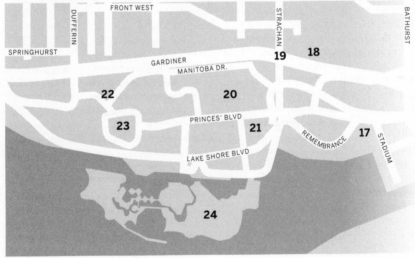

Walk 23: Waterfront West

**1 Toronto Ferry Co. Waiting Room, 145
Queens Quay W., 1907; renovations, Natale
Scott, 1990.** This modest structure with its
wide overhangs represents the earliest wave
of port buildings. Once located at the foot of
Bay Street, it became in 1911 the waiting
room for ferries to Toronto Island; it serves a
similar purpose for tour boats, as well as
supplying visitor information, today. *AB*

**2a Queen's Quay Terminal, 9 Queens
Quay W., Moores & Dunford, 1926–27;
renovation, Zeidler Partnership
Architects, 1979–83.** Canada's largest
warehouse building—a million square feet of
cold and dry storage, pierced by CP and CN
trains—was largely out of use by the 1970s,
and Harbourfront Corp. had to find a way to
repurpose this behemoth. Eberhard Zeidler's
scheme inserted the Fleck Dance Theatre,
capped the building with four floors of condo
apartments, and made dramatic use of its

elegant structure. In opening up three atria, Zeidler made the most of the interior viable for commercial use and conjured a three-dimensional forest of columns, one of Toronto's most fantastical architectural experiences. *AB*

2a | Queen's Quay Terminal

2b Jack Layton Ferry Terminal and Harbour Square Park, 25 Queens Quay W., KPMB, West 8 (landscape architects) + Greenberg Consultants, ongoing. A truly visionary project, and badly needed: a welcoming access point to the Toronto Islands. This competition-winning design would interweave landscape and architecture, with a park of grassy hillocks extending on top of a wood-framed pavilion—both more capacious and more beautiful than what is now here. The existing Harbour Square Park, by local architects Natale Scott Brown, is the result of a 1985 international design competition chaired by Rem Koolhaas—but was never fully implemented. Hopefully this time is different. *AB*

2c Centre Island Park, Project Planning Associates (landscape architects and architects); four wave-roof shelters, Venchiarutti & Venchiarutti, 1956. Concession buildings and bathhouse, Hancock, Little, Calvert Associates, c. 1961. Olympic Island pavilion and theatre, Irving Grossman, 1964. This much-visited site is perhaps Toronto's most visible Modernist landscape, the work of Macklin Hancock's Project Planning Associates **[see 26/5a]**. Manicured lawns and sculptural plantings line the way across Centre Island to the formal Avenue of the Islands, which

originally had strongly graphic plantings of flowers. Along the way are three interesting shelters by Venchiarutti & Venchiarutti, their wavy roofs reflecting the lakeside setting; the mushroom-columned ones over on Olympic Island are by Irving Grossman, and the flat-roofed pavilions by Hancock—as is the remarkable hexagonal restaurant, now called Carousel Café, which is crying out to be refurbished. *AB*

3 The Power Plant, 231 Queens Quay W., Moores & Dunford, 1926–27; renovation, Lett/Smith Architects, 1987. These two hardy brick volumes served the Terminal Warehouse **[23/2a]**, housing ice to the north and refrigeration equipment to the south; after the latter ceased operation in 1980, the buildings were repurposed as a theatre and art gallery respectively. Lett/Smith's renovation preserved the exterior's austere majesty while wrapping the theatre in a glazed entry pavilion. *AB*

4 Ontario Square and Canada Square, 235 Queens Quay W., Michael Van Valkenburgh Associates, 2013. This pair of plazas caps an underground parking garage, which is built around a lightwell and the installation *Light Cascade* (2013) by artist James Carpenter. In Ontario Square, MVVA's elegant ipe benches and patterned pavers harmonize with tightly planted quaking aspens, doses of natural beauty in boldly artificial containers. *AB*

5 Bill Boyle Artport, 235 Queens Quay W.; renovation, 1974; renovations, Natale and Scott, 1986–95. Once a garage for trucking company Direct Winters, this found a second life in the arts as one of Harbourfront's two main buildings, first called York Quay Centre. After many low-budget renovations in the 1980s and '90s by Natale Scott Brown, it retains a garage-chic sensibility. The interior is choppy but charming. The 1995 addition on top houses all of Harbourfront's administrative and curatorial staff, and its steel-truss structure left most of the earlier building untouched. *AB*

6 | Simcoe WaveDeck

6 Simcoe WaveDeck, Queens Quay W. and Lower Simcoe St., West 8 and DTAH, 2015. Local landscape architects DTAH and Dutch counterparts West 8 won an international competition in 2006 to rethink the central waterfront. The WaveDecks—there are others at Spadina Avenue—are the poetic showpieces of that scheme: swells of ipe decking that invite you to come and play. The steel railings on top send the opposite message; a courageous City Hall will remove them someday. *AB*

7 Queens Quay Revitalization, West 8 and DTAH, 2015. How Toronto's grand streets should look. The design for this street installed hardy London plane trees, a continuous separate bike lane, and paving with high-quality materials. The wide promenade, elegantly detailed, is made from three shades of granite cobbles. Its subtle, kitschy pattern of maple leaves is suitable for a tourist-heavy zone. *AB*

8 HTO Park, 339 Queens Quay W., Claude Cormier Architectes Paysagistes, Janet Rosenberg + Associates, and Hariri Pontarini, 2007. A landscape inspired by Seurat's *Sunday Afternoon on the Island of*

La Grande Jatte. Round hills topped with silver maples and willows, a tight rectangle of beach, and grand yellow umbrellas for shade and colour. The predecessor to Cormier's Sugar Beach **[24/3]**. *AB*

9 Harbour Terrace, 401 Queens Quay W., Li Architect, 1987. The most urbane of the 1980s Harbourfront-era condos. Its restrained High-Tech cladding, skilful massing, and modest scale have let it age more gracefully than most of its peers. *AB*

10 Toronto Music Garden, 479 Queens Quay W., Julie Moir Messervy, 2000. Landscape as frozen music. Created by the Boston landscape architect along with Yo-Yo Ma, its plan represents a Bach cello suite. The nuanced design provides places of refuge and a venue for live performance. *AB*

11 Kings Landing and Carsen Centre for National Ballet of Canada, 470 Queens Quay W., Arthur Erickson Architects, 1982; interior, Kuwabara Payne McKenna Blumberg, 1997. A pioneer on the block, this is a cousin of Erickson's terraced Evergreen Building (1978) in Vancouver. The stepped form responds to the water and the Gardiner—the highway-facing north end holds a pool and tennis court while, Erickson wrote, "we opened the apartments fully to the lake and light." Also on the lower floors is a 100,000-square-foot institutional space that lay vacant until 1996, when the Ballet moved in. *AB*

12 Canada Malting Silos, John Metcalf Co., 1929; E.C. Miller and T. Pringle and Son Limited of Montreal, 1944. The renewal of Toronto's grain trade in the late 1920s created these stolid concrete towers—examples of a North American

8 | HTO Park

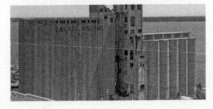

12 | Canada Malting Silos

building type Le Corbusier hailed as "the first fruits of a new age." Like others of their kind, they remain in search of a new use. *AB*

CityPlace, the final buildout of the railway lands, is no Metro Centre [see 3/16], but remains among the largest private-sector redevelopments ever carried out in Canada. Developer Concord Adex imported the tower-and-podium model from downtown Vancouver, but didn't bring the excellent urban design and public realm. These are Toronto's typical mean streets, with concrete sidewalks and sad plantings. The project began east of Spadina in the 1990s; the west part remains in the works. An upcoming community centre and school, by ZAS Architects and The Planning Partnership, promises to raise the architectural standard.

13a Toronto Public Library, Fort York Branch, 190 Fort York Blvd., KPMB, 2014. Mouth of the Creek Park, PUBLIC WORK (landscape architects) and ERA, ongoing. Quiet in colour and material, this library offers two levels of varied spaces for storytime, working, and hanging out. On the outer façade is part of a Margaret Atwood poem from *The Journals of Susanna Moodie*; Charles Pachter's accompanying illustration is perforated into the metal fins above, and reveals itself from just the right angle. Angles are important; the building's wedgy geometry alludes to the ramparts at Fort York, to which it will connect once the adjoining park is finished. This is where Garrison Creek once emptied into the lake; though shore and creek are now buried, they will be memorialized here. *AB*

13a | Toronto Public Library, Fort York Branch

13b Library District Condominiums, 170 Fort York Blvd., KPMB Architects with Page & Steele/IBI Group, 2014. Blues and greens: cool colours, but very welcome in this greige precinct. The low pavilion to the west reaches out toward the library. *AB*

14 Canoe Landing (park), 95 Fort York Blvd., PFS Studio with The Planning Partnership (landscape architects), 2010. The grand park is necessary—and well-used—but not as good as it should be. The central arcade lines up with the gap in Parade **[23/15]**, a couple of hills add topographical drama, a splash pad cools down sweaty kids, and Douglas Coupland's big red canoe and fishing bobbers provide landmarks and visual interest. Still: scrawny trees, the usual concrete paths, and plantings that are already going out of control. Developer Concord Adex surely made a mint in this neighbourhood, and the public didn't land much in return. *AB*

15 Parade (residential and retail), 15 and 21 Iceboat Terrace, KPF with Page & Steele/IBI, 2013. This massive agglomeration of units shows how very big buildings can go wrong. Two mid-rise towers and two high-rise towers, joined by low slabs of apartments and—in the middle—by a bridge 32 floors in the air. This gimmick fails to liven up the towers, which are dull, and it sure doesn't fix the inward-looking, activity-killing mass of the project. *AB*

16 150 Dan Leckie Way (rental apartments), Kuwabara Payne McKenna Blumberg, 2012. Full of family-sized apartments for Toronto Community Housing, a 41-storey tower and mid-rise buildings surround a private elevated courtyard where kids can play safely. Those buildings have "skip-stop" units, with corridors and doors on every other floor. This harks back to the Diamond Myers Hydro Block **[14/17]** and Peter Dickinson's vanished buildings in Regent Park. All this is neatly clad in standard precast and spandrel glass, yet these are the best-looking buildings in the neighbourhood. *AB*

17 Tip Top Lofts/originally Tip Top Tailors Building, 637 Lake Shore Blvd. W., Roy H. Bishop, 1929–30; alterations and addition for residences, architects-Alliance with ERA, 2006. This Art Deco pile was a factory, warehouse and headquarters for the garment makers and retailers Tip Top. The condo conversion, one of the best so-called "hard loft" projects in Toronto, took advantage of its massive windows and tall ceiling heights—and reinstalled the neon sign at a jaunty angle. *AB*

18a Fort York Visitors Centre, 250 Fort York Blvd., Patkau Architects and Kearns Mancini Architects, 2014. This competition-winning design is rich with meaning: its massing marks the original shoreline of Lake Ontario, and its weathering-steel ramparts evoke the War of 1812 while presenting a tough face to the behemoth Gardiner Expressway. Up a ramp and out the north side, the building presents a delicate façade of cast glass to historic Garrison Common and the fort. *AB*

18a | Fort York Visitors Centre

18b Fort York, 250 Fort York Blvd., 1793. Fort York is, literally, where Toronto began: John Graves Simcoe established the fort here in 1793 (with an eye to controlling the waters of Lake Ontario) and then the town to its east. When the War of 1812 began, American leaders saw the fort as a weak target and invaded; they won the 1813 battle, but British commander Sir Roger Sheaffe blew up the fort's gunpowder reserves, killing many of the invaders. After the Americans left, having destroyed what remained of the garrison, the British rebuilt, increased the fort's defences, and deterred a later American attack.

After the war, New Fort York (later Stanley Barracks) became the city's primary defence; the old fort, however, remained a British garrison until Confederation, and then a Canadian military base until 1932, when it became a historic site. It became an island surrounded by railroads, the Gardiner Expressway, industry, and now a new dense neighbourhood. But as a historic site and civic space, it is only gaining in importance. *AB*

i) Defences
The west wall, the moat, and the south side's circular battery date to 1811, when the British strengthened defences in anticipation of an American invasion.

ii) Officers' Brick Barracks and Mess, 1815
Staid Georgian brick at a low, defensible scale; the colourful period-reconstruction interior hints at the social complexities of military life.

iii) Centre and East Blockhouses, 1815
The first components in the rebuilding of the fort, these small buildings were defensible in themselves. The walls of old-growth square timber could stop a bullet and even some artillery fire. Today, these nearly windowless structures retain a solid beauty.

iv) Stone Magazine, 1815
The narrow coursing of the rough-stone walls reflects the care of the military masons, and their work stood up; this building housed munitions until World War II.

v) Fort York Armoury, 660 Fleet St., Marani, Lawson & Morris, 1935
An Edwardian Classical volume surrounds the vast double-height drill hall—which is capped by a type of parabolic structure called a lamella roof and spans a remarkable 123 feet from end to end. *AB*

19 The Bentway, PUBLIC WORK (landscape architects) and Greenberg Consultants (urban design), ongoing. Can you make vibrant public space under an expressway? That's the challenge and promise of this new trail, which will extend (for now) from Strachan Avenue to Spadina

Avenue. The design details are still taking shape, but a sculptural pedestrian bridge at Fort York Boulevard and an open amphitheatre at Strachan should be high points. Built on a limited budget, it won't be especially polished, but the idea of a unified hub for art and recreation that spans this dense area is inspired. It will certainly bring new life to Fort York. *AB*

20a Exhibition Place, 100 Princes' Dr.

This site was once home to Fort Rouillé, the original French settlement, and Stanley Barracks—the fort that supplanted Fort York but has been largely wiped from the map. After the Toronto Industrial Exhibition was first held here in 1879, this became a place for Ontario's largely rural population to gather, ride the rides, and marvel at the riches of the province's agriculture and the innovations of industry.

Between 1904 and 1912, G.W. Gouinlock added a crop of highly refined buildings influenced by the 1893 Chicago Exposition; Chapman and Oxley created a new City Beautiful plan in 1920, punctuated by their Princes' Gate, completed in 1927.

The grounds served military purposes in World War I, World War II, and then, starting with the new CNE Grandstand in 1948, a campus of Modernist buildings was developed that embodied the consumerist pizzazz of the era. George A. Robb's Shell Oil Tower (1955, now demolished) shone above the Midway. Where the Gardiner took down George Gouinlock's old Beaux Arts Dufferin Gate, Philip Brook's 1959 replacement was a suitably modern riff on Eero Saarinen's Gateway Arch in St. Louis.

It's been downhill from there. A lack of imagination by the city has allowed the grounds to lie fallow much of the year and be taken over by parking lots and car-oriented entertainment uses. The 1997 Enercare Centre introduced a new, uncomfortably massive scale to the site, while the later BMO Field and Hotel X fail miserably to live up to the architectural standard of the first 60 years. *AB*

20b Ricoh Coliseum, 45 Manitoba Dr., G.F.W. Price, 1921; Livestock Pavilion addition, J.J. Woolnough, 1926–27; renovations and additions, Parkin Architects and Brisbin Brook Beynon, 2003. Direct Energy Centre/originally National Trade Centre, Zeidler Architects and Dunlop Farrow Inc., 1997.

The Coliseum complex was originally designed by city architects Price and Woolnough for the CNE and the Royal Agricultural Winter Fair; it has been substantially rebuilt, but the restored north facades retain the craft and grandeur of the original Beaux Arts structures. After 1927 the centre became (so claims a plaque on the site) the largest enclosed exhibition space in the world. Clearly that is no longer the case; it's dwarfed by the current trade centre to the south. The latter makes gestures to its context, including a new partial façade that matches the rhythm of the Automotive Building across the street and a set of Postmodern "lanterns" that provide visual landmarks. (The Coliseum originally had a set of towers along its south side, to match those on the north side.) Yet that massive complex, with its massive garage, brought Exhibition Place a scale and volume of car traffic that are inherently unfriendly and un-urban. *AB*

21 Automotive Building (now Allstream Centre), Douglas E. Kertland, 1929; renovations, NORR Architects, 2009.

Kertland, trained in Britain and formerly of John Lyle's office, beat out 30 other submissions to win a design competition in 1928 with his design—which blended an establishment-friendly modern classicism with Art Deco detailing, including a frieze ornamented with winged wheels, that suited its very modern purpose. The building rose (in just four months) the next year, with outer walls of cast artificial stone. *AB*

21 | CNE: Automotive Building

22a | CNE: Queen Elizabeth Building

22a Queen Elizabeth Building, Page & Steele (Peter Dickinson, design architect), 1955.
Dickinson at his most expressive. In the lobby, a folded-plate concrete roof zips up and down above a spiral stair; that same roof, engineered by the local sages Morden Yolles and Roly Bergmann, continues invisibly above the 1,300-seat hall, which retains much of its original detail. The large, single-storey exhibition hall has its own, larger folded-plate roof; the concluding row of leaning columns, capped with flagpoles, expresses the outward thrust of the forces from the roof. *AB*

22b Horticulture Building, G.W. Gouinlock, 1907.
The centrepiece of Gouinlock's Baroque classical ensemble. Its grand dome echoes the previous building on the site, Toronto's own Crystal Palace, which burned in 1906. Its current use, as nightclub Muzik, has been rough on the building. *AB*

23 Better Living Centre, Marani, Morris & Allan, 1962.
A fervently Modernist work from an old Toronto office, founded in 1919, who were also the designers of the (long-gone) 1948 CNE Grandstand. Essentially a shed, this is a graceful container for a chaotic cornucopia of consumer goods: a five-acre roof floats above curved volumes of glazed white brick, separated by narrow clerestories. The multi-coloured ornamental tower on top adds a De Stijl flavour. *AB*

24 Ontario Place, 955 Lake Shore Blvd. W., Craig Zeidler Strong and Hough Stansbury and Associates, 1971.
Ontario's jealous response to Expo 67 allowed the young Michael Hough and Eb Zeidler the job of a lifetime: creating an urban park, and indeed a city district, out of nothing and in a hurry. Hough's artificial reef placed a hilly Modernist landscape on top of sunken barges and construction debris, studded with innovative adventure playgrounds. Zeidler's domed Cinesphere builds on the innovations of Buckminster Fuller, while his network of elevated "pods" evokes the Japanese Metabolists and other utopian streams of Modernism—as did the Frei Otto–inspired fabric roof on the Forum, the concert venue with a rotating stage that was insensitively replaced by the Molson Amphitheatre. Indeed all of Ontario Place was poorly maintained until it closed in 2012, and is now in flux, awaiting a new mixture of uses. The William G. Davis Trail, by West 8 and Land Inc., is the first step in what should be a reverent reworking of the site. *AB*

24 | Ontario Place

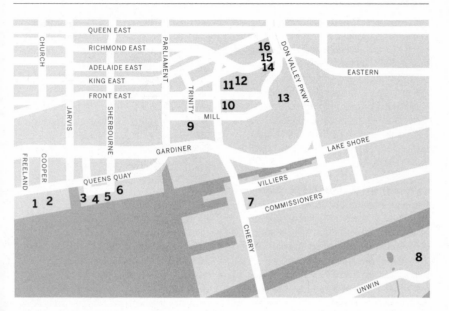

Walk 24: Waterfront East

1 Pier 27, 29 and 39 Queens Quay E., architectsAlliance, 2014. These two pairs of high-end condo buildings make an unusual contortion: the design by aA lifts some of their bulk into three-storey bridges, leaving the ground unobstructed but creating an awkward composition. The complex's east wall blocks noise from its long-established neighbour Redpath. *AB*

2 Redpath Sugar refinery, 95 Queens Quay E., Gordon S. Adamson Associates with H.G. Acres & Co. Ltd., engineers, 1957; additions later. One of the few places where maritime trade touches the city in a visible way: ships still come and go as they

have since the 1950s, sliding up to the massive storage shed that will soon be surrounded by new residences and offices. The prominent local Modernist Adamson designed an efficient ensemble of brick-clad boxes, which have been enlarged but retain their Bauhausian refinement and their cladding of (almost) sugary-white brick. *AB*

3 | Sugar Beach

3 Sugar Beach, 11 Dockside Dr., Claude Cormier Architectes Paysagistes Inc. and The Planning Partnership, 2010. In 2010 this playful concoction by Claude Cormier was the first new park to open on this part of

2 | Redpath Sugar refinery

the waterfront. The granite boulders and Ohio white sand set a playful, populist tone, along with the pink umbrellas—which are in fact custom-fabricated, weatherproof pieces of street furniture that include light fixtures. For all its beachy trappings, Cormier's design is in effect a skilfully proportioned and designed public plaza, seasoned with maples and golden weeping willows. The design will soon extend across the street with Sugar Beach North. *AB*

4 Corus Quay, 25 Dockside Dr., Diamond Schmitt; interior, Quadrangle, 2010. The area's pioneering office building, developed by a city agency in 2010 to bring jobs into the then sleepy neighbourhood. The building's envelope is competent but uninspired Diamond Schmitt; still its restaurant and radio studio activate Sugar Beach and the waterfront promenade. The liveliest element of Quadrangle's interior, an atrium pierced by pedestrian bridges and a tube slide, lies within a lobby accessible to tenants only. *AB*

5 George Brown College Waterfront Campus, 51 Dockside Dr., Stantec Architecture and KPMB in joint venture, 2012. An elegantly detailed "vertical campus" for health-related disciplines. A series of public, open stairs ascends to the top of the building, culminating in a "learning landscape" of bleachers that spans the 6th and 7th floors. The rooftop terrace enjoys fine prospects over the Port Lands and the adjacent Sherbourne Common. From the outside, a pair of interlocked stairs on the north side offer a bit of bravura form-making. *AB*

6 Sherbourne Common, 61 Dockside Dr., PFS Studio and The Planning Partnership with Teeple Architects, 2011. A two-part plaza that anticipates adjacent tower developments, this space provides a smartly woven mix of lawns, square, and playground space. The design tells a story about water: it is treated within the sinuous pavilion building (designed by Teeple), emerges from sculptures (by the artist Jill Anholt) to the north, and then winds back, purified, toward the lake. *AB*

6 | Sherbourne Common

7 Hydro Substation, 281 Cherry St., 1930. 309 Cherry St., 1935. This modest Edwardian Classical substation reflects the effort by the Toronto Harbour Commission to draw industry here; the Moderne building at no. 309, for shippers William McGill and Co., is one rare result. *AB*

8 Hearn Generating Station, 440 Unwin Ave., Stone & Webster (engineers), 1951. One of the largest buildings in Canada. Its single main room of 400,000 square feet once housed coal-fired generators, and is for the moment a glorious ruin used for film shoots and the Luminato arts festival. The concrete and brick volume, along with the 770-foot stack added in 1971, could and should have a future in the redeveloped Port Lands. *AB*

8 | Hearn Generating Station

Distillery District millers William Gooderham and James Worts established one of Toronto's first waterfront industries here in 1832; its windmill became a landmark in the young town. The site operated—including through Prohibition—until 1990; a decade later it began its second life as a retail, cultural, and residential neighbourhood, a likely precedent for 21st-century downtowns. At the moment, it feels slightly Disneyfied, but the brawn and patina of the architecture give the place some soul.

Distillery District

9a The Stone Distillery, 2 Trinity St., David Roberts Sr., 1860; renovated in 1870 after a fire; renovation, ERA, 2003.

The oldest surviving building in the Distillery, this once faced the wharves where materials and products came and went. A fire in 1869 did not touch its outer walls, and distillery employees soon rebuilt it; production continued here until 1957. Today the brawn of the building's wood structure and stone walls serve as atmospheric backdrops for creative-class professionals. Interpretive panels and exhibits in the stairwell explain the distillery processes. *AB*

9b Fire Pump House, Trinity St., David Roberts Jr., 1895; renovation, ERA, 2002.

The last building added here in the Victorian era, this has lost most of its tall chimney but retains much of its deliciously elaborate brickwork. *AB*

9c Pure Spirits, 15 Trinity St., David Roberts Jr., 1873.

The fine glassy façade at 15 Trinity had a very serious practical intent: the front of the building housed stills, and any explosion would dissipate its energy out the windows. The fact that William Gooderham could see this façade from his office may have inspired a certain level of quality. Today that volume is handsome office space (all private) and retail at ground level. *AB*

9d | Clear Spirit

9d Pure Spirit, Clear Spirit, and The Gooderham, 70 Distillery Ln., architects-Alliance, 2008 and 2013.

Three crisp Neo-Modernist glass towers—the latter two, at the east end, enlivened by variegated and kinked balconies—rise in contemporary counterpoint to the Distillery District. The bases, with their cladding of long red bricks and punched windows, engage with the 19th-century form and materiality. (A set of canted concrete columns on the east side of Clear Spirit hit the ground with poetic force.) *AB*

9e Young Centre, 50 Tank House Lane, David Roberts Jr., 1883 and 1888; renovation, KPMB, 2006.

The two tank houses, built for the storage and aging of spirits, feature solid massing and intricate brickwork; their open volumes have lent themselves well to theatre uses. The renovation shows the hand of KPMB's Thomas Payne, channelling Louis Kahn in the deep doorway details and hefty oak benches around the lobby hearth. *AB*

10a Canary District and Canary Park (condominium apartments), 398 Front St. E. and 120 Bayview Ave., KPMB, 2015. Curved buildings are rare in Toronto, but this pair of towers responds sinuously to their park-front site. A tailored façade of ironspot brick and glass is capped with Aalto-esque curved penthouses; with elegant townhouses at ground level and a through lobby, this is sensitive urbanism. *AB*

10b Canary District, precinct plan and block plans, Urban Design Associates and du Toit Allsopp Hillier, 2004; public realm and urban design, The Planning Partnership and Phillips Farevaag Smallenberg, 2015. A rare master-planned neighbourhood in Toronto, this district was expropriated in 1987 for an affordable-housing scheme that came to be called Ataratiri; then the land sat fallow for nearly 20 years before being rebuilt in a hurry to serve as the athletes' village for the 2015 Pan Am and Parapan Am Games. A Canadian dream team of architects and planners assembled a coherent mid-rise district that expresses the best of architecture and urbanism of its period: walkable, tightly detailed, formally coherent, and very grey. A consistent, six-metre ground floor creates strong retail and public spaces, while the public realm includes wide sidewalks with granite curbs. The plaza along the north side of Front Street (positioned to catch sunlight) includes two fine works of public art, Tadashi Kawamata's *Untitled (Toronto Lamp Posts)* and *The Water Guardians* by Jennifer Marman and Daniel Borins. *AB*

10b | Canary District

11 Cooper Koo Family Cherry Street YMCA/George Brown College Student Residence, 461 Cherry St., MacLennan Jaunkalns Miller, 2015; architectsAlliance, 2015. A complex and urbane ensemble, capped by a 500-bed student residence and ringed by sophisticated public space. The Y's interior is rational, tightly organized, and beautifully daylit, typical of the deeply competent MJM. The Cherry Street façade is marked by a bold red protrusion full of angled screens for sunshading; on Front Street, aA's irregular cluster of columns forms a dynamic composition while supporting the mass of the residence above. *AB*

11 | Cooper Koo Family Cherry Street YMCA

12 Affordable housing, Wigwamen and Fred Victor, 75 Cooperage Lane and 20 Palace St., Daoust Lestage, 2015. There are few cues that these two buildings are affordable housing, but some playful notes—the Supergraphic numbers on the façades and the hits of red—mark the touch of Quebec's Daoust Lestage. Townhouses for families are set apart formally from the buildings but share systems and a parking garage. *AB*

13 Corktown Common, 155 Bayview Ave., Michael Van Valkenburgh Associates (landscape architects), 2015. Public space and a tool of urban resilience, this 18-acre park sits on a flood protection landform that protects the adjacent area, including much of the downtown core, from 350-year floods of the Don River. The elevation produces remarkable vistas of the nearby rail tracks and of the downtown skyline; MVVA has taken advantage of this high ground with a playground, a splash pad, and a fine pavilion (by Maryann Thompson Architects). The hardscape is MVVA's signature circa 2010, with ipe-and-steel benches and interlocking paving stones in a complex pattern—but the bulk of the experience is of flora and fauna, largely native species; these thrive in and around an artificial marshland fed by stormwater runoff. It's hard to imagine that this site was, for more than a century, home to noxious industries. *AB*

13 | Corktown Common

14 Cube House, 1 Sumach St., Ben Kutner, 1996. A long-shot experiment in modular housing. Kutner, an Ottawa architect, licensed the design from the Dutch architect Piet Blom, who built a cluster of these houses in Rotterdam in 1984. The project demonstrated one way to build on leftover scraps of land—a dream associated to this day with prefab housing—but failed to become a viable prototype for larger development. Getting a building permit took Kutner and his partner eight years. *AB*

15 Underpass Park, 29 Lower River St., The Planning Partnership and PFS Studio (landscape architects), 2015. A thoughtful, even revolutionary remaking of found space beneath off-ramps to the Don Valley Parkway. Dark, covered areas become basketball courts and a skate park; the uncovered area between ramps, a playground, accented by the shimmering magic of Paul Raff's public-art installation *Mirage*. *AB*

15 | Underpass Park

16 River City, 51 Trolley Cres., Saucier + Perrotte with ZAS, 2013 (phase 1); 2015 (phase 2); ongoing. This complex, which will include four residential towers spanning the adjacent expressway ramp, commands a prominent site with views to downtown and the Don Valley. With their dynamic forms and minimal material palette, these buildings prove it's possible for developer housing to vary the window-wall formula. *AB*

16 | River City

For the past century, there have been two Torontos: the historic core and the suburbs—the vast area beyond which has evolved into a continuous city region. This process of suburbanization began a century ago, and while it has been chaotic at times, a strong planning regime centred around the former Metropolitan Toronto hosted expressions of grander visions. There have been versions of the Garden City; car-based Modernist planning of cul-de-sac neighbourhoods; and regional policy that scattered North America's second-largest number of high-rise buildings across the city. And in recent years, there are hints of a 21st-century post-car suburbanism.

The growth of what we see as Toronto's suburbs—the former Etobicoke, York, North York, East York, and Scarborough—plus the surrounding municipalities, was initially shaped by the same patterns as downtown Toronto. First came the colonial surveyor's grid of farm lots and concession roads. In the 19th century, those roads became the spines for rural settlements such as Weston. Then, in the 20th century, individual farms were bought by developers and subdivided into new neighbourhoods that would, eventually, be annexed by the city and become a part of it, echoing the pattern in earlier areas such as the Annex and Yorkville. In a few cases, this expansion looked like suburbia as we imagine it today: a master-planned, pastoral redoubt from the city, made for discerning middle- and upper-class residents. There were a few such planned suburbs early on, including Lawrence Park, laid out in 1909 by the English-Canadian engineer Walter S. Brook. In the following years, the landscape architect Frederick Gage Todd, a former employee of Frederick Law Olmsted, laid out a plan for Leaside for the Canadian Northern Railway. Shaped by the Garden City movement, the plan proposed curved streets and a separate zone for industry. But the place was remote and it lacked transit and, crucially, servicing; Toronto refused to annex it and it remained rural. Yet 25 years later, Todd's vision for Leaside would be largely built out, with a rapid construction of houses and apartments including Garden Court **[25/47]**, some of Toronto's finest architecture of the period.

Area XIII
Walk 25: Suburbs West
Walk 26: Suburbs East

In the interim, another more anarchic sort of building also shaped the growing city: working-class people buying land and building their own homes, establishing what journalists of the 1900s and 1910s called "shacktowns." The geographer Richard Harris estimates that 40 per cent of all Toronto's new houses between 1900 and 1913 were built by their owners. This left behind an uneven fabric in places like Earlscourt and what is now called Leslieville. These would create opportunities for Torontonians to find their way onto the property ladder and, in a few cases, to innovate [see 26/12c].

Most of the new neighbourhoods, up to 1950, had one thing in common: they were dense and walkable, comparably so to the old city itself. Along the shore of Lake Ontario, Long Branch, New Toronto, Mimico, Leslieville, and southern Scarborough all grew up along streetcar networks, shaped by transit and scaled for walking. Often specific neighbourhoods were built up around industry, such as the Boxer Building as early as 1891.

But then came, in the years after 1945, a series of changes that turned Toronto inside out. For one thing, there were the new arrivals: more than 500,000 immigrants landed in the city between 1945 and 1965, and instantly created strong Eastern European and Southern European presences in the city. In 1951, 31 per cent of city residents were foreign-born; that number was 42 per cent a decade later. These new Torontonians helped spur the economy, brought building skills that would transform the city's construction sector, and needed places to live.

This population growth and the development pressure that came with it arrived at the same time as widespread car ownership. And so, the car-oriented suburb, with curvy streets and (relatively) big lots. Toronto's most prominent (though not first) example was Don Mills [26/5a]. The brainchild of the tycoon E.P. Taylor, this development remade 2,000 acres with a master plan that drew on Garden City thinking and on the Modernist planning that young landscape architect Macklin Hancock had absorbed from his Bauhaus-trained professors at Harvard.

For observers of architecture, the most interesting aspect of Don Mills is Taylor's insistence on Modernism. Houses, office buildings, and schools were shaped with a remarkably up-to-date aesthetic standard, equalled in no other Toronto district. And the planning of Don Mills was equally interesting, informed as it was by the progressive politics of its architects: the place was designed for a mix of classes, with housing for sale and rent, and detached houses, row houses, and multifamily buildings. "The advantage to a family of being able to move about within the area, as income and family status change, was obvious," wrote Murray V. Jones, Metro Toronto's commissioner of planning and a Don Mills resident, in a rather ambivalent article in 1957. That vision of upward mobility quickly vanished as Don Mills became fashionable and uniformly middle-class.

Don Mills's real influence, for better and worse, came through its separation of residential and industrial uses, separation of pedestrian and vehicle traffic. Jones asked, presciently, "What urban form has been produced? . . . There still seems to be no dominating force linking these ['neighbourhood'] units together." There was, in other words, no centre.

Yet most contemporary observers viewed this growth with an optimism shared by local politicians in rapidly suburbanizing Metropolitan Toronto, where the parallel growth of industry and housing promised prosperity. The civic centres built in Scarborough [26/17] and in North York [25/39] capture the breezy ambition of the 1970s: a car in every driveway, and gathering places with plenty of parking.

However, the real picture is more complicated than that. After Metro was formed in 1953, it became responsible for the planning of the area within and somewhat beyond its borders. In part, Metro allowed for developers to push car-oriented, low-density development, and provided the infrastructure and planning to support this (no small feat). Yet, in addition, a relatively strong planning culture also shaped Metro in unique ways. Planners insisted on high population densities, and developers responded with high-rise apartment towers. By 1965, 26 per cent of all Toronto dwellings were in apartment buildings, which were concentrated in the suburbs. Today there are nearly 1,200 such buildings housing a million Torontonians, numbers unmatched by any city in North America other than New York.

These concrete-slab towers tended to follow the Modernist orthodoxy of towers-in-the-park with banal architectural and urbanistic results. Uno Prii's Jane Exbury Towers [25/19] are a rare example with some flair. And today, these clustered towers present a planning problem for the city, in that their residents are increasingly new Canadians, less than wealthy and without cars. Still, most of these communities function well, and apartment living has been a part of life for Torontonians for more than half a century; the truth is that Toronto is just as much a city of slab towers as it is of Victorian houses.

It is also—though this is too often forgotten by the residents of red-brick downtown—a city largely built in the Modernist era. The architectural fruits of that can be seen in public buildings: schools, hospitals, cultural and civic structures, and higher education facilities provided an endless stream of work for architects at mid century. The Parkin office's Sunnylea School, completed in 1943, imported au courant modern ideas into the city, and it became a template for hundreds of such schools [19/22] where Torontonians came of age.

Architectural ambition peaked around the centennial year of 1967. Raymond Moriyama's Ontario Science Centre [26/11b], epic in scale and profound in its engagement with the landscape, has a boldness that would be inconceivable in today's Toronto. York University [25/22a] attempted, among farmers' fields, to re-create a pedestrian campus with a Modernist design language. John Andrews's design for the Scarborough College campus [26/21a] was globally acclaimed for its innovation and ambition; what is now University of Toronto Mississauga did not achieve the same heights, but it later became a hub for ambitious architecture [25/4c, 25/4d].

For the most part, innovative architecture in the suburbs has been limited to such public and educational buildings, from Andrews's remarkable Bellmere Junior Public School of 1965 [26/19] all the way to the Centennial College Progress Campus and the Ashtonbee Library and Student Centre [26/15].

Housing, on the other hand, has been overwhelmingly developer-driven, largely low-density, banal in execution, and unimaginative in its form. The occasional non-profit experiment [26/14], or showpiece building such as Absolute Towers [25/6], is the exception that proves the rule.

All that, however, is beginning to change. Condos are now a major part of the housing mix in the 905 suburbs, while policy including the provincial Growth Plan for the Greater Golden Horseshoe of 2006 has begun steering toward a new consensus that denser development, served by transit, is an economic and ecological necessity. This change will be slow in coming, and it's not clear what architectural form it will take. What is clear is that suburban areas such as Scarborough and cities such as Mississauga must see themselves building new places that will encourage citizens to get out of their cars. The Mississauga Civic Centre and its precinct perhaps point the way to a future that's oddly familiar: more crowded, more mixed, more varied, more like the old city that went out of fashion 60 years ago and is now, again, full of life. The two Torontos may be starting a productive new conversation.

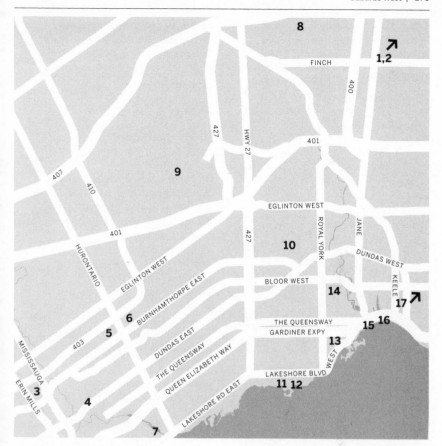

Walk 25: Suburbs West

1 Vaughan City Hall, 2141 Major Mackenzie Dr., Vaughan, Kuwabara Payne McKenna Blumberg, 2011. The initial piece in a long-term plan to build a "civic campus," this is an extraordinarily refined building. A symbolic tower provides a visual landmark, while two low wings define a courtyard. Despite these familiar gestures, the architecture has not a hint of historicist detail; it draws its strength and warmth from the fine proportions of its lowrise boxes, the control of light through atria and high-quality limestone, maple and walnut. A saucer-shaped council chamber, the one exception to the grid, draws inspiration from Toronto City Hall **[7/18]**. A 2012 Governor-General's Medal winner. *AB*

1 Vaughan City Hall

2 Vaughan Civic Centre Resource Library, 2141 Major Mackenzie Dr., Vaughan, ZAS, 2015. Next to City Hall, this takes a decidedly different tack—swoopy instead of boxy, with façades that both lean and curve. The transparent design welcomes both pedestrians and drivers stuck in traffic; hot colours articulate a welcoming, child-friendly atmosphere. *AB*

3 Carlo Fidani Peel Regional Cancer Centre, Credit Valley Hospital, 2200 Eglinton Ave. W., Mississauga, Farrow Partnership, 2005.

Thanks to a deliberate effort by hospital leadership, this wing's public spaces are as elegant and humane as hospital architecture gets. The public lobby, brightly sunlit, is lined with both actual trees and treelike, curving wood columns—complex compositions in glue-laminated Douglas fir. The rest of the wing includes an unusual amount of natural light, which is, belatedly!, being seen as a tool of healing. *AB*

3 | Carlo Fidani Centre, Credit Valley Hospital

The suburban campus of the University of Toronto Mississauga, originally known as Erindale, was designed in the wake of the acclaimed U of T Scarborough College, and Scarborough's architect John Andrews drew an initial plan; in the end, Raymond Moriyama worked with A.D. Margison & Associates on a design that had the megastructural character of Scarborough but less finesse. Later additions have been mixed in quality. Here are the highlights.

4a Student Centre, U of T Mississauga, 3359 Mississauga Rd., Mississauga, Kohn Shnier, 1999.

The product of a national design competition, this multi-purpose building bridges the space between the main academic buildings and a cluster of residences. Its large portico (punched by a round oculus) provides space to linger in warm months; the spare, Modernist public spaces do the same, despite an agglomeration of furnishings that fight with the original design. *AB*

4b Erindale Hall Student Residence, 3359 Mississauga Rd., Mississauga, Baird Sampson Neuert, 2005.

A long, skinny, slightly bent residence hall, clad in friendly brick and nubbly capstone. Yet the building also provides a covered outdoor pedestrian passageway, lined with columns that resemble Le Corbusier's pilotis, and visual links to the public spaces and complex network of stairs and corridors within. *AB*

4c Communication, Culture, and Technology Building, 3359 Mississauga Rd., Mississauga, Saucier + Perrotte, 2004.

This complexly programmed building, despite its bulk, is highly transparent. A glassy ground level, atrium, internal bridge, and ceremonial stair encourage interaction and communication, aptly so for the programs housed within. A black-and-white palette puts the emphasis on the building's spatial complexity, which carries through onto the expressive protruding boxes on the long façade. The building won a Governor General's Medal in 2008. *AB*

4c | Communication, Culture, and Technology Building

4d Terrence Donnelly Health Sciences Complex, 3359 Mississauga Rd., Mississauga, Kongats, 2011. A series of five slabs, offset to dramatic effect, and wrapped in a skin of stainless-steel panels that variously shades, shimmers, and conceals. The interior of labs and classrooms is less remarkable, but the complex is the finest architectural object on the campus. *AB*

4d | Terrence Donnelly Health Sciences Complex

5a Mississauga City Hall, 300 City Centre Dr., Mississauga, Jones & Kirkland, 1987. This design won a national competition in 1982 and remains perhaps the best Post-Modern building in Canada. Hence the abstracted references to architectural history in its design. The drum-shaped council chamber is a sort of silo; the skinny, shallowly gabled administration building echoes a barn or a suburban house; the clock tower is an obelisk, and the glass roof of the atrium a pyramid. And yet these allusions are deftly handled, and the materials are surprising: the yellow-brick exterior channels Gunnar Asplund's Nordic Classicism, the marbled

atrium a 1980s Adolf Loos. And most importantly, the adjacent Celebration Square (redesigned as such by Janet Rosenberg and Associates Landscape Architects and CS + P Architects) has the proportions and adjacencies of a good piazza. *AB*

5b The Living Arts Centre, 4141 Living Arts Dr., Mississauga, Zeidler Roberts Partnership, 1997. Zeidler picks up on the massing of City Hall here. The tall atria are clearly on view, cutting across the front of the building and through it. The network of bridges, stairs, and internal windows evoke Zeidler's Eaton Centre **[5/11]**. *AB*

5c Scholar's Green Park, 275 Prince of Wales Dr., Mississauga, gh3, landscape architects, 2012. A sophisticated square that extends the pedestrian realm northward from City Hall into the nascent Sheridan College campus. A sculptural pavilion, copses of beech with moveable tables, and a rubberized purple conversation pit provide elegant places to gather. *AB*

6 Absolute Towers, 60 Absolute Ave., Mississauga, MAD Architects with Burka Architects, 2011. The products of an international design competition, the swoopy 50- and 56-storey towers by the Chinese firm led by Yansong Ma set a new standard for formal experimentation in condo housing and gave Mississauga new icons. The design of the base and the adjacent towers, however, is both banal and clumsy. *AB*

5a | Mississauga City Hall

6 | Absolute Towers

7a Port Credit Village, Giannone Associates Architects with Young + Wright Architects, 2005. New Urbanism without the usual faux-historic grammar. This coherent ensemble of retail, live/work spaces and mid-rise condos creates strong street walls, a lovely, walkable square, and a real sense of place. *AB*

7a | Port Credit Village

7b Mississauga Public Library, Port Credit Branch, 20 Lakeshore Rd. E., Mississauga, Brook & Banz, 1962; renovation, Rounthwaite Dick & Hadley, 2011. A fine example of adaptive reuse. This mid-century glass pavilion was designed by Massey Medal winner Philip Brook; RDH's addition opened up sightlines, improved the lighting and materials, and added a bravura set of canopies that make the building even better. *AB*

7b | Mississauga Public Library, Port Credit Branch

8 BAPS Shri Swaminarayan Mandir, 61 Claireville Dr., Etobicoke, Papadopoulos & Pradhan, 2007. Perhaps the most intensely handcrafted building in the city's history. This complex includes a social hall ornamented with carved teak, and the *mandir* or Hindu place of worship itself whose architecture represents the proportions of the Divine's bodily features. Its outer façades and holy spaces are lined with 24,000 pieces of limestone, sandstone, and marble carved in traditional style by Indian artisans. *AB*

9 Terminal 1, Toronto Pearson International Airport, 6301 Silver Dart Dr., Mississauga, Airport Architects Canada (joint venture by Skidmore Owings & Merrill, Adamson Associates, and Moshe Safdie Associates), 2007. An intelligently organized response to the complex problem of the 21st-century airport terminal. The main space—a vast, arched, crescent-shaped, all-white shed—provides plenty of natural light and intuitive navigation. The strong public art program, including Sol LeWitt's rainbow-hued domed mural, offers counterpoint to the High-Tech detailing. *AB*

9 | Pearson Terminal 1

10 Toronto Public Library Eatonville Branch, 430 Burnhamthorpe Rd., Elken & Becksted, 1964; renovation, Teeple Architects, 2001. Who'd expect to find a fine object building here? The curved band of zinc evokes the "parametric" digital-design experimentation of Zaha Hadid, and provides a gesture towards—or is it a fortification against?—the East Mall and Highway 427. This zinc lands atop a domestically scaled stone wall; the tension between big and little, bold and cozy, carries through to the spiky dropped ceiling. *AB*

11 Robert A. Gordon Learning Centre, Humber College (Lakeshore Campus East), 2 Colonel Samuel Smith Park Dr., Etobicoke, Kivas Tully, 1900; renovations Taylor Hazell, 2008; Lakeshore Commons building, HOK, 2011. This adaptive reuse of the former Lakeshore Psychiatric Hospital links 11 stately High Victorian structures with a finely wrought brick-and-concrete promenade, turning a place of confinement into one of gathering. The later Lakeshore Commons is the elephant in the room. *AB*

11 | Humber College Robert A. Gordon Learning Centre

12 Rotary Park Pool, 25 Eleventh St., Etobicoke, MacLennan Jaunkalns Miller, 1997. A modest building with a masterfully controlled sequence of spaces. The change rooms and lobby form a long bar, pierced by linear skylights above and windows partially screened by wooden slats. *AB*

13 Mimico Centennial Library, 47 Station Rd., Banz, Brook, Carruthers, Grierson, Shaw, 1966. A 1967 Massey Medal winner, this is a sleeper: the staid orange-brick façades hide surprising spatial complexity. The dramatic open volume of the first and second floors is bridged by a mezzanine and staggered windows lined by brick piers. Architect Phillip Brook wrote in 1978 that "the character, scale, and atmosphere of spaces in [a] library should vary as widely as its users." That's true here. The building's mass wraps around a front garden designed by landscape architect Michael Hough, while a parking lot is stashed a level below at the rear. *AB*

14 Sunnylea School, 35 Glenroy Ave., Toronto, John B. Parkin Associates, 1943. An early example of Modernist elementary school design—inspired by the then-recent Crow Island School in Winnetka, Illinois, by Eliel Saarinen with Perkins, Wheeler & Will. The details and materials are drawn from International Style modernism, applied here to an asymmetrical building whose large-windowed classrooms are suited to child-centred learning. *AB*

15 Palace Pier Condominium, 2045 Lakeshore Blvd. W., E.I. Richmond, 1978. One of the city's first luxury condo developments. The brown glass and chamfered corners mark the complex as a product of the Late-Modernist 1970s—and a very fine one, from the staggered siting of the two towers to the proportions of the windows. The grim jumble of high-rise condos that joined it a generation later, some by Richmond's firm, should have learned some lessons here. *AB*

16 Humber River Bicycle and Pedestrian Bridge, Montgomery Sisam, 1996. A grand piece of civic design marks the mouth of one of Toronto's two great rivers with a 100-yard span. The triangular motif in the upper structure alludes to the Anishinaabe symbol of the Thunderbird. *AB*

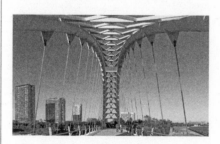

16 | Humber River Bicycle and Pedestrian Bridge

17a Colborne Lodge, 11 Colborne Lodge Dr., John Howard, 1836. John Howard was one of Toronto's first architects—best known for the Provincial Lunatic Asylum at 999 Queen St. West—and an early city engineer. For this, his own house, he chose a prime site overlooking the lake and built a bungalow with wide veranda, borrowing both from India for Toronto's unexpectedly hot climate. (His lawns and gardens are now largely forest.) Topped up and altered before his death in 1890, the house is now a museum; it displays some of Howard's own drawings and retains some of his innovations, including indoor plumbing and a "dumb stove" that helped warm the master bedroom. The house sits within his own estate, which he deeded to the city and which became half of High Park. *AB*

17a | Colborne Lodge

17b Museum of Contemporary Art Toronto Canada/formerly Tower Automotive Building, 158 Sterling Rd., J. W. Schreiber with C.A.P. Turner (engineer), 1919; architectsAlliance and ERA, 2017. A new home for the city's ambitious contemporary art museum, whose shift from Queen West reflects the dispersal of the city's visual arts community. It will occupy five floors in this building, constructed for the Northern Aluminum Company and the sole remnant of what had become an auto-parts plant. The gallery becomes the anchor of a residential-and-office project here, a rare case of development generating new space for culture. The gallery's space promises to be an unflashy repurposing of the spacious concrete-boned structure, and will engage an adjacent privately owned public space and park. *AB*

18 Eglinton Crosstown Mount Dennis Station, 3500 Eglinton Ave. W., Daoust Lestage and IBI Group, ongoing. Incorporates Canadian Kodak Company Employees' Building, Wells & Gray (engineers and contractors), 1940. Even in the early 20th century, Toronto had pockets of industry scattered far from the core.

Kodak opened a manufacturing plant here, next to the Grand Trunk Railroad line, in 1916; the complex became known as Kodak Heights and was central to the Mount Dennis community until it closed in 2004. This Commercial Style building included social facilities for staff, including a large auditorium and facilities for the employee camera club. It is the only one of 12 buildings in the complex to survive; having been moved 200 feet from its original site, it is becoming the hub of the Crosstown and UP Express station here, renovated with a minimalist design language and generously proportioned concourses. This, like the other Crosstown stations and associated public realm, comes with serious design ambitions; if built as promised this line should set a new bar for transportation projects in Toronto. *AB*

19 Jane Exbury Towers, 2415 Jane St., Uno Prii, 1969. The Estonian-born Prii gave a sculptural spin to these five apartment slab towers; the projecting shear walls, curved and top-pointed, give them a singular presence. They are similar to his Prince Arthur Towers **[17/25]** in this way, but otherwise entirely generic. There are over 1,000 such slab towers in Toronto, generally built with the same flying-form concrete construction, faced with brick and aluminum windows and lined with balconies. They are the products of thoughtful, top-down planning and now house over a million Torontonians. And yet many, like the Jane Exbury Towers, are aging and isolated from the economic and social fabric of the city. Knitting them back in, currently the object of Toronto's Tower Renewal Program, will be a major challenge for city leaders over the next quarter-century. *AB*

19 | Jane Exbury Towers

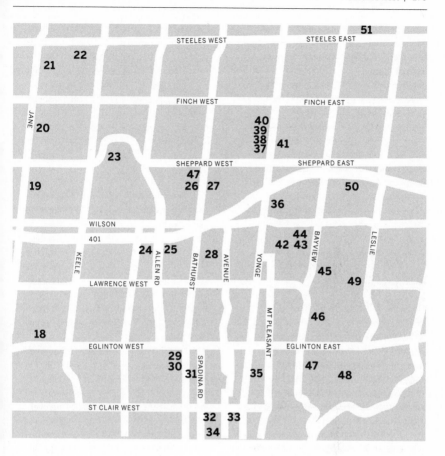

20 Oakdale Community Centre, 350 Grandravine Dr., Patkau Architects with Ralph Giannone, 1999.

A palpably public landmark in this dense tower neighbourhood: the dramatic canopy, its poetic steel structure tricked out in hot-yellow paint, both provides generous shelter and reaches for the sky. Windows reveal the pool beyond, surrounded by sinuous concrete benches. *AB*

21 Edgeley in the Village (apartments), 4645 Jane St., Irving Grossman, 1968.

Grossman designed these towers of market apartments as well the adjacent lowrise public housing. The muscular, protuberant concrete channels the sculptural Brutalism of Paul Rudolph, whose Yale Art and Architecture building of the 1960s was hotly controversial—and has now been lovingly restored. *AB*

22a York University (master plan), 4700 Keele St., UPACE, 1965–66.

A parable of 1960s planning. Toronto's new suburban university was a product of that era's optimism and the industry of local architects. "UPACE" was a consortium of Gordon S. Adamson and Associates, John B. Parkin Associates, and Shore & Moffat—who designed the campus along with the Harvard professor and landscape architect Hideo Sasaki and his local collaboraor Richard Strong.

These busy modernists delivered an agglomeration of buildings, predominantly Brutalist, organized in "clusters" by discipline and linked by walkable plazas and quadrangles. Cars—most people would drive here—would be kept to the periphery. The goal, the architects wrote, was to capture "the concentrated activity and intense development of the city." Yet there wasn't enough activity or intensity: too few residents, too little retail, and the buildings were not really very close together. Later additions have introduced a mix of styles and materials, as well as mixed-traffic streets, to the centre of campus, trading austere beauty for a more lively mess. *AB*

22b York University subway station, 4700 Keele St., Foster + Partners with Adamson Associates, ongoing.

Still very much cooking, this promises to be one of the strongest pieces of architecture on the campus. Two entrances will flank a broad, dug-out amphitheatre and be linked by a single sail-like roof. The day-lit concourse will include an installation of screens by British artist Jason Bruges. *AB*

22c Ross Building, 4700 Keele St., UPACE, 1962.

A megastructure, like Scarborough College [26/21a], that contains classrooms, office space and amenities. Originally a massive ramp led from York Boulevard up through the centre of the Ross slab onto its elevated terrace; this was the literal and symbolic centre of the campus, meant as a place for graduations as well as everyday use. That was destroyed in favour of Vari Hall [25/22f], which creates something like a traditional streetwall, thanks to a new 1980s master plan. This leaves the terrace as a dead zone, and the adjacent Central Square, with its elegant enclosed courtyard, somewhat forlorn. All the street life you'd expect to see is in fact indoors. *AB*

22c | Ross Building

22d | Scott Library

22d Scott Library, UPACE, 1971; Learning Commons alterations, Levitt Goodman, 2012.

An inverted ziggurat that recalls the very influential Boston City Hall. [See 12/5.] The atrium, with its planter boxes and theatre-like protruding balconies, is a tour de force. Levitt Goodman's later alterations provide social space for a post-2000 generation of students and warm up the tough interior with colour, textiles and booths for studying. *AB*

22e Schulich School of Business, 111 Ian Macdonald Blvd., Hariri Pontarini with Robbie/Young & Wright, 2003.

If York's first wave of buildings were aspiring radicals in the sixties, this is their grandson with an MBA and elite-flyer status. Schulich combines an undergraduate business school and a mid-career executive program, including a hotel; both wear the same dress code of limestone, milky glass and copper (tailored into flattering curves), and meet around courtyards. The spaces within are uniformly well-planned and refined. This approach would be a bit too sleek for an entire campus, but it is exceptionally handsome here. Winner of a 2006 Governor General's Medal in Architecture. *AB*

22e | Schulich School of Business

22f Vari Hall, 100 York Blvd., Moriyama & Teshima, 1992; rotunda renovation, Gow Hastings, 2011. This building effectively destroyed the original York campus plan, but it is a solid expression of Postmodernism's turn to history. The dome, which reaches a height of 18 metres, sits on an axis with the entrance to the campus, in keeping with Classical precedent. The bands of stone and brick bring to mind the work of the influential British architect James Stirling. Inside, the space is grand and unadorned, with exposed concrete columns contrasting the maple panelling. It works very well as an informal gathering place, especially after a renovation that added handsome benches and lots of electrical outlets. *AB*

22g Computer Science and Engineering, 120 Campus Walk, Van Nostrand Di Castri with Busby & Associates, 2001. One of Toronto's first consciously green buildings, this facility employs some now-standard features such as green roofs and recycled concrete and aluminum, but also natural ventilation—carefully designed atria and operable windows allow hot air to move by itself. This is, sadly, still not standard practice. *AB*

22h Honour Court and Welcome Centre, 55 York Blvd., Teeple Architects, 2000. A wedge of architectural creativity at the gateway to the university, in concrete, Tyndall limestone, Cor-Ten steel, cedar and mahogany. Its form draws on the digitally derived shapes that architects such as Zaha Hadid and Greg Lynn began developing in the 1990s. Aside from the small enclosed welcome centre this is essentially a walled garden: an example of what is rare in Toronto, a built form with minimal utility and maximal poetry. *AB*

23 Downsview Park/formerly CFB Downsview/originally De Havilland Aircraft of Canada, 35 Carl Hall Road, 1929-ongoing. De Havilland Canada began making and maintaining planes here in 1929, and Mathers & Haldenby designed an assembly plant—at 65 Carl Hall Road—which grew repeatedly through World War II. The RCAF and Canadian Forces arrived here in 1946, and the 640-acre site continued to play overlapping roles for de Havilland and the military until the mid-1990s. The military built a 27-acre supply depot (at 40 Carl Hall Rd.) in 1954, designed to survive a nuclear blast; it endures, along with a fascinating mixed bag of remnant military and de Havilland buildings that date from 1929 to 1971. The post-military history, when the site has been split into land for development and Parc Downsview Parc, is murky: the Dutch architects OMA and Bruce Mau Design won an international design competition for the park in 2000, but their "Tree City" scheme has been largely abandoned. *AB*

24 Yorkdale Shopping Centre, 3401 Dufferin St., John Graham with John B. Parkin Associates, 1964. A decisive signal from competing retailers Eaton's and Simpson's, here in cooperation, that Toronto was embracing car-oriented suburbs. The enclosed mall, the city's first, was overseen by shopping-mall pioneer John Graham; the most dramatic piece of architecture, then and now, was the Simpson's store (now ·Hudson's Bay Yorkdale), designed by John Andrews while he was at the Parkin office. Its language captures the quasi-classical "New Formalism" current in Modernism; New York's Lincoln Center complex, designed under the direction of Philip Johnson, was influential. Andrews's glass tile and flashy, curvaceous interior court are largely buried under the mall's ever-growing mountain of luxury generica. *AB*

25 Yorkdale subway station, Arthur Erickson, 1974. Erickson's above-ground station is a tube in concrete and steel echoing the shape of a train, and is clearly legible to drivers of fast-moving cars on the Allen. Artist Michael Hayden's neon *Arc en Ciel*, an integral part of the original design, will soon return after a long absence. *AB*

25 | Yorkdale Subway Station

26 Beth David B'Nai Israel Beth Am Synagogue, 55 Yeomans Rd., Irving Grossman, 1959. One of several synagogues the young Irving Grossman designed as the city's Jewish community moved north from downtown in the 1950s and 1960s. This one features panels of precast concrete made with the artist Graham Coughtry, in which the bas-relief ornament interlocks with the building's irregular windows. The slab building is fronted by a drum-shaped entry pavilion which, like the ornament with its echoes of the Brazilian Roberto Burle Marx, introduces some curves to the stolid modern box. *AB*

As Metropolitan Toronto grew, North York under long-time mayor Mel Lastman had visions of establishing its own "downtown" to rival Toronto's. Today it is the closest thing in the city proper to a second centre.

27 Betel Residence, 33 York Downs Drive, Irving Grossman, 1957. This early work by Grossman is, for now, remarkably well preserved. Its white brick and bold, sculptural composition—a glass-ended box sitting crosswise on a horizontal white-brick box—echoes the Bauhaus ideas of the "Harvard Five" in suburban New Canaan, Connecticut. Its ravine-side site could make it a teardown, like most of its contemporaries on the Bridle Path, but let's hope not. *AB*

27 | Betel Residence

28 Ledbury Park Skating Pavilion and Pool, 146 Ledbury St., Shim-Sutcliffe and G + G Partnership with NAK (landscape architects), 1997. Patronage from the City of North York allowed the young architects Shim-Sutcliffe to alter the site's topography and channel their ideas about space and materiality into a complex public park: a swimming pool and change room, a water play area, and a canal for skating. The 1999 Governor General's Award winner looks a bit scruffy today: plywood soffits and cedar slats are rotting, and the fountain is out of service. But the spatial logic remains strong, as do the custom steel light standards (channelling Carlo Scarpa). A gem worth polishing. *AB*

29 Holy Blossom Temple, 1950 Bathurst St., Chapman & Oxley with Maurice D. Klein, 1938; school wing, John B. Parkin Associates, 1960. Alteration and addition, Diamond Schmitt, ongoing. One of Toronto's first major buildings to use exposed concrete, this grand synagogue achieved a rare proto-modernism combining Romanesque arches with a near-total lack of ornament. (It is a stripped-down variation on their east wing for the ROM **[8/43]**.) The later school wing continued that tradition with its board-formed concrete exterior walls; the current project will add a large, skylit atrium and clean up the connection between the two wings. After much discussion, the renovation will leave one important aspect intact: the sanctuary faces west, rather than east toward Jerusalem as is traditional. *AB*

30 Beth Tzedec Congregation, 1700 Bathurst St., Harry B. Kohl with Page & Steele, 1955. Altered later. Alteration and addition, Hariri Pontarini, ongoing. Among Toronto's great Modernist buildings and its great religious buildings, this complex was overseen by Peter Dickinson in collaboration with engineer Morden Yolles. Clad in yellow brick and limestone, it includes a grand sanctuary with striking bas-relief murals by the artist Ernest Raab (and diagonal walls filtering light toward the central ark, an idea borrowed from Basil Spence's 1962 Coventry Cathedral); an interesting octagonal chapel; and a series of other surprises, including the bravura curving stair in the main lobby. The back end, which houses a school and the daily entrance, is being substantially rebuilt and will add a new material, Siamak Hariri's favoured limestone **[8/46]**, to the mix. *AB*

31 | Lawren Harris House

31 Lawren Harris House, 2 Ava Cres., Alexandra Biriukova, 1931; renovation, Drew Mandel, 2011. A founding member of the Group of Seven and an heir to the Massey-Harris fortune, Harris commissioned one of Toronto's most remarkable houses from an equally remarkable figure: Biriukova, Russian-born and Italian-trained, the first woman to register in Ontario as an architect. This would be her only work in the city, and it bridges Art Deco ornament with stripped Moderne massing and silky stucco. *AB*

32 Richard G.W. Mauran House, 95 Ardwold Gate, Taivo Kapsi, 1968. Bloomberg residence, 70 Ardwold Gate, Hariri Pontarini, 2014. One of the few genuinely Brutalist houses in Canada, the bold essay at no. 95 by Estonian-Canadian architect Kapsi suggests an architectural road not taken. Kapsi died young, but the house remains one of the most serious pieces of architecture on the street, which was subdivided in the 1930s from the short-lived estate of Sir John Craig Eaton and Lady Eaton. Its most noble neighbour is the over-scaled but well-honed home of Lawrence Bloomberg. *AB*

33 Imperial Oil Building, 111 St. Clair Ave., Mathers & Haldenby, 1957; renovation, OneSpace and ERA, 2015. In the mid 1950s, the city commissioned a design for a new city hall from well-connected local firm Mathers & Haldenby; that slab was so uninspired that it helped build support for an international design competition, and the rest is history [7/18]. The M&H design was plenty good enough for Imperial Oil, who adopted it for their headquarters here. The building has found a welcome new life as luxury residential. The penthouses are now dressed in ungainly cladding; but the shaft of the building looks spiffy, and retail spaces have retained much of the lobby's character, including York Wilson's mural *The Story of Oil*. AB

34a Benvenuto Place, 1 Benvenuto Pl., Page & Steele, 1955. 561 Avenue Rd., Page & Steele, 1959. At Benvenuto Place, Peter Dickinson worked with engineer Morden Yolles on what Yolles called "one of the first, if not the first truly modern building constructed in Toronto." The innovation was in its structural system of flat concrete floor plates, soon ubiquitous; the layouts of the luxury apartments, and Dickinson's chic interweaving of buff brick and plate glass, have helped the building maintain its status for 60 years. The same team would use similar principles up the street a few years later, setting a high-style standard for slab apartment towers that would soon spring up across the city. AB

34a | Benvenuto Place

34b The Claridge (apartments), 1 Clarendon Ave., Baldwin & Greene, 1927-28. The Balmoral (apartments), 150 Balmoral Ave., S.B. Coon & Son, 1928–29. The Clarendon (apartments), 2 Clarendon Ave., Charles B. Dolphin, 1927. Mayfair Mansions (apartments), 394–398 Avenue Rd., H.C. Roberts, 1931. This hilltop on Avenue Road holds a cluster of grand apartment buildings from the Roaring Twenties—and one just after the crash. The Claridge speaks a Venetian dialect, through the hand of architect Lawrence Baldwin. Baldwin, who would go on to become director of the Art Gallery of Toronto (later AGO), invited Group of Seven member J.E.H. MacDonald to decorate the lobby ceiling with zodiac- themed murals; these survive in fine condition. MacDonald's nearly contemporaneous decoration of the Concourse Building [see 6/24] downtown has also been restored. The Balmoral, the showiest of the group, has a standard H-shaped plan and lovely Tudor fancy-dress. Interesting to think that Trinity College [8/39] was being rebuilt almost at the same time. And when Mayfair Mansions was completed a few years later, the apartment-building specialist H.C. Roberts took a stripped-down Deco approach. Where the Balmoral is all horizontal stone stolidity, these buildings and their bold pilasters emphasize the vertical. Onward and upward. AB

35 Girl Guides of Canada Headquarters, 50 Merton St., Toronto, Carmen Corneil with William McBain, 1968; addition, Carmen Corneil, 1970. Carmen Corneil was a major figure in Toronto architecture and architectural education for the last half of the 20th century; he was also a devotee of the Finn Alvar Aalto, in whose office Corneil worked from 1958 to 1960. Here he pays homage to Aalto with the textured brick and floating rectangular masses of the skylit front wing; the concrete-and-glass rear wing is in another register entirely. AB

36 St. John's York Mills Anglican Church, 19 Don Ridge Dr., John G. Howard, 1844; alterations and additions, Molesworth Secord & Savage, 1949; alterations and additions, Page & Steele, 1968; alterations and additions, Parker Architects, 2014. Lodge, B. Napier Simpson, 1958. Perhaps the oldest standing church building in the city and the second oldest such institution, after St. James' **[1/13]**, this is still very much in use. Howard designed this white-brick Gothic building for a rural congregation with a low-church character; the building's relative modesty and low ceiling reflect the lack of pomp and ceremony in its early days. It has been altered repeatedly, and the interior has a woodsier character than it did in Victorian times. (Some of the beams in the narthex were recovered from the 1816 log church.) Still, Howard's work survives, along with one of the prettiest churchyards in Toronto—now an unlikely remnant between subdivision houses. *AB*

37 Joseph Shepard Building, 4900 Yonge St., DuBois & Associates with Shore Tilbe Henschel Irwin Peters, 1977. A grand public building that opens sociably to the streets on each side, and is cut by a tall and complex set of atria that provides many routes for vertical and horizontal circulation. Yet the massive structure also has a moody quality, with its pyramidal massing and mix of ruddy clay brick and exposed concrete structure— all of which is balanced by the subtlety of its details, integrated artworks, and beautifully modulated light. *AB*

37 | Joseph Shepard Building

38 Toronto District School Board/North York Board of Education, 5050 Yonge St., Mathers & Haldenby, 1970. An open-plan office building whose prefab steel walls are dressed in ruddy aluminum cladding. Built for the old North York school board, and now the citywide headquarters, this has none of the refinement of its predecessor **[8/11]** but does enclose Mel Lastman Square. *AB*

39 North York Civic Centre, 5100 Yonge St., Gordon Adamson & Associates, 1976. An ambitious coming-out for the nascent city of North York, this centre is designed around a 300-foot-long interior street, capped by a diagonal ceiling of steel trusses, glass, and bronzed aluminum sheathing. Balconied offices and a strong suspended public art exhibit emphasize the building's soaring vertical dimension, while it connects to the earlier Board of Education building and the later library through bridges and indoor passageways. *AB*

40 | North York City Centre and North York Public Library

40 North York City Centre and North York Public Library, 5120 Yonge St., Moriyama & Teshima, 1987; interior renovation, Diamond Schmitt, in progress. The heart of North York's 1980s downtown development—and a period piece, for better and worse. A bland glass-and-granite office tower, designed for developer clients, is studded with some Deconstructivist details (including the half-a-clock tower). Inside, the library is built around a tall atrium, much like the Scarborough Civic Centre **[26/17]** and Toronto Reference Library **[5/47]**. *AB*

41 | Claude Watson School for the Arts

41 Claude Watson School for the Arts, 130 Doris Ave., Kohn Shnier, 2007.
A subtle and complex building, and an apt home for an arts-focused institution. The outside bleachers-slash-staircase link the school building with the adjacent park; the brise-soleil with a hexagonal pattern signals that this is a hive of creativity. *AB*

42 Viva House/Originally Berman House, 54 Plymbridge Rd., Irving Grossman, 1956; altered, AGATHOM, 2005.
Hoggs Hollow is full of custom houses spanning more than half a century; many from the 1950s and 1960s have been knocked down for fake chateaux. This elegant white-brick box, designed by Irving Grossman for the developer Joseph Berman around the time of the Betel Residence **[25/27]**, shows the influence of R.M. Schindler, for whom Grossman worked. It survives in the hands of illustrator and graphic designer Frank Viva, who commissioned a sensitive reno by AGATHOM. *AB*

43 Sharp House, 36 Green Valley Rd., Peter Dickinson, 1960.
When Isadore Sharp was founding the Four Seasons hotel chain, his architect of choice was Peter Dickinson: the young Brit designed the first Four Seasons (now demolished) behind a fieldstone wall on Jarvis Street, in 1961. Dickinson also designed this house for Sharp and his wife Rosalie at the edge of Rosedale Golf Club; it had its own fieldstone front wall, this one curved. Was that a nod to the local vernacular, or Marcel Breuer houses in Connecticut? Either way it was just one of many modes adopted by Dickinson in his short career. This house is divided into two wings, one at the front for public rooms, a larger one at the back for bedrooms; despite its considerable size it is likely to be treated as a teardown by its next owner, which should not be allowed to happen. *AB*

44 Weathering Steel House, 87 Highland Cres., Shim-Sutcliffe, 2001; interior alterations, Atelier Kastelic Buffey, 2016.
Surrounded by McMansions on a ravineside street is this seminal house by Shim-Sutcliffe, wrapped in "weathering steel"; often known by the trade name Cor-Ten, this material acquires a deep red colour over time **[see 25/28]**. With its sunken courtyard, integrated water feature and Douglas fir cladding, the house is an influential piece of Toronto architecture. Publication of this house brought David Bowie and Iman for a visit, sparking a long friendship between the famous couple and the architects and plans for a house, never built, in New York State. *AB*

45 Originally the Frank Wood House. Crescent School, 2365 Bayview Ave., Delano & Aldrich, 1931. Later additions and alterations; addition for Centre for Creative Learning, CS&P, 2004; addition for Lau Family Middle School Wing, CS & P, 2011.
Banker and art collector Frank P. Wood commissioned this interesting house from the distinguished New York architects Delano & Aldrich—a grand symmetrical building, in the Adamesque style or what was in America called the Federal Style, but faced with smooth-cut limestone. The building passed in 1970 to Crescent School, which has made the house the centre of a gracious campus. *AB*

46 Holland Bloorview Kids' Rehabilitation Hospital, 150 Kilgour Rd., Montgomery Sisam with Stantec, 2007.
Toronto's most

46 | Holland Bloorview Kids' Rehabilitation Hospital

beautiful medical facility. Serving a complex knot of functions including a hospital, rehab centre, and school, it is elegantly resolved and fully accessible architecture. Transparent public spaces; terraces and gardens that engage with the ravine-side site; and a warm material palette of cherry wood, zinc, and brick allow the building to escape the expected institutional coldness. *AB*

47 | Garden Court Apartments

47 Garden Court Apartments, 1477 Bayview Ave., Forsey Page & Steele with landscape architects Dunington-Grubb and Stensson, 1941. Leaside was laid out Garden City–style by the Olmsted student Frederick G. Todd in 1913, but not developed until the late 1930s and early 1940s. This Deco complex is the best architecture of that era, gently integrated with the landscape by prominent local firm Dunington-Grubb and Stensson, who would design University Avenue's central boulevards **[7/16]**. The complex provides several types of town-house and apartment units, in buildings featuring corner windows and dapper ornamental brickwork. These apartments, still rental for now, are in high demand. *AB*

48 Longo's/originally Canadian Northern Railway shops, 93 Laird Dr., c. 1919; renovation Scoler Lee & Associates, 2012. The Canadian Northern Railway that planned Leaside **[see Introduction, Area XIII]** built this locomotive shop just before it failed and became part of CN Rail. The Leaside facility closed in the 1930s and this building became a packaging plant for much of the 20th century; the current renovation shows off much of its remaining character, though it's buried in the parking lot of a big-box mall. *AB*

49 Toronto Botanical Gardens, 777 Lawrence Ave. E., Raymond Moriyama, 1964; Jerome Markson, 1976; Montgomery Sisam with landscape architects PMA and Thomas Sparling, 2005. First opened to the public in 1956, this city-run centre has some of the most remarkable planted landscapes in the city; its buildings are also of high quality, from Moriyama's temple-like monolith to Montgomery Sisam's green-roofed glass jewel. *AB*

50 Temple Emanu-el, 120 Old Colony Rd., Irving Grossman, 1963. Another synagogue by Irving Grossman **[25/26]**, this grand but inward building is unusual for its village-like form. A row of low, tent-like forms defines the front façade; behind this a tall, nearly cubical volume holds the sanctuary, and it is flanked by two low wings, one of them pierced by an enclosed courtyard. These spaces, largely intact, read as attractive period pieces today. The sanctuary, though, is timeless: its interior is almost without ornament, and a stained-glass window and narrow clerestories invite sunlight to play across its tall brick walls. A remarkably austere and yet warm place of worship. *AB*

51 Wong Dai Sin Temple, 378 Steeles Ave. E., Markham, Shim-Sutcliffe, 2015. A singular alien and exquisite object in a banal suburban context. The building's mass rests on a cantilevered concrete slab, allowing room for required parking below. The forced perspective of the Cor-Ten panels wraps a warm, wood-clad sanctuary one level above ground. *AB*

52 Richmond Hill Central Library, 1 Atkinson St., Richmond Hill, A.J. Diamond, Donald Schmitt, and Company, 1993. A bit mean when seen from the road, but inside this is a public building that offers both comfort and a ceremonial quality. Light is skilfully channelled and modulated by shading devices and skylights that bounce light off of protruding cones and down into the building. This won a 1994 Governor General's Award of Excellence. *AB*

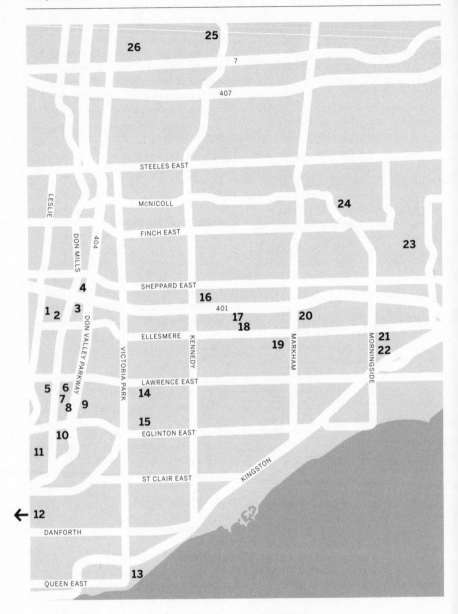

Walk 26: Suburbs East

1a OPSEU Headquarters, 100 Lesmill Rd., North York, Carmen Corneil, 1991. Most industrial buildings in this area have been one-story slabs; this office for Ontario Public Service Employees Union harks back to 19th-century factory lofts, in two long, skinny, tall bars linked by an atrium. The proletarian details and materials—with galvanized metal siding and exposed concrete block—mark this as a late iteration of High Tech [5/11]. But the interior is spatially complex, with mazy stairs that ascend through the atrium and transparency everywhere to bring people together. A 1992 Governor-General's Award winner. *AB*

1b Originally Ceterg offices, 2 Duncan Mill Rd., North York, Fairfield and DuBois, 1967; later addition. Moody and fortress-like, bermed into a hill and punctuated by a Corbusian tower: This was originally the home of an engineering company, whose drafting staff enjoyed north light through narrow clerestories. Architect Macy DuBois designed custom, notched concrete blocks for this project, adding texture and interest to a dull material. Winner of a 1967 Massey Medal. *AB*

2 OAA Headquarters, 111 Moatfield Dr., North York, Ruth Cawker, 1992. How do architects build for themselves? In this, the winner of a 1989 design competition, very subtly. The building houses meeting space and offices; you reach them from the hidden parking beneath the building, up an outward-facing stair and then into a office block pierced by a double-height open space and capped by a pergola. White-painted exposed steel echoes the early International Style and 1980s Richard Meier, but neither material nor colour dominates here: it's about space. Cawker herself cited "planes and lines of materials that do not meet, but pass . . . providing a sense of relative light-weightedness." The association is now working on a retrofit to make the facility carbon-neutral by 2030. This important effort is undercut by the location in a car-oriented suburb. *AB*

3 Graydon Manor, 185 Graydon Hall Dr., North York, Allan George and Walter Moorehouse with Dunington-Grubb & Stensson (landscape architects), 1936. "Every important window in this handsome Georgian house opens to literally miles of view," began a 1938 story in Canadian Homes & Gardens. The estate, funded by owner Rupert Bain's success promoting gold stocks, sat on 150 acres, and included a private golf course and formal gardens by the pioneering landscape architects Dunington-Grubb. The site of its 400-foot-long formal lawn is still legible in the allée of trees running south from the house into the park. The building itself retains some of its original, stuffy charm in its current role as an event space. The views are gone, however;

Bain sold the land in 1951, and in the 1960s it was surrounded by highrise apartments and condos, as well as the 401 and the Don Valley Parkway. *AB*

4 Emerald City (residential towers and townhouses), Forest Manor Road, Parkway Forest Drive and George Henry Boulevard, WZMH, ongoing. Parkway Forest Community Centre, 55 Forest Manor Rd., North York, Diamond Schmitt, 2016. Some apartment-tower neighbourhoods now seem ripe for development: the private green space that surrounds these towers is underused, and today's urban design favours buildings that address the street. The solution in this 14-hectare precinct: add townhouses, highrise and midrise buildings to fill in the gaps. The four townhouse blocks off Forest Manor Road are well-detailed; otherwise, developer modernism of the 1970s meets its contemporary equivalent with no clear winner. The combination of street-facing and set-back buildings creates some awkward corners, but the pedestrian paths and the scattering of colourful Douglas Coupland sculptures make it clearly more walkable. The new community centre, developer-funded, adds recreational facilities and also a dose of craftsmanship and colour, its fashionable grey-purple brick punctuated with dashes of blue and green mosaic tile. *AB*

5a Don Mills master plan, planner Macklin Hancock, architect Douglas Lee, 1953. The young, Harvard-educated Hancock designed this community (with architect Lee) for the brewer and developer E.P. Taylor. It drew on Ebenezer Howard's Garden City model and the best Modernist thinking of the day—plus Taylor's willingness to pay for infrastructure, which brought the city onside and opened the dam for a river of development profits. The site was divided into four walkable neighbourhood quadrants surrounded by a ring road, the Donway; commercial and industrial uses were separated from the homes (in many configurations) that lay on wide lots on curvy streets; and the developer enforced Modernism as the house style, creating a unique continuity of vision that was executed by ambitious young architects, including Henry Fliess, James A. Murray, and Irving Grossman. The city's leading Modernist firm, John B. Parkin Associates, set up their own office here and designed public and private buildings **[26/5b, 26/6, 26/7]**. The Modernist character of the area has been much degraded but remains alive in the culs-de-sac and office parks. The scale and business model of Don Mills shaped many future suburban developments in the region but, sadly, without the attendant design standards. *AB*

5b Bank of Montreal, 877 Lawrence Ave. E., John B. Parkin Associates, 1957; altered later. Scotiabank, 885 Lawrence Ave. E., John B. Parkin Associates, 1957, altered later; altered, Our Cool Blue Architects with Barbara Szewczyk, 2016. Once upon a time, these two matched: Miesian glass-and-steel pavilions for rival banks. To Scotia's credit, its branch retains some of that spirit, with a grid of columns that extend beyond the building edge and an interior renovation that borrows the lightness and openness of the original. The BMO branch has suffered a grimmer fate, receiving a cheap cladding of stucco. Which will look better in another 50 years? *AB*

5c Shops at Don Mills, 939 Lawrence Ave. E., North York, Rudy Adlaf in collaboration with Giannone Petricone Associates and Pellow & Associates, 2009. This "lifestyle centre," Toronto's first of the genre, replaced the seminal Don Mills Convenience Centre, a Modernist outdoor mall by John B. Parkin Associates and Macklin Hancock, that in 1955 was among the first and best of its kind. The current design speaks a muted Modernist language worthy of Don Mills, and tries to conceal car traffic and parking on its fringes; sadly, this effort is half-hearted. The centre has a functioning, walkable "town square" and a clock tower by Douglas Coupland that riffs on 1950s suburban houses; yet the place feels dominated by cars and car infrastructure. *AB*

6 Don Mills Collegiate and Don Mills Middle School, 15 The Donway E., North York, John B. Parkin Associates, 1959. Addition, Teeple Architects, 1997. The Parkin office's rational modernism applied to a high school and middle school complex, sharing a library, auditorium and snazzy squared canopy. This should be read as an ensemble with two other Parkin projects, Ortho Pharmaceutical **[26/7]** and the now-demolished Don Mills Convenience Centre. Here the expressed concrete structure was filled in with white glazed brick, brown brick and glass; insensitive new windows reduce the effect. The interior is unfussy and well made: two varieties of terrazzo add some flavour to the right-angled rectitude. *AB*

7 Janssen Inc./Originally Ortho Pharmaceutical offices and plant, 19 Green Belt Dr., North York, John B. Parkin Associates, 1955. Additions, 1966 and 1969. Front addition, the Austin Company, Architects and Engineers, c. 1992. A 1958 Massey Medal winner by the designer John C. Parkin, this was the archetype of corporate Don Mills—and of Canada's suburban corporate headquarters, self-contained buildings set on broad green lawns. It originally consisted of the office wing at the northwest, with its exposed concrete frame, and the plant, with white brick between its concrete structure, at the southeast. Later additions enlarged the building considerably in a respectful manner. You can still read the original pavilion-like offices as an orthodox expression of the International Style, what would become the architectural lingua franca of big business. Later John C. Parkin would compare himself

7 | Janssen/Ortho Pharmaceutical

to I.M. Pei, arguing that their highly ordered, rational modernism "is mainstream 20th-century architecture . . . It's the mainstream and will continue to be so for the balance of the century." He was largely correct. *AB*

8a | Aga Khan Museum

8a Aga Khan Museum, 77 Wynford Dr., North York, Moriyama & Teshima with Maki & Associates, 2014. An unexpected gift to Toronto from the Ismaili community, this museum is part of a 16.8-acre site master-planned by the Japanese Modernist Fumihiko Maki. The museum building, wrapped in white Brazilian granite, encloses a glass courtyard whose walls carry ornament based on Middle Eastern *mashrabiya*. Solid, rational gallery spaces and a fine domed auditorium add public amenities, making up for the building's slightly fortress-like stance to the city around it. *AB*

8b Ismaili Centre, 49 Wynford Dr., North York, Moriyama & Teshima with Charles Correa Associates; interior design, Arriz & Co. and Gotham Nottinghill UK, 2014. The second component in the Aga Khan campus lies across a set of formal gardens by Lebanese landscape architect Vladimir

8b | Ismaili Centre

Djurovic. Less public than the museum, it holds some fine moments orchestrated by the prominent Indian Modernist Correa: the central glass-roofed prayer hall, or *jamat khana*, is one of the great sacred rooms in Canada and a credit to all its architects. *AB*

8c 39 Wynford Dr., North York, Peter Dickinson Associates and Webb & Menkes, 1963; altered later. 90 Wynford Dr., Bregman & Hamann, 1968. 100 Wynford Dr., Webb Zerafa Menkes, 1969. This trio of office buildings is among the dwindling stock of high-design corporate redoubts that once lined Wynford Drive. (The Aga Khan Museum replaced the best of the bunch, John B. Parkin Associates' derivative but lovely headquarters for Bata Shoes.) Dickinson's building, for AC Nielsen, has been doubled in height but retains its elegant proportions of slab, window, and louvres. No. 100, designed for Bell Canada by Dickinson's former colleagues at Webb Zerafa Menkes, makes an unusual blend of Brutalist concrete and ribbon windows. No. 90, for Texaco Canada, is a similarly deft slab of concrete, brick, and glass. Each deserves renewal. *AB*

9 Noor Cultural Centre, 123 Wynford Dr., North York/originally Japanese Canadian Cultural Centre, Raymond Moriyama, 1963; renovation, Moriyama & Teshima, 2011. A seminal project for the young Moriyama, this signalled the Japanese-Canadian community's deliberate effort to "become re-established in the main stream of Canadian life," as Moriyama wrote in 1964. His design delivered a Japanese character through its use of redwood and careful relationship to site,

9 | Noor Cultural Centre

while the façades of precast concrete and ashlar speak a personal, Modernist language. The renovation by Moriyama's firm introduced new wood screens, derived from Islamic architecture, which harmonize beautifully with the original building. *AB*

10 Housing, St. Dennis Dr.; Deauville Lane to Don Mills Rd., Rochefort to St. Dennis. Irving Grossman, architect; Project Planning Associates, master plan, 1961–62.

One of the biggest modernist housing schemes in Toronto, overseen by the young Grossman for the American developer William Zeckendorf, this combines a variety of house and apartment types along a network of slightly elevated walkways and greens. It is a modernist update of the Garden City ideal, also seen at Alexandra Park [15/16]. Grossman wrote proudly in 1961 of "people strolling along the landscaped pedestrian malls while cars move unseen in the garages below." This model is anathema in today's urban design, with good reason: these "malls" belong to nobody in particular, and here have become somewhat run-down and hospitable to street crime. The privately owned houses at 61 Grenoble Drive, arranged in a spiral pattern, are the worst offenders and yet you can see the almost medieval character the architect intended for these spaces, an intimate connection between domestic space, plaza and greenery.

Unit types are varied, which has allowed the place to evolve. The midrise building at 1 Deauville Lane contains two-level apartments on its ground and second floors; "maisonette-apartments" at 1 Vendome Place split the difference between house and apartment; units throughout the blocks vary from one-bedrooms to houses. And even the rounded brick apartment tower at 35 St. Dennis, now poorly maintained, has proved adaptable. Like much of the area it is a landing point for immigrants from around the world, who occupy the building at much higher densities than were intended. Architects make plans; then other people make theirs. *AB*

11a Fraser Mustard Early Learning Academy, 82 Thorncliffe Park Dr., Kohn Shnier, 2013.

With the existing Thorncliffe Park Public School overcrowded, Kohn Shnier deftly transformed this fragment of its site into a new school for nearly 700 kindergartners. A sunken garden provides secure play areas; a central atrium, both security and freedom of movement for the students; and a work by artist Micah Lexier offers a message of welcome on the north-side brick. The building is capped by car parking, the result of regressive city planning requirements. *AB*

11b Ontario Science Centre, 770 Don Mills Rd., North York, Raymond Moriyama, 1969; renovations, Zeidler Roberts Partnership, 1996; renovations, Diamond Schmitt, 2006.

Another milestone for the young Moriyama, the centre steps down from tableland deep into the Don Valley. Its Brutalist language and closed exhibit halls are skilfully punctuated by views and experiences of the valley. Unsympathetic additions may one day be removed, when this is properly recognized as a classic of 20th-century Canadian architecture. *AB*

11b | Ontario Science Centre

11c | Residence for the Sisters of St. Joseph and Taylor House

11c Residence for the Sisters of St. Joseph, 101 Thorncliffe Park Dr., Shim-Sutcliffe, 2013. Taylor House, David B. Dick, 1885; restoration, ERA Architects, 2013. The residence is a highly expressive building designed to provide long-term and hospital care for an aging order of nuns. The façade of green aluminum and weathering steel fronts a sinuous plan borrowed from Alvar Aalto, and the central chapel—oak-clad, with transcendent views of the Don Valley—is one of Toronto's great sacred spaces. The adjacent Queen Anne house was built for John F. Taylor, founder of the Don Valley Brick Works, and in its current freshened state it shows off the material and craftsmanship of 1880s Toronto. *AB*

12a Centennial College Story Arts Centre/ Formerly Toronto Teachers' College, 951 Carlaw Ave., Page & Steele, 1954; renovation Kongats Architects, 1994. Amid the modest postwar houses of East York sits this jaunty educational building. Organized around a quadrangle and filled with light, the building has adapted well to its current arts-education use. The crisp and occasionally expressionist original design (check out the central ramp) clearly shows the hand of Peter Dickinson. The addition and renovation respect the proportions of the original curtain wall and two-over-one windows, and leave the exposed stack-bond yellow brick and terrazzo intact; the front addition for the library leans to one side, breaking the grid of the original façade with something clearly new but equally spirited. *AB*

12b Laneway House, 1 Leslie Garden Lane, Shim-Sutcliffe, 1993. Designed by the young architects as their own home, it proved that Toronto's laneways are an untapped resource for housing and that such development requires architectural finesse. Just 1,350 square feet, the house feels spacious thanks to its walled courtyard, whose floor is sunken below ground, creating near-total privacy within. Rich mahogany counterpoints humble concrete block. *AB*

12b | Laneway House

12c Craven Road House and Studio, 1007 Craven Rd., Shim-Sutcliffe, 1996/2005. A challenging site on an unusual thoroughfare (half lane, half street) allowed Shim-Sutcliffe to design this house, and then the studio, for an architect-archivist colleague, with modest materials—the house is clad in plywood but detailed with great care. Its compact main floor is capped by a grand, loft-like library and the ensemble is elegantly sited. *AB*

13 R.C. Harris Water Filtration Plant, 2701 Queen St. E., Thomas Pomphrey, 1941. Built as one of Toronto's crucial pieces of infrastructure, it remains in service and testifies to a design ambition in public works that has rarely been matched in Canada. Pomphrey was a journeyman architect with the engineering firm Gore, Nasmith & Storrie, but this project commissioned by and named for the city commissioner of works Roland Caldwell Harris found Pomphrey at his best. The utilitarian concrete interior has hallways of finely crafted marble and terrazzo, and it's wrapped in an Art Deco shell of buff brick and Queenston limestone that utterly commands its hilltop site. Its nickname, "the Palace of Purification," is well earned. *AB*

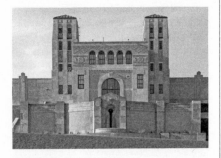

13 | R.C. Harris Water Filtration Plant

14 Salvation Army Scarborough Citadel and Housing, 2015 Lawrence Ave. E., Scarborough, Garwood-Jones Van Nostrand Hanson Architects, 1993. The Salvation Army has been a patron of modernist architecture, hiring Le Corbusier in Paris in the 1920 and the Parkin office for its Canadian headquarters on Albert Street (built 1956, demolished 1998). This sophisticated building follows that tradition, nodding to Corbusier through the elevation of its bulk on columns (what Corbusier called pilotis) and the strip windows in its chapel. You can read three separate elements—the tower of 158 residential units, school and daycare, and chapel—artfully arranged and linked. *AB*

15 Centennial College Ashtonbee Library and Student Centre, 75 Ashtonbee Rd., Scarborough, MacLennan Jaunkalns Miller, 2014. A gorgeous building-as-bridge, both highly accessible on foot and legible at driving speed with its brawny steel trusses and textured glass façades. Yet while this campus is shaped by car culture, the building anticipates a more walkable urban form with strong street walls. *AB*

16 Umbra World Headquarters, 40 Emblem Ct., Scarborough, Kohn Shnier, 1999. Kohn Shnier took a generic factory and added two exterior elements: a glass penthouse, where the Umbra logo is visible by drivers on the adjacent Highway 401; and a new, angled outer skin to address visitors, made from panels of perforated plastic that echo Umbra's housewares product line. *AB*

17 Scarborough Civic Centre, 150 Borough Dr., Scarborough, Moriyama & Teshima, 1973. Inside, this building expresses a late–Jet Age collective optimism. Its curving atrium is lined with terraced balconies studded with plants and Op Art textiles, an agora with lots of carpet. The building's great bulk, like a deep pie that's been cut away from two sides, is elegant from a distance. Up close it's another story. The centre was meant to open out sociably in two directions, bringing activity into a plaza to the north and open space to the south; these outdoor spaces never became as lively as Moriyama intended. This reflects the mall urbanism of the precinct but also some flaws in the design. The civic centre's level changes, and its expanses of impermeable concrete and black glass, have not helped. *AB*

17 | Scarborough Civic Centre

18 | Toronto Public Library Scarborough Civic Centre

18 Toronto Public Library, Scarborough Civic Centre Branch, 156 Borough Dr., Scarborough, LGA Architectural Partners with Phillip H. Carter, 2015. An exemplar of the 21st-century library as active social space: its one grand room wraps around a forest-like assemblage of glue-laminated spruce beams. Its irregular form and translucent glass walls provide a fine, lively, messy counterpoint to the monolith next door [26/17]. *AB*

19 Bellmere Junior Public School, 470 Brimorton Dr., Scarborough, John Andrews, 1965. A genuinely novel approach to elementary-school design: a one-storey collection of classrooms that are each shaped like houses, gathered into intimate clusters around a wood-ceilinged, clerestoried gym. From outside, the school has a monumentality and modularity that echoes Louis Kahn; inside, the brick walls and woodsy, intimate classrooms show empathy for the experience of young children. *AB*

20 Centennial College Progress Campus, 941 Progress Ave. Student Centre, Kongats Phillips, 2001. Athletic and Wellness Centre, Kongats Architects, 2012. Library and Academic Facility, Diamond Schmitt, 2011. Three distinguished projects that present a bold face to the traffic on the 401. First, the Student Centre, elegantly reclad by Kongats. Then its addition and renovation of the athletic centre add a new façade of concrete-and-glass half-cylinders, evoking a colonnade and also a particularly elegant variety of plastic packaging. Diamond's library and classroom building has an agreeably spiky aspect; those north-facing bays bring light deep into the building. *AB*

21a Scarborough College master plan, 1265 Military Trail, Scarborough, John Andrews, Michael Hugo-Brunt (planner), Michael Hough (landscape architect), 1963. One of Toronto's boldest and most lasting products of the 1960s public-sector building boom. The Australian Andrews, barely 30 and an instructor at U of T, snagged this seminal commission; he worked with contemporaries Hough and Hugo-Brunt (all "hungry as hell," Andrews later wrote) to develop a scheme in just six weeks. They imagined a long, linear campus that hugged the edge of the Highland Creek valley; it would be Brutalist in its language, and would bring together diverse departments and functions in one enormous envelope, "a microcosm of a small town," in Andrews's words. It would protect faculty and students from winter weather and the especially harsh, windy microclimate on the site. This then fashionable idea of the "mega-structure" is strongly and consistently expressed in the Andrews Building [26/21c], but the university later abandoned it through decades of scattered and deliberately incoherent additions to the campus. *AB*

21b Centennial HP Science and Technology Centre, 755 Morningside Ave., Scarborough, Kuwabara Payne McKenna Blumberg with Stone McQuire Vogt, 2004. A faceted, metallic form that reads not like a shard but a jewel. The massing of this building is unusually aggressive for KPMB, and successfully so in holding the sloped corner site. Inside, the complex network of atria, stairs, and a set of what the architects call "Spanish steps" are beautifully lit and highly refined. Strategically placed windows help you to imagine this place as sitting in a virgin forest and to ignore the gas station across the street. *AB*

21c Andrews Building (Science Wing and Humanities Wing), 1265 Military Trail, Scarborough, John Andrews Architects and Page & Steele with Michael Hough (landscape architect), 1966. Among the most-published and critically revered Canadian Modernist buildings. The two original structures are each triangular in section, and at their hearts are long internal "pedestrian streets"; lined with bush-hammered concrete and paved with terracotta tile, these spaces are rich in texture and atmosphere, and they're punctuated by grand, moody, skylit atria. These "streets" don't always serve their intended function as social gathering and mixing spaces, and yet the buildings are packed with spatial complexity, finely crafted details, and a grandeur that both acknowledges its site and transcends it absolutely. *AB*

21c | Andrews Building

21d Arts and Administration Building, 1265 Military Trail, Scarborough, Montgomery Sisam, 2005. A quiet, elegant reply to Andrews's quasi-industrial rhetoric, this is a sculpted box of buff brick—a traditional Toronto material that's too little used by Modernist practices. It captures a variety of functions, including classrooms, a welcome centre, and a new Council Chamber, in an unfussy envelope. Most importantly, it successfully imposes some traditional urbanism onto the site, making strong pedestrian connections from the edge of campus toward the Andrews complex. *AB*

21e Academic Resource Centre, 1265 Military Trail, Scarborough, Brian MacKay-Lyons with Rounthwaite, Dick & Hadley, 2003. One of a few Toronto buildings by the celebrated Halifax architect MacKay-Lyons, this is a knitting together of four existing buildings with a new envelope and open corridors. It speaks a language of standing-seam copper cladding, stack-bond concrete blocks, and exposed services that responds to, but does not mimic, Andrews's *béton brut* **[see 26/21c]**. *AB*

22 Miller Lash House, 130 Old Kingston Rd., Scarborough, Green & Wicks, 1913. The businessman Miller Lash began building this house as a summer getaway on his 375-acre estate in the Highland Creek valley. Buffalo architect Edward B. Green Sr. designed a gabled, beamed, Arts and Craftsy manse with that movement's emphasis on local materials. The stones laid into the walls come from the bed of Highland Creek; the floor tile and Spanish Colonial–style roof tile were made from local clay. The architecture couldn't have less to do with local traditions, but the house (which can be seen from the public gardens around it) is a welcome interloper. *AB*

22 | Miller Lash House

23 | Toronto Zoo Indo-Malayan pavilion

23 Toronto Zoo master plan, 2000 Meadowvale Rd., Scarborough, African Pavilion and Indo-Malayan Pavilion, The Thom Partnership with Crang & Boake and Clifford & Lawrie, 1974. Your first experience of the zoo is of a rolling rural site loaded with enough road and parking infrastructure to accommodate an army. The zoo itself, planned by Ron Thom, is much more nuanced: it forms a promenade through a 75-acre site of tableland flanked by two ravines, and is organized around the concept of grouping animals and flora by their native geographic locations. Some of the lesser structures, made with heavy timber, show a West Coast Thom sensibility that fits the forested milieu. But the highlights are the Indo-Malayan and African pavilions: each is a multi-level green landscape, capped with a faceted roof which is formed from a weave of squares, rhombuses, and triangles. *AB*

24 Thomas L. Wells Public School, 69 Nightstar Rd., Scarborough, Baird Sampson Neuert, 2005. A sophisticated Modernist composition in friendly orange brick despite the quasi-Victoriana of the area. Baird Sampson Neuert fought successfully for all classrooms to get a southern exposure, and organized the school around courtyards and an indoor "main street" that provides orientation and natural light. The project was an early Toronto example of sustainable building, employing radiant heat and passive solar and ventilation strategies. *AB*

25 Unionville Public Library, 15 Library Lane, Unionville, Barton Myers, 1984; renovation, Luc Bouliane, 2014. Myers working in full Post-Modern mode, to great effect. The library's skin of red and yellow brick echoes Victorian traditions in this quaint historic context. And yet the jazzy patterning of the brick and the asymmetrical massing suggest something else is going on. In fact, the building is broken down into eight square "houses" of books; these are visible more clearly inside, where their stage-set-like façades address the open court at the middle of the building. This is washed by square skylights and the ceiling is lined with cloth, another layer of material and conceptual richness that nods to Myers's hero, Louis Kahn. *AB*

26 | Markham Civic Centre

26 Markham Civic Centre, 101 Town Centre Blvd., Markham, Arthur Erickson with Richard Stevens, 1990. A dowdy 1980s garb of big pink precast slabs disguises artful siting and a thoughtful embrace of Post-Modernism. There are historical references here, in the Po-Mo mode, including a rotunda and a colonnade; and there are also pure rectangles and a cylinder that hint at Aldo Rossi. The building is J-shaped in plan, and it steps down from the entrance level toward an array of reflecting pools that sit within the crook of the building. On a big, featureless site, Erickson was able to create grandeur through massing and careful deployment of landscape elements. Inside, the building is straightforward and well crafted. Its biggest space borrows the formula of the Law Courts Complex in Vancouver with a steel-and-glass atrium rich with trees and greenery. *AB*

Glossary

Adamesque. After Robert Adam (1728–92), English architect and designer known for his refined, elegant classicism.

apse. Semicircular or polygonal projection at the chancel end of a church.

arcade. 1. A range of arches supported on columns or piers, either freestanding or blind (applied to a wall). 2. Covered passage lined with shops.

arch. Structural device arcing an opening supported only from the sides. Various configurations include: **round** or **semicircular; segmental; S-shaped** or **ogee; horseshoe;** and **pointed** or **lancet.**

architrave. 1. In classical architecture, the lowermost division of an entablature above which is the frieze and cornice. 2. Moulding around the top and sides of a rectangular door or window. Also called a **surround.**

ashlar. Blocks of horizontally laid rock that have been hewn with square edges and rough-cut faces, as opposed to unhewn rubble on the one hand and smooth-sawn stone on the other.

atrium. 1. In early Roman architecture, a courtyard in the centre of a house covered only along the sides. 2. In contemporary architecture, an enclosed vertical space welling the interior of a multi-storey building.

baluster. Support for a railing on stairways, balconies, etc., originally partially bulb-shaped or similarly turned.

balustrade. A series of balusters supporting a railing.

bargeboards. Decorative, often scroll-sawn boards edging a gabled or overhanging roof. Also called vergeboards or gingerbread.

bartizans. Small tower-like structures at and overhanging the top corners of a building. Originally for defence.

base. In classical architecture, a supporting foundation of a column on which the shaft rests.

batter. Outward slant of the bottom of a wall. Originally the thickening of the base of a tower as fortification against battering.

bay. Vertical division of a building as delineated by some regular, recurring feature such as windows, buttresses, columns, etc.

bay window. A bay that projects from a building and contains one or more windows. If a bay window projects from an upper storey only, it is called an **oriel.**

Beaux Arts. After the École des Beaux Arts in Paris, the French state school of art education renowned as the training place for architects worldwide. The principles of design expounded there, particularly those dealing with craftsman-like construction, appearance of strength, visual order, and urban drama, were a major influence on those practising neoclassical architecture and town planning in the late 19th and early 20th centuries, especially in the United States.

bellcote. Small gabled structure for hanging bells atop a roof.

belvedere. Small covered structure on a roof for looking at a view.

board-and-batten. Butting flat boards topped with flat trim strips covering the joins.

bond. Patterns of brick (see also header), **English bond** is one course of headers (long sides) followed by one course of stretchers (short sides); **Flemish bond** alternates headers and stretchers in each course. In **Running bond**, courses of stretchers are offset by half a brick per course. In **Stack bond**, courses of stretchers are aligned with the joints aligning.

boss. Ornamental knob.

bracket. Wooden or metal member projecting from a wall to help support an overhanging weight such as an extended roof.

brick. Hardened clay, block-shaped in a mould, may or may not be baked in a kiln. **Pressed brick** is made of very fine clay forced into the mould under great pressure to form an especially smooth hard brick. **Clinker brick** is an uneven and vitrified brick that has become misshapen in firing; often used for an "artistic" effect. **Tapestry brick** is a random arrangement of different coloured brick, usually black and dark red; popular in the early 20th century.

bungalow. A house, relaxed in style, often asymmetrical and showing the hand of the builders who made it; often associated with the Arts and Crafts or Craftsman movements, and with the California houses of Greene and Greene.

buttress. Masonry support built against a wall to give it added strength.

capital. In classical architecture, the uppermost division of a column crowning the shaft.

cartouche. Bas-relief in the form of an ornamental tablet.

cast-in-place concrete. A material that is mixed on site, or transported to the site as ready-mix, then cast in forms. Compare precast.

chancel. That part of the central space of a church that contains the main altar and is reserved for clergy and choir, as distinct from the nave.

classical architecture. Formal, symmetrical, codified architecture of Ancient Greece and Ancient Rome, and architecture derived thereof.

clerestory. Upper windowed walls of a church or other building that rise "clear" of all other structural parts to provide light to the interior.

colonnade. A row of columns supporting an entablature, roof, or arches.

colonnette. Small slender decorative column.

column. In classical architecture, an upright support consisting of base, circular shaft, and capital; situated below and carrying the entablature. Variously proportioned and ornamented depending on the order.

Composite. One of the Roman classical orders, similar to the Corinthian but with larger volutes (spirals) in the capitals.

console. Ornamental S-shaped bracket.

corbel. Stone or clay member projecting from a wall to help support an overhanging weight such as an oriel.

corbel table. A range of corbels in courses, each course built out beyond the one below.

Corbusian. After the Swiss-French architect, urban designer and artist Le Corbusier (born Charles-Édouard Jeanneret), 1887–1965, one of the pioneers of Modernism in architecture and closely associated with the International Style as well as the use of exposed concrete and with the growth of Modernist city planning; his 1925 Plan Voisin for Paris, which proposed replacing much of the city with cruciform towers surrounded by parkland, is an important source for the "tower-in-the-park" model so common in public and private housing developments of the 1950s through 1970s.

Corinthian. One of the classical orders, distinguished by columns with high bases, tall slender fluted or unfluted shafts, and ornate foliated capitals. The entablature uses dentils, modillions, and a fascia.

cornice. 1. In classical architecture, the uppermost division of the entablature below which is the frieze and architrave. 2. Projecting moulding at the top of a building, wall, etc., or over a door or window.

course. Horizontal row of bricks or stones in a wall. A **string** or **belt course** is a decorative coloured, moulded, or projecting row.

crenellation. Parapet with alternating voids and solids. Originally intended for warriors to shoot through or hide behind. Also called **battlement.**

cresting. Ornamental ridge atop a roof or wall, generally of filigreed metal.

crockets. Projecting foliate ornaments, usually stone, found on Gothic spires, pinnacles, gables, etc.

cupola. Small, domed structure crowning a roof or tower. (See also belvedere).

curtain wall. Exterior, screening wall situated in front of a load-bearing frame. In modern steel-frame buildings, all exterior walls are non-load-bearing curtain walls.

dentils. Very small rectangular blocks ranged in a series to form a tooth-like moulding.

Doric. One of the classical Greek orders, distinguished by columns with no base, short fluted shafts, and plain, saucer-shaped capitals. The Roman Doric order has a simple base and the shaft may be unfluted.

dormer window. Window and its roofed enclosure rising vertically atop a roof.

double house. Single building comprising two distinct dwellings, one *beside* the other, sharing a common or party wall that separates the two. Each distinct dwelling is called a **semi-detached house.**

dressings. Finely finished stone trim.

drip-mould. Projecting moulding around the top of an opening, nominally to protect it from rain. Also called **hood-mould, dripstone,** and if rectangular, **label.**

Eastlake style. After Charles Lock Eastlake (1836–1906), English architect and writer, whose interior design books showing furniture with knobbed and spindled lathe-turned members as well as latticework influenced similar decoration on late 19th-century picturesque houses.

eaves. Underside of an overhanging roof.

egg-and-dart. Moulding with a pattern of alternating ovals and arrowheads.

entablature. In classical architecture, the horizontal beam consisting of architrave, frieze, and cornice; situated above and spanning the columns. Variously proportioned and ornamented depending on the order.

fanlight. Semicircular or semi-elliptical window above a door or another window, originally with radiating glazing bars suggesting a fan.

fascia. 1. In classical architecture, plain horizontal band constituting part of some architraves. 2. Plain wide board edging a gabled or overhanging roof. If decorated, called a bargeboard or vergeboard.

fenestration. Arrangement of windows in a building.

finial. Ornament at the tip of a gable, pinnacle, etc.

frieze. 1. In classical architecture, the middle division of an entablature between the cornice and architrave, often figurally sculpted in bas-relief. 2. Any decorated band around the top of a wall.

gable. The wall or other area demarcated by the triangular configuration of a peaked roof. Ornamental variations include: **Dutch gable** (curved sides topped by a pediment); **shaped gable** (multi-curved sides); and **stepped** or **Flemish gable** (angular, step-like increments).

gallery. Part of an upper floor open on one side, either to an interior courtyard, auditorium, etc., or to the exterior street, garden, etc.

grotesque. Carving or painting of highly fanciful human/animal forms. Antique examples were first discovered in grottoes, hence the name.

half-timbering. Exposed wooden framing on the outside of a wall, usually filled in with some kind of non-load-bearing plasterwork.

hammerbeam. Wooden roof construction in which the horizontal beams are cut away in the centre, the ends then supported from the top of the roof by hammer posts, forming a kind of bracket.

header. Short end of a brick as it appears on the face of a wall. Various distributions of headers and stretchers (long sides) result in different patterns called **bonds.**

impost. The structural point at which an arch begins and ends.

inglenook. A seating recess beside a fireplace.

Ionic. One of the classical orders, distinguished by columns with moulded bases, tall slender fluted shafts, and capitals with volutes (spirals). The entablature is relatively plain, with dentils.

keystone. Centre voussoir that locks an arch into place, often outsized and ornamented.

label-stop. An ornamental knob, often figural, at the end of a drip-mould.

lights. The openings or divisions in a window created by the intersecting mullions and transoms.

lintel. Horizontal wooden beam or stone over an opening.

lunette. A semicircular or half-moon window, opening, wall surface, etc.

mansard. In North America, commonly a steep, storey-high roof with two planes on all four sides, the first plane almost vertical, pierced by dormers, and variously convex, concave, or straight-sided; and the second plane nearly flat. Named for François Mansart, 17th-century French architect, who developed the form.

Miesian. After Ludwig Mies van der Rohe (1886–1969), Bauhaus-trained master of Modernism, whose dignified "less-is-more" aesthetic of formal, precise glass-and-steel buildings ranks as a foremost influence on the architecture of the 20th century.

modillions. Small ornamental-shaped blocks ranged in a series to form a decorative band, normally located under a classical cornice.

mullion. Vertical bar dividing a window into lights. Horizontal dividers are called transoms.

nave. That part of the central space of a church that is flanked by the aisles and intended for the congregation, as distinct from the chancel.

Neo-Grec. Type of simplified linear classical detail popular in the mid 19th century; often incised.

order. In classical architecture, the structural unit comprising columns and entablature. There are five orders, each with its own established proportions and ornament: Doric, Ionic, Corinthian, Tuscan, and Composite.

oriel. (See bay window.)

Palladian. 1. After Andrea Palladio (1508–1580), North Italian architect known for his harmonious Renaissance villas and other buildings. 2. Arched opening flanked by two smaller, straight-topped openings, a design associated with Palladio.

parapet. Low wall around the edge of a roof, bridge, etc.

pavilion. 1. Ornamental, generally lightly constructed building. 2. Unit of a building projecting from the main mass.

pediment. In classical architecture, the area above the entablature of a portico demarcated by the triangular configuration of a peaked roof. Also any similar triangular section used as decoration above a window, door, etc. Ornamental variations may be: **segmental, open-topped,** or **broken-based.**

pendant. Elongated ornamental post or knob hanging from a roof, bracket, etc.

picturesque architecture. Informal, asymmetric, diverse architecture. First defined during late 18th century formulations on the nature of the Beautiful and the Sublime, the Picturesque being pronounced somewhere between the two.

pier. 1. Solid, upright support; freestanding or part of a wall. Term is generally used to describe structural members that are square or rectangular in plan as opposed to circular. 2. A square or clustered pillar of a Gothic or Romanesque church.

pilaster. Classical column as if squared and flattened and then attached to a wall as decoration.

pillar. General term for an upright support; may be circular, rectangular, triangular, etc.

pinnacle. In Gothic architecture, a miniature tower-like member crowning a buttress, gable, etc.

porch. Partly open, floored structure attached in front of a door and sheltered by a roof carried on upright supports.

portico. In classical architecture, a large porch with its roof carried by an entablature and columns and often having a pediment.

precast. Concrete that has been cast and cured in a factory environment, then transported to a site for installation. Compare cast-in-place concrete.

quatrefoil. Design resembling a cloverleaf made up of four lobes or foils. Found in Gothic church tracery, on Gothic Revival bargeboards, etc.

quoins. Dressed stones, or bricks implying stones, that alternate long side, short end, etc., at the corner of a building; originally structural but later often merely decorative.

relieving arch. An arch built flush in a wall above the top member of a framed opening to relieve it of superincumbent weight; usually constructed of radial brick treated decoratively.

roof. The cover of a building, in various configurations, including: **bell-cast** (concave, bell-like profile); **conical** (cone-like profile); **gable** (two opposite sides have a triangular profile); **gambrel** (two opposite sides have a double-sloped profile, with steep lower plane and less steep upper plane); **hipped** (all four sides have a single-sloped, flat-topped profile); **mansard** (all four sides have a double- or triple-sloped profile with steep lower plane and less steep or nearly flat upper planes); **pyramidal** (all four sides have a triangular, peaked profile); and **tent** (eight sides with a peaked profile).

roughcast. Cement cladding made of lime, water, and cows' hair, with fine gravel thrown on by the plasterer as a last coat.

row. Single building comprising four or more distinct dwellings, one *beside* the other, sharing common or party walls that separate them. Also called a **terrace.** Each distinct dwelling is called a **row house,** and by those who wish to be fancy, a **townhouse.**

rustication. Masonry with deep-set joins to exaggerate the look of weight and scale, generally used to delineate a base storey. If of stone or implied stone, surface may also be roughened.

shaft. In classical architecture, the cylindrical fluted or unfluted middle division of a column, between the capital and the base.

sidelights. Narrow vertical windows, usually fixed, flanking a door or another window.

sill. Horizontal member at the base of a window or door opening.

spandrel. 1. Unit of wall between two windows, vertically, from floor to floor. 2. Unit of wall between two adjacent arches.

spire. Tall pointed roof of a tower.

steeple. The combined tower and spire of a church.

stretcher. Long side of a brick as it appears on the face of a wall. Various distributions of stretchers and headers (short ends) result in different bonds. (See bond.)

Sullivanesque. After Louis H. Sullivan (1856–1924), American architect and a father of the modern skyscraper; also known for his distinctive geometric/naturalistic ornament.

terracotta. Hardened clay, shaped in a mould as tiles, paving, decorative panels, or other architectural ornament and then baked (literally "cooked earth" in Italian). Harder than brick. Around the turn of the century, terracotta was manufactured to look like stone and used for its fireproofing qualities as cladding on steel-framed skyscrapers as well as for interior casing.

toplight. Window, usually fixed, above a door or other window.

tower. A building or structure higher than its diameter. May be freestanding or attached to another structure.

tracery. Ornamental separations in a Gothic window. May be of stone, wood, or iron.

transept. Transverse arms of a cross-shaped church.

transom. 1. Horizontal bar dividing a window into lights. Vertical dividers are called mullions. 2. Horizontal window above a door or another window.

trefoil. Design resembling a cloverleaf made up of three lobes or foils. Found in Gothic church tracery, on Gothic Revival bargeboards, etc.

trophy. Relief ornament on a building, usually depicting arms and armour as a memorial to some victory, but may be any similar collection of symbolic objects.

turret. Small slender tower, usually round.

Tuscan. One of the Roman classical orders, similar to the Roman Doric but the shaft of the column is always unfluted. The entablature is very plain.

tympanum. A wall or other area demarcated by a lintelled opening and an arch above it.

vault. An arched ceiling or roof, usually of stone, brick, or concrete. Various configurations, including: **barrel** (continuous unbroken semicircle); **domical** (dome atop square or polygonal base); and **groin** (four-part intersection of two barrel vaults).

veranda. Partly open, floored structure attached alongside a house and sheltered by a roof carried on upright supports. Sometimes called a loggia.

verdigris. The natural patina that forms, through oxidation, on copper, bronze or brass; or the greenish colour characteristic of that patina.

vergeboards. (See bargeboards.)

vermiculation. Worm-track-like squiggles randomly cut into dressed stone as decoration.

voussoirs. Wedge-shaped blocks of stone, clay, etc., forming an arch.

window. 1. Opening in a wall to ventilate and light an enclosed space. Various configurations, including: **straight-topped; round-arched; lancet** (narrow and pointed at the top); **French** (carried to the floor like a door); and **rose** (circular). 2. The framework and fittings which close a window opening. Of various types, including: **casement** (hinged at the sides to open inward or outward); and **sash** (hung by cords to slide up and down, one section in front of the other).

window head. Protective and/or decorative member projecting at or around the top of a window. Of various configurations, including: cornice, eyebrow, segmental-pedimented, and triangular-pedimented.

woonerf. ("Living yard" in Dutch.) A street in which pedestrian, cycle, and vehicular traffic share a common surface with no curbs and, usually, a consistent paving material.

Suggested Reading

Online resources

City of Toronto Archives. www.toronto.ca/archives

City of Toronto's Heritage Property Search. app.toronto.ca/HeritagePreservation/

Architectural Conservancy of Ontario, *TOBuilt*. http://www.acotoronto.ca/tobuilt_new.php

Biographical Dictionary of Architects in Canada, 1800–1950. Editor, writer and webmaster: Robert Hill. http://dictionaryofarchitects incanada.org/

The TORONTO PARK LOT PROJECT. Editor and webmaster: Wendy Smith. http://wendysmith-toronto.com/parklotproject

Historical Maps of Toronto. Editor and webmaster: Nathan Ng. http://oldtorontomaps.blogspot.ca/

Goad's Toronto. Editor and webmaster: Nathan Ng. http://goadstoronto.blogspot.ca/

Toronto Reference Library Architectural Index for Toronto. http://archindont.torontopubliclibrary. ca/Arch/main.do

Periodicals

Azure

Building

Canadian Architect

The city

Careless, J.M.S. *Toronto to 1918: An Illustrated History*. Toronto: James Lorimer, 1984.

Dendy, William. *Lost Toronto*. Toronto: Oxford UP, 1978.

Fulford, Robert. *Accidental City: The Transformation of Toronto*. Toronto: Macfarlane Walter & Ross, 1995.

Gatenby, Greg. *Toronto: A Literary Guide*. Toronto: McArthur, 1999.

Glazebrook, G. P. de T. *The Story of Toronto*. Toronto: University of Toronto Press, 1971.

Harris, Amy Lavender. *Imagining Toronto*. Toronto: Mansfield Press, 2010.

Hayes, Derek. *Historical Atlas of Toronto*. Vancouver and Toronto: Douglas & McIntyre, 2008.

Kilbourn, William. *Toronto Remembered: A Celebration of the City*. Toronto: Stoddart, 1984.

Levine, Allan. *Toronto: Biography of a City*. Madeira Park, BC: Douglas & McIntyre, 2014.

Mays, John Bentley. *Emerald City: Toronto Visited*. Toronto: Viking, 1994.

Scadding, Henry. *Toronto of Old*, 1873. ed. F.H. Armstrong. Toronto: Oxford UP, 1966.

Van Nostrand, John. "Second Nature." *Toronto: A City Becoming*, ed. David MacFarlane. Key Porter, 2008. 117-141.

Neighbourhoods and places

Batten, Jack. *The Annex: The Story of a Toronto Neighbourhood*. Erin, Ont.: Boston Mills, 2004.

Benn, Carl. *Fort York: A Short History and Guide*. Toronto: Toronto Culture, City of Toronto, 2007.

Bonnell, Jennifer L. *Reclaiming the Don: An Environmental History of Toronto's Don River Valley*. Toronto: University of Toronto Press, 2014.

Coopersmith, Penina. *Cabbagetown: The Story of a Victorian Neighbourhood*. Toronto: James Lorimer, 2004.

Desfor, Gene, and Jennifer Laidly, eds. *Reshaping Toronto's Waterfront*. Toronto: University of Toronto Press, 2011.

Donegan, Rosemary. *Spadina Avenue*. Toronto: Douglas & McIntyre, 1985.

Gibson, Sally. *Toronto's Distillery District: History by the Lake*. Toronto, 2008.

Lorinc, John, ed. *The Ward: The Life and Loss of Toronto's First Immigrant Neighbourhood*. Toronto: Coach House, 2015.

McClelland, Michael, and Brendan Stewart. "University Avenue: Toronto's Grand Boulevard." *Ground* 26, Summer 2014, 28-31.

Myrvold, Barbara. *Historical Walking Tour of Kensington Market and College Street*. Toronto Public Library Board, 1993.

Old Town Toronto: Images of Past and Present. Toronto: Enoch Turner Schoolhouse, 2003.

Richards, Larry Wayne. *University of Toronto: An Architectural Tour*. New York: Princeton Architectural Press, 2009.

Stinson, Jeffery, and Michael Moir for the Royal Commission on the Future of the Toronto Waterfront. *Built Heritage of the East Bayfront*. Toronto, 1991.

Thompson, Austin Seton. *Jarvis Street: A Story of Triumph and Tragedy*. Toronto: Personal Library, 1980.

———. *Spadina: A Story of Old Toronto*. Toronto: Pagurian Press, 1975.

Architecture, landscape, and planning

Armstrong, Christopher. *Making Toronto Modern: Architecture and Design 1895–1975*. Montreal & Kingston: McGill-Queen's UP, 2014.

Arthur, Eric. *Toronto: No Mean City*. 3rd ed. Revised by Stephen A. Otto. Toronto: University of Toronto Press, 2003.

Bernstein, William, and Ruth Cawker. *Building with Words: Canadian Architects on Architecture*. Toronto: Coach House, 1981.

———. *Contemporary Canadian Architecture: The Mainstream and Beyond*. Toronto: Fitzhenry & Whiteside, 1982.

Bureau of Architecture and Urbanism. *Toronto Modern Architecture 1945-1965*. 2nd ed. Toronto: Coach House, 2002.

Byrtus, Nancy, Mark Fram, and Michael McClelland. *East/West: A Guide to Where People Live in Downtown Toronto*. Toronto: Coach House, 2000.

Cruickshank, Tom. *Old Toronto Houses*. Toronto: Firefly, 2003.

Dendy, William, and William Kilbourn. *Toronto Observed: Its Architecture, Patrons and History*. Toronto: Oxford UP, 1986.

Dobney, Stephen. *Barton Myers: Selected and Current Works*. Books Nippan, 1994.

Exploring Toronto. Toronto: Toronto Chapter of Architects, 1972.

Fraser, Linda, et al. *John C. Parkin, Archives and Photography*. Calgary: University of Calgary, 2013.

Freedman, Adele. *Sight Lines: Looking at Architecture and Design in Canada*. Toronto: Oxford UP, 1990.

Goodfellow, Margaret, and Phil Goodfellow. *A Guide to Contemporary Architecture in Toronto*. Vancouver: Douglas & McIntyre, 2010.

Gowans, Alan. *Building Canada: An Architectural History of Canadian Life*. Toronto, Oxford UP, 1966.

———. *Looking at Architecture in Canada*. Toronto: Oxford UP, 1958.

Gruft, Andrew. *Substance over Spectacle: Contemporary Canadian Architecture*. Vancouver: Arsenal Pulp Press, 2005.

Harris, Richard. *Creeping Conformity: How Canada Became Suburban: 1900-1960*. Toronto: University of Toronto, 2004.

———. *Unplanned Suburbs: Toronto's American Tragedy, 1900 to 1950*. Baltimore: Johns Hopkins, 1996.

Kalman, Harold. *A History of Canadian Architecture*. Toronto: Oxford UP, 1994.

Kapelos, George Thomas. *Competing Modernisms: Toronto's New City Hall and Square*. Halifax: Dalhousie UP, 2015.

Kapusta, Beth, and John McMinn. *Yolles: A Canadian Engineering Legacy*. Vancouver: Douglas & McIntyre, 2002.

McClelland, Michael, and Graeme Stewart. *Concrete Toronto: A Guidebook to Concrete Architecture from the Fifties to the Seventies*. Toronto: Coach House, 2007.

Moore Ede, Carol. *Canadian Architecture 1960-1970*. Toronto: Burns & MacEachern, 1971.

Myers, Barton, and George Baird. *Vacant Lottery*. Volume 108 of *Design Quarterly*. Walker Art Center, 1978.

Osbaldeston, Mark. *Unbuilt Toronto: A History of the City That Might Have Been*. Toronto: Dundurn Press, 2008.

———. *Unbuilt Toronto 2: More of the City That Might Have Been*. Toronto: Dundurn Press, 2011.

Ricketts, Shannon, Leslie Maitland, and Jacqueline Hucker. *A Guide to Canadian Architectural Styles*. Peterborough: Broadview, 2004.

Rochon, Lisa. *Up North: Where Canada's Architecture Meets the Land*. Toronto: Key Porter, 2005.

Sewell, John. *The Shape of the City: Toronto Struggles with Modern Planning*. Toronto: University of Toronto Press, 1993.

———. *The Shape of the Suburbs: Understanding Toronto's Sprawl*. Toronto: University of Toronto Press, 2009.

Simmins, Geoffrey, ed. *Documents in Canadian Architecture*. Toronto: Broadview Press, 1992.

Stanwick, Sean, and Jennifer Flores. *Design City Toronto*. London: John Wiley & Sons, 2006.

Toronto Society of Architects. *TSA Guide Map: Toronto Architecture 1953-2003*. Toronto: Toronto Society of Architects, 2003.

White, Richard. *Planning Toronto*. Vancouver: UBC Press, 2016.

Whiteson, Leon. *Modern Canadian Architecture*. Edmonton: Hurtig, 1983.

Williams, Ron. *Landscape Architecture in Canada*. Montreal & Kingston: McGill-Queen's UP, 2014.

Individual architects and firms

Baird, George, et al. *Kuwabara Payne McKenna Blumberg Architects*. Basel: Birkhauser, 2013.

"Benjamin Brown: Architect." Exhibition texts, 2016. Toronto Ontario Jewish Archives, Blankenstein Family Heritage Centre.

Brown, W. Douglas. *Eden Smith: Toronto's Arts and Crafts Architect*. Mississauga, Ont.: W. Douglas Brown, 2003.

Carr, Angela. *Toronto Architect Edmund Burke: Redefining Canadian Architecture*. Montreal & Kingston: McGill-Queen's UP, 1995.

Diamond, A.J., et al. *Insight and On Site: The Architecture of Diamond Schmitt*. Vancouver: Douglas & McIntyre, 2010.

Erickson, Arthur. *The Architecture of Arthur Erickson*. Montreal: Tundra Books, 1979.

Fulford, Robert, and Edward Burtynsky. *Frank Gehry in Toronto: Transforming the Art Gallery of Ontario*. Merrell, 2009.

Kapusta, Beth, et al. *Place and Occasion: Montgomery Sisam Architects*. London: Artifice, 2013.

Lambert, Phyllis, et al. *The Architecture of Kuwabara Payne McKenna Blumberg*, Basel: Birkhauser, 2013.

LeCuyer, Annette, ed. *Shim-Sutcliffe: The Passage of Time*. Halifax: Dalhousie UP, 2014.

Litvak, Marilyn M. *Edward James Lennox: Builder of Toronto*. Toronto: Dundurn Press, 1995.

Markson, Jerome. *Jerome Markson Architects: Twenty-Five Years of Work*. No date.

Martins-Manteiga, John. *Peter Dickinson*. Toronto: Dominion Modern, 2010.

McArthur, Glenn. *A Progressive Traditionalist: John M. Lyle, Architect*. Toronto: Coach House, 2009.

Neal, Carolyn. *Eden Smith, Architect, 1858–1949: A Biography*. Toronto: The Branch, 1976.

Shadbolt, Douglas. *Ron Thom: The Shaping of an Architect*. Vancouver: Douglas & McIntyre, 2005.

Sisam, David. *Jeffery Stinson Architect: Building, Drawing, Teaching, Writing*. Toronto, 2015.

Superkül. *Rain Gravity Heat Cold*. Toronto, 2015.

Taylor, Jennifer. *John Andrews: Architecture, A Performing Art*. New York: Oxford UP, 1982.

Teeple, Stephen. *Near/Far: Teeple Architects*. L'Arca Edizioni, 2007.

Thomsen, Christian W. *Eberhard Zeidler—In Search of Human Space*. Berlin: Ernst & Sohn, 1992.

Weder, Adele, ed. *Ron Thom and the Allied Arts*. West Vancouver Museum, 2013.

Photo Credits

Photographs are all copyright © 2017 by Vik Pahwa, except the following, listed by page number:

C.S. Richardson: 15 (bottom), 50, 60, 69 (left), 72, 102 (left), 104 (right), 112 (right), 119 (right), 141 (left), 141 (bottom right), 142 (top left), 161, 212, 213, 226, 227, 228, 229, 230, 231 (top), 232, 233, 234, 237, 238, 240, 243, 244, 245, 246, 247, 248, 250, 252, 253, 254 (left), 257, 266 (bottom right), 268 (right), 269 (top right), 269 (bottom right)

The National Archives of the UK (item: CO 700 Canada no. 60): 1

Toronto Public Library: 4

City of Toronto Archives: 3 (Fonds 1498, Item 1), 5 (Fonds 200, Series 372, Sub-series 32, Item 187)

Canadian Architectural Archives, University of Calgary: 7 (Toronto City Hall; Panda Associates fonds; PAN 61881-207); 116 (left) Massey College/Ron Thom fonds/Photograph by Peter Varley [THO D52W23 2A/75.02]

Nicola Betts: 8

Alex Bozikovic: 10 (left), 12 (left), 14 (left), 15 (top right), 16 (left)

Shai Gil: 119 (top), 124, 141

Darius Himes: 119 (bottom)

DTAH: 22 (left), 254 (right)

Elizabeth Gyde: 51, 164 (right)

Tom Arban Photography: 97 (right), 98 (right), 115 (right), 118 (left), 194 (bottom left), 204 (left), 268 (left), 286 (left)

Ben Rahn/A-Frame Studio: 109 (right), 295

Brian Boyle © Royal Ontario Museum: 118 (right)

Robert Moffatt: 135

Lisa Logan: 141 (top right)

Bob Gundu: 179

Kohn Shnier Architects: 188 (right), 286 (left)

Diamond Schmitt: 195

Doublespace Photography: 231 (right)

Jan Becker: 260 (bottom left)

James Brittain: 231 (left), 261

Courtesy of Waterfront Toronto: 266 (top)

Claude Cormier + Associés Inc.: 265 (right)

Connie Tsang: 269 (left)

Maris Mezulis: 273

Giannone Petricone Associates Inc.: 276 (top)

Drew Mandel Architects: 283

Scott Norsworthy: 291 (left, top and bottom)

Moriyama Teshima: 294 (right)

Nic Lehoux: 131 (left)

Acknowledgements

I am writing this acknowledgement on behalf of Patricia McHugh, my mother, who passed away in September of 2008. Patricia's absence presented a unique challenge to this new edition of her book— first published in 1985, and followed by a second edition in 1989. The cityscape of Toronto has evolved substantially since that time, and the task now has been to incorporate recent structures, trends, and ideas with the legacy material and Patricia's commentary from the 1980s editions. Co-author Alex Bozikovic has enlivened the book with his equally passionate voice and informed perspectives—not only his assessments of the new, but also his reconsiderations of the old. Alex's attention to current developments, future proposals, and the city beyond downtown has given the volume fresh dimensions. The end result is a sensitive interweaving of the two authors' narratives.

At McClelland & Stewart I would like to thank Doug Pepper, and in particular Jenny Bradshaw for her smart, ever-thoughtful shepherding of this multifaceted tome through all the stages of editing and production.

Thank you to Vik Pahwa and CS Richardson for their robust visual interpretations of the book's content.

A special note of recognition is due to Ben McNally, proprietor of Toronto's Ben McNally Books, for his foresight in recognizing the value of reviving this book for the 21st century.

In her acknowledgements for the first edition Patricia gave distinct thanks to a number of individuals who had an impact on the book. I name them again here, as their influence has undoubtedly carried on: George Baird, Jim Bitaxi, William Dendy, Susan Ford, Ken Greenberg, Robert Hill, Stephen Otto, Douglas Richardson, and George Rust-D'Eye.

Joshua McHugh
New York, March 2017

I would like to thank: Jocelyn Lambert Squires, who as researcher played a critical role in the shaping and the making of this book. Likewise at McClelland & Stewart, Jenny Bradshaw and Doug Pepper. Robert Hill, whose *Biographical Dictionary of Architects in Canada* is an indispensable resource, and whose research informs much of this book. Stephen Otto, for his advice, his generosity and for his selfless commitment to Toronto and its history. Larry Richards, for valuable critiques and encouragement. George Baird, who offered much insight into the city that he has helped to shape. And for incisive comments on parts of the book, Paul Bedford, Howard Cohen, Roger Keil, John Lorinc, Stephen McLaughlin, Shawn Micallef and Zack Taylor.

For research help: Mary MacDonald and Yasmina Shamji of Heritage Preservation Services, City of Toronto. Catherine Nasmith. Michael McClelland, Scott Weir and Evan Manning of ERA Architects, for sharing their work and their advice. Andrew Blum, Ian Chodikoff, Elsa Lam and Chris Bateman for critical insights.

Toronto Reference Library; the Shore + Moffat Library; University of Toronto Libraries; City of Toronto Archives; Archives of Ontario; Ontario Jewish Archives; CNE Archives; and their staffs, librarians, and archivists.

The many architects and firms who provided information about their work; Naomi Kriss and Kriss Communications.

My editors at the *Globe and Mail*, especially Jared Bland.

For suggestions and information, Adam Sobolak, Adele Weder, Alex Josephson, Amy Lavender Harris, Brendan Cormier, Bryan Gee, Catherine Osborne, Chris Pommer, Craig White, Dave LeBlanc, Dieter Janssen, Doug Saunders, Elizabeth Pagliacolo, Geoff Kettel, Heather Dubbeldam, Helena Grdadolnik, Jay Pitter, Jenny Francis, Jesse Colin Jackson, John Monteith, John Shnier, Marc Ryan, Mason White, Meg Graham, Omar Gandhi, Robert Moffatt and all those whom I've forgotten.

Vik Pahwa, CS Richardson and Joshua McHugh.

Most of all, Liv Mendelsohn, who makes so many things possible.

This book is dedicated to Benjamin and Joel.

Alex Bozikovic
Toronto, March 2017

Index of Architects

Adlaf, Rudy, 290
Adamson Associates, 22, 27, 44, 74, 85, 104, 105,
    111, 120, 227, 228, 236, 276, 280, 285
AGATHOM, 286
Airport Architects Canada, 276
A.J. Diamond. See Diamond, A.J.
A.J. Diamond, Donald Schmitt, and Co., 111, 236
A.J. Diamond & Barton Myers, 55, 114, 148, 177, 195,
    198, 222, 244
A.J. Diamond & Partners, 34, 72, 157, 177
Allward & Gouinlock, 70, 105, 108, 115
Alsop Architects, 175
Altius Architecture, 245
A.M. Ingelson & Associates, 70
Andrews, John, 46, 295
Annau Associates, 180
architectsAlliance, 32, 33, 42, 48, 50, 51, 52, 57, 68,
    109, 115, 140, 153, 157, 160, 168, 192, 193, 230,
    265, 267, 268, 278
architectsAlliance/John van Nostrand, 254
Arcop Associates, 33
Armstrong, Norman A., 50, 168
Armstrong & Molesworth, 217
Arriz & Co., 291
Arthur, Eric, 2, 22, 41, 106
Arthur Erickson Architects, 260
AS + GG, 97
Atelier Kastelic Buffey, 286
Audax, 52
Austin Company, Architects and Engineers, 290
Aylesworth, Marshall B., 122

Babington, Edwin R., 167
Badgley, Sidney Rose, 64
Baird Sampson, 85
Baird Sampson Neuert, 108, 131, 274, 297
Baker, Francis S., 81, 84, 115
Baldwin, William W., 24
Baldwin & Franklin, 67
Baldwin & Greene, 56, 85, 86, 284
Banz, Brook, Carruthers, Grierson, Shaw, 277
Barnett, R.E., 187
Barott, Marshall, Merrett and Barott, 82
Barrett, Arthur C., 227
Barton Myers Associates, 18, 47, 115, 148, 175, 192, 297
BBB, 44, 103, 166. See also Brisbin Brook Beynon
Beck & Eadie, 87
Beggs, Neil G., 230
Behnisch, Behnisch and Partner, 109
Beman, S.S., 222

B+H, 45, 89, 97, 102, 104, 117, 118, 207. See also
    Bregman & Hamann
Binder, David, 224
Bird, Eustace G., 81, 251
Biriukova, Alexandra, 283
Bishop, Charles H., 110, 138, 142, 218
Bjarke Ingels Group, 54
BKL, 153
Black & Moffat, 209
Blackwell, Adrian, 100
Blair, William W., 32
Bogdan, Joseph, 70
Boigon, Irving D., 218
Bond & Smith, 34, 67, 80, 247, 251
Bortolotto, 104
Bouliane, Luc, 297
Boultbee, Alfred E., 240, 243
Bregman & Hamann, 33, 44, 47, 62, 64, 79, 80, 89,
    90, 103, 111, 195, 208, 244, 291
Brennan, Frank, 121
Brennan & Whale, 121
Brisbin Brook Beynon, 47, 97, 263
Brook & Banz, 276
Brown, Benjamin, 56, 57, 58, 67
Brown, J. Francis, 54, 55, 237, 247
Brown, Murray, 102
Brown + Storey, 67, 114
Brudnizki, Martin (interior designer), 87
Burden & Gouinlock, 252
Burdi, Diego (interior designer), 204
Burdi Filek, 204
Burka Architects, 153, 180, 206, 275
Burka Varacalli, 23
Burke, Edmund, 41, 62, 134, 224
Burke & Horwood, 41, 55, 62, 80, 118, 122, 221, 237,
    239, 249
Burke Horwood & White, 47, 61, 62, 66, 155, 174,
    229, 241, 251
Burston, H.D., 207
Burt, Joan, 36, 48
Busby & Associates, 281

Calatrava, Santiago, 80
Cannon Design, 102
Carmen Corneil, 288
Carmichael, William John, 187
Carrère & Hastings, 81
Carruthers Shaw & Partners, 23, 30, 164. See also
    CS&P
Carter, Phillip H., 178, 295
Caspari, Peter, 166, 207
Cawker, Ruth, 289

Chadwick, Bryan, 41, 243
Chadwick, Vaux, 23, 41, 243, 252
Chadwick & Beckett, 53, 102, 217, 218, 219, 221, 223, 243, 249, 250, 251, 253
Chapman, Alfred H., 110
Chapman, Howard D., 110, 148
Chapman & McGiffin, 111, 236
Chapman & Oxley, 62, 70, 84, 85, 86, 110, 117, 118, 164, 283
Charles Correa Associates, 291
Cheng, James K.M., 97
Chong, Williamson, 179
Clarke Darling Downey, 23
Claude Cormier Architectes Paysagistes, 260, 265. *See also* Cormier, Claude
Claude Cormier + Associés, 254. *See also* Cormier, Claude
Clifford & Lawrie, 207, 297
Clifford Lawrie Bolton Ritchie, 207, 209
Cobb, Charles S., 61
Cobb, Henry Ives, 29
Connolly, Joseph, 37, 162
Coon, Burwell R., 165
Cooper, Kenneth R., 104, 221
Corban & Goode (landscape architects), 114
CORE Architects, 49, 50, 51, 54, 75, 103, 133, 140, 180, 207
Cormier, Claude (landscape architect), 28, 48, 56, 193. *See also* Claude Cormier + Associés
Cormier, Ernest, 121
Corneil, Carmen, 285
Cowan, James M., 197
Cowle, John, 131
Craddock, David, 235
Craig & Madill, 109
Craig Zeidler Strong, 260
Crang & Boake, 47, 68, 164, 207, 208, 221, 222, 249, 297
CS&P, 142, 286
Cumberland, Frederic W., 111
Cumberland & Ridout, 24, 29, 30, 165
Cumberland & Storm, 35, 41, 106, 107, 127
Curry, Samuel G., 75, 83, 149
Curry & Sparling, 87, 163, 240
Curry Sproatt & Rolph, 87, 162, 224

Daoust Lestage, 268, 278
Darling, Frank, 108, 109
Darling & Curry, 79, 104
Darling Curry Sproatt & Pearson, 219
Darling & Pearson, 42, 55, 63, 81, 89, 104, 107, 108, 109, 111, 117, 118, 126, 140, 175, 186, 202, 223, 240, 253

Darling Sproatt & Pearson, 247
Davidson, Jocelyn, 218
Davie, James M., 132
Delano & Aldrich, 286
DeLeuw, Cather & Co. (engineers), 135
Denison, A.R., 226
Denison & King, 69
Designing and Draughting Co., 249
Diamond, A.J. (Jack), 111, 177. *See also* A.J. Diamond entries
Diamond & Myers/A.J. Diamond, 113
Diamond Schmitt, 36, 51, 54, 58, 67, 98, 107, 111, 113, 131, 140, 141, 154, 155, 164, 254, 266, 283, 285, 289, 292, 295
Dick, David B., 29, 33, 43, 106, 107, 115, 117, 150, 157, 164, 177, 293
Dick & Wickson, 71, 74, 196
Dickinson, Peter, 28, 81, 82, 86, 110, 143, 264, 286
Dolphin, Charles B., 44, 284
Donald Schmitt and Co., 111
Downey, Stanford, 81
DTAH (landscape architects), 21, 35, 73, 254, 260. *See also* du Toit Architects
du Toit Architects, 209, 254
DuBois & Associates, 285
DuBois Plumb Partnership, 221
Dunington-Grubb & Stensson (landscape architects), 99, 287, 289
Dunker Associates, 112, 163
Dunlop Farrow Aitken, 216
Dunlop Farrow Inc., 263
Dunning, Max, 155
Dyson, C.E.C., 158

Eden, Emslie, 222
Eden Smith & Son, 116, 221, 250. *See also* Smith, Eden
Eden Smith & Sons, 131, 243
Edward Durell Stone Associates, 89
Edwards, Robert J., 237
Edwards & Saunders, 222
Edwards & Webster, 68
Elken & Becksted, 277
ERA, 26, 29, 34, 35, 50, 63, 66, 67, 73, 85, 86, 95, 106, 108, 111, 130, 173, 175, 204, 221, 229, 231, 254, 261, 262, 267, 278, 284, 293
Erickson, Arthur, 43, 282, 297
Esenwien & Johnson, 29
Etherington, F.C., 110
Ewart, David, 75
Ewart, John, 41

Fairfield & Du Bois, 112, 289
Falloon, John, 230
Farrow Partnership, 275
Farrugia, John J., 121
Faulding, Heather, 244
Ferris & Associates (landscape architects), 180
FGMDA, 95
Finney, Percy H., 237
Fisher Dachs, 98
Fisher Tedman Fisher, 102
Fleury & Arthur, 120
Fleury Arthur & Barclay, 135
Forsey Page & Steele, 287
Foster + Partners, 109, 207, 280
Fournier Gersovitz Moss, 185
Fraser, William, 55
FRCH Design Worldwide, 62
Fuller, Thomas William, 95, 188

G + G Partnership, 282
Garwood-Jones Van Nostrand Hanson Architects, 294
Gehry International, 55, 173, 175
Gensler, 51
George, Allan, 289
George & Moorhouse, 91, 116, 117
George Moorhouse & King, 244, 252
gh3 (architects and landscape architects), 49, 117, 240, 275
Giannone, Ralph, 279
Giannone Associates Architects, 276
Giannone Petricone, 30, 64, 141, 245
Giannone Petricone Associates, 290
Gibson, Charles J., 34, 48, 61, 158, 203, 222, 224, 247, 248, 250, 251
Gibson & Pokorny, 142
Giller, Marvin, 75
Gillies, Kenneth Stevenson, 58
Goldsmith Borgal, 21, 64, 75, 86, 153, 156, 197, 240
Gordon Adamson & Associates, 285
Gordon & Helliwell, 61, 68, 71, 117, 134, 184, 222, 242, 249
Gordon S. Adamson Associates, 27, 74, 105, 120, 228, 236, 265
Gotham Nottinghill UK, 291
Gouinlock, George W., 23, 54, 56, 75, 82, 103, 105, 183, 263
Gouinlock & Baker, 23, 55
Govan Ferguson Lindsay, 175
Govan Ferguson Lindsay Kaminker Maw Langley & Keenleyside, 103
Govan Kaminker Langley Keenleyside Melick Devonshire & Wilson, 108

Gow Hastings, 23, 111, 165, 281
Graham, John, 281
Grand, James, 72
Grant, Robert, 43
Grant & Dick, 29, 202
Gray, J. Wilson, 63, 83, 133
Graziani & Corazza, 70, 71, 140
Green & Wicks, 296
Greenberg Consultants, 259, 262
Greenspan, Howard M., 180
Gregg, William R., 71, 219
Gregg & Gregg, 55
Grossman, Irving, 31, 110, 259, 279, 282, 286, 287, 289, 292
G.S. Baldine Associates, 74
Gundry & Langley, 34, 157, 158, 162, 173, 175, 188, 246

Hall, Mark, 188, 237
Hamilton, Peter, 36
Hancock, Little, Calvert Associates, 259
Hancock, Macklin (landscape architect and planner), 289. See also Hancock, Little, Calvert Associates and Project Planning Associates
Hancock & Townsend, 193
Hankinson, E.L., 64
Hariri Pontarini, 24, 48, 53, 63, 73, 97, 115, 117, 119, 142, 149, 160, 175, 194, 200, 206, 208, 226, 231, 260, 280, 283. See also Taylor Hariri Pontarini
Harper, George Robinson, 57
Harvey, James A., 49, 168, 227
Havill, James L., 85
Hay, William, 65, 66, 80, 121
Hazell, Taylor, 41, 74, 278
HDR, 131
Heakes, Francis R., 41, 105, 108, 109, 183
Henriquez Partners, 231
Herbert, Frederick H., 34, 36, 80, 83, 166, 177, 184, 201, 217, 218, 219, 221, 226, 227, 228, 229, 247, 249
H.G. Acres & Co. Ltd. (engineers), 265
Higgins, Spencer, 79, 80, 157
Hoare, John E. Jr., 140
HOK, 277
Holman, Hugh G., 204
Holmes, Arthur W., 114, 121, 175
Horwood & White, 62, 156, 175
Hosoya Schaefer Architects, 96
Hough, Michael (landscape architect), 101, 295, 296
Hough Stansbury and Associates, 264
Hounsom, Eric, 206
Howard, John G., 24, 126, 243, 277, 285
Hugo-Brunt, Michael, 295
Hutchins, Edward F., 177

Hynes, James P., 152, 247, 249
Hynes Feldman & Watson, 49
Hyslop, Kirk, 206

IBI Group, 24, 26, 28, 44, 45, 46, 51, 55, 67, 68, 70, 73, 96, 204, 261, 278
I.M. Pei & Partners, 89
Irving, William, 72, 156, 177, 183
Irwin/Beinhaker Associates, 113. *See also* IBI Group

Jacobs, Bob, 230
Janet Rosenberg & Associates (landscape architects), 30, 192, 231, 260
Jarosz, George, 151
Jarvis, E. Beaumont, 21, 251, 253
Jeffrey, J.M., 187
John Andrews Architects, 296
John B. Parkin Associates, 62, 90, 98, 100, 113, 135, 209, 245, 277, 281, 283, 290
John Metcalf Co., 260
Johnson Chou (interior designer), 196
Johnson/Burgee, 47
Jones, Hugh G., 95, 96
Jones, Jedd, 167
Jones & Kirkland, 275
Jurecka, Lobko, Tregebov Architect, 49

Kaplan & Sprachman, 58, 73, 231
Kapsi, Taivo, 283
Kearns Mancini, 23, 89, 140, 262
Keith, A.G., 135
Kennedy & Holland, 139
Kertland, Douglas E., 263
Kirkland Partnership, 56
Kirkor, 51, 71, 174
Klein, Maurice D., 283
Klein & Sears, 31, 138, 184, 200, 207
Kneider, George E., 164
Knox & Elliot, 149, 155, 157, 178
Knox Elliot & Jarvis, 83
Kohl, Harry B., 283
Kohn Pedersen Fox, 44, 86
Kohn Shnier, 106, 110, 120, 167, 173, 187, 188, 274, 286, 292, 294
Kongats, 275, 293, 295
Kongats Phillips, 295
KPF, 261. *See also* Kohn Pedersen Fox
KPMB, 45, 64, 73, 85, 98, 114, 115, 118, 119, 131, 152, 156, 204, 221, 259, 260, 261, 266, 267, 268. *See also* Kuwabara Payne McKenna Blumberg
Kucharski, Brian, 35

Kuhn, Monica, 132
Kutner, Ben, 269
Kuwabara, Bruce, 36
Kuwabara Payne McKenna Blumberg, 24, 28, 43, 45, 51, 91, 100, 114, 116, 254, 273, 295. *See also* KPMB

Lamb, Thomas W., 63, 66, 75
Landini Associates, 166
Lane, Henry Bowyer (interior design), 21, 35, 41, 65, 173
Lane Fox, Martin, 116
Langley, Henry, 24, 80, 129, 161
Langley & Burke, 25, 150, 179, 183, 228, 229
Langley & Howland, 166, 242
Langley & Langley, 122, 217, 239, 241, 249
Langley Langley & Burke, 23, 24, 47, 48, 118, 150, 156, 158, 160, 236, 247
Langton, William A., 188, 250
Law, Frederick C., 152, 162
Leaning, John, 224
Lebedinsky, Boris A., 31
Lee, Douglas, 289
Lemay Michaud, 48
Lennox, E.J., 28, 29, 33, 63, 75, 83, 99, 104, 105, 158, 159, 209, 215, 216, 222, 237, 252
Lett Architects, 164
Lett/Smith, 55, 120, 165, 259
Levitt Goodman, 71, 186, 280
LGA Architectural Partners, 58, 185, 254, 295. *See also* Levitt Goodman
Li, Daniel, 206
Li Architect, 260
Liaigre, Christian, 241
Libeskind, Daniel, 28
Lobko, Joe, 254
Ludlow & Fleury, 72
Lyle, John M., 43, 67, 69, 87, 95, 113, 122, 204, 244

MacDonald, Ian, 113
Macdougall, Henry, 30
Macdougall & Darling, 27
MacKay-Lyons, Brian, 296
Mackenzie, John A., 82, 167
MacLennan Jaunkalns Miller, 115, 141, 147, 150, 268, 277, 294
MacVicar & Heriot, 80
MAD Architects, 275
Makepeace, Stanley, 63
Maki & Associates, 291
Mandel, Drew, 283
Marani, Ferdinand H., 83

Marani, Lawson & Morris, 262
Marani Lawson & Paisley, 220
Marani & Morris, 99, 102, 103, 208, 209, 210, 221
Marani, Morris & Allan, 29, 264
Marani Rounthwaite & Dick, 103, 209, 210
Markson, Jerome, 25, 31, 73, 184, 287
Martel, Paul, 216
Massey, Hart, 117
Mathers & Haldenby, 41, 43, 87, 101, 105, 106, 107,
    108, 109, 113, 118, 121, 131, 147, 226, 236, 242,
    243, 251, 253, 284, 285
Matsui Baer Vanstone, 27, 178
Matsui Baer Vanstone Freeman, 31
Maw, S.H., 91
MBTW (landscape architects), 156. *See also* Milus
    Bollenberghe Topps Watchorn
MCA, 207
McBain, William J., 117, 284
McCallum, Robert, 192
McCaw & Lennox, 72, 186
MdeAS, 207
Medwecki, Joseph A., 221
Mekinda Snyder & Weis, 163
Mendelow, Martin, 186
Merrick, Paul, 245
Mesbur, David K., 66
Messervy, Julie Moir, 260
Michael Van Valkenburgh Associates (MVVA), 259,
    268
Mies van der Rohe, Ludwig, 90
Miller, E.C., 260
Miller, George M., 64, 114, 117, 119, 120, 156, 158, 177,
    209, 221
Miller, Maxwell, 155
Milus Bollenberghe Topps Watchorn (landscape
    architects), 85
Mitchell & White, 66
Moed de Armas & Shannon, 89
Moffat Kinoshita, 109, 117
Moffat Moffat & Kinoshita, 118, 175
Molesworth, West and Secord, 110, 134
Molesworth Secord & Savage, 285
Montgomery Sisam, 178, 277, 286, 296
Moody, Alan E., 23, 70
Moores & Dunford, 258, 259
Moorehouse, Walter, 289
Morgan, Earle C., 28
Moriyama, Raymond, 76, 287, 291, 292
Moriyama & Teshima, 26, 76, 120, 220, 281, 285,
    291, 294
Morphosis, 112
Morton, J. Gibb, 74, 161

Moshe Safdie Associates, 276
Murray, James, 151

NADAAA, 111
NAK Design Group (landscape architects), 204,
    254, 282
Nakashima, Hiro, 209
Natale Scott, 258, 259
Netkin Architect, 188
nkArchitect, 223
NORR Partnership, 37, 41, 95, 263
Northgrave, Paul H., 155, 207
Northgrave Architect, 43, 154

Oberst, Paul, 187
O'Connor, John, 134
Ogilvie, Robert M., 227
Ogus & Fisher, 207
Oleson Worland, 51, 194
OneSpace, 284
Ostiguy, André, 68
Ott, Carlos, 121
Ough, Richard, 74
Our Cool Blue Architects, 290

Page & Steele, 28, 41, 67, 81, 82, 83, 86, 89, 102, 110,
    143, 155, 195, 204, 205, 206, 208, 264, 283,
    284, 285, 293, 296
Page & Steele/IBI Group, 28, 44, 45, 51, 55, 67, 68,
    73, 85, 155, 168, 204, 261
Page & Warrington, 243
Paine, A.J.C., 98
Papadopoulos & Pradhan, 276
Parker Architects, 285
Parkin Architects, 210, 263
Parkin Millar & Associates, 64
Parkin Partnership, 64, 97, 175, 210
Parrott Tambling & Witmer, 150
PARTISANS, 95
Patkau Architects, 115, 262, 279
Paull, Herbert George, 185
Pellow Associates, 37, 62, 290
Pennington, Peter, 135, 139, 188
Peter Dickinson Associates, 291
Peter Lindsay Schaudt Landscape Architecture, 100
PFS Studio, 254, 261, 266, 269
The Planning Partnership (landscape architects),
    50, 105, 207, 261, 266, 268, 269
PLANT Architect Inc., 100, 118
PMA (landscape architects), 287
Pomphrey, Thomas, 293
Popper, George, 222

Post, A.A., 121
Price, G.F.W., 174, 263
Priest, Margaret, 85
Prii, Uno, 203, 226, 229, 278
Pringle. *See* T. Pringle and Son Limited of Montreal
Project Planning Associates, 259, 292
PUBLIC WORK (landscape architects), 44, 54, 111, 261, 262

Quadrangle, 35, 52, 72, 195, 197, 230, 266
Quadrangle Architects, 61, 174
Queen's Quay Architects International Inc., 64
Quinn Dressel (structural engineers), 46

R. Varacalli Architect, 204
Radford, Edward, 209
Radford, George, 209
RAN International, 45
RDH, 95
Read, Charles J., 153
Redmond & Beggs, 150
regionalArchitects, 150
Reno C. Negrin Architects, 98
Revell, Viljo, 100
Revington, Dereck, 134
Richard Hodgins Architect, 48
Richmond, Edward I., 70, 157
Ridgely, Gordon, 251
Robb, George A., 83, 195
Robbie/Young + Wright, 175, 280
Robert A.M. Stern Architects, 206
Roberts, David, 26, 27, 32, 153, 159, 220
Roberts, David Jr., 114, 267
Roberts, H.C., 284
Roberts & Caunter, 227
Roberts Duncan, 106
Robinson, Gerald, 173, 205
Robinson & Heinrichs, 31
Rogers, Richard, 22
Rogers Stirk Harbour & Partners, 22
Rosen, Sheldon, 196
Rosenberg, Janet (landscape architect), 192. *See also* Janet Rosenberg & Associates
Ross, Townsend, Patterson & Fish, 96
Ross & Macdonald, 70, 81, 95, 96, 166
Rounthwaite, Dick & Hadley, 116, 164, 276, 296. *See also* RDH
Ryrie, Jack, 166

SAKS Fifth Avenue team, 62
Saucier + Perrotte, 112, 269, 274
Saunders & Ryrie, 41, 253

S.B. Coon & Son, 86, 284
Scherman, Tony, 85
Schofield, John S., 96
Schreiber, J.W., 278
Schwartz/Smith/Meyer (landscape architects), 194
Scoler Lee & Associates, 287
Scolozzi, Francesco, 83
Scott, Sir Giles Gilbert, 117
Scott Associates, 47
Searle, Wilbee, and Rowland, 98
Seymour, Allan, 81
SGH Design Partners, 87
Sheard, Joseph, 61, 156, 162
Shepard & Calvin, 248
Shim, Brigitte, 293
Shim-Sutcliffe, 50, 116, 196, 245, 282, 286, 287, 293
Shore & Moffat, 105, 158
Shore Tilbe Henschel & Irwin, 102
Shore Tilbe Henschel Irwin Peters, 71, 285
Shore Tilbe Irwin & Partners, 100, 120
Shulman, Wilfrid, 62
Siddall, John Wilson, 21, 57, 164, 238, 252
Sievenpiper, J.E., 31
Sillaste & Nakashima, 31
Simpson, B. Napier, 243, 285
Simpson, Henry, 53, 63, 150, 242
Simpson and Young, 134
Skidmore, Owings and Merrill, 80, 276
Skywalk, 96
Smith, Eden, 176, 198, 217, 222, 223. *See also* Eden Smith & Sons
Smith, James Avon, 182
Smith & Gemmell, 29, 37, 80, 111, 150, 157, 182, 205, 219, 246
Snøhetta, 68
Somerville McMurrich & Oxley, 108, 116, 117, 142
Sparling, Thomas (landscape architect), 287
Sprachman, Mandel, 63, 66, 75, 187
Sproatt & Rolph, 23, 48, 68, 69, 70, 87, 96, 101, 102, 103, 107, 114, 120, 159, 176, 209, 228, 238, 241, 243, 248
Stantec, 34, 103, 110, 131, 266, 286
Starck, Philippe, 50
Stevens, Richard, 297
Stewart, William, 184
Stillman, H.N., 63
Stinson, Jeffery, 186
Stokes, Peter John, 173
Stone McQuire Vogt, 295
Stone & Webster (engineers), 267
Storm, William G., 35, 41, 43, 111, 120, 183

Strickland, Walter R., 27, 173
Strickland & Symons, 34, 219
Stringer, Archibald J., 243
Strong Associates, 29
Studio Daniel Libeskind, 118
Studio NminusOne, 132
Superkul, 110, 187, 201, 242
Swadron, Wayne, 180
Swan, Douglas, 48
Swartz, Benjamin, 186
Sweeny, Dermot J., 35
Sweeny, Sterling, Finlayson & Co, 44
Sweeny & Co., 57, 96
Sweezy, Larremore V.V., 167
Syme, Paul, 27
Symons, William L., 129
Symons & Rae, 158, 237, 249
Szewczyk, Barbara, 290

T. Pringle and Son Limited of Montreal, 260
Tampold & Wells, 205
Tan de Bibiana, Scott, 90
Taylor Hariri Pontarini, 119
Taylor Hazell, 41, 74, 277
Taylor Smyth, 21, 228
Teeple Architects, 52, 112, 161, 179, 185, 266, 276, 281, 290
3rd Uncle, 27, 175
Thom, Ron, 35, 37, 116, 245
Thom Partnership, 27, 31, 83, 165, 297
Thomas, William T., 22, 25, 80, 121, 130, 162, 164, 250
Thompson Berwick Pratt, 116
Toronto Board of Education, 110, 136, 139, 188
Townsend, S. Hamilton, 221, 227, 239, 240, 241, 250, 252
Tully, John, 47, 163
Tully, Kivas, 41, 173, 277
Turner, C.A.P. (engineer), 278
Turner, Peter, 128, 152, 178
Turner Fleischer, 166, 185

UPACE, 279, 280

Vaclav Kuchar & Associates, 31
Valjus, Seppo, 98
Van Elslander & Associates, 112
van Ginkel, Blanche Lemco, 100
Van Nostrand Di Castri, 281
Venchiarutti & Venchiarutti, 259
Ventin Group, 130, 162
Wagland, Keith, 119

Wagner, Charles F., 163
Wagner, Ferdinand A., 132, 149
Waite, Richard A., 105
Walker, Howard V., 110, 148
Wallman Architects, 24, 56
Wallman Clewes Bergman, 50
Walton, Charles A., 62
Warner Burns Toan & Lunde, 113
Waters, Mackenzie, 102, 166, 238
Webb & Menkes, 291
Webb Zerafa Menkes, 103, 165, 184, 194, 291
Webb Zerafa Menkes Housden, 28, 45, 61, 70, 83, 86, 88, 91, 97, 174, 196, 205. *See also* WZMH
Wells & Gray (engineers), 278
West 8 (landscape architects), 259, 260
Westervelt, John C., 67
Wickson, A. Frank, 37, 74, 122, 236, 237
Wickson & Gregg, 23, 49, 56, 73, 110, 219, 239
Wilkes, F. Hilton, 35, 87, 101
Wilkinson Eyre, 44
William Strong Associates, 102
Williamson Chong, 179, 230
Willmot, Mancel, 193
Wilson Newton, 106
Windeyer, Richard C., 148, 188, 230
Winkreative (design consultants), 96
Wodkiewicz, Wieslaw, 178
Wong, Michael K., 187
Woolnough, J.J., 263
Wright, Bruce, 235
WZMH, 34, 62, 63, 85, 86, 91, 155, 289. *See also* Webb Zerafa Menkes Housden

Yabu Pushelberg, 195, 244
Yolles Chapman & McGiffin, 48
Yolles & Rotenberg, 56
York & Sawyer, 89
Young, Allan M., 164
Young + Wright Architects, 74, 175, 276
Young & Wright/IBI Group, 24, 26

ZAS Architects, 50, 150, 269, 273
Zeidler, 32, 64, 67, 68, 87, 89, 95, 96, 102, 103, 113, 114, 160, 195, 258, 262
Zeidler Roberts, 103, 160, 174, 210, 275, 292

Index of Buildings

Every building described in the guide is listed below by present name and/or street address. Original and former names that are still in common use, as well as those that perhaps should be, are also given.

Absolute Ave.
  No. 60: 275
Absolute Towers: 275
Academic Resource Centre: 296
Ace Hotel: 50
Adelaide St. E.
  No. 2-6: 82
  No. 8-12: 82
  No. 20: 83
  No. 31: 29
  No. 57: 30
  No. 252: 24
  No. 258: 24
  No. 264: 24
  No. 300: 23
  No. 333: 33
  No. 363-365: 23
Adelaide St. W.
  No. 11: 83
  No. 100: 86
  No. 192-194: 97
  No. 312-318: 56
  No. 317-325: 56
  No. 338: 52
  No. 345: 56
  No. 366: 56
  No. 461: 54
Admiral Rd.
  No. 12: 224
  No. 13-15: 224
  No. 14-16: 224
  No. 57: 224
  No. 58-60: 223
  No. 59: 223
  No. 62-64: 223
  No. 77: 223
  No. 101: 223
Affordable housing, Wigwamen and Fred Victor: 268
Aga Khan Museum: 291
Aikens, Hon James Cox residence: 73
Air Canada Centre: 44
Albany Ave.
  No. 69: 230
Alexander St.
  No. 40: 166

No. 50: 166
Alexander, William house: 247
Alexandra Park: 184
Alexandra Park townhouses: 185
All Saints Church-Community Centre: 148
Allan Gardens: 147
Alliance Française de Toronto: 226
Allstream Centre: 263
Alpha Ave.
  No. 1-17: 128
  No. 2-18: 128
Alumnae Theatre: 37
Alumni Hall (University of St. Michael's College): 121
Amelia St.
  No. 50: 134
Ancroft Place: 248
Anderson Building: 55
Andrews Building (Science Wing and Humanities Wing): 296
Annesley Hall: 120
Annex Lane
  No. 16: 225
Annex Lane: 225
Arcade Building: 62
Architectural Science Building (Ryerson): 165
Ardwold Gate
  No. 70: 283
  No. 95: 283
Army & Navy Clothing Store: 25
Art Gallery of Ontario: 175
Arts and Administration Building: 296
Arts and Letters Club: 68
Ashtonbee Rd.
  No. 75: 294
Asquith Park: 209
Asquith St.
  No. 14: 209
Atkinson St.
  No. 1: 287
Atrium on Bay: 67
Augusta Ave.
  No. 25: 184
Aura: 70
Austin Terrace
  No. 1: 215
Automotive Building: 263
Ava Cres.
  No. 2: 283
Avenue Rd.
  No. 4: 204
  No. 38: 195
  No. 55: 196

No. 102: 200
No. 104: 200
No. 106: 200
No. 394: 284
No. 396: 284
No. 398: 284
No. 561: 284

Bahen Centre for Information Technology: 111
Baillie, Sir Frank house: 238
Baldwin, Mrs. William Augustus house: 203
Baldwin St.
No. 110-112: 178
No. 123-125: 179
No. 160: 187
Balfour Building: 57
Balmoral Ave.
No. 150: 284
Balmoral, The: 284
Bank of British North America: 80
Bank of Canada: 99
Bank of Montreal: 63, 79, 184, 290
Bank of Nova Scotia: 87
Bank of Upper Canada: 24
BAPS Shri Swaminarayan Mandir: 276
Barberian's Steak House: 68
Barton Myers house:198
Bata Shoe Museum: 220
Bathurst St.
No. 202: 186
No. 783: 231
No. 1700: 283
No. 1950: 283
Bay Adelaide Centre: 85
Bay/Charles Tower: 207
Bay Park Centre: 44
Bay St.
No. 40: 44
No. 81-131: 44
No. 161: 80
No. 181: 80
No. 200: 91
No. 222: 90, 91
No. 234: 91
No. 243: 89
No. 302: 87
No. 303: 87
No. 320: 87
No. 325: 87
No. 330: 86
No. 333: 85
No. 347: 85

No. 350: 86
No. 372: 84
No. 401: 62
No. 483: 64
No. 595: 67
No. 1166: 207
Bayview Ave.
No. 155: 268
No. 550: 254
No. 1477: 287
No. 2365: 286
Beardmore Building: 27
Beardmore, George residence, 176
Bedford Rd.
No. 121: 200
No. 123: 200
Bellair St.
No. 10: 206
Bell Trinity Square: 64
Bellemere Junior Public School: 295
Bellevue Ave.
No. 103: 188
No. 132: 188
Bentway, The: 262
Benvenuto Place: 284
Benvenuto Place
No. 1: 284
Berczy Park: 28
Berczy, The: 26
Berkeley Castle: 34
Berkeley Church: 37
Berkeley St.
No. 2: 34
No. 26: 34
No. 55-79: 36
No. 70: 37
No. 106-108: 37
No. 110-112: 37
No. 115: 37
Berkeley Street Theatre: 34
Bernard Ave.
No. 10: 199
No. 19: 199
No. 18-20: 199
No. 24-26: 199
No. 28-30: 199
No. 32-34: 200
No. 36-38: 200
No. 62: 223
No. 63: 223
No. 112: 218
Berryman St.

No. 19: 198
Betel Residence: 282
Beth David B'Nai Israel Beth Am Synagogue: 282
Beth Tzedec Congregation: 283
Better Living Centre: 264
Betty Oliphant Theatre: 157
Beverley Mansions: 176
Beverley Place: 177
Beverley St.
    No. 18: 180
    No. 25: 180
    No. 70: 179
    No. 133-135: 176
    No. 136: 176
    No. 137-139: 176
    No. 141: 176
    No. 145-147: 176
    No. 152: 176
    No. 186: 177
    No. 196: 177
    No. 198: 177
    No. 200: 177
    No. 206: 178
Bible & Tract Society Building: 61
Bill Boyle Artport: 259
Bird, Eustace G. house: 251
Birge-Carnegie Library; 120
Black Bull Tavern: 182
Blaikie/Alexander house. 157
Blaikie, John house: 247
Blake, Hon. Edward house: 157
Bleecker St.
    No. 55: 138
    No. 85: 138
    No. 101: 138
    No. 135: 138
Bloor Hot Docs Cinema: 231
Bloor St. E.
    No. 1: 208
    No. 2: 208
    No. 117: 208
    No. 120: 208
    No. 121: 208
    No. 160: 208
    No. 200: 209
    No. 227: 209
    No. 250: 209
    No. 321: 210
    No. 350: 210
    No. 600: 135
    No. 711: 135
Bloor St. W.

No. 1: 207
No. 2: 207
No. 50: 207
No. 55: 207
No. 100: 206
No. 110: 206
No. 130: 193
No. 131: 205
No. 150: 205
No. 157: 119
No. 162: 205
No. 200: 204
No. 206: 204
No. 246: 221
No. 252: 221
No. 273: 118
No. 300: 219
No. 315: 221
No. 321: 115
No. 327: 220
No. 427: 227
No. 506: 231
No. 581: 231
Bloor Street United Church: 219
Blue Jays Way
    No. 1: 45
Bond St.
    No. 51: 162
    No. 57: 162
    No. 82: 163
    No. 105: 163
    No. 110-112: 163
    No. 115: 164
    No. 116: 163
    No. 122: 164
Boone, Charles house: 237
Borough Dr.
    No. 150: 294
    No. 156: 295
Boswell Ave.
    No. 41: 201
    No. 46-48: 201
    No. 49-51: 201
    No. 54-56: 201
    No. 58: 201
    No. 60-62: 201
Branksome Hall: 153, 246, 247
Brant Park Condos: 51
Brant St.
    No. 39: 51
    No. 60: 58
Breadalbane St.

No. 15: 72
Bremner Blvd.
    No. 55: 45
    No. 120: 45
    No. 255: 45
    No. 288: 45
Brennan Hall: 121
Bridgepoint Health: 131
Bridgepoint Dr.
    No. 1: 131
Bright St.
    No. 19-21: 35
Briomorton Dr.
    No 470: 295
Brookfield Place: 80
Brougham Terrace: 139
Brown, George Chefs' House: 23
Brown, George College: 23
Brown, George College Waterfront Campus: 266
Brown, George residence: 177
Brown, George School of Hospitality: 23
Brownley, The: 168
Brunswick Ave.
    No. 324-326: 229
    No. 328-330: 229
    No. 332-334: 229
    No. 343: 229
    No. 345: 229
    No. 348: 230
    No. 350: 230
    No. 352-354: 230
    No. 356: 230
    No. 358-360: 230
    No. 385: 230
B.streets: 231
Burnamthorpe Rd.
    No. 430: 276
Burroughes Building: 185
Burwash Hall, 120

Camden St.
    No. 29: 51
    No. 51: 50
Campbell House: 42
Campus Walk
    No. 120: 281
Canada Life Assurance Building: 101
Canada Malting Silos: 260
Canada Permanent Building: 87
Canadian Imperial Bank of Commerce: 89, 140, 166, 183
Canadian Music Centre: 74

Canadian National Express Building: 96
Canadian Pacific Building: 81
Canadian Pacific Roundhouse: 45
Canadiana Building: 108
Canary District: 268
Canary District master plan: 268
Canary Park: 268
Canoe Landing: 261
Capitol Building: 56
Carlaw Ave.
    No. 951: 293
Carl Hall Rd.
    No. 55: 281
Carlo Fidani Peel Regional Cancer Centre: 274
Carlton St.
    No. 2: 70
    No. 14: 70
    No. 165-179: 137
    No. 181-183: 137
    No. 185: 137
    No. 187-189: 137
    No. 191: 137
    No. 195: 137
    No. 218: 137
    No. 219: 137
    No. 220: 137
    No. 222-224: 137
    No. 226-228: 137
    No. 230-232: 137
    No. 242-250: 140
    No. 245: 140
    No. 286: 132
    No. 288: 132
    No. 294-296: 132
    No. 295: 133
    No. 297: 133
    No. 298-300: 132
    No. 314: 132
Carr Hall: 121
Carsen Centre for National Ballet of Canada: 260
Casa: 168
Casa Loma: 215
Casey House: 160
Castle Frank Rd.
    No. 8: 252
    No. 32: 251
    No. 43: 251
    No. 48: 251
    No. 65: 250
Castle Frank subway station: 135
Castlemere Apartments: 242
Cathedral Church of St. James: 24

Cawthra, John house: 176
Cayley, Francis residence: 250
CBC Broadcast Centre: 47
Cecil Community Centre: 178
Cecil St.
    No. 20-22: 178
    No. 24-26: 178
    No. 28-30: 178
    No. 37: 178
    No. 39: 178
    No. 41: 178
    No. 43: 178
    No. 45: 178
    No. 58: 178
Centennial College Ashtonbee Library and Student
    Centre: 294
Centennial College Story Arts Centre: 293
Centennial College Progress Campus: 295
Centennial HP Science and Technology Centre: 295
Central Building: 85
Central Christadelphian Church: 209
Centre Island Park: 259
Ceterg offices: 289
Chamberlin Block: 137
Chamberlin Terrace: 137
Charles St. E.
    No. 33: 168
    No. 42: 168
    No. 45: 168
    No. 61-63: 168
    No. 68-70: 168
    No. 101: 160
    No. 110: 160
Charles St. W.
    No. 10: 119
    No. 55-57: 207
    No. 89: 120
    No. 93: 120
Charlotte St.
    No. 11: 51
Chaz: 168
Cherry St.
    No. 281: 266
    No. 309: 266
    No. 461: 268
Chestnut Park Rd.
    No. 1: 241
    No. 15: 241
    No. 20: 240
    No. 22: 240
    No. 27: 240
    No. 39: 240

    No. 43: 240
    No. 45: 240
    No. 50: 240
    No. 56: 239
    No. 77: 239
    No. 82: 239
    No. 86: 239
Childs Restaurant: 67
Chinese Consulate: 222
ChumCity: 174
Church-Isabella Co-operative: 168
Church of St.-Alban-the-Martyr: 230
Church of St. George-the-Martyr: 173
Church of the Holy Trinity: 65
Church of the Holy Trinity rectory: 65
Church of the Redeemer: 205
Church St.
    No. 35: 25
    No. 191-197: 163
    No. 200: 162
    No. 322: 164
    No. 325: 165
    No. 432: 166
    No. 438: 166
    No. 484: 166
    No. 519: 167
    No. 551-555: 168
    No. 561-571: 168
    No. 573-575: 168
    No. 580-582: 167
    No. 625: 168
    No. 634-636: 168
    No. 728: 209
CIL House: 195
Cinema Tower: 51
City Adult Learning Centre: 135
City Centre Dr.
    No. 300: 275
City Hall: 98, 99, 100
City Park Apartments: 166
Claireville Dr.
    No. 61: 276
Clarendon Ave.
    No. 1: 284
Clarence Square
    No. 5-16: 48
Clarence Terrace: 48
Clarendon Ave.
    No. 2: 284
Clarendon, The: 284
Claridge, The: 284
Clear Spirit: 267

Cloud Gardens: 85
Cloud Gardens Conservatory: 85
Cloverhill Apartments: 74
Cluny Dr.
  No. 2: 243
  No. 9: 243
  No. 37: 241
  No. 52: 241
CN Tower: 46
Cody, Maurice Hall: 209
Colborne Lodge: 277
Colborne Lodge Dr.
  No. 11: 277
Colborne St.
  No. 41-45: 29
  No. 47-55: 28
Cole St.
  No. 1: 140
  No. 25: 140
College Park: 70
College St.
  No. 2: 71
  No. 14: 71
  No. 22: 71
  No. 30: 71
  No. 40: 71
  No. 67: 104
  No. 101: 104
  No. 144: 109
  No. 149: 104
  No. 150: 109
  No. 155: 110
  No. 160: 109
  No. 164: 109
  No. 170: 108, 109
  No. 184-200: 110
  No. 214: 110
  No. 230: 110
  No. 239: 178
Colonnade, The: 205
Colonel Samuel Smith Park Dr.
  No. 2: 277
Commerce Court: 89
Commercial Bank of the Midland District: 77, 80
Commodore Building: 56
Communication, Culture, and Technology Building: 274
Computer Science and Engineering: 281
Concourse Building: 86
Confederation Life Building: 83
Confederation Life Insurance Co.: 210
Confederation Square: 83

Convocation Hall: 108
Cooper Koo Family Cherry Street YMCA: 268
Cooper, James house: 153
Cooperage Ln.
  No. 75: 268
Corktown Common: 268
Corus Quay: 266
Counsel Trust: 29
Courthouse Square: 30
Court St.
  No. 10: 30
"Craigleigh": 253
Crashley, J. Douglas Residence: 245
Craven Rd.
  No. 1007: 293
Craven Road House and Studio: 293
Crescent Rd.
  No. 60: 241
  No. 68-70: 242
  No. 75: 242
  No. 76-78: 241
  No. 80: 241
  No. 84: 241
  No. 88: 241
  No. 95: 242
  No. 108: 242
  No. 146: 238
  No. 164: 238
  No. 166: 237
  No. 170: 237
  No. 180: 237
  No. 182: 237
Crescent School: 286
Crocker's Block: 184
Croft St.
  No. 54: 188
Crown Life Insurance Co.: 208
Cube House: 269
Cumberland Court: 194
Cumberland, Frederic W. residence: 111
Cumberland St.
  No. 115: 194
  No. 155: 195
Currie Hall: 167

"Dale, The": 249
Dale Ave.
  No. 21: 249
Dalhousie St.
  No. 155: 155
Danforth Ave.
  No. 1: 135

Dan Leckie Way
  No. 150: 261
Daniels, John H. Faculty of Architecture, Landscape,
  and Design: 111
Daniels, John house: 193
Daniels Spectrum: 141
D'Arcy St.
  No. 84-100: 177
Darling Building: 58
Davenport Ave.
  No. 277: 200
David Mirvish Theatre: 66
Davies, William residence: 236
De La Salle Institute: 24
Delta Hotel Toronto: 45
Denison Ave.
  No. 12: 184
Denison Square
  No. 28: 186
Derby, The: 35
Devonshire House: 116
Devonshire Pl.
  No. 3: 116
  No. 4: 116
  No. 15: 116
  No. 20: 117
  No. 100: 115
Dineen Building: 83
DiPede, Tony Residence: 150
Distillery Ln:
  No. 70: 267
District Lofts: 57
Dixon Building: 27
Dockside Dr.
  No. 11: 265
  No. 25: 266
  No. 51: 266
  No. 61: 266
Dominion Public Building: 95
Don Jail: 130
Don Mills Collegiate: 290
Don Mills master plan: 289
Don Mills Middle School: 290
Don Mills Rd.
  No. 770: 292
Donnelly Centre for Cellular and Biomolecular
  Research: 109
Don Ridge Dr.
  No. 19: 285
Donway E.
  No. 15: 290
Doris Ave.

No. 130: 286
Downsview Park: 281
Dragon City Mall: 187
Drake 150: 87
Draper St.
  No. 3-5: 49
  No. 4-6: 49
  No. 7-9: 49
  No. 8-10: 49
  No. 11-13: 49
  No. 12-14: 49
  No. 15-17: 49
  No. 16-18: 49
  No. 20-24: 49
  No. 23-25: 49
  No. 26-28: 49
  No. 30-32: 49
"Drumsnab": 250
Drumsnab Rd.
  No. 5: 250
Dufferin St.
  No. 3401: 281
Duncan Mill Rd.
  No. 2: 289
Dundas St. E.
  No. 80: 163
  No. 155: 155
  No. 200: 155
  No. 585: 141
  No. 640: 141
Dundas St. W.
  No. 20-40: 67
  No. 55: 67
  No. 210: 102
  No. 255: 102
  No. 317: 175
Dundas Square
  No. 10: 67
  No. 19: 67
  No. 21: 67
Dundas Square Gardens: 155
Dupont subway station: 216

Earl Court: 152
Earl St.
  No. 30-38: 152
Early Learning Centre: 112
Earth Sciences Centre: 111
Eaton Centre: 64
Eaton's College Street: 70
Edgeley in the Village: 279
Edition Richmond: 52

Eglinton Ave. W.
No. 2200: 274
No. 3500: 278
Eglinton Crosstown Mount Dennis Station: 278
18 Yorkville: 192
Elementary Teachers' Federation of Ontario: 152
Elephant & Castle: 69
Eleven Apartments: 74
Eleventh St.
No. 25: 277
Elgin Ave.
No. 2: 202
No. 25: 201
No. 27: 201
No. 27A: 201
No. 45-47: 201
No. 52: 201
Elgin Theatre: 63
Elm Ave.
No. 1: 247
No. 2: 246
No. 3: 247
No. 4: 247
No. 10: 247
No. 14: 247
No. 16: 247
No. 18: 247
No. 20: 247
No. 21: 247
No. 23: 247
No. 24: 247
No. 25: 247
No. 26: 247
No. 44-46: 248
No. 45: 249
No. 47: 249
No. 49: 249
No. 50: 248
No. 51: 248
No. 53-55: 248
No. 61: 249
No. 88: 252
No. 89: 252
No. 93: 252
Elm St.
No. 7-9: 68
No. 8-12: 68
No. 14: 68
No. 18: 68
Elmsley Place
No. 1: 122
No. 2: 122
No. 3: 122
No. 5: 122
No. 6-8: 122
Elmwood Club: 68
Emblem Ct.
No. 40: 294
Emerald City (residential towers and townhouses): 289
Emmanuel College: 120
Erindale Hall Student Residence: 274
Ernescliffe: 150
Ernst & Young Tower: 91
Esplanade, The: 27
No. 8: 28
No. 25: 27
No. 250: 34
Essex Park Hotel: 156
Eva's Phoenix: 58
"Evenholm": 253
Evergreen Brick Works: 254
Exhibit Residences: 204
Exhibition Place: 263
EY Tower: 86

Factor-Inwentash Faculty of Social Work: 221
Faculty of Law (U of T): 117
Fairweather's: 59
Falconbridge, John house: 240
Fashion Building: 58
Fashion House: 54
Festival Hall: 56
Fieldstone Co-op: 138
52 Division Headquarters Toronto Police: 102
56 Lippincott: 188
Fire Pump House: 267
Firehall No. 3 (Yonge St.): 72
Firehall No. 4 (Berkeley St.): 37
Firehall No. 8 (Bellevue Ave.): 188
Firehall No. 10 (Yorkville Ave.): 193
First Canadian Place: 89
First Church of Christ Scientist: 222
First Lutheran Church: 163
Fisher, Edward house: 237
FitzGerald Building: 109
Fitzroy Terrace
No. 1: 187
Five Condos: 73
500 Wellington West Condos: 49
519 Community Centre: 167
Flatiron Mural: 27
Flavelle House: 117
Fleet St.
No. 660: 262

Forestry Building (U of T): 111
Fort York: 262
Fort York Armoury: 262
Fort York Blvd.
    No. 95: 261
    No. 170: 261
    No. 190: 261
    No. 250: 262
Fort York Visitors Centre: 262
401 Richmond: 57
Four Seasons Centre for the Performing Arts: 98
Four Seasons Hotel and Residences: 193
Frank, John Place: 163
Fraser Mustard Early Learning Academy: 292
Fraser Residence: 245
French Quarter (condominiums): 154
Front St. E.
    No. 1: 28
    No. 27: 27
    No. 35-39: 27
    No. 41-43: 27
    No. 45-49: 27
    No. 63: 26
    No. 67-69: 26
    No. 71: 26
    No. 77-79: 26
    No. 80: 25
    No. 81A: 26
    No. 81-83: 26
    No. 85: 26
    No. 87: 26
    No. 91: 21
    No. 139-145: 32
    No. 165: 32
    No. 219-221: 33
    No. 223-237: 33
    No. 239: 33
    No. 398: 268
Front St. W.
    No. 1: 95
    No. 18-22: 80
    No. 65-75: 95
    No. 100: 96
    No. 123: 97
    No. 160: 97
    No. 250: 47
    No. 255: 47
    No. 410: 48
Frye, Northrop Hall: 120
Fudger, Harris Henry house: 249

Gagnier, Harold house: 239

Galbraith, William house: 72
Garden Court Apartments: 287
Gardiner Museum of Ceramic Art: 119
Garibaldi House: 36
Garner, Hugh Housing Co-operative: 138
Geary, George Reginald house: 236
George Brown School of Hospitality: 23
George St.
    No. 105: 24
    No. 112-116: 24
German Consulate: 223
Gerrard Building: 69
Gerrard St. E.
    No. 62-66: 165
    No. 78-80: 165
    No. 130: 156
    No. 550: 130
Gerstein Science Information Centre: 107
Gilead Pl.
    No. 7-15: 35
Girl Guides of Canada Headquarters: 284
Glas: 51
"Glen Hurst": 246
Glen Morris St.
    No. 7: 112
Glen Rd.
    No. 51: 249
    No. 55: 249
    No. 57: 249
    No. 97: 253
    No. 105: 254
Glenroy Ave.
    No. 35: 277
Global House: 103
Globe and Mail Centre: 36
Gloucester Mews: 74
Gloucester St.
    No. 86: 168
    No. 100: 160
Gluskin, Max House: 115
Goldring Centre for High-Performance Sport: 115
Gooderham, Alex house: 243
Gooderham Building: 26
Gooderham, Charles H. house: 153
Gooderham, Edward D. house: 248
Gooderham, George house: 220
Gooderham, George H. house: 159
Gooderham, The: 267
Gooderham and Worts Distillery: 153
Gordon, Robert A. Learning Centre, Humber
    College: 277
Gould St.

No. 50: 165
Gradient House: 187
Graduate House: 112
Grandravine Dr.
    No. 350: 279
"Grange, The": 173
Grange Ave.
    No. 13-17: 179
    No. 19-21: 179
    No. 22: 179
    No. 23-25: 179
    No. 27-29: 179
    No. 51: 179
    No. 69: 179
Grange Triple Double: 179
Granite Club annex: 167
Grant, Lewis house: 250
Graphic Arts Building: 84
Graydon Hall Dr.
    No. 185: 289
Graydon Manor: 289
Greenbelt Dr.
    No. 19: 290
Green/Green house: 165
Green Valley Rd.
    No. 36: 286
Grosvenor St.
    No. 20: 72
    No. 25: 72

Halo: 72
Harbour Terrace: 260
Harbord St.
    No. 60: 112
Harris, Lawren House: 283
Harrison, Dan Social Housing Complex: 148
Hart House: 107
Hart House Circle:
    No. 7: 107
    No. 12: 107
Haultain Building: 109
Hawthorn Ave.
    No. 44: 251
    No. 46: 251
    No. 48: 251
Hawthorn Gardens
    No. 2: 252
    No. 4: 252
    No. 5: 251
    No. 6: 251
Hazelton Ave.
    No. 30: 197
    No. 33: 196
    No. 35: 197
    No. 49-51: 197
    No. 53-55: 197
    No. 57-59: 197
    No. 61-63: 197
    No. 65: 198
    No. 68: 198
    No. 77-81: 198
    No. 85: 198
    No. 88-90: 198
    No. 92-94: 198
    No. 101-105: 198
Hazelton Hotel and Residences: 195
Hazelton House: 196
Hazelton Lanes: 196
Hearn Generating Station: 266
Heaslip House: 164
Heintzman Hall: 63
Hermant Building: 67
Highland Cres.
    No. 87: 286
Hillcrest Ave.: 129
Hilton Toronto: 98
Hincks-Dellcrest Centre: 158
Hoare, John house: 249
Hockey Hall of Fame: 79
Holland Bloorview Kids' Rehabilitation Hospital: 286
Holt Renfrew Centre: 207
Holy Blossom Temple: 283
Honour Court and Welcome Centre: 281
Horn, Thomas W. house: 221
Horticulture Building: 264
Hoskin Ave.
    No. 5: 117
    No. 6: 117
Hoskin, John residence: 249
Hospital for Sick Children: 103, 104
Hotel Le Germain: 48
Hotel Winchester: 139
Howard, J.S. house: 24
Howland Ave.
    No. 21-23: 230
    No. 67-69: 230
    No. 71-73: 230
    No. 100: 230
    No. 120: 230
Howland, Mrs. Peleg house: 242
HTO Park: 260
Hudson's Bay Centre: 208
Hudson's Bay Co. and Saks Fifth Avenue: 62
Hudson, The: 51

Humber River Bicycle and Pedestrian Bridge: 277
Huron-Madison Project: 216
Huron St.
    No. 122: 178
    No. 124-126: 178
    No. 300: 112
    No. 478: 219
    No. 480-482: 219
    No. 496: 219
    No. 500: 219
    No. 532: 219
    No. 534: 219
    No. 541: 218
    No. 571-573: 218
    No. 610: 218
Huron Street School: 218
Hutchison Building: 28
Hydro-Electric Building: 103
Hydro Place: 104
Hydro Substation: 266

Ian Macdonald Blvd.
    No. 111: 280
Iceboat Terrace
    No. 15: 261
    No. 21: 261
Imperial Oil Building: 284
INDX: 85
Inglenook Community High School: 35
Innis College: 114
Institute of Child Study: 228
Integral House: 245
Irwin Ave.
    No. 6-14: 75
Isabella St.
    No. 40-42: 162
    No. 72: 168
    No. 81-83: 168
    No. 105: 160
    No. 108: 160
    No. 136: 152
Ismaili Centre: 291
Italian Consulate: 176

Jane Exbury Towers: 278
Jane St.
    No. 2415: 278
    No. 4645: 279
Janssen Inc: 290
"Janus House:" 132
Jarvis Collegiate Institute: 158
Jarvis, Edgar residence: 246, 253

Jarvis St.
    No. 160: 154
    No. 207-213: 154
    No. 215-219: 154
    No. 222: 155
    No. 285-291: 155
    No. 300: 156
    No. 311: 155
    No. 337: 156
    No. 354: 156
    No. 372: 156
    No. 383: 156
    No. 400-404: 157
    No. 440: 158
    No. 441: 157
    No. 445: 157
    No. 449: 157
    No. 467: 157
    No. 495: 158
    No. 504: 159
    No. 510: 159
    No. 512: 159
    No. 514: 159
    No. 515: 158
    No. 519: 159
    No. 571: 160
Jarvis Street Baptist Church: 156
Jarvis, William Botsford residence: 243
Jesuit Fathers residence: 252
John St.
    No. 55: 47
    No. 126-132: 56
    No. 165: 173
    No. 203: 173
    No. 205: 173
Juvenile and Family Courts Building: 155

Kay, John Co.: 83
Keele St.
    No. 4700: 279, 280
Keg Mansion Restaurant: 158
Kelly, John M. Library: 121
Kensington Market: 186
Kensington Market Lofts: 187
Kerr Hall: 165
Kiever Synagogue: 186
Kilgour Rd.
    No. 150: 286
King Charlotte: 51
King East Centre: 37
King Edward Hotel: 29
King George Square: 23

King James Place: 24
King St. E.
    No. 1: 81
    No. 2: 81
    No. 37: 29
    No. 106: 24
    No. 107-111: 25
    No. 115: 25
    No. 125: 25
    No. 133-135: 25
    No. 145: 24
    No. 151: 22
    No. 150-154: 23
    No. 167-185: 23
    No. 168: 23
    No. 172: 23
    No. 187: 23
    No. 200: 23
    No. 215: 23
    No. 280: 37
    No. 298-300: 36
    No. 302: 36
    No. 334: 36
    No. 351: 36
    No. 359: 36
    No. 393: 35
    No. 399–403: 35
    No. 417: 35
    No. 425: 35
King St. W.
    No. 1: 81
    No. 2: 82
    No. 25: 89
    No. 30: 88
    No. 36-38: 83
    No. 44: 87
    No. 50: 89
    No. 55: 90
    No. 100: 89
    No. 150: 97
    No. 189: 43
    No. 200: 97
    No. 212: 42
    No. 224: 42
    No. 260-270: 55
    No. 260: 43
    No. 274-322: 55
    No. 284: 55
    No. 300: 55
    No. 322: 55
    No. 350: 51
    No. 431: 55

    No. 438: 51
    No. 441: 55
    No. 445: 55
    No. 455: 55
    No. 460: 51
    No. 461: 55
    No. 469: 54
    No. 489-539: 54
    No. 489: 54
    No. 500-522: 54
    No. 511: 54
    No. 560: 54
    No. 572: 54
    No. 600: 53
    No. 602: 53
    No. 620: 53
    No. 636: 53
    No. 642: 53
King's College Circle
    No. 1: 108
    No. 7: 107
    No. 15: 106
    No. 23: 111
    No. 27: 108
    No. 31: 108
King's College Rd.
    No. 5: 108
Kings Landing: 260
Klaus by Nienkamper: 36
Knox College: 111
Koffler Student Services Centre: 110
Krangle Building: 55

L Tower, The: 28
Laird Dr.
    No. 93: 287
Lake Shore Blvd W
    No. 637: 262
    No. 955: 264
    No. 2045: 277
Lakeshore Road E.
    No. 20: 276
Lamb, Daniel house: 129
"Lambton Lodge": 177
Laneway House: 293
Larkin, Gerald Academic Building: 116
Larkin, Gerald house: 252
Laurier Ave.
    No. 1-21: 127
    No. 2-22: 127
Lawrence Ave.
    No. 777: 287

No. 877: 290
No. 939: 290
No. 2015: 294
Layton, Jack Ferry Terminal and Harbour Square
   Park: 259
Ledbury Park Skating Pavilion and Pool: 282
Ledbury St.
   No. 146: 282
Lee, George house: 198
Lennox, John House: 134
Leonard Pl.
   No. 5: 186
LePage, A.E. Building: 28
Lepper's Block: 140
Leslie Dan Pharmacy Building: 109
Leslie Garden Ln.
   No. 1: 293
Lesmill Rd.
   No. 100: 288
Lewis/Haldenby house: 242
Library District Condominiums: 261
Lillian H. Smith Branch Library: 178
Lippincott St.
   No. 56: 188
Library Lane
   No. 15: 297
Little Trinity Annex: 35
Little Trinity Church: 35
Little Trinity House: 35
Little York Hotel: 23
Living Arts Centre, The: 275
Living Arts Dr.
   No. 4141: 275
Loew's Uptown Theatre: 75
Lombard St.
   No. 120: 154
Longo's: 287
Lord Lansdowne Public School: 188
Loretto Lane
   No. 10-20: 231
Loretto, The: 230
"Lorne Hall": 236
Lower River St.
   No. 29: 269
Lower Simcoe St.
   No. 75: 45
Lowther Ave.
   No. 9: 202
   No. 16: 202
   No. 23-29: 202
   No. 26: 202
   No. 30-32: 202

No. 36: 203
No. 46: 203
No. 50: 203
No. 60: 224
No. 75: 224
No. 80: 219
No. 82: 219
No. 84: 219
No. 86: 219
No. 188: 229
Lukes, Lewis house: 216
Luminous Veil: 134
Lumsden Building: 82

MacInnis, Grace Co-operative: 168
Mackenzie, William Lyon house: 163
MacLean Building: 56
Maclean Publishing Co.: 102
Madison Ave.
   No. 12: 216
   No. 14: 216
   No. 16-18: 216
   No. 17-19: 216
   No. 20: 216
   No. 21-23: 216
   No. 24-26: 216
   No. 25: 216
   No. 30-32: 216
   No. 37: 216
   No. 47: 217
   No. 54: 217
   No. 64-66: 217
   No. 69-71: 217
   No. 78: 217
   No. 88: 218
   No. 93-99: 217
   No. 138: 218
   No. 140: 218
   No. 145: 218
Maitland Place: 157
Maitland St.
   No. 36-42: 166
   No. 37: 72
   No. 55: 166
   No. 111: 167
Maitlands, The: 166
Major Mackenzie Dr.
   No. 2141: 273
Manhattan Apartments: 168
Manitoba Dr.
   No. 45: 263
Manufacturers Building: 56

Manufacturers' Life Insurance Co: 209
Manulife Centre: 207
Maple Ave.
    No. 33: 249
    No. 35: 249
    No. 39: 249
    No. 40: 249
    No. 41: 249
Maple Leaf Gardens: 166
Maple Leaf Square: 45
Maple Terrace: 140
Market Square Condominiums: 25
Market St.
    No. 1: 32
Market Street: 21
Market Wharf: 32
Markham Civic Centre: 297
MaRS Centre: 104
Mason and Risch: 53
Massey, Chester D. house: 159
Massey College: 116
Massey Hall: 64
Massey, Hart residence: 158
Massey, Lillian Department of Household Science: 205
Massey Tower: 63
Mauran, Richard G.W. House: 283
Mayfair Mansions: 285
McCaul St.
    No. 49-105: 174
    No. 100: 175
    No. 131: 175
    No. 141: 175
    No. 240: 178
    No. 263: 110
McClelland and Stewart Building: 102
McDonald, Ronald House: 178
McKenzie Ave.
    No. 2: 250
    No. 10: 250
    No. 20: 250
    No. 49: 250
McKinsey & Co: 119
Meadowvale Rd.
    No. 2000: 297
Mechanical Engineering Building (U of T): 108
Medical Arts Building: 220
Medical Sciences Building (U of T): 108
Mercer St.
    No. 15-31: 47
    No. 24: 47
    No. 30: 48
Meredith Crescent

    No. 3: 236
Merlan, The: 168
Merton St.
    No. 50: 284
Metcalfe St.
    No. 1-3: 133
    No. 5-7: 133
    No. 6-18: 133
    No. 9-11: 133
    No. 13-15: 133
    No. 17-25: 133
    No. 20-32: 133
    No. 37: 133
    No. 39-43: 134
Metro Hall: 47
Metropolitan Place: 97
Metropolitan Toronto Police (52 Division
    Headquarters): 102
Metropolitan Toronto Police Headquarters: 71
Metropolitan United Church: 161
Metropolitan United Church parsonage: 162
Mickleborough, James house: 239
Military Trail
    No. 1265: 295, 296
Miller Lash House: 296
Millichamp Building: 29
Millington St.
    No. 7: 133
Mimico Centennial Library: 277
Mirvish + Gehry: 55
Mirvish Village: 231
Mississauga City Hall: 275
Mississauga Public Library, Port Credit Branch: 276
Mississauga Rd.
    No. 3359: 274, 275
Moatfield Dr.
    No. 111: 289
Monarch Building: 48
Monteith St.
    No. 2-36: 167
Morningside Ave.
    No. 755: 295
Mooredale House: 238
Morgan, The: 52
Morrison, James L. house: 133
Moss Park Apartments: 142
Moss Park (park and community centre): 147
Mount Pleasant Rd.
    No. 1: 160
    No. 129: 236
Mount Sinai Hospital: 103
Mozo: 33

Munk Centre for International Studies: 116
Munk School of Global Affairs: 221
Museum House: 204
Museum of Contemporary Art Toronto Canada: 278
Mutual St.
    No. 281-285: 157
Myers, Barton house: 198

Nassau St.
    No. 21: 187
National Ballet School: 156, 167
National Building: 85
National Club: 87
Native Canadian Centre of Toronto: 225
Native Child and Family Services: 71
New City Hall: 100
New College: 112
New College residence: 112
New York Life Centre: 208
Newman Centre of Toronto: 114
Niagara St.
    No. 10: 50
    No. 20: 50
Nicholas Residences: 75
Nightstar Rd.
    No. 69: 297
Niles, Charles house: 243
Noble, The Block: 182
Noor Cultural Centre: 291
Normal and Model Schools: 165
Northern Ontario Building: 86
North St. Lawrence Market: 22
North St. James Town proposal: 153
North York Board of Education: 285
North York City Centre and North York Public
    Library: 285
North York Civic Centre: 285

OAA Headquarters: 289
Oak St.
    No. 1: 140
Oakdale Community Centre: 279
"Oakham House": 164
O'Brien house: 71
Occident Hall: 186
O'Keefe Centre for the Performing Arts: 28
Old City Hall: 99
Old Colony Rd.
    No. 120: 287
Old George Pl.
    No. 3: 245
    No. 4: 245

Old Kingston Rd.
    No.130: 296
Old York Lane: 195
Olivet Congregational Church: 196
One Bedford: 204
One Bloor: 208
One Cole: 140
One Park Place: 142
One Park West: 140
One, The: 207
OCAD University: 175
Ontario Heritage Centre: 82
Ontario Hydro Building: 103
Ontario Institute for Studies in Education: 221
Ontario Medical Association: 222
Ontario Place: 264
Ontario Research Foundation: 121
Ontario Science Centre: 292
Ontario Square and Canada Square: 259
Ontario St.
    No. 481-483: 138
    No. 484-490: 138
    No. 497-503: 138
    No. 505-511: 138
    No. 550: 138
OPSEU Headquarters: 288
Ord, Lewis house: 238
Origami Lofts: 186
Osgoode Hall: 41
Our Lady of Lourdes Roman Catholic Church: 152
Our Lady of Mt. Carmel: 175
Owl House Lane: 128
Oxford St.
    No. 91: 187
Oxley St.
    No. 25: 51

Pace: 155
Pachter House: 179
Paintbox Condos: 141
Palace Pier Condominium: 277
Palace St.
    No. 20: 268
Pantages Theatre: 66
Parade: 261
Parisian Laundry Building: 53
Park Hyatt Hotel: 204
Park Rd.
    No. 50: 209
    No. 100: 236
    No. 104: 236
    No. 105: 235

No. 107: 235
No. 108: 236
No. 110: 236
No. 114: 236
No. 120: 236
No. 124: 236
Parliament Building: 105
Parliament St.
    No. 45: 34
    No. 51: 34
    No. 433-443: 140
    No. 519-527: 140
    No. 531: 139
    No. 549-563: 139
    No. 583-585: 139
    No. 635: 126, 127
Paul Bishop's Buildings: 23
Paul Lane Gardens
    No. 1-25: 185
Peter St.
    No. 125: 56
    No. 134: 57
Peter Street Condominiums: 52
Phoebe, The on Queen: 180
Picasso: 52
Pier 27: 265
Pilkington Bros. Ltd.: 47
Piper, Noah L. house: 199
Plymbridge Rd.
    No. 54: 286
Polish Combatants' Hall: 178
Port Credit Village: 276
Portland St.
    No. 66: 50
    No. 75: 50
Post Offices
    Seventh: 29
    First: 24
Postal Station F: 75
Post House Condos: 24
Power Plant, The: 259
Power St.
    No. 93: 37
Pratt, E. J. Library: 120
Prince Arthur Ave.
    No. 20: 203
    No. 25-27: 203
    No. 29-31: 203
    No. 35: 203
    No. 94: 219
Prince Arthur, The: 195
Prince Arthur Towers: 203

Prince Edward Viaduct: 134
Princes' Drive
    No. 100: 263
Princess Margaret Cancer Centre: 103
Prince of Wales Dr.
    No. 275: 275
Princess of Wales Theatre: 55
Progress Ave.
    No. 941: 295
Prospect St.
    No. 15: 138, 139
Provincial Ombudsman: 205
Provincial Parliament Building: 105
Prudential Building: 82
Public Libraries
    Mississauga: 276
    Scarborough Civic Centre Branch: 296
    Unionville: 297
    Yorkville: 192
Public Reference Library: 110
Public Schools
    Bellmere Junior: 297
    Huron Street: 218
    Nelson Mandela Park: 142
    Wells, Thomas L.: 297
    Winchester Street: 138, 139
Pure Spirit: 267
Pure Spirits: 267

QRC West: 57
Queen Elizabeth Building: 263
Queen Portland Centre: 185
Queen St. E.
    No. 1: 83
    No. 2: 63
    No. 56: 161
    No. 315: 37
    No. 2701: 293
Queen St. W.
    No. 60: 99
    No. 100: 100
    No. 116-138: 41
    No. 123: 98
    No. 145: 98
    No. 160: 42
    No. 234-240: 174
    No. 280: 182
    No. 298: 182
    No. 299: 174
    No. 315: 174
    No. 328-330: 182
    No. 342-354: 182

No. 356-356A: 182
No. 371-373: 182
No. 378: 183
No. 388-396: 183
No. 440-450: 183
No. 441-443: 183
No. 472-474: 183
No. 484: 183
No. 486-492: 183
No. 489-491: 183
No. 493-495: 183
No. 500-504: 183
No. 506-514: 184
No. 577: 184
No. 588: 186
No. 589: 185
No. 639: 185
No. 651: 186
No. 999: 277
Queen's Park
No. 1: 105
No. 14: 108
No. 73: 120
No. 75: 120
No. 78: 117
No. 95: 120
No. 100: 118
No. 111: 119
Queen's Park Building (University of St. Michael's
College): 122
Queen's Park Crescent E.
No. 23: 105
No. 53-59: 121
No. 73: 120
Queen's Park Crescent W.
No. 14: 108
Queens Quay Revitalization: 260
Queens Quay Terminal: 258
Queens Quay
No. 25: 270
Queens Quay E.
No. 27: 265
No. 29: 265
No. 39: 265
No. 95: 265
Queens Quay W.
No. 9: 258
No. 25: 259
No. 145: 258
No. 231: 259
No. 235: 259
No. 339: 260

No. 401: 260
No. 470: 260
No. 479: 260

Radio City: 157
Ravine House: 254
R.C. Harris Water Filtration Plant: 293
RCMP Building: 180
Redemptorist Fathers residence: 175
Redpath Sugar refinery: 265
Regent Park Aquatic Centre: 141
Regent Park Blvd.
No. 55: 142
Regent Park Community Recreation Centre and
Employment Centre: 142
Regent Park North: 140
Regent Park South: 143
Reid, John B. house: 47
Renaissance Centre: 205
Residence for the Sisters of St. Joseph: 293
Residences of 488 University Ave, The: 103
Richmond Hill Central Library: 287
Richmond St. E.
No. 20: 83
No. 60: 161
No. 115: 154
Richmond St. W.
No. 73: 84
No. 80: 85
No. 111: 86
No. 145: 98
No. 259: 56
No. 318: 52
No. 364: 57
No. 388: 57
No. 438: 52
No. 505: 58
No. 850: 52
Ricoh Coliseum: 263
RioCan Hall: 56
Ripley's Aquarium: 45
Ritchie/Forneri house: 149
Ritz-Carlton, residences: 44
River City: 269
Riverdale Park: 130
Robarts, John P. Research Library: 113
Robert St.
No. 33: 188
Robert A. Gordon Learning Centre, Humber College:
277
Robertson, John Ross residence: 149
Rogers Centre: 45

Rogers headquarters: 160
Ronald McDonald House: 178
Rosar-Morrison Funeral Residence: 150
Rose Ave.
　No. 1-11: 139
Rosebrugh Building: 109
Rosedale Presbyterian Church: 236
Rosedale Ravine: 235
Rosedale Rd.
　No. 1: 244
　No. 16: 244
　No. 19: 244
　No. 23: 243
　No. 27: 259
　No. 30: 244
　No. 34: 243
　No. 35: 242
　No. 36: 243
　No. 40: 243
　No. 41-43: 242
　No. 44: 243
　No. 45: 243
　No. 47: 242
　No. 48: 243
　No. 52: 243
Rosedale School of the Arts: 135
"Rosedale Villa": 243
Ross Building: 280
Rotary Park Pool: 277
Rotman, Joseph L. School of Management: 114
Roxborough Dr.
　No. 51: 244
　No. 194: 245
Roxborough St. E.
　No. 141-147: 239
　No. 170: 238
　No. 171: 238
　No. 172: 238
　No. 174: 238
　No. 176: 238
Royal Alexandra Theatre: 43
Royal Bank: 81
Royal Bank Plaza: 91
Royal Canadian Military Institute: 102
Royal Canadian Mounted Police Building: 180
Royal Canadian Yacht Club: 221
Royal Conservatory of Music: 118
Royal Ontario Museum: 118
Royal York Hotel: 96
Rundle, Charles R. house: 159
Ryerson Image Centre: 164
Ryerson Student Learning Centre: 68

Ryerson University Architectural Science Building: 165
Ryerson University Learning Resources Centre: 165
Ryerson University Student Campus Centre: 164
Ryrie Building: 66
Ryrie, James house: 241

Sackville St.
　No. 19: 35
　No. 21-33: 35
　No. 180: 141
　No. 225: 141
　No. 246: 140
　No. 260: 140
　No. 298A: 131
　No. 298B: 131
　No. 306: 131
　No. 377: 132
　No. 483-485: 128
SAS Canada: 37
St.-Alban-the-Martyr Church: 230
St. Andrew's Lutheran Church: 156
St. Andrew's Manse: 43
St. Andrew's Presbyterian Church: 43
St. Andrew's United Church: 156, 208
St. Basil's Church: 121
St. Basil's College: 121
St. Basil's School: 197
St. Clair Ave.
　No. 111: 284
St. Dennis Dr.: 292
St. Felix Centre: 184
St. George St.: 114
　No. 33: 111
　No. 40: 111
　No. 45: 111
　No. 59: 111
　No. 73: 113
　No. 75: 113
　No. 85: 113
　No. 89: 114
　No. 97: 114
　No. 100: 113
　No. 105: 114
　No. 111: 114
　No. 119: 115
　No. 130: 113
　No. 135: 220
　No. 139: 221
　No. 150: 115
　No. 163: 222
　No. 165: 222
　No. 169: 222

No. 170: 220
No. 174: 221
No. 176: 221
No. 178: 221
No. 180: 221
No. 182: 221
No. 186: 221
No. 190: 221
No. 196: 222
No. 212: 222
No. 228: 222
No. 230: 222
No. 234: 222
No. 240: 222
No. 260: 223
St. George's College: 230
St. George's Greek Orthodox Church of Toronto: 164
St. Hilda's College: 117
St. James' Cemetery: 126
St. James Square: 165
St. James Town: 151
St. James-the-Less Chapel: 127
St. John's York Mills Anglican Church: 285
St. Joseph St.
  No. 5: 73
  No. 6-14: 73
  No. 11: 74
  No. 11-19: 74
  No. 18-20: 74
  No. 26: 74
  No. 50: 121
  No. 95: 121
  No. 96: 122
  No. 100: 121
  No. 113: 121
  No. 121: 121
St. Lawrence Centre for the Arts: 27
St. Lawrence Hall: 22
St. Lawrence Lofts: 26
St. Lawrence Market: 21, 22
St. Lawrence Neighbourhood: 31
St. Luke's United Church: 150
St. Michael's Cathedral rectory: 162
St. Michael's College: 121
St. Michael's Roman Catholic Cathedral: 162
St. Nicholas St.
  No. 45-63: 75
  No. 75: 75
St. Patrick St.
  No. 196: 175
St. Patrick's Church: 175
St. Patrick's Market: 174

St. Paul's Anglican Church: 209
St. Paul's Roman Catholic Church: 37
St. Stanislaus Roman Catholic Church: 184
St. Stephen-in-the-Fields Anglican Church: 188
St. Thomas
  No. 1: 206
  No. 7: 206
St. Thomas House: 217
St. Thomas St.
  No. 18: 206
Salvation Army Scarborough Citadel and Housing: 294
Salvation Army Harbour Light: 154
Samuel Building: 55
Samuel, Sigmund Library: 107
Scadding, Rev. Henry house: 66
Scarborough Civic Centre: 294
Scarborough College master plan: 295
Scholar's Green Park: 275
Schulich School of Business: 280
Scollard St.
  No. 72-76: 196
  No. 92: 196
  No. 94-104: 196
Scotia Plaza: 61, 83, 88
Scott Library: 280
Scrivener Square
  No. 10: 240
Seagram, Norman house: 252
Seventh Post Office: 29
Severn St.
  No. 25: 198
Sharp House: 286
Shell Oil Building: 103
Shangri-La Hotel and Residences: 97
Shepard, Joseph Building: 285
Sheraton Centre: 98
Sherbourne Common: 266
Sherbourne Lanes: 148
Sherbourne St.
  No. 223: 148
  No. 241: 149
  No. 241-285: 148
  No. 260-262A: 149
  No. 280: 149
  No. 283-285: 149
  No. 291: 149
  No. 355: 150
  No. 380: 150
  No. 467: 150
  No. 490: 150
  No. 495: 150
  No. 520: 152

No. 582: 153
No. 592: 153
Sherbourne St. N.
    No. 1: 248
    No. 27: 248
    No. 35: 237
Shops at Don Mills: 290
Shuter St.
    No. 15: 64
    No. 68-70: 163
    No. 112-120: 148
    No. 122-136: 148
    No. 138-140: 148
    No. 142-152: 148
    No. 402: 142
    No. 440: 142
Siddall, J. Wilson house: 238
Silver Dart Dr.
    No. 6301: 277
Simcoe Hall: 108
Simcoe St.
    No. 60: 43
    No. 73: 43
Simcoe WaveDeck: 260
Simpson, Napier house: 130
Simpson, Robert Co.: 62
Simpsons-Sears: 155
Small, Ambrose house: 249
Small Row: 36
Smith, Lillian H. Branch Library: 178
Smith, Sidney Hall: 113
Society of Friends Meeting House: 167, 224
Soho Square: 180
Soho Street
    No. 11-25: 180
    No. 14-24: 180
Soldiers' Memorial Tower: 107
Sony Centre for the Performing Arts: 28
South Dr.
    No. 48: 236
    No. 54: 236
    No. 67: 237
    No. 69: 237
    No. 73: 237
    No. 74: 236
    No. 75: 237
    No. 79: 237
    No. 103: 237
    No. 132: 254
    No. 134: 254
    No. 144: 253
    No. 146: 253

No. 157: 253
No. 160: 253
South St. Lawrence Market: 21
Southcore Financial Centre: 45
Spadina Ave.
    No. 49: 48
    No. 96-104: 58
    No. 106-111: 58
    No. 119-121: 57
    No. 130: 58
    No. 241: 179
    No. 280: 187
    No. 285: 187
Spadina Crescent
    No. 1: 111
Spadina Gardens: 226
Spadina House: 215
Spadina Rd.
    No. 9-11: 225
    No. 16: 225
    No. 24: 226
    No. 25: 226
    No. 41-45: 226
    No. 50: 227
    No. 69-71: 227
    No. 85: 227
    No. 106: 227
    No. 151: 227
    No. 285: 215
Spruce Court Apartments: 131
Spruce Court
    No. 1-32: 131
Spruce St.
    No. 35: 132
    No. 39: 132
    No. 41: 132
    No. 56: 132
Standard Theatre: 187
Star Mansions: 168
Station Rd.
    No. 47: 277
Steeles Ave.
    No. 378: 287
Sterling Rd.
    No. 158: 278
Sterling Tower: 84
Stewart St.
    No. 20: 50
    No. 32: 50
    No. 38: 50
Stinson House: 186
Stone Distillery, The: 267

Strathy, Gerald residence: 251
Struthers/Ross house: 202
Student Centre, U of T Mississauga: 274
Studio Building: 198
Sugar Beach: 265
Sullivan St.
    No. 11: 180
    No. 24-26: 180
    No. 28-30: 180
    No. 32-34: 180
    No. 53-83: 180
Sumach St.
    No. 1: 269
    No. 52: 35
    No. 330: 131
    No. 384: 129
    No. 404-408: 129
    No. 410-412: 129
    No. 420-422: 129
    No. 425-435: 129
    No. 437-439: 128
    No. 441-443: 128
    No. 442-444: 128
    No. 446-448: 128
    No. 450-452: 128
    No. 454-456: 128
Summerhill LCBO: 240
Sun Life: 98
Sun Life Centre: 97
Sunnylea School: 277
Superior Loan: 71
Sussex Ave.
    No. 2: 114

Tableau: 56
Tanenbaum, Joey and Toby Opera Centre: 33
Tank House Ln.
    No. 50: 267
Ted Rogers School of Management: 67
Temperance St.
    No. 2: 83
    No. 9: 83
    No. 14: 85
    No. 17: 83
    No. 70: 85
Temple Emanu-el: 287
Terminal 1, Toronto Pearson International Airport: 276
Terrence Donnelly Health Sciences Complex: 275
Terroni: 30
Theatre Park: 42
Thomas L. Wells Public School: 297
Thomas, William residence: 164

Thompson Hotel and residences: 50
Thomson, Roy Hall: 43
Thorncliffe Park Dr.
    No. 82: 292
    No. 101: 293
Three Streets Co-op: 134
TIFF Bell Lightbox: 51
Tip Top Lofts: 262
Toronto Baptist Seminary: 156
Toronto Botanical Gardens: 287
Toronto Camera Centre: 67
Toronto Chinese Baptist Church: 179
Toronto Convention Centre: 47
Toronto Dance Theatre: 134
Toronto District School Board: 285
Toronto-Dominion Bank: 63
Toronto-Dominion Centre: 90
Toronto Ferry Co. Waiting Room: 258
Toronto General Hospital: 104, 131
Toronto Heliconian Club: 197
Toronto Hydro-Electric System: 70
Toronto (Don) Jail, The: 130
Toronto Music Garden: 260
Toronto Necropolis Chapel: 129
Toronto Pharmacol Building: 55
Toronto Police Service, 51 Division: 34
Toronto Police Service, 52 Division: 102
Toronto Public Library:
    Eatonville Branch: 276
    Fort York Branch: 261
    Scarborough Civic Centre Branch: 295
    St. James Town Branch: 150
Toronto Reference Library: 76
Toronto Sculpture Garden: 25
Toronto Silverplate Co.: 54
Toronto Stock Exchange: 91
Toronto Street: 29
Toronto St.
    No. 10: 29
    No. 17: 29
    No. 25: 30
    No. 36: 29
Toronto Sun Building: 37
Toronto Zoo master plan: 297
Tower Building: 58
Town Centre Blvd.
    No. 101: 297
Traders Bank of Canada: 81
Traders Building: 168
Tranby Ave.
    No. 11: 200
    No. 33-35: 200

No. 37-39: 200
No. 43-45: 200
No. 47-49: 200
No. 51-53: 200
No. 66-68: 200
No. 70: 200
No. 71-73: 200
Tranby Terrace: 200
Trefann Court: 142
Trinity College: 117
Trinity College Library: 116
Trinity Mews: 132
Trinity-St. Paul's United Church: 229
Trinity Square: 65
Trinity St.
    No. 2: 267
    No. 15: 267
    No. 105-109: 35
    No. 106: 34
    No. 115-127: 35
Trolley Cres.
    No. 51: 269
Trump International Hotel and Tower: 87
Turnbull Elevator Manufacturing Co: 56
Turner, Enoch residence: 149
Turner, Enoch Schoolhouse: 34
12 Degrees Condos: 180
Twenty Niagara Condos: 50

Umbra showroom: 173
Umbra World Headquarters: 294
Underpass Park: 269
Union Building: 42
Union Station: 95
Unionville Public Library: 297
University Ave.
    No. 1: 97
    No. 188: 97
    No. 200: 98
    No. 250: 99
    No. 330: 101
    No. 375: 102
    No. 382: 101
    No. 426: 102
    No. 480: 103
    No. 481: 102
    No. 488: 103
    No. 505: 103
    No. 555: 103
    No. 600: 103
    No. 610: 103
    No. 620: 104
    No. 661: 104
    No. 700: 104
University Avenue landscape: 99
University Club of Toronto: 101
University College: 106
University of Toronto Health Sciences Building: 110
University of Toronto Library: 107
University Theatre: 191, 206
Unwin Ave.
    No. 440: 266

Vanauley St.
    No. 41-97: 185
Vari Hall: 281
Vaughan City Hall: 273
Vaughan Civic Centre Resource Library: 273
Victoria College: 120
Victoria Hospital For Sick Children: 104
Victoria Memorial Square: 50
Victoria St.
    No. 244: 66
    No. 252: 67
    No. 297: 164
    No. 350: 165
    No. 380: 165
Victory Building: 85
Village by the Grange: 174
Village Green: 166
Village of Yorkville Park: 194
Viva House: 286
Vu: 24

Wales Ave.
    No. 29: 186
Wallberg Memorial Building: 110
Walmer Rd.
    No. 21: 229
    No. 35: 226
    No. 44: 229
    No. 45: 228
    No. 53: 228
    No. 70: 228
    No. 81: 228
    No. 83-85: 228
    No. 87: 228
    No. 91-93: 227
    No. 95-97: 227
    No. 109: 227
Walmer Road Baptist Church: 229
Ward, Sheldon house: 37
Warren, H.D. house: 158
Waterworks, The: 58

Watson, Claude School for the Arts: 286
Weathering Steel House: 286
Well, The: 48
Wellesley Ave.
    No. 1-3: 128
    No. 2-4: 128
    No. 5-7: 128
    No. 6-8: 128
    No. 9-11: 128
    No. 10-12: 128
    No. 13-15: 128
    No. 14-16: 128
    No. 17-19: 128
    No. 18-20: 128
Wellesley Cottages: 127
Wellesley Community Centre: 150
Wellesley On the Park: 73
Wellesley Park: 129
Wellesley Pl.
    No. 2: 158
    No. 4: 158
Wellesley St. E.
    No. 27: 73
    No. 77: 167
    No. 95: 158
    No. 195: 150
    No. 314: 127
    No. 316-324: 127
    No. 326-334: 127
    No. 376-380: 128
    No. 390: 128
    No. 398-402: 128
    No. 414-416: 128
    No. 418-420: 128
    No. 422-424: 128
    No. 426-428: 128
Wellesley St. W.
    No. 11: 73
Wellington St. E.
    No. 36-42: 28
    No. 49: 26
Wellington St. W.
    No. 5: 80
    No. 7: 80
    No. 9: 80
    No. 11: 80
    No. 13-15: 80
    No. 79: 90
    No. 100: 90
    No. 155: 44
    No. 181: 44
    No. 422-424: 48

No. 438: 48
No. 462: 48
No. 482-488: 49
No. 495: 49
No. 500: 49
No. 517: 49
No. 550: 50
Wesley Buildings: 174
West Neighbourhood House: 186
Westbank King Street: 54
Whitney Hall: 113
Widmer St.
    No. 21: 51
Willcocks St.
    No. 40: 112
Wilson, Sir Daniel Residence: 113
Winchester Block: 139
Winchester Square: 138
Winchester St.
    No. 7-11: 139
    No. 21: 139
    No. 77: 134
    No. 80: 134
    No. 85: 134
    No. 92: 134
    No. 94-96: 134
    No. 98: 134
    No. 156: 129
    No. 200: 129
Winchester Street Public School: 138, 139
Windsor Arms Hotel: 206
Wolf House: 244
Wong Dai Sin Temple: 287
Wood, Frank House: 286
Wood Gundy & Co.: 83
Woodsworth College: 115
Woodsworth College Residence: 115
Wycliffe College: 117
Wynford Dr.
    No. 39: 291
    No. 49: 291
    No. 77: 291
    No. 123: 291

X Condos: 160
X2 Condos: 160

YC Condos: 71
Yeomans Rd.
    No. 55: 282
YMCA of Greater Toronto: 72
Yonge-Dundas Square: 67

Yonge St.
No. 30: 79
No. 33: 28
No. 36: 80
No. 38-40: 80
No. 42-44: 80
No. 46: 80
No. 49: 80
No. 55: 81
No. 61-67: 81
No. 83: 61
No. 100: 61
No. 102-104: 61
No. 118: 85
No. 137: 62
No. 140: 83
No. 160-184: 62
No. 173: 63
No. 189-191: 63
No. 193: 63
No. 197: 63
No. 199: 63
No. 205: 63
No. 221-223: 64
No. 229: 66
No. 241: 66
No. 263: 66
No. 279-283: 67
No. 340: 67
No. 341: 68
No. 363-365: 69
No. 378: 69
No. 385-395: 69
No. 386: 70
No. 401-405: 69
No. 444: 70
No. 460: 71
No. 480: 71
No. 484: 72
No. 502-508: 72
No. 526-528: 72
No. 527-529: 72
No. 531: 72
No. 533: 72
No. 535: 72
No. 565-571: 73
No. 588: 73
No. 590-596: 73
No. 601: 74
No. 606-612: 73
No. 614: 73
No. 616: 73
No. 618: 73
No. 634-644: 74
No. 664-682: 75
No. 675: 75
No. 726-728: 75
No. 764: 75
No. 764-766: 75
No. 789: 76
No. 4900: 285
No. 5050: 285
No. 5100: 285
No. 5120: 285
York Belting Building: 25
York Blvd.
No. 55: 281
No. 100: 281
York Club: 220
York County Magistrates Court: 30
York Downs Dr.
No. 33: 282
York Square: 195
York St.
No. 20: 96
No. 150: 87
York University: 279
York University subway station: 280
Yorkdale Shopping Centre: 281
Yorkdale subway station: 282
Yorkville Ave.
No. 18: 192
No. 22: 192
No. 34: 193
No. 60: 193
No. 77: 193
No. 80: 194
No. 99: 194
No. 100: 194
No. 117: 195
No. 118: 195
Yorkville Public Library: 192
Yorkville Village: 196
Young Centre: 267
Young People's Theatre: 32
YWCA: 68

About the Authors

PATRICIA MCHUGH (1934–2008) was an architectural journalist and a member of the Toronto Historical Board. She published two editions of *Toronto Architecture: A City Guide*, which was a finalist for the Toronto Book Award.

ALEX BOZIKOVIC is the architecture critic for the *Globe and Mail*. He has won a National Magazine Award for his writing about design.